AT THE MERCY — OF THE — STATE

By Robert Coleman

Published by:

True American Publications
P.O. BOX 488
Huron, SD 57350-2944

www.michigancorruption.com

Design Credit, Janet Coleman

Production Credit, Kayleen Wharton

Library of Congress Cataloging -in- publication data.

Coleman, Robert
At the Mercy of the State

Library of Congress Control Number: 2012938127

ISBN: 978-0-615-61218-8

ISBN: 978-0-615-61218-8

FORWARD

When I look at this world and see the criminal elements that not only exist in it, but who are, in fact, *protected* by our own governments, who either conceal facts or simply look past the crimes of these perpetrators, I have to ponder why it is that I find myself on the list of *criminals* in our society. It seems to me that we have much more visible, much worse criminal elements to concern ourselves with, whose crimes (which are real) far surpass the severity of what my crime was reported to be. The local, state, and federal governments continually protect their own, while going out of their way to prosecute the weak, the poor, the ones whose crimes do not even compare to their own. You see people like Dick Cheney, who has started up, operated, and served as CEO of corporations whose business is war. His actions are a direct result in the deaths of thousands of Americans, as well as many thousands of other people in countries other than our own. Yet he walks free, no punishment even considered for him. He is but one example. The mass number of Wall Street thieves who literally stole the savings of thousands of Americans is another. One or two were imprisoned, probably because they offended someone in their own ranks. The rest have been totally ignored by prosecutors.

My crime? I spanked my child. Why? Precisely because I don't want my child to eventually become another Wall Street thief or a Dick Cheney. I do believe in the lost art of discipline, including spanking, so long as it is done in a corrective manner, and not in an abusive manner. In my case, a vindictive tenant accused me of abuse (to a state that was willing to listen) even though the facts were completely falsified. As a poor person in this country, however, I immediately am an evil offender, and in a child abuse accusation particularly, because this type of case gives the state an added opportunity to make money. This book covers that, as well as how the states go about setting up what you might call *legalized kidnapping rings.*

What the state of Michigan did not plan on, however, is that my wife Janet and I might fight back. We did, and we are not through yet. You see, the undeniable truth is that I *love* my children and will not stand by idly while anyone attempts to take them away from me, be it the state or anyone else. My wife shares my views.

If, indeed, I were a true child abuser or molester, as the state of Michigan attempted to establish, it would have been a justified action. My step daughter, Caitlyn would indeed have been rescued. But if my *intent* were really to hurt her, I would not *bother* with corrective spanking. I would, instead, simply turn her over to Dick Cheney and let him take her on a hunting trip. He could then shoot her in the face, and the government would protect him. Moreover, he would probably find it quite sporting, as he doesn't care much about the members of poor families anyway.

The system of justice in this country is a cruel joke on the American people. The cruelty extends from local governments right on up to the federal government, exemplified in the case of Dick Cheney. Perhaps I should describe the whole thing as a true *crime*, as opposed to a cruel *joke*, because surely the atrocities committed by public officials (in the pretense of performing public services) far exceeds the severity of crimes committed by the general populous, most of whom spend years in prison for their less severe offenses. This is what we call *justice.*

With that, we come to the *point* of this book. It is my intent, in divulging my own experiences, to *expose* the state of Michigan for the atrocities they allowed to be played out in my case, and to refer readers to many other cases, like my own, where *Child Protective Services,* allegedly set up to *protect* children, are instead *hurting* the children, by allowing the states to set up and operate *child kidnapping rings* all across this great country, with the purpose of *making money.*

—Robert Coleman—

PREFACE

Imagine a scene where police officers from a number of departments block off the entrances to a hotel and begin a raid on one of the rooms on a Sunday at three o'clock in the morning. Bystanders at the scene would probably suspect it was a drug raid, or perhaps something even more sinister. Would it surprise those bystanders to find out it was merely a child custody raid, conducted by overzealous officials to remove two small children from the custody of their parents?

Imagine the agony and pain of the parents when they find out later in the process that their children have been abused by the people the state then turned them over to. All under the pretense of protecting them from their abusive parents.

Then consider what in fact the state said constituted this so-called child abuse. A spanking! Because that is why this raid actually happened in 2008. This was not a case of us, as parents, beating our children, or sexually abusing them, not even a case of belt spanking as the state accused us of, but could never offer undeniable proof. They instead produced two very unreliable witnesses, who had grievances with us as their former landlords. One was a mentally challenged individual, the other his wife, and a spurned lover. Both of these people had severe personal problems of their own, yet the state was willing to use their false accusations to bring this case against us. Why would a state do this? For money! It goes on all the time!

Is it right to spank your child? Some argue against doing that under any circumstances, and it is the opinion of many that because a lot of people support that argument, we have the rise in crime we do have over the past few decades, and our children are growing up with no respect for any authority. But ever since the advent of the "Thou shalt not touch thy child" concept, this rise has continued. Many people across America support the other theory which says that a spanking now and then, for disciplinary purposes, done modestly, without intent to harm the child, is indeed a good thing because it teaches right from wrong. I happen to support this latter theory, which is why I found myself on the wrong side of the state.

Whichever side of this argument you agree with, I think that most of us can agree that children should be loved and protected from real harm. But when you remove a child from a family, where there is love, even if they do believe in spankings, you do much more harm to the children than what spankings could ever do. You cannot make a comparison. If matters are so serious in a home that a child should be taken away, then I agree it should be done. But in that event, the harm should also suffice to bring criminal charges against the parents. But it doesn't work that way under the disguise of child protection involving Child Protective Services, simply another government bureaucracy that is not needed by the people. If you make it a criminal matter, as it should be, you need only your local police and the courts. Then let the adoption agencies fend for the children, because in the event of criminal conviction, a child really should have another home. But we don't need agencies seeking to make money draining our national budget while falsifying the need of protection for the sake of money! And that's just what we have under CPS. As a result, kids and parents who are not criminals suffer emotional scars that can never be mended.

For many who feel that critics of CPS are few and far between and that something like this only occurs to parents who, indeed, cross the line of abuse, let me express how easy it is for something like this to happen to you, as it did to me. Put simply, if you ever spank your child, you could be subject to the same type of events my wife and I experienced. In some cases, parents win their children back, as we were able to do. In other cases, they never see them again until they turn eighteen, at which time the state boots them out of foster care programs to become homeless on the streets. Why? Because the states at that point, no longer get federal dollars for them! All that care and concern the state professes, suddenly vanishes!

This book goes into all of that and more. In my view, and the view of thousands of other parents who have gone through the agony of dealing with CPS, the states should be held accountable for this wrongful kidnapping of their children. Some parents fight back, as we did, and the states retaliate strongly when you do. But the need to fight back is so important, that we never let it stop us, and that is what all parents in this country must do to put a stop to the government supported kidnapping rings existing under our current legal system, a system run amock, and headed by Child Protective Services (CPS).

In my view, any state that takes custody of any person's child, should be required to justify their actions publicly and should have to answer each of the following two questions with a firm yes answer before they are given the authority to do so:

(1) Is the removal of the child to be placed in foster care really needed and in the best interest of the child?

(2) Is the state willing and prepared to be a subject of legal lawsuits in the event their decisions is proven wrong?

If they cannot firmly say yes to each of those questions, they have no basis for disrupting the lives of any family in this country.

Contents

This book is lovingly dedicated to my girls Caitlyn and Ashley for having been unwillingly taken away from their loving family to endure this traumatic experience.
And to all those children who have been torn from their loving families that were loved and needed in their lives, to one day be reunited with their loved ones.
To all those who helped make this book a reality.
To my loving wife, who stood by and supported me through the entire process.
I Love You!

—Chapter One—

The Life Of A Landlord

Don't ever think that owning apartment buildings is an easy way of life. While it can be profitable, if you run your business appropriately, it brings with it a set of adversarial problems that can, at best, be difficult to cope with. It would be a good idea, if you are contemplating entering in to this kind of business, that you first bone up on legal issues and if possible, seek a good attorney to provide you with legal advice.

In most cases, eviction of tenants is carried out because either a tenant did not pay his rent or engaged in activities resulting in property damage. But in our case, it was the vindictive action of disgruntled tenants that created the basis for our problems. These vindictive efforts, in our case, included the gathering of several tenants at a local bar to discuss how to make life difficult for us, as their landlords. It was, to say the least, an *organized effort* by a group of tenants who were unhappy because we had evicted friends of their group. I walked in on them at one of their meetings, to find them discussing how they could hit back at us. One of them popped off to me at that time, that they could nail us as landlords, by merely charging us with child abuse. They knew we had children, and although at this point in time, none of them had actually gone so far as to do this, it was now out in the open that it was their intent to do so. I dismissed it at the time as merely a collective voice of a group of drinkers, but would later find out, some were serious in this sinister method of inflicting revenge. In this bar meeting, the *seed* had indeed been planted. It would only be a matter of time before one truly disgruntled and vindictive tenant would actually try to do this. So, vindictive or not, such claims by disgruntled people can be of value to a corrupt state government, when the desire of such a government would be to misconstrue or manufacture *facts* with which they can pursue a child abuse case against their chosen target. My own case with the state of Michigan is the basis of this book, but it is one of only *many* such cases in Michigan state. So many came to the front, that the state became the subject (shortly after our case concluded) of a well publicized class action lawsuit from people such as myself— a case the state lost! What we would discover, through our own experience, was that the state would seize upon the manufactured charges of vengeful people in our lives to break up our family and remove our kids for well over a year, while we fought the battle to get them back. They would go so far as to use the hearsay of biased tenants, going back to the time well before our case came to fruition, to try to justify the state's own unlawful actions.

I should start by telling you, as the reader of this book, that I have *never* abused my kids. Not with my biological kids that I've had with my wife Janet, nor with my step child Caitlyn, who was the focus of the state kidnapping story I'm about to unveil. I love my children beyond all else in life, and when I display anger in this book, forgive me, but it is in response to the phony claims of child abuse this state made against me and my wife. When a state goes against you, it was my experience that they will pull out all the stops to *make you guilty,* whether or not you actually are. If you make it to their most wanted list, they will invent their own set of facts to shade a truth, distort facts, or plain out lie to make it *appear* to a jury that you have been a terrible, abusive parent, not fit to retain the custody of your children. They will make you appear to be *dangerous,* whether or not you actually are. In my case, I am big, have a booming voice, contentious (yes, I will admit that), but not at all dangerous. I have never so much as ever had a physical fight in school. But due to some of those outward appearance factors I just cited, it is quite easy for a cunning prosecutor to paint me as dangerous, particularly if they introduce lies to support their theories, which is exactly what this state did. Their intent, of course, is the present things in a way that will make you *appear* guilty to a jury they wish to influence. They will do anything to win a case, as I found out, with their ultimate objective to win the money which the federal government provides, to care for the children they kidnap.

In my case, I made the state's *hit list* due to their unsuccessful effort to prosecute me in the case of my neighbor, John Cain, as you will read about in chapter two. So the state needed a stronger case, hopefully based on statements from someone who would not appear to have conflicts of interest, as happened in the Cain affair. Their chance came when they were able to use some very *unstable acquaintances* of mine, along with the history of the first group of disenchanted renters, to bring bogus charges against my wife and I. I made the biggest mistake of my life in attempting to help this couple, Rebecca and Bobby Payne, and in allowing myself to become close enough to Becky (Rebecca) to result in a short affair. I will always regret that mistake.

As you will see, when we discuss the events of 2008 and 2009, the years that followed those initial bogus charges, it took only the word of a government official, with no physical proof whatsoever, to cast the kind of shadow that would allow the state to take my kids hostage. As you read the ensuing chapters, you will see how the events played out, and how the state of Michigan was able to manipulate the events, claiming to exercise "protective rights" as the basis for committing a kidnapping of my children. When I fought it, and confronted them with arguments my wife and I made, they tried to cover it up and shape the events to suit their own purposes, even to the extent of instructing a court on how to behave. A court, they, in fact, controlled. You might *think* your state is answerable to a court. But don't be too certain. In Michigan, at least in the county where our case was heard, it was a case of a court working hand in hand with a prosecutor to establish a case result that would favor the state's false claims, resulting in revenue building for the state.

—Chapter Two—

The Cain Incident

John Cain and his family were neighbors, sitters for our kids, and I *thought* our friends. But on January 29, 2006, I would learn the hard truth of the matter. My step daughter, Caitlyn, was in their care that night. When I came to pick her up that night, she decided (as children sometimes do) to play hide and seek in the kitchen. Caitlyn did not want to come home. When she still refused, I went in, picked her up, and administered a disciplinary spanking. When I left for home, I thought that was the end of that. But the next morning would prove differently. I woke up about 9:00 a.m., and as we began dressing the kids and preparing for the day, I discovered some abrasions on Caitlyn's back. Naturally, I asked her what happened. She told me she fell off a ball at "grandma's house" (the way she referred to the Cain household). I then visited the Cain residence, leveling a little criticism because they did not tell me about the incident. That resulted in some unpleasant exchanges. When I left the Cain house that morning, I called the police (the Ironwood Public Safety Department or IPSD). I was not aware at that time that the Cains had also reported me to the Ironwood Public Safety Department for spanking Caitlyn that same night. Perhaps they feared I might blame them for the ball incident, and in fact, report them. It could account for the *gross exaggerations* contained in their own report, filed with the Ironwood officials. That report was enough to result in officials visiting our family the following day, after they had first visited the Cain house.

Public Safety Officer (PSO) Chad Novascone and Police Sargeant Ron Carpenedo were sent out for the visit, and the resulting Carpendo report was both shocking and a total surprise to me. To me, his report was blown so far out of proportion, that it was at once an obvious *slant* intended to express his views in the manner he intended for them to be interpreted, and far from the truth. Were those *slants,* contained in his report, put there out of loyalty to his friend, John Cain, who was a city commissioner he knew well? I did not know. But I did know that attempts were being made to portray me as a vicious and violent parent, a sexual pervert, and a danger to my kids. I am none of these things.

There was more to my acquaintance with Ron Carpenedo than this visit, however, so perhaps it was more than his friendship to Cain that inspired his volatile attack on me in his report. In nearly my first day in Ironwood, he stopped me to ticket me for a minor violation— my introduction to him. He was arrogant to me then, and we established a common feeling of dislike for each other, even from that day. I would soon find out he was to be involved in nearly every aspect of the events to come surrounding the state kidnapping of my children.

Little did I know at the time the state of Michigan had a history for presenting these types of children's cases. There were numerous reports at the time my case unfolded and the state was thriving on these cases, building false cases as they went about prosecuting them, and greatly exaggerating the details contained in their cases. I was learning about the state's child kidnapping ring, condoned and supported by the medical profession, state protective officials, law enforcement officials, and even the courts themselves. Perhaps that explains Carpenedo's portrayal of me in such a light. As a member of the system, it strikes fear in your heart. Who, in their right mind, would dare to oppose such a large, coordinated system, of which you are a mere pawn? Perhaps it is not until you become such a pawn, and lose everything dear to you in life, that you might not care about your own security any longer and might choose to fight back. I think that is what happened in our case. I had no idea at the time, but in future events, I was about to lose my children to the state, my business, and possibly my wife due to a bad choice in the events to come. And Ron Carpenedo would play a huge part in this later case.

The effort to frame us in this event, however, might also explain why, when we requested our own doctors check out our kids, the state intervened and insisted on having their own doctors do it. In ensuing medical reports, from their state doctors, views other than medical found their way into the reports. I found this intriguing, and it was clear that law enforcement was attempting to influence the medical findings.

Of course, when an event such as this one is unfolding, parents are first, confused, frightened, and without an understanding as to what is happening. No parent would imagine, or foresee, the corrupt methods that would be used against them to set them up as perceived *perpetrators.* It is impossible in the beginning to see how one element of the kidnapping ring works with the other to *characterize* and *victimize* the parents. What is most shameful is that tax dollars, collected from these same parents (as well as other unknowing taxpayers) are used to support their corrupt activities.

Was John Cain, the commissioner who lived next door to us, aware of the state's great scam? Was his fear of a state that could be so ruthless, the motivating factor in his reporting me, before, as he might have feared, I might report him? I would not presume to answer that question, but I do know the state saw this an opportunity to go after Robert Coleman, considering they now had the word of a commissioner to back up any bogus charges they might produce. It appeared ironclad, in that they now had someone within their own circle, who they could all support, bringing about the abuse claims. Ironically, this same Cain, who was so concerned about my spanking of Caitlyn had previously defended one of my former tenants, charged with killing his own baby! Yet, because I dared confront him over an injury to my daughter, he became hell bent to go after me. So you see, when a political figure becomes personally involved, the police, the medical establishment, the state protective agencies, and even the courts tend to bond together in their attempts to persecute the person they seek to exert their powers on. To this day, I'm not sure how I escaped their wrath in this single event, but they were only waiting until they had a second opportunity to go after me, to lay a better plan.

The events to come in my life taught me well. They say that experience is the best teacher, and for sure, that holds true in this case. I wanted, throughout the course of these events to be able to tell my side, to reveal to people what I was learning first-hand, but there was no platform for doing it. It has become my challenge, since the return of my children, for me to be able to tell others about the rings, to show them the degree of state collaboration in framing innocent (or mild offending) parents. I wanted to illustrate just how far the state will go to fight you if you choose to fight back. But how? I finally settled on the writing of this book. It would illustrate how they went about it in my case, and using the references I will include also, you can also see how they have gone about it in other cases, and to what extent they will go to protect their kidnapping rings.

So please indulge me for a moment, as I explain to you the makeup of these state rings. The first thing your ring needs, if you are the operator of ring, is a good police report that highlights the personified abuser in a negative manner. A manner that can be shown to a jury later during the trial phase of the operation. In this case, Sergeant Carpenedo was the exact thing the state needed to launch their phony case. In his report, he made sure to include his opinions, statements conveyed by him, indicating the Cain family had told him that Caitlyn was afraid of me and that the slap (spank) given to Caitlyn was loud enough for John Cain to hear in the next adjacent room. The truth is, it doesn't take that loud of slap (spank) to make such a thing possible. Carpenedo saw fit to state that one person at the Cain home discussed other past incidents they had heard about involving my disciplinary actions. These were not verified, nor documented, but they still managed to find their way into Carpenedo's report. Why would an officer even include such hearsay comments unless it was his full intent to frame me as a dangerous villain? But his efforts did not end there. He elaborated on his views (his views) indicating I became very upset and that it was his opinion that Caitlyn had been coached on what to say. Why? Because she would not directly tell him what he wanted to hear? Carpenedo made a major emphasis in his report, highlighting the movements of members of our family in our home on the night of the baby sitting incident, as well as on the following morning. To cite an example, he questioned Caitlyn as to who gave her a bath. When it was confirmed it was me, he wanted to know if I did this in the nude. The only way that becomes a factor, is if his intent is to then report me as a sexual child molester. I would learn later, that was indeed his intent. After all, that would be reason to keep the kids forever, and make a lot more money. It was unfortunate for the state that their own medical exams would not support that. The point, however, is that an effort was made to try to set me up for charges a lot more serious, perhaps even criminal. How wonderful it would be if they could get a state kidnapping that produced money, and nail Robert Coleman with a criminal charge at the same time! In any case, in the state's hope to find something more serious, they use a dummied up police report as the basis for later court ordered medical testing, which is precisely what took place in our case a little later. Still not satisfied, Carpenedo added more opinions, allegedly relating to Caitlyn's comments.

As any parent recognizes, a child will become somewhat contradictory when they feel pressure or feel they might be in trouble. So did Caitlyn fall on the exercise ball, as she told us (and investigators), or was she, in fact, injured by my spanking abuse (the case the prosecutors wanted to make)? Most kids will tell you (if asked) that spankings hurt, which is what Caitlyn told investigators, but she reiterated that she fell on the ball. Somehow, though, the ball issue did not seem important to the investigators, who were hell bent on making spanking the central issue.

Secondary, in a corrupt kidnapping ring, following the procurement of a favorable police report, would be a good medical report, supporting the drummed up police and social service reports. Such a report can then be used to take to the next level. Every effort was made to show this in Caitlyn's medical examination, given by Dr. Leaann Schroeder, the chosen physician of the state in this case. Her report, on February 1, 2006, followed the Cain incident and the police and social service interviews of the PSO. The state made certain that Elizabeth Fyle, a representative of the Michigan Family Independence Agency, which is an arm of CPS (Child Protective Services), would accompany my wife and I to have Caitlyn examined. It was clear she was there to try to influence a finding for something that might suggest a sudden discovery by this doctor of some form of child abuse. Why would she not wait first for an independent examination by a physician of our choosing, before insisting on the need to accompany us to a medical exam? When you know the entire procedure of the kidnapping rings, it becomes much more clear. Her purpose, from my observation, was simply to try to influence what could later become prosecutorial evidence, via her suggested list of things for the doctor to look for. So it was not too surprising, following the visit, once we discovered what she was about, that she would bring the pressure she did to the final version of the doctor's examination. As with the drummed up police report, the doctor's report included comments totally unrelated to a simple medical examination. They made sure to ask Caitlyn if she had been touched or fondled in her private area, I'm sure, with the hope she would confirm such a thing so they could implicate me. It was most unfortunate for the state's effort that Caitlyn denied any such thing had occurred, and in her report, the doctor had to report she saw no evidence to support such a thing either. It must have been very disappointing to them, following the best efforts of a police opinion and a CPO effort to find something—anything—they could to bolster their case. As for the injury itself, which is what they were supposed to be checking for, the doctor stated it was most likely caused by what she described as a classic rug burn. That was consistent with the story Caitlyn told about falling over the big ball. This doctor says it was her suspicion was that the injury probably occurred on the morning following the babysitting incident. Now why would she suspect that? That makes no sense at all! The rugs were in the Cain house, not ours! And the ball she rolled over was their ball as well! It all seems like a well planted theory—perhaps suggested by Ms. Fyle? You will discover as we go through the events of this entire story, it was not one bit beneath her dignity to lie about this, or anything else, as she did in so many other elements of our future case. In any case, it appeared to me the doctor had help developing her suspicions. She did have the sense to qualify her statement a bit, however, by adding, "It is conceivable it could have occurred the night prior." How about probable, since, from the onset, it was what Caitlyn was claiming. Again, though, you must remember the purpose was to set me up for character assassination, so they could build a false case for their child kidnapping effort. Also, remember, it was a duel purpose: they also had to subdue any allegations against one of their own—John Cain. That was probably the reason this case was dropped. The real remaining question though, is if these were opinions only—why did they feel the urgent need to put that in writing?

Even more intriguing about her report was another opinion she felt compelled to include. She said that while we were there, I did ninety-nine percent of the talking. Why did she need to say that? It's true, I talk a lot. Is there something wrong with that? She is the one given the privilege of writing the final report. I don't get to. So what difference does it make as to how much I had to say while the medical exam was taking place? Was this just another deliberate attempt to characterize Robert Coleman? Were they setting me up to appear uncontrollable to a future jury? In conflicting statements in her report, the doctor quoted Caitlyn as stating the injury occurred at grandma's house, when she slipped off the exercise ball. Yet in her report, the doctor also indicated it was not likely the injury occurred that night - the very night she was at grandma's house. It was apparent to me later, that this was a concentrated effort to try to show the injury occurred in the morning at my house, so they could then frame my wife and I as abusive, or inattentive or neglectful.

Finally, there was this quote, inserted by the doctor. It was regarding a question to Caitlyn, in which she asked Caitlyn if she was otherwise injured or hurt in any way, other than falling over the ball. She said that Caitlyn responded to her by saying, "Yes, my daddy always spanks me." So the question becomes, when there is only one injury to look at, and she had already ascertained it was a classic rug burn, why did she find it necessary to include that statement in her report? Certainly, this was not at all related to the injury she was asked to look at, but it would surely influence a non-suspecting jury who are being told by Elizabeth Fyle that Robert Coleman is a dangerous man.

As it turned out, the very next day, on February 2, 2006, Sergeant Carpenedo called Trooper Steve Koskela of the Department Of State Police, asking him to meet at the Ironwood Public Safety Department. Once there, he asked Trooper Koskela to take over this investigation of child abuse, indicating he wanted to avoid any conflict of interest, because John Cain, the complainant in the case, was on the Ironwood City Council. It is funny how that was not an important factor when he first came to my house and did his initial interview and report. Perhaps he had second thoughts about that.

Trooper Koskela then met with Chief Assistant Prosecutor Tracie Wittla regarding the complaint. She requested that he re-interview my wife and I. In his report, on February 16, he reported that I was not willing to take a polygraph test, citing correctly my opinion that it was a waste of time. A month after that, Trooper Koskela spoke again with Wittla, regarding the complaint, and she advised him to close it out, saying there was not enough evidence to prosecute. She advised Trooper Koskela she would let DHS (the Department of Human Services) know of her decision, and for the time being, this was behind us. We would learn later, however, that it was not forgotten, and would be resurrected when the time was right.

—Chapter Three—

The Affair

Rebecca (Becky) Payne and Robert (Bobby) Payne entered our lives as tenants at one of our apartments in July of 2007. Call it pity, or any other term you might care to apply to it, but in my quest to assist them during their difficult times, my life would take a new turn.

It was in that same month the Paynes moved in that a bad rain storm damaged a portion of an addition we were building. Rebecca and Bobby both came and assisted with our cleanup effort, and we were most appreciative. One thing led to another, and soon we found them helping out with other small odd jobs, after indicating to us they were bored and had nothing better to do. It wasn't long until they were going to church with us, and at the end of the month, I recall Janet broke a tooth. Since Janet's dentist could not schedule her, Rebecca was able to get Janet in to see her dentist. Although Janet did not consider Becky's dentist to be a good one, she still went, and we appreciated the good will effort extended to us by Rebecca.

Meanwhile, to me, Don and Rosemary Christopher were like substitute parents. After the death of my mother, they stepped in and helped my wife and I in every way you can imagine, including with assistance in establishing my business. At the very end of July, 2007, after the Paynes had become tenants, the Christophers came to visit us, and during that time we took time out to have fun and travel to Ashland and Duluth. Rosemary observed Becky and Bobby and I still recall her expressing at that time that she regarded Becky as *trouble.* I saw it a bit differently, perhaps choosing not to see it. It is quite possible even that I may have found Rebecca's *flirting* to be somewhat enjoyable. In any event, I could never have known how right Rosemary's assessment would turn out to be. To describe the Paynes, I guess you might think of Bobby as a bit *slow,* and for sure a bit of a mental case. My step daughter, Caitlyn, always called him dit-dit because it took him so long to complete his words and sentences. It was a nickname that stuck, and it became difficult to know him by his real name as time went on. As for Becky, my step daughter today still describes her as never being able to tell the truth - a chronic liar, and my take, once I got over my infatuation with her, was exactly the same. Perhaps I didn't see it at first, due to my own unwillingness to see it, but before this case was anywhere near completion, it became crystal clear! As we would learn, the Paynes were both also very vengeant, as well as deceitful. Just a few years after the events described in this book, I hired a private investigating company to check out the backgrounds of the main players, who were instrumental in ruining our lives, destroying our business, and putting us all through what can only be describe as pure hell. I want to take the time here to thank *Duvall Group Investigations, P.O. Box 1822, Monroe, Michigan,* for helping me uncover some interesting things about Becky, to illustrate some of the fine qualities I've just mentioned. Residing in five different cities, covering the years 2003 to 2011, she used five different names. Probably so she could cover up her one crime on her record, which we discuss in more detail when we cover her testimony in our trial for child abuse. But those names, in case anyone should be looking to find her, are as follows:

Rebecca J. Petersen

Rebecca J. Jensen

Becky J. Payne

Rebecca J. Payne

Becky J. Jensen

The cities she lived in over the years I related are:

Lincoln, Nebraska

Santa Maria, California

Oceano, California

Burt, Michigan

Ironwood, Michigan

We bring this up because during our trial she claimed on the stand that she was not wanted for any crimes, when in fact, she did have an active warrant out at that time for an offense in Nebraska. So it was this kind of deceit, mixed with vengeance that resulted in events which would transcend the lives of everyone in my family.

It was September of that year when the Payne's moved into one of our apartments. Later on, they would change their original apartment to one directly above our own. Near the end of October, at the time my wife Janet became aware of her pregnancy with our daughter Britney, Becky tagged along with Janet for her scheduled doctor's appointment. Once home, following that visit, Becky began gossiping to Janet's friends that she was also pregnant—with a baby that I had fostered! It was not the case, but nevertheless it was a claim that stereotyped the type of personality we were dealing with. This discussion of course led to a series of conflicts between Janet and Becky, and although I had not admitted it to this point, I was having a sideline affair with Becky. Janet, of course, had reason to suspect it.

In early January, at a time when both my wife and I visited our doctors, both sick and under great stress, Janet's doctor advised me to get Rebecca out from under Janet's feet. It seemed to Janet, by now, that Rebecca was attempting to take over her house.

Becky, however, was only part of our problem. At just about the same time things were coming to a head with her and my wife, we began to become involved with the psychological problems of Bobby, Becky's husband. Janet became Bobby's payee for his disability due to his own inability to cope, culminating in his doctors' visit in Watersmeet in February. Bobby's treatment was pertaining to suicidal thoughts and behavior. It was on January 21, 2008, that Bobby's problems seemed to become quite acute, when a police report described his possible suicide attempts. He was admitted the next day to Marquette General Hospital for in patient treatment. Earlier that week I called there and the girl I spoke with on the phone referred to Bobby as the Nascar driver, and said, "Yes, he is here." It was quite clear to me at that point, that he was not just suicidal, but delusional as well, because he never was a Nascar driver.

In February, 2008, the Paynes requested permission to move into our basement, indicating their intent to move back to California in short order, after Bobby got his disability check. I said she needed to talk to Janet about that, but Janet said, "No." Despite my wife having told them that, Rebecca began sneaking her things in to the basement anyway, just prior to Valentine's Day. Had I done what I should have, I would have tossed them out, but adding to the bad decisions I was making at the time, I allowed them to stay.

Everything came to a head on March 10 of that year. That was the day Janet had had enough of the arguing and other chaos of the couple. Bobby began arguing with Becky about her affair, in the process throwing a glass frame at her, which contained their wedding license. Naturally, it broke all over, and Caitlyn, in her effort to move out of the way, stepped on the glass, severely cutting her foot. That was all for Janet. She ordered them both out of the house. This time Janet would have her way. We advised them that we were going to Walmart, and that upon our return we would devise a way for them to leave. While we were at Walmart, the Paynes left our house, taking my police scanner and my wallet, so that I would not be able to hear their phone call to the police, nor have access to my own identification.

The very next day, all hell broke loose! It started with a call from the police requesting me to come into the department. I quickly responded, and upon arrival I was served a personal protective order (PPO). It had been filed by the Paynes, who had also reported us for child abuse! I knew for a fact it was actually in retaliation for our actions the day prior, but police and other state officials were not about to hear any of that. It was, after all, just another *opportunity* to nail Robert Coleman, after their failed efforts in the past. Even though, this time, it was based only on the word of the spurned Payne couple, and even though neither was exactly a stable complainant, the officals seemed almost thrilled at this opportunity to pursue us again.

Devastated, I felt the need to level with Janet. So I admitted the affair, and began to realize at that moment what a terrific woman I had in my life. Her great strength in handling my infidelity, coupled with her strength throughout all the hell we were about to encounter from the state of Michigan, would be trying, to say the least. The trials were so unwarranted, for her especially, because she was guilty of nothing. The very largest regret of my life is that I ever put her through this. It is a position she never deserved to be in. I will spend the remainder of my days in an attempt to make amends for this undeserved fate.

—Chapter Four—

The Investigation

Janet and I had our long talk, discussed our own personal problem, and then began wondering, together, how seriously anyone could take this *wacky couple* we had just kicked out of our household. A couple seemed bent on revenge. The charges they had filed were completely false, exaggerated to such a degree that it seemed improbable that *anyone* could consider them as valid. The complainants (the Paynes) in the police log, indicated they had personally witnessed me hit my step daughter, Caitlyn, with a leather belt on her bare buttocks, leaving marks. They also indicated I had struck my younger daughter, Ashley. Had that been the extent of the complaint, we would probably have had nothing to worry about, in that it came from the sources it did. But the Paynes went above and beyond in filing their complaint, feeding the frenzy of a state already seeking me as a prime target due to their failed missions in the past to make a charge stick. Thus, when the Department of Human Services and the Ironwood Public Safety Department officer visited our house to do their investigation, it was their prime mission, so it seemed, to find something—*anything*—with which to go after us.

What Rebecca and Bobby had reported to DHS could have reflected a dangerous home life environment for my children, had any of it been true. But an amateur investigator would have been able to see through it, much less people who are supposed to be professionals. It further illustrates the *will of the state* to create and manufacture *false evidence* that can later be used in a court of law to win a conviction, with *profit* the usual goal, but in our case, *revenge of the state* another of their goals in bringing this case. Many state abuse cases have been widely reported in Michigan, in which similar claims were presented, which would support our allegations. (See my website referred to under *references* in the back of this book). So in that it is not just *my* case, but in fact a multitude of others, perhaps you'll keep an open mind as you read about my own experiences.

What was most intriguing to me was what the DHS put into their *investigative findings report* following their visit to our house. Included were quotes my kids and I had allegedly made in Bobby's presence. Remember, this was the guy who was put into the Marquette Hospital mental ward, and thought, among other things, that he was a Nascar driver, and was constantly under observation for suicidal thoughts. He was quoted in the DHS report as having said that I had threatened Caitlyn because she would not eat her rice. In his words, he told DHS I was "going to give her the belt." And he said that at that point, Caitlyn backed up and said, "No, daddy, no!" Well, of course this was all manufactured. What was even more remarkable to me however, was that in later formal reports, those filing the reports used those *same words* having supposedly heard them from Caitlyn. But as of this writing, Caitlyn (then 6, now 10 years of age) says she never said those things. Bobby even told them that I instructed *him* to go get the belt, which he says, I used. He indicated he did it, out of fear of me (another lie). So it was this sort of thing that both he and Rebecca were manufacturing in order to seek their vengeance. It was falsified, of course, but nonetheless made good, quotable material for an anxious state to put in a report. It is quite interesting to discuss this now with my step daughter, Caitlyn, who is at the time of this book writing, ten years of age. Her comments about the *rice reports* are that those charges make her laugh, because she *loves* rice. And she says now that she thinks Bobby created those outlandish belt remarks because *he* would have enjoyed seeing her get hit with a belt! Interesting concept? Yes, I think so!

Probably even more outlandish in the *investigative findings report* of DHS, was their own description of the visit they made to our home. Officer Sheryl Saippa from the local City Of Ironwood Public Safety Department (IPSD) showed up for the home visit, accompanied by DHS case workers Bob Ross and Elizabeth Fyle, who is probably the number one head-hunter for the state in that area, and whose lies and exaggerations are quoted throughout this book. You might recall, in our earlier experience, she was the one who went with us to the state doctor to examine Caitlyn at that point. And it was her comments that were opinionated, as we have already pointed out. It is interesting that it was *she* who, in this latest case, chose to come to the house to do the investigation! Was it because she wanted to make sure this time that her *manufactured comments* would be more apt to stick? After all, this time she would not be up against a conflict of interest, as she was with the first case, where Carpenedo and Cain could clearly be shown as friends. And rather than getting her personal views incorporated into a medical report, as she attempted to do in the first case, she could instead *manufacture* what my step daughter said to her behind closed doors, knowing full well she would not testify in a trial. Therefore, she could just take the words of Bobby and Becky, knowing they were simply statements of revenge, and *manufacture* them into something Caitlyn was supposed to have said. As an interesting tidbit to our story, it should be noted that while Ross and Fyle were busy interviewing our children in another room, Officer Saippa let it slip to me, and I quote: "You know, the chief of police (Robert Erspamer) has got it in for you!" So now you had two cops who wanted to see me go down—Carpenedo and Erspamer! This was not a great revelation to me, of course, because the chief and I had an altercation at a City Council meeting on September 10, 2007. At that time, angry with me, he physically pushed me out of the meeting because I had dared voice my feelings that I would not tolerate the type of treatment I had received during the course of that meeting. It was all centered over my meeting complaint that the IPSD was not enforcing the barking dog ordinances. Mayor Bruce Noren stated in that meeting that the City of Ironwood ordinance did not address barking dogs. But the City Attorney, Dennis Cossi, who disliked me in any case because of lawsuits he had brought in previous cases against me, including my divorce case, tried his best to make little of my remarks, adding such comments as, "Robert always complains about something," and "he likes to complain." He informed the meeting that I had "other issues" and that barking dogs was not the only one. It is irritating to be treated in this fashion at any public meeting, but even more so if the motive for it is revenge. Hence my comments regarding my treatment in that meeting. My main contention at that meeting, of course, was my stated view the police department was having problems writing out tickets for these offenses. As it was, one of the ladies complained about was a relative to one of the city's police officers. Gosh, you don't think that might have had something to do with an officer looking the other way, do you? Could it be the police chief took exception to my statements and felt the need at the conclusion of my testimony, as I returned to my seat, to sneer at me? I informed him, quite verbally, that I would not tolerate abuse from him either. At that moment, he jumped up, grabbed me, pushing me out of the door and out of the meeting. Since I am not one to take this lying down, the very next day I brought my complaint of his pushing incident to the state police. Nothing came of it, of course, but it should explain *clearly* what the *motive* of this police chief was in creating a child abuse case against me when the opportunity presented itself.

In any event, Bob Ross and Elizabeth Fyle, with Fyle virtually forcing her way into our house, began the process of interviewing my step daughter, Caitlyn. Having expressed our concerns about our *parental rights* in this matter, an expression they seemed bent to ignore, we managed, about three minutes into the interview, to get our attorney on the phone. This, after we were refused the right to sit in on the interview. Our attorney at the time (Mike Pope) told us someone had to be present at the interview, so Janet walked in on the interview, being conducted in an Caitlyn bedroom. Bob Ross got up quickly, and escorted Janet out of the room, leaving Fyle alone in the interview with Caitlyn. Their meeting concluded some five minutes or so later, at which time they brought our youngest daughter, Ashley, into the room. After another few minutes, they emerged, commenting, "She didn't say much of anything"—adding, "Ashley only showed us her bed," which I am sure was true because Ashley was immensely proud of her new toddler bed! For Fyle this must have been an expression of her disappointment, which might explain why, in later court hearings, it would take Fyle two hours to explain what took place in roughly ten minutes of interviewing time?

The *investigative findings report* resulted in the DHS describing us as *hesitant* at first. Gee, can anyone understand why that might have been the case? First, they *shove their way* into your house, *deny your parental rights,* and basically *ignore you* as they go about their invasion of your home. They indicated in their report that Caitlyn stated she had to *go to the corner* when in trouble and that she also *gets the belt.* Asked to explain about the belt, the DHS report says Caitlyn replied, "He smacks me," indicating it was me (daddy) doing the "smacking." And the report says she said it happened "many times." The truth is, words contained in that report were words that were not even a part of Caitlyn's vocabulary. Never had she ever heard or used the word "smack." That is but one example of the words planted by Elizabeth Fyle to build a false case. If you read the report, and what is purported to have been said, there are many cases of misstatements, total fabrications, and third party claims that could obviously be traced to the lies and claims made directly by Bobby and Becky in the initial complaint lodged with officials. Why, unless an attempt was being purposely made by DHS to *create a case* would third party claims be inserted into an investigative report, falsely claiming they were comments of my step daughter, who could not possibly have used those words? Let me cite just some of the false claims and quotes, with the quotes supposedly from my step daughter, that were first, impossible; and second, quite apparently taken directly from the Paynes:

(1) The DHS report said Caitlyn was *willing* to speak to them. That was a direct lie, as in reality, she was *frightened* to speak to them. At this writing, in fact, Caitlyn claims that what happened, after entering the bedroom, she and her sister played with toys for the entire discussion. (Fyle stated that did not happen, that she was not *distracted* by toys). Caitlyn says Elizabeth sat her on the bed, and Bob was trying to make sure she did not leave—which Caitlyn says *scared her.* Bob started by saying to her, "How are you doing?" Caitlyn's response was "Great." It was then Elizabeth's turn, and she asked her, "How is your family? What is going on?" Caitlyn says again she said, "Good, and it's fine." At which point Elizabeth asked her, "Does your mom or dad hit you with a belt?" Caitlyn says she told them no, but that the state workers tried to scare her into saying yes . As her parent, and knowing now what I know about this state, I do believe that if Caitlyn had said "yes" at that very point, the state would have taken them that very day. It was about this time, according to Caitlyn, that Janet came in, and Bob left her alone with Elizabeth. Elizabeth, according to Caitlyn, then laid down on the bed with her feet still on the floor, running her fingers through her hair, and making what Caitlyn now describes as a *sighing* sound. She then got up, and began playing with the dolls with Caitlyn. She then asked Caitlyn, "Does your father love you?" Caitlyn acknowleged that her father did love her, and then, according to Caitlyn came one more question, and we quote, "Does your dad beat you on your tush?" Caitlyn says she answered, "No, why?" Elizabeth gave no answer and got up, leaving the room.

(2) The DHS report said that when in trouble, Caitlyn was made to go to the corner and that she

also gets *the belt.* Once this report was made available to us, long *after* this initial invasion of our house, it became crystal clear to us that this quote came directly from the Paynes, not Caitlyn. In the first place, we never used a belt on our kids. But we *did* have conversations with the Paynes in which we discussed differing forms of discipline we had all grown up with. Among the methods discussed were the belt, but also the use of wooden spoons, brooms, and so on. Oddly, *all of those items* made their way into this DHS report, yet Janet and I did not even *own* most of these items. And why, when DHS was *searching* our house, as they *did do,* were these items not uncovered? It was quite obvious these were third party *planted ideas,* contributed by the Paynes—not by Caitlyn. We understood the motives of the Paynes (revenge). But why would Bob Ross or Elizabeth Fyle make up such lies, using input from third parties they claim came from our step daughter? Unless, of course, it was to support their local law enforcement people who wanted to "take us down." Or to support Fyle's own desire to do so, having failed in her first attempt at getting doctors to insert *opinions* in state medical reports which would support Fyle's own desired version of events to allow for bringing a stronger case in the Cain matter? I question still what kind of professional would ever write into a report such third party information under the guise of it originating from a child who could not possibly make such claims? Is that not a *criminal act* on the part of a case worker?

(3) The DHS report said I used an orange belt. I did not even own one then, nor have I ever. The one belt they dug out of my dresser, which Elizabeth Fyle described as orange, was in fact, brown. But it was the largest and thickest one. It was conveniently coincidental that this was the belt Elizabeth Fyle focused on since it would be the best to try to use as an abuse weapon. It was also coincidental that they found my belts in that dresser drawer, because I did not even know where they were. I hardly ever used a belt, and the only way they could know where they would find them is if they were advised by someone who had lived in the house that I kept them there (which Fyle admitted to in the trial). The Paynes knew where I kept everything, having basically lived in my house, and I'm certain told the DHS exactly *where* to look, and the DHS did, in fact, *ask* about the drawer when they were doing their search. Why would they *ask,* unless they already *knew* where my belts might be found. And I don't think that the idea I did own belts amounts to much—most people do own belts. But as it was described as an *orange belt* in both their report and the complaint lodged by the Paynes, it would not look too good if they wrote they found a brown one, would it? Not if you are in the process of trying to *create a case.* And we should also remember, Bobby thought he was a Nascar driver. It was quite possible he thought I spanked my kids with an orange belt, even if it did not exist. So Fyle would later expand on her report to say Caitlyn told her and perhaps Caitlyn viewed a brown, faded belt, as orange. Our supposition is, that description came from the Paynes, and was inserted into this report as though it were from Caitlyn.

(4) The DHS report claimed my wife and I were presented the allegations when they came to the house. We were not. We were only told a complaint had been filed. That was all. The long list of *allegations* was not presented to us at the time this visitation was made. Likewise their report claimed that correct protocol had been followed. It was not.

Had these so-called *investigators* actually been trying to do their jobs, instead of trying to build a false case against us, they could easily have seen the fraudulent efforts of the Paynes to mislead them. They could have easily followed up on why we suddenly found audits being conducted by virtually all of our utility companies, told by *unnamed sources* that we were committing fraud in the usage of our electricity, cable, and more. Isn't it odd? The timing of this was at the very same time that the child abuse claims came in— immediately after the Paynes were asked to leave our household. In addition to that, there were also witnesses, who the state seemingly could not find, who heard Becky proudly claim that she wanted to adopt my kids, and that she was happy her and Bobby screwed us over via their child abuse accusations. But if a state is in the business of child kidnapping, I guess it all makes sense.

—Chapter Five—

"The Raid"

It never ceases to amaze me how a state can get so worked up over child abuse when there is no proof it is actually occurring with ordinary people, yet remain so aloof when there is evidence of it in one of their foster homes. We will discuss the latter part of that in subsequent chapters, but to set the plate for this one, let's just say it was apparent we were already tried and convicted in the mind of Michigan authorities based on the claims of two very vengeful and unreliable people who were obviously biased and bent on revenge.

Not knowing that at the time, of course, we continued to go on with our daily lives as best we could, so we headed for our previously arranged doctor visit for Janet in Houghton, just a few hours drive from our home in Ironwood. Elizabeth Fyle, after her unannounced surprise visit to our home, had not addressed the matter of whether or not we could go out of town. So we just went about our normal daily planning, figuring we would hear from them when they were ready to contact us for whatever might come next, if anything. We decided to include some rest and relaxation time with Janet's doctor visit, so we could clear our minds over these recent events. The state had never indicated to us that they might become *paranoid* if we took a little time for travel, and since we did not have any court orders indicating we should not do so, in our minds, the entire *lie* or *invented episode* was behind us. Our visitors had warned us that if any further charges surfaced, we would lose our kids, so to us, that is where the matter stood. So we headed out, keeping with our original plan to stay in a hotel with a pool as a gift to our girls for Easter. Janet's mother was willing to spring for the cost. So on March 13, 2008, when the DHS case worker, Bob Ross, called us, we informed him that we had an attorney and that we were out of town until Monday, March 17. Asked by Ross why we had a local phone number, I explained to him that our Ironwood phone number was ported to our cell phone. Apparently not understanding that, Ross thought he was calling a local number when he talked to us, out of town, on our cell phone. Following this call, we contacted our attorney, who then advised us to stay put until Monday, at which time he would handle it, saying that until the kids got back to town, DHS could do nothing. What we *did not know* is that DHS case worker Elizabeth Fyle stated she had attempted to call us that same night (March 13) following the call from Bob Ross, saying she attempted to leave us a message. But why was it that we never had a message from her on our voice mail, or her number on the caller I.D.? Whether she did or did not actually attempt this, we simply did not receive her message. So on we went with our plans, as we had already set out to do, checking in to a nice motel in Houghton, complete with swimming pool. And of course we were not at all aware of the activities of Elizabeth Fyle, who was seizing this moment to make the first major move to kidnap our children. According to remarks placed in that same DHS *investigative findings report,* following her visit to our home, my initial phone call on our trip requested us to call a DHS worker as soon as we returned. The report errantly said, however, that I had said we would be home that night, which was the *first* of her long list of *fabrications.* As I said, I had told Bob Ross we would be home Monday. My wife Janet explicitly told Ross that, before I completed my own call myself to Ross. Yet somehow, here it was, in her report, completely fabricated by someone. The question is, who put it there? Fyle or Ross? I'd bet my money on Fyle. It seems to me, that purposely falsifying a report would be a criminal act, and if I can ever *prove* which one of them did it, I will bring them up on criminal charges at a later time.

I learned a lot more from reading this *investigative findings report,* which of course I never saw for some time after the house visit. In one entry, dated 3/13/2008, it stated that they had left a message on my phone to call through IPSD when we returned to the area for another interview. The time on that report as listed as 6:00 pm. Yet another entry, the same date, at 7:30 pm, stated that the DHS had spoken to an officer, explained the situation, and asked *them* to call my phone as I was not *responsive* to their call. The ISPD had told this worker they would check my home and notify them if our family returned. I found this to be interesting for a number of reasons. First, if the DHS workers already knew where we were, why the need to check my home when we had already indicated the time we would be back? Why deceive the IPSD? Second, if they left a message, as indicated by the 6:00 pm entry, why a need for a follow up call? (Unless they *knew* the message had not been received). Thirdly, how can you expect a *response* to any message in only an hour and a half? But another entry was also made, indicating the DHS worker was contacted at 9:30 pm by IPSD, who had checked my home and stated I had not returned. This seems to make it quite clear that DHS was *tracking* us to be sure we were where we said we were. That would give them the time they needed to go about getting an illegitimate court order on the very next morning. I would learn later that is exactly what they did, and they were all together in this effort, with Ron Carpenedo spearheading the alleged *search* for the missing Colemans. They could twist this story to make it seem we *had not* told Bob Ross we would be back on Monday, go about getting their phony search warrant in the meanwhile, allowing Ron Carpenedo to trace our cell phone calls to make it appear we were trying to run, so they could legitimize their effort by presenting it to the judge in court, so they could receive their long sought-after child removal order!

In trying to make it all look good, there were several other entries on the *investigative findings report* that make clear the state's true intent. First, an entry at 8:00 am the following morning, stating simply, "The family has not returned yet." Why put that in any report, unless, of course, the *motive* is to produce a paper trail to show a *justification* for their illigitimate court action, which could or could not involve pre-planning by the court as well. What I am finding as I delve deeper and deeper into my research of the Michigan system of *justice* is that oftentimes, one state agency holds hands with the other, working together to reach a common objective. With child abuse cases, the *objective* is to set things up so there can be a *conviction,* whether or not there is actual, unquestionable truth in the facts they work to manufacture, fabricate, or exaggerate in building their case. In many of the *setups* they arrange, relatives can be found working together, in separate but linked agencies, to act upon actions of one agency to another. A conflict of interest? You bet it is! In any case, at 8:20 am, according to the report, they checked Caitlyn's school, to find she was not in school. Did they *really expect* she would be? My wife had already informed the school she would *not* be there due to our travel plans. The state claimed later in court the school was not informed that Caitlyn would not be there, yet our lawyer unveiled in court that, in fact, their own school records prove the opposite to be true. There seemed to be some confusion about it by the school, as Caitlyn's teacher had been out of school herself due to a family matter, and had only just returned before the police, at the instruction of Ms. Fyle came pounding on her classroom door! So leave it to Elizabeth Fyle to over dramatize the entire thing, and go running to the courts expressing her opinion (and only an opinion) that we were running away with the kids! How stupid! This was yet another example of the *falsification of paperwork,* which Elizabeth could then *fabricate as fact* to the judge, and it needed to be done fast, because otherwise, we might have an attorney representing us in the matter! She wanted to get this done before we got back on Monday. So Elizabeth went running to the court with her wild story, in her attempt to obtain an order to remove our children. She would tell the court that our attorney at the time, Mike Pope, was no longer taking these cases, which was true, but at that point, we were still acting on his advice to remain where we were until Monday. If we were to retain a new and different lawyer, he would have advised us of that when we saw him on Monday. Fyle, of course, had other ideas. We had not understood how this all transpired, until a few years after we got our kids back and we got the transcript of her court pleas to a biased judge, who was as much a part of this entire charade as were the other participants in this child kidnapping effort. Here now is that complete transcript, as it went down in court, for you to see for yourself:

Bessemer, Michigan

March 13, 2008 @ 11:07 A.M.

THE COURT: Okay we're on the record in file Number 08-93 NA, in the matter of Ashley Coleman and Caitlyn Brag, ah; we're here on an emergency request by the DHS for a removal of children, with allegations of, ah, child abuse. Ms. Fyle is, I'm sorry, from the DHS, the Prosecutor's office has signed as co-petitioner, Ms. Wittla is participating by, ah, telephone; she's not in the office today. Ms. Fyle, would you raise your right hand; do you swear to tell the truth, the whole truth, and nothing but the truth, so help you God?

MS. FYLE: I do.

THE COURT: State your name for the record.

MS. FYLE: Elizabeth Fyle.

THE COURT: And how are you employed?

MS. FYLE: I'm a CPS worker through DHS.

THE COURT: And are you the primary investigator and the person who prepared the petition on this file?

MS. FYLE: I am.

THE COURT: And to the best of your knowledge, information and belief, those allegations are true?

MS. FYLE: Yes.

THE COURT: Um, Ms. Wittla, did you want to ask any questions of Ms. Fyle?

MS. WITTLA: Ah, just a couple questions your Honor. Um, Ms. Fyle, when was the first time you interviewed the child in this case?

MS. FYLE: It would have been Tuesday, the 11th of March.

MS. WITTLA: And was it your intention to interview her again after that date?

MS. FYLE: Yes.

MS. WITTLA: Was there anything that prevented that from taking place?

MS. FYLE: Yeah. Yes, we called yesterday, well, we went yesterday to the school, to interview Caitlyn at school; she was not at school, so then I called, well, actually my co-worker, Bob Ross, called Rob Coleman's phone; he stated they were up in Marquette, but would be returning last night, and this was—

happened yesterday. Um, and that they would, but they would be returning last night, um, and so, Bob Ross, um, informed Mr. Coleman that he needed to contact, um, contact us, or whatever for this interview to take place last night.

Just a note here! Nobody *ever* said when such an interview was to take place. In fact, it appears quite clear here that the state intended to do it at school, without our knowledge!

MS. FYLE (continuing): I called Rob Coleman at six o'clock last night, and left a message on his cell phone; I called IPSD approximately 7:30 and asked them to leave another message on his cell phone, um, to see if we would get any other different results. Um, IPSD reported that Rob was not at his home; the last call I got was 9:30 last night, um, that the Colemans had not returned to their home. This morning I called again just about eight o'clock; um, they said, again, they had been checking the home throughout the night and there did, did not appear to be any life in the home and didn't see any cars that were returned to the home. Um, Caitlyn was not at school when I called this morning at 8:20, and I don't know where the family currently is.

MS. WITTLA: Thank you. That's all I have.

THE COURT: Okay, I'm, ah, Ms. Wittla, I'm, guess I'm going to inquire and I know you're not in the office, but your office has not currently issued any criminal charges in conjunction with this or with the other case involving the, the people mentioned; the Paynes; is that right?

MS. WITTLA: That's correct your Honor, that case is currently under investigation, ah, because of the, ah, I guess the nuances of financial transactions and all that sort of thing; they're waiting to hear back from a couple of different sources, before the, um, investigation be considered complete.

THE COURT: But it is currently under investigation, correct?

MS. WITTLA: Yes it is.

THE COURT: Okay, and I would assume that's one case; um, on the allegations that are included in this petition, by which, by the way have you seen or are you aware of the allegations of this petition?

MS. WITTLA: Um, yes your Honor, um, Ms. Fyle started drafting it yesterday, and um, I believe she's added things to it since I saw the original draft version yesterday, but I, um, she read the additions to me.

THE COURT: I mean, are there criminal components to that that are also being considered by your office?

MS. WITTLA: You're speaking of child abuse?

THE COURT: Yeah.

MS. WITTLA: Regarding Caitlyn?

THE COURT: Yeah. Right, right.

MS. WITTLA: Well that was part of the reason I believe for having a second interview with her, to see if that could be pursued. And unfortunately that never took place, and I think it's fairly doubtful that it will.

Let me interrupt right here! Now, WHY? Why would she tell the judge that she doubted that a second interview would ever take place? That is crazy! Maybe it would not take place when they planned for it to, because they never told us about it, but it isn't like it could not take place! She simply *deceived* the judge with that remark!

THE COURT: Okay and my only other question, Mr. Pope is mentioned in the petition, um, and what I'm trying to determine here is whether or not he's on board negotiating with your office; does he need to be contacted on this case or, can you give me a status, or?

MS. WITTLA: The only one who's ever mentioned Mr. Pope as being part of this case was, ah, I believe, the reference that the Colemans made when the little girl was originally being interviewed. To my knowledge he has made no contact with my office, and frankly, in the past, has told me he doesn't take these kind of cases.

While it may be true he did not take those types of cases, we were not aware of it, as he had always *been our attorney in all of our other business related cases, personal cases, etc. Since we had never been brought up for child abuse with Pope as our lawyer, we were not aware, and that is why we called him when Elizabeth Fyle made her surprise attack on our home before, as well as when Ross contacted us after the home visit. At that point, he was our attorney.*

THE COURT: All right, so he's not actively involved in....

MS. WITTLA: ... Not that I'm aware of.

THE COURT: We, we don't know if he'll be appearing or not at any given time, huh?

MS. WITTLA: Considering what he's told me about child abuse cases, I would be surprised if he appeared on this case.

THE COURT: All right then, and there also, I mean, there also is the issue that this is being considered an emergency in the, and you know, I don't know that anybody wants to alert anybody; I guess I'd ask Ms. Fyle; it's pretty clear to you; does it appear pretty clear to you that this is just not a— they just happened to be out of town, misunderstanding situation?

MS. FYLE: No, no! When Bob Ross spoke yesterday to them, um, the Colemans explained that they would be back yesterday afternoon; that they were going to be attending this OB appointment, but then they would be back. Um, like I said, several messages were left on his cell phone, um, most cell phones work throughout, at least, chunks of the U.P., especially in larger cities where he alleges that he would have been; and nobody has heard from him.

Once again, there was *no reason* for this to be an emergency. It was only what this broad wanted it to be, because she knew I could not be represented at this hearing!

For goodness sake, I had a *business* in Ironwood. Was I just going to pull out and run away, over some lunatic's accusations about child abuse? It would still have to go to court before I would panic in that manner. But then, if she waited for it to go to court, she couldn't just *snatch* the kids, in order to avoid a court hearing first, could she? She wanted the judge's quick permission to legally kidnap my children!

THE COURT: All right, um, based upon the record, then, I find there's an unreasonable risk of harm to these children in terms of the fact that the allegations include physical abuse, um, including use of the belt in more extreme situations, and I find that, ah, an emergency exists, and therefore, I will issue an order to remove the children from the custody of the parents pending further proceedings; immediately after which, assuming that they are located, ah, we would, ah, come into court and commence this by a preliminary hearing and take it one step at a time from there. I also take judicial notice of the fact that I did sign personal protection orders in this, ah, involving these respondents, um, on the allegations of, of, ah, taking advantage of basically people who are developmentally disabled or the like; which includes sexual abuse type of, ah, allegations earlier this week, and the court takes judicial notice of the same, and finding a potential danger to these children. I will therefore issue the order as indicated, making any other findings as part of my written order; is there anything else for the record, um, Ms. Wittla?

MS. WITTLA: No, your Honor.

So simply put, from reading these transcripts Becky had also tried to hang me for a rape charge, which never materialized because it never happened. My lawyer, later on in court, would indicate that if she did what she said she did, it would amount to prostitution, which would be a crime on her part. The truth is she just wanted sex and loved to flirt, but in retaliation for me breaking it off and asking her to leave our home, she wanted to fry me for everything she could charge me with. And this prosecutor and Elizabeth Fyle were both in on the plot!

THE COURT: Okay, all right, we're going to recess then, and as I said we'll come back, ah, to court if and when these folks are located. We are in re— Ms. Fyle? Were you going to say something?

MS. FYLE: I was just going to ask, you Honor, that, that if, if possible that that it be in the order that we be able to enter the home, and at least, either (a) check on the locations of the children and/or (b) to, um, obtain personal belongings for them in the event that they are removed?

In the event? Ms. Fyle! It's already in your game plan!

THE COURT: And that's at 400 South Suffolk Street in Ironwood?

MS. FYLE: Yes, yes.

THE COURT: Yeah, that's pretty standard. So ordered, um, and it will be included in the written order. Anything further? Thank you, we are in recess, and you can put your phone away. Thank you.

So the plot was laid. It was now only a matter of *how* they would remove our kids, and *when.*

Back to the *findings report,* there was one other *huge mistake,* or should I say *insertion,* in the *investigative findings report* that I found of interest. DHS stated that we had apparently taken Janet to her doctor in Marquette. We never went to Marquette, nor did we plan to. Why would they make that entry? It could not have been a simple mistake. Did they, in fact, insert that *on purpose* to justify their *false accusation* that we were in the process of *fleeing* with our children? Or to support the *false claim by Ross* that we had told him we were in Marquette and would be home that night? That is just plain stupid. If running would have been in our thoughts, we surely would never have spent the night in that motel in Houghton, with Canada only about two short hours away. Why would we do that?

In any case, that set the stage for the big *show.* After a wonderful day with the kids on Friday, shopping and swimming, we called it a night and retired in our hotel room in Houghton. At three o'clock in the morning, we were awakened by a knock on our door, accompanied by a voice claiming to be maintenance. Janet, going to the door, cautiously opened the door slightly, the chain still in place. But in moments, nine police officers had forced their way into the room! All entrances to the hotel were blocked, as well as the street and the entire parking lot! Observers stumbled out of their hotel rooms to observe the chaos, and must certainly have thought it was a drug bust, or something much more sinister! It scared the living hell out of my kids, and when the dust settled a bit, police handed Janet the court paperwork, allowing them to kidnap our kids. As the kids continued to show their terror over the incident, my wife, Janet, *pleaded* with police officers to at least allow her the right to say a proper goodbye. Once the kids were buckled into the car they were to be taken away in, Janet was finally granted that right. Caitlyn asked about the Easter bunny, and Janet said she would call him and let him know, and have him wait until they got home. Janet kept telling the children to be strong and that she loved them, but the shock was apparent in all of us! Janet, caught up in all the events, was not aware that police had taken our keys without our knowledge. They had already removed our kids' car seats from our car before those keys were turned back over to Janet, and to this day, we still don't know how they obtained them. We would like to know. Did they steal them while making their raid of our room? If so, we would like to add a charge of theft to the kidnapping charges they were already guilty of.

In my own case, this event landed me in the hospital. After going down to the car to see to the concerns of my children, I was sent up to get a bottle and a blanket for Ashley, and collapsed when I got upstairs. I simply could not breathe, and later came to realize I had experienced a nervous breakdown. And while I was lying up there, needing help, these so-called servants of the public refused to provide it until they could first see that my kids had been removed and that their raid could be termed successful. Caitlyn was never told of my collapse, and upon hearing about it at her current age, she says that had she seen the ambulance, which didn't arrive until later, she would surely have jumped out of the car.

As to what transpired in the car, when you later read an account of Bonnie Huttunen's testimony at trial, it completely contradicts what our daughter, Caitlyn, now age ten (at the writing of this book) tells us. Huttunen was the children's services worker who accompanied the raid team at our hotel. Huttunen had the jury believing that Caitlyn was perfectly calm, walking hand-in-hand with her to the car, conversing the entire time, and that she continued to do so throughout the ride in the car, to her first foster home. But Caitlyn now gives us a completely different account of that story. According to Caitlyn now, both of our kids were crying really hard when they left, and were scared, thinking they would never see us (their parents) again. They both fell asleep, exhausted from crying. Caitlyn says upon their arrival at the home, she was taken by the arm to a room with Sponge Bob décor... a boy's room, as she describes it. She was told to sleep on a lower bunk bed, with a boy sleeping above her. They told her to call the foster mom "Auntie." Ashley slept in a crib in the foster mom's bedroom. They were crying in bed and the boy told Caitlyn to shut up.

Supposedly, during this brief period from the kidnapping to the first time we were allowed to see our children, Caitlyn made further admissions to Elizabeth Fyle, which she testified to later in court. These so-called *admissions* by Caitlyn (according to Fyle) supported her claim of Caitlyn's so-called earlier *admissions* at our home—all of which Caitlyn denies took place voluntarily. With all Fyle had to say, one has to wonder how it all could possibly have taken place. The first time Caitlyn saw Bob Ross and Fyle was at our home. The second time was at the DHS office before we had our visit that first day (a Friday). And the third time was at the foster home *after* our visit. So how could Fyle say in a court room that Caitlyn said all these things in the foster home on Monday, when the first time Caitlyn saw Fyle and Ross at the foster home was on Friday—*after* our visit? Not only that, but when Fyle *did* interview Caitlyn in the foster home, even Bob Ross indicated it was not for more than one half hour. All of those things could *never* have been covered in that time, given the nature of the protocol they said they follow, which would have to take at least half of that time in preparation and followup.

In the end, however, it is our *children* who suffered the most—the ultimate *victims* of this totally *unnecessary* raid. They will suffer for the remainder of their lives due to the reign of terror then, and later to follow, initiated because DHS workers were intent upon *creating a false case* of child abuse.

—Chapter Six—

"Bogus Charges"

While I was recuperating in the hospital from my nervous breakdown, a result of the raid on our hotel room, Janet left the hotel on her way to the emergency room. After numerous attempts, she was finally able to contact our attorney, Michael Pope, who was no longer taking defense cases. Still offering some friendly advice, however, he was somewhat dumbfounded when told of our incident, expressing his surprise that authorities would go to another county in order to conduct such a raid. By now, of course, I had developed a strong distrust for all public officials, and decided that my best course of action in dealing with them was to record everything we did or said in the presence of any state official. It would also give me ironclad proof of what they said. I am glad I developed this habit, because it proved to be so very beneficial, and a pivotal part of my ability to write this book. Every claim I am able to make regarding the statements of child service providers and other public officials (i.e., police, doctors, state workers, etc.) in ensuing chapters are backed up by either these tapes, memos they created, or transcripts of the hearings and trials themselves. I have them all, in order to back up what I've said in this book. Their only defenses would be to try to lie even more, disclaiming what these records clearly show they said. Perhaps it was even more clear to me that I needed to continue this, after our March 17, 2008 meeting with Gogebic County DHS worker Robert Ross. At that meeting, he stated, "I want birth certificates, social security cards, immunization records, and your signature. You're done." In this same meeting, I asked Ross to see our kids on Easter, as it was a special event for our family. He said he would do that, but it did not materialize. Many of his promises would be made, in fact, but never delivered upon, and several statements made by Ross proved simply untrue. On March 20 and March 24 of that year, we met once again with Ross. It appeared, at that time, we were in a more cordial meeting, but we view it now in a different light. It is clear to me, in reviewing a series of my tape recordings of those conversations, the true intent of the conversations were not to *help* in reuniting us as a family, as he portrayed it, but rather for him to dig for more information that could, in fact, be used against us, perhaps even opening up his possible pursuit of *criminal actions* against us.

The most remarkable comment Ross made, as we were to go forward in this process, was that I should *not talk* about the case with our children. *Why?* Were they in fear of us allowing our children to know what was happening to them? As players in the event, I felt they *should* be made aware of what was going on with the case. It didn't take me long, however, to understand more clearly what the *state's motives* were in taking this position. If the parents don't discuss the case with their children, it gives the state unchecked opportunities to influence or brainwash their children, without opposition, using the *power of suggestion* in a heavy handed manner to obtain the comments or statements from their children that can be turned against them as parents. They can elicit comments or statements kids otherwise might not be willing to make. A child under pressure can oftentimes be influenced to say or do most anything that they think will keep them or those they love out of trouble. If they are frightened, a complete lie would not be unusual from them, simply so they could get out of the threatening condition they find themselves in. The state, in many child abuse cases, likes to present to the court their scenario of the kids in a case being *frightened or fearful of their parents*—and in some cases, that may be factual. But in many cases, including our own, it was not factual. But the state of Michigan *did try* to present it in our case as well. It was, in fact, *the state,* that my children feared the most. Our recordings support this as well, making it *evident* as to who our children were most fearful of. Even at this writing, at age ten, Caitlyn (as does Ashley) lives with a deep rooted *fear* of being taken in the middle of the night, and they often relive the fear in recurring nightmares of the state coming to take them away in the middle of the night. So the question remains, *why* the state would fear the truth coming out? If, as they might suggest, kids feel *fear and intimidation* from their parents, it should not *matter* that the case be brought up and discussed in visitations, which the state *does monitor.* What better way to truly observe and see for themselves their *suspicions of fear from parents?* Surely, in such a setting, they will be able to clearly see it, if a parent threatens or intimidates their kid in any manner. It seems to me that would prove advantageous to the state, if indeed, they really did have a true abuse case. But again, if you are attempting to build a *false case,* as I do believe the *large majority* of state child abuse cases are, you would not *want* the child to express anything that might jeopardize the case you have concocted, would you?

Another point of contention with the state was over the placement of the kids. I had requested that if my kids were to be placed in foster care, that some consideration be given to placing them with my brother. I think many parents, who find themselves in the same plight, would choose to have a relative, as opposed to a stranger, look after their children. In response to my request for such, Ross indicated they would initiate a *home study* of my brother's family—a study which was never done. As I would learn later, it is a response Ross used consistently, apparently to put people off as to what his true intentions would be.

Then came the initial question we had as to where our children were being housed. Ross stated he did not know. For a man in charge of an agency, I found this to be rather unbelievable. How in the world would he *not know,* given the kids had been *brought* to our initial visitation to meet us? It was not very difficult to conclude that this was a direct lie.

In the March 24 visitation, Ross indicated he needed to complete a *funding determination* that would allegedly make it possible for us to be paid for our required mileage costs in making our visitations to a visitation facility the state would set up in another city. This sounded good to us, but what they didn't tell us is that it would take so long for reimbursement, that it would prove a hardship to be able to travel the distances the state made us travel, in order to see our children. By now our business was in trouble financially, due primarily to the bad image we had developed—the result of the disgruntled tenants and the invented allegations which the state had allowed to surface against us. With the help of the state, those elements opposing us were banded together to try to bring us down, and quite frankly, they were succeeding. Some of our current tenants, in reaction to the bad public outcries began not paying their rents, engaged in thefts against our property, vandalized the apartments, and basically did all they could do to ruin our reputation and business in Ironwood. They really needed only for that one good knockout punch to be thrown. It was, of course, thrown by the mental case who was one of our accusers in this case. For county and state officials, it was not important what his mental condition was, for he had put it in writing that Robert Coleman had abused his kids, and that was good enough for both the county and the state to finally go after me, big time, in their quest to settle a score with me for having beaten back their efforts in the past. When I discussed with Robert Ross, the mental state of Bobby Payne, I indicated that I wanted it as part of the record in my effort to get my children back. He responded by saying, "It's all going to help." It sounded good and I had the feeling he was going to assist, but that assistance never came.

As one might also expect, in such a case, there were questions surrounding the *needs of our kids* while all of this was playing out. Ashley, our youngest, was only two years of age at the time, and quite accustomed to drinking from a bottle at night. Authorities took it upon themselves to just *coldly stop this practice,* providing no weaning time at all, *forcing her* to take her drinks from a sippy cup. Had I not asked Robert directly about this, I would never have been made aware of it by the state. We were later to learn that a number of gifts we had brought for our children during visitations, were, in fact, *confiscated,* and not given to the children at all. *Why would the state see fit to do that?* Those items were only returned to us as their parents, when we finally got our kids back many months later.

When it came to education, we were led to believe that Caitlyn, my step daughter, was being placed in school so she would not fall behind. This was a big concern for us, and I was reassured the state was taking care of that. We would later discover she was, in fact, out of school for most of a month, so the state could use educational difficulty in future court matters as a claim of poor parenting on our part as well. In her schooling, which she was having difficult times with while in state custody, she had both academic and behavioral difficulties, which we assess to her direct response to her having been *involuntarily kidnapped* by the state. It was only in her later counseling efforts, as we worked through this nightmare, that she began to gain some in her schooling difficulties. Today, now that she is home, she is a good student with normal difficulties, but still somewhat playing catch up to what was missed due to the state's failure to keep her in school in the early weeks of foster care.

Other issues were discussed in those early meetings as well. One regarded the subject of a pair of $300 earrings belonging to Caitlyn, which were snatched by the state at the time of the raid. We were assured by Ross that the state would document everything, and we were fine with that at the time. Later, however, the earrings would become an issue, as they came up missing at the same time foster care problems began to escalate.

There was another element of our initial discussions that came as a complete and total surprise to me. It was the comments and questions put to me by Ross, dealing with my business. He stated that it was *safe to assume* I was not making a profit, with all the difficulties of my present situation. Quick to respond to that, I shot back that I had a very rich family and that if I were in need of help, they would come to my aid. He indicated that it was his intent to make the entire family eligible so the state would pick up costs, as opposed to the county. But I wonder. Could his real intent have been to *set me up for fraud charges for filing false paperwork* in this case? I was putting nothing past Ross or the entire system as this juncture.

The March 24 meeting concluded with Ross stating, "We will not hurt your kids." My response was very direct, my look even more so perhaps, when I said, "I hope not, Bob." I think I drove that point home clearly. Nothing more needed to be stated, because in my manner, I think he recognized that hurting my kids would result in a lot more serious consequences for them than just being at the brunt of a book I would write about them. I think most caring parents understand my point here. As it was, the state *did* hurt my children, most dramatically in an emotional way, and without just cause. It is why I felt compelled to write this book.

—Chapter Seven—

"The Accomplices"

When states commit crimes, such as legal kidnapping, they do so with willful consent from a number of accomplices, most of whom stand to *gain* from their transgressions. As we have indicated prior, a good kidnapping ring needs to have a willing group of *accomplices* in order to succeed in their efforts. Some do it for the money, some do it for other reasons. Revenge or power oftentimes enter into it, and perhaps one of those with the biggest cross to bear against us in our case was police Sergeant Ron Carpenedo, who had no love for me since the day I showed up in Ironwood. When my neighbor, John Cain, was unable to prove his case against me, it must have been difficult for Ron, as they were good friends, and perhaps that does explain his zest to see me fry this time around. Our day had already been very destructive, as on April 7, 2008, we had our pretrial hearing, and 77 charges of child abuse were unveiled. Most, of course, were *bogus charges,* in fact, were only basic statements given by Bobby Payne, in his quest to destroy us. That did not alter the fact that each of them needed *responses,* which would come later in coming hearings of the court. Inasmuch as I had already pointed out that these bogus charges were being launched by someone with a verifiable past of mental problems, it seemed that social services had paid no heed to what we had revealed about Bobby and his vindictive and scorned wife, Rebecca. All the state needed to lend *credence* to their outrageous claims of abuse was the ear of a law enforcement accomplice, who would be anxious to destroy Robert Coleman. It was my opinion that the ear they chose was Sergeant Carpenedo.

If my wife and I were truly the *monsters* the state was attempting to paint us up to be, portrayed by the Paynes—and if we had in fact, been guilty of those 77 so-called *charges* we were confronted with, I would wonder why, at visits with my kids, in the many visits we were permitted, the kids always cried when we left, but squealed with delight when we showed up to see them. Does that sound like the reaction you would expect from children who been so brutally abused? It was fortunate for me and my wife that we had the presence of mind to *record* all of these events that dealt with either social workers and/or law enforcement. I learned from our experiences that these people *fear* the truth—possibly because the truth has a way of coming out and exposing them. As these truths are *undeniable* in unedited tape recordings, it is therefore, a procedure they all abhor. I've concluded it is because their agendas are not based on truth, therefore, it is very difficult for them to defend their actions when bringing their *false accusations* in front of a court. It is somewhat easier when that court is playing ball with them as well, of course, but there comes a point where even a corrupt court has to stand on law, for the shear reason that all of their procedures (in court) are, in fact, documented. And since a lower court cannot stop an appeal to a higher court, in the end, if they do not follow some guidelines, it will look very bad to be exposed for the failures at their own level. It is for that reason, I make *all* of my documentation and recordings available via links from my website, which I invite all readers of this book to explore.

Enter Sergeant Ron Carpenedo, in my mind a valued *accomplice* in this case. This case was aided, by among others, Sergeant Carpenedo, and it should come as no surprise that on April 7, 2008, following our pre-trial hearing, I was pulled over by none other than this same police sergeant, allegedly because of the placement of my plates on my truck. They were displayed in the truck windows, as opposed to the license plate fixtures on my truck. Explaining my reasons for it, I told Carpenedo that in consideration of our financial difficulties at this time, due to the circumstances we were in, Janet and I had decided to let the truck go back, as opposed to trying to continue to keep it and continue to make payments on it. As is normal in most traffic stops, I was asked to produce identification, which I produced, even though he knew full well who I was. His questioning then began, which was his true motive for having stopped us. He asked about my wallet, which I had reported stolen prior to my trip to Houghton, where the raid took place. The Sergeant started by asking when I noticed my wallet missing. I told him it was prior to going to Houghton, so he then wanted to know how it was, if my license was stolen (as I had reported) that I was able to supply an identification to the Houghton police at the time of the raid. Janet had given them an older identification I had while waiting for my replacement of that with my new identification. It was not clear to Carpenedo (so he said) how I could have current identification, as Houghton police reported, when, in fact, my license had been stolen. I thought about this a lot, later, and it made me *wonder* why Carpenedo was so anxious to raise this subject at all, or why he seemed so anxious to debunk claims I had made earlier about the theft of my wallet. As the trial would later show, since I was sure that Bobby Payne was the thief, they had to somehow try to make him look more legitimate when our case got to court. After all, what jury is going to believe claims of a mental case who is also a thief? So if you can cast doubt on either or both of the aspersions I was making, it would bolster their own state case against me and my wife. If the state could prevail in showing Bobby Payne was neither the mental case nor a thief, they could emphasize even more powerfully that Robert Coleman was indeed, a child abuser. The state had to illustrate that the Paynes' drummed up *charges* were taken seriously. To do less would be to allow for their kidnapping effort to fail. Of course, at this time, I had no knowledge as to how widespread such child kidnapping efforts were—that, in fact, they were *national* in scope. Nor did I then understand to what extent state officials would go in order to carry out such kidnapping efforts.

I would reiterate that in order for a kidnapping ring to work, you need the help of the *accomplices.* These accomplices must benefit in some way. If not financially, then at least in some form of power entitlement, or, perhaps even more motivating, they must stand to *lose* somehow. The thought of financial loss, job loss, etc., are strong motivating factors. I think it is quite possible that many who are helping the rings do know their actions are wrong, or questionable at least. And they might not be criminally motivated themselves. But that fear of losing a job, or position, as I stated, can be very motivating to act in a certain manner. It would be great if, in today's society, people in all walks of life would choose to use their consciences to guide their actions, and would then expose or refuse those who abuse our public trust. If that were to happen in police departments, hospitals, agencies, the courts, etc., the rings could be broken and the perpetrators brought to justice.

I think what scares me most is that under the banner of *Child Protective Services,* these kidnapping rings are not only protected and supported, but condoned by the state and federal governments.

Most people think you have to *do something bad* to gain a state's interest in making you a target as a child abuser. The truth is, more often than not, you don't have to actually abuse a child. In my subsequent study of cases from all over the country, I'm learning that in the majority of instances, it is more because of some public figure's animosity towards a family member, or simply an opportunity to make money, and not a matter of child abuse, that parents become targeted by a state. In our social circle today, we find one level of authority that is in collusion with the other levels of authority—to such a point that if one says something happened, the other will concur without much question. They do this just to protect each other. When you add to that, the public's *indifference* as to what they do (unless it directly affects them), it is no small wonder corruption flourishes, and in fact, even spreads to larger and larger geographical boundaries. In this instance, *Child Protective Services, or CPS,* purportedly in place to *protect children,* is instead allowed to go unchecked in disrupting lives of families, and their mission, in fact, *harms* as many or more children than it protects. The sad part is that most of it is done purely for the sake of making *money* for state governments, or to satisfy some personal vendetta.

Let's take a moment and examine the 77 *allegations* we were presented with in our case. In truth, they were *not* real allegations, although the prosecution in this case chose to call them that. They were merely *statements* that either Bobby or Becky Payne made, and notations from a subsequent interview conducted by DHS and IPSD. The statements given by the Paynes were, simply put, mostly statements, and if they did contain some form of allegation, they were out and out lies. As for the comments of investigators, much of what they indicated was, likewise, invented, exaggerated, or simply total lies. Sometimes a glimmer of truth is tossed in, just to try to instill some *believability* in their presentations. I did, in fact, spank my children, in a disciplinary fashion, but *not* with a belt nor in an abusive manner as prosecutors and the Paynes set out to show. It was somewhat of a challenge, actually, to even *read* the so-called *allegations,* simply because of the nonsensical illiterate wording they consisted of. When you could distinguish a clear meaning, they were not at all charges, but mere statements. To cite an example, here was the first one given on their list:

"Whose parent or other person legally responsible for the care and maintenance of such child, when able to do so, neglects or refuses to provide proper or necessary support, education, medical, surgical or other care necessary for his or her health or morals, who is subject to a substantial risk of harm to his or her mental being, who is abandoned by his or her parents, guardian, or other custodian, or who is without proper custody or guardianship."

Can any of you tell me what that *allegation* was? Or where or to whom any of it was directed? I have difficulty even trying to understand what it all relates to. Certainly *none* of this applied to our situation in life. Abandonment was not an issue. Maintenance was no issue. Medical care was no issue. Substantial risk of harm to mental being? I don't know, does a spanking fall into that statement? To my thinking, I found *nothing* in that paragraph of half-sentences that warranted the removal of my children from my home. None of it applied, and I wondered why it was even on there. It is like God saying, "Here are my ten commandments. Some nut has charged you with breaking one, but I won't tell you which one. Just read them and determine for yourself, which one you are being accused of."

There were, of course, the direct *accusations* given by the Paynes that were a bit more clear to discern, even if crazy. These amounted mostly to *"he said"* or *"she said"* accusations, but can easily bring the *number* of so-called *allegations* to a higher number, so you can paint a picture of a much more villainous defendant. After all, in a child abuse case, 77 sounds a lot better than 2 to an unsuspecting jury, doesn't it? Of course, all of these so-called *allegations* are accepted readily by anxious prosecutors, police officials, court officials, and social workers, all recognizing the opportunity before them. Many of them had knowledge of Bobby's mental state. But why waste the opportunity to go after one of their prime targets? (Me!) So never mind the *preliminary* investigations to see if, indeed, there was any legitimacy in pursuing this action. It was *show time, baby!*

Time to get on with the *show (raid).* But in case you would like to review what some of the mental case *accusations* were, let me list a few:

(1) "Bobby stated that Rob (me) is very harsh with Caitlyn, age 6, and screams at her often."

(2) "Bobby stated that around January 26, 2008, while eating dinner, Caitlyn did not want to eat rice, as she doesn't like rice. Bobby stated that Rob told Caitlyn he was "going to give her the belt." Bobby says she backed up in her chair and said, "No, daddy, no." Bobby said Rob instructed him to go get the belt, and Bobby did it because he was afraid to not do as Rob said."

Of course none of that second allegation ever happened. And in the first instance, what constitutes *very harsh?* A reprimand? And whose interpretation is it, as to how harsh an action is? A lunatic witness? A disgruntled lover? Who? Rebecca also cited events of fiction, such as the one alleged to have occurred on February 16 of 2008. In that one, she said Janet held Caitlyn's legs while I held her hands above her head and pulled off her pants, then I used a belt to strike her twice. OK, first, it did not happen. Second, had it occurred, I can't help wondering why it is that two tenants who could never remember to pay their rent could suddenly be so *enlightened* as to recall exact dates and times? And to remember them several weeks later. It also puzzles me, when I could not even recall where I kept belts, as I rarely used one, *they* knew exactly where to tell *investigators* where to look for mine. Yet when those investigators came to my house, they *knew* precisely where to search to find my belts in a dresser drawer. Could it be they had *inside knowledge* of where I kept things because it was given them by either Bobby, Becky, or both? They were the only two who had any knowledge of where I kept things in the house. As I said, even I was not sure where I kept belts. And even then, I did not own an orange one, and they never did find one. That was relayed to them by Bobby and Becky also, and was a great example of the kind of *reliable information* they were building this case on. (As I said earlier, Fyle did admit to this in court)

As to the *allegations* specific to me, there was the fact that I owned belts. So to any of you who have children, if you are reading this book, *get rid of your belts now!*

If the state visits your house and a mental case says you use belts to spank your kids, you will lose your children via this kind of *evidence.* Until this event ruined our lives, I had no idea it was criminal to own belts—or, for that matter, brooms or wooden spoons! (Which we did *not* own)

I could go on here and *dwell* on the *stupidity* of these so-called *allegations.* But to do so would only bore you into turning your TV set back on. Suffice to say, these charges were all bogus, exaggerated, even created in order to make a case. But in case you still insist on such boredom, and would want to examine the complete list of these *allegations,* they are shown in a later chapter of this book that covers the actual trial transcripts. I am also gladly making them available to read for yourself on a link to my website. So just go to the actual trial chapters (18 through 21) or visit my website and explore them for yourself.

—Chapter Eight—

The War Begins

Our girls squealed with delight when we began our visitation with them on April 8, 2008. As nice as it was to see the girls, it also marked the start of our war with DHS. A war we would fight much longer than we originally anticipated. When your children are first abducted, and you are accused of abusing them, it adds more salt to the wounds to find out that those entrusted with their care are far more abusive than you ever were. That became starkly clear to us during that April 8 visit. Caitlyn repeatedly questioned us during that visit, wanting to know when she could come home, asking repeatedly, "Why did they take me?" Ashley, in the meantime, became unusually quiet, seemingly shy, where previously she chattered a lot. As we were preparing to leave, we told Angela Andriacchi, the child welfare worker on duty, that we would be willing to bring more clothes to the kids in our next visit because the clothes they had on were becoming too small. Her response was that it was not necessary, because in a couple of weeks they would receive additional funding to pay for more clothing. During our visit Janet noticed some bruises and other things on Caitlyn, starting with a bruise in the area of her right inner elbow, as well as another on her right wrist area. Thus, when Caitlyn indicated she had to go to the bathroom, Janet took her, and it actually gave her a few moments alone with her. While they were in the rest room, Caitlyn started crying and asked Janet, "Why are they doing this? They are making me say daddy beats me!" Janet told her to be strong, and about that time, Angela stormed in. Janet quickly changed the subject and began telling Caitlyn she loved her and that everything was going to be OK. During this private time, though, Janet lifted Caitlyn's shirt and noticed also what appeared to be bruises on her legs and arms. We observed in this visit that Caitlyn's eyes looked droopy, as though not sleeping well; her hair was uncombed; and she had slight body and breath odors. When we first asked Caitlyn about the elbow, she looked first at the case worker, who was listening intently, and Caitlyn hesitated, and then stated she had bitten herself. We could tell she was not being truthful, in fact, appeared to be covering up something. Asked about the ankle, she again looked first at the case worker before responding. This time she merely said she did not know what happened. We asked the case worker to seek medical attention for this injury, due to the swelling, but it appeared to us the case worker was much more interested in getting the kids back to the foster home than to seek treatment for her injuries. In Ashley's case, there was a bump on her head and her right wrist also contained a bruise. Her lower leg had a deep cut that had healed over, and her back contained multiple scratches. Again, as with Caitlyn, there was body odor, and her nails had not been trimmed for apparently, some time. The case worker appeared to hurry, hastily applying their coats, but failing to button them or place gloves or a hat on them. Both children were in tears, as you might expect, as they were being led away. So, too, were we, as parents.

For me, the abuses we had witnessed signs of, at the hands of our so-called *protectors,* marked the opening salvo of our war with the system. Like any parent, I am deeply disturbed if *anyone* harms my children, and the evidence was all there. I made it my mission from that point forward to challenge anyone in the system who abused their authority, refused to carry out trusts granted to them under the system, or who used the system for their own selfish gain. Little did I realize this was only the *beginning* of an all-out war, and that even once concluded, it would become a lifetime commitment for me to put a *stop* to corruption wherever I might encounter it.

On April 14, 2008, at our request, we had an emergency hearing with Judge Joel Massie because of the conditions we had observed in our April 8 visitation. At that hearing we presented photos of the bruises our children had developed while in the state's care, which we snapped at the visit. At first the judge seemed to be a bit sympathetic, asking the state for an explanation for what he was viewing in the photos. It was our first real taste for the despicable manner of the prosecutor in the case, Tracie Wittla. Quick to accept the hearsay of the mental case who fed her the lies with which to prosecute this case, she wasted no time in attacking us and denying the true photo evidence in front of the court. She tossed it all off as *normal child's play.* When it appeared the judge was not buying any of that, she used what we would discover was a favorite tactic of hers—she would throw out something else, and see how that would play with the court. So she then introduced, almost in the manner of an afterthought, allegations of sexual molestation. Our attorney, Michael Findlay, countered that an emergency room doctor reported *no such abuse* following their initial check of the children, which followed their abduction in the raid of our motel room. Thus, Findlay argued, and justifiably so, if there had been any such abuse, it would have had to be at the hands of the foster parents—and not by us. In making his rebuttal, however, he used the wording *horrible specter of sexual abuse* in disclaiming the prosecutor's accusations. And even though there was no merit to any of this, and my attorney had properly pointed out this impossibility of that applying to us, the judge showed his true colors early as well, seizing upon this opportunity to rule that, indeed, it was, as our own attorney had described it, a *horrible specter*—and he wanted it to be checked out further. (In other words, they were all doing there best to try to *find something* they could pin on Robert Coleman. If it were *criminal,* so much the better!)

There is little doubt that this was all in response to my first real offensive action in this case, which came some three days prior to this court hearing. As I said, any parent willing to fight back on one of these state kidnappings, is immediately targeted for retaliation. I was now encountering such retaliation from the sytem, for my actions three days prior. I had placed a phone call to the Department Of Human Services, Region 1 Service Center. It was my contention then, as now, that *surely* people must be held *accountable* for their actions. I learned, after voicing my complaint, that agencies of the government go out of their way to *cover up* abuses within the system and rarely ever deal with the problems presented by the common people, oftentimes the *real victims* in these types of cases. The only exception to that rule is if it is a big enough case to make headlines and create a notable impact on the society at large. In any case, the reply to my call came some two weeks later, long after our court hearing, and was typical of the type of cover up that goes with such case complaints. They make a lot of *promises* to *look into the matter—but do nothing!* But this is how the letter, when they did finally reply, was worded:

April 23, 2008

Mr. Robert Coleman

205 East Vaughn Street

Apt. 1A

Ironwood, Mi. 49938

Dear Mr. Coleman:

This letter is in response to your phone call on 4/11/2008 during which you indicated allegations of physical abuse by the foster parents of your children. You also alleged that the children were starving and that they were not being bathed properly and their clothes were tight and not fitting properly. I've looked into your concerns and have spoken with the supervisor in Gogebic County. After reviewing all the issues you have addressed, I do believe that Gogebic County has acted in accordance with agency policy and relevant to statutory requirements. Abuse/neglect allegations are currently being investigated by Marquette County DHS and the allegations pertaining to licensing violations are being investigated by Child And Family Services.

During your phone call you also expressed dissatisfaction with your visitation schedule and a home study request for a relative. I have discussed those issues with the Gogebic County director and he is reviewing the case to insure that appropriate actions were taken. During this phone conversation I also encouraged you to discuss your concerns with your attorney and bring up these issues at your next court hearing that was scheduled for April 14, 2008. My advice continues to be that you speak with and utilize your attorney so that issues can be brought forward at court hearings. I also advise that you regularly talk with the DHS specialist involved with the case and to work with them to bring this case to an appropriate conclusion.

You are entitled to the CPS investigation summaries after the completed investigation. Please contact Gogebic County CPS supervisor, Daniel Borth, for a copy of that investigation.

Thank you for sharing your concerns.

Sincerely,

Marilyn Dutkavich

Region 1 Services Specialist

In other words, folks, I was to talk to the fox that was guarding the hen house. I would ask him if any other fox was going after the hens (my kids) and he would tell me no, so the case would be resolved. Sorry, not that easy. Not when it came to my kids.

Clearly, by now, we knew we were in a dog fight. The state, in effect, had declared war on us by attempting to try to establish phony molestation charges and to elevate our made up spanking abuse case to a higher, *criminal* level. In their haste to *cover up* abusive actions of the very foster parents they had chosen to *protect* our children, they were willing to *fabricate the case* to an even higher extent, in order to cover their ineptness. It did not matter to them that this could totally destroy my life or that of my family, including the lives of my children. What was important to them was to *win*. It was never so clear to me that we had to fight with everything we had if we were ever to see our children again. I made up my mind that if it was a war they wanted, that we, too, must declare war on the state.

It came as no surprise then, when the GAL (guardian ad litem) petitioned the court for our visits to be *cancelled* until a further examination could be done on Caitlyn. The GAL is *supposed to be* a protector of the children, but most often, as in our case, is merely and added prosecutor, which gives the state a two to one advantage in court lawyers for child abuse proceedings. That, it turned out, was the ruling of the court, so now it was a question of when we would be able to resume visitations.

—Chapter Nine—

The Medical Complicity

As we indicated in an earlier chapter, in the kidnapping rings, participation from many organizations, working as a team, is needed to support state crimes. The medical field is an important link to the state's crime efforts for many reasons. First, and foremost, they provide the *information* a prosecutor will use in a court case. A corrupt prosecutor is able to *manufacture* a reason for a corrupt judge to issue an order via the court for *abducted children* to be *examined* by the corrupt medical authorities, who can word their reports in such a way as to allow this prosecutor to return a written report as *evidence* in a case. In many instances, the *evidence* lacks any real merit, and is, in fact, simply a *conclusion* given by the physician doing the examination. A doctor, as an example, can indicate an injury *appears* to be either positive or negative, without any real scientific proof that it is so. An unethical prosecutor can twist that in a court room to convince a jury that because the doctor said so, it must be so. And thus, this unethical prosecutor easily advances his or her *invented theory* as hard evidence, convincing an unsuspecting jury it is true. In many cases, a doctors' statements do not have to be conclusive to sway a jury. When a doctor is asked to do a checkup by the state, he is generally advised by the state to look for specific case related details. (Or, told to include case related details that shine a light on their case) In so doing, if the doctor is at all in collusion with the state, it can generally result in something that can be worded in such a way as to support a state's *ficticious theory*. As you might recall, in our first run in with the state, Elizabeth Fyle was right there insisting that her state doctor do the exam on Caitlyn. As we pointed out, a lot of *personal observations* found their way into her report at that time, in addition to the doctor's *could-be assessements,* all designed to frame Robert Coleman. It failed, but the effort was made. Now it is quite interesting to note that once again, Elizabeth Fyle is right there to take the reigns of this second effort to nail Robert Coleman. So too, of course, was police Sergeant Ron Carpenedo. This would become a trend throughout our ordeal, but in this second instance, they played it a bit different, having the foster parent, Tara Fleis and an *unidentified case worker* from Child & Family Services bring Caitlyn in for a physical. This was the result of our complaint, filed against Marc and Tara Fleis, for the abuse we suspected as a result of our visit on April 8 in our visitation, as we noted in Chapter eight. Among Dr. Terry Hayryne's report of the visit was a comment that "on visual exam of the vaginal area, there is no lesions or scars. *I do not think the hymen is completely intact."* Now, seemingly, this could be the state's opportunity to go after Robert Coleman again, saying this took place long ago most likely, so he must be the abuser! I'm sure that is why somebody probably offered their *encouragement* for the doctor to say upon *visual exam* that the dear doctor *did not think* they hymen was intact. Now, as reader, I would ask you, would you not think if they were looking for that they do an in-depth determination of that? But as it was *not* the actual fact, if they wanted to *pursue* this later in court, they would have to word it that way. In fact, they *did* try to pursue this, but as my lawyer was able to quickly point out, since we did have our own examination of Caitlyn done with our own private doctor, which disproved this, if there were such abuse, it would have had to occur while Caitlyn was in foster care, and not with us. So that matter was quickly abandoned. Still, we were curious as to what was in the medical report, since it was not made available to us, so we fought to get it. The state and the doctor of the clinic tried their best to conceal it from us, and we had to fight, as we did with every medical record of Caitlyn while she was in state custody, and it was not until much later we would be able to see it.

What is important for readers of this book to understand is that parents have the right to all records contained in the medical files of their children. It does not matter if a parent does or does not have custody, so long as parental rights have not been terminated. So when a state takes custody of children, it is incumbent upon the state to keep parents informed where it comes to medical matters. It is not practiced that way in many states, even though it is the law. That is one of the main reasons that child kidnapping has been allowed to flourish and become a nationwide epidemic. (Discussed in chapter 22)

In our case, we found the so-called medical *professionals* to be corrupt and dishonest, concealing, uncooperative, and totally enveloped in the Michigan state child kidnapping ring. To this day when we request information on the childrens' medical files (and we do now have custody of our children), we still get strong resistance from the medical facilities we were forced to do business with in those dark and difficult days when our children were in state custody. That is why I encourage all parents in my state of Michigan, as well as in other states where these rings flourish, to complain loudly and with resolve to federal authorities to put a stop to the abuse that is inflicted by the states on children (all in the name of making money for their state coffers). If the feds, who fund these criminals, truly want to cut the budget, this is a good place to start. They need only cut funding to *Child Protective Services,* turning it over to states, making it an *expense* in each state, as opposed to an *income opportunity* in which states steal federal money, and just watch then how dramatically the reports of child abuse will go down all over the country.

But hiding information isn't all they do. Information is also passed from one medical provider to another (at a state's request). *Private patient information,* theoretically protected, whether it is yours or your children's health information, is invaded by the state. We were not aware of this until we won a hard fought battle to see what was in the doctors' reports from the unauthorized visits the state took it upon themselves to set up, in their zest to *create a case* against us. They were seeking to find something that might allow them to pursue sexual molestation charges against either my wife and I, or just me, and what we found is that they went into our medical histories as parents as well. We discovered this when we were finally able, after a lengthy battle, to get copies of some of the treatment information we sought on our children. Mind you, this is information we should have been given free as a part of this process of our children being *protected* in foster care. We should have had easy access to it. But because of the secretive nature of what they were doing, they fought us, revealing nothing. We did finally get some information during the process, but nothing would have supported the type of testing we found they did on Caitlyn, which included performing a rape kit, and when we asked why the state had proceeded in such a fashion, we got nothing but denials from all parties concerned. In the medical report we finally did get our hands on, written by Dr. Patricia M. Callahan, it stated that she did order tests, which was verified in the April 17th report and later a subsequent lab report documented by the Marquette General Health System. But we were denied a copy of any of it when we requested it, and had to fight to get the information which should have been freely given up to us. The question then becomes, "Why did they order such testing?" Was it just a shot in the dark to try to produce a case? Recall, Bob Ross, when asked when the state stops looking for prosecutable information, replied by saying, "Never." As it was, *all* of their efforts, it would seem, turned up nothing, and no medically supported child abuse findings could ever be substantiated, despite massive efforts on the part of this state to manufacture them.

—Chapter Ten—

The Resumption of Visitation

April 24, 2008 marked the resumption of our parental visitations, but certainly not the beginning of the end for the war. While our visitation rights were being restored to a certain extent, the prosecutor was still waging new battle, following our court hearing of April 14. Two days prior to our scheduled visitation of April 24, the prosecution pulled another fast one. On that day, Ms. Wittla filed a motion for admission of Caitlyn's *alleged comments* in her efforts to further her case against us for child abuse. In her motion she asked for admission of statements made by Elizabeth Fyle and by both foster parents of our children (obvious retaliation efforts). The foster parents had now allegedly made the same false allegations that Elizabeth put forth following her so-called *investigation* of our home, in which she flatly lied about what she said Caitlyn said. Gee, do you think it possible that the two of them might have *talked about doing this?* In any case, the foster parents were now saying too, that I had spanked her with a belt. In both such claims, the court was unable to allow the admission of the statements, simply because, in fact, the witnesses themselves (the kids) did not provide the testimony. But that wasn't going to stop a relentless prosecutor and vindictive social workers from trying in any case. And later, even though not admitted, the court would show a position of having accepted that theory. But to make the record clear, once again, I never used a belt on my children. That was Bobby's assertion—remember? The Nascar driver? And if you ask my step daughter, Caitlyn, about this at this printing, at age ten, she will deny it ever happened. And no, she is not living in fear of me at this time.

In any case, we did get our visitation on April 24, 2008, which was insignificant so far as events flaring up any more. But the girls did take our leaving to go home very hard again, as there was a lot more crying on their part as well as our own. I guess I could never express, except to another parent, what the feeling is. You feel defenseless, unable to help your child as she reaches out to you, and that is a feeling that cannot possibly be written down on paper. In any case, as a means of attempting to *console* my children, I told them they would be coming home in 17 days. *HOW DARE I DO THAT!* While it did offer her a sense of security for the moment, which was my intent, it totally set off Andrea Andriacchi and DHS! So on April 28, 2008, I would hear all about it in a follow up discussion, as we entered for our next visit. When we arrived for that visit, DHS had already called police, and tried to *scare us* into signing a set of *ground rules for visitations* they had printed up for us. We were then advised of other *requirements* DHS had for us, such as being told we should provide diapers and other items when we visited. It's kind of funny, because in any sports event, the organization that rules over the sport creates the ground rules and makes them clear to the participants *before* any actual game action commences. They do this so a certain *standard* can be followed by all in the game. But here, it was different. In the game of *child kidnapping* the state's *standards* are made up as they go along. So here is the list of rules we were presented with and were forced to sign off on as we entered the facility on that day:

(1) You should provide a nutritious snack for all the children. This includes food, drink, and/or formula.

(2) You should provide diapers and wipes during the supervised visits.

(3) You should use no form of physical punishment or humiliation during visits.

(4) You should watch the children at all times and not leave that responsibility to someone else.

(5) You will not discuss any concerns you have regarding the case while visiting with your children.

(6) You should make sure the areas you and the children use are cleaned up by the end of the visit.

(7) You should make sure that discussions, topics, and situations during the visits promote a healthy environment and are in the best interests of the children.

Now, in baseball, such ground rules, as I said, are put in place to try to establish a level playing field for all of the players in any one game, no matter what team they may play. It doesn't vary from game to game. It would seem that the purpose in the game of child kidnapping, however, is not to set rules for the game, but rather to make sure the players behave in a way suitable to the sport. So the rules in one game (or visit) may be altered by time you play the next game (make the next visit). And as a player, you are allowed no input, you cannot complain, object, or otherwise express yourself. In baseball, at least, you can point to the rules and get a questionable play overturned if it is called wrong. Not so in child kidnapping. There are no questionable calls. If the state says it is so, it is so. (We would call this a dictatorship if a government was doing it, would we not?) Oh, wait! A government *is doing it!* Well, anyway, we were to understand that under their own corrupt system, we were to have no input, follow the rules they set down, and keep our thoughts to ourselves! To do otherwise would be to put your children at risk! I think in common terms, that amounts to a thing called *blackmail.*

In any case, once given our list of rules and requirements, Ms. Andriacchi got right to the scolding for having given hope to my children on the previous visit. We were not to discuss the case in any way, so that was a no-no. Not able to keep my big mouth shut, I reversed the tables and chided her for them telling Caitlyn to keep secrets from us. Again, a no-no. She quickly denied she did this, so I related to her that we were still the parents, and that we noted where previously, while at home, when she returned from school Caitlyn was very open and willing to tell us how her school day went. Now, it seemed, she didn't want to say, expressing that it was a *secret.* I added to that, saying there was no court order saying we could not talk to our children. I asked her what was wrong with putting *hope* in my daughter's heart.

She remained adamant that putting a date out was not good. Especially when it was uncertain what that date would be. I fired back that a six year old has no concept of calendar dates, and there could be no harm in providing some hope. I elaborated then, expressing that DHS was saying one thing, while the perception we had was a lot different from what they were saying. An example of that was when Caitlyn had expressed to us that she had been told (regarding our house), "that home was dangerous." We wondered just *who* had been telling her this. Was it Elizabeth Fyle? Or was it the foster parents? *Who?* So why was the state instilling thoughts in the minds of our daughters that our home, and we, as parents, were *dangerous*. More importantly, *why?*

So now it was on to the next point. Caitlyn, it seemed, was seeing a counselor, and we wanted to know why, and who had authorized this. Ms. Andriacchi quickly stated that Caitlyn was under court jurisdiction and that the Guardian Ad Litem (GAL) had the authority to send her to doctors, etc. My wife Janet challenged that on the spot, as she informed Ms. Andriacchi they only had the authority to determine where she lived, and that federal laws prevented anything else. (And at this point, in fact, the court still did not have jurisdiction over the kids—that had not been determined yet). So I then advised Ms. Andriacchi that we had a civil liberties lawyer, and that there were a *lot* of rights that had been violated already. I told her we would engage them in that at a later time, but for now, we just wanted to see our children. I expressed to her that our visitation time had been diminished a lot already because some *stupid idiot* said we spanked our kids or whatever, which would be a court decision to come in a trial next month. I expressed disappointment that we had been promised more visiting time as well as phone calls, but have received neither one. Her rebuttal was that she had not been made aware of any such promises. I replied, "Well, *we* are!" She then indicated it would all be worked out the next month, in that they did not as yet have jurisdiction as far as we were concerned, but we could do something if we chose to do it. I should have replied that what we would choose to do is take the children home, since she now admitted they had no jurisdiction. But unfortunately, that thought did not pop up in my mind at the time. But truthfully, what right did the state have to kidnap our kids? And to hold them without jurisdiction?

It was at this point I began my full assault. We had done nothing wrong, I asserted, and the government comes into our life, telling us how to raise our children. That, despite the fact the law clearly states they have no right to do that. I told her she could try to get all the jurisdiction she wanted the next month, but as where we had done nothing wrong, we were not about to take *services* from the state for something we did not do. I went on to say that even if the court were to find us guilty, we would not stop, and as a next step, we would be appealing any such local decision. I told her we would not stop until every court resource had been exhausted. Again, defensively retaliating herself, she said, "Well, it is your decision, but it only prolongs matters." This really enraged me, as a red flag would do to a mad bull. "Then it does," I shot back, "and we are not going to bow down to the government."

The conversation then reverted to Caitlyn. I told Angela that if Caitlyn wants to talk, I was going to talk. I insisted I was the only dad Caitlyn ever knew. Then I pointed out that it was not our *wish* to fight, that, in fact, we were all exhausted over this. I included the kids in that. My concluding statement to her was, "You folks feel that we are not good parents, so you took our kids out of our home for *imminent danger.* Then I come in here and see our kids covered in bruises. Now *who* is the culprit here?" I went on to tell her that I had problems with that because there was no *imminent danger.* "There was no evidence, nothing," I told her, "only two witnesses who had lied, and their lies will be proven in court."

Angela, still in a retaliation state, responded that we had not communicated with them either. But that was a complete lie. We had been *begging* for more visits, phone calls, etc., from day one of this charade! She insisted she had received no phone calls from us, which I promptly challenged because we had never been advised we *could* do that. She shot back that we *had* been told in the very beginning of the process, and that she had transcripts to prove it. It was time now for me to pull out the tape recorder I had been using and I challenged her to see how her lies held up to my recordings. Oddly enough, all of the *transcripts* she talked about somehow came up missing. This all made her very angry, and she stated that if we continued to record, the visitation would be cancelled. I refused to stop recording, and then asked her why the DHS was *sneaking* our kids over to doctors. Still angry, she denied that, and coldly stated she was not going to go any further with our conversation (this is what they do when they know *they* are the ones being monitored, as recordings would illustrate). With that I reiterated we wanted to see our children. She responded by again insisting I first stop recording. I again refused, and she immediately cancelled the visitation. I informed her promptly that she had just violated a court order and we would be dealing with that the very next day. As she ushered us out of the building, knowing my girls were in the next room, I yelled, "Bye Caitlyn. Bye Ashley. I love you!" My gut told me that they would lie to my girls and try to sell them the idea that we didn't love them and didn't show up. So that's why I yelled, so that they would *know* we *were there* and that we would do everything we could to get them back.

—Chapter Eleven—

Leading Up To The Trial

On April 29, 2008, we found ourselves back in court for the protective proceedings motions leading up to our trial, which was to begin in approximately two weeks time. This was primarily a hearing to determine patterns to be followed in the actual trial which would take place, with little testimony given, the exception that which was given by Elizabeth Fyle, the Child Protective Services worker for the Gogebic County DHS office. The prosecutor, Tracie Wittla, began questioning of Ms. Fyle by asking her if she had interviewed our daughter, Caitlyn in the case. It was affirmed that she had. The testimony then continued as follows:

MS. WITTLA: Did you draft a petition in this case?

MS. FYLE: Yes I did.

MS. WITTLA: Did you read the motion that I submitted for you to testify about what Caitlyn told you?

MS. FYLE: Yes I believe I did.

WHOA! Hold it here! "BELIEVE I DID?" You either DID or DID NOT. This is not a gray area question, and you are testifying before a judge in a court! How can any judge accept this answer? Or how can any subsequent questions be accepted as EVIDENCE in this case if the woman cannot say for SURE if she did or did not read the motion the prosecutor was asking about? Well, back to their "testimony":

MS. WITTLA: In the motion I had cited Paragraphs 29 thru 38 and 44 thru 54, and if you look at the petition can you tell me if those are the paragraphs that correspond with things that Caitlyn told you?

MS. FYLE: Yes they are.

(How could she be sure if she wasn't sure if she read it or not?)

MS. WITTLA: Did Caitlyn tell you anything beyond what's in those paragraphs; I guess at her first interview with you?

MS. FYLE: Um, I believe that that contains most, if not all, of what she had told to me.

(If you didn't read it, perhaps it may have even contained MORE....)

MS. WITTLA: Okay —

MR. FINDLAY: — may I, only cause I want to make sure I'm on that same page; where were you indicating that there were references to — I'm sorry, I'm, never mind, sorry about that. I, I see it now, sorry.

MS. WITTLA: Um, when you interviewed Caitlyn, what did you do when you interviewed her?

MS. FYLE: I utilized the Forensic Interview Protocol.

MS. WITTLA: And when you say you used, utilized the Forensic Interview Protocol, does that mean that you asked her questions in a certain way?

MS. FYLE: Yes.

Stop again for a moment. Does it seem to anyone, other than myself, that the way this question was raised by the prosecutor that she and the witness might have talked about this already, prior to this court hearing? And a further question would be whether or not the witness was tutored in her answering of this question. If this technique had to be explained in court, as was to be done next, how is it that a witness would already know exactly what the prosecutor meant when she asked what she did when she interviewed Caitlyn? The more this case progressed, the more it seemed the questions and answers had quite a lot of rehearsing before ever being served up in court.

MS. WITTLA: Can you describe just briefly what that means?

MS. FYLE: Um, it means we insure that the child knows the difference between the truth and a lie, and we, um, we discuss the fact that the child needs to be truthful. Um, I go through a few of things as far as if, if I say something incorrectly back — I'm paraphrasing what I've been told. Um, the child can correct me if I say something incorrectly; I call them the wrong name; if I, whatever, ah, should happen they can correct me. And, um, I also go through the explanation that if I ask a child a question and if they don't have the answer to it, they say "I don't know." Um, the Forensic Interview Protocol also provides for us to ask open-ended questions; such as, you know, can you tell what happened? What happened after that? And then what happened? And they just tell us what happened, tell us their story.

MS. WITTLA: Did you have any problems talking to Caitlyn?

MS. FYLE: No.

MS. WITTLA: Was she willing to talk to you?

MS. FYLE: Yes.

MS. WITTLA: Did she seem afraid or scared to talk to you?

MS. FYLE: No.

MS. WITTLA: Was anyone else there when you had this interview with her?

MS. FYLE: Bob Ross was in the room.

MS. WITTLA: Did you give her anything while you were talking to her?

MS. FYLE: No.

MS. WITTLA: Make her any promises?

MS. FYLE: No.

MS. WITTLA: You interviewed her a second time on March 17th?

MS. FYLE: Yes I did.

MS. WITTLA: Where were you when you talked to her?

MS. FYLE: At the, the first foster home.

MS. WITTLA: And that was in Ontonagon?

MS. FYLE: Yes.

MS. WITTLA: Okay and the first foster home was Laverne Pestka's?

MS. FYLE: Yes.

MS. WITTLA: When you spoke to her; well when you went there to see her that day, how did she react when she saw?

MS. FYLE: Um, she looked at me and she smiled, and I said, "Hi"to her, and then she took off running down the hallway, down to her bedroom.

MS. WITTLA: Was there a point in time when you did actually talk to her?

MS. FYLE: Yes.

MS. WITTLA: And what she tell you, ah, about her parents when she talked to you?

MS. FYLE: Well when she, when she came out of the bedroom, that she had been in, um, she told me that, or I, I heard her saying as she was walking out of the — down the hallway anyways; that they are cops and my daddy says that I, that I'm not supposed to talk to them. And so then, I explained to her, I said, "Well Caitlyn, you know I'm not the cops." And so she was building a puzzle on the floor, so I sat down with her and I began building a puzzle with her; just chit-chatting, and then she asked me if I wanted to see her room; and I said sure. So we went down into her room, and I asked her; I said, "Caitlyn I have to ask a few more questions — of you." Whatever, and so I again followed the Forensic Interview Protocol; went through the rules of Forensic interviewing and she again agreed to tell me the truth, etc., and then I asked her, I said, "Well what, you know, what was said after the last time we talked?' And she said that "My daddy said that I'm not supposed to talk about spanks because you're going to trick me, and you, and that you're going to take me away."

MS. WITTLA: Did you ask her anything else about how life was going or how she felt about things?

MS. FYLE: I asked her, I said, "You know, can you tell me, or how, how, you know, how are things here?" And she goes, "Hoa, really good."

MS. WITTLA: I said, well, what do you mean by really good?

MS. FYLE: And she says, "Well, you know when I get in trouble,I have to ah, I just have to sit in a timeout chair for a few minutes. And I said, "Well, how is that different from how things usually, you know, how things, how things before?" And she said that when she was at home, she would have to stand in a corner for a really long, long time or she would get the belt; and she was in trouble.

MS. WITTLA: Now you just stressed words when you were quoting here, you said, things were really good; is that the way she said it to you?

MS. FYLE: Yes.

MS. WITTLA: Have you spoken to her since then?

MS. FYLE: Yes.

MS. WITTLA: Ah, did you see her face to face since then, to talk to her or....?

MS. FYLE: Yes, I've seen her since then.

MS. WITTLA: Okay, when you've spoken to her since, have you used the Forensic Interview Protocol any time since then to have an interview with her?

MS. FYLE: Not that I recall; not that I can think of, no.

MS. WITTLA: So how would you describe the other contacts that you've had with her then?

MS. FYLE: Fairly, fairly, you know, casual. You know, "Hi, how are you?" That kind of thing.

MS. WITTLA: Okay, nothing where, um, you would describe it as her being interviewed?

MS. FYLE: No not that I can recall.

MS. WITTLA: During the times that you have see that, has she mentioned anything else about her parents, one way or the other?

MS. FYLE: I can't recall specifics off the top of my head right now.

MS. WITTLA: Okay, I have nothing further.

THE COURT: Mr. Findlay?

MR. FINDLAY: Forensic Protocol, um what is that and where could I get it; well I won't make a compound question. What is Forensic Protocol?

MS. FYLE: It's, it's a state, um, from what I recall, off the top of my head, it was designed through the Michigan Children's Task Force, and it's basically a protocol for how to interview children, and allow them to tell your story; you don't ask leading questions; you don't offer, you know, bribes or promises or, you just basically ask open ended questions and allow them to tell you their story.

THE COURT: Just to interrupt for a minute, um, and, and to answer Mr. Findlay's questions; the Court takes judicial notice the Forensic Interview Protocol as having been promulgated and adopted by the State of Michigan is the method where interviewing children in child abuse cases. Um, for you to have a copy, I think the Court had several and before you came back I had distributed some books to all defense attorneys and guardian ad litems, and it's contained in those books. I think it's also in the Lawyer, Lawyer/Guardian ad Litem handbook; if your office doesn't have that, we'll make that available for you, if you want to pick up from there.

MR. FINDLAY: Um, and the Court, I've may have the missed recording date, it has been accepted by the State of Michigan, or has not?

THE COURT: Well I, the State of Michigan put it out as, as the way of doing interviews, and it's been a generally accepted, and, I'm not saying there's any court case that says it's infallible; it's just the methodology that is currently in use in the state of Michigan.

Does it strike ANYONE at all funny at this point that all three — the prosecutor, the witness for the state, and the judge seemed to lean on the importance of this protocol, and so willing to be forthcoming in describing it for all in the court room to hear? Why such importance to the "procedure?" Doesn't it seem obvious that a clear attempt was being made here to "make a case" against us by suggesting all of the comments from my daughter were totally "unsolicited" and simply volunteered to them? And why is it the judge was so anxious to add his two cents and not simply just listen? It smells of plots and pre-planning among all three in my interpretation of what was going on.

MR. FINDLAY: And that does answer my question, where I can get a copy of it. Ah, and I knew what it was but just wanted some more particulars. (Then, to FYLE) Um, do you recall what the specific questions you asked her were? I was referring, first of all, to the, ah, statements that are alleged and made in the petition. Um, all it, all the petition contains are what Caitlyn said. Do you remember what your questions were?

MS. FYLE: Well, specific to what, which items, I mean?

MR. FINDLAY: Well, um, I think you wanted to admit 29 to 38, and 29 is what Caitlyn stated when she was in trouble, she has to stand in the corner.

MS. FYLE: Uh-hm, I, so I believe I would have asked her something to the effect of, you know, can you tell me what happens when you get in trouble. What, you know, happens?

MR. FINDLAY: Okay so, um, referring to the interview at the Pestka's home, um, do you — you're indicating that you used the Forensic Protocol at that time too?

MS. FYLE: Yes.

MR. FINDLAY: But that was all done after the petition was filed, to remove and the petition was filed?

MS. FYLE: Right.

MR. FINDLAY: That would be Pestka's home?

MS. FYLE: Right.

MR. FINDLAY: Nothing, nothing further.

THE COURT: Ms. Wittla?

MS. WITTLA: Um, just one point to clarify? In the motion as I filed it, I believe in Paragraph 9, oh sorry, 10. Um, the paragraph reads that Ms. Pestka went into Caitlyn's room to ask what was wrong, and Caitlyn stated, "They are cops, my daddy said I'm not supposed to talk to them," and I am not sure if you just said today that you heard her say that?

MS. FYLE: Right.

MS. WITTLA: Okay so you, you actually heard Caitlyn say that?

MS. FYLE: Yes, yes.

MS. WITTLA: But she was responding to a question you asked; she was responding to Laverne Pestka?

MS. FYLE: Right, I believe Bob, Bob's heard that statement as well; we'd both gone up to the Pestka home that day.

With that, after my attorney once again clarified with Ms. Fyle that Ms. Pestka was not using the Forensic Protocol when she asked that question, Ms. Fyle was excused. Robert (Bob) Ross was then called, and his testimony echoed much of the same question responses as Ms. Fyle had given. Bob did establish that he was there as an observer, not a direct interviewer. In explaining this, his testimony was as follows:

MS. WITTLA: Is it fair to say that at this stage of the case that you and Ms. Fyle have some of the similar objectives, but you each have your own separate things you have to cover?

MR. ROSS: Yes.

MS. WITTLA: Okay so from the outside looking in, it might like why do you need two, two of you guys there, but you each have to do different things?

MR. ROSS: Yes I — initially we partnered up on the case, as I said for worker's safety. Now the case is kind of split; she handles the PS part of the case; and I'm insuring, I'm overseeing the, ah, the care of the kids in the foster care situation.

MS. WITTLA: I have nothing further your Honor.

THE COURT: Mr. Findlay?

MR. FINDLAY: Um, and I should have asked this of Ms. Fyle as well; the purpose of the, using the Forensic Protocol, I mean, is done as investigation tool, correct? I, I'm asking you Mr. Ross, I should have asked Ms. Fyle.

MR. ROSS: Yes it is.

MR. FINDLAY: And it's done with the purposes of developing evidence for discovering evidence, um, in these type of cases?

MR. ROSS: Correct.

That in itself tells you the state had no case. They had to try to "create" evidence in order to charge us with child abuse. In other words, their "witnesses" (Bobby and Becky Payne) were not strong enough to merit this case on their own. Any good judge would have dismissed at this juncture alone, if that were the case. And a prosecutor of worth would have refused to bring the case in the first place if the Payne claims were so worthless and weak. But not in the state of Michigan. Wittla continued on redirect:

MS. WITTLA: Mr. Ross when do you stop looking for evidence in child protective cases?

MR. ROSS: Never.

I rest MY case. He said it all in that response alone. The state of Michigan is in it for the money, and will look for any angle to try to prosecute parents, whether or not they have solid evidence that abuse ever occurred in the first place.

Tracie Wittla had finished with her escapades at this point, but my lawyer was not quite finished. He began with his argument that the use of testimony Forensic Protocol violates the right of confrontation under the United States constitution:

MR. FINDLAY: Although this isn't a criminal case, I think that's still at issue in this case, and the case law I've read indicates that there's, ah, a right of confrontation in these cases, that the respondents, the parents, have a right to see the evidence against them, and the witnesses against them and to have them cross-examined and, and to do all the things that — almost that they're done in a criminal case; and that's because the, I think as the court has acknowledged previously that, that the Supreme Court has said the parents do have a liberty interest in their, their children. So that's why the constitution and the due process rights kick in; so, as it's a confrontation issue, I would direct the court to the, um, United States Supreme Court case of Crawford vs. Washington, it is a 2004 case out of the U.S. Supreme case, court, it isn't a criminal matter, but it, it sets forth, um certain new standards, and it kind of turns — prosecuting it at the time, and that it sort of turned everything on its head in terms of making it actually more difficult for Prosecutors to get hearsay. What would ordinarily be viewed as hearsay evidence, um, into court because it violates the confrontation issue. And I guess I just go through the, what I believe is the appropriate analysis in, in when the court is looking at determining whether Crawford is an issue is: (1) Is the witness available; um, and if there's — and that is the crux of it, the witness availability in this case; obviously this child witness is not going to be available if we're using the Tender Years exception as the whole purpose of the Prosecutor wanting to do that, so they don't have to have the witness testify. Um, then the court needs to look at whether the, there was a prior exam — opportunity to cross-examine the witness; obviously nobody on the parents' side has access to the children other than the limited visits that they've had with them. I certainly had — haven't had any opportunity to cross-examine them, and that makes it sound much more harsh than even to question them or to independently, um, talk to them about these events; and nobody has and I don't know if there's an illegal means for that to happen. Um, then the next thing you go to is whether the statements are testimonial, and, and that is where most of the case law, subsequent to Crawford is, has gone in trying to figure out what is testimonial; but I think in this instance there's no question that the questions asked and the information and statements made; um, by a child in this circumstances are testimonial because they are done in anticipation of litigation. I mean, that's why I asked Mr. Ross about whether they're done as part of the investigative process; I mean, it's clearly done as an investigative tool; it's not, it's not like an excited utterance hearsay; it's somebody just, you know, a child blurting out somebody beat me or, or a child crying and somebody coming up to them and saying, you know what happened. And they make an excited utterance; those wouldn't be testimonial statements, but here, there's no question that these statements are done in anticipation of litigation; and actually to further the litigation. Um, and when those factors exist in that chronology, then Crawford stands for the proposition that those statements, hearsay statements, which are out-of-court statements should be inadmissible as a violation of that person's right to confront the evidence against them. And so based on that, I would argue that the Tender Years exception, um, basically violates Crawford. And I, I have looked to try and find a case that even mentions Crawford, um the child abuse, and to be honest I haven't found one. I don't know if anybody's ever — I don't, wouldn't be so presumptuous to think that I'm the first one that's raised it. But it hasn't made it up to a, um, appeal, appellate level that I'm aware of at this point, so thank you. I have the case if the court is interested in the case itself; I have a copy of the case here.

THE COURT: No, I mean, I am interested but just let me say, um, I guess Crawford takes another turn in criminal law as indicated, but what we are dealing with here is the child protective law, which has been basically made, made major changes in late 80's and early 90's with the Brimer and Brock cases in Michigan which continue to recognize the parent has a liberty interest in the right to parent their child. There are however some exceptions that are made or distinctions that are made between the criminal law and the child protective law because constitutionally the courts weigh the rights of the child and the need for society's need to protect the child vrs. the rights of the parents. Again, the parents' rights certainly do exist in our constitution and are protected. But because of that things are different in child protective cases and the current law in the State of Michigan continues to allow this Tender Years exception to exist. As a matter of fact there's even been a, um, if you will, reduction in the parents' protection in this Tender Years exception in that a number years ago it used to be a two prong analysis of adequate indicia of reliability, followed by further corroboration of the statements. And in at least one case, I have refused to admit a statement because it wasn't corroborated by anyone else, other than the State Police trooper that took the statement. Um, they've removed that now, and the only issue is the indicia of, of reliability which in this case is bolstered by the use of the Forensic Interview Protocol, adopted by the State for the very reason of, of making not such a leading, trapping type of question, ah, go on. It was done in a comfortable environment; it was done in an environment where apparently the child appeared to be comfortable and happy. Um, apparently the responses were somewhat spontaneous, all of which add to the, ah, adequate indicia of reliability; I will therefore grant the Prosecutor's motion as to those issues that were indicated on the record of Ms. Fyle, or in the presence of Ms. Fyle, any statements contained or proffered in her motion where the — Ms. Fyle was not there and were made to the social workers will not be allowed because, ah, we don't have the foster parents here, and so we have no establishment or adequate indicia spontaneity. But let me see now because there was some question about what came up here, so, um —

MR. FINDLAY: — I think Paragraph 10 which is the — they are cops, my daddy said I'm not supposed to talk to them — that was not a response to a —

THE COURT: — No, but it was still done within the presence, and I find that it was an adequate indicia situation, even though it wasn't responsive to the protocol it was still consistent with prior, ah, statements or the plan scheme, whatever in this case, so I, ah, I'd allow that.

Now, let's stop for just a moment. You will notice how quickly this judge made the effort to discuss "indicia of reliability" because it could quickly separate criminal cases from the Michigan-preferred child protection law. You could say it is one way to circumvent the constitution, which is done frequently in our courts. And you have to *love* the way court and other professionals choose their pet little words, such as *indicia*. Why don't they just use the words that mean the most to most people? In this case, where they say "indicia of reliability" they could just say "indicators of reliability". But it is the professionals' way of conning the public into believing they are a bit smarter than everyone else. Or, in this case, a crutch the judge can use to say he is going to ignore the constitution because of his own desire to pursue a case based on his own interpretation. It helps him in his effort to continue illegal kidnapping schemes. Constitution be damned.

From that point on, the hearing turned to other rule proceedings for the pending trial, or in the case of the prosecutor, to an opportunity to launch her attacks on us. The judge indicated first that support persons could be included, namely the guardian-ad-litem named on behalf of the children (who frankly represented the state and not the children). They discussed the possibility of video or screening, which the judge then indicated had been brought up in preliminary discussions in his chambers. The judge indicated he didn't like screening, finding it "inefficient" in prior use. He seemed open minded about video, but asked Ms. Wittla where she was going on that subject:

MS. WITTLA: Well your Honor, um, as the court is aware the guardian-ad-litem can't be here today, and to some extent I'm making this request regardless of who calls Caitlyn as a witness. So I would request that, um, close circuit television be used regardless of who calls this child, um, just as a protective measure for her. I can't say that I plan on calling her right now because that's not true; I don't plan on calling her; but I can't say that something wouldn't change that I would need to; I also can't predict what they parents are going to do; whether or not they're going to call her as a witness. I don't believe that the guardian-ad-litem intends to call her as a witness, but to be completely honest with you; I didn't ask him the question either. So my request would be that if Caitlyn is called as a witness because I don't think anybody would call Ashley, she's just too darn little, but if Caitlyn is called I would still request that a close circuit television be made an option for her. I also wanted to let the court know that although I've had voice mail tag going on back and forth between me and her counselor, Mr. Kitchen, I haven't had a conversation with the man to really fair it out whether or not he really believes this would be the worst thing in the world or not. It would be, it would be surprising to me if he was in favor of anything less than closed circuit television and screens and the like, because I've never met a counselor who didn't think that that was necessary.

THE COURT: Okay but, I mean you kind of answered a question I was going to ask, I mean, you have to acknowledge it is your burden to — you can't just ask and have it for convenience, you have to have —

It was at about this point that the prosecutor, from my perspective, began to "lose" it. It was as though when she could not have her way, her behavior was like that of a small child throwing a temper tantrum. And it was at this point, as the judge held her in question as to her motives, that she began her personal attacks on us, as the ensuing testimony revealed:

MS. WITTLA: — Well, it's not so much convenience your Honor as it is the fact that, um, the proofs as they've come in so far indicate that this child; if the petition is to be believed was subject to a severe form of physical abuse. Ah, further that she was told not to talk about this, and Ms. Fyle was the one who saw her and knows that she's not supposed to talk to them; she's not supposed to talk to the police because her father said that they would take her away, blah, blah, blah.

Blah, blah, blah? Is that the way you explain things to a judge? More like tantrum display to me. She continued:

MS. WITTLA: I don't think that that's going to encourage her to be forthright and speak about what has happened to her if she is in a room where she sees the very man who told her not to talk about these things.

THE COURT: But at the very least don't you have to establish there's going to be some harm to her, I mean, which you proffered, but we don't have a Craig Kitchen here?

MS. WITTLA: I don't have Craig Kitchen here, no, but I would I guess argue from a common sense approach since that's all I have for today that she would be harmed because she has already been coached and told do not talk about these things. I would argue to the court that even if she had not that any child who would have to testify at the age of six years old, in front of a parent who physically abused them, about that abuse would have a hard time talking about it, and that would emotionally be upsetting for them and potentially psychologically damaging to them.

What? Was I convicted already? How could she state emphatically that I abused my own daughter? And why did this so-called "judge" just sit there and allow her to do that? It was our contention the STATE abused her. It was not us, and that had already been established via the medical exams done PRIOR to the state taking custody! In any case, this inept judge, ignoring her preposterous accusation, which, at this point was totally unproven, continued the discussion:

THE COURT: Okay, I, ah, I know you've gone through this, ah, recently in a criminal case, and, ah, which would shed a tangent — tangential, not tangential but a companion case here. But I mean, I guess don't you acknowledge that the cases say you have to do something more than a general statement about what happened to any kid or, it's more or less conjecture what you're saying, I, I guess. It may be common sense, but, but you have to have something — you've proffered Craig Kitchen which I would indicate for the record would probably be enough, but....

MS. WITTLA: Mr. Kitchen left me a voice mail where he indicated that he thought that protective measures should be used, but he did not give me any detail as to why or what types; he just said, you know, yes, I agree with you; I'll call you back. And then every time I called him, I don't get in touch with him. I, I can't tell you exactly how the decision came about in the other case, in the criminal version of it, but to some extent I believe that the judge also relied on a somewhat common sense approach, that yeah, if a little kid were to talk about this subject, (the kid) would have a hard time talking about it in an open court room; that you know, so to speak. Um, that case obviously was a sexual assault case, and that would be much easier to believe from a common sense point of view that anybody would have a hard time talking about that. So I certainly understand the court's opinion that to some extent I'm labeling all kids as being unable to have this conversation in front of their parents. I think to some extent that's true, but for Caitlyn she's only six years old. For Caitlyn she has been physically restrained so that she could be beaten by her father.

WHOA! Let's stop it right here! And the judge should have stopped it right there! A person with mental problems made that *allegation* in his original statements to the police, but those charges were *never* substantiated, and this prosecutor just delivered this to the court as though it were *fact*. She knew this was an out and out *lie*, and yet she had the audacity to do this in court. She should be disbarred for such outrageous behavior. The truth is we *never* restrain our kids to exact discipline on them, and that was supported by our vindication early on.

MS. WITTLA: For Caitlyn she was told "Don't talk about this." (She said), "I'm not supposed to talk about spanks, I'm not supposed to talk to you because you're the police."

So here again, we see how this prosecutor took things out of context to build her own version of the case. First, I did advise Caitlyn not to talk to them *because of the phony allegations they were attempting to build into facts.* We knew what they were doing, and this prosecutor's efforts to reestablish what we had already overcome in those earlier hearings only confirms I was right in telling my daughter not to trust them. All that we, as parents, wanted, and our kids wanted, was to be reunited again, yet here was this prosecutor attempting through lies and distortion to make it appear we were guilty of things we had never done.

MS. WITTLA: I think that the foundation is already there so that we know that this kid is not going to want to talk about this stuff at all if she has to be eyeball to eyeball with her dad. And I don't think if she sees her mother it's going to be any more helpful to her.

What Ms. Wittla really meant was that it was not going to be any more helpful to the state.

THE COURT: I keep, I keep — I'm kind of making the argument for you here, just give me a minute. I'm not — I, I'm reading the cookbook, but I'm also, you know, in Brock which led the way in opening up, if you will, easier procedures for the prosecution in these cases; even in that case they had a counselor testify. In the cookbook that we use here, you know, Michigan Child Protective Proceedings, they quote from Maryland vrs. Craig, and they talk about the confrontation issue and the requisite finding of necessity must be a case specific. The trial court must hear evidence and determine that the use of, of a closed circuit television is necessary to protect the welfare of a particular child witness who seeks to testify; must find that the court, the child witness would be traumatized, not by the courtroom, but by the presence of the defendant. Um, it's more than an argument on common sense; it's, it's you gotta' have something. So okay, all right, I've — let's go on further, go ahead Mr. Findlay.

MR. FINDLAY: Your honor, I, I, I mean the things that Ms. Wittla has indicated are the allegations which remain to be proven, um, that I understand that's their position, but, um, even if she was told these things about not testifying or not talking to them, obviously it wasn't very effective because she did. Um, and it appears from that, you know, even on the other issue the, the issue that statement from Mr. Ross indicated that the interview was done in the home with the parents present and she went ahead and talked to them, I don't think there's been any showing that, um, he's shaking his head that —

MR. ROSS: — parents were not present when we did the interview.

MR. FINDLAY: Not in the room, but wasn't it done at the home?

MR. ROSS: It was done in the home, Ms. Coleman — Ms. Coleman interrupted the interview twice.

MR. FINDLAY: Okay, she, she continued the talking in spite of that, um, and I don't think there is any showing that this child, Caitlyn, would suffer any kind of harm as a result of it. I think that, you know, the extent that they have the statements coming in; sort of indicate otherwise she seems to be pretty free about talking about this. Um, there hasn't been, and although visits have been supervised and, you know, hasn't been any allegations that she's afraid of the, the parents on those visits or, or afraid to, you know, be affectionate with them, um, I don't think the -

and especially the screen situation, and even the, the video conferencing, um, situation, and even the, the video conferencing, um, situation, I don't think the prosecution has met its burden in terms of using those measures.

THE COURT: Okay, the court's concern in protective, in a case like this has to be protection of the witness. There's also a broad court rule on the court's ability to take whatever methods necessary to protect the witness from fear or harassment, etc., etc. Um, and you know I don't want people — I guess for the better of the prosecutor, it's, it's oh, it's Michigan Rule of Evidence 6.11, court exercises reasonable control and, ah, over the mode in order of interrogating witnesses and also to protect witnesses from harassment or undue embarrassment. That's cited in again the Child Protective Handbook; um bench book has broad authority to do what we need to do. But we still have this confrontation issue, um, don't do that stuff please so —

At about this point the judge rendered a ruling on the idea of monitoring testimony of Caitlyn's testimony:

THE COURT: So what I'm going to do is, at this point, I'm not allowing closed circuit or screening, but I'm going to allow the prosecution, at some point between now and trial, um, to establish that need through, apparently, Mr. Kitchen or if she has another witness, another counselor, ah, that can do that, I'll allow her to do that, and I'm telling the defense that, you know, I, I think it's a foregone conclusion with a six year old, if somebody says that about this case specific particular child, um, that's going to be allowed. So, you still have that ability, but if you just let it go all the way through the trial, if you, if you let it go all the way through the trial and we're like at the end of the prosecution's case, and then you've decided to use these means, um, and you are still don't have Craig Kitchen, they're not going to come in. If between now and then either by contacting counsel, setting up some kind of hearing, ah, or even doing it during the trial, out of the presence of the jury, we will, we will deal with it as it comes up. However, because we're still at the adjudicated phase, rules of evidence do apply unless both parties agree, um, more or less it falls under the specific exception of the interactive video rule, we'll have to check on that cause there's been some changes in that over the past year or two. So you're going to need a live witness, like Craig Kitchen, I don't know, am I making myself clear?

MS. WITTLA: Yes.

THE COURT: So nothing to support the harm to the child, then no protective measures. Um, we get Mr. Kitchen or some other case specific person's testimony, then yes, as a matter of course I have allowed these in the past. And frankly, a lot of times, I think it's come up because counsel has kind of let it go and nobody's really contested it before. Okay, any other issues that I missed?

MS. WITTLA: There was a request to have witnesses filed by next Monday.

THE COURT: Thank you.

MR. FINDLAY: Yeah, we stipulate to that.

THE COURT: Counsel are ordered to have any witnesses filed by next Monday, we will relay that to Mr. Perhalla; if for some reason he has somebody independent, I'm just going to indicate I recognize he's engulfed in a trial right now and if something comes up between next Monday and the following week's trial we hay have to deal with that on an emergency basis.

MR. FINDLAY: And one other, just a — more of a query then, is there a means that the court is aware of that, that there can be an independent or even I can talk to the child; obviously with CPS or DHS present; I wouldn't ask that — I - I don't know that, that it's our intention to call her to testify; I don't want to, I don't think anybody wants to put the child through, you know, anything that's difficult, but I guess I just —

THE COURT: Okay Ms. Wittla can you spark my memory; it's come up before; we've done it before?

Why was the court asking *her?* This certainly sounds like these two (the judge and the prosecutor) had been down this road a few times together, doesn't it?

MS. WITTLA: Their request needs to be made to the guardian ad litem; typically, and the guardian ad litem usually responds to whether or not they're going to make their client available.

Does this mean the guardian ad litem has more *power* than the court? What the hell is the court for, if it cannot decide on this?

THE COURT: (continuing to ask the prosecutor's position on this): But we've done it, right? Haven't we done it like at DHS with a worker and a —

MS. WITTLA: — No we haven't ordered it, um, the guardian ad litem in, at least, one case that I know of said that her child client who was 15 or 16 years old would not have a problem talking to the defense attorney and she said she had no problem with it; she'd just make it happen.

Ok, so are we to understand that *any* attorney — no matter *who* they represent can decide who will or will not testify? Maybe that is one thing that is *wrong* with our current judicial system! We hire judges to make determinations on these matters, so why are they not making those determinations? If that is the way the law reads at the present time, it needs to be *changed* in order to eliminate *game playing* by the attorneys in the court room.

MS. WITTLA (continuing): Um, depending on the age of the child, sometimes they have determined they do not want to meet with someone else, so, that hasn't been a CPS case; that's been a criminal case. My familiarity with criminal cases where typically the family and the child themselves make that decision — determination whether they're going to, um, allow themselves to be interviewed by the defense or not.

THE COURT: I guess what I'm saying is I'll make myself available to what counsel wants. I'm clearly not for the two year old.

MR. FINDLAY: Yeah, I'm, I'm not even requesting that.

THE COURT: But, um, if it were to be done it would be done under controlled circumstances, I guess, I have to review the law, I'll do like an off the record conference with counsel, with all counsel, no exparte, um, I'm not talking about exparte but to find out where people are at on this and it's come up before; I'm not aware of any firm law on the matter, um, and we'll determine whether it can be done. If it is to be done, it would be under extremely controlled circumstances, like, ah, at DHS with a worker observing or possibly the guardian ad litem observing. Maybe between now and the next couple days we'll be able to get Mr. Perhalla's input on it. We would also, as indicated, want his input as guardian ad litem. Anything further for the record?

MR. FINDLAY: No.

MS. WITTLA: No your Honor.

With that, the judge discussed jury selection procedures briefly and then recessed the court.

—Chapter Twelve—

Resumption of the CPS Battles

By now we were chomping at the bit to see our children again, following the failed effort of April 28th, and in anticipation of doing so, we were relaxing at home on Sunday, May 4th, the day before our next scheduled visitation. I was advised I had a phone call while I was out from Angela Andriacchi, so when I got home I got my tape recorder ready and called her back. By now I knew I was in a war, so every single word from this point on would be recorded, despite the wishes of any of the child kidnappers. I was delighted that I chose to record the call, because it was indicative of the attitude that prevailed at CPS, among others in collusion with a ring of, to my way of thinking, common criminals.

The conversation rambled a lot, and for those who want to hear the entire ramble, it is available on my web site. For the benefit of those who do not want to listen to the excessive rambling, the following excerpts pretty well cover the more important elements of what we discussed:

ANGELA: What I was calling about was in regard to parenting time tomorrow. Due to the concerns in the behavior in the last one, I have to consult with the GAL (guardian ad litem) on how we proceed from here, so it would be postponed until I can get ahold of the guardian ad litem tomorrow.

ROBERT: OK, so you're calling me on a Sunday in the afternoon and you're finally coming up with this decision?

ANGELA: Well, I am at work today. That's why I'm calling today.

ROBERT: So you normally work on a Sunday?

ANGELA: Sometimes, yeah.

ROBERT: So what's happening? We're not allowed to see our children tomorrow?

ANGELA: Not tomorrow.

ROBERT: Why?

ANGELA: Because of the concerns that we have from our last event.

ROBERT: What concerns are those?

ANGELA: Well, I'll discuss it with the GAL and then I can discuss it with you further or you can call your attorney and have your attorney call me.

ROBERT: We spoke with our attorney and I'd like to know what excuse is this as to why we can't see our children.

ANGELA: Because of the behavior at the last visit.

ROBERT: What behavior is that?

ANGELA: The behavior of walking out of the visit.

ROBERT: Angela—you told us the visit was over because we wanted to record.

ANGELA: No, there was the option of not taking that into the visit.

ROBERT: But do you realize that it was RECORDED that YOU SAID that we were not allowed to see the kids because we were recording?

ANGELA: If you took the tape recorder in, yes.

ROBERT: OK, but YOU cancelled the visit, not us. You could have said, "Fine, go see your children."

ANGELA: Without the tape recorder, yes.

ROBERT: OK, but that was YOUR choice for us to not have the visit.

ANGELA: No, it was YOUR choice whether to take the visit, to shut the tape recorder off, and go into the visit— or to have the visit cancelled with the tape recorder. There is a difference.

ROBERT: Well, what are you HIDING then? Why would you CARE if we recorded the conversations?

ANGELA: I'm not going to discuss this any further right now. But I will call the GAL and get back to you.

ROBERT: I just have a question. Why are we doing this on a Sunday? At three in the afternoon? You couldn't have told us this a couple of days ago?

ANGELA: This was determined after discussing it with my supervisor. That's why it's now. I'm in the office today, and wasn't yesterday.

ROBERT: I still don't understand why we can't have a visit tomorrow.

ANGELA: I need to determine with the GAL how we are going to proceed as far as using tape recorders and cameras and those kind of things.

ROBERT: Oh, I see. Okay. So you're concerned about us recording anything?

ANGELA: That's not what I'm saying. But I'm going to discuss it with the GAL and then I will get back to you.

ROBERT: I see. Meanwhile, my children don't get to see their parents.

ANGELA: Not tomorrow.

ROBERT: Then explain to me this: the judge said we have the right to see our children.

ANGELA: Correct.

ROBERT: You're holding us from seeing our children because we have a recording device. So why is that? I mean, I'd like to know what law substantiates you holding our visitation, from us recording a conversation. You're taking transcripts during the whole time. Why can't we use some kind of documentation as a recorder?

ANGELA: We don't tape the visit. We write it up and you can see the notes. There's not an issue with that. I can show you the last...

ROBERT: But that is YOUR version typed up.

ANGELA: Actually, if you follow the last one, they weren't bad. I know you think things get made up, but really, they don't.

ROBERT: I don't understand why if it doesn't really matter, then, if you're recording all this at the time, then....

ANGELA: The problem with recording things, is that they can be ALTERED—or they can be.... I mean, different things can happen with those. We don't record here.

ROBERT: (Laughing) I'm sorry. You mean to tell me that your transcripts CAN'T be altered, but yet a hearing of something being digitally recorded CAN be altered? Is that what you just said?

ANGELA: No, I said that we... when we supervise... do not use recording devices.

Let's stop it here for just a moment. Governments *often* resort to *closed meetings,* as any news reporter could tell you, to keep confidential what they say, so the media, for instance, cannot know what they are talking about behind those closed doors. At the same time, down throughout our history, when some of the comments have been obtained and released, we have found corruption, altered facts, etc., to be a part of the business they did. Why would we think it might not apply in this case? It should also be noted that governments consistently try to hide facts by blacking out what they do release in public documents, and try to claim things such as national security as a reason. So an argument against recording is a bad argument, and in my view, recording should not just be allowable.... but a requirement! Ok, back to the conversation:

ROBERT: But you said that it can be altered.

ANGELA: Yes, but they can be... well, I'll discuss this with the attorney and I'll get back to you.

ROBERT: Well again, you're punishing us. That's what you're doing. You know, we have the right to see our children.

ANGELA: It's not to punish. It's to sort it out. The GAL has been in trial all week and I haven't been able to get ahold of him.

You mean this man had no answering machine or secretary? No way to get back to you if you left a message? What if you NEVER got ahold of him? Would that mean we would NEVER see our kids? This was a baseless argument, which I was not about to accept.

ROBERT: Don't you guys have attorneys as well, or do you need to talk to THEIR attorney?

ANGELA: Well, I don't have my own attorney. The GAL is the kids' attorney.

ROBERT: You guys are making this up as you go along, aren't you!

ANGELA: Absolutely not.

ROBERT: OK, well, I am highly disputing the fact that we are not allowed to see our children for the single fact that a little half inch by three inch long tape recording device. I just can't believe that we would go to this level.

ANGELA: It's also about the behavior. I don't want you coming in with a recorder, I say no, and then, when you guys yell to the kids as you're leaving—that's not fair to them.

ROBERT: Angela! You cancelled the visitation. We didn't. You could have said, "OK, fine. Keep the recorder. Just go visit your kids." You know, our main goal is to see the children. We don't understand why we are being punished now. Our children have the right to see us.

ANGELA: If you had taken the recorder out, the visit would not have been cancelled.

ROBERT: Oh, I see! So basically you were going to see how LEGALLY you were going to strip search us before we go in there so you can hide stuff.

ANGELA: No, I do not strip search though.

ROBERT: I know that. But it's not against the law to bring a recorder in.

ANGELA: It is against the law, without permission, to record somebody.

ROBERT: Michigan has a one-sided law. As long as one person knows, you can record. Don't you check the laws? I mean, you guys should check the laws when you take my kids to the doctors and you don't consult us. Don't you realize that you're breaking the law every time you do that? You know, Angela, you're not a government agency. You are umbrellaed under CPS as far as anything goes. You guys are subject to a lawsuit. OK? You're not under a government shelter! You are a sub-contractor. I want you to remember that every time you say and do stuff to us, OK? Because the outcome will be brought upon those who have done the most wrong. OK? Have a good day! (Pause) Hello?

ANGELA: Bye....

ROBERT: Goodbye.

So with that, we waited...again.

—Chapter Thirteen—

Caitlyn's Perspective

To this point the book you are reading has been presented from my own first person perspective. But I wanted to devote one chapter to allow for the viewpoint of Caitlyn, my step daughter, who was one of the primary *victims* of the state of Michigan. Too often, we concern ourselves only with our own points of view, and not those who are the most affected. So I asked a friend, whose wish it is to remain a confidential interviewer, but has a media past, if he would do an interview with Caitlyn, now that the tragedy is over, and he was perfectly willing to do so if I agreed that the questions he would ask of her would include private questions that even I would not be privy to in advance. He did that primarily because he wanted to be sure that her answers would go unrehearsed, and would reflect her views from a fact-laden series of events, my own desired slant of what took place not to influence her answers. I could not be present when he did the interview. With that agreed to, these are the transcripts he recorded in his interview with Caitlyn:

INTERVIEWER: Let's start with Elizabeth Fyle. Do you remember her?

CAITLYN: Yes.

INTERVIEWER: Do you remember Elizabeth Fyle interviewing you at home, or at any of the foster homes?

CAITLYN: (At first not remembering her by name, the interviewer reminded her that she was the one who talked to her at home prior to the raid at the motel) Yes, I remember her.

INTERVIEWER: Were you frightened of Elizabeth Fyle?

CAITLYN: Yes.

INTERVIEWER: Do you recall her coming to visit you at any of the foster homes?

CAITLYN: Yes.

INTERVIEWER: Do you recall what she asked you during these visits?

CAITLYN: Questions like: (1) Did your dad spank you? (2) Did your dad chase you with a broom? (3) Does he touch you in the private? (4) Does he cheat?

INTERVIEWER: How did you feel about the questions she asked?

CAITLYN: I just didn't want to talk to her because she asked me all those questions.

INTERVIEWER: What else can you recall about her? What she might have said to you, or done?

CAITLYN: Just.... she was always WATCHING me.

INTERVIEWER: Do you recall when you were taken from the custody of your parents at the motel?

CAITLYN: Yes.

INTERVIEWER: Were you afraid?

CAITLYN: Yes.

INTERVIEWER: Can you remember what you were first told by authorities as they took you away?

CAITLYN: Come with me. Your family will be OK. Just come with us. You could be safer.

INTERVIEWER: Do you remember anything they said later that might have had an effect one way or another about your fear or your feelings?

CAITLYN: Lorie (her last foster parent) locked me in the basement when I didn't do anything wrong. When I tried to tell other kids something and they didn't want to do it, they went to Lorie to tattle and she put me in the basement. When I complained about the other kids bothering me, she put me in the basement.

INTERVIEWER: Let's turn to your foster parents. Did you like them?

CAITLYN: No.

INTERVIEWER: None of them?

CAITLYN: No.

INTERVIEWER: Why?

CAITLYN: Because they were not my parents.

INTERVIEWER: Were you afraid of your foster parents?

CAITLYN: Yes.

INTERVIEWER: Did you feel comfortable in the foster homes?

CAITLYN: No.

INTERVIEWER: At one time at the FLEIS foster home, you had a bruise on your shin that concerned your parents, as well as one on your inner arm. It was explained that the shin injury was from normal child's play, and that you ADMITTED you bit yourself on your arm. Was that the truth?

CAITLYN: No. One grabbed my arm and said, "Let's go to the store." She gave my arm a really hard twist.

INTERVIEWER: So you never said you bit yourself?

CAITLYN: No.

INTERVIEWER: What about the shin?

CAITLYN: She knocked me over.

INTERVIEWER: During this entire process, were you EVER threatened or made to think you would not get to come home if you revealed things to your parents?

CAITLYN: I overheard the guy and the girl say it. They didn't know I heard it but I did.

INTERVIEWER: Now, what about Bob Ross and Angela Andriacchi - do you remember them? The ones who oversaw your visitations with you and your parents?

CAITLYN: Yes.

INTERVIEWER: How did you feel about them?

CAITLYN: First - worried about my parents. I tried to ask where my parents were and why I could not see them. Their answer was, "That's OK. They are OK. We are just not letting you be there so you won't get hit. Stuff like that."

INTERVIEWER: Did they EVER tell you what you should or should not say to your parents?

CAITLYN: Yes. They said not to talk to them. Don't tell them about the rug burn Lorie gave me.

INTERVIEWER: Lorie? She was your last foster parent, right?

CAITLYN: Yes.

INTERVIEWER: How did she give you the rug burns?

CAITLYN: I didn't want to eat my onions. She said, "Eat them... eat them!" I didn't want to so she slapped me and dragged me all the way upstairs to my room on my foot and on my arm too. I was screaming to get me out of there. Once I tried to escape by climbing on a ladder outside my window. Half way down she caught me and locked me in the basement. It was dark there, and I'm still afraid now of the dark.

INTERVIEWER: Turning now to your parents. Truthfully now, are you afraid of your parents?

CAITLYN: No

INTERVIEWER: Your parents, particularly your Dad was accused of many things. Just tell me if any of these things were true, OK?

CAITLYN: OK.

INTERVIEWER: Your dad was accused of spanking you with a belt. Did he, in fact, do that?

CAITLYN: No.

INTERVIEWER: Your Mom was accused of holding you down for him while he used the belt. Did she, in fact, do this?

CAITLYN: (Kind of laughing) No, never.

INTERVIEWER: How do you feel about your family life now?

CAITLYN: Kind of safer. More comfortable. But still kind of fearful of the dark.

INTERVIEWER: Are you fearful of people coming in the night to take you?

CAITLYN: A little, yes.

INTERVIEWER: OK, let's talk now about Bobby and Becky... they were the ones living with your family and brought the allegations against your parents. Do you remember them?

CAITLYN: Yes.

INTERVIEWER: Did you feel they were honest?

CAITLYN: No.

INTERVIEWER: Trustworthy?

CAITLYN: No.

INTERVIEWER: How was it to have them living in your house?

CAITLYN: Very dangerous. They were going to break up and they fought. One time they broke a glass and I cut my toe on the broken glass. They were bossy and made me feel threatened.

INTERVIEWER: Did you ever hear what some of the allegations were that they made against your parents?

CAITLYN: No.

INTERVIEWER: About the doctors you went to visit. Did they touch you with their hands? Do you think they did anything that seemed a little bit more than what your thoughts were as to what a doctor should do?

CAITLYN: They did that. At the hospital. I can't remember what doctor. There were lots of people there. I felt scared. Now I feel comfortable with my doctors. But they were looking inside of me. They cut up a pill, put it in a tube, and dumped it in my private.

INTERVIEWER: How do you HONESTLY feel about the writing of this book?

CAITLYN: I feel a little nervous. Like my dad's going to be fired or sued.

INTERVIEWER: Is there anything you would WANT to see with the writing of this book?

CAITLYN: People should gather a big group and fight back.

INTERVIEWER: Against the state (the system)?

CAITLYN: Yes.

INTERVIEWER: Is there anything you DO NOT WANT to see in the writing of this book?

CAITLYN: My dad and I in jail.

Today Caitlyn says there are no statements in this interview that she is not willing to see included in this book, and if she could have her testimony presented today in the case, she indicates the lies of the state would be exposed. Suffice to say, as you review her answers here, you will be able to determine this was not a good experience for either her or her sister. The scars that the Michigan authorities created will likely be with her for life, and it was all needless. Had they actually done their job and checked out the sources doing the complaining, they would have easily found their credibility was zero, and no case would ever have come forth. But when you have a state interested only in making a fast buck from the free money dispensed by the Federal Government to them for providing "services", you learn that not only does the statistical abuse case number increase, but that a lot of what goes on in implementing the "services" becomes so corrupt that even those working in the system are sickened by it.

—Chapter Fourteen—

The Trial That Wasn't

The trial was to begin on May 12, 2008. Oddly, it did not happen. The excuse was that the prosecutor was sick and unable to go to trial on that day. Maybe she had a case of "guilt" and could not figure out a way to forge any more false charges. More likely, she needed more time to prepare her falsified claims. In any case, it was now postponed, so our week consisted of trying to celebrate Mothers' Day in some fashion, and we included a move to Calumet on the 17th, so we could be closer to our children's visitation sites. The driving was terrible, and it is my contention the state made it that way on purpose so as to discourage us from seeing our children. After all, the longer they could keep them in custody, the more they stood to make from the Feds. So in any case, the new trial start date would be on June 24th, which would allow Child & Family Services (CFS) workers to rig the game even further.

On May 19th, we were finally able to visit our children, but not before the state sent us our *guidelines* as to how we were expected to behave. Their memo read as follows:

To: Robert and Janet

From: Angela Andriacchi

Child Welfare Worker

Tracey Compton

Child Welfare Supervisor

Date: May 9, 2008

Re: Parenting Time Guidelines

Below are the parameters for visitation. Child and Family Services would like you to have regular visitation with your children however, the requirements below must be followed in order for visitation to occur:

* *At no time will any video or audio recording devices including cameras be used during parenting time and/or during contact with the caseworker or service providers. Failure to comply will result in your visit being terminated.*

* *There will be no questions or concerns regarding this case discussed in the presence of the children. All concerns will be directed toward the caseworker and/or your attorney in private. Failure to comply will result in your visit being terminated.*

* *Parents will ensure that discussions, topics, and situations during supervised visitation promote a healthy environment and are in the best interests of the children. Failure to comply will result in your visit being terminated.*

* *Comments made to the children that are deemed inappropriate at any time may result in postponement of future visits.*

** All visitation is to be supervised by Child and Family Services staff. Any additional supervision must be approved by the court.*

** Parenting time is designated for parents. At no time will an unauthorized party attend parenting time. And additional parties must be authorized through Child & Family Services, the Department of Human Services, and/or the court.*

** A nutritious snack, food or drink for the children will be provided by the parents. Diapers and wipes will also be provided by the parents during the supervised visits. Bags containing contents required for visitation will be subject to examination prior to visitation.*

** No other personal items will be brought into Child and Family Services under any circumstances. Failure to comply will result in your visit being terminated.*

** No form of physical punishment or humiliation during the visits. Failure to comply will result in your visit being terminated.*

** Supervision of the children is the responsibility of the parents. Parents are expected to watch the children at all times and not leave that responsibility up to service providers.*

** The visitation room will be cleaned up by the end of the visits.*

** Parents are required to provide one business day notice of a request to cancel visitation.*

The primary goal is to have a cooperative relationship between the caseworker and parents in order to achieve family reunification. Your full cooperation is required to proceed with parenting time. Please acknowledge receipt of this email stating your willingness to follow the parameters set forth for visitation. Additionally, upon arrival for visitation, parents will sign an acknowledgement stating their agreement to follow the parameters outlined.

Sincerely,

Angela Andriacchi

Child Welfare Worker

The next day, May 10, 2010, we emailed our response. It read as follows:

Dear Angela,

We received your letter in regards to the parameters for visitation. You stated that "Child and Family Services would like you to have regular visitation with your children, however the requirements below must be followed in order for visitation to occur." If that statement were true and correct, then you would not continue to cancel our scheduled visits with our children. Why didn't we receive these parameters for visitation before now, if they were in existence, wouldn't we have been given them before our first visit?

Included in your parameters you state that "There will be no questions or concerns regarding this case discussed in the presence of the children. All concerns will be directed toward the caseworker and/or your attorney in private." We don't control our childrens' thought process. Caitlyn has a free will, and she wants and deserves answers! We can't possibly stop her from asking questions about her life and future. Why is it OK for you to question Caitlyn under your guise of "it's a secret", yet we are not allowed to exchange normal questions between parent and child?

You also stated that "Parents will ensure that discussions, topics, and situations during supervised visitation promote a healthy environment and are in the best interests of the children. Failure to comply will result in your visit being terminated". Caitlyn was obviously coached, before our visits, as to what she is and isn't allowed to say. Normally a free spirited, outspoken child, Caitlyn was in fear of disclosing the truth to us under the watchful eye of you as the caseworker.

We have absolutely no problem bringing the necessities for our children. But we do have a problem with you trying to continuously violate our Constitutional rights and us. You stated that "Bags containing contents required for visitation will be subject to examination prior to visitation". Again, these are new rules that you are making up as you go along. We were never informed of this, and you never searched anything we brought in before. Do you have a search warrant for these searches you want to conduct?

In your closing paragraph you state "The primary goal is to have a cooperative relationship between the caseworker and parents in order to achieve family reunification. Your full cooperation is required to proceed with parenting time." You mention reunification, and make continuous threats with canceling our visitation time with our children if we don't comply, yet we've done nothing to deserve this abuse from you. We have cooperated with everyone that we've come in contact with since our children were viciously removed away from us. Regardless of how much we cooperate with you, you continue to cancel our visits.

You tell us not to ask our children any questions. Caitlyn and Ashley are our children, we have every right to inquire about their mental and physical well-being, and it's not in our nature to not have concerns for them. Our parental rights have not been terminated. We wish to continue making all decisions pertaining to the rearing and upbringing of our children. We have not, nor do we intend to forfeit any legal right afforded to us as parents. With that being said, we refuse to sign off on any of our constitutional rights, therefore we will not comply with your ficticious parameters for visitation. You are cancelling the visit you schedule for Monday, due to our refusal to give up our rights to an illegal search.

At this time, we'd like to also make you aware of the fact that we are in the process of reviewing our options for other sources of supervision during our visits. We are also filing a motion for more frequent and meaningful visitation. In addition, we will also be filing a grievance with the Department of Human Services, in regards to your inappropriate behavior and continuous threats. You are supposed to be looking out for the best interest of the children, but instead worry needlessly about us recording family moments.

Thank you for your immediate response.

Sincerely,

Robert and Janet Coleman

Anyone dealing with Child Protective Services knows the lengths they will go to make their case seem a lot more "protective" than it really is. As we continued our battles with Child And Family Services, the Child Protective Services work horse for Ironwood, Michigan, where we were living, it became increasingly clear that the surveillance on us was increasing. That only became more apparent as we went from one fight to another trying to see our kids. So it was, that following the most recent letter exchange (described in the opening of this chapter), we decided on a move to Calumet, a city located in a different county. You had to cross over the bridge to get to this island city in Houghton County, and it seemed more like a sanctuary than it did a city to us. We can still recall the watch put on us by the city police in Ironwood, as we hurriedly moved all we could, moving first the most important things in anticipation of someone going through our things in our absence. That did happen, but fortunately, we had grabbed the most important documents, etc., as we went about the speedy move. I can still recall how they followed us all the way to the county border. The sense of *relief* we felt upon crossing that border into our new home is hard to describe. Although if I think back, I don't know *why* we felt this way because that did not stop them from crossing county lines at the time they kidnapped our children. Still, somehow, it felt different — even comforting — to be out of Ironwood and Gogebic County.

—Chapter Fifteen—

Escalation Of War

With our Child And Family Services battle now reaching a fever pitch, we did finally get a reprieve, and were allowed another visitation on May 19th. As it was, it only resulted in another round of fighting, however, this time with both CFS and the foster parents where my kids had been reassigned. As we entered to visit our children, we were greeted with demands for submitting to a search and to sign that we had no taping devices. Of course I did have recording devices, and was not willing to relinquish my constitutional rights no matter what they said or did. We spent some time before our visit arguing with them regarding this procedure, and finally settled by telling them we did not plan to tape. We countered that they should not transcribe either. They did transcribe and we did tape. In any case, we were allowed in to see our children, and the visit went well, except that during the visit we detected bruises on Caitlyn's shin as well as her under arm. Now enraged, we concluded the visit and went directly to the sheriff's department to file a complaint. We were passed on to the central dispatch of the Michigan Department of State Police, and the officer assigned to look into it met us in our van outside of the courthouse. Our complaint, against the foster parents Marc and Tara Fleis, was for child abuse. According to the official investigative report of Ed Deyo of Child Protective Services in Marquette County, he advised he did in fact open a file and investigated the allegations we made. He ascertained that the bruise on Caitlyn's leg was that of normal child's play, and said he did not feel the children were being abused. He stated that the bruise on her inner arm was where she bit herself, and he advised that she admitted to that. So, as usual, when anyone on the CFS side of the fence is accused, they just write it off, but when a mental case accuses someone on the other side of the fence of abuse, the verdict is *guilty until proven innocent.* Not one to settle for their cover up, on May 26 I followed up by requesting a well being check from the State Police. They did comply, but their report was quite remarkable. Here is what the report said:

INTERVIEW MARK FLEISS: I met with Fleiss at his residence and advised him of the nature of the complaint. Fleiss was aware Coleman had filed complaints against them. Fleiss let me inside the residence and was very cooperative.

OBSERVATIONS: His wife Tara was present, as were Caitlyn and Aura Coleman upon my arrival. Caitlyn and Aura seemed to be playing and having fun. Nothing seemed out of the ordinary. Nothing would lead me to believe there was any type of abuse going on in the home.

Nice report. And his thoroughness in following up on this would, to the state, be unquestioned. But how thorough was he? Well, notice first, that my daughter's name, which is Ashley, was not even reported correctly. If he can't even get the names right, why should we believe he got anything else right?

Prior to the report of the police, we found ourselves in court due to requests of the GAL (guardian ad litem). It seems that while our back was turned, this *protector of the children* had decided to request of the court that our parenting time be suspended. With my girls crying every time we had to leave a visitation, it should have been quite apparent to anyone that his request would not be best for the kids. Quite a guy, right? Further, he requested that parenting time "prohibit" the audio and video recording of the minor children. Now, correct me if I'm wrong, but this is a constitutional issue, not one a judge can rule unchecked on. Yet in this case, it is precisely what the judge did do. Seems to me it is just a nice way to *protect the state* from villains like me who insist on their constitutional rights. Well, our response was to counter with a request to the court to return the children to us and to disqualify the prosecutor. Additionally we requested increased and more meaningful parenting time. Well, as you might have expected from this group of kidnapping thugs, we were denied the return of the children. The judge did, however, reschedule our other motion for increased time to another hearing on May 27th. (Most likely so they could cook up something else together before that date). It was comforting though that the judge denied the GAL's request for suspending our parenting time. So I guess in every dark cloud there is a silver lining somewhere. The GAL did prevail though, on the request to prohibit our recording of the children. But if the state felt relief in that, they should not have! Because while I was told we could not record the *children,* nothing was said about not doing recordings of the state officials as they went about their corrupt activities. I surely planned to keep doing that! And that brought us to the ER hearing of May 27th.

In his opening remarks, the judge again showed his colors:

THE COURT: I had indicated, frankly, off the record, um, to cousel here that I am not likely to grant the motion to disqualify the Prosecutor on the allegations in the motion. I just, I guess, ah, find the cross allegations contained in the pleadings basically indicate some manner of aggressive advocacy, by all counsel, and maybe there's some sarcasms here and there, but that's not nearly enough to disqualify an attorney on any side.

OK, so what the judge just did was to admit that the prosecutor had indeed shown the behavior we had charged. But because we *dared* to fight back, now *our* attorney becomes a part of this judge's "aggressive advocacy." So because we would not go along with the state, and decided we should fight for our children, the prosecutor would not be disqualified. That is what I got from his words. Continuing:

THE COURT: My intention is to deny the motion, so I guess we don't need to spend too much time on that, um, but we did have an issue left of parenting time with the parents and how that was going to work. So I guess we're back in court after four days. Mr. Findlay, what's your position on what's transpired since?

MR. FINDLAY: Um, your Honor, just now that the court's decided that motion to disqualify the prosecutor, I don't want to make any additional argument, I just want to assure the court I don't make the motion lightly and it's not a frivolous matter for me to do so. I'd let it stand on its own and I understand what the court's ruling is going to be. As to the parenting time, your Honor, I guess some intervening time is, is happened in that there was a scheduled visit, from all the information I have, and all the information my clients have, for Monday, yesterday. Um, it was on paper, um, and told to my clients and they showed up for the visit, I believe at noon, yesterday, and nobody else was there. Nobody else, so obviously the children weren't there for the visit. It certainly doesn't go very far towards improving a spirit of cooperation when on scheduled visits they children aren't there. I realize the court wants to have it so that basically it's in discretion and in under the direction of DHS. But if they can't be made available on dates that its been scheduled and my clients are told they are going to be there, they drive a significant way with costs of gas now; probably close to a hundred bucks for the round trip for them, I believe from Houghton; you know, it's just — they need to be made available when they're supposed to be. In addition to that, I'd be asking for additional visitation time, up to three times a week. I think there's probably a plethora of information out that indicates that children need to see their parents as much as parents need to see their children. This goes to the rights of children in this matter and they have a vested interest in their family life, to the same extent that the respondents, and my clients. It is about the best interest of the children that is even a higher value in terms of their rights to have their family life preserved to the greatest extent possible. The lack of time spent with their parents has got to be hurtful and harmful to any child for whatever the reason is. The number of visits are relatively low. I'd ask the court to order DHS to provide additional and meaningful parenting

time and visitation time, which allows them some meaningful interaction with their children on a more liberal schedule than what there is now.

Following further discussion regarding the exact means and distance of travel, etc., the judge picked up on the date where the state failed to deliver with presentation of the children for our scheduled visit:

THE COURT: OK, they show up and apparently nobody's.... I mean.... the whole place is shut down apparently?

MR. FINDLAY: Apparently, yes.

THE COURT: The reason the building itself is shut down is Memorial Day, I presume. And I guess Mr. Ross or Ms. Fyle, are either one of you aware what happened here or... ...

MR. ROSS: We weren't given a copy of the visitation schedule; that's coordinated between Child and Family (services) and the Coleman family. There must have been an oversight or something for them to schedule a visit on a Federal and State holiday, where normal business hours are not even in operation. So I don't have an explanation. I will contact Child and Family and attempt to reschedule the visit, because if they traveled that way, it's wrong. They should have had their visits.

Nice move to just "toss it off" as "oversight." So in other words, every time Child & Family Services wants to jab us with lack of follow through, they can be rescued in court by having another agency simply indicate they were "not aware" of what took place. After some further discussion regarding requested time, the judge asked the prosecutor what *her* position was on all of this, and this is where it got interesting:

MS. WITTLA: Well a couple of things your Honor. My best guess, and it's just a guess, because I have not spoken to Tracie Compton at Child and Family Services, is that they suspended parenting time. Because looking at the dates that they were; that they actually showed up for parenting time; they were there on May 19th, and they were told that they needed to sign the parenting time guidelines; at that time. Tracie Compton did not notice that they signed the word "refused" on both of them, both mom and dad. So the visit went ahead, and then afterwards they looked at the form and said, "Oh my gosh, they signed refused; we didn't look at this close enough." Or my expectation is that they wouldn't have had the visit on the 19th at all. Since they have had conversations with the guardian ad litem and since his position was to actually suspend parenting time, to me it would not be unreasonable that they actually had suspended parenting time; waiting to find out the decision of this court, which was last Friday. I did not talk to anybody at Child and Family Services last Friday, but they knew that there were motions on the books for that day regarding whether or not parenting was even going to occur. So it wouldn't surprise me if they were under the impression that parenting time was, in fact, suspended because of both mom and dad's refusal to abide by the parenting time guidelines. And both because the GAL had filed to have it suspended. So until they heard the results of that, I don't know that they would have accommodated parenting time anyway. Now that was as clear as mud from the parents' perspective; they thought they had a visit. It didn't happen; that's unfortunate, and I certainly wouldn't want to set them up and have them go all the way to Marquette for a visit that wasn't going to happen. But I'm also convinced that they made their displeasure known to the parents on the 19th that, hey, you know, I can't believe you signed refused or something to that effect as far as the conversation went. And that leads into my stance as far as parenting time; if the parents aren't going to take advantage of the parenting time that they are allotted to this point in time; it makes zero sense to me to increase it. They have been given an opportunity to have parenting time on a once a week basis for two hours; and they have decided that other things are more important. To me the most egregious is when they left on April 28th calling out goodbye to Caitlyn and Ashley because they were told they couldn't record the visit; and that was more important than seeing their kids that day.

OK, let's stop it right here! This bitty stated that our call of goodbye to our children was more important than seeing them — and outright *lie*. It was Child & Family Services that would not let us see them because we would not submit to their blackmail. Yes, it was important we would not let them blackmail us, but not more important than seeing our kids. But you see, this is how these state agencies operate. They threaten you via blackmail to get you to submit to their methods. When someone has the gall to fight back, they try to intimidate and scare them into submitting to the unreasonable demands they produce — regardless of whether or not those demands are constitutional, legal, etc. We would *not* be intimidated, but it surely did not mean we placed values ahead of our children. What the state forgets is that in many cases they illegally kidnap kids to begin with, and when that occurs, people have the *right* to fight back — and should do so!

In any case, the prosecutor continued to try to illustrate that Child & Family Services did no wrong and that we should have been willing to comply with their rules, even if we did regard them as unacceptable. She tried to illustrate that we were not like *average people* who would go along with the agency guidelines, and here I would say she was right for a change. You see, average people can be scared out of their wits and intimidated. It just happens we were willing to fight. Thus it was, that she used this opportunity to bring up her next pet peeve with us, which was the recording and our posting of the state's kidnapping methods on the internet. I had posted my comments regarding these methods on the internet, and it had apparently come to this prosecutor's attention. Picking up on Ms. Wittla's continued request of the court:

MS. WITTLA: Your Honor, the other request I would have, in this case, would be for the Colemans to provide a copy of all the internet postings that they've made to each counsel and to this court.

MR. FINDLAY: We were here last week, I offered to do that.

THE COURT: Okay.

MS. WITTLA: You offered to give it to the court, but nobody ever asked me if I wanted a copy, and I didn't think of it at the time.

THE COURT: But you're saying that you are willing to offer?

MR. FINDLAY: I just don't understand why that request wasn't made when we were here last when we had the laptop here to do it, and were willing to let the court view it to make it's own decision; it just seems sort of like it's —

THE COURT: — Yeah, the court didn't want to do it.

MR. FINDLAY: — Well, and we weren't made aware anybody else wanted to do it either. I'd like to respond to a couple of points your Honor.

THE COURT: Yeah.

MR. FINDLAY: It sounds like what Ms. Wittla is saying is that Child and Family Services decided they're going to go ahead and suspend parenting unilaterally without the approval of anybody else. That to me is troubling. To do so without letting the parents know seems rather vindictive. You know, people are human beings. I realize, and I'm sure Angela Andriacchi, at this point, doesn't like Robert and Janet Coleman very well but I guess I'd ask the question, who are the professionals and whose job is it to act professionally in this matter? Who are the people who have had their children taken away and who should be given a little bit of latitude for being upset and distraught over that? The second point is they keep bringing up that the Colemans refused to see their kids because they weren't allowed recording and it was more important that they record than see their children. I want to know why the reverse isn't true also. That it's more important for Child and Family Services; they're not being recorded. I mean, why does Child and Family Services get to make that determination? And then there is this: I'm hearing that Child and Family Services even wants to prohibit the photographing of their kids.

THE COURT: — Well the answer to your question is because I said so. That's a determination I made that they didn't get to video, so that's going to have to be good enough for now. I mean it was either yes or no, and which

way it went.

MR. FINDLAY: No, but this was before the court had even -- the issue didn't even come up.

THE COURT: I thought you were arguing now.

MR. FINDLAY: No, no, no. Child and Family Services makes the decision unilaterally that it's more important that they not record, than these children be allowed to see their parents.

THE COURT: All right, um, well then I am not going to speak for them because of the general distaste over, over that kind of a procedure. I didn't get to share last week what I meant to. I've shared with counsel here my general distaste for video and audio recording because to me it reminds me of past cases where it has been done by other parties in this and other courts; and reeks basically of a type of paranoia.

Now, for the sake of argument, how does this judge define "paranoia"? Is it the same thing as "truth" because in my opinion recording does not lie. People do. The truth always comes out if a complete recording is allowable. The only time it is any kind of problem is if, as the media often does, they use only "clips" from recording, which can distort the real meaning of a recording. But if done in its entirety, it is cannot reflect "paranoia", but rather the true meaning of what people say. Anyway, back to the judge's comments:

THE COURT: What I find interesting is last week when I was in Houghton on another very difficult case, a guardian ad litem actually recommended that a mother be able to tape record for the protection for the mother because of differences between the parent and the DHS in terms of interpretation of the final plan. The guardian ad litem basically agreed with the parent whose child was removed, and in which jurisdiction is clear, but basically agreed with the parent that a worker was seeing things different from the way the mother saw it, and the way it got into the service plan had a different slant. I'm only saying that because I find it to be interesting, and it kind of gives pause in my general feeling that we shouldn't be tape recording or video recording. So I guess there's two sides to every story. Okay, I'm going to look at a calendar here for a reason I will tell you in a minute, just so I can have a visual look at things. Then I'll tell you where we are coming down on this matter. For the purposes of the record I'm referring to, I didn't read the Colemans' letter, I mean it's two pages. I was really concerned with parameters of Child and Family Services, and that was a memo to the Colemans dated May 9th of 2008, called parenting time guidelines, which are indeed initialed refused at the bottom, but they come from the worker Angela Andriacchi.

MR. FINDLAY: And your Honor, I had received a provision at one point where they'd indicated that in order to see their children, they would be required to subject themselves to searches of their belongings; I don't know if that one has it on there....

THE COURT: — Yeah, yeah, nutritious food snack or drink will be provided; bags containing contents required for visitation will be subject to examination prior to visitation, if that's what you mean?

MS. WITTLA: — Your Honor, I'd ask that Ms. Comparin mark those as exhibits.

THE COURT: Do you want them both marked?

MS. WITTLA: Unless she just wants to mark them all as one, it doesn't matter to me.

With that, the judge decided we should be entitled to two periods of parenting time during the three week period preceeding the trial, so that we could "make up" for the missed session because of the mixup. The judge emphasized strongly that he then expected DHS and Child and Family Services to comply with his order. He said that "the court has decided that the Colemans get parenting time; and they get parenting time." The judge indicated that we could not be refused visitation time if we refused to sign something, but because the court had mandated it, we could be denied visitation if we failed to allow the search of our bag. Also he indicated that we could not violate certain rules, such as talking about the case to the kids, etc., which we did not do anyway. Thus, our preparations began for our trial, now set for June 24th.

—Chapter Sixteen—

The Last Minute Backstabbing

It would have been a surprise to us if there were not some last minute backstabbing on the part of the state. So as not to disappoint, they did comply, with some very petty moves before trial.

The first came on the part of Rudy Perhalla, the GAL (guardian ad litem), who decided the state should be the ones to make our kids' medical decisions, rather than us, when he filed to have the court allow dental procedures he wanted to see done. What was requested was full anesthesia, in the nature of surgery. While we, of course, loved our children and wanted to see to their best care, it was our opinion as well that we, as their parents, should be making medical decisions on their behalf. In the same context, we did not feel the state should be making these decisions without first consulting us. The state, of course, would try to use our stance to signify that we were unfit parents and had no concern for the welfare of our children. Fortunately, our attorney was on top of this one, and in his letter to the judge, he got the desired outcome, which was the denial of the ad litem's motion. But just the mere effort, on the part of the state, is indicative of the type of deceit they use to try to paint a picture that is totally false. Anything to try to build a case as opposed to getting at the truth. That is the problem with CPS in general, and of course the CFS local services who support their corrupt activities. All in the name of money because the longer they can keep your kids the more federal dollars they can collect. The timing was quite interesting also, in that the GAL made his request at the time our attorney was going out of town, knowing full well that the judge was to make a ruling soon. Here was my attorney's letter to the judge, exactly as it read:

Dear Judge Massie,

As you know, when I left your courtroom this morning at approximately 11:00 a.m., the plan regarding the Coleman's dental issues was for Bob Ross to facilitate a phone conference with the Colemans and the dentist proposing to put a two year old under general anesthitic to discuss the procedure and determine if the Colemans would consent to the same. Immediately upon my return to my office I called the Colemans and informed them of that procedure and to wait for Bob Ross' call.

At 3:45 p.m., while on a recess from an all afternoon parenting time hearing in circuit court I saw Ms. Wittla in the hallway and asked what she had heard about the dental issue. It needs to be clear that I initiated this contact. I was then informed that the plan had been changed and now required me to call the dentist with my clients. No one informed me of this change of plans and I would not have been made aware of it if I hadn't happened to be on a break at that moment and inquired of Ms. Wittla. I did not receive a telephone call, email message or any form of communication from anybody at the court, Bob Ross or anyone else. Further I was in circuit the whole afternoon and am writing this letter at 6:00 p.m.

I am willing to accept that there may have been something lost in the shuffle, but Ms. Wittla is correct that I was, and I am not, happy with the change in plans. I am also not happy about the way this whole issue was handled. It was exceedingly unfair for DHS to ask my clients to consent to a procedure (putting a two year old under general anesthetic for dental work), on less that 24 hours notice. A procedure that DHS has known about for two weeks, and that I have been requesting information from during that entire time.

I am not available for a conference call with the dentist as I will be out of town until next Monday afternoon. I have instructed, by the email, the Colemans to try calling the dentist tomorrow to discuss the procedure and it is my hope that Bob Ross will have explained to the dentist the importance of talking about this procedure with the parents.

However, in light of all things considered, my proposal is that the procedure currently scheduled for Tuesday, June 10, 2008 be cancelled and an appointment made with a new dentist in Delta County. The new dentist should be required by DHS to consult with the Colemans' previous dentist, Dr. Herford, (I may not have the name spelled right), and then have Dr. Herford consult with the Colemans. Surely some pain medication can be prescribed for Ashley in the interim.

If necessary I can be reached by cell phone (XXX-XXX-XXXX), depending on where I am on my drive across the U.P. I can also be reached at my Cheboygan number (XXX-XXX-XXXX) on Friday afternoon or Monday morning.

Sincerely,

Michael D. Findlay

Attorney At Law

I should point out, the court was not happy about rendering this decision. So their bias again was very evident to us, even though we prevailed in this one matter.

Here was the court's Ex Parte Order, expressing that bias:

The Guardian ad Litem moved the Court, ex parte, to allow certain dental procedures. The Court discussed the matter with the Prosecutor and Defense counsel together in chambers and indicated the parties should communicate, including having the parents consult with the proposed dentist. The Court has received cross letters from counsel and apparently that has not effectively happened. The Court is then left to review the applicable law.

MCLA 722.124a(1) authorizes a court PRE DISPOSITION to consent to ROUTINE non-surgical medical care of EMERGENCY surgical treatment of a minor. No other law addresses the issue pre-jurisdictionally. In this case, what is requested is full anesthesia in the nature of surgery. Indeed, the dentist report indicates OR as a necessity. No sufficient showing has been made by the GAL of an emergency. Interestingly, the same statute authorizes the "department" to seek such care and make the determination of their own. The Court cannot advise the DHS legally on that issue, but notes it as a matter of interest.

The Court is not saying that upon proper showing of emergency it would not issue such an order, only that there is not a sufficient showing at this time. Obviously this child is in pain and the dental records show a clear need for care. The parents, counsel and the DHS should find a way to communicate and achieve that. The Court is disappointed in the continuous polar battling of the parties which causes this child to continue her discomfort. The Court can only follow the law. Therefore, the motion is denied.

And so, that was the order on June 6, 2008. This, of course, could have been averted if the state were not playing Gods and would have contacted us out of concern for our children, asking us to recommend what to do. We may desire our own doctors and dentists for our own personal reasons, but certainly we would not deny our own kids the treatment they need. But if you are God, you don't have to ask permission from the parents, right? If CPS ever wants to have a better kind of relationship with the parents they kidnap kids from, they should start by treating the parents with a little bit of respect. Especially when they don't really have a case against the parents, and are only trying to frame one.

Other than the dental issue, an unnecessary dispute, there were a couple of other issues the state tried to pull before the trial. Both counsel submitted their lists of witnesses they intended to call while the prosecutor tried to squeeze in the issues before the opening of the case. One request of the court was for us to provide the video and audio recordings previously posted on You Tube and the Yahoo Group True Americans of Ironwood. I guess those postings really bothered them because, after all, exposure to corrupt activities conducted by governments is a problem when it comes election or budget time. But the other effort by the prosecutor was of more interest, in that they wanted to be able to have Craig Kitchen, a therapist, be able to testify by way of video conference in a hearing set for June 17, 2008. It was allowed, but isn't it interesting how the prosecutor had no problem with electronic devices when it suited her, but definitely did not want us using them! In any case, the conferencing was allowed, and on June 17th we found ourselves back in court for his testimony. His direct examination began with questions from the prosecutor:

MS. WITTLA: Would you please state your name for the record?

MR. KITCHEN: Craig Kitchen.

MS. WITTLA: And your current occupation?

MR. KITCHEN: A therapist.

MS. WITTLA: And whose agency do you work out of now?

MR. KITCHEN: Child and Family Services.

MS. WITTLA: Did you have an opportunity to work with Caitlyn Brag?

MR. KITCHEN: Yes I did.

MS. WITTLA: And approximately what time span did that cover?

MR. KITCHEN: About a month and a half.

MS. WITTLA: Okay, and when did it end?

MR. KITCHEN: Ah, the end of May, 2008.

MS. WITTLA: During that period of time, would you say that she opened up to you?

MR. KITCHEN: No. No, she was very guarded through the whole time that we worked together. And it had got to a point where, for the most part, I wouldn't ask of her very much information. I just worked with her on social skills, such as playing with the other kids. And most of that was an attempt to get her so that she was more comfortable with me in a non-therapeutic setting. It was a therapeutic setting, but I mean it was directed more at social skills instead of working on trust issues and stuff like that.

MS. WITTLA: We're here today, Mr. Kitchen, because I filed a motion asking for protective measures for Caitlyn, if she's called to testify as a witness in the trial next week. At that trial her parents would be present, as well as a jury and various other entities in the room. In order to make it the best scenario for Caitlyn to feel comfortable and give her testimony about her life experiences, what do you think she'd need to do that?

MR. KITCHEN: The first thing is the setting is to have to be feeling non-threatening for her, and I think in the courtroom, where she had to look at other people, a live number of people, I think that would cause her a great deal of stress. And I think she's probably.....

MS. WITTLA: .... Would you repeat that last thing, you kind of, we kind of got a little.....

MR. KITCHEN: I think she, she would, um, close down and not give any valid information if she was in a situation where she was very threatened.

MS. WITTLA: If we were able to set something up where she was, ah, by closed circuit TV in another room where she only saw the person who was asking her questions, and didn't see everyone else; would that be helpful to her or harmful?

MR. KITCHEN: I think it would be the most helpful of any of the situations, whether it be the screen that you had talked about or whether it just be open in the courtroom. I think the closed circuit TV like what we're doing here would probably be the most non-threatening to her. I'm not saying it wouldn't be threatening to her, but I think it....

MS. WITTLA: Okay, could you repeat that last bit again?

MR. KITCHEN: Ah, I think any time that you're trying to get any information on a case when she's extremely guarded, and that's going to threaten her in itself. But I think that the situation like what we're doing here now is probably going to be the most non-threatening of all the scenarios. Her being asked to give information may be threatening in itself.

MS. WITTLA: Do you think Caitlyn would be more guarded if she had to see her parents while she was testifying?

MR. KITCHEN: Oh, definitely.

MS. WITTLA: And why do you believe that?

MR. KITCHEN: Because I think that would be a threat to her. Especially if she thought that she was giving up any information that might be damaging to them.

MS. WITTLA: I have nothing further.

THE COURT: Mr. Perhalla?

MR. PERHALLA: Thanks your Honor.

MS. WITTLA: (to Perhalla): I'm looking at your records. It seems you had about five sessions with Caitlyn?

MR. PERHALLA: Right.

MS. WITTLA: You no longer are seeing Caitlyn because she's been moved to another county?

MR. PERHALLA: Right.

MS. WITTLA: Ok, had she remained in Marquette County, would the plan have been to stay seeing you?

MR. PERHALLA: Yes, it would have been.

MS. WITTLA: And I take it you had started working on trust building with Caitlyn between herself and you?

MR. PERHALLA: And what I was doing with that is backing off on the therapeutic issues, and working more on social skills, so that she was seeing me more as a person who was teaching her instead of a person who was trying to get information from her. And the way I did that was to talk with her about her behavior and talk with her about that in terms of her needing skills to learn.

Like adding one and one equals two, instead of talking with her about you've been bad. I was trying to gain more of a relationship where she would see me as somebody that was helping her.

MS. WITTLA: You hadn't been able to reach that point yet with her?

MR. PERHALLA: No, it was just too early.

MS. WITTLA: Do you believe had you had more time, eventually you may have reached that point, at least, hopefully?

MR. PERHALLA: I would hope so, yes.

MS. WITTLA: And it is my understanding you did not see the other child, Ashley, at all?

MR. PERHALLA: She was oftentimes in the room at the same time that Caitlyn was, and that was the play scenarios that we would set up. It would be like children in there and they would all be playing. What we'd be doing is talking, but then, like for instance, Caitlyn began to be bossy towards one of the other kids; we would redirect that, and we would teach her about interacting in a cooperative way instead of a bossing way. That's what I mean by teaching social skills.

MS. WITTLA: Would those have been two children though during your sessions?

MR. PERHALLA: Pardon?

MS. WITTLA: Was there to have been other children present during your sessions, or just Ashley and Caitlyn?

MR. PERHALLA: Ah, Tara's child was there also.

MS. WITTLA: OK, was Tara present during this time or did she stay out of the room?

MR. PERHALLA: Yes, she was there. For the same reason that I was, to work on trust issues with her and she was also there at the same time we were working. I was helping show her how to do the social skills instruction with Caitlyn and with the girls.

MS. WITTLA: And for the record, Tara was the foster mother at that time?

MR. PERHALLA: Yes, she was.

MS. WITTLA: Nothing further, your Honor.

THE COURT: Mr. Findlay?

MR. FINDLAY: Thank you. From your notes, you had five sessions with Caitlyn?

MR. PERHALLA: Yes.

MR. FINDLAY: OK, and from what you've just indicated, for each of those sessions there were other individuals present besides just you and Caitlyn?

MR. PERHALLA: Yes, Tara, the foster mom was there, and often her daughter was there also.

MR. FINDLAY: OK, so none of this was individual counseling then?

MR. PERHALLA: No.

MR. FINDLAY: OK, and you indicated that what you worked on was social behaviors?

MR. PERHALLA: Social skills, yes, teaching her to play cooperatively with the other children, and also teaching her to follow directions.

MR. FINDLAY: OK, so you didn't talk about her parents or her relationship at home or anything like that?

MR. PERHALLA: No, any time I tried to do anything like that I would get, "I don't know." That's all she would answer. That's why I backed off.

MR. FINDLAY: Ok, when you say any time, how often was that topic brought up?

MR. PERHALLA: Probably the first three sessions.

MR. FINDLAY: And so any request for information from you was met with an "I don't know?"

MR. PERHALLA: I could ask her what did you have for lunch today and she's say, "I don't know." And that's an example of her feeling of being threatened by giving me some information.

MR. FINDLAY: So she was just generally threatened of giving you information in general?

MR. PERHALLA: Yes.

MR. FINDLAY: OK, so it didn't matter what you were talking about, she was generally threatened?

MR. PERHALLA: Yeah, as I said I could ask her what she had for lunch and she wouldn't answer.

MR. FINDLAY: Ok, so regardless of who was in the courtroom, you believe that she's respond that way, correct?

MR. PERHALLA: I do. I do.

MR. FINDLAY: So it really doesn't really have anything to do with whether her parents or there or not? It's just the fact that she would be in a court room and she would.....

MR. PERHALLA: And she would feel threatened right now.

MR. FINDLAY: Is it fair to say that there was no individual counseling regarding her parents and her relationship with them?

MR. PERHALLA: No, it's not.

MR. FINDLAY: It's not fair? Ok, so then what? Explain to me how that counseling took place?

MR. PERHALLA: Well, again, what we did is we talked. Kind of why I feel like I got through with her was social skills education. Ah, following directions, playing with the other kids appropriately, without bossing them around, accepting feedback. If somebody corrected her instead of arguing about it, just saying "Okay."

MR. FINDLAY: And what did that have to do with her parents and her relationship with them?

MR. PERHALLA: What it had to do was to developing trust with her, and also some interest in skills, but the main part of it is getting her so she has some trust in me so that she would work on issues that she felt threatened about.

MR. FINDLAY: I'm still puzzled by how that has anything to do with her parents or her relationship with them?

MR. PERHALLA: It has to do with relationships with authority figures. And that's what we were working on. It's just so she would be appropriate in the foster homes.

MR. FINDLAY: OK, so that was the focus of your counseling. Getting her to be appropriate in foster homes?

MR. PERHALLA: Yes, it was.

MR. FINDLAY: So you weren't dealing with issues then that may have happened in the past with her?

MR. PERHALLA: No I was not. Oftentimes with children it takes a long time to start getting into anything that's going to be of any substance.

MR. FINDLAY: Nothing further, thank you.

THE COURT: Mr. Kitchen, I have a few questions. Once in a while you're kind of breaking up on us, are we breaking up on you?

MR. KITCHEN: Sometimes, yes.

THE COURT: Just give us a brief curriculum vitae. What's your educational background?

MR. KITCHEN: Ok, I have a Masters in community counseling through Winona State University in 1990. I've been working with kids since about 1982 and on a Masters level since 1990. I have worked at Child and Family Services for the last year. I've worked with teaching family homes in Marquette for ten years, and I worked with a variety of places in LaCrosse, Wisconsin before I moved up here.

THE COURT: Ok, and I know the answer to this because you testified in this court before, but have you testified before as an expert?

MR. KITCHEN: Yes, I have.

THE COURT: And have you dealt with this issue about protective measures for children?

MR. KITCHEN: Yes, I have.

THE COURT: The kind of thing about whether you use a screen? Whether to use video? You've dealt with that before?

MR. KITCHEN: I've dealt with that, yes. In fact the last time I dealt with it, it was around two weeks ago in almost the same situation.

THE COURT: Ok, when you use the word that she's threatened or there's a problem with the way she's testified, is that because it could cause her psychological harm to be in a courtroom setting?

MR. KITCHEN: I think it could cause psychological harm from the standpoint that it would, with the trust issues, it's lack of trust that she already has. I think it would continue to damage trust in authority figures. She would feel threatened by all of those people out there, and she's not familiar.

THE COURT: But I mean could it harm her psychologically, is that right or not right?

MR. KITCHEN: Yes, yes.

THE COURT: Ok, and does that include the presence of her parents in the courtroom?

MR. KITCHEN: Definitely.

THE COURT: If the parents weren't there at all, is it different than if her parents are there?

MR. KITCHEN: I would have to say it wouldn't. She would still be threatened by it.

THE COURT: More or less or the same or.....

MR. KITCHEN: Maybe a little bit less, but she'd still be threatened.

THE COURT: All right, thank you. Ms. Wittla? Any follow up?

Does it seem strange to anyone else why a judge would have inserted questions of his own is this type of case? It did to me. It was as though he were trying to establish "credibility" of Mr. Kitchen, something perhaps the prosecution had failed to do at this juncture. Also, it appeared my lawyer had destroyed the prosecutor's effort to make the case that the presence of myself and my wife would be intimidating to our children (primarily Caitlyn). Did this judge feel he needed to reverse that damage on the record so it could be later used in court more effectively. In my opinion, this judge was very biased, and the friendship he had with the prosecutor, Mr. Kitchen, and the rest of the state kidnapping ring came through crystal clear.

The prosecutor and Mr. Perhalla both had no further questions, but as you might well expect, my lawyer seized on the moment to try to once again undo the damage the prejudiced judge had just inserted into the hearing on behalf of the prosecution:

THE COURT: Mr. Findlay?

MR. FINDLAY: Based on those five sessions, how long was each session with Caitlyn?

MR. KITCHEN: About an hour.

MR. FINDLAY: Based on those five one-hour sessions, how do you know she'd suffer psychological harm?

MR. KITCHEN: I'm just basing it on what I've seen clinically over the years.

MR. FINDLAY: So it's not based on individual findings with Caitlyn; it's based on your overall experience with all children?

MR. KITCHEN: Yes.

MR. FINDLAY: Nothing further, thank you.

Now, Ms. Wittla had more questions, since once again, my attorney had shot down the attempted frame of her and her prejudiced co-conspirators in child kidnapping:

MS. WITTLA: Your Honor, I have some followup if that's okay.

THE COURT: Ms. Wittla, go ahead.

MS. WITTLA: Mr. Kitchen, obviously (?) you've had a lot of training on dealing with kids, the things they go through. Would you say that your training that other children would be threatened or suffer psychological damage if they had to testify in front of their parents would also hold true specifically for Caitlyn?

Hold on a minute!! Review his previous testimony and it was never said they would suffer such damage because her parents were there. In fact, Mr. Kitchen had already contradicted that by saying that the damage (if any) would be due to the entire courtroom atmosphere, whether or not her parents were there. So his next reply was, in fact, perjury:

MR. KITCHEN: Yes, I do believe it would be specifically true for Caitlyn.

There you have it. He said no first, and now yes. Continuing:

MS. WITTLA: And why do you believe it would also be specifically true for Caitlyn?

MR. KITCHEN: Ah, I think that what she, she would feel like, um, especially if the parents were there, um, she's already guarded about giving information, and I think she would feel threatened about, ah, is she going to get somebody in trouble; or is she going to get in trouble. I think she'd use a lot of what does, if she's not doing right; she questions what she does, and so her way of dealing with that is she shuts down or she tries to take control.

What did he just say? I've never heard such babbling in all my life! And if you can make any sense out of what he just said, you are far superior in your interpretation of the English language than I am! I think he said the overall court atmosphere would be intimidating to Caitlyn and she would, therefore, make her attempt to take control. Whatever that is supposed to mean. I might add that, if you have not already seen it, a lot of the questions directed to Mr. Kitchen were leading questions by the prosecutor, whose primary effort was to lead the witness. My lawyer should have objected more often based on her doing that, and any judge would never allow it (unless of course you have a prejudiced judge, which I had already determined we did have). In any case, she now began to insert some very leading questions to try to salvage the testimony:

MS. WITTLA: So it is her coping skill (nice wording to lead) then, so she doesn't get in trouble or get anyone else in trouble to just do nothing at all?

MR. KITCHEN: Not do anything at all; not, um, either, um, act out and try to take control by her own behavior, by bossing people around. That would be an example, the bossing of the other children or even trying to boss the foster parents around. Um, those are the things that I think you would see that would show you that she was, ah, feeling threatened by the situation in court; by closing down or trying to take control of it.

MS. WITTLA: Thank you.

THE COURT: Follow up again? Go ahead.

What? The judge didn't like for my lawyer to respond to her obvious leading form of questioning? Damn, judge, he is a lawyer! He has the right to follow up!

MR. FINDLAY: Is it possible that her lack of trust , uncomfortableness with strangers, and all these things is a result of being removed from her family and being forced into the company of strangers?

MR. KITCHEN: I would say that it's possible. But again, over time, even over a short period of time, what we see, as they do come into foster care, is they develop a very trusting relationship to those caregivers; she didn't.

Seems to me he just admitted that she broke the trend pertaining to the other kids the prosecutor had attempted to lump Caitlyn in with—doesn't it seem?

MR. FINDLAY: Is it, this is a general proposition, is the forcible removal from one's parents a damaging factor for a child this age?

MR. KITCHEN: In some cases, I believe it is.

This was our case and there is very little doubt that it has been damaging to Caitlyn and Ashley. Even today, at age ten, and Ashley at age six, they still have bad dreams about being taken in the middle of the night, and are still frightened of the dark. The questioning of Mr. Kitchen ended at this point, but nobody can convince me that our case was unique in the damage the state of Michigan has inflicted on so many parents and children. There is a long list of cases cited on my web pages, illustrating the length this state was willing to go to illegally kidnap the kids of unsuspecting parents. And in each case, money was the motivating factor. And it is not only the state of Michigan. As you review the cases I cite in my web pages, refer also to other states, and see just how far some of the states would go to make their case or eliminate their opponents. In one case, it is suspected officials at some level even committed murder of a state politician for speaking out against the national arm of CPS (Child Protective Services). We take that up in another chapter.

Following the testimony of Mr. Kitchen, there was discussion about if or not there would be allowance for the use of video or screening, and the judge decided he would allow it.

We thought, at this juncture, that the hearing was over, and that we could prepare for the coming trial, due to commence in about a week. But now we would see the collusion of the Guardian Ad Litem in this case— the person who was supposed to protect the interests of our children. Instead, it would be his turn to try to manipulate the case and influence a jury by demonstrating through his deceit, how bad we were as parents, with his timing of his surprise "issue" he wanted the judge to now hear.

—Chapter Seventeen—

The Collusion of My Kids' Lawyer

When an attorney is appointed to represent your children after they are taken away by the state, you would assume they would represent them with their best interests at heart. We learned in Michigan that it is not the best interest of the kids these so-called Guardians of the state (Guardian Ad Litems) represent, but rather the best interests of coffers of the state they guard so devoutly. So approaches such as lying, deceit, or any other successful method of keeping the children away from their parents is just an ordinary procedure.

With our trial only a week away, and the hearings not going the way the state might like, it needed a boost from someone, so they could try to slander the Colemans, who apparently were putting up too good of fight in their effort to keep their kids. Janet and I had fought bad treatment, illegal kidnapping, harassment efforts, and phony charges from the onset, and yes, were in the fight of our lives. Now it would enter a new phase, as before our latest hearing was to conclude (as we discussed in the last chapter), the Guardian Ad Litem in the case would show his true colors. Instead of considering the state might be wrong, and moving to give our children back, he chose instead to introduce his own effort to join forces with the prosecutors and other conspirators as they fought to keep our children for their own profits and conspiratorial purposes. It started with his request before the hearing could conclude:

MR. PERHALLA: Your Honor, I had an issue I wanted to bring up that hasn't been noticed for today.

MR. FINDLAY: I object to bringing it up.

THE COURT: Okay, but let's hear what it is first.

MR. FINDLAY: You know you're putting me on a— your Honor.

MR. PERHALLA: ...Thank you your Honor.

THE COURT: Is it about teeth or?

MR. PERHALLA: Your Honor, I don't know if the court knows but the children were first placed in Ontonagon County and then transferred to a foster home in Marquette County. While at that foster home in Marquette County, I have police reports here that the parents made unsubstantiated complaints, what I will classify as frivolous complaints against those foster parents.

Who made Mr. Perhalla the one to do such "classification"? Continuing:

MR. PERHALLA: As a result of that I believe that is a factor in those foster parents refusing to keep the children. And thus, we had to rush to find another foster home that is now, I believe, in Escanaba County or Delta County where these children are.

You mean he had all this information for the judge but did not know where they were? Continuing:

MR. PERHALLA: It's my understanding that the parents have again made complaints to DHS and SA in Delta County. In my motions at this time, your Honor, those complaints have been made. I believe they're being investigated. At this time your Honor, the parents (the Colemans) do not know who the foster parents are. I am moving at this time to ask for an order that the address, the name, and telephone number of those foster parents not be given at this time to the parents. And I have, I would like to have put in the police reports, I'd like to have marked as an exhibit your Honor.

Two things: first, was this so that bad foster parents, which the state of Michigan seemed to enjoy employing, could go about their abuse undetected? And second, did he want it marked for exhibit so he could try to label us as villains to the coming jury? We were sure of it. Continuing:

THE COURT: Okay, now are you talking about a police report or a report that came out of DHS following an investigation?

MR. PERHALLA: I am talking about the police report that came out of Negaunee and Michigan State Police as a result of the investigation on the foster parents in Marquette County where the children are no longer.

THE COURT: Ok, well let me see it; I thank you.

He thanks them? Could it be he was prepared for what was a surprise last-minute effort to slander the Colemans? Continuing:

MR. PERHALLA: I didn't have it marked yet you Honor; I did provide Mr. Findlay and I think the Prosecutor has a copy.

What a joke! Of course the prosecutor had a copy because they cooked it up together! And Mr. Findlay was given the copy only at the time the hearing was to begin! (With no time to prepare his response) Continuing:

MR. PERHALLA: I am fearful that once they know, the Colemans will then.....

THE COURT: ...Well, I see, when I asked you about a complaint and my mind may be crossing between different cases here; you're not talking about an administrative complaint against the foster parents to DHS saying they're bad foster parents and shouldn't be foster parents; you're saying actual abuse, neglect complaints that they are abusive or neglectful.

MR. PERHALLA: The Colemans made against the foster parents in Marquette County. Yes your Honor, and I believe even now.

THE COURT: ...To fill me in, I think you said they're making the same complaint against the people in Escanaba.

MR. PERHALLA: Yes.

THE COURT: Well, can they if they don't know who they are or where they are?

MR. PERHALLA: Based upon their visits with their children.

THE COURT: Oh, got yah; you're not asking....

MR. PERHALLA: The visits are at the Escanaba DHS.

THE COURT: You're not asking to stop the visits?

MR. PERHALLA: Oh,no your Honor, we would just ask to withhold that information at this time.

THE COURT: Well, that's good; that's a new one.

Indeed! So the judge recognized that, but still allowed this man to slander us, as he did with his next out and out lie:

MR. PERHALLA: In Republic (the Marquette County foster home) the Colemans drove by their home on more than one occasion; what I would state to this court is "stalking."

MR. FINDLAY: There's no evidence of that on this record; obviously the court knows the attorney's GAL statement that happened is not evidence and I'd ask that it be stricken because....

MR. PERHALLA: ... It's just my statement, based on what I've gathered your Honor, but there would be no reason for them, on their way to Marquette, to even go to Republic, and they were there, and I'm just concerned, scared. To frighten another foster family and moving these children again at this time.

Just your statement? Based on what you've gathered? You mean, lies you have gathered? What did you gather? From whom? Proof? Lawyers should be subject to perjury just as witnesses are! The truth is, if you drove me by that house today I would not know it was the house my kids were in! I've never seen it! So this accusation was nothing short of total fabrication! It was also said we did this in a white pickup. While we did have a white pickup at one time, we had to let it go back. As you might recall in another chapter I explained that we were letting it go back at the time Ron Carpenedo stopped us to question me about my wallet. Gee, does it seem that perhaps there was some collusion between Carpenedo and Mr. Perhalla here? It's the only place Perhalla could have gotten this bogus information because the Paynes were long gone by now. But what is new? This was contrived by all of them! Guess they were not informed that I didn't have that truck any longer when I supposedly stalked the Fleis family! But it was a nice try, wasn't it? If Mr. Perhalla was basing his information from what he gathered, it had to be from the foster parents themselves, Marc and Tara Fleis, and it appears, Ron Carpenedo. The Fleis' own background is, in fact, quite suspect. But to make this short, Mr. Perhalla simply fabricated this! Continuing:

THE COURT: OK, Mr. Findlay, this was kind of brought on on an emergency basis. I heard Mr. Perhalla's statements. What do you have to say?

MR. FINDLAY: I am taken by surprise. I object to the one filing the police reports, at least for the time generally considered, as evidence. I mean, you can make the motion based on whatever he wants to; I'd object to the timing of the motion, I guess the court's hearing on an emergency basis. I thought that the policy was, from the very beginning, they didn't divulge the foster care names. Isn't that correct?

THE COURT: Ok, you got me on that one too.... is that....

MR. ROSS: ... That was the plan your Honor, but based on the fact that there was a complaint made last week, a general complaint made at the foster parents; nothing would stop the Colemans at the end of the line here from doing a FOIA request and ask for the CPS records, which would automatically have the foster parents name and address on it.

THE COURT: Oh, I got you.

MR. ROSS: So in order to protect the safety of the foster parents and their family, we're just asking for an order, at least until the investigation is completed down the line, that none of the information pertained to in the specific foster family is to be made available for the Colemans.

Oh! So now we were a dangerous couple, capable of anything! Even though to this point we had only taken steps to protect our children, and never threatened any kind of violence towards anyone! Here again, was the collusion effort by all the state parties to slander us and paint us as dangerous people. Continuing:

THE COURT: All right, not being a lawyer, somebody probably advised you not to put the strategies forward to the family because I never thought about the FOIA request.

MR. ROSS: That's how they got that information on the first, previous foster family.

THE COURT: Well, like I say, you're all way ahead of me.

That is the understatement of the year! Of course they were, because they had it all planned out! Including the "when" to surprise the court with it. Continuing:

THE COURT: All right, here is the situation. I have been very careful in the case based on the fact it is a hotly contested case. A jury is going to determine, based upon the facts put before the jury, whether or not it comes within jurisdiction. So I have been somewhat sanitized to the extent of not reviewing the You Tube broadcast.

Not going to go into this, but it is absolutely clear that they Colemans have entered into an aggressive counter attack; more than just in the court proceedings, which they have the absolute right to do.

Really? Then why is it when you take steps to fight the system for its abusive action towards your family and your kids, that they try to punish you for it? Continuing:

THE COURT: They don't have the right to harass as is being claimed by the foster parents.

That was a complete lie.

THE COURT: In order to make sure that they are protected, I'm going to enter the order as requested that they (the Colemans) not be allowed to have that, even after a FOIA request. That they not be allowed to have the foster parents name and address. Now, if they find it out anyway in the next seven days, and something else happens, it's reasonable that the foster parents would not want to have anybody constantly driving by their house wherever it may be, and I don't know where it is. Frankly, based on what I'm hearing here, I'm not sure I want to know either, and so I'm trusting the agency to have adequate placement; this should not interfere with the Colemans' right to have parenting time with their children; which is scheduled. How is that going right now?

MR. ROSS: We are doing it every Thursday and Friday your Honor. They're coming down from Calumet, doing a 3 to 5 visit on Thursday afternoon; they're staying the night in Escanaba; we're reimbursing them for the lodging for the night; and they're doing an 8 to visit on Friday morning. So they're getting the two visits back to back.

THE COURT: All right, that will be up until the time of the trial, which is next Tuesday.

MS. WITTLA: Your Honor, the only request I would make is that your order address law enforcement as well. It's not just a DHS order.

THE COURT: Oh, ok, because a FOIA request comes into law enforcement, is that what you are saying or what?

MS. WITTLA: Absolutely. If an allegation of abuse is made in Escanaba, if it goes to the local police department or Michigan State Police or whatever. They're going to have cover sheets that say this was reported by X person.....

THE COURT: ... I got yah... ok, I will indicate for now and between next week that nobody disclose only the names and address of the foster parents; I'm not interfering with any other procedural steps in the abuse neglect process. If they report it DHS is going to follow up, do investigation, do all the things that they have to do under the law. I'm not getting in the way of that.

MS. WITTLA: Well, and my caveat would certainly be that if local law enforcement anywhere does an investigation and finds abuse then clearly all bets are off.

THE COURT: And frankly, they always have to under the law, no matter who makes a complaint, no matter when, no matter how.

MR. FINDLAY: And also to the FOIA law the ongoing investigation is the exception to FOIA and the police can basically indicate we not release anything because there's an ongoing investigation. So they already have an exception to release information.

THE COURT: Ok, so I've learned a lot today, but for purposes of keeping again, a sanitized situation where they don't get accused of stalking, then it should not be disclosed to them pending the next proceeding. Parenting time has been arranged. Anything else?

From that point on, it was only a discussion of how to get the order written, and the hearing came to a close.

So now the setup was nearly complete. The state still had some "stacking" work to do, which would come at the beginning of trial during the jury selection process. The next step in The State Guide to Legal Kidnapping.

Meanwhile, we still had a visitation left before the trial, which surprisingly enough produced no controversy. Perhaps the state and the agencies needed to get ready for trial and didn't have time for more controversy at this juncture. Whatever the reason, it was a welcome change for us, given we knew we had the fight of our life upcoming in the trial.

—Chapter Eighteen—

The Trial—Day One

The time had come at last. With all of the false accusations submitted, it was time for the state to prove their case against us. Or, so we thought. As we were about to learn, in a civil case in the state of Michigan, it is not really a case of a defendant being innocent until proven guilty. Rather, it is a case of a defendant being guilty until proven innocent. This was made very clear in the line of questioning pursued by the prosecutor, Tracie Wittla, during the jury selection portion of this case. In our best effort to put that line of questioning into context, let me make a list of her favorite questions she put to prospective jurors during the jury selection phase of this trial:

1.) Do you believe we should have laws that protect children from abuse?

2.) Even if that abuse comes from the parents?

3.) What is your feeling on corporal punishment? (Applying physical punishment to a child)

4.) Do you feel objects (such as a belt) should be used in applying this punishment?

5.) Do you know we are here for a civil trial and not a criminal trial?

6.) You are aware that this is a civil case with a lower standard of proof?

7.) Would you hold me to a higher standard than what the judge instructs you to do?

(i.e., if the judge instructed you that the standard of proof was preponderance of evidence, which is essentially a fifty-one percent level; would you insist that I prove my case beyond that level to your satisfaction?)

8.) Would you be able to accept the testimony of the interviewer of the child in this case?

9.) Would it be okay with you then, if the child herself did not come in to testify?

10.) Is there any reason why you wouldn't want to make a decision in this case?

11.) If you believe the witnesses testimony and that the petition has been proven to be true, would you be able to return a verdict of giving this court jurisdiction?

In order to illustrate we are not trying to just put my slant on it, we invite any and all readers of this book to go to my website and read the complete transcript of that first day in court, so readers can see for themselves how she actually worded this to each and every juror she questioned. It gets quite redundant to read though, and frankly, quite boring, so we won't quote it all in this chapter. Likewise, the other transcripts of the trial (days 2, 3, and 4) are also available on my website. We have nothing to hide, so please do read it for yourself if you feel the need to do so.

I think the reasons for the prosecutor's questions are fairly obvious. It was her effort to set them up and brainwash them in order to remove any doubts or questions in their minds that any of this actually happened. By asking these questions, she can force them to think in the terms she wanted them to think in terms of, and remove the idea that perhaps, in truth, the main accusers (Bobby and Rebecca Payne) as well as the state's chief investigator (Elizabeth Fyle) were all lying. My step daughter was not even capable of making most of the statements Ms. Fyle testified she made, but it was quite clear those so-called statements Ms. Fyle did present came directly from the Bobby and Rebecca playbook, as they were quoted nearly word for word from the complaint that stated the allegations. There was never much emphasis on the basic truth: that these allegations were made in retaliation for us having kicked the pair out of our apartments and because Rebecca was in fact, a spurned lover who was bent on revenge. The stability of this pair was never pursued to any degree, yet again, Bobby was the one who was being treated in mental health centers and claimed he was a NASCAR driver and was on suicide watch, as was confirmed in police reports.

So let's take Ms. Wittla's questions, listed above, and see if we can't find reasons why this prosecutor was so insistent upon building her jury around the false information she was so matter-of-factly presenting as fact:

(1) Question #1 above is an obvious yes or no question. And of course everybody does believe we should have laws to protect children from child abuse. But a prosecutorwants first, to get the jury members agreeing with them, so your first question must naturally be one that they would all agree on. And of course if they did not, any judge in the land would automatically disqualify them from being on the jury. It is vital, however, to get all of the jury nodding their heads yes from the very start.(2) Question #2 above was designed to insinuate, without proof, that we, as parents,had indeed, abused our children. But by tying it in with #1 above, the obviousreply, again, would be a yes, implying to the jury that we were in fact, guilty in this case.

(3) Question #3 above was designed to size up jury members. Anyone who supported any form of corporal punishment would be stricken from the jury by prosecutors.(4) Question #4 was designed for two purposes: first, to insert, without proof, the lietheir entire case was built on; that I had used a belt on my daughter in a vicious and abusive way, rather than disciplining without a belt and with love (which was the way I actually disciplined my children). Secondly, this question was inserted to support the lies of Elizabeth Fyle, who merely took the word of Bobby and Rebeccathat any of this ever actually took place, and then framed their statements into thestatements she presented as having been made my step daughter. The entire belt thing was one big lie, and in fact, was the major push the prosecution would use to claim I abused my step daughter. And even if it had occurred, why would a court remove my step daughter from custody from my wife, unless she too, were guilty ofassisting in the abuse. The prosecution did try to show that too, using lies of the Paynes to bolster that idea, but when you ask Caitlyn today (at age 10) about such claims, she laughs at the suggestion of such a thing.

(5) Question #5 was obvious. She had a weak case, and if she were held to a higher standard, as in a criminal case, she would have no prayer of achieving any form of conviction. So she hammered that point home, time and time again, so those who were judging the case would come in with a guilty verdict, based on perhapsjust one or two issues, such as spanking with a belt. Just that belief could result inthe state succeeding in removing the children from the custody of the parents. Thisis very serious, and one place where I feel the law is wrong. And all parents should think about this: why is it that the idea of taking peoples' children away from afamily should not be as serious of matter as would be a criminal case? Most anyparent, if thinking about this,

would agree that before such a drastic action shouldbe taken, that the proof of the need should be strong enough to justify such action.In civil courts, however, that is NOT the case, and that is why there is so muchrage among parents who have had their kids taken unjustly by states, all acrossthis country. It is sad to say these cases get little or no publicity, and virtually noneof the general public understands these states are doing this, as much as anything,to make MONEY. So it is important for states to keep this at a civil level, so their burden of proof can go virtually unchecked. In fact, should they need to prove thecases beyond a reasonable doubt, the number of child abuse cases would reduce drastically.

(6) Question #6 was inserted to just reinforce question #5. You must make the jury understand it should be an easy conviction.

(7) Question #7 was inserted to make sure the jurors understood and supported the #5 and #6 questions. Should any juror NOT support the prosecutor with this question, the prosecution would challenge, based on prejudice to the defendant, and thus, have that juror excused. (It did happen in our case)

(8) Question #8 was obvious. Elizabeth Fyle wanted to lie. But she had to have her lie supported as though her claims actually came from my children. Our biggest mistake in this trial was in not making my step daughter (Caitlyn) testify. But you do what you think you should do to protect your kids, if you are a good parent, and the state knows this, so they will gladly have you produce your kids as witnesses if you wish, so they can further frame you as an uncaring parent, who has no regard for your own kids. So we failed to do this, thinking it was for the good of Caitlyn. It left Ms. Fyle totally able to insert Bobby and Rebecca's words into an alleged interview statement from Caitlyn.

(9) Question #9, again, was to support the efforts of #8.

(10) Question #10, again, was simply to size up jurors.

(11) Likewise, #11, again, was simply to size up jurors.

Suffice to say, from my perspective, this trial was decided before it ever began. We were guilty. The jurors already had that feeling, from just the so-called huge number of allegations the prosecutors had pretended to be presenting them with. The local rag that some would refer to as a newspaper was a mirror voice for the city officials and of course the state when they prosecuted in the city of Ironwood, and our case was no different. Unfortunately I have no pre-trial articles of this rag to quote for you, but one of the potential jurors unveiled their prejudicial coverage in a few remarks he made during the trial itself. It prompted my lawyer to call for a mistrial, but of course the prejudicial system would not allow that to occur, in order that we could indeed have a fair trial. We'll get into that in another part of this chapter. Though we tried to obtain those articles, they no longer can be found on the internet, nor were we successful in obtaining them prior to the publication of this book. People should insist that the Daily Globe, located in Ironwood, Michigan, make all of their pre-trial articles on the Robert Coleman case available on the internet. As it is now, you can find post trial articles, but if you try their search for the dates of this trial on their site, they say they are not available. WHY NOT? If they put on their site that you can research stories, why is it they do not have them on their site?

Maybe the best way to describe the jury selection would be to give you the names of the potential jurors who were seated on the jury in one grouping, and the names of those rejected, and why, when possible, in another grouping. That way you will not have to be bored with repetition of the same tired old questions over and over again, yet you get the jest of what each juror's views were as they were questioned by the legal teams.

So let's start with those who were rejected for being seated on this jury, and why:

Matthew Jacobsen. This prospective juror was excused by the judge for "cause", but as it was done over a break, we had no written reason this was done, nor was any kind of reason given by the court. But this happened very early on, so perhaps it was due to some kind of medical or scheduling conflict. We don't know, nor did we hear any type of questions directed to him. His was the only case where a cause excuse was not heard by all in the court room.

Chongkol Schrandt. My lawyer used one of his challenge preemptions to excuse this prospective juror. One exchange with my lawyer went like this:

MR. FINDLAY: And you're saying Ms. Schrandt they (the Colemans) need to prove they DIDN'T do it?

MS. SCHRANDT: Definitely. Okay, your example is it's not raining. It's raining outside and it's not—so that is an ALLEGATION.

But we heard the allegations are up to what number? In the sixties? I mean, how could government come up with that many numbers?

While my lawyer and us, as defendants, of course, agree it is impossible to come up with such numbers legitimately, it was not taken into consideration, it seemed, by this court. And as we've pointed out, most of the allegations were mere statements, mainly by vengeful accusers, and many without substance. This witness also stated such things as use of the belt was "too much" - even at age 6; and law enforcement should step in. So it came as no surprise my lawyer challenged her, as she was obviously biased.

Kyle Ramme. This prospective juror was excused for "cause" by the court. He admitted his nephew worked for the Gogebic County Sheriff's Department and that his best friend was an Ironwood Police Officer. He admitted it might influence him a little. He also admitted he would give preference to testimony from an officer over anyone who was not.

Crystal Heil. Here, the court showed their bias in the case. Fortunately, we were still able to see this prospective juror excused. In her case, she admitted she knew Tracie Wittla (the prosecutor) and that Tracie had been working on her case on behalf of the juror's kids. (That should have been enough for the court already) But she then admitted she knew Bob Ross and that he was a good friend of her husband, and he was also her daughter's probation officer. She admitted to my lawyer, upon questioning, she would tend to side with Bob Ross. Needless to say, my lawyer tried to get her excused for "cause", but the judge denied it, despite all of the obvious bias that we just pointed out. I was shocked by this, and no doubt my lawyer would have later been forced to use one of his preemption challenges to get rid of her (which I believe was the judge's intent - to force him to do so). But in what was one of the biggest surprises of this trial, to me, she was excused when Rudy Perhalla, the GAL in this case, exercised one of his preemption challenges to have her excused. I do not know why he did this, as she seemed to be one of the best potential government witnesses being interviewed. I admit this came as a total surprise to me, and to this day, I still do not understand why Rudy did that. But we were elated!

Sandra Stevens. This prospective juror was excused by the court for "cause"—and even though she would obviously been a juror we would have preferred, it came as no surprise because she openly admitted she would favor us, having sat previously in our position herself.

Robbie Williams. It seemed to me that this prospective juror was intimidated by the prosecutor. First, he told the prosecutor he would need more than a 51% standard of proof to find us guilty, but upon ensuing questioning, conceded it would be his choice.
But his questioning was interesting, to say the least. Most revealing was his statement that he knew us, by name only, and from the "newspaper stuff" he had read in the rag of a newspaper in Ironwood, the Daily Globe. He also indicated he knew where we lived. He indicated that a co-worker of his, James Tumin, who was a previous tenant of ours, had told him he did not like the way I treated my child. He said that Tumin told him that if he were not a tenant, he probably would have said something. All of this prompted my lawyer to request, in chambers, a mistrial based on the juror bias and his disclosures, all of which my lawyer claimed would prevent us from getting a fair trial. Again, the judge's bias was shown here, as he denied the request. My lawyer then asked for this juror to be stricken for "cause"—and once again, the judge denied my attorney's request, saying that even though Mr. Williams had gotten this information and even though he discussed it, the jury was very clear he could be fair and an impartial juror. Naturally, when the time came, Mr. Williams was excused via my lawyer's preemptory challenge, but again, in my view, the judge wanted that to happen, so my lawyer could not use this action on yet another biased juror.

Roger Jacobsen. This prospective juror was immediately excused for "cause" by the court when he admitted he knew me and said he sold firewood to me. He further stated that what he saw me going through was "outrageous" and a waste of taxpayer money.

Kelly Parker. This prospective juror was excused for "cause" at the request of my lawyer after some very revealing testimony indicating (to me) she was already brainwashed by the prosecution. First, she stated she was "cringing in her seat" when she heard the allegations... especially the part about the vinegar bath (a complete lie). She admitted she "partially believed" those allegations (which in itself would have been enough to convict us based on the easy proof system of civil cases). She told my attorney she did not see why anyone should use "that much force", referring to those same unproven allegations, and she indicated she felt law enforcement should step in. She finally went so far as to say that from what she had heard, it put a "feeling" in her that the children had been abused and that she did not know if she could be fair in the deciding of this case. She finished by ASKING who made the allegations—a fair question in my mind, which should have been pursued more fully by the court. If the people making the initial accusations had been properly investigated, they would have found out they were maliciously attacking my wife and I out of revenge, and that Bobby, in particular, was mentally unstable and should not be taken seriously when he made his accusations. Yet none of this mattered. Likewise, there was no real pursuit of Elizabeth Fyle in this case, which there should have been, to ascertain where she got her information. Claiming my step daughter confirmed it, it was never revealed that it was done using pressure on her part to get a desired statement from my step daughter... something that now, at the writing of this book at age ten, my step daughter claims did happen. She indicated among other things, that Fyle told her that if she did not admit to the belt useage, she would not be allowed to go home again.

Tabitha Amore. This prospective juror was also excused for "cause" based on my attorney's challenge. My lawyer made it clear she would be biased in favor of the government due to her working background. She admitted she could not be very fair in this case because she was a licensed childcare provider in the state of Wisconsin.

Brian Trekas. My attorney was forced to use one of his preemptory challenges to excuse this prospective juror, as soon as he told the court he knew Ironwood police officer Ron Carpenedo and was a friend of his. Carpendo hated me, and had been after me for some time, just waiting for an opportunity to come after me. He was in on the early failed investigation of us for child abuse, brought by my neighbor, John Cain (see the Cain Chapter)—an event he was not happy with the results of. So naturally, when Fyle sought her removal order from the court, Carpenedo was all too eager to assist her in tracking us down, as to our current location, using our cell phone to do it... and to assist her in claiming we were RUNNING, when in fact we were on a combined doctor's visit and vacation. It was no surprise they wrote the report they did following that visitation because they were seeking reasons to go after me again.

Robert Mattila. This prospective juror scared prosecutor Tracie Wittla, because he did not show the aggressive nature that would indicate he would be willing to go after me, based on pre-conceived views. I think she was afraid he might not pay close enough attention, as early on he said he had a physical problem in that he needed his nap every day. He also indicated he could have a hard time making a decision in the case, because he was not a decision maker. Tracie attempted to have him excused for "cause"—but that request was denied by the judge. So she later used one of her preemptory challenges to have him excused. In truth, he probably would have made a pretty fair juror because, even though he might have gone against us, he also was not so easy to convince that he would make a decision lightly—and that was something that Tracie could not take a chance on. After all, the truth was the last thing she was interested in.

Roger Bachand. This prospective juror was excused for "cause" at the request of my lawyer following his statements. He admitted he had a couple of people he knew who were state policemen—not indicating if they were family or friends. After stating that he felt it would be better if he heard testimony directly from my step daughter, indicating he also had a 6-year-old daughter who would tell the truth, he then reversed himself and said he didn't want to subject a child this age to the court process. He did say he would "trust" the Department of Human Services (Elizabeth Fyle) to let us know what my step daughter said. And he told my lawyer he thought a person should "never" be hit, and that if he heard spanking was used it might make him biased in the case.

Amanda Delich. If there was one prospective juror I might have disagreed with my lawyer over, it might have been this one. She was excused on a preemptory challenge by my lawyer. She had stated she was spanked as a child and did not consider that to be child abuse. She insisted she did not know where she stood on the subject of corporal punishment, but that she was against using objects for any physical crime. To my lawyer, perhaps that meant the use of a belt, even if limited, might fall into her description of "crime"— I'm not certain. But in any case, my lawyer was not comfortable with her, so he used one of his preemptory challenges to remove her as a prospective juror.

So now, at last, with all challenges completed, we were left with 7 jurors... 6 of whom would judge our case, and a 7th to serve as an "alternate" juror in the event we needed that person to fill in for one of the other ones. So the jury was empanelled. So let's look now at the jurors who did decide our fate:

Clinton Gustafson. This juror was selected, probably because my lawyer was out of preemptive challenges. It is all I can figure, because this juror admitted to the court that he knew prosecution witness Jamie Perlich. Asked if knowing her would result in his not being able to work fairly and weigh the evidence and sit as a juror, his reply was, "A little bit." He indicated to my lawyer he would probably side with her a little bit because he knew her.

Danny Maki. Here again, a juror was selected simply because the law limits the number of challenges a lawyer can make, even when it was apparent in this case that the selection of this juror would favor the state. This juror admitted that his sister worked for the Department of Human Resources in Iron County, Wisconsin. He also admitted he was "disturbed" when he heard the "allegations." In particular, he cited the vinegar bath (the one that never happened). He did say the trial could be fair if the spankings referred to were by hand. But if he believed already that the baths took place, why would he not believe the belt lies as well?

Dean Strubble. This juror's dad worked on the police force, his cousin worked on the police force, and Mr. Strubble himself had worked as a dispatcher's aide for the Eau Claire, Wisconsin police department. Although he stated none of that would prevent him from sitting as a fair and impartial juror, it wasn't convincing to me. He admitted during questioning that the interviewer's version of what my step child said would be acceptable as "evidence" in this case. Most all jurors subscribed to this, with all subscribing to the theory that because of her position, Ms. Elizabeth Fyle would never lie! I wonder now how many other child kidnappings she helped arrange for the state, and how many others she fabricated the charges in. The state of Michigan was sued monumentally for false kidnapping cases, and lost a big lawsuit in that process. I wonder how many of those were her cases?

Judy Pietrocatelli. Other than telling my lawyer she did think belt use would probably be abuse, and agreeing that law enforcement should step in when belt use occurred, she told the GAL (Mr. Perhalla) that her grandson had been involved in a child abuse case, but that in his case, her son was exonerated. My question is "why" he was exonerated. Perhaps because he KNEW someone? In any case, just her mere statements regarding belt use and her acceptance of law enforcement stepping in was proof enough to me that she was a stacked juror.

Thomas Pallin. This juror admitted he knew us through a church event about 4 years prior our trial. Or was it 3 years, as he later adjusted it to. More important, of course, was that he knew Bob Ross, having gone to college with him. No doubt, he was going to be impartial, wasn't he?

Holly Kostac. Holly did believe in spanking, she said. So maybe one juror that might side with us? Doubtful, since she also had a cousin who was a state police officer in Marquette!

So there you have it. That was the jury we had to rely on to find us not guilty. We had the same chance as a snowball in hell.

I think it noteworthy to mention that my lawyer had told all the jurors that my wife and I did not have the burden (under the law) of proving anything. That, was, in fact, the responsibility of the government (the state). But it seems that escaped the jurors due to the excessive efforts of both the judge and the prosecutors to make it clear they did not have to present a preponderance of evidence due to the civil nature of this case. That, in itself, was a bias that should never be allowed in a court of law. It reverses the basic principle that a defendant is considered innocent until proven guilty.

There was one point made by the judge in his instructions the newly selected jury that I did accept. He stated that, "When the case is over, you may, if you wish, discuss the case with anyone." I haven't forgotten that, which is why I am writing this book. It may be that the court took away all of our other rights in hearing the drummed up case against us, but we still have our constitutional rights, of which this is one. And I will never quit fighting the corruption of CPS (Child Protective Services) which is tearing apart families at their roots all across this country.

THE TRIAL BEGINS

With the deck stacked, the actual trial began immediately after a break from the completion of jury selection. The judge had made it clear, even in our last pre-trial hearing, that he wanted this case to be heard in the shortest possible period of time, because he had more pressing matters to be heard. In other words, our case was not a primary focus and its outcome had already been predetermined. But you still have to go through the motions.

So now, we were ready. Or were we? It seems that from the point where the judge called a break after jury instruction, to this point, the prosecutor had pulled one of many last minute tricks she would pull throughout this trial and beyond. She had tried to get introduced into the trial my posted web page accounts of what I stated and what I felt about CPS and other personal and political views. She had apparently printed off a large number of these things from my web site, and wanted to be able to incorporate that as evidence in this trial. My attorney argued strongly that none of that had anything to do with the petition of this trial, and argued it should not be allowed. The court asked for specific exhibits, which she could not produce. She only had some 700 pages of stuff she had printed from my web pages, not singling out any of it for my lawyer to see. Ms. Wittla tried to argue that we were aware of it because it was my group discussions on my site. Ms. Wittla showed the judge a package containing these pages, and the judge recoiled and made it very clear he would not hear each and every page of that, because he was not interested in my personal political views. He did allow that if any of it pertained to the case at hand, he may allow some of it, but that it all may be subject to objection or to relevance to the case. He stressed he would limit her and prohibit her from bringing any of it up unless she first alerted the court before she did it.

Having gotten past that, the court was ready to proceed, with each side agreeing first to sequester the witnesses. In the next four chapters, which include this one, the testimony will be cited from the actual transcripts of the court proceedings. In some cases, we have left out an "ah" or some word repetition, added a word that was obviously either left out by a witness or was a typing error of the clerk who typed the transcripts. But in no instance have we changed any meanings of what was stated. Keep that in mind as you read all transcripts cited in this book. The actual transcripts, as they were transcribed word for word by the clerks are visible on my web site links, so feel free to go to them if you have any difficulty with what we state in this book. So it was, at 3:07 pm, the jury was allowed to enter into the court room, and the prosecutor, Ms. Tracie Wittla, began her opening statement, which will quote from the transcripts:

MS. WITTLA: Hi, you already know I am Tracie Wittla; I represent the petitioner in this case.

THE COURT: I'm going to interrupt you just for a second, cause I was reminded at the break; if anybody can't hear, again, remember that goes for witnesses or lawyers, raise your hand to make sure you're getting everything from us. Thank you. That's exactly what we're looking for. Okay, proceed.

MS. WITTLA: Hi, take two. I'm Tracie Wittla, I am the assistant Prosecutor for Gogebic County, and I represent the Petitioner in this case. Parenting is one of the toughest jobs there is, and those of you who are parents can probably agree that there have been times when this 24-7 hour job can take it's toll on a person. And sometimes

even the combination of life stresses and the bad behavior of a kid can push even the best of parents into making a bad decision. But those parents typically realize somewhere along the line that they're going over the line; that they're messing up; that they, you know, aren't doing this the way they really want to do it. And because they are human beings and because they're fallible and they were able to make these mistakes; sometimes they make decisions that, um, on later reflection, they wished they hadn't. And most of those good parents will take the time to do some introspection and look inside of themselves and say, "You know, should I have really done that?" You know, maybe they'll seek advice from a professional or a friend on parenting issues, ah, maybe they'll just make a heartfelt apology to the child involved in the situation. But most of the time parents who are good at being parents, will understand internally that they've done something that crosses a line and they need to make it right; a do-over or a mulligan, if you will. Because parents understand, good parents understand, that kids aren't property; they're people. And as people, they deserve to have love and care, kindness, compassion, direction and discipline. But they don't deserve to be abused or treated cruelly in the name of discipline, and that's what this case is about. Having heard the petition read to you by Judge Massie, you already have some idea of what we are going to be talking about over the next few days. And this case began like any other case; there was a report of abuse; it was sent to the Department of Human Services; they went out, they did an investigation; interviewed some people; determined they had enough evidence to file a petition, with this court, not in this courtroom; downstairs, and asked for jurisdiction over these children. The question before you as the fact finder is whether or not you find one or more of the statutory grounds described in the petition have been proven by a preponderance of the evidence. And we talked about the preponderance of the evidence standard a little bit during voir dire; so we know that we are talking about tipping the scales in favor of the petition allegations; the statutory grounds being proven as true. So what statutory grounds are we talking about? First, that the Colemans neglected or refused to provide proper care or necessary support or other care necessary for Caitlyn and Ashley's health and morals. Second, that Caitlyn and Ashley are subject to a substantial risk of harm to their mental well-being. And third, that Caitlyn and Ashley's home, by reason of neglect, cruelty, criminality, or depravity on the part of their parents is an unfit place for them to live. You'll hear testimony from Elizabeth Fyle, the protective services worker who interviewed six-year-old Caitlyn Brag and how she described her step father, Robert Coleman, hitting her with a belt while her mother, Janet, restrained her. You'll hear how Caitlyn's mother interceded, not to protect Caitlyn, but to protect her husband from the scrutiny of DHS by reminding him not to leave any marks when he hit her. You'll hear how Caitlyn was kept in a vinegar bath for hours to get rid of the strap marks left on her bottom by her step father's belt, to keep her abuse a secret. You'll hear how Elizabeth Fyle's first interview with Caitlyn, on Tuesday, March 11th, was interrupted twice… sorry, perhaps once… by Janet Coleman, and how Elizabeth and Bob Ross decided to re-interview Caitlyn at school on Thursday, March 13th, approximately 36 hours later, only to find that she wasn't there. You'll hear about the conversation Bob Ross had with Robert Coleman, on that Thursday, asking where he was; and Mr. Coleman's response, that they were in Marquette for an OB visit, and they'd return later in the day and contact DHS. And then you'll hear about the realization that they didn't come back on Thursday; and how law enforcement was looking for them at their house, and DHS tried to contact them at their house, and was not able to do so on Thursday. Then you'll hear about how through a bit of detective work done by Sergeant Carpenedo of the Ironwood Public Safety Department, that they were located by finding out where their cell phone was bouncing off of the towers. That led them to the Hancock/Houghton area, and Houghton County law enforcement, and the Department of Human Services there interceded; located the children at a local hotel, and took them into custody. Finally, you'll hear about how Caitlyn was coached by her step father in those few days not to talk to DHS because they would trick her and take her away. But Caitlyn still chose to talk to Elizabeth Fyle and told her that being at a foster home was really good, and added that when she got in trouble there, she only got time-outs. And my belief, ladies and gentlemen, is that after you hear from all the petitioner's witnesses; that you will believe the allegations in the petition have been proven true; and that statutory grounds do exist to grant the Court the ability to intercede on behalf of these children; and decide what to do about their family. Thank you.

THE COURT: Mr. Perhalla, do you want to open or reserve?

MR. PERHALLA: I would open, thanks your Honor. Ladies and gentlemen of the jury, again, my name is Rudy Perhalla, and I thank you here today for your service on this jury. As you already know, this is a protective service case, in other words, as you already know, allegations have been brought against the parents, Robert and Janet Coleman. I will discuss those allegations in general in a couple of minutes, but for now I want to talk to you about my role in this case. Ladies and gentlemen, I am the guardian ad litem for the children, for Caitlyn and Ashley. The guardian ad litem is responsible both for protecting the legal rights of the children, and the children are and independent party in this case, in this lawsuit, and as for serving as an independent voice for what is in those two little girls' best interest. That is my role ladies and gentlemen. It makes the most sense to look at my role and say that I am the kids' attorney; I have looked at some of the facts, and I will be here advocating for what I believe is in their best interest. But then let's turn to the factual allegations and obviously you've heard them. You've heard them read to you, but I'd just like to speak to them; speak to them in summary and focus on what I see as the key to this case. The key to what the factual allegations are; the key to what factual allegations will be proven to you; and they will no longer be allegations, but facts after you hear the witnesses. First, ladies and gentlemen, I believe it will be proven to you that on one or more occasions, Robert and/or Janet Coleman struck Caitlyn, a little six-year-old girl with either a belt, a broom, or a spoon. I believe that will be a fact proven to you, ladies and gentlemen, and I believe that fact alone would be enough to grant this Court jurisdiction to intercede; to look out for what is truly in the best interest of these two little girls. Secondly, a second general fact that I believe will be proven to you ladies and gentlemen, is that on one or more occasions Robert and/or Janet Coleman struck Ashley; and Ashley is just a two-year-old toddler, basically a baby. I believe even the proof of the case; that fact alone will be sufficient for you to give this Court jurisdiction to intercede; to act for what's in the best interest of both of these little girls; these two sisters. Ladies and gentlemen, what I see as our task here today, and the days that follow, is basically two-fold. First, you have to look and make a determination on credibility, on what you believe from the witnesses right here in the witness stand. And I'm very confident, ladies and gentlemen, that what you will believe are the allegations that I just stated to you. I believe that you will come back, and in your mind, even more than fifty-one percent; that in your mind you'll completely believe that on one or more occasions, Caitlyn was struck with some object. And I firmly believe that you will come back and find believable that on one or more occasions the two-year-old, Ashley, was struck. That is what one of the two tasks, I believe, you have to, to decide here in this case; and that's essential, what everybody calls credibility. Who do we believe? What do we believe coming out of the mouths of the witnesses here? Our second task then, ladies and gentlemen, is that you must make a decision based upon the preponderance of the evidence; that one or more of the statutory grounds has been met; have been met. And just one or more of them have to be established, not both, but one or more. Now I know this can get a little bit confusing; statutory grounds is probably something you're not accustomed to hearing in your everyday affairs. How I like to look at it, ladies and gentlemen, is on one hand you have the facts; you have the evidence, you have the testimony, you have what you are to hear to decide this case. And on the other hand you have these statutory grounds; the law; what has to be met in order to grant this Court jurisdiction over these two little girls. And the question I look at, is how do we connect these facts to this law of statutory grounds? And that's what I think is the—the standard of proof—the burden of proof. And as you have already been told in this case, the standard of proof is just merely fifty-one percent. The standard of proof in this case is proof by a preponderance of the evidence; and proof by a preponderance of the evidence means that the evidence that a statutory ground alleged in the petition is true. The evidence that the statutory grounds alleged in the petition is true outweighs the evidence that the statutory ground is not true. And that's when we say fifty-one percent; that's what, that's what we're talking about. That you have to believe the testimony is true and that it meets the statutory grounds; that the truth of it outweighs the untruthfulness of it. Now what are the statutory grounds? They've been read to you in the jury instructions already, and the petition, basically, has two statutory grounds; or at least two paragraphs that; one contains multiple grounds. And they are again, ladies and gentlemen, and these are the statutory grounds what, what may be something you can't—little bit; something unusual for you. I'm sure by the time this is over, you'll have heard the word many, many, many times. But as far as coming in here today, I'm sure the term statutory grounds is new to you. And how they read are: (1) Whose parent or other person legally responsible for the care and maintenance of such child, when able to do so, neglects or refuses to provide proper and necessary support, education, medial, or surgical or other care necessary for his or her health or morals; who is subject to a substantial risk of harm to his or her mental well-being; who was abandoned by his parents; his or her parents, guardian or other custodian; or who is without proper custody or guardianship. That is the first paragraph; the first statutory ground that is set forth in the petitiion. The second reads: (2) Whose home or environment by reason of neglect, cruelty, drunkenness, criminality, or depravity, on the part of the parent, guardian, non-parent, adult, or other custodian is an unfit place for the juvenile to live in. Ladies and gentlemen, that is; that's a mouth full of the statutory grounds. But suffice it to say that it's my position, ladies and gentlemen, first, that a parent who beats his or her children is not providing proper care; or a parent who beats his or her children is simply cruel. Ladies and gentlemen, let us now listen to the testimony, what you'll hear, and when it's over, when the testimony is done; we can talk in a little more detail about how that testimony, what you've heard, fits into the petition, how it fits in to those statutory grounds. And I believe that once you've heard all this, ladies and gentlemen, I feel very confident we'll grant this Court jurisdiction to these two little girls. Thank you.

THE COURT: Mr. Findlay, do you care to open or do you want to reserve it?

MR. FINDLAY: I'm going to open, thanks your Honor. Now you KNOW what a parent is up against when the allegation of child abuse is made. It's an ALLEGATION. You were here for jury selection; you heard peoples' attitudes; all it takes, basically, is SAYING it happened, and a parent is just about found guilty of it. So what it does is SHIFT THE BURDEN. It's that once the allegations are made, the parents then have to come back and PROVE that they DIDN'T DO THIS. That's not the way the system is supposed to work. The government is supposed to prove that the parents DID THIS. Parents don't have to prove they didn't. And I want you to keep that in mind when you're listening to all evidence, and when you're listening to everything going on in this trial. The Colemans have NOT hit their children with a belt. That said, it's in the allegations in the petition. All over the place it's been said by numerous people. They deny adamantly that they've EVER hit their children with a belt or any objects. They will admit that they have spanked Caitlyn, with their hand on the bottom; they've never taken a hand, all all, to Ashley. She's only two years old. Let me tell you what happens to parents, at least these parents, when they're accused of this kind of abuse. Now we can get into a little bit about who the accusers are. The first thing that happened was that police officers and DHS show up, unannounced, at their door of their house demanding to see their children. They're told if they don't cooperate during the course of this demand to see the children, that "we'll get a court order and make you do it." They're basically not given a choice. DHS comes in with these two DHS personnel, police officers come into the house, start making accusations or saying that you've done these things; this has been reported to us that you've done these things. And keep in mind that these reported incidents had happened previously; I mean, so that then when you're evaluating the reporter; the person that reported these things originally; the first one was on January 26th is when this happened. Police show up on March 11th. Okay, the DHS would have been March 11th. The other is February 16th. I mean, so whoever is reporting this took their own sweet time to do it. They waited. That's—you may interpret why they waited. Maybe you can figure that out after hearing all the evidence. Anyway, the police show up on March 11th, demanding entry with DHS; get in the house and start making the accusations. In the house, they take Caitlyn aside, in her room, and then do this interview with her. Now you're going to hear testimony, and I mentioned a little bit in voir dire about this forensic protocol. It's a protocol that's been designed to interview children; it's designed and then put in place because, at least in this field, although it, the parent from voir dire that made while obvious people don't understand it; children are not always the most reliable witnesses. And children have a very strong tendency, some children more than others, have a tendency to basically tell adults, especially strange adults who they don't know, in a situation where they're barged in on, what they want to hear. And so if questions (are) asked in a certain way, you can get a child to say what you want them to say. Now they're going to tell you that they used the forensic protocol interview. Well, you're going to have to decide how well that was followed and how well that was done… done at the house itself as opposed to a neutral location. We'll get into all that in the testimony. So they make these allegations, apparently, obviously, they believe that these allegations are true—DHS does. So what does DHS do? They leave; they don't take the children then. They—the petition, what was defined in the petition that are—were subject to substantial risk of harm that, I guess if, you know, it was substantial but not substantial enough to do anything that day? That's what, I guess, you would have to believe what DHS believes. That it was, you know, substantial, but not substantial enough to remove the kids, because they didn't. They left. They didn't do anything on the 12th; then on the 13th, they decided they were going to start looking for the kids again. And do you want to know WHY they didn't do something on the 12th? They had training! DHS had training! So it terms of DHS's priority, their training on the 12th takes precedence *over the safety of these kids, apparently. So they go to their training. On the 13th, they start looking for the Colemans; they get hold of Mr. Coleman, asked him where he is. You know, this is one of those deals where there's a difference in the stories. Mr. Coleman is going to tell you that he told them they were in Houghton for a pre-arranged OBY-GYN visit with Janet Coleman's doctor, who's obviously pregnant; she's pregnant then; pre-arranged. The absence from school was excused; they went to the elementary school in Ironwood. That was excused; the records show that was an excused absence. They had gone up for this doctor appointment and decided to make a weekend out of it up in Houghton. DHS takes this and tries to twist this into they FLED the jurisdiction, and so they go the length of finding out their cell phone number and bounce it off towers and finding out where they are. Apparently they couldn't do that on the 13th. No, they couldn't do anything then. They couldn't do it, and I think I got my dates right; I think the 11th was a Tuesday, the 12th was a Wednesday, 13th is a Thursday, and 14th a Friday; didn't do anything then, but then on the morning of, I think it was Saturday morning; so the morning of the 15th, and I'm not talking nine o'clock in the morning, I'm not talking ten o'clock in the morning; I'm talking about three o'clock in the morning! They barge into their hotel up in Houghton and take their kids! Again, it wasn't important enough to do this on the 12th, that they could have these interviews; it's they could wait to deal with that, and you know, there are allegations the Colemans fled. You also hear that, at this hotel in Houghton, the Colemans certainly weren't doing a very good job in hiding their tracks; their car was parked out front. Again, a "pre-scheduled" doctor visit. Now I suppose DHS is going to tell you that they had an obligation to let DHS know their every whereabouts. You know, maybe I'm off in left field; maybe I'm— I don't think the citizens of this country has responsibility to inform the government of their whereabouts at all times. And they didn't do it this time, and then they called and didn't do it. I hope we haven't gotten to the point where we have to do that. But that's how the kids get taken away, and that's just, you notice that hasn't been mentioned by the people in the government yet. The Colemans haven't had their children since that morning of March 15th; their children have been in foster care since then. They've had relatively limited visits, you know, so I ask the question, I guess, who is getting punished? I mean, is it the— if somebody, like I said, previously your children also have a right in this, you know, who is getting punished here? Now I'll turn to who the accusers are; and this is why at the voir dire I asked the question about whether if you can set aside something you hear bad about somebody; and still evaluate the case fairly? The accusers, the reporting parties who brought this in are government's witnesses, Bobby and Becky Payne. They lived in the Coleman's residence; they were kind of a tenant's relationship. Janet Coleman was actually Bobby Payne's representative payee, they had been considered friends. But in the relationship, Robert Coleman had an affair with Becky Payne. Now Janet knows about that; it's been something obviously that on top of all this it's painful for them that they've had to work through, but that's between them. Again, I don't think the government's business about that; that's between them. And as Mr. Coleman himself said to me, "You know I'm not—I haven't been a good husband, but I have been a good father. So the reason I'm bringing this up is to show you that these reporting people have a motive; they have a reason to accuse the Colemans of this, and you're going to hear evidence of just what they think about this proceeding and evidence of that motive; in order to screw over the Colemans; I'm using THEIR words. And I'd say they pretty much succeeded, at least, so far at this point, and you're the ones that I guess—that are standing in the way of it going further. In addition to the affair, they (the Paynes) were also evicted on the date, right about on the 10th. The date that the Colemans said "We have enough, you got to get out, we can't do any more." Bobby Payne had an espisode where he kind of threw a fit, broke their wedding ceremony license on the ground, and Caitlyn actually cut her toe on it, and the Colemans said, "That's enough….*

we're done with that and you got to get out." The day after is when the Paynes went and ran to DHS and the police to report this stuff. So you've got that… that motive, that late reporting, all these things that weigh into whether these allegations can actually be proven; or if the alternative explanation is true that this didn't happen; that the reason the Colemans are here is because they are people that had an axe to grind against them; who don't like them; and who want to see them in trouble, and that's why they've made these allegations. Here's some things you won't hear, is they allege that she was hit by a belt; you're not going to see this belt. And wouldn't that be evidence? Don't you want to see that evidence of what the instrument of abuse was? I, as far as I know, you're not going to see anything, they should have been; it should, the presence of should have been known to us. I don't believe you're going to see it. This other indication of a spoon, a spoon or that's supposedly something Caitlyn says, there's none of that. They may show you some pictures, but we're going to show you pictures too, and then you decide, you know, how much weight you give each set of pictures. As a parent myself, I'm not sure what more, what worse thing you could do to me and, and I say this because this is a civil proceeding; and the burden of proof is lower than a criminal proceeding; but I can tell you right now, I would much rather do time in jail than have my children taken away from me. No question; I'll serve years; don't take my kids away; that's what's happened to the Colemans in this case. That's what they've had to go through while this was going on. They've been put in a situation now where they've got to, basically, they've got a tough hill to climb in terms of proving, I'm afraid, they're going to have to prove they didn't do this. And you're the last line of defense so to speak in terms of what, how far, the government goes in this. Another question I ask, I didn't ask this on voir dire, but just to want you to think about it; if the Colemans are— really did these things to their children; I mean, all those allegations are pretty bad; shouldn't they be charged criminally? Isn't that—doesn't that—go beyond just, you know, the civil matter? Shouldn't that be a crime? They haven't been charged criminally. And you know why I think that is? It's because that's a higher burden to prove; it's much tougher to prove a criminal accusation than it is a civil one. You have to prove that beyond a reasonable doubt—government knows—they'd be hard pressed to do that. They couldn't do it. And so they can use this in terms of charging them with a crime; if they really did these things, you know, that sounds like criminal activity; that sounds like child abuse, which is a crime in Michigan; but they haven't done that. I hope that communicates volumes to you about—even what the government views about this case. This will be a difficult case because you have, one, the interest of these children and what they are alleging happened shouldn't happen to these children. I don't think anybody is in here saying that that's legitimate. I know I asked on voir dire, you know, what about spanking with an object? Do you spank with an object? I just want to know where you're at in terms of, you know, how just the fact that anything was demonstrated by the questioning and the back and forth was just that you just hear these allegations and, man, the bells and whistles go off, and, you know, somebody's got to face these allegations. Well those allegations have to be proven, and that's your job as fact finders to believe; to discern and decide whether they are proven. Right now they are just allegations; the judge has said and will say again; at least once more if not a couple of times; what we say here and who— what I say right now, much like who she was—it's not evidence. The others you're going to hear from that stand and any exhibits that have been admitted—that's what you have to listen to; evaluate the people that are making these statements; evaluate their motives for making them. And I ask you to remember what this case is about. Hopefully, this case isn't about the legal parameter, the back and forth of who can prove what; it's about a family; the Colemans. And what we're doing here is, this what shouldn't happen to a family, based on the allegations, and the nature of the allegations. I'm hoping you're going to be fair. I'll be honest with you, I was worried after we started doing this voir dire. I said, "Oh, they're not going to have a chance; people have already convicted them just based on hearing the allegations." I'm asking you to restore our faith in the jury system and give this a fair hearing; don't make it a decision, don't make up your mind what this is until you've heard all the evidence. Thank you.

THE COURT: We will now begin with the proofs. Ms. Wittla, who is your first witness?

MS. WITTLA: Robert Coleman.

THE COURT: Okay, Mr. Coleman, would you step up to the front here. Before you are seated, please raise your right hand. Do you swear to tell the truth, the whole truth, and nothing but the truth, so help you God?

MR. COLEMAN: I do your Honor.

THE COURT: Be seated and Ms. Wittla, if you would proceed.

MS. WITTLA: Would you please state your name for the record?

MR. COLEMAN: Robert Coleman.

MS. WITTLA: I'm just going to move the microphone your Honor, it's pointing the wrong way. What is your current address?

MR. COLEMAN: It's 707570 Caledonia Street, Calumet.

MS. WITTLA: That's in Houghton County?

MR. COLEMAN: Yes.

MS. WITTLA: You live there with anyone else?

MR. COLEMAN: Yes I do.

MS. WITTLA: And who do you live there with?

MR. COLEMAN: My wife, Janet.

MS. WITTLA: How long have you lived there?

MR. COLEMAN: Lived there for a month and a half.

MS. WITTLA: Do you plan to live there indefinitely? Are you going to stay there forever?

MR. COLEMAN: For the time being.. or, I'm sorry, can you rephrase that?

MS. WITTLA: Ah, you own property in the city of Ironwood?

MR. COLEMAN: Yes ma'am.

MS. WITTLA: And it's called Coleman Estate?

MR. COLEMAN: Yes.

MS. WITTLA: And that consists of your apartment building, and some houses that you rent out?

MR. COLEMAN: That's correct.

MS. WITTLA: And you used to live there?

MR. COLEMAN: Yes, I did.

MS. WITTLA: Do you plan to go back to living there?

MR. COLEMAN: No, I don't.

MS. WITTLA: Okay, so you're disposing of that property then?

MR. COLEMAN: It's for sale.

MS. WITTLA: Okay, so you moved, you're not coming back; is that fair to say?

MR. COLEMAN: Not at this time.

MS. WITTLA: Not at this time. Does that mean yes or does that mean no?

MR. COLEMAN: No, I'm not coming back.....

MR. FINDLAY: ... your Honor, just, I'm going to object as to the relevance of this.

THE COURT: All right, this is somewhat preliminary, I guess. I'll give you a little room, but I don't know where we need to go, and he also can't be pinned down to a yes or no answer. I'm not sustaining any objection, just probably if we keep going too much with the where he lives and his plans, where he'll live will not be relevant.

MS. WITTLA: Is it fair to say then that not at this time means you could move back to Gogebic County?

MR. COLEMAN: I could.

MS. WITTLA: Did you live at the Coleman Estates when this case began?

MR. COLEMAN: Yes.

MS. WITTLA: What was the apartment number of the apartment that you lived in within your building?

MR. COLEMAN: 205.

MS. WITTLA: And approximately how long did you live at apartment number 205 at the Coleman Estates?

MR. COLEMAN: 8 years.

MS. WITTLA: How many units are there?

MR. COLEMAN: There's four, including mine, in my apartment building.

MS. WITTLA: And then houses in addition to that that you rent out?

MR. COLEMAN: Two other apartment buildings and two houses.

MS. WITTLA: Okay, so the total number of units that you rent out to the public on any given time is ball park, how many?

MR. COLEMAN: Ten apartments and two houses.

MS. WITTLA: Have you ever evicted anyone from your rental units?

MR. COLEMAN: Yes I have.

MS. WITTLA: Your attorney indicated in opening remarks that Bobby and Becky Payne were evicted from your rental units. Is that accurate?

MR. COLEMAN: Yes it is.

MS. WITTLA: What apartment number did they have?

MR. COLEMAN: They stayed with us.

MS. WITTLA: You evicted them from your apartment?

MR. COLEMAN: Yes I did.

MS. WITTLA: Mr. Coleman, isn't it true that at one point in time they had their own apartment in your building?

MR. COLEMAN: Yes it is.

MS. WITTLA: Isn't it also true that you encouraged them to leave that apartment and live in your basement?

MR. COLEMAN: No it's not.

MS. WITTLA: Isn't it true that the only time that the Paynes spent with you was for dinner or to take care of your children?

MR. COLEMAN: I'm sorry?

MS. WITTLA: Mr. Coleman, isn't it true that the only time that Becky and Bobby Payne spent in your apartment building with you, was to take care of your children or dine with you?

MR. COLEMAN: No, it's not true.

MS. WITTLA: So your testimony today is that they lived with you?

MR. COLEMAN: Yes, they did.

MS. WITTLA: And their belongings were within your apartment?

MR. COLEMAN: Yes, they were.

MS. WITTLA: How many bedrooms are in your apartment?

MR. COLEMAN: There is one bedroom and the rest is under construction.

MS. WITTLA: So who had the bedroom?

MR. COLEMAN: The children did.

MS. WITTLA: Okay, and the children— you mean Caitlyn and Ashley?

MR. COLEMAN: That's correct.

MS. WITTLA: So where did everybody else stay?

MR. COLEMAN: My wife and me stayed in the living room.

MS. WITTLA: Okay, and where did Becky and Bobby stay?

MR. COLEMAN: Becky and Bobby stayed in the basement.

MS. WITTLA: In the basement?

MR. COLEMAN: That's correct.

MS. WITTLA: That's where they had their mattress?

MR. COLEMAN: That's where they had all their belongings.

MS. WITTLA: Okay, you understand that just a moment ago you told me that they lived within your apartment and they had their belongings in your apartment?

MR. COLEMAN: That is my apartment.

MS. WITTLA: The basement is your apartment?

MR. COLEMAN: That's correct; that's part of my apartment.

MS. WITTLA: It's part of the apartment building?

MR. COLEMAN: It's part of my apartment.

MS. WITTLA: The basement you consider to be part of your personal apartment that you have at the Coleman Estates?

MR. COLEMAN: Yes ma'am.

MS. WITTLA: So was the basement fixed up like your apartment?

MR. COLEMAN: It was under construction.

MS. WITTLA: So when you evicted them, you evicted them from the basement part of your apartment?

MR. COLEMAN: That's correct.

MS. WITTLA: Why did you evict them?

MR. COLEMAN: Because they were fighting.

MS. WITTLA: With who?

MR. COLEMAN: Each other.

MS. WITTLA: Was that because of the affair that you had with Becky?

MR. COLEMAN: Part of it.

MS. WITTLA: When you're talking about an affair, are you talking about a sexual affair you had with Becky Payne?

MR. COLEMAN: That's correct.

MS. WITTLA: How long was this affair?

MR. COLEMAN: Since January.

MS. WITTLA: Of 2008?

MR. COLEMAN: This year.

MS. WITTLA: When did your affair with Becky Payne end?

MR. COLEMAN: There never was a relationship; it just ended when I asked them to leave.

MS. WITTLA: Well how would you describe an affair then; what does that mean?

MR. COLEMAN: Affair, I feel, is cheating on your wife; and that's what I did, I cheated on my wife.

MS. WITTLA: Does that mean you had sex with Becky Payne?

MR. COLEMAN: Yes ma'am, I did.

MS. WITTLA: And you believe that that is the reason that Becky and Bobby were fighting?

MR. COLEMAN: They were fighting when we first met them; they always fought.

MS. WITTLA: Would you classify them as violent people?

MR. COLEMAN: Yes, I would.

MS. WITTLA: Do you know any of the things that they would fight about?

MR. COLEMAN: Cigarettes... um, little things like things Becky would do; she'd bring home some shoes;

Bobby wouldn't like them. They'd fight over that.

MS. WITTLA: Did they both smoke?

MR. COLEMAN: Yes, they did.

MS. WITTLA: Cigarettes were important to them?

MR. COLEMAN: Yes, they were.

MS. WITTLA: When did you stop collecting rent from Becky and Bobby Payne?

MR. COLEMAN: When Becky moved all of her belongings down to our basement; she pretty much just kind of moved herself in, and we stopped rent on them. They wanted to go back to California.

MS. WITTLA: And when was that?

MR. COLEMAN: That was in March.

MS. WITTLA: In March they moved down to the basement?

MR. COLEMAN: That's correct. Um... no, I'm sorry. I don't recall when they moved down in the basement.

MS. WITTLA: I believe it was indicated that you evicted them sometime in the month of March, is that accurate?

MR. COLEMAN: It was on March 10th, that's correct. I told them that they had to leave because of all the arguing.

MS. WITTLA: So were they in the basement for a few days, weeks, longer than that?

MR. COLEMAN: A couple of weeks.

MS. WITTLA: Couple of weeks? Does this basement area connect directly up to your apartment?

MR. COLEMAN: Yes it does.

MS. WITTLA: It's not through a common hallway or anything?

MR. COLEMAN: No, it's not. It's in our apartment.

MS. WITTLA: Okay, and by common, I mean like your specific unit, not the entire building?

MR. COLEMAN: That's correct.

MS. WITTLA: How many children do you have?

MR. COLEMAN: I have two.

MS. WITTLA: And what are their names?

MR. COLEMAN: Caitlyn and Ashley.

MS. WITTLA: How tall would you say Caitlyn is?

MR. COLEMAN: Caitlyn is all thirty-two inches tall.

MS. WITTLA: Any idea of how much she weighs?

MR. COLEMAN: She weighs fifty-two pounds.

MS. WITTLA: How about Ashley?

MR. COLEMAN: Ashley is about, take twenty-eight inches tall, thirty inches; and she weights about twenty-five pounds; thirty pounds. She was twenty-six pounds when they had taken her.

MS. WITTLA: Okay, you indicate she is how tall?

MR. COLEMAN: She's about two foot, three inches.

MS. WITTLA: How tall are you?

MR. COLEMAN: I'm six foot four.

MS. WITTLA: When were Caitlyn and Ashley placed in foster care?

MR. COLEMAN: They day they had taken them on March 15th.

MS. WITTLA: And when you say they; who is they that took them?

MR. COLEMAN: It was about twelve police officers and a CPS worker.

MS. WITTLA: Why do you believe Caitlyn and Ashley were place in foster care?

MR. COLEMAN: Why do I believe it?

MS. WITTLA: Yes.

MR. COLEMAN: I don't, um, think they should be in foster care. I believe the state took them unlawfully.

MS. WITTLA: Why would the state take them unlawfully?

MR. COLEMAN: Because I feel they jumped the gun.

MS. WITTLA: How?

MR. COLEMAN: Like they did in Texas. They didn't have all their facts, they just came in and acted.

MS. WITTLA: Like they did in Texas?

MR. COLEMAN: That's correct.

MS. WITTLA: Did you live in Texas before?

MR. COLEMAN: No ma'am, I haven't.

MS. WITTLA: What are you referring to?

MR. COLEMAN: I'm referring that when I spoke with Bob Ross on the phone, and I told him that I had an attorney, he was satisfied with that until we got out to our motel and they barged in at 1:40 in the morning on a Saturday.

MS. WITTLA: Okay, I think you shifted off of Texas with me here, but let's follow up with where you're going. So you acknowledge that Bob Ross called you on Thursday, March 13th?

MR. COLEMAN: It was at six o'clock he called.

MS. WITTLA: Would that be six o'clock in the morning?

MR. COLEMAN: It was six o'clock in the evening.

MS. WITTLA: Bob Ross called you at six o'clock at night on Thursday, March 13th?

MR. COLEMAN: No, it was not March 13th.

MS. WITTLA: Okay, tell me when Bob Ross called you at six o'clock?

MR. COLEMAN: Ma'am I don't know what the day was for Thursday; I'd have to find that date out.

MS. WITTLA: Well then let's back up a little bit more, do you know what day this investigation started with Caitlyn and Ashley?

MR. COLEMAN: It started the day they knocked on our door, on the 11th.

MS. WITTLA: The 11th of March?

MR. COLEMAN: That's correct.

MS. WITTLA: And do you know why they knocked on your door on March 11th?

MR. COLEMAN: I didn't at first, but I kind of figured it out after awhile.

MS. WITTLA: And what did you figure out?

MR. COLEMAN: Well, I figured out that they were investigating us.

MS. WITTLA: They didn't tell you that when they showed up?

MR. COLEMAN: They came and they said they needed to talk to Caitlyn.

MS. WITTLA: Okay, and the "they" that you were referring to now is?

MR. COLEMAN: That was on March 11th.

MS. WITTLA: Yes.

MR. COLEMAN: That's correct.

MS. WITTLA: Yeah, but who? Who came to talk to Caitlyn?

MR. COLEMAN: It was Bob Ross, Elizabeth Fyle, and Officer Saippa.

MS. WITTLA: So did one or all of these people talk to Caitlyn that day?

MR. COLEMAN: Two of them did.

MS. WITTLA: Okay, which two?

MR. COLEMAN: It was Bob Ross and Elizabeth Fyle.

MS. WITTLA: And how do you know that Bob Ross and Elizabeth Fyle talked to Caitlyn?

MR. COLEMAN: Because they walked in our bedroom and they shut the door; they wanted to talk to her.

MS. WITTLA: What did you think of that?

MR. COLEMAN: I felt they needed a warrant, but I cooperated with them. I called my attorney and he told me that we should be in there with Caitlyn.

MS. WITTLA: So then what happened?

MR. COLEMAN: My wife walked into the room and told them that our attorney advised us that she should be in there.

MS. WITTLA: Was it explained to you and your wife that you could not be present during the interview?

MR. COLEMAN: It wasn't explained until after they had said that they would just go get a court order and remove our children.

MS. WITTLA: Okay, so what was explained to you about the interview with Caitlyn?

MR. COLEMAN: That they had to do an interview with her by themselves.

MS. WITTLA: Okay, just because, or did they tell you why, or?

MR. COLEMAN: I don't recall that. My wife went into the room and.....

MS. WITTLA: ... She's the one who had been told that?

MR. COLEMAN: She interrupted the interview.

MS. WITTLA: Okay, were you ever told that according to the law they'd have to interview Caitlyn without her parents presence?

MR. COLEMAN: Bob Ross had stepped out, and he left Elizabeth Fyle in the room, and then he, ah, explained that to Janet that they just need to talk to her for a few minutes; they have questions to ask.

MS. WITTLA: Okay, but what I'm asking you is did it ever become apparent to you that the reason you weren't allowed to be there was because they had to follow protocol which prevented you from being there?

MR. FINDLAY: Your Honor, I'm going to object; that, I guess assumes.....

THE COURT: .... Grounds?

MR. FINDLAY: Assumes facts not in evidence to the protocol and the.....

THE COURT: .... I'm assuming you're going to connect, offering that you're going to connect that up later or?

MS. WITTLA: Ah, well, yes, your Honor, but I'm just asking if he ever knew that was the reason why he couldn't be there.

THE COURT: Okay, so if you want to restate that, I don't think the question was under... oh, let him....

MR. FINDLAY: Yeah, I mean, he does... it would also be with outside the scope of his knowledge, he's not a lawyer; now I guess she can ask was he told that, but whether he knew that or not is... I don't think he's quali-

fied to answer that question.

THE COURT: Well I guess he's not qualified to understand the protocol, but he may be qualified to understand whether somebody told them they were using it, that... that's the real question?

MR. FINDLAY: That, right, and that's fine along with distinction.

THE COURT: So if you could rephrase that, then if you understand what we're saying; I mean, he can't talk about compliance with the protocol, but he can, he can say they told him whether they're following this protocol; is that what your question was?

MS. WITTLA: To some extent, but I'll rephrase it since it's kind of gotten out of hand. Mr. Coleman, what I'm essentially asking you if if you were ever told a reason why you and your wife could not be present when Caitlyn was interviewed by CPS?

MR. COLEMAN: No. That's why I called my attorney.

MS. WITTLA: Okay, and then after you talked to your attorney, did Mr. Ross at some point in time explain to you why you and your wife could not be present when Caitlyn was interviewed?

MR. COLEMAN: No. I did what my attorney told, asked. He said that we had the right to be in there.

MS. WITTLA: Okay, what were you told regarding the court order for this interview?

MR. COLEMAN: I'm sorry. What court order?

MS. WITTLA: Were you ever told anything about CPS getting a court order to interview Caitlyn, if you would not allow her to be interviewed?

MR. COLEMAN: They told, when my wife walked in there, they told her that if she did not allow them to interview her, they would get a court order and remove our children.

MS. WITTLA: Okay, and the court order would be to remove the kids; the court order would not be to interview the kids?

MR. COLEMAN: That's correct. That's what we were told.

MS. WITTLA: Do you remember a point in time after the interview with Caitlyn that Bob Ross called you on your cell phone?

MR. COLEMAN: I'm sorry. What day was this?

MS. WITTLA: Well I'm asking you what day that was. Did Bob Ross call you on your cell phone, after the day that Caitlyn was interviewed.

MR. COLEMAN: It was on Thursday.

MS. WITTLA: Okay, two days later, the 13th?

MR. COLEMAN: That's correct, if that's what day Thursday was.

MS. WITTLA: Okay, well Tuesday was the 11th.

MR. COLEMAN: Okay.

MS. WITTLA: And Thursday would have been the 13th. It was the same week?

MR. COLEMAN: Wednesday would be the 12th—that's correct.

MS. WITTLA: Where were you when he got a hold of you on your cell phone?

MR. COLEMAN: I was in a mall in Houghton.

MS. WITTLA: And where did you tell Mr. Ross you were?

MR. COLEMAN: I told him that I was in Houghton.

MS. WITTLA: Did you tell him when you'd be returning to the area?

MR. COLEMAN: On Monday.

MS. WITTLA: And did you tell him why you would be returning on Monday?

MR. COLEMAN: Yes I did.

MS. WITTLA: And what was it?

MR. COLEMAN: We were on vacation. It was spring break and I told him that we would meet up with him on Monday.

MS. WITTLA: So your intention was when you returned to town on Monday, that you would get in contact with Mr. Ross?

MR. COLEMAN: The attorney. We would have an attorney present at this time; I explained to him that I have an attorney.

MS. WITTLA: What hotel did you stay at in Hancock?

MR. COLEMAN: Best Western.

MS. WITTLA: And what name were you registered under?

MR. COLEMAN: Janet Coleman.

MS. WITTLA: Do you know anyone by the name of Russell Brag?

MR. COLEMAN: I'm sorry. Russell Brag?

MS. WITTLA: Yes.

MR. COLEMAN: Do you mean David Brag?

MS. WITTLA: I'm sorry, did you say David Brag?

MR. COLEMAN: Yes.

MS. WITTLA: Actually I asked about Russell, but do you know someone named David Brag?

MR. COLEMAN: No, I don't know anybody of Russell Brag; I know that Janet's mom and dad paid for the room.

MS. WITTLA: And Janet's mom and dad's names are?

MR. COLEMAN: It would be Kathy and David Brag. B-R-A-G. It's Brag.

MS. WITTLA: Do you know how you were located at the Best Western?

MR. COLEMAN: Yes I do.

MS. WITTLA: And how were you located?

MR. COLEMAN: Well, when I was in the mall, Mr. Ross asked me how could I be calling; how could he get a hold of me because my phone was 906-932-7400; and how could I be in Houghton if I had a 932 cell phone. And I explained to him it was ported from my business; and when I was in the motel room after the police had raided it; they told me that they located me from my cell phone.

MS. WITTLA: If you already told Mr. Ross that you were in Houghton, why would anybody try to track you down with cell phone records, if you were eventually found in Hancock which is a sister city?

MR. FINDLAY: Objection your Honor, I don't know how... that calls for speculation on the part of the witness. He can't get inside the head of DHS and why they do things.

THE COURT: I'll overrule, I mean the question is if which I presume you intend to connect up later with a different statement, that if he was indeed in Houghton, why was that necessary? It will be made relevant, I presume, is that right? There was some discussion of it; frankly, there was some discussion of it in the voir dire about where Mr. Coleman had said he was, as well as being in the petition. So you intend to connect that up later I believe, that your allegation is that he was in Houghton; that he didn't say he was in Houghton?

MS. WITTLA: Yes, your Honor.

THE COURT: All right, overruled. Proceed.

MS. WITTLA: Do you recall the question?

MR. COLEMAN: I'm sorry. Could you please repeat it?

MS. WITTLA: If Mr. Ross already knew that you were in Houghton, then why search for you through cell phone records?

MR. FINDLAY: Your Honor, I'm going to object again, I'm sorry to, but that's a relevance objection; it's scope of knowledge. How does he know why Bob Ross did a cell phone search?

THE COURT: That's true and if that's his answer, that's his answer, but in terms of admissibility, I don't find a valid objection. It's overruled, so proceed. You may have to ask it again, I don't know.

MS. WITTLA: Well, let's try something new. Isn't it true, Mr. Coleman, that when Bob Ross called you on Thursday morning that you told him that you were in Marquette for an OB visit?

MR. COLEMAN: No, it's not true.

MS. WITTLA: Isn't it true, Mr. Coleman, that you told Bob Ross that you'd be returning Thursday evening?

MR. COLEMAN: No, that's not true.

MS. WITTLA: You indicated that the officers came to the room and picked up Caitlyn and Ashley with their twelve officers and a CPS worker. Is that accurate?

MR. COLEMAN: No ma'am, I said nine.

MS. WITTLA: Nine. Okay, nine officers and a CPS worker, right?

MR. COLEMAN: That's correct.

MS. WITTLA: What did you do when they came to your door?

MR. COLEMAN: I was in bed sleeping. All of us were asleep, and they had the door open and they were trying to break it in with the chain on it; and my wife got up and opened, took the chain off, and wouldn't allow me to get out of bed. Um, they just came in and they grabbed the kids and went through and grabbed whatever they thought they needed, and then they left, and after they left, and after the children were out of the room; then they had given us a piece of paper stating that they had the right to take them.

MS. WITTLA: Okay, so if I'm understanding you, when the police officers arrived at your room, they're trying to bust down the door, but the chain is hooked?

MR. COLEMAN: Yes, there's a safety chain that goes on the door.

MS. WITTLA: And Janet got up and unlatched the safety chain?

MR. COLEMAN: Yes ma'am.

MS. WITTLA: And then the police came in, grabbed the kids, grabbed whatever they wanted, and left?

MR. COLEMAN: With the children, the other officer stayed to serve us some papers.

MS. WITTLA: And what were you doing at this time?

MR. COLEMAN: I was sitting; they, they wouldn't let me get out of the bed.

MS. WITTLA: And what was Janet doing?

MR. COLEMAN: Janet was standing there.

MS. WITTLA: Did either of you say anything to the police?

MR. COLEMAN: I told them I, I said that I wanted to know why they were taking our children; and they said that they were, ah, under, ah, for abuse and, ah, I told them that I wanted them to look the children over right then and there; and they didn't want to do that; they just took them and left with them.

MS. WITTLA: Were the girls awake or asleep when the police arrived?

MR. COLEMAN: They were asleep.

MS. WITTLA: And who escorted the girls out of the hotel?

MR. COLEMAN: The DHS; I didn't even know who it was, just, she just took the kid, um, she took the baby I,

I'm pretty sure, and then an officer had taken Caitlyn; and they carried them out of the room.

MS. WITTLA: So at the time you didn't know that she was a CPS, but a woman carried Ashley and a police officer carried Caitlyn; is that accurate?

MR. COLEMAN: It's vague, but I, I'm a very hard sleeper so I was still half asleep when this was going on.

MS. WITTLA: Okay, so you're not clear on who took the kids out of the room?

MR. COLEMAN: No, our children was just removed.

MS. WITTLA: Okay, but you do recall saying that you wanted them to look over the kids for, I'm assuming signs of abuse? You said this to the police officers?

MR. COLEMAN: Yes ma'am.

MS. WITTLA: And they didn't want to do that?

MR. COLEMAN: No. I told them to take the kids and strip them right there and see if there was any bruises on them. And they said no.

MS. WITTLA: Did you send anything of a personal nature, along with the children when they were taken from the room?

MR. COLEMAN: I didn't get a chance.

MS. WITTLA: Okay, did any of their personal stuff end up leaving with them?

MR. COLEMAN: They had taken our car keys and grabbed our car seat out of our truck, and they had gone through everything and took what they felt that they needed.

MS. WITTLA: Okay, so when you refer to they, this is law enforcement and CPS took your car keys?

MR. COLEMAN: The police officers did. There were state police, there were sheriff, there was Houghton, there was Hancock.

MS. WITTLA: And when you say they took whatever else they wanted, they took whatever else they wanted from your vehicle?

MR. COLEMAN: They took our car seat out of the truck; they they took out of the motel room, my diaper bag or whatever they had for the children.

MS. WITTA: Okay, they just took it.

MR. COLEMAN: Yes.

MS. WITTLA: Did you go out to the car with the kids?

MR. COLEMAN: Yes, I went down afterwards, after this officer had served us papers, Janet and me walked downstairs.

MS. WITTLA: You went down together?

MR. COLEMAN: Yes.

MS. WITTLA: Did you say anything to the kids when they were leaving?

MR. COLEMAN: I did, yes.

MS. WITTLA: Do you recall what you said?

MR. COLEMAN: Yeah, I said I love you Ashley and I'll miss you.

MS. WITTLA: Were the children upset?

MR. COLEMAN: They were crying.

MS. WITTLA: When did they start crying.

MR. COLEMAN: As they were going downstairs.

MS. WITTLA: So after they left the room as they were going down the hallway, or, I'm not sure where your hotel room was in relation to the stairs.

MR. COLEMAN: To go down, ah, just probably about three rooms and then you go down the stairs, and the motel was designed so that you park underneath of it... and our truck was just right in the front, and that's where all the police cars were; they had the whole place surrounded; and we walked down the stairs to say goodbye to our children. Janet was pleading with them to let us say goodbye. I wanted to say goodbye as well.

MS. WITTLA: So getting back to when the kids started crying; they started crying at what point in the removal process?

MR. COLEMAN: They were very upset and they started crying when they were; ma'am they came in and they just grabbed them out of bed; they pulled the sheet off and they just grabbed them both; and they put their jackets on them, and out they went; pajamas and all.

MS. WITTLA: So it is your testimony today that the children were upset when they were still in the room with you?

MR. COLEMAN: Yes, they were upset to get pulled out of bed and to get their coats put on them and be taken by total strangers down to a vehicle.

MS. WITTLA: And you know that they were upset? How?

MR. COLEMAN: Because they are my children and I could see that they were upset.

MS. WITTLA: By facial expression.... because they were crying?

MR. COLEMAN: I could hear them and I could see them, them taking out of the children out of bed, and I was laying there in bed. They wouldn't let me get out of my bed, and the beds were next to each other, so their bed was the farthest to the wall, and they just put their coats on; their jackets were not even zipped up or anything, and their hoods were not put on, and they just took them right out the door. That was their main priority is to get those children out of that motel room, and then after they were removed out of there, then things had calmed down.

MS. WITTLA: When you state that things had calmed down, who calmed down?

MR. COLEMAN: The police officers did. They were armed with tasers, and they had tasers and guns. I mean they're... after the children were removed out of the room, they seemed to have calmed down.

MS. WITTLA: Okay, are you saying that the police officers had their weapons drawn when they came into your room?

MR. COLEMAN: I talked to the police later, and they told me that they were ready; so they told me that they had their hand ready, and they were armed with tasers.

MS. WITTLA: Okay, but it didn't end up going in that direction, is that fair to say?

MR. COLEMAN: No. If I had gotten out of that bed, I'm sure I would have probably gotten hit with whatever they had to restrain me. I just laid there until the children were removed. After they did, then they allowed me to get up and things were more calm.

MS. WITTLA: So where was Janet during this period of time when the kids were being taken out of the room?

MR. COLEMAN: She was standing on the other side of the bed, and they went by her with the children.

MS. WITTLA: And at this point in time, as the kids were woken up, had their jackets put on them, they're already upset as they're leaving the hotel. That's your testimony?

MR. COLEMAN: That's correct.

MS. WITTLA: When you went down to the car to say goodbye to them, was that an attempt to comfort them in some way?

MR. COLEMAN: Yes.

MS. WITTLA: When was the next time you saw them?

MR. COLEMAN: At child... um... at the DHS office in Bessemer.

MS. WITTLA: Do you remember how many days that was?

MR. COLEMAN: It was on the 20th.

MS. WITTLA: After Caitlyn's first interview with Elizabeth Fyle and Bob Ross, did you talk to her about her interview?

MR. COLEMAN: At the dinner table.

MS. WITTLA: Did you warn her not to talk to DHS?

MR. COLEMAN: No.

MS. WITTLA: Did you warn her not to talk about spanks?

MR. COLEMAN: No.

MS. WITTLA: Isn't it true, Mr. Coleman, that you told Caitlyn that DHS would try to trick her and take her away?

MR. COLEMAN: No.

MS. WITTLA: Are you aware of Caitlyn making any statements to that effect?

MR. COLEMAN: She kept saying at the dinner table that she had a secret, and finally I just played into her game, and I said "What kind of secret?" And she says, "Daddy they told me if you... if I tell them that you spanked me they won't take me."

MS. WITTLA: Are you aware of Caitlyn making statements while she was in foster care that you were upset with her after her first interview?

MR. COLEMAN: I'm not aware of that.

MS. WITTLA: How would you describe yourself, Mr. Coleman?

MR. COLEMAN: I would describe myself as very kind, loving, generous person that goes out of their way to help people.

MS. WITTLA: Do you believe you have any problems withholding your emotions?

MR. COLEMAN: Yes, I have problems.

MS. WITTLA: Does that fit with the kind, loving, generous person aspect of your character then?

MR. COLEMAN: Yes, because when I get hurt, I cry.

MS. WITTLA: What do you believe is accepted punishment for a kindergartner?

MR. COLEMAN: For a kindergartner?

MS. WITTLA: Yeah.

MR. COLEMAN: For as far as a child?

MS. WITTLA: A six year old child, a kindergartner, yes.

MR. COLEMAN: I believe in putting them in a corner and redirecting him.

MS. WITTLA: Are you aware of Caitlyn stating that your nickname for her was Corner Lover?

MR. COLEMAN: No, I'm not aware of that.

MS. WITTLA: Is that true?

MR. COLEMAN: That was a statement that Bobby and Becky had made up for her.

MS. WITTLA: So that's a lie. You didn't, you didn't call her that?

MR. COLEMAN: I didn't call her that. They would tease her when I'd ask her to go to the corner if she got out of line.

MS. WITTLA: So in this entire case, the bad people are Becky and Bobby Payne in your opinion?

MR. COLEMAN: Yes ma'am, I would perspect it to be that way.

MS. WITTLA: Doesn't that seem a bit convenient?

MR. FINDLAY: Your Honor, I'm going to object; it's argumentative.

THE COURT: I suppose it is; sustained.

MS. WITTLA: Mr. Coleman, who had control of Becky's food stamp card.

MR. COLEMAN: They did.

MS. WITTLA: So there are not any DHS records that would show that you guys used it; you and your wife?

MR. COLEMAN: We went shopping with them.

MS. WITTLA: So you helped them use their food stamp card?

MR. COLEMAN: They got their groceries; we helped them shop.

MS. WITTLA: Okay, and when you say you helped them shop; what did you have to help them with?

MR. COLEMAN: We showed them the value of money and how to spend money and how to make things last.

MS. WITTLA: Would you say that they wouldn't be able to figure that out on their own?

MR. COLEMAN: I would say that they were very wasteful.

MS. WITTLA: Okay, just crazy, live for the moment kind of people?

MR. COLEMAN: Pretty much.

MS. WITTLA: So if Rebecca Payne came in and testified that you had control over her food stamp card, through the DHS, she would not be telling the truth?

MR. COLEMAN: That's correct.

MS. WITTLA: And if she came in and said, "We moved out of that apartment that we had at Coleman Estates after Christmas, 2007 because Robert Coleman wanted to re-rent our apartment to somebody else; that would also be false?

MR. COLEMAN: That's correct.

MS. WITTLA: Do you recall inviting anyone to your basement to view the Paynes' belongings after they left your building?

MR. COLEMAN: On what day would that be?

MS. WITTLA: I don't know. Did it ever happen?

MR. COLEMAN: We moved their belongings out of the apartment.

MS. WITTLA: Mr. Coleman, isn't it true that you invited Jamie Perlich and her boyfriend Eli Wells to come down and peruse through all the things that the Paynes had left behind in the basement?

MR. COLEMAN: That's incorrect.

MS. WITTLA: How did that go then?

MR. COLEMAN: They were down there as….

MR. FINDLAY: … Your Honor, I'm going to object just to the relevance. I'm not sure what the relevance of….

THE COURT: I guess we are…. well, what is relevant? What's your response?

MS. WITTLA: Your Honor, this line of questioning is an attempt to prove that Robert Coleman controlled several aspects of the Paynes' lives, including their belongings which they left; which were behind; when they chose to leave in a hurry.

THE COURT: I'm presuming some, some time in the future with the Paynes' testimony or Mr. Coleman's further testimony this is going to be connected up. I mean it's vaguely in touch with the allegations, the Paynes are certainly the original reporters in the matter… but…

MS. WITTLA: Actually, I can't say that is accurate.

THE COURT: You can't say that it's... that what's accurate?

MS. WITTLA: I can't say that reporters have ever been identified; this court has never ordered the release of who reported this incident to.....

WHOA! WHOA! WHOA! We'll stop it right here! At this point in the trial, the

judge should have demanded that Ms. Wittla reveal who the accusers were! If this petition was filed by someone else, we, as defendants have a constitutional right to face our accusers! That was denied to us in this case, and judge should be serverly reprimanded for having this allowed to go on. Back to the testimony:

THE COURT: What I'm referring to is the allegations of the petition that says Rebecca says or Becky says, or Rebecca says, Bobby says; I mean they become the main, initial people in your petition. I guess I don't know either who the original reporters would be, but what I'm saying is what you're doing now is somewhat tangential to those allegations of the physical discipline, alleged abuse, and it... it very well may be relevant as the Paynes' testify as to the situation and are cross examined. But right now I'm— it's getting a bit too far away is what I am saying. And there's actually been some legal issues that have been addressed, prior to this that question the relevance, I guess, which if counsel wants to spell out later on the record, we can make clear. But go ahead:

MS. WITTLA: Mr. Coleman, then, would you deny that you had control over Becky and Bobby Paynes'

Benefits from the DHS?

MR. COLEMAN: That's correct.

MS. WITTLA: Would you deny that you have financial control over Becky and Bobby Paynes' social security benefits?

MR. COLEMAN: That's correct.

MS. WITTLA: Would you deny that you had control over where Becky and Bobby lived in your apartment building?

MR. COLEMAN: That's correct.

MS. WITTLA: Mr. Coleman, isn't it true that you wanted Becky and Bobby Payne to refer to you as Daddy?

MR. COLEMAN: That's incorrect.

MS. WITTLA: Were you aware that they refer to you as Daddy?

MR. COLEMAN: Yes I was.

MS. WITTLA: This was not at your bidding?

MR. COLEMAN: It freaked me out.

MS. WITTLA: Mr. Coleman, is it your testimony that you believe that Becky and Bobby Payne made up this story about you abusing Caitlyn?

MR. COLEMAN: Yes.

MS. WITTLA: And their motive for making up this story would be what?

MR. COLEMAN: Revenge.

MS. WITTLA: And they want revenge because of what?

MR. COLEMAN: I slept with Becky.

MS. WITTLA: So Becky would want revenge on you because you slept with her?

MR. COLEMAN: She wanted me. She wanted a relationship with me.

MS. WITTLA: So Becky would want revenge only because that relationship ended?

MR. COLEMAN: She realized she couldn't have me when we told them to leave.

MS. WITTLA: Okay, so Becky wanted revenge on you because she's a scorned woman; she wanted but she can't have you; that's your testimony? That's your belief?

MR. COLEMAN: Yes ma'am.

MS. WITTLA: And Bobby Payne would want revenge on you because you had sex with his wife?

MR. COLEMAN: That's correct.

MS. WITTLA: Have you ever used physical punishment for Caitlyn?

MR. COLEMAN: Yes I have.

MS. WITTLA: And what did you do?

MR. COLEMAN: I spanked her.

MS. WITTLA: Describe what that means.

MR. COLEMAN: Open hand swat on the butt.

MS. WITTLA: And what kinds of things would Caitlyn do to deserve to get this open hand swat on the butt?

MR. COLEMAN: It was very far from few, but when it was .... she took, um... Janet was taking a shower and she had taken a porcelain Duluth Business University mug that she had on the desk and had thrown it at Janet in the shower. It shattered all over the bottom of the porcelain tub and I spanked her butt for that.

MS. WITTLA: She threw a porcelain mug at her mother while she was taking a shower, and it smashed on the porcelain tub?

MR. COLEMAN: It smashed inside, it hit the curtain and then it went down inside the curtain and it smashed on the floor.

MS. WITTLA: How long ago did that happen?

MR. COLEMAN: That was probably about two years ago.

MS. WITTLA: Anything more recent that you would have spanked her for?

MR. COLEMAN: There was a time where she took her sister and threw her down and started just getting pretty rough with her. I asked her to stop and after a couple of times I gave her a swat on the butt.

MS. WITTLA: And when was that?

MR. COLEMAN: That was probably around September.

MS. WITTLA: September of 2007?

MR. COLEMAN: Yes ma'am.

MS. WITTLA: Anything more recent than that?

MR. COLEMAN: Not that I can recall.

MS. WITTLA: Have you ever struck Caitlyn with a belt?

MR. COLEMAN: No I have not.

MS. WITTLA: Have you ever grabbed your daughter Ashley by the face?

MR. COLEMAN: No I have not.

MS. WITTLA: How many belts do you own Mr. Coleman?

MR. COLEMAN: I couldn't tell you ma'am.

MS. WITTLA: More than one?

MR. COLEMAN: Yes.

MS. WITTLA: When the Child Protective Services workers were at your house, when they interviewed Caitlyn, did they locate belts in your possession?

MR. COLEMAN: They directed me to where they knew they were at.

MS. WITTLA: And where were they at?

MR. COLEMAN: They were in a drawer in my dresser.

MS. WITTLA: Okay and the drawer in your dresser was which drawer?

MR. COLEMAN: They were in the second drawer in my dresser.

MS. WITTLA: Were they the only things in that drawer?

MR. COLEMAN: I had clothes in there.

MS. WITTLA: Do you remember like sweaters, socks?

MR. COLEMAN: That was my t-shirt drawer.

MS. WITTLA: Were you surprised that belts were located in your t-shirt drawer?

MR. COLEMAN: Yes ma'am, I was.

MS. WITTLA: Why were you surprised?

MR. COLEMAN: Because I don't keep them there.

MS. WITTLA: Where did you keep them?

MR. COLEMAN: I keep them in my armoire.

MS. WITTLA: How do you think they got into your belt drawer; did you move them?

MR. COLEMAN: No, I did not.

MS. WITTLA: Did you see anybody else move them?

MR. COLEMAN: No, I did not.

MS. WITTLA: Did you tell Ms. Fyle that day that you thought they were planted there?

MR. COLEMAN: Yes I did.

MS. WITTLA: Who do you think planted them there?

MR. COLEMAN: Becky.

MS. WITTLA: Why would Becky have access to your t-shirt drawer?

MR. COLEMAN: Because they were in our apartment when they left.

MS. WITTLA: So when you would go somewhere Becky might still be in your apartment?

MR. COLEMAN: The day that they left, and they had gotten into a fight, Bobby pushed, he went to go push Becky, and he pushed me, and I hit my head on the door jam, jammed my neck, and he smashed the marriage license on the floor, and Caitlyn cut her foot. And we told them that we were going to leave, and when we come back, we need to make different arrangements for you to get out. So they were in the apartment when we left.

MS. WITTLA: Okay, and you think that one of their mean spirited acts was to move your belts on you?

MR. COLEMAN: There were a lot of belts in the drawer; they weren't even all mine and my wife's. They were there, and they were all put into this drawer.

MS. WITTLA: You told Becky and Bobby to leave on March 10th. Is that accurate?

MR. COLEMAN: That's correct.

MS. WITTLA: Are you aware of any of the statements that Caitlyn made to Ms. Fyle in that interview on the 11th?

MR. COLEMAN: In her bedroom?

MS. WITTLA: Yes.

MR. COLEMAN: Ms. Fyle told me when we were talking in the kitchen that she said that your daughter said that you hit her with a belt, and I looked at her and I said, "No ma'am, I don't believe that; my daughter wouldn't lie like that."

MS. WITTLA: So which then becomes true; that Ms. Fyle was telling you a lie?

MR. COLEMAN: Yes, I believe that.

MS. WITTLA: Okay, because Caitlyn never said that to Ms. Fyle?

MR. COLEMAN: Okay, she told me that in the kitchen.

MS. WITTLA: What I'm asking you is whether or not you believe that Caitlyn ever made that statement to Ms. Fyle?

MR. COLEMAN: I don't believe that.

At this point, the judge interrupted and called a recess for the trial for the next day. Day one was behind, but the fight was only beginning!

—Chapter Nineteen—

The Trial—Day Two

It was day two, and having undergone just a little of the off-the-wall crap of the state prosecutor in my first day, I came in prepared for more the second day, knowing now that this was a personal attack from her against me more than it was a matter of pursuing a child abuse case. With that in mind, I took my place on the stand once again, and decided to fight back with the bitch I was confronting. After having been sworn in once again, the assault began:

MS. WITTLA: Mr. Coleman, we talked a little bit yesterday about Rebecca Payne; would you say Rebecca Payne is of average intelligence?

MR. COLEMAN: Yes.

MS. WITTLA: Same as you?

MR. COLEMAN: Average intelligence? Could you rephrase the question?

MS. WITTLA: Would you say Rebecca Payne is of average intelligence, same as you, me, anybody else?

MR. FINDLAY: Your Honor, I'm going to object to this, and I don't think he's at the least qualified to assess Becky Payne's....

THE COURT: .... Well, he can give his personal view if he has one; I don't know that we're sitting here doing an IQ test, but, overruled, proceed.

MR. COLEMAN: I'd say she's smart.

MS. WITTLA: How about Bobby Payne? Is he smart too?

MR. COLEMAN: He's smart.

MS. WITTLA: Are you aware of Bobby Payne being on social security disability?

MR. COLEMAN: Yes.

MS. WITTLA: Do you know why he's on disability?

MR. COLEMAN: That wasn't brought clear to me.... why he is.

MS. WITTLA: Wasn't your wife his rep payee?

MR. COLEMAN: Yes.

MS. WITTLA: How long was she in charge of his money, if you know?

MR. COLEMAN: That I can't recall.

MS. WITTLA: How long have you known Becky and Bobby Payne?

MR. COLEMAN: Since last year.

MS. WITTLA: 2007?

MR. COLEMAN: Yes.

MS. WITTLA: Do you remember approximately what time in the year? Spring, Summer, Fall?

MR. COLEMAN: It would be Spring.

MS. WITTLA: Spring of 2007?

MR. COLEMAN: From my knowledge, yes.

MS. WITTLA: And how long after meeting them in Spring of 2007 did they start living in your apartments?

MR. COLEMAN: That's how I met them. They moved into our apartments.

MS. WITTLA: Okay, and how was their rent paid?

MR. COLEMAN: It was paid, the first time through her mom; she had paid the rent and the security deposit on it.

MS. WITTLA: Okay, and then afterwards they just paid it themselves?

MR. COLEMAN: Yes.

MS. WITTLA: Okay, it wasn't vendored through MSHDA or anything else?

MR. COLEMAN: No.

MS. WITTLA: Was the rent payment taken out of Bobby Payne's disability? Out of his disability income?

MR. COLEMAN: My wife handles the financial situation in our company.

MS. WITTLA: Okay, so that's not a question you'd be able to answer; I'd have to ask her?

MR. COLEMAN: That's correct.

MS. WITTLA: Do you know how much your apartments are rented out for?

MR. COLEMAN: Approximate.

MS. WITTLA: Okay, approximately what is it?

MR. FINDLAY: Your Honor, I'm going to object to relevance.

THE COURT: Well, I guess we don't know at this point. What is the relevance?

MS. WITTLA: Your Honor, Mr. Coleman has described Becky Payne as a woman scorned who would make up this story against him. And it's my belief that Becky Payne was a person who had no control over her own financial life because it was controlled by the Colemans.

THE COURT: Well, I guess if it's your belief isn't the point... the point will be what the evidence shows, but it's somewhat tangential. But it relates to the relevant's evidence; overruled, proceed.

MS. WITTLA: The approximate rent for your apartments?

MR. COLEMAN: The apartments vary from apartment to apartment.

MS. WITTLA: How much rent would the Paynes' apartment be worth?

MR. COLEMAN: Ma'am, I do not handle the financial situation with my company. My wife does. I'm sorry I can't answer that.

MS. WITTLA: Mr. Coleman, yesterday when I was questioning you, you mentioned something that happened in Texas. What were you referring to?

MR. COLEMAN: The FLDS; the removal of all those children.

MS. WITTLA: And why would you mention that is this proceeding?

MR. COLEMAN: Because I'm LDS.

MS. WITTLA: Because you are FLDS?

MR. COLEMAN: I am LDS. Latter Day Saints.

MS. WITTLA: And the Texas case had something to do with what's happened here?

MR. COLEMAN: I feel that they've a national sweep; taken up a lot of children because of our religion.

MS. WITTLA: Mr. Coleman, haven't you identified yourself as being Lutheran?

MR. COLEMAN: That's correct.

MS. WITTLA: So you're Lutheran and Latter Day Saints?

MR. COLEMAN: That's correct. You're not welcome in this town if you're not Lutheran, so we became Lu-

theran for a cover.

MS. WITTLA: Okay! (Her voice inflection reflecting her usual sarcastic attitude)

Even had my lawyer not objected at this point, I should like to point out that this line of questioning violated my right to worship under the freedom of religion portion of the United States Constitution. This judge should never have allowed this line of questioning. My lawyer did object, but not to what he should have objected to. As it was throughout this trial, I was denied my Constitutional rights, while the Prosecutor got only slaps on the wrist for her bad behavior:

MR. FINDLAY: Your Honor, I object to the Prosecutor's utterance; and it has to be stricken. It's not appropriate.

THE COURT: (Making light of my lawyer's words) The Prosecutor's what?

MR. FINDLAY: Utterance. I mean, saying okay with that inflection in her tone of voice; I don't think it's appropriate. And I'd ask for an instruction to not be commenting on the questions or the answers.

THE COURT: You'll get an instruction.... I'm sorry, the JURY will get an instruction that the questions again are not evidence; the only evidence is what you hear as an answer; and I would caution the Prosecutor not to comment upon the answers of the witnesses. Proceed.

MS. WITTLA: When did you determine that you were in need of cover?

MR. COLEMAN: When I moved to Ironwood.

MS. WITTLA: And how long ago did you move to Ironwood?

MR. COLEMAN: I moved to Ironwood in 1998.

MS. WITTLA: So in 1998 you decided that you needed to go underground through religion.....

MR. FINDLAY: Your Honor, I'm going to object. This is getting way off the field. This is, she's done what, 1998 when he moved to Ironwood. This is a petition of allegations that have happened in 2008. I understand what she's trying to do. It's not relevant and I'd ask that it be discontinued, and find a question.

THE COURT: Well, as they say, he opened the door and indicated a belief that this is a result of some national sweep. (Now the judge was showing his sarcastic views) I'm going to allow the question and to continue in that direction.

MS. WITTLA: Mr. Coleman, the children involved in this case weren't born until 2002 and 2006; that's accurate?

MR. COLEMAN: That's correct.

MS. WITTLA: If you have told people that you're Lutheran, why would a nationwide sweep apply to you?

MR. COLEMAN: The LDS believes in genealogy and it's very easy to locate and to find us.

MS. WITTLA: If I'm understanding your response you believe that they trace genealogy records to find you?

MR. COLEMAN: I'm not saying that ma'am.

MS. WITTLA: Okay then why would it apply to you?

MR. COLEMAN: Because I believe that sometimes people get singled out for certain beliefs.

MS. WITTLA: Okay, and if I understand what you just said, you believe you've been singled out for your beliefs and that's why we're here today?

MR. COLEMAN: No, ma'am, I didn't say that.

MS. WITTLA: A few minutes ago you testified that you thought there was a nationwide sweep regarding children of Latter Day Saints. Is that correct?

MR. COLEMAN: Yes ma'am.

MS. WITTLA: Do you believe that you were part of that nationwide sweep?

MR. COLEMAN: It's a possibility.

MS. WITTLA: Are there other possibilities as to why you're here today?

MR. COLEMAN: In my opinion, I'm here because I feel that I've been set up.

MS. WITTLA: And who set you up?

MR. COLEMAN: Bobby and Becky Payne.

MS. WITTLA: And I believe we went over some testimony yesterday where you believe that Ms. Payne would have set you up because of the affair that went badly; and Mr. Payne would have set you up because you had an affair with his wife?

MR. COLEMAN: That's correct.

MS. WITTLA: So it could be that or it could be bad luck with the nationwide sweep; is that true? Is that your belief?

MR. COLEMAN: That's my belief.

MS. WITTLA: Mr. Coleman, is it your belief that the government is trying to persecute you?

MR. COLEMAN: Yes.

MS. WITTLA: Mr. Coleman, is it your belief that Elizabeth Fyle has lied about you?

MR. COLEMAN: I would say fabricated a lot of the truth.

MS. WITTLA: Has anyone else fabricated a lot of the truth in this case?

MR. COLEMAN: Yes ma'am.

MS. WITTLA: And who would that be?

MR. COLEMAN: That would be a lot of members in the government.

MS. WITTLA: Well who are they?

MR. COLEMAN: Well, it would be Angela Andriacchi, Bob Ross, anybody that would be involved in taking my children.

MS. WITTLA: Did you say anyone that would be involved in taking your children?

MR. COLEMAN: Yes ma'am.

MS. WITTLA: Okay, and you're referring to DHS people, law enforcement people?

MR. COLEMAN: I'm referring to CPS (Child Protective Services), along with DHS, that's correct.

MS. WITTLA: And me?

MR. COLEMAN: Yes ma'am, I would think so also.

MS. WITTLA: Bonnie Huttunen works for the Department Of Human Services in Houghton County. Do you recall who she is?

MR. COLEMAN: Yes ma'am.

MS. WITTLA: Would she be part of this.... people who fabricated the truth?

MR. COLEMAN: She's part of your system, yes.

MS. WITTLA: My system?

MR. COLEMAN: Yes ma'am.

MS. WITTLA: Is there anyone else who is part of my system that fabricated the truth?

MR. COLEMAN: Would just be part of the system of what the government's doing right now to make money.

MS. WITTLA: And what is the government doing right now to make money?

MR. COLEMAN: They're taking children out of safe homes, putting them into foster care for federal funding.

MS. WITTLA: Do you believe that's what happened with your children?

MR. COLEMAN: Yes I do.

MS. WITTLA: How much money are we talking about?

MR. COLEMAN: Thousands.

MS. WITTLA: Thousands like two thousands; thousands like ten?

MR. COLEMAN: The government gets bonuses to adopt out children; they have no reason to bring the children home. Their money and the way they make things is what keeps them functioning. The State of Michigan is broke; that's how they get money. They take children from safe homes; then they turn around and adopt them out.

MS. WITTLA: So it is worse right now because the State is broke?

MR. COLEMAN: This has been going on for years.

MS. WITTLA: Do you believe that there's an uptake in this activity because the State is broke right now, or just that it's always been going on?

MR. COLEMAN: I believe that if the Federal Government right now stopped your funding, my children would be home right now.

MS. WITTLA: The only reason that they're not in the house is because my system is making money off of your children?

MR. COLEMAN: That's correct ma'am.

MS. WITTLA: Mr. Coleman, what do you consider to be the conditions of your children right now? What do you consider foster care to be?

MR. COLEMAN: I consider foster care to be making money; foster parents basically just take the children in to make money.

MS. WITTLA: Do you think that they're taking care of your children?

MR. COLEMAN: No ma'am, I don't.

MS. WITTLA: Do you think your children are being harmed by being in foster care?

MR. COLEMAN: Yes ma'am, I do.

MS. WITTLA: Have you visited your children since this case began?

MR. COLEMAN: Yes ma'am.

MS. WITTLA: How many times?

MR. COLEMAN: It's a total of; I have the statistics; I believe it was 18 times since they've been in foster care for three months.

MS. WITTLA: And in what settings have those visits taken place?

MR. COLEMAN: They've been in basically a fish bowl with me and my children interacting with somebody transcribing our every move and watching over us.

MS. WITTLA: Transcribing your every move?

MR. COLEMAN: Yes ma'am.

MS. WITTLA: In this fish bowl environment, was that at a DHS office?

MR. COLEMAN: The first time it was a DHS office.

MS. WITTLA: And after that?

MR. COLEMAN: Then the children were transferred out to Marquette.

MS. WITTLA: And your visits in Marquette were where?

MR. COLEMAN: They were at Child and Family Services.

MS. WITTLA: In their office somewhere?

MR. COLEMAN: They have like a little playroom in there that we visit with our children.

MS. WITTLA: And where do your visits take place now?

MR. COLEMAN: They're being taken out in Delta County. We drive four hours to see our children.

MS. WITTLA: And then you stay overnight and see them again the next day?

MR. COLEMAN: That's correct.

MS. WITTLA: And the visits in Delta County take place where?

MR. COLEMAN: They take place inside the DHS office; they're no longer in the care of Child and Family Services because they're under investigation.

MS. WITTLA: Do you believe that your children were removed from the care of Child and Family Services because Child and Family Services is under investigation?

MR. COLEMAN: Yes ma'am. I have a letter to prove it.

MS. WITTLA: A letter that was sent to you?

MR. COLEMAN: Yes, that's correct.

MS. WITTLA: As a result of a complaint you made against Child and Family Services?

MR. COLEMAN: Ma'am I came in to visit my child and she was covered in bruises, so I filed a police report. The foster family is under investigation right now as well.

MS. WITTLA: Do you know the result of that investigation?

MR. COLEMAN: It's at the Prosecuting Attorney's office.

MS. WITTLA: Mr. Coleman, isn't it true that the Michigan State Police told you that they didn't find anything wrong?

MR. COLEMAN: No, that's not true.

MS. WITTLA: Isn't it true, Mr. Coleman, that you originally went to the Marquette Department of Human Services to make this complaint; and then not being satisfied with their response, then you went to the Negaunee Post of Michigan State Police to make these complaints that turned out to be false both times?

MR. COLEMAN: Ma'am these cases are right now under investigation; DHS failed to investigate their own; so I called the State Police and asked them to do whatever they could to protect my children in foster care.

MS. WITTLA: Mr. Coleman, isn't it true that you have subsequently made an allegation of abuse against the current caregivers of your children in Delta County that has also been shown to be false?

MR. COLEMAN: Ma'am there was no doctor to stipulate that. I come in and my kid was covered in bruises. They said she fell face forward down a flight of stairs; they're not watching her; they're not tending after her. My daughter also said that she is having sex, and that there was an older girl beating her up in the foster home.

MS. WITTLA: And where was this supposedly taking place?

MR. COLEMAN: In the foster home.

MS. WITTLA: Well which county are we in now?

MR. COLEMAN: The one you just stated, Delta County.

MS. WITTLA: So when you say your daughter is telling you this; you're referring to who?

MR. COLEMAN: I'm referring to an investigation that I had requested from the Sheriff's Department to have them look into the fact that Caitlyn claims that she is being pinned down and beat up in the foster home by a teenager.

MS. WITTLA: Again, Mr. Coleman, aren't you— haven't you been made aware by the Delta County DHS that they investigated your claim, and found it to be unsubstantiated?

MR. COLEMAN: No ma'am.

I would just insert here for a moment, that not only was I not made aware of this claim by the Delta County DHS, but that in their so-called investigation, they never even talked to my step daughter, who will verify that today! If she had been able to testify, all of this would have become crystal clear to even a trumped up jury!

MS. WITTLA: So to your belief as we're sitting here today that Delta County DHS and the Delta County Sheriff's Department is actively investigating a claim of abuse against Caitlyn?

MR. COLEMAN: We haven't pursued that any further at this time.

MS. WITTLA: You didn't report it to the Delta County Sheriff's Department?

MR. COLEMAN: Yes ma'am, I did.

MS. WITTLA: Then what happened?

MR. COLEMAN: The caseworker told us the next day that Ashley had fell down a flight of stairs and she bruised up her face, and she didn't get into the fact about the teenager, and she said that (she had) what looked like cigarette burns on her left wrist, which were bug bites. I asked them to take her to a doctor to verify that, but they refused, but it was infected, and they weren't taking proper care of her wrist.

At age ten, Caitlyn today, tells us about this Delta County incident, of which the state was very secretive. They would not even reveal to us the names of the foster parents there. But Caitlyn not only confirms the bullying of the teenager, but in fact, described the burn truth. The bites were in fact, a tick, and Caitlyn now reveals the foster parent tried to burn it out with a cigarette lighter, but that it failed. This was a very serious matter, as ticks are dangerous. Yet this state tried its best to conceal this from us, obviously for fear of retaliation via a lawsuit. We will follow up on that once this book is released.

MS. WITTLA: Mr. Coleman, aren't these the same kind of allegations that you made when your kids were in Marquette County? That they were covered in bruises and you wanted them to be taken to a doctor?

MR. COLEMAN: That's correct. In Marquette they were— Caitlyn had bruise marks on her arms that were grab marks.

MS. WITTLA: Mr. Coleman, you've been provided with the reports from the doctors. They do not indicate any kind of abuse. How do you explain that?

MR. COLEMAN: My further investigation found that the doctor's office, Child and Family Services owns a medical facility that's a subsidiary insurance company. These people make money on taking my children to the hospital. These doctors work for them. I feel they're not going to claim in the best interest for anybody but for them.

MS. WITTLA: So after you made the claim that Caitlyn was covered in bruises in Marquette, and she was taken to a doctor at your request; that doctor was tainted because they worked for Child and Family Services?

MR. COLEMAN: That's correct.

MS. WITTLA: So that doctor wouldn't have found abuse ever because they know who pays them, so to speak?

MR. COLEMAN: They photographed the pictures and they looked at the bruises that were on her arms. Those were grab marks. I've had other doctors look at those photographs. Those are grab marks.

Did anybody notice she got away from the subject here once it was pointed out that other doctors viewed the photos differently than did her selected state doctors? But I leave it to you as the reader. Go to my website and view the photos for yourself. You tell me whether you think they look like normal child's play or grab marks!

MS. WITTLA: Mr. Coleman, would you describe yourself as technically savvy?

MR. COLEMAN: I would describe myself as a very caring parent and very worried about my children.

MS. WITTLA: Okay, that's not answering my question though. I'm talking about whether or not you're familiar with technology. Computers?

MR. COLEMAN: Yes I am.

MS. WITTLA: Websites?

MR. COLEMAN: Somewhat.

MS. WITTLA: Digital photography?

MR. COLEMAN: No, I'm not very good into the electronic part of it.

MS. WITTLA: How many visits did you refuse to attend with your children?

MR. COLEMAN: None.

MS. WITTLA: Mr. Coleman, isn't it true that you were offered a visit with your children in Marquette and chose to leave?

MR. COLEMAN: They told us to leave.

MS. WITTLA: Why did they tell you to leave?

MR. COLEMAN: Because I had a recorder.

MS. WITTLA: And they told you to leave because you had a recorder?

MR. COLEMAN: That's correct.

MS. WITTLA: Didn't they give you the option of shutting off your recorder and having your visit with your children?

MR. COLEMAN: We told them that it wasn't in the court order to shut off our recorder. We had the right to record. She told us if we don't shut the recorder off our visit is over.

MS. WITTLA: And subsequent to that your choice was to leave?

MR. COLEMAN: Subsequent to that is what they are hiding. Why would it matter if I record? And I told her I'd like to see my children. And she said if you don't shut the recorder off, you'll have to leave.

MS. WITTLA: And you chose not to shut the recorder and forego your visit?

MR. COLEMAN: It's not— it's set up in the visitation; that's correct.

MS. WITTLA: Mr. Coleman, is there anybody involved with the governmental process regarding this case that you feel is being honest?

MR. COLEMAN: I haven't found one yet.

MS. WITTLA: Do you think there are any problems within your family that need to be addressed?

MR. COLEMAN: Yes, there is.

MS. WITTLA: Do you think those problems involve the parental discipline as you call it, of your children?

MR. COLEMAN: No I don't.

MS. WITTLA: You mentioned having to travel four hours to see the children in Delta County. Have you been reimbursed for them?

MR. COLEMAN: No I haven't.

MS. WITTLA: Why haven't you?

MR. COLEMAN: Because they're refusing to reimburse me.

MS. WITTLA: Mr. Coleman, isn't it true the DHS cannot reimburse you until you actually submit receipts for your expenses?

MR. COLEMAN: The mileage report has nothing to do with the receipts for our expenses; we've not received any mileage since this whole incident has happened. We feel this is a ploy to break us down so that I can't afford to see my children; otherwise, why would they move our children so far away? The judge had upped our visits to two times a week. Next thing you know my children are being moved to another location four hours away instead of two. So why haven't we received any money? When I was out in the hallway with the attorney during a court session, Bob Ross started talking money. He said we need you to fill out paperwork for Federal taxpayers' dollars to reimburse us. And I said, "Mr. Ross, you plan on keeping my children that long?" And I quote, he says, "I've had enough of your bullshit, just do as you're told." And I said to him, "Sir, I just want to know exactly what's going on with my children." And we were then proceeded to not talk to Mr. Ross after that. But we have not been informed of any type of funding at all to be reimbursed. I've asked Mr. Ross several times and when I've tried to speak with him on the phone, he gets very violent with me and he has told me to just talk to my attorney from now on, and he'll deal with it through there.

MS. WITTLA: Do you have any idea why Mr. Ross doesn't want to talk to you on the phone?

MR. COLEMAN: Well ma'am, that's his job to talk to me on the phone.

MS. WITTLA: I comprehend Mr. Ross's job. I'm asking if you know why he doesn't want to talk to you on the phone?

MR. COLEMAN: No ma'am, I don't.

MS. WITTLA: You mentioned recording visits. Have you recorded anything else?

MR. COLEMAN: I've recorded every time I've come in contact with the State.

MS. WITTLA: Is it possible that Mr. Ross does not want to be recorded on the telephone, and that's why he does not want to speak with you on the telephone?

MR. COLEMAN: Is it possible Mr. Ross does not want to be caught in the many lies like I have caught him in; like he said that my children would be placed with family immediately, and they're still in the care of foster care?

MS. WITTLA: I guess it would make this a lot quicker if you actually answered my question. So do you think that Mr. Ross doesn't want to talk to you because he doesn't want to be recorded?

MR. COLEMAN: It's never occurred to me ma'am. If I have nothing to hide, why would I care if I was recorded?

MS. WITTLA: What have you done with the recordings?

MR. COLEMAN: Given them to you.

MS. WITTLA: Anyone else?

MR. COLEMAN: I'm sorry. As far as what?

MS. WITTLA: Have you done anything else with the recordings? Are they just for your personal use or have you done something else with them?

MR. COLEMAN: I've given them to my attorney.

MS. WITTLA: And that's it?

MR. COLEMAN: We've used other recordings for certain devices.

MS. WITTLA: And what have you used the other recordings for, for certain devices?

MR. COLEMAN: To prove to people that the State lies.

MS. WITTLA: How did you do that?

MR. COLEMAN: I've used them in group meetings and talking with people.

MS. WITTLA: So you've used the recordings that you've made during the pendency of this case when you've had meetings with other people?

MR. COLEMAN: That's correct.

MS. WITTLA: Have you used them for anything else?

MR. COLEMAN: I've used them to talk to other people. We've counseled other people that are going through this, like us, today.

MS. WITTLA: And what medium did you use?

MR. COLEMAN: Well, I spoke with the news.

MS. WITTLA: Well did you just send in a copy of them— a disk for their computers? Where they see these recordings? How did you get this information to these other people?

MR. COLEMAN: Through email and through correspondence through, we belong to a group that (says) children need both parents. And we've spoken with them and we've posted that on our site there.

MS. WITTLA: Your website?

MR. COLEMAN: It's a blog.

MS. WITTLA: But it's on the Worldwide Web through the internet?

MR. COLEMAN: That's correct.

MS. WITTLA: So to sum up, you've recorded things from this case and posted them on the internet, accurate?

MR. COLEMAN: No, that's not accurate. It was just basically recordings of conversations with Bob Ross and me. Other recordings that would prove that we've been brought into things being twisted.

MS. WITTLA: Okay, but those things were posted on the internet?

MR. COLEMAN: That's correct.

MS. WITTLA: And you indicated that they were posted on the blog "Children Need Both Parents?"

MR. COLEMAN: That's correct.

MS. WITTLA: Did you post it anywhere else?

MR. COLEMAN: They were posted on Youtube.

MS. WITTLA: Youtube?

MR. COLEMAN: Yes.

MS. WITTLA: Do you think Mr. Ross was aware of the fact that his conversations with you were posted on Youtube?

MR. COLEMAN: I didn't need her permission ma'am.

MS. WITTLA: I didn't ask that question. I asked if you knew whether or not Bob was aware that his conversation with you was on Youtube?

MR. COLEMAN: Yes, he was aware.

MS. WITTLA: Do you think that might be why he doesn't want to talk to you on the phone?

MR. COLEMAN: No I don't.

MS. WITTLA: What do you think is the reason that Mr. Ross does not want to talk to you on the phone?

MR. COLEMAN: Because I feel he has a temper, and I feel that he does not want to talk to me and try to communicate with me to try to bring my children home. He's claiming that children need to be home with their parents; they need to be with their family; yet he continually cancels visits, moves our kids far away from us, and fails to reimburse us for mileage that costs us a lot of money.

MS. WITTLA: And going back to the mileage issue. You're telling me today that you've submitted the documents you need to the DHS to get reimbursed for that?

MR. COLEMAN: We have submitted everything that we needed to. He told us to go on a website and join that; we did that. They have tracks, he said he goes under some kind of Yahoo, Google, or something for mileage, and then he figures out that and then we get reimbursed according to that.

MS. WITTLA: Thank you, I have nothing further.

THE COURT: Mr. Perhalla, do you care to question at this point?

MR. PERHALLA: You've heard; you've read the petition, correct?

MR. COLEMAN: Yes, I have.

MR. PERHALLA: And you're aware in the petition that there are several allegations that Caitlyn said whatever, correct?

MR. COLEMAN: Could you define whatever please?

MR. PERHALLA: Let's go through them. Are you aware that the petition states that Caitlyn stated that when she gets in trouble, she has to go in the corner. You've heard that before?

MR. COLEMAN: On the petition?

MR. PERHALLA: Yes.

MR. COLEMAN: Yes I have.

MR. PERHALLA: Do you agree with that or is she lying or is someone lying there?

MR. COLEMAN: Well, I believe that she's... ...

MR. PERHALLA: .... Okay, so that allegation is....

MR. FINDLAY: ... Your Honor, can he finish the question? He was in the middle of his answer and he didn't.... he cut him off.

THE COURT: Okay, he was cut off. If you will please let him finish the question. Mr. Coleman, you may finish your answer.

MR. COLEMAN: I believe that, as a form of discipline, we would ask Caitlyn to go into the corner for less than whatever her age would be, and she's six now, but usually when she calms down within three minutes, she's allowed to go out after we had spoken to her as to why she's gone to the corner.

MR. PERHALLA: So that allegation is true?

MR. COLEMAN: I would suppose, yes.

MR. PERHALLA: The next one states that Caitlyn says she also gets the belt?

MR. COLEMAN: That is untrue.

MR. PERHALLA: And why, again, is that untrue?

MR. COLEMAN: Because I've never hit my daughter with a belt or any other object.

MR. PERHALLA: And then why would Ms. Fyle put that allegation in the report after interviewing your child?

MR. COLEMAN: That, I don't know sir.

MR. PERHALLA: Okay, yesterday you said because Liz would lie, correct?

MR. COLEMAN: That's correct.

MR. PERHALLA: Okay, do you have any basis of how much you believe she would lie?

MR. COLEMAN: I believe that she would sir. I don't know, I wasn't in the room with Caitlyn and Elizabeth Fyle so I don't know what was said. But I believe that my daughter would not say that.

MR. PERHALLA: You believe your daughter would not say that. And is that your only basis for that being a lie?

MR. COLEMAN: During visits Caitlyn would say to us that they're making me say that you spank me, daddy.

MR. PERHALLA: And then you recorded these conversations during these with your daughter?

MR. COLEMAN: Yes I have.

MR. PERHALLA: Anything else?

MR. COLEMAN: No sir.

MR. PERHALLA: Just so I'm clear on this. You believe it's a lie because your daughter wouldn't say that, and she has said things to you during the recent visits, correct?

MR. COLEMAN: That's correct.

MR. PERHALLA: And nothing else?

MR. COLEMAN: Three months after she's been in your care, my daughter sat on my lap and said she wanted to have sex with me.

MR. PERHALLA: My care?

MR. COLEMAN: State's care.

MR. PERHALLA: And I'm part of the State too?

MR. COLEMAN: You're there to protect my children.

MR. PERHALLA: Correct, but I'm part of the State?

MR. COLEMAN: You're there to protect my children.

MR. PERHALLA: Okay, and in your opinion we're not really protecting your children in foster care. Correct?

MR. COLEMAN: That's correct. I feel especially you.

MR. PERHALLA: Especially me?

MR. COLEMAN: Yes sir.

MR. PERHALLA: So the allegations in the petition that earlier this year your daughter wouldn't eat what she was supposed to be eating and you gave her the belt; that's a lie?

MR. COLEMAN: That's correct.

MR. PERHALLA: Even though that's the same allegation comes out from Becky Payne?

MR. COLEMAN: My understanding that was three months later.

MR. PERHALLA: Even though that same allegation comes from Becky Payne, correct? Becky Payne makes the same statement.

MR. COLEMAN: May I see a copy of that petition please, so I may follow along?

THE COURT: Mr. Findlay, you have…..

MR. FINDLAY: I've got my copy here.

MR. COLEMAN: Thank you your Honor. Sir, can you please tell me what line you're on?

MR. PERHALLA: Okay, line 6. But I might have said, "Becky, Bobby stated around January 26th while eating dinner, Caitlyn did not want to eat rice as she doesn't like rice."

MR. COLEMAN: That's not true.

MR. PERHALLA: Okay, but you understand what paragraph I'm referring to, correct?

MR. COLEMAN: Yes.

MR. PERHALLA: The next paragraph after that, item 7, Bobby stated that Rob told Caitlyn he was going to give her the belt? And you're stating that's untrue?

MR. COLEMAN: That's correct. This was Caitlyn's birthday sir; Caitlyn's birthday is January 26, 2008, at this particular day.

MR. PERHALLA: Then paragraph 52, second page. Caitlyn also confirmed the story as getting smacked for not eating her rice; do you see that?

MR. COLEMAN: Yes sir, I do.

MR. PERHALLA: Do you understand what is said in those three paragraphs that we just talked about? You may disagree with it, but do you understand what is being said?

MR. COLEMAN: I disagree with what's being said.

MR. PERHALLA: Okay, do you understand the words though. You can read words and you know what's being said, correct?

MR. COLEMAN: Yes, I understand.

MR. PERHALLA: So we have the Paynes, Bobby Payne on one hand saying you struck, he recalls you striking your child for not eating food, for eating rice, correct?

MR. COLEMAN: That's what Bobby states.

MR. PERHALLA: You understand that as to what he states, correct?

MR. COLEMAN: Yes sir, I understand.

MR. PERHALLA: And then the other paragraph your daughter Caitlyn is make the same statement that she's getting smacked for not eating her food, you understand that, correct?

MR. COLEMAN: May I answer to that question?

MR. PERHALLA: Sure.

MR. COLEMAN: It doesn't state in here what day, and it doesn't state in here anything was hit with the belt, and I understand the question though.

MR. PERHALLA: Well what do you, what do you interpret getting smacked for?

MR. COLEMAN: What would I interpret?

MR. PERHALLA: Yeah.

MR. COLEMAN: The smack?

MR. PERHALLA: Yeah.

MR. COLEMAN: I would interpret that she said that I swatted her one.

MR. PERHALLA: You struck her? You touched her?

MR. COLEMAN: If that happened that particular day.

MR. PERHALLA: So my question is, you have your child saying that she got hit for a certain event, which corroborates or is the same as what the Paynes are saying, correct?

MR. COLEMAN: Sir, I don't know that my child said that. This is basically going off of what Bobby and Becky had stated.

MR. PERHALLA: Is it your understanding that paragraphy 52 is what DHS is reporting to us after an interview with your daughter?

MR. COLEMAN: Where did this interview take place?

MR. PERHALLA: Isn't it, when did you first get the petition you're looking at?

MR. COLEMAN: The day we had an emergency hearing.

MR. PERHALLA: Okay, so what—March 9th? No, early March of this year, correct?

MR. COLEMAN: Says here— it doesn't state the day that we received this.

MR. PERHALLA: Okay, well you said it was during the emergency hearing, correct?

MR. COLEMAN: Yes sir.

MR. PERHALLA: You have already that your children were removed in Houghton County?

MR. COLEMAN: That's correct.

MR. PERHALLA: And it was days, weeks, months after the removal? When was this hearing approximately?

MR. COLEMAN: It was, I believe this was Monday.

MR. PERHALLA: Okay, so that Monday in early or mid-March of this year, you received the petition, correct?

MR. COLEMAN: That's correct.

MR. PERHALLA: And the petition is how many pages?

MR. COLEMAN: It's three pages of the petition and one just docket heading letter.

MR. PERHALLA: Did you review the petition back then?

MR. COLEMAN: Have I reviewed the petition?

MR. PERHALLA: Yes.

MR. COLEMAN: Yes I have.

MR. PERHALLA: It seems to be your testimony now, you're not sure where or what is said in the petition; is that a fair summary of how you testified?

MR. FINDLAY: Your Honor, that's mischaracterizing his testimony completely. He basically said he doesn't agree with what's in the petition but when asked a question about whether he understands it, he said that yes, he understands that's what was said there.

THE COURT: I mean I'll sustain that. I didn't get out of it that what you said. I didn't get exactly the way you phrased it so, I'm going to indicate the objection is sustained. If you want to rephrase, or keep going.

MR. PERHALLA: Do you understand paragraph 52, which simply reads Caitlyn also confirmed the story of getting smacked for not eating her rice?

MR. COLEMAN: I understand that.

MR. PERHALLA: Do you understand that to mean something your daughter said?

MR. COLEMAN: I understand that that would be something that she—that you are claiming she had said.

MR. PERHALLA: But it's your position now that she's lying there too, or that that's not a true statement because your daughter wouldn't say it?

MR. COLEMAN: Sir, if I walked up to my daughter and asked if she went to the moon, she'd probably agree.

MR. PERHALLA: So you're saying your daughter would lie?

MR. COLEMAN: I'm saying she was probably coached.

MR. PERHALLA: Coached. And the reason for this coaching is this federal funding; the State is broke and they need the federal funding, correct?

MR. COLEMAN: Yes sir.

MR. PERHALLA: Okay, where did you come up with that?

MR. COLEMAN: I've done a lot of investigating on it.

MR. PERHALLA: Well where did you come up with it?

MR. COLEMAN: Well, for example, Mike's Lemonade. A guy accidentally gave his kid a Mike's Lemonade. They took his child. Fifty children were taken all at once in Detroit; taking children left and right. Beds are being over full in foster care homes. The government gets money to take children. They get this money if they're only kept in foster care, and they get bonuses when they are adopted out. I would say that that's making money.

MR. PERHALLA: So that's how DHS funds itself?

MR. COLEMAN: That's correct. That's partially.

MR. PERHALLA: And you came up with that so that's what you believed happened here to you, correct?

MR. COLEMAN: Yes sir, I believe that.

MR. PERHALLA: You don't have any other facts than that's your opinion?

MR. COLEMAN: I have statistics.

MR. PERHALLA: So any time in the petition that your daughter states that you hit her or your wife hit her or struck her with a belt of some other object, again, it's a lie, correct?

MR. COLEMAN: Again, I feel she was coached.

MR. PERHALLA: Okay, in other words it's a lie; someone's lying?

MR. FINDLAY: Your Honor, he answered the question. Maybe Mr. Perhalla doesn't like the answser, but that's his answer.

THE COURT: Proceed.

MR. PERHALLA: What do you mean coached?

MR. COLEMAN: I mean by misleading. Caitlyn is six years old, she's very well misled.

MR. PERHALLA: Do you have any evidence that she was misled?

MR. COLEMAN: I don't have to have any evidence that she would be misled.

MR. PERHALLA: Let's talk about the Paynes for a while. It's your testimony you don't know how they paid their rent, correct?

MR. COLEMAN: My wife handled all the financial.

MR. PERHALLA: You also testified that they moved into your apartments in approximately last Spring of '07?

MR. COLEMAN: Into one of my apartment buildings, that's correct.

MR. PERHALLA: Into which one?

MR. COLEMAN: Into 207 East Vaughn Street; they lived in Apartment 1B.

MR. PERHALLA: That's not the basement where you moved them to later, correct?

MR. COLEMAN: I didn't move them to the basement sir.

MR. PERHALLA: That's not the apartment where; that's not the basement, correct?

MR. COLEMAN: That's correct.

MR. PERHALLA: You did not ask them to move to the basement?

MR. COLEMAN: No sir, I did not.

MR. PERHALLA: And the basement is, a basement, correct?

MR. COLEMAN: It's a new addition on our home. We just put a new addition up.

MR. PERHALLA: So it's refinished down there?

MR. COLEMAN: We were working on it.

MR. PERHALLA: When Becky and Bobby Payne moved in there, was it refinished?

MR. COLEMAN: Partially.

MR. PERHALLA: So it had running water?

MR. COLEMAN: As far as, I'm sorry, could you please rephrase that?

MR. PERHALLA: Did it have running water in the basement; obviously a sink, showers, bath tub?

MR. COLEMAN: They used our bathroom.

MR. PERHALLA: Upstairs?

MR. COLEMAN: In our apartment.

MR. PERHALLA: Which is upstairs, I assume, of the basement?

MR. COLEMAN: Yes sir.

MR. PERHALLA: So they did not have running water down there?

MR. COLEMAN: It was a room.

MR. PERHALLA: Pardon?

MR. COLEMAN: It's a room that they were in.

MR. PERHALLA: They were in one room. So they went from a fairly nice apartment to a basement?

MR. COLEMAN: They wanted to move back to California; so that's why they had wanted to get out of their lease; so we allowed them to—we were going to give them the money back.

MR. PERHALLA: To move back to California?

MR. COLEMAN: That's correct.

MR. PERHALLA: So you did give them money?

MR. COLEMAN: I'm sorry, give what money?

MR. PERHALLA: You did give them money to move back to California?

MR. COLEMAN: No, they did not leave for California.

MR. PERHALLA: Okay, they just left?

MR. COLEMAN: Sir, could you please rephrase? We're jumping around from day to day, I don't know where we are going.

MR. PERHALLA: Okay, well you had the Paynes, you got to know the Paynes in a landlord-tenant relationship, right?

MR. COLEMAN: That's correct.

MR. PERHALLA: So they move into a separate apartment. Not your apartment, but a separate apartment, right?

MR. COLEMAN: That's correct.

MR. PERHALLA: So somehow I take it that you and your wife and the Paynes somehow got to know each other, better than a landlord-tenant relationship, correct?

MR. COLEMAN: They always hung around us.

MR. PERHALLA: Hung around enough so that you or your wife took control of Mr. Payne's income; his money?

MR. COLEMAN: I did not take control of anything of theirs.

MR. PERHALLA: Your wife did, correct?

MR. COLEMAN: My wife didn't take control of their lives.

MR. PERHALLA: She was the representative payee of his Social Security, correct?

MR. COLEMAN: Yes sir, she was. She was probably the fifth payee that he's had.

MR. PERHALLA: Did they have any other source of income other than his SSI?

MR. COLEMAN: Becky worked at some kind of medical facility. Plus we have provided them with whatever they needed; we were giving them money for shoes or clothes or whatever they needed.

MR. PERHALLA: Did they ever work for you?

MR. COLEMAN: They were helping me.

MR. PERHALLA: What do you mean by helping?

MR. COLEMAN: It was part of the contingency in their lease that they would help me for a certain percentage of their rent.

MR. PERHALLA: And help? Helping you do maintenance of your chores around your apartment buildings or in your own home? What do you mean, what kind of help?

MR. COLEMAN: I had a handyman service.

MR. PERHALLA: And it is your testimony that their rent was not vendored through MSHDA, correct?

MR. COLEMAN: To the best of my knowledge, no, it was not.

MR. PERHALLA: Okay, let's talk about Caitlyn for a while. How long has Caitlyn lived with you?

MR. COLEMAN: Since she was three.

MR. PERHALLA: And you are her step father, correct?

MR. COLEMAN: Yes sir, I am. I'd like to consider myself as her only father.

MR. PERHALLA: Okay, and then I take it Ashley was born while Caitlyn, Janet, and yourself were living together, correct?

MR. COLEMAN: That's correct.

MR. PERHALLA: Did Caitlyn ever go to any type of daycare?

MR. COLEMAN: No sir, she did not.

MR. PERHALLA: She stayed in the home?

MR. COLEMAN: She went to preschool.

MR. PERHALLA: Where did she go to preschool?

MR. COLEMAN: Up at, ah... I'm sorry I don't recall the school. It was Sleight School, up on Lowell Street.

MR. PERHALLA: Near Sleight School.

MR. COLEMAN: It was in Sleight School.

MR. PERHALLA: Sleight School?

MR. COLEMAN: Yes sir.

MR. PERHALLA: And that's where she was this past school year or was it before then?

MR. COLEMAN: She was in kindergarten this year.

MR. PERHALLA: Now in your disciplining of her, did you ever yell at her?

MR. COLEMAN: Yes sir I have.

MR. PERHALLA: Did you actually raise your voice?

MR. COLEMAN: On occasion.

MR. PERHALLA: Would you lose your temper with her?

MR. COLEMAN: Yes sir, on occasion.

MR. PERHALLA: And even though you would lose your temper, it didn't reach the point where you'd hit her, correct?

MR. COLEMAN: That's correct. I'd just go outside, take a walk, and Janet would take over.

MR. PERHALLA: And you never hit your other child, Ashley?

MR. COLEMAN: No sir, I have never hit her.

MR. PERHALLA: Your visits now with them, since they've been moved to Escanaba, you've maintained those visits with your daughters?

MR. COLEMAN: Every visit they allow us to, we see our children.

MR. PERHALLA: Okay, so the twice a week, you've been doing since they moved to Escanaba, correct?

MR. COLEMAN: That's correct.

MR. PERHALLA: Now you testified you moved to Calumet recently, correct?

MR. COLEMAN: That's correct sir.

MR. PERHALLA: Who is operating the rental units in Ironwood?

MR. COLEMAN: We have somebody that operates them for us.

MR. PERHALLA: So you are paying rent somewhere else in Calumet?

MR. COLEMAN: That's correct.

MR. PERHALLA: I guess the question I have is why would you leave your business here in Ironwood, and move somewhere else?

MR. COLEMAN: For relocation for more jobs, for more better future, there's more of a career out there.

MR. PERHALLA: So you have a new job up there?

MR. COLEMAN: Not at this time.

MR. PERHALLA: Now you had ten apartments and two houses, did I quote that correctly, here in Ironwood that you rented?

MR. COLEMAN: From my knowledge sir, yes.

MR. PERHALLA: Were they not producing income for you?

MR. COLEMAN: They were producing income; we lost quite a few tenants in the past couple of months.

MR. PERHALLA: More than normal or no, tenants come and go all the time?

MR. COLEMAN: Would you like to know why we lost our apartments' tenants?

MR. PERHALLA: You're losing more now than you did before?

MR. COLEMAN: We did.

MR. PERHALLA: So you're telling me that you did not lose tenants before but now you are or the number is less?

MR. COLEMAN: It was stable. Tenants would move out, we would refill the leases immediately.

MR. PERHALLA: I assume your reason is because of this protective service case, people don't want to rent from you?

MR. COLEMAN: Because Becky was talking to all my tenants; telling them to move out.

MR. PERHALLA: So you decided to give up your source of income here in Gogebic County?

MR. COLEMAN: I did not give up on it sir.

MR. PERHALLA: You also said that Becky and Bobby are violent people?

MR. COLEMAN: That's correct.

MR. PERHALLA: What was so violent about Becky?

MR. COLEMAN: Becky would always get into fights with Bobby and she'd throw things.

MR. PERHALLA: When did you realize you thought she was violent?

MR. COLEMAN: Pretty much upstairs when they had moved into our building, because they moved from 207 into our apartment building up in 205, upstairs.

MR. PERHALLA: When was that they moved into 205?

MR. COLEMAN: That I can't recall sir, I don't have the records.

MR. PERHALLA: Did you have Becky or Bobby then take care of your kids ever, baby sit, watch your kids?

MR. COLEMAN: At first we did.

MR. PERHALLA: And at some point then you decided you didn't want them any more?

MR. COLEMAN: With Becky, we had asked her to watch Caitlyn, and all that she had to do was call or when she arrived off the school bus and she failed to do so. And we were enormously worried about her. I was out of town and I had to call one of my friends to go locate her and pick her up and bring Caitlyn to her house to watch her.

MR. PERHALLA: So Becky couldn't do a job; couldn't do the job watching; so that's why you cut off having her watch your daughter?

MR. COLEMAN: Becky would treat my daughter like she was hers, and she felt that she could do whatever she wanted. So we didn't feel it was in her best interest for our child, and for her safety, to be in Becky's care alone.

MR. PERHALLA: When is this that you made this decision?

MR. COLEMAN: It was when we had an appointment up in Houghton for a doctor's appointment.

MR. PERHALLA: Okay, in the winter, and do you know, what about the month?

MR. COLEMAN: I would say it was probably about January.

MR. PERHALLA: And it's after that date, it's after January of '08 that they moved into the basement?

MR. COLEMAN: Sir, Becky moved herself into the basement. I had an affair with her in January, and after that she pretty much just moved all of her belongings into our apartment.

MR. PERHALLA: And you did not stop her?

MR. COLEMAN: I wasn't there.

MR. PERHALLA: Okay, eventually you found out she was there though, correct?

MR. COLEMAN: When I came home, that's correct.

MR. PERHALLA: But you didn't kick her out of the basement?

MR. COLEMAN: She said to me that she wanted to stay down there, she felt safer down there. And as far as Bobby, if I could answer that question sir? One time we came home, Janet and me, and Bobby was watching Ashley and we had come into the house and there was no heat on in the house. Bobby was in flannels and a snowsuit and boots and a coat and a hoodie, and he comes walking out to greet us, and I could see my breath in the room. And here comes Ashley with just a t-shirt and a diaper on, and I asked him why is there no heat on in the house? Well, we do have a fireplace, but we also have radiator boards that he could have turned on, but he was too interested in playing video games. I said Bobby, I didn't appreciate this with you, and he had stepped back. Bobby has a size nine shoe and he wears size thirteen boots, so when he stepped back he fell backwards over his feet, and then I got accused of pushing him.

MR. PERHALLA: So he's not too reliable either for a baby sitter?

MR. COLEMAN: That was the last time he watched our daughter. For her safey we put an end to that.

MR. PERHALLA: Now you testified earlier that, yesterday I believe, that when you were up in Hancock when the police— before the police came into that hotel, that somehow your wife's parents paid for the room?

MR. COLEMAN: Janet's mom and dad. They paid for the room.

MR. PERHALLA: Okay, they were there with you?

MR. COLEMAN: No sir they were not.

MR. PERHALLA: Okay, how did they pay for the room?

MR. COLEMAN: They put it on their credit card.

MR. PERHALLA: So you have their credit card?

MR. COLEMAN: No sir, we do not.

MR. PERHALLA: At that time, I'm sorry.

MR. COLEMAN: They had called their credit card numbers in.

MR. PERHALLA: They called the motel and arranged it for you?

MR. COLEMAN: Janet had asked her mom and dad; she told her that we were staying out of town and her mom said, well, we'll pay for that for the children for the spring break.

MR. PERHALLA: So the room was not.... was it in their name or your name? Or you're not sure?

MR. COLEMAN: It was in our name, and they paid for the room.

MR. PERHALLA: That's all I have your Honor.

THE COURT: Okay, were you going to question at this time or are you going to reserve that right to later Mr. Findlay?

MR. FINDLAY: I'll reserve that right till later.

THE COURT: Are you going to ask any more questions, Ms. Wittla?

MS. WITTLA: Just a few.

At that point the judge took the mid-morning recess, and it was during this time that the shifty little prosecutor prepared to attack again, using my blogs to assassinate my character as court resumed:

THE COURT: Okay, we're back on the record. We had taken a mid-morning break. Shortly before coming back counsel alerted me that Ms. Wittla, actually, has some exhibits. Some printings off of, I guess, what I generically refer to as the blogs that have been referred to of Mr. Coleman's statements. In chambers, counsel had already been supplied copies before I believe; but we reviewed them and I omitted without any further ruling emails to Mr. Coleman that prompted a response in those blogs; one from Heather Hicks and one from a Josh, unidentified. Those people are not identified as witnesses in this case. Their statements are hearsay and peripheral and irrelevant; so I'd indicate on the record that we would not include the messages from those two to Mr. Coleman. The issue remains then, are you objecting to the balance of them?

MR. FINDLAY: Yes.

THE COURT: Okay.

MR. FINDLAY: Thank you your Honor. My objection is two-prong. One is first the relevance of it. We had touched on that a little bit previously, but I'm just going to read the Michigan Rule Of Evidence 401. "Relevance— evidence having any tendency to make the existence of any fact that is of consequence to the termination of the action more probable or less probable than it would be without the evidence." I would submit that Mr. Coleman's political views and views towards the government, even his attitude towards DHS after the incidence or the allegations were made in the petition; after the petition was filed; are not relevant to whether the allegations in the petition are true or not. And it does not indicate one way or the other whether they are more or less probable. Basically his obvious displeasure with DHS and distrust of them is not relevant to whether the things in the petition actually happened. So on that ground , I'd ask that it be excluded as being relevant. I also believe it's an end around way of getting into admitting character evidence which is not admissible pursuant to Michigan Rule Of Evidence 404. It's pretty clear to me that what the government is trying to do is basically engage in character assassination of Mr. Coleman and paint him out as a whacko, an antigovernment nut job frankly, is what they are trying to make him out to be, and their hope is that the jury is going to think that of him, and because they think that of him, then make the next step into saying, "Well, if he's that nuts about the government, then he probably, you know, he's more likely to have engaged in abuse of his children." So on those two prongs, I would object to the admitting of these documents and this evidence. Thank you.

MS. WITTLA: Your Honor, it's already put into evidence that Mr. Coleman has a belief that this entire case is based on a government conspiracy to take children that belong to Latter Day Saints people; to make money off of these children. These documents indicate further proof of his belief that that is so. He's already essentially opened the door on these types of issues by his responses to questioning today and yesterday. The other document, that ROBERT AND JANET COLEMAN STORY, appears to be a synopsis of what happened when the children were removed from the Colemans' care up in Hancock on March 15th. His version of events has come through to some extent during questioning, but I believe that he is the author of this document, and it would make it clearer for all involved to know what his version of events is.

THE COURT: Okay, and is it exactly the same as been testified or has there been some differences?

MS. WITTLA: I don't know that there are differences; I know there are additional things in here that I don't believe he's already testified to. I mean, my intention in using these documents would be to show them to Mr. Cole-

man and ask if he was the author of these documents, and to identify them, and then to question him on them.

THE COURT: All right, as I said, we edited them somewhat before coming in. It goes to the crux of the case as it has developed so far that Mr. Coleman has challenged the State on the basis of a number of possibilities and the word possibility was used. One of which is that the statements were false; they were coached from the children; that the State indeed is doing this as part of a money-making process that they follow to gain Federal funding. There was also a mention, a reference to Texas and the LDS case in Texas and the LDS nationwide sweep. I shouldn't say.... an "alleged" nationwide sweep of the LDS came out on the record. All of these he has put his feelings as to what the motivation for the case is, and that is the crux of this case. Why is it brought? Is it brought because facts are true and the children were abused? Or is it brought because it is either a lie or a political conspiracy, and he has to put that into play? Therefore, it is a proper subject to cross examination on the story. It's a prior statement of a witness. I don't know if it's inconsistent or consistent but it is his prior statement. I will therefore overrule the objection and you may introduce them and question him on these matters. We will get the jury.

MS. WITTLA: If I intend to have them entered as exhibits would you like me to ask the court reporter to mark right now?

THE COURT: Yeah, if you do that while the jury is coming back. You can get the jury in, we'll be doing that while you're doing that. Be seated, thank you. Mr. Coleman, if you would resume the stand, I would remind you, you are under oath, and Ms. Wittla is marking a few exhibits, and you may proceed.

MS. WITTLA: Your Honor, may I approach the witness?

THE COURT: Sure.

MS. WITTLA: Mr. Coleman, I'm handing you a document that's been marked as Plaintiff's Exhibit #1. At the top it says THE ROBERT AND JANET COLEMAN STORY. Have you ever seen that document before?

MR. COLEMAN: Yes ma'am, I have.

MS. WITTLA: Okay, and were you the author of that document?

MR. COLEMAN: No ma'am, I wasn't.

MS. WITTLA: You did not write it?

MR. COLEMAN: No ma'am, I did not.

MS. WITTLA: Okay, at the end of it, it would give the impression that you did. It looks like it was kind of signed by you.

MR. COLEMAN: No ma'am, it was not.

MS. WITTLA: Okay, do you know who the author of that document is?

MR. COLEMAN: Yes I do.

MS. WITTLA: Was it Janet Coleman?

MR. COLEMAN: No ma'am, it was not.

MS. WITTLA: Who was the author of that document?

MR. COLEMAN: Martha Hine.

MS. WITTLA: Can I see it?

MR. COLEMAN: Yes ma'am.

MS. WITTLA: So at the end of this document it says we swear that our statements are true, Robert and Janet Coleman; she's writing this pretending to be you?

MR. COLEMAN: No ma'am. She had took it upon herself to write that document and posted it on the internet.

MS. WITTLA: Okay, did she show you that document?

MR. COLEMAN: Yes ma'am, she did.

MS. WITTLA: Did you consult with her in its creation?

MR. COLEMAN: I'm sorry, could you please rephrase the question?

MS. WITTLA: Did you give her information so she could write the ROBERT AND JANET COLEMAN STORY?

MR. COLEMAN: We had just had phone conversations.

MS. WITTLA: She knew your story because you had told her your story, is that fair to say?

MR. COLEMAN: That's correct.

MS. WITTLA: I'm going to switch backwards with you. This one's been marked Plaintiff's Exhibit #2.

MR. COLEMAN: Okay, thank you.

MS. WITTLA: Can you tell me if you've ever seen that document before?

MR. COLEMAN: Yes, I have.

MS. WITTLA: Are you the author of that document?

MR. COLEMAN: Yes ma'am, I am.

MS. WITTLA: Have there been any changes made to that document at all? It's what you wrote?

MR. COLEMAN: It doesn't appear to be that there's any changes; this was written on 04-22-2008. It's been quite a while. Doesn't appear to be.

MS. WITTLA: And what is this document about?

MR. COLEMAN: Would you like me to read the document ma'am?

MS. WITTLA: Well, not necessarily read it out loud, but review it yourself; and tell me what it is about. What is the gist of it?

MR. COLEMAN: It's basically how I feel the government has treated us.

MS. WITTLA: Would you say that that's an accurate description of how you feel the government has treated you?

MR. COLEMAN: It is now.

MS. WITTLA: And how is it that you believe the government has treated you?

MR. COLEMAN: Before I trusted in the system; but then after going through this, I can see for myself that I do not have any faith in the system.

MS. WITTLA: And you're referring to going through this as this case we're talking about right now?

MR. COLEMAN: I have a lot of friends that are going through the same thing as well.

MS. WITTLA: What I'm asking you though, is you're describing an event that took place that cause you to lose faith in the system. Is this case that event? Or are you speaking of something else?

MR. COLEMAN: I would say I just about justified the whole system of how I felt I feel, and my dealings with the government.

MS. WITTLA: That this case made you feel this way? Or you already felt this and this case just proved it's true?

MR. COLEMAN: No ma'am. I had faith in the system until this case came about.

MS. WITTLA: All right, and this case started in March of 2008?

MR. COLEMAN: No. I'd lost faith in the system a little bit before that.

MS. WITTLA: In 2008 or previous to that?

MR. COLEMAN: Just pretty much 2008.

MS. WITTLA: Mr. Coleman, do you believe that the system was designed to systematically destroy the family?

MR. COLEMAN: It appears that way ma'am.

MS. WITTLA: Is that, in essence, what you wrote in that document?

MR. COLEMAN: The point I was trying to get across is there is no incentive to bring children home; government is allowing the State to make money in giving them bonuses. Bill Clinton signed an act that clearly was stated for older children that were in foster care to get them placed with people and good families that were in foster care. The states have used that as a tool to make money by taking younger children and getting bonuses and incentive programs to take younger children, because those are easier to get adopted out. Children with blonde hair, blue eyes are the main targets, and average age of two to six. And these are a lot of children that they (government) has been taking from families; all for the sake of money.

MS. WITTLA: Your Honor, at this time, I would move for admission of Plaintiff's Exhibit #2.

THE COURT: Okay, we've discussed the evidentiary issues off the record. Any other objection?

MR. FINDLAY: No, I mean nothing but what we've already done.

THE COURT: Based upon that ruling then, Exhibit #2 is admitted. You don't appear to be offering Exhibit #1, right?

MS. WITTLA: No, I don't believe I'd offer Exhibit #1.

THE COURT: Okay, if you would keep possession of that Exhibit then, there's an issue now under the Court rules with exhibits, where actually the Court holds on to them only for the length of the case. Since it's not coming in, hold on to Exhibit #1. Exhibit #2 we'll make sure it comes back to within the court files for as long as this case goes on. Proceed.

MS. WITTLA: Mr. Coleman, I have a third document that's called Plaintiff's Exhibit #3. Mr. Coleman have you seen that document before?

MR. COLEMAN: Bits and pieces of it. It's not all here. There's some of it on the last page that has been chopped off.

MS. WITTLA: I believe that the piece that was at the end was a response that you've had to someone else who had written to you. Does that make it clearer?

MR. COLEMAN: So you purposely took the ending of it off, is that what you are saying?

MS. WITTLA: Yes.

THE COURT: Just, just for the record, with counsel in chambers, we had identified that was somebody else's letter to you, and that's what we chopped off.

MR. FINDLAY: That's correct.

THE COURT: So what is chopped off is, is the, when I say letter, the email or the communication to you that's what was, that's why it's a half a page. And the court's ruled it is hearsay and it is inadmissible.

MR. FINDLAY: I agree, just I'm not objecting or not disputing the court's rule.

MS. WITTLA: Mr. Coleman, aside from that piece that's been taken off of that document, is the rest of it accurate and something you wrote?

MR. COLEMAN: I did not write the second part here, ma'am.

MS. WITTLA: Okay.

MR. COLEMAN: This foster care abuse in Michigan. That is an article that was written on a blog from a website.

MS. WITTLA: Okay, so how did it get there then?

MR. COLEMAN: It's called copy and paste ma'am. It's copied and pasted.

MS. WITTLA: And you did that? I mean, you took from one place and put it on here?

MR. COLEMAN: On a web log, if somebody else had made a comment, you can add to the top of that. So if somebody had made a comment, you can reply to that, and it would keep their comment on there, and it would keep stacking, so that when you got that, you could see.

MS. WITTLA: What parts of that document are things that you wrote?

MR. COLEMAN: I didn't write this ma'am.

MS. WITTLA: You didn't write any of it?

MR. COLEMAN: No ma'am. These are bits and pieces of things that I had wrote, the plan and destruction of family is part of this medic re-engineering not only civilization of humanity itself. I wrote that. I think of it as the revolution in action; I feel the government is trying to repopulate the people and the country to take them away from their families, and reunify them with other families.

THE COURT: Unless there's a better pattern, I guess, to expedite it; if you do intend to use it, I've got a red pen here. Maybe we can make marks on what are his and what are not—or—I question I guess adds into... did you put the whole thing together Mr. Coleman? I mean, did you pull in those pieces other people did and paste them in yourself?

MR. COLEMAN: No sir. I added to the blog on the top. There was bits and pieces that were mine. Other people have my user name that have logged in under my user name and have added things.

THE COURT: So I guess if, if you do intend to use it, we should somehow identify what are his and I have a red pen you can do that with, or if you have another method.

MS. WITTLA: Well, we will probably be done in a second, your Honor. Mr. Coleman, at the beginning, it looks like a response to a person named Heather. Did you write that part?

MR. COLEMAN: I believe that was Melissa that wrote that.

MS. WITTLA: Okay, well, who is Melissa?

MR. COLEMAN: Melissa is a user that goes on my blog.

MS. WITTLA: Okay, so Melissa would have said, "I'll tell you they have one and they're trying to destroy my family." Melissa's family is trying to be destroyed by the system currently?

MR. COLEMAN: Yes ma'am, they are.

MS. WITTLA: Okay, so you didn't respond to Heather at all when she made postings on this web log?

MR. COLEMAN: Heather had her children abducted from the State as well, and I have talked to her in reference to that. She just lost one of her children, eleven, to the State forced adoption. They told her that if she gave up one child, they would let her keep the other two.

MS. WITTLA: So you had this conversation with Heather, and yet in this document it says, "Heather has emailed me for years and you told me on the phone that you know I could never be capable of child abuse." She didn't have that conversation with you? This is some other woman who is responding to Heather?

MR. COLEMAN: I also talk to these people on the phone ma'am. So there's bits and pieces that people have access to my blog. They log in, they'll type in things, add things.

MS. WITTLA: Okay, so just to kind of speed this up a little bit, did you have a conversation with Heather through the internet where you are telling, "Hey Heather, you know, I would never hurt my kids?"

MR. COLEMAN: That was over the phone ma'am.

MS. WITTLA: Oh, that was on the phone. Not over the internet?

MR. COLEMAN: That's correct.

MS. WITTLA: So at the part where it says, "I'll tell you they have, now these fuckers are saying I am a bad parent, they took my children, where is their proof? I'll tell you, they have none, and they are trying to destroy my family." That's a conversation you had with Heather on the phone, on the internet, or it never happened at all?

MR. COLEMAN: No ma'am. I discussed it with a couple of people on the phone and they must have posted that under my name; my user name.

MS. WITTLA: The next bit goes on to say, "I was saying that I'm not like you; I will not lie down and take it in the ass like you did. They've messed with you for years and they are not going to do that to me. I'll show you, I'll show you that CPS hears you prove, photos taken while I was visiting my children in your care." Is that something you wrote?

MR. COLEMAN: No. Again, Melissa wrote that.

MS. WITTLA: So she's pretending to be you on your web log?

MR. COLEMAN: There are people that have typed logs up in regards to my defense that they feel, but I would not have said that kind of vulgar language on the internet.

MS. WITTLA: But you're the one who took the pictures at the visitation?

MR. COLEMAN: Yes ma'am, I did, and those were posted under a different post of mine.

MS. WITTLA: Towards the middle of this document there's a page that looks like a page that has two photographs on it, and I presume that this is Caitlyn and Ashley, and at the bottom it says "I can't say much more about the case or what is going on; I will tell you that I have dug up more abuse on my children, and other children in foster care that the State would've ever had on me because there is none." Is that something you wrote?

MR. COLEMAN: Again, ma'am, Melissa had wrote that post. Bits and pieces out of that were from my statements.

MS. WITTLA: Well, is it true that you dug up more abuse.....

MR. FINDLAY: ... Your Honor, I have a new objection, based on the Michigan Rule of Evidence, 403, I suppose if it's relevant and the Court has ruled it is, but basically relevant evidence can be excluded also on the grounds of among three things; one, being prejudiced, and the other two, and I'm basing it on this to confusion or waste of time. We're going to be here forever if we keep messing around with this; he's already said how he feels about what the government's done. It's cumulative, I mean, it just has no value, and I'd ask the court to have us move on.

THE COURT: But I guess we need to define what you're intending to use in there, if anything. I mean you are questioning him based on it but we still have the status of, it's somebody else's, it's not his, so unless you are able to connect up that he did it... well, let me ask this though: there's a reference Mr. Coleman to, you say, you keep saying my blog, so is this your sight?

MR. COLEMAN: Sir what I was indicating is that's my user name. That was probably used.

THE COURT: Right, but you can blog the Detroit Free Press. The sight that this is coming on to is known as a blog; is that right?

MR. COLEMAN: It's called a web group.

THE COURT: Okay, and who owns and controls that?

MR. COLEMAN: I have three people that were working under it, to control it.

THE COURT: Okay, you say you have. Did you start this blog?

MR. COLEMAN: I did. Yes, your Honor.

THE COURT: And that's why you call is "my" blog?

MR. COLEMAN: It's called a web group; it's Yahoo web group; it's called True Americans of Ironwood, and basically it states a lot of things that go on in Ironwood.

THE COURT: Okay, but you are the person that started it?

MR. COLEMAN: Yes sir.

THE COURT: Okay, based on that, I'm going to allow it. I'm still not going to allow the first one because it's.... has different, I guess, authorship or whatever, but go ahead, proceed, but let's, again, kind of get to the point of it.

MS. WITTLA: Mr. Coleman, as the person who set up the Yahoo group, do you control the contents on it?

MR. COLEMAN: No ma'am, I don't.

MS. WITTLA: You can't kick people off?

MR. COLEMAN: People are free to join and leave any time they want. It's a free group.

MS. WITTLA: But the question I have is do you have the ability to kick people off?

MR. COLEMAN: As far as a member?

MS. WITTLA: Yes.

MR. COLEMAN: I would probably say that I've never kicked anybody off of there. I don't really know how to do that.

MS. WITTLA: Is it your testimony today, Mr. Coleman, that you set up a Yahoo group called True Americans of Ironwood and that you didn't really know how it worked?

MR. COLEMAN: Yes ma'am. That was new group that I had started probably back in November.

MS. WITTLA: Mr. Coleman, you indicated that Becky and Bobby helped you for a certain percent off their rent, is that accurate?

MR. COLEMAN: That's correct.

MS. WITTLA: Do you know what percent off their rent they received for working for you?

MR. COLEMAN: No ma'am I don't.

MS. WITTLA: Then how do you know it happened?

MR. COLEMAN: Because my wife and me talk, and my wife had told me that they were to work off a percentage of our rent.

MS. WITTLA: But I thought they were employed by you in your handyman business?

MR. COLEMAN: They worked with me. They weren't employed by me.

MS. WITTLA: So Janet is the one that was the bookkeeper for all that stuff?

MR. COLEMAN: We just pretty much handled as far as the just basic maintenance of things, mainly around the apartment buildings.

MS. WITTLA: Okay, but as far as the financial arrangements, you would not know anything about that; Janet took care of all that?

MR. COLEMAN: Yes ma'am.

MS. WITTLA: Mr. Coleman, just a little bit more about this room in the basement; when Mr. Perhalla was asking you questions, he asked you if there was running water, and I believe your response, it was a room; could you describe the room?

MR. COLEMAN: There's two rooms down in the basement, and one of them was a room that they had set up. Becky had put a dresser and a bed and they had everything they needed. TV cable, everything was in there. So that's.... it's a room.

MS. WITTLA: So the furnishing was a dresser and what else?

MR. COLEMAN: It was dresser, TV, DVD player, Cable TV, anything that I guess they needed.

MS. WITTLA: You'd never been in there to see what they had or?

MR. COLEMAN: Yes, I have.

MS. WITTLA: When they left the basement, did they take all their stuff with them?

MR. COLEMAN: Did they take all their things with them?

MS. WITTLA: Yes.

MR. COLEMAN: No, they did not.

MS. WITTLA: Did they eventually get them back?

MR. COLEMAN: Yes ma'am, they did.

MS. WITTLA: Were things, I believe, returned to them at the Ironwood Public Saftey Department?

MR. COLEMAN: I'm sorry.

MS. WITTLA: Were their possessions returned to them at the Ironwood Public Safety Department?

MR. COLEMAN: We were told to drop them off at the Ironwood Public Safety Department.

MS. WITTLA: And you did?

MR. COLEMAN: Yes ma'am.

MS. WITTLA: Mr. Coleman, isn't it true that you actually asked Becky and Bobby to move out of their apartment within your building; continued to collect rent from them, and then collected rent from somebody else who lived in that same apartment?

MR. COLEMAN: That's untrue.

MS. WITTLA: Mr. Coleman, isn't it true that when you had them move out that they left a number of small appliances behind for the new tenants to use so you could rent it as fully furnished?

MR. COLEMAN: Could you please rephrase that?

MS. WITTLA: Didn't you encourage Becky and Bobby Payne to leave behind a number of their personal belongings in the apartment they lived in, in your building, so that you could in turn rent that apartment out and list it as fully furnished?

MR. COLEMAN: No, I did not.

MS. WITTLA: So it's your testimony today that things that the Paynes' moved in with; they moved out with. They got all their stuff back.

MR. COLEMAN: Everything they wanted, yes ma'am.

MS. WITTLA: I have nothing further.

THE COURT: Mr. Perhalla, do you have any questions based on her questions?

MR. PERHALLA: Thanks your Honor, just briefly. You just testified that someone by the name of Heather told you that they had; that she had to give up one child and could keep two?

MR. FINDLAY: Objection, your Honor. This is going to be hearsay.

MR. PERHALLA: He testified to it your Honor. He didn't object then.

MR. FINDLAY: Yeah, well, it's still hearsay. It was on her questions in terms of what's on the blog, but now he's asking him to testify what Heather said. It's hearsay.

THE COURT: Sustained. It's hearsay.

MR. PERHALLA: I'd have nothing further then.

THE COURT: Okay, again, you've already reserved, you're going to have the right to recall your client if you choose later.

MR. FINDLAY: I'm going to reserve.

THE COURT: All right, Mr. Coleman, you are free to step down, thank you. And Ms. Wittla, your next witness is?

MS. WITTLA: Janet Coleman.

THE COURT: Ms. Coleman, if you would step up to the front?

At this point, my wife Janet was sworn in, followed by her direct examination:

MS. WITTLA: Would you please state your name for the record?

MS. COLEMAN: Janet Coleman.

MS. WITTLA: And I believe your current address is up in Calumet with your husband?

MS. COLEMAN: Yes.

MS. WITTLA: Do you intend to live there indefinitely?

MS. COLEMAN: As far as right now, I'm planning to stay there.

MS. WITTLA: How long did Becky and Bobby Payne live in Coleman Estates?

MS. COLEMAN: They moved in the middle of July and they left on March tenth.

MS. WITTLA: July of 2007?

MS. COLEMAN: Seven.

MS. WITTLA: And during that period of time, where did they live?

MS. COLEMAN: First, they moved into 207 East Vaughn Street, an apartment in that building, and then I believe either the end of August or September, somewhere around that time they moved to 205 East Vaughn Street, which is an apartment above ours.

MS. WITTLA: Do you remember the apartment number?

MS. COLEMAN: 1B.

MS. WITTLA: And your apartment number would be?

MS. COLEMAN: 1A.

MS. WITTLA: Do you know what they paid for rent?

MS. COLEMAN: In 2007, the first apartment, they paid around $400; and then, when they moved to 205, since that was a brand new apartment, it was approximately $500, but we made an agreement with them that if they helped around Coleman Estates, we would take off a hundred dollars from their rent; so what they actually paid was the same.

MS. WITTLA: As the previous apartment?

MS. COLEMAN: Yes.

MS. WITTLA: How did their rent get paid?

MS. COLEMAN: Through Bobby Payne's social security disability.

MS. WITTLA: And you were the representative payee for his social security?

MS. COLEMAN: For a short amount of time.

MS. WITTLA: When did you start becoming his payee?

MS. COLEMAN: I believe it was the end of November or beginning of December.

MS. WITTLA: Did you first meet the Paynes in July of 2007?

MS. COLEMAN: Yes.

MS. WITTLA: So from July to November, approximately four—maybe five months social security was....

MS. COLEMAN: ... His mother-in-law was his payee.

MS. WITTLA: His mother-in-law was his payee?

MS. COLEMAN: Yes, Diane Peterson, I believe, was her name.

MS. WITTLA: Okay, but you became his payee?

MS. COLEMAN: Yes.

MS. WITTLA: And knowing him for five months was okay with social security for you to be his rep payee?

MS. COLEMAN: Yes.

MS. WITTLA: So when you were his rep payee, you just paid Coleman Estates the amount of rent out of that check?

MS. COLEMAN: Yes.

MS. WITTLA: And where did the balance of it go?

MS. COLEMAN: Went to his cell phone account, his charter cable TV account, any other bills that he had.

MS. WITTLA: And you paid those for him?

MS. COLEMAN: Yes, and every month when I went through his bills, I also sat him down and informed him of what, where his money was going.

MS. WITTLA: Is there a reason he didn't do this himself?

MS. COLEMAN: He couldn't manage his money, according to social security.

MS. WITTLA: And how about Becky? Becky couldn't manage it for him?

MS. COLEMAN: They wouldn't allow her to.

MS. WITTLA: Why not?

MS. COLEMAN: I don't know.

MS. WITTLA: So after the bills were paid, the rent, phone, cable, was there any money left that you just gave him straight out, just to have?

MS. COLEMAN: Actually, his bills were more than what he would receive in disability, so there was quite often, a few times where additional money that were owed for his cell phone or his Charter, we paid out of our own Coleman Estates checking.

MS. WITTLA: Were you aware of Becky Payne having a food stamp card?

MS. COLEMAN: Yes.

MS. WITTLA: Did you have anything to do with how they used it?

MS. COLEMAN: At first, no. When she first received it when she first moved to Michigan, every time she would get her monthly allowance, Bobby would take it and they'd spend it right away. So then after a week they would have no food, and Becky came up to me and asked me if I can help her stretch her dollars more wisely.

MS. WITTLA: And how did you do that?

MS. COLEMAN: I went grocery shopping with her.

MS. WITTLA: So you went together to pick out things that they needed?

MS. COLEMAN: Yes. Yes.

MS. WITTLA: Did they have, like, a separate stash of food?

MS. COLEMAN: Yeah.

MS. WITTLA: Even when they lived with you?

MS. COLEMAN: Yeah.

MS. WITTLA: And when did they move in with you guys?

MS. COLEMAN: It was right before Valentine's Day, beginning of February.

MS. WITTLA: You heard your husband's testimony here?

MS. COLEMAN: Yeah.

MS. WITTLA: And he testified that they lived in the basement which is connected to your apartment 1A?

MS. COLEMAN: Yes.

MS. WITTLA: Was that accurate?

MS. COLEMAN: Yes.

MS. WITTLA: So you considered that basement area to be living space within your own apartment?

MS. COLEMAN: Yes.

MS. WITTLA: And that's essentially where they lived?

MS. COLEMAN: Yes, there was a bedroom area down there.

MS. WITTLA: How much did they pay for rent when they moved into the basement?

MS. COLEMAN: I don't think they paid anything. The money from March went towards his bills.

MS. WITTLA: Well if they moved in at the beginning of February, where would the rent money have gone for February?

MS. COLEMAN: For the apartment upstairs.

MS. WITTLA: So they paid rent in the apartment upstairs for February, even though they didn't live there?

MS. COLEMAN: Well the apartment was empty until the beginning of March.

MS. WITTLA: And then in March, when his disability check would have come in, did you pay yourself for them living in the basement?

MS. COLEMAN: No, I don't believe so.

MS. WITTLA: Well would anybody else know better than you?

MS. COLEMAN: I used that money for, ah, I think Becky had some medical bills that she had before, miscellaneous bills that they left back in California. So I tried to get them caught up on all their other bills.

MS. WITTLA: Okay, because you were in charge as to how that money got disbursed?

MS. COLEMAN: Yes.

MS. WITTLA: Is Caitlyn's father involved in her life?

MS. COLEMAN: No.

MS. WITTLA: Has she ever met him?

MS. COLEMAN: When she was first born a couple of times.

MS. WITTLA: Since, has she seen him?

MS. COLEMAN: No.

MS. WITTLA: Do you have an extended family in the area?

MS. COLEMAN: What do you mean, like how close?

MS. WITTLA: Are you related to anybody in Gogebic County?

MS. COLEMAN: No.

MS. WITTLA: Are you related to anybody in the U.P.?

MS. COLEMAN: No.

MS. WITTLA: Is Robert related to anybody in the area?

MS. COLEMAN: Not that I know of.

MS. WITTLA: Where is your family located?

MS. COLEMAN: North Dakota.

MS. WITTLA: Aunts, uncles, cousins. Everybody is there?

MS. COLEMAN: Most of them. I have some relatives down in Minneapolis and Iowa.

MS. WITTLA: Do you know where Robert's family is from?

MS. COLEMAN: Lower Michigan.

MS. WITTLA: Like just below the bridge, or way far?

MS. COLEMAN: Detroit. Dearborn.

MS. WITTLA: Ms. Coleman, how far did you go in school? Did you graduate high school?

MS. COLEMAN: Yes.

MS. WITTLA: Do you share your husband's belief that the State makes money off of foster children?

MS. COLEMAN: The group and the things, the stories that I've read, I do believe so.

MS. WITTLA: The case we're here on right now began on March 11th of this year... correct?

MS. COLEMAN: Yes.

MS. WITTLA: Why do you think it began?

MS. COLEMAN: Over false allegations.

MS. WITTLA: And the false allegations were from the Paynes?

MS. COLEMAN: Yes.

MS. WITTLA: When did you find out that your husband had an affair with Becky?

MS. COLEMAN: March 10th.

MS. WITTLA: Is he the one who told you?

MS. COLEMAN: Yes.

MS. WITTLA: Is that the day the Paynes were told to leave?

MS. COLEMAN: Yes.

MS. WITTLA: Is that the reason?

MS. COLEMAN: No. Actually, March 11th, that morning when Robert went to the police station, he came home and told me about the affair. March 10th is when Becky and Bobby had the fight and that's when I said I had enough, they had to leave.

MS. WITTLA: So when they were having this fight on the 10th, you don't know what it's about? You just know it was a fight?

MS. COLEMAN: Well, seems like they were always fighting.

MS. WITTLA: If they were always fighting, why would you want them to live with you?

MS. COLEMAN: Becky needed help with dealing with Bobby. Bobby, numerous times had threatened to kill himself. She couldn't deal with his mental or emotions by herself, so we agreed to help her until he had saved up enough money with his disability and that, so we can help them go back to California.

MS. WITTLA: Both of them to go back to California?

MS. COLEMAN: Yes.

MS. WITTLA: Becky wouldn't need help in California?

MS. COLEMAN: Well, his family lives in California.

MS. WITTLA: So they would help her with him?

MS. COLEMAN: Yeah, I would assume so.

MS. WITTLA: That was the plan at any rate?

MS. COLEMAN: Yeah, that was the plan.

MS. WITTLA: Was there anyone else that could have helped Becky?

MS. COLEMAN: I'm assuming so, but she asked me and Robert to help her... so....

MS. WITTLA: Would you consider the relationship you had with Becky to be that she was your friend?

MS. COLEMAN: At the time, to a point. I tried to keep a tenant/landlord relationship, but I know there was times that she was more of a friend.

MS. WITTLA: Is that why you would have let her move in with you? Because she was becoming more of a friend then?

MS. COLEMAN: I didn't let her move in.

MS. WITTLA: How did she end up in your house?

MS. COLEMAN: I believe it was the beginning of February, Becky and Bobby had come up to me and Rob and said that they want to move back to California. What they wanted, is, you know, the blinds they didn't want; just to leave them in the apartment where we could re-rent and then, you know, they said, "Well, why don't we move down into your basement?" I said no, and I'm not sure exactly what Robert said. I'm assuming that Robert disagreed with it, and then the next thing I know Becky had already moved her stuff down into the basement.

MS. WITTLA: Well if the basement is connected to your apartment, how did they get in?

MS. COLEMAN: There's a back door.

MS. WITTLA: Oh, there's independent access to the basement?

MS. COLEMAN: We have three doors that enter into our apartment.

MS. WITTLA: Okay.

MS. COLEMAN: And I spend the majority of my time in the front part of the apartment.

MS. WITTLA: Are you telling me they snuck in the back when you weren't looking?

MS. COLEMAN: Basically.

MS. WITTLA: And moved all their stuff in and you didn't notice?

MS. COLEMAN: Yeah. They didn't have that much stuff.

MS. WITTLA: What did they leave behind in the other apartment?

MS. COLEMAN: I think a couch... they had two beds and they left one up there... tables and chairs... some miscellaneous kitchen supplies.

MS. WITTLA: Microwave, toaster, blender?

MS. COLEMAN: Stuff like that, yeah.

MS. WITTLA: Why wouldn't they want those things?

MS. COLEMAN: They said they didn't want to take them back to California.

MS. WITTLA: To your knowledge, have they gone back to California?

MS. COLEMAN: I don't know.

MS. WITTLA: Did you hear Robert's version of what happened on March 11th when the DHS and Sheryl Saippa came to your house?

MS. COLEMAN: Yes.

MS. WITTLA: Is that fairly accurate, what he described?

MS. COLEMAN: I believe so, yeah.

MS. WITTLA: Are there any changes you would have made in it or additions?

MS. COLEMAN: Not that I can recall.

MS. WITTLA: So is it fair to say then that Caitlyn was interviewed by Elizabeth Fyle, Robert Ross in her bedroom and you and Robert weren't in there?

MS. COLEMAN: No.

MS. WITTLA: At one point in time you actually interrupted the interview?

MS. COLEMAN: Yes.

MS. WITTLA: And you did this on advice of your attorney?

MS. COLEMAN: Yes.

MS. WITTLA: Were you told why you couldn't be there during the interview?

MS. COLEMAN: No. I walked in there, Caitlyn was sitting on the floor playing with some toys. Elizabeth was sitting on Caitlyn's bed; and Bob Ross was standing by the door, and the only thing I was told is you don't allow us to talk to Caitlyn, we'll get a court order and take your kids.

MS. WITTLA: Is it true that you never wanted Caitlyn to talk to the DHS?

MS. COLEMAN: No.

MS. WITTLA: Then why interrupt the interview?

MS. COLEMAN: Our attorney said I had a right to be in there.

MS. WITTLA: Have you come to believe since that point in time that you didn't have a right to be there?

MS. COLEMAN: I still have a right to know. I have a right to either have myself or a witness present.

MS. WITTLA: Okay, so as we are sitting here today, if this interview was going to take place right now, your opinion today is, "Hey, I have a right to be there?"

MS. COLEMAN: Yes.

MS. WITTLA: You don't believe there is a law to prevent you from being there?

MS. COLEMAN: Don't think so.

MS. WITTLA: And you were never told about this law?

MS. COLEMAN: No.

MR. FINDLAY: Your Honor, under Rule 403 I think this is leading some to confusion; I think the state of the law is that if they did refuse the interview, then DHS would have to do a court order to do an interview. I think that a parent , if there's a court order, then .....

THE COURT: Well the question is whether or not under the interviewing requirements, we're not going to get into the technicalities of all that I don't believe unless you're going to submit something. But I would just indicate to the jury that I will instruct you on the law that applies to this case. Any references to the law by the lawyers, you should not consider as evidence. So with that, were you still on that point Ms. Wittla, or?

MS. WITTLA: No.

THE COURT: All right, then move on please.

MS. WITTLA: Mrs. Coleman, did you write letters to Angela Andriacchi up in Marquette?

MS. COLEMAN: Yes.

MS. WITTLA: Was one of them entitled PRESERVATION OF PARENTAL RIGHTS?

MS. COLEMAN: Yes.

MS. WITTLA: This letter looks like it is an outline of how you want your child to be taken care of while in foster care. Is that fairly accurate?

MS. COLEMAN: Yes, yes.

MS. WITTLA: And knowing that she's in Marquette, you wanted her to go to a physician in Watersmeet?

MS. COLEMAN: Yes, that was our family doctor.

MS. WITTLA: And a dentist in Ironwood?

MS. COLEMAN: Yes.

MS. WITTLA: Wouldn't it be kind of a long ride for her?

MS. COLEMAN: Well, why was she in Marquette?

MS. WITTLA: Because she was placed in foster care, right?

MS. COLEMAN: Yeah.

MS. WITTLA: Okay, well since her location changed, wouldn't it make more sense for her to go to somebody closer to where she was?

MS. COLEMAN: You would think that she'd want to go to a doctor or a dentist that she's familiar with.

MS. WITTLA: How many times did she see Doctor Herfort?

MS. COLEMAN: Like two or three times.

MS. WITTLA: So if his dental records show that he only saw her once, would that surprise you?

MS. COLEMAN: Yes, because she's been there at least twice.

MS. WITTLA: And at six years old, seen a dentist twice, she's got a relationship with him?

MS. COLEMAN: Well, a lot better than a complete stranger.

MS. WITTLA: And Doctor Pusateri in Watersmeet, she had seen him several times before?

MS. COLEMAN: Yes.

MS. WITTLA: And what about Ashley? How many times did Ashley see Doctor Herfort?

MS. COLEMAN: I don't believe she had.

MS. WITTLA: But you still wanted her to see Doctor Herfort in Ironwood?

MS. COLEMAN: Yes, he's familiar with our family.

MS. WITTLA: But not Ashley, I mean, he never treated Ashley?

MS. COLEMAN: No.

MS. WITTLA: Did Ashley actually go to see Doctor Pusateri?

MS. COLEMAN: Yes.

MS. WITTLA: At the beginning of your letter it states, "I am the traditional and legal parent." What does that mean?

MS. COLEMAN: I'm her legal parent. I'm the one that gave birth to her. I'm her mother.

MS. WITTLA: Well I understand the legal part. What's the traditional part? What does that mean?

MS. COLEMAN: I carried her for nine months. I was the one that carried her and delivered her and took care of her.

MS. WITTLA: So you're referencing biology in that you are her biological and legal mother?

MS. COLEMAN: Yes.

MS. WITTLA: Okay, and you put that in both letters; the one regarding Caitlyn and the one regarding Ashley?

MS. COLEMAN: Yes.

MS. WITTLA: Do you recall writing a letter to the school principal up in Republic?

MS. COLEMAN: Yes.

MS. WITTLA: And you indicated in your letter, your parental rights have not been modified or terminated, correct?

MS. COLEMAN: Yes.

MS. WITTLA: Weren't your parental rights modified when your children were put into foster care?

MS. COLEMAN: They were not terminated. I still had the right to know where and what my children's activities were.

MS. WITTLA: Okay, but your parental rights were modified because they were not with you?

MS. COLEMAN: Basically, and that was the only right I didn't have is for them to be with me. I still had the right to know where and what they were doing.

MS. WITTLA: Well doesn't your letter kind of imply that you're putting these people on notice that nothing's changed and you're still in charge?

MS. COLEMAN: Basically.

MS. WITTLA: But that's not accurate, is it?

MS. COLEMAN: I had every right as a legal parent, except for her to live with us.

MS. WITTLA: Okay, but that's a pretty big thing, right? That the DHS had control over where Caitlyn and Ashley lived; that's correct?

MS. COLEMAN: Where she lived, yes.

MS. WITTLA: And they were making arrangements for them to be fed and clothed and go see doctors and dentists and stuff, right?

MS. COLEMAN: They were supposed to get my consent that they were doing it.

MS. WITTLA: You go on in your letter to be fairly clear that you don't want the foster care providers to be given any information regarding Caitlyn's school. Is that fair to say?

MS. COLEMAN: I'm not sure.

MS. WITTLA: Well, it states in here, "My child's education should not be discussed with the foster caregiver without me present." So just to modify that, as long as you're there, you're okay with them knowing....

MS. COLEMAN: Yes, exactly.

MS. WITTLA: Okay, but otherwise, you don't want them to know anything?

MS. COLEMAN: No.

MS. WITTLA: Does that seem reasonable considering they're in Marquette and you are here?

MS. COLEMAN: I have the right to know what her education is. Before they took Caitlyn and Ashley, I was very involved in Caitlyn's education. Her every activity that she did, I was very involved in, and knew what was going on.

MS. WITTLA: But we're talking about Caitlyn, not you, so if Caitlyn is having an issue at school, does it make sense for the school to sit on that information until they can coordinate a meeting with you and the foster care providers? Or does it make more sense for Caitlyn that they just tell the foster care providers, "Hey, here's what's going on."

OK, I need to break away from the testimony on this point, just to point something out! First, the snide prosecutor, in her usual unprofessional manner, slid into this the statement that we were not talking about Janet. That is WRONG! We were very much talking about Janet, because following reunification, who did she think was going to have to pick up with Caitlyn's education? The FOSTER PARENT? I believe also, there is a thing called the TELEPHONE which would have worked just fine for the school to call Janet, informing her that they would also be calling the foster parents. Not a big deal at all, except in the mind of a sick prosecutor!

MS. COLEMAN: They could quick pick up the phone as well and call me and tell me what's going on.

MS. WITTLA: So your stance today is that it would be reasonable under any set of circumstances to keep you in the loop because you're her mom?

MS. COLEMAN: Exactly.

MS. WITTLA: You also indicate that, "Any papers that my child would bring home should be mailed to me, rather than sent to the foster caregiver." That also doesn't strike you as unusual?

MS. COLEMAN: What do you mean?

MS. WITTLA: Well kids bring home a lot of stuff that has to be sent back. Right?

MS. COLEMAN: Yes.

MS. WITTLA: Fairly timely fashion. I need a permission slip; I got to finish my homework; you want all that stuff shipped to Ironwood?

MS. COLEMAN: Yes.

MS. WITTLA: How does Caitlyn typically address adults?

MS. COLEMAN: What do you mean?

MS. WITTLA: If you were introducing her to somebody who is an adult, what would she typically call that person?

MS. COLEMAN: By their name.

MS. WITTLA: Okay, what? Their whole name, first name, last name?

MS. COLEMAN: Well, like if I was introducing her to you, I'd say, "Well, this is Tracie." You know, usually by their first name.

MS. WITTLA: Do you understand why a child who's living in a home environment with adults might refer to them as mom and dad?

MS. COLEMAN: Yes.

MS. WITTLA: Is that okay?

MS. COLEMAN: As in like, in the foster parents?

MS. WITTLA: Yes.

MS. COLEMAN: No.

MS. WITTLA: Why not?

MS. COLEMAN: Mom and dad are a sacred word.

MS. WITTLA: But if the kids feel comfortable when referring to the foster parents as mom, that's not okay?

MS. COLEMAN: No, because they are not their mom.

MS. WITTLA: And in your letter, you wanted to make sure that the foster caregivers were not called mom and dad?

MS. COLEMAN: Exactly.

MS. WITTLA: Our Auntie, or anything like that?

MS. COLEMAN: They had a first name.

MS. WITTLA: Just Bob? Just Judy? That's all they're allowed to call them?

MS. COLEMAN: Exactly.

MS. WITTLA: At six years old and two years old?

MS. COLEMAN: Yeah.

MS. WITTLA: Doesn't that seem a little cold?

MS. COLEMAN: No.

I can't let this go! The prosecutor was again showing her arrogance here! Besides, nobody was as cold as this woman! Who is she to throw this in, and where was the judge when she did it??? Were we there to tend to the sensitivity of the caregivers? Or try to reunite my kids with our family? And how many parents would want to have someone else referred to by their own children as mom and dad?

MS. WITTLA: Have you ever used physical punishment with Caitlyn?

MS. COLEMAN: I guess.

MS. WITTLA: I'm sorry?

MS. COLEMAN: A swat on the butt, yes.

MS. WITTLA: You've never struck her with a belt?

MS. COLEMAN: No.

MS. WITTLA: You've never restrained her while somebody else struck her with a belt?

MS. COLEMAN: No.

MS. WITTLA: You've never watched your husband strike Caitlyn with a belt?

MS. COLEMAN: No.

MS. WITTLA: What would you do if he did?

MS. COLEMAN: I would probably be calling for help. I stated on March 11th when Bob Ross and Elizabeth Fyle came to our home; I stated in the kitchen that if myself or my children were in any danger, I would be the one to report it, and be fleeing and asking for help.

MS. WITTLA: But what if you didn't report it. How would you feel?

MS. COLEMAN: Probably guilty.

MS. WITTLA: Well what if this had been going on hypothetically for months, years, and you didn't say anything?

MS. COLEMAN: It wouldn't have happened.

MS. WITTLA: That's not what happened; that's your testimony….

MS. COLEMAN: If I knew my children were seriously being harmed I would have done something immediately.

MS. WITTLA: Do you think that the allegations in the petition where Caitlyn—restraining her arms over her head; her legs held down; her body exposed and struck with a belt; would have consisted of harm?

MS. COLEMAN: If that would have happened, yes.

MS. WITTLA: That would have harm?

MS. COLEMAN: Yes.

MS. WITTLA: And you'd have called?

MS. COLEMAN: I would have called or fled, or I would have done something.

MS. WITTLA: Have you ever used physical punishment for Ashley?

MS. COLEMAN: No.

MS. WITTLA: Your husband described the situation where Caitlyn threw a porcelain cup into the porcelain tub where you were taking a shower.

MS. COLEMAN: Yes.

MS. WITTLA: Do you recall that happening?

MS. COLEMAN: Yes.

MS. WITTLA: How old was Caitlyn?

MS. COLEMAN: Maybe four… five…. I'm not sure exactly.

MS. WITTLA: And there was one other incident that he described where Caitlyn had pushed her sister down, was hitting her. Do you recall anything like that ever happening? I'm assuming you're going to say?

MS. COLEMAN: Yes.

MS. WITTLA: Yes, okay, they're say fighting?

MS. COLEMAN: Yeah.

MS. WITTLA: Those are the kind of things that would get Caitlyn in trouble for, you know… get the swat on the butt or something like that?

MS. COLEMAN: Yes.

MS. WITTLA: Your husband also testified that another punishment would be that she had to stand in the corner for an amount of time that was less than her age; so she's six, so she'd stand in a corner for five minutes?

MS. COLEMAN: About six minutes. Depends. Usually when she had to go in the corner, we, you know, until she calmed down, which is probably just a couple of minutes, and we would just let her out and talk to her about what had happened. But we wouldn't leave her in there for more than six minutes.

MS. WITTLA: So if Caitlyn would have ever said that she had to stand in the corner for a really long time till her feet hurt; that really long time is really just six minutes?

MS. COLEMAN: Yeah.

MS. WITTLA: Do you think that your family needs foster care for Caitlyn and Ashley?

MS. COLEMAN: Do I need help parenting Caitlyn and Ashley?

MS. WITTLA: Yes.

MS. COLEMAN: As in me and Robert?

MS. WITTLA: Yes.

MS. COLEMAN: No, I don't believe so.

MS. WITTLA: I believe your husband testified about being reimbursed by the State for travel expenses; are you aware of the arrangements that were made?

MS. COLEMAN: Yes.

MS. WITTLA: To your knowledge, have you submitted all the documents you need to get reimbursed?

MS. COLEMAN: Yes.

MS. WITTLA: And you have not been reimbursed?

MS. COLEMAN: No, we have not.

MS. WITTLA: Have you missed any visits with your children that you have been offered?

MS. COLEMAN: Yes.

MS. WITTLA: Why were they missed?

MS. COLEMAN: Because Angela or the guardian ad litem cancelled them.

MS. WITTLA: Do you know why Angela cancelled them?

MS. COLEMAN: Because she refused to let us record or take photographs.

MS. WITTLA: Did you hear me talking to your husband about that?

MS. COLEMAN: Yes.

MS. WITTLA: And I believe my question would have been— well, my question is now, were you offered the chance to have a visit as long as you shut off the recording device?

MS. COLEMAN: She gave us an ultimatum. Either turn off the recorder or your visit is cancelled.

MS. WITTLA: And what was your choice.

MS. COLEMAN: To continue to record.

MS. WITTLA: Which meant no visit?

MS. COLEMAN: She cancelled the visit.

MS. WITTLA: Okay, but by definition you got an ultimatum. It's one or the other, right?

MS. COLEMAN: Yeah.

MS. WITTLA: So you can have a visit or you can record; by choosing to record, you lost the visit?

MS. COLEMAN: Yes.

MS. WITTLA: Thank you, I have nothing further.

I should note right here, that our choice, no matter what it would have been, would have resulted in the state violating our constitutional rights. We had a court order allowing the visit, which the state did violate, on the one hand, and of course, along with that, we had our constitutional right to information obtained at the visit. So our right to freedom of information was also an issue. Whether or not we submitted to their demand, they would have violated our right to freedom of information via our desire to record. We refused to give up our constitutional right, which they insisted we must do in order to see our children.

THE COURT: Mr. Perhalla?

MR. PERHALLA: Thanks your Honor. (To Janet) Do you recall an incident earlier this year where Caitlyn may not have been eating her food and was punished?

MS. COLEMAN: She wouldn't have been punished for it.

MR. PERHALLA: Okay, you're aware the petition alleges that she was hit with a belt for not eating her rice, correct?

MS. COLEMAN: Yes.

MR. PERHALLA: What would you do if she did not eat all her food. Nothing? Or would you do something?

MS. COLEMAN: Usually, what we would do if I made something that was new to her; she'd at least have to try it, if she liked it she would eat it. If she didn't, at least as long as she would try it. But if something that we've had before, she has such a small portion, you know?

MR. PERHALLA: Would she be yelled at by either Robert or you if she didn't eat everything off her plate?

MS. COLEMAN: No, we would just, you know, eat.

MR. PERHALLA: So nothing would ever be mentioned if she didn't eat her food?

MS. COLEMAN: Basically, as long as she tried it and made an attempt to eat it. We wouldn't push it.

MR. PERHALLA: So when there's an allegation in the petition that she was hit with a belt; that she says she was hit with a belt; Caitlyn, for not eating her rice; you would disagree with that?

MS. COLEMAN: Yes.

MR. PERHALLA: And why would you disagree with that?

MS. COLEMAN: Because we would not punish her physically for not eating.

MR. PERHALLA: And you share the same opinion as to why Caitlyn would even say that, or do you have another opinion?

Had I been asked this question in this manner when I was on the stand, the answer would have been simple: "Yes, I have another opinion. The state lied." And I'd have been correct to say that, because, in fact, they did lie about this. They took this right out of the Bobby Payne playbook, and Caitlyn never said this. I know that for certain, because at the time of the writing of this book, Caitlyn is ten years of age. She read these transcripts and literally laughed at this assertion! "Dad," she said, "I loved rice!" But as the state made sure that Caitlyn could never take the stand, under the guise of protecting her, they could put all the words they wanted in her mouth, which we have effectively found to be true since the days of the trial. Continuing with my wife's answer to the GAL questioning:

MS. COLEMAN: And what's that? That she's being coached?

MR. PERHALLA: Correct.

MS. COLEMAN: Yes, I do believe that.

MR. PERHALLA: Did you have a problem with Caitlyn lying?

MS. COLEMAN: No, not really.

MR. PERHALLA: Anywhere in the petition's allegations that she was struck two times with a belt and then had to take a vinegar bath? You aware of those allegations in the petition?

MS. COLEMAN: Yes.

MR. PERHALLA: Did you ever give your... any.... ever a vinegar bath?

MS. COLEMAN: No.

MR. PERHALLA: So again, that's being coached?

MS. COLEMAN: I do believe so.

MR. PERHALLA: Have you ever talked to your daughter about the allegations in the petition?

MS. COLEMAN: No, not really. After I was presented the allegations, we haven't been able to really talk to Caitlyn.

MR. PERHALLA: So during visits she's never mentioned anything about any of the allegations?

MS. COLEMAN: Well, that evening on March 11th until Friday night when she went to bed, on the 14th, she repeated that she had a secret, and after we had—okay, what's the secret? She had stated that that lady told her that if she said that you spanked me with a belt, then they won't take me away. And then there was another incident at a visit where I took her to the bathroom and she said, "Mama, why did they take me?" I said I don't know, but we have a lot of people helping us to get you back as soon as possible, and she said, and I quote, "Well, they're making me say you spank me."

MR. PERHALLA: So she's told you this on two occasions and you cannot recall any others?

MS. COLEMAN: I know in Escanaba she had made a comment similar to that to Robert.

MR. PERHALLA: So again, the allegations in the petition that she is smacked with a belt and it has happened many times, that's being coached again?

MS. COLEMAN: She wouldn't use the word "smacked."

MR. PERHALLA: Pardon?

MS. COLEMAN: Ah, smacked. She wouldn't use that word. If anything, swat or a spanking, and she doesn't call me mommy, she calls me mama.

MR. PERHALLA: Now you've never seen your husband, first of all, strike either child with first, his hand?

MS. COLEMAN: They've received a swat on the butt, or Caitlyn has. Ashley hasn't.

MR. PERHALLA: But never with a belt or....

MS. COLEMAN: No, never. No objects. No belts. No nothing.

MR. PERHALLA: I'm going to show you, are you familiar with the petition?

MS. COLEMAN: The allegations?

MR. PERHALLA: Yeah, the allegations.

MS. COLEMAN: Somewhat, yes.

MR. PERHALLA: I'm going to show you, I'll give you a copy so you have it. In item 58, it states that Rob acknowledged that he does use a belt for spanking at times.

MS. COLEMAN: That's untrue.

MR. PERHALLA: So you believe whoever put that in there is just simply lying?

MS. COLEMAN: I believe when we were in our kitchen with Bob Ross and Elizabeth Fyle on the 11th, he had said that he does not use a belt, and they just twisted it.

MR. PERHALLA: They changed his words around?

MS. COLEMAN: Yes.

MR. PERHALLA: Now there's allegations in here about an orange belt?

MS. COLEMAN: Yes.

MR. PERHALLA: Okay, and Caitlyn stated that she's hit with an orange belt in the petition, correct?

MS. COLEMAN: In the petition, yes.

MR. PERHALLA: And you believe that's being coached?

MS. COLEMAN: Yes.

MR. PERHALLA: And isn't it true that an orange belt was found in the home?

MS. COLEMAN: It wasn't orange, it was brown.

MR. PERHALLA: To a child, was it turning to color orange, from brown to orange?

MS. COLEMAN: No, I don't believe so.

MR. PERHALLA: Do you still have the belt that you think might be this orange one?

MS. COLEMAN: I don't know. We just recently moved, so everything's kind of still in boxes.

MR. PERHALLA: Have you rented out your apartment in Ironwood?

MS. COLEMAN: Not yet.

MR. PERHALLA: So you absolutely do not intend to get back to Ironwood?

MS. COLEMAN: No.

MR. PERHALLA: And the reason is there's employment in Calumet?

MS. COLEMAN: In our opinion they have better employment in that area, better medical facilities, and the school in Calumet has higher standards.

MR. PERHALLA: Any other reason?

MS. COLEMAN: We like the area. The country area.

MR. PERHALLA: And you did that just since removal of the children, correct?

MS. COLEMAN: Yeah, the end of May I think is when we moved up there.

MR. PERHALLA: I guess a question I have is if you were going to move anyway, why wouldn't you move closer to where at least the children are now?

MS. COLEMAN: Well, they are in Escanaba right now, and it seems like they keep moving them every few months, so should we relocate everything every few months? We plan on staying in Calumet for some time too.

MR. PERHALLA: It's true your children were moved from Marquette to Escanaba, correct?

MS. COLEMAN: Yes.

MR. PERHALLA: And do you know the reason why?

MS. COLEMAN: For what I was informed, there's no beds.

MR. PERHALLA: No beds?

MS. COLEMAN: And the investigation with Child and Family Services.

MR. PERHALLA: It had nothing to do with either you or your husband?

MS. COLEMAN: No.

MR. PERHALLA: As to the reason that.... Moved, would that be a fair statement?

MS. COLEMAN: No, other than the investigation of the bruises we've seen.

MR. PERHALLA: And it is your understanding that that investigation is not completed?

MS. COLEMAN: No, it's not. The last I heard it was still in the prosecutor's office in Marquette County.

MR. PERHALLA: The Negaunee State Police didn't inform you that they completed their investigation?

MS. COLEMAN: Last time I spoke to Negaunee, they said it was still open at the prosecutor's office.

MR. PERHALLA: Have you spoken to that prosecutor's office?

MS. COLEMAN: No.

MR. PERHALLA: There's allegations that you hit Caitlyn with a spoon. Do you recall those allegations in the petition?

MS. COLEMAN: Yes, the wooden spoon?

MR. PERHALLA: Yes, did you ever hit her with a wooden spoon?

MS. COLEMAN: No, because I don't own a wooden spoon.

MR. PERHALLA: How about any other type of spoon?

MS. COLEMAN: No.

MR. PERHALLA: Are you saying that you never even swatted Caitlyn with your hand, and it was always left up to Robert?

MS. COLEMAN: No, I've given her a swat on the butt periodically.

MR. PERHALLA: You've heard Mr. Coleman testify that he does lose his temper at times?

MS. COLEMAN: He doesn't lose his temper. He gets frustrated or angry, or raises his voice, but it's very seldom with the children.

MR. PERHALLA: How about with others? Does he get frustrated and raise his voice with others?

MS. COLEMAN: Well, I know there was some disputes with Bobby and Becky.

MR. PERHALLA: (FOLLOWING A SHORT COURT BREAK): I have a few questions about the Paynes. Who made the decision to rent to them?

MS. COLEMAN: I believe I did. That was before they moved from California and I was working with Becky's mother.

MR. PERHALLA: So you knew Becky's mother before hand or?

MS. COLEMAN: Well, she had contacted us because we had an opening.

MR. PERHALLA: Okay, was it just an advertisement or something?

MS. COLEMAN: Yes.

MR. PERHALLA: Then the decision to move and let them reduce their rent or pay part of their rent by working. Who made that decision? You, too?

MS. COLEMAN: Yes.

MR. PERHALLA: Who came up with the amount? To reduce it by a hundred?

MS. COLEMAN: Me and Rob kind of came up with a mutual agreement.

MR. PERHALLA: Were you satisfied with whatever work they were doing for that hundred dollars?

MS. COLEMAN: Yeah, it was just basic chores.

MR. PERHALLA: Chores around the....

MS. COLEMAN: .... The Coleman Estates and.....

MR. PERHALLA: Did they also do some work in other apartments too? Cleaning?

MS. COLEMAN: Yeah, they were like, you know, if we had someone who would move out they'd help us clean to get it ready for a new tenant.

MR. PERHALLA: How about for other realtors or tenants that went to realtors? Would they help clean for them too, through you?

MS. COLEMAN: I know through Handyman, we had an account, and part of the account was to clean.

MR. PERHALLA: For your Handyman business too?

MS. COLEMAN: Yes.

MR. PERHALLA: How many hours a week were they doing this cleaning?

MS. COLEMAN: I'm not sure. I took care of the financial part and Rob kind of managed the work aspect.

MR. PERHALLA: Then after you moved into the basement, you told us Rob and you didn't make the decision to let them move there, but once you found out they were down there, why didn't you tell them to move?

MS. COLEMAN: I guess we just mutually agreed well, as soon as they get their next month's disability, we'll just give them enough money, or you know, try to get them out of..... back to California.

MR. PERHALLA: And the disability that he was receiving. It was enough to at least pay the rent?

MS. COLEMAN: Yes.

MR. PERHALLA: Why didn't they or you help them get MSHDA to pay for part of the rent?

MS. COLEMAN: I know when they first moved into our place, I did mention a few times to Becky about, you know, why don't you go check into MSHDA? That was her responsibility to see if she qualified or not; if she did or not, then it was up to her.

MR. PERHALLA: You didn't think maybe you should drive them there or help them get to the office to apply?

MS. COLEMAN: If they wanted transportation, all they had to do was ask.

MR. PERHALLA: Now the night your children lived in the Hancock hotel, I assume you remember that night?

MS. COLEMAN: Yes.

MR. PERHALLA: So when the police knocked on the door, what did you do?

MS. COLEMAN: I heard some loud banging and I got up and the door was already open, but I had to undo the chain. And as soon as I undid the chain, the door flew open and cops swarmed in there.

MR. PERHALLA: And they showed you an order to get the children?

MS. COLEMAN: Not at first. It was so early in the morning, but they hurried up and grabbed the kids and as soon as they were dressing the kids is when they threw a piece of paper in my face.

MR. PERHALLA: Who grabbed the kids?

MS. COLEMAN: I know the DHS worker and there was a couple of officers that were putting the boots and a coat on.

MR. PERHALLA: So the only people that arrived were police officers and then one DHS worker?

MS. COLEMAN: Yes.

MR. PERHALLA: Do you recall how many officers?

MS. COLEMAN: I know there are statements of at least nine, but it looked like there was a whole lot more outside.

MR. PERHALLA: Then did you help them get the children ready?

MS. COLEMAN: No. They wouldn't let me have any contact with them.

MR. PERHALLA: Did you gather anything for them to take for the children?

MS. COLEMAN: Not when they first came in. I noticed one State officer had a handful of diapers. I noticed that they were just kind of grabbing clothes, you know, at their leisure, just grabbing things and going.

MR. PERHALLA: So they just came in, took the children, grabbed some of their stuff and left?

MS. COLEMAN: Yes.

MR. PERHALLA: And what did you do?

MS. COLEMAN: I was, I remember talking to the head officer who was in charge of it; and I was asking him, trying to ask him why, what's going on? And he just said that they have a court order to get the kids.

MR. PERHALLA: After they took the children, did you see the children again that night?

MS. COLEMAN: When they were buckled in the vehicle.

MR. PERHALLA: So you stayed with the children; they just took the children. They didn't give you a chance to say goodbye the first time?

MS. COLEMAN: I know I was at the door of our room and I begged a DHS worker to say a proper goodbye.

MR. PERHALLA: And then you got to see them in the car?

MS. COLEMAN: Yeah, and then I got my coat on and we went downstairs.

MR. PERHALLA: Did you have any other contact with the DHS worker?

MS. COLEMAN: I know after I talked to Caitlyn and Ashley, I gave her my phone number.

MR. PERHALLA: What did you say to Caitlyn when she was in the car?

MS. COLEMAN: When I first got in there, I told her that.... I said, "I love you." She asked about the Easter Bunny, and I said don't worry about that, I'll contact the Easter Bunny and I'll let him know to wait to come to our house until you're home. She kept asking what's going on, and I said I don't know. I kept repeating I love you, and we're going to get you home as soon as possible.

MR. PERHALLA: So your next contact with your children would have been, then, in the visits?

MS. COLEMAN: The next—first visit.

MR. PERHALLA: Okay, and you've already testified that you decided not to take one, at least exercise, one visit because you didn't want to give up your recording device, correct?

MS. COLEMAN: That was... yeah, I guess that was a choice.

MR. PERHALLA: Were there other visits that you had to give up because you didn't want to give up the recording equipment?

MS. COLEMAN: The following visit, that Sunday before the visit, Angela Andriacchi had called us and said the visit was cancelled.

MR. PERHALLA: And this was after they found out you were recording?

MS. COLEMAN: Yes. Can I get a tissue?

MR. PERHALLA: Who made the decision to bring the recording devices into visits?

MS. COLEMAN: After the emergency hearing, me and Rob decided that we needed to protect ourselves so we had gotten a recording. We both decided, agreed upon each other.

MR. PERHALLA: Yet you never told anyone you were recording them, at least, initially. Correct?

MS. COLEMAN: No.

MR. PERHALLA: Did you ever tell anyone you were recording them?

MS. COLEMAN: Our attorney was aware of it.

MR. PERHALLA: Just your attorney? No one else?

MS. COLEMAN: No. Not at the beginning.

MR. PERHALLA: No one from Child and Family Services?

MS. COLEMAN: No.

MR. PERHALLA: So the recording devices were not kept in the open; they were hidden in parcels, your bags, or whatever you were taking into places. Correct?

MS. COLEMAN: Yeah. Well, our bags had openings in them so, if you can look clearly, you would have seen them.

MR. PERHALLA: That's all I have, thank you.

THE COURT: Mr. Findlay, are you going to reserve the right to call her?

MR. FINDLAY: I'm going to reserve, yes.

THE COURT: Do you have questions for Mrs. Coleman?

MS. WITTLA: Just a couple, your Honor.

THE COURT: Proceed.

MS. WITTLA: Mrs. Coleman, isn't it true that the conversation about the Easter Bunny happened at the first supervised visitation in Gogebic County?

MS. COLEMAN: No. I told her in the car.

MS. WITTLA: The night that they were.....

MS. COLEMAN: ... the night they were removed.

MS. WITTLA: Mrs. Coleman, isn't it also true that the night that Caitlyn and Ashley were removed, that you went downstairs and told Caitlyn, "I'm never going to see you again?"

MS. COLEMAN: No.

MS. WITTLA: And then she started cyring?

MS. COLEMAN: She was crying. I heard her and Ashley crying all the way down the stairs, when they first left the room.

MS. WITTLA: They started crying when they first left the room?

MS. COLEMAN: Yes.

MS. WITTLA: They cried all the way down the stairs?

MS. COLEMAN: I heard children crying, so I'm assuming it was our children that were crying.

MS. WITTLA: Because at three in the morning there weren't any other kids around that you saw?

MS. COLEMAN: Yeah.

MS. WITTLA: When the police officers were taking things for the children from the room; did they ask you at any point in time if you would help them?

MS. COLEMAN: Not at first. But I remember being downstairs, I think before I spoke to the kids, they had asked for some personal belongings, and then I gave them their blankets. And Caitlyn had two ponies, my little pony toys, that she was playing with. And Ashley had her baby doll.

MS. WITTLA: Because you got those things for the children?

MS. COLEMAN: I can't remember if I went up to get them or if Robert came down, but I remember going into the car and giving Caitlyn her ponies and telling her to hold on to those and keep them close to her.

MS. WITTLA: Who was it who got the car seats out of your vehicle to give to the DHS?

MS. COLEMAN: I don't know. I'm assuming it was one of the police officers. When I got to the car where the kids were, the car seat was already in there, and then when after the kids had left, when I went back up to the room, a police officer handed me the car keys.

MS. WITTLA: So is it your testimony then, that the police got your car keys without your knowledge?

MS. COLEMAN: Yes.

MS. WITTLA: And you're not sure if they took the seat out of your car because it wasn't you?

MS. COLEMAN: It wasn't me.

MS. WITTLA: Did you give anybody permission to take the car seat out of your vehicle?

MS. COLEMAN: No.

MS. WITTLA: When the police officers first entered the room, you indicated that you're the one who took a chain off the door?

MS. COLEMAN: Yeah.

MS. WITTLA: So you were standing when they first came in?

MS. COLEMAN: Yes.

MS. WITTLA: Where was Robert?

MS. COLEMAN: He was still in bed. I think he was still sleeping or half asleep.

MS. WITTLA: Was there a point in time when he got out of bed?

MS. COLEMAN: Yeah, after everyone barged in. I know when the police first walked in, I was calling for Rob to wake up.

MS. WITTLA: Did he wake up?

MS. COLEMAN: Yeah, well obviously, with all these... everyone barging in your room, you would think you would wake up.

MS. WITTLA: Were they being loud?

MS. COLEMAN: Well lights being, you know, turned on when it's pitch dark, and I'm assuming, it was loud.

MS. WITTLA: Well, you were there. You don't have to assume, do you?

MS. COLEMAN: No.

MS. WITTLA: Was it loud or no?

MS. COLEMAN: I think so. I....

MS. WITTLA: How many police officers entered your room?

MS. COLEMAN: At least nine that were.... that I've read in reports. There was quite a few.

MS. WITTLA: And you think there were more than that?

MS. COLEMAN: The entire motel was surrounded; so if there was nine that went into our room, and then when I went outside there was more around the building, so all the police reports I've read, there was a least nine listed.

MS. WITTLA: But your testimony today is that you think that they had more than that?

MS. COLEMAN: Yeah, there were.

MS. WITTLA: After Rob woke up and I guess got up, did he get out of bed, move around the room?

MS. COLEMAN: No. There was like two police officers that stood right next to Rob, not allowing him to get up.

MS. WITTLA: So what was he doing when the police officers came into the room then, and were there for a while?

MS. COLEMAN: He just sat there.

MS. WITTLA: You mentioned a document that was handed to you, or I think you said they threw a piece of paper at you?

MS. COLEMAN: Yeah.

MS. WITTLA: The piece of paper was the order allowing for the removal of the children?

MS. COLEMAN: Yes.

MS. WITTLA: Did you keep that paper?

MS. COLEMAN: Yes.

MS. WITTLA: Okay, Robert didn't read it?

MS. COLEMAN: Well I didn't read it at the time either.

MS. WITTLA: Nobody read it then?

MS. COLEMAN: No one read it. He just gave me a piece of paper and said I've got a court order to take your kids and.....

MS. WITTLA: Okay, so you get this piece of paper, you set it down somewhere or something....

MS. COLEMAN: ... I had it in my hand. Everything was in such a hurry that I didn't have a chance to sit down and read it.

MS. WITTLA: And you were there the entire time?

MS. COLEMAN: Yes.

MS. WITTLA: And you didn't see Robert reading it either?

MS. COLEMAN: No.

MS. WITTLA: So Robert's sitting on the bed. Do you remember telling Robert that he should call your attorney?

MS. COLEMAN: Yes, I kept telling him, "Call Pope"— who was our attorney at that time.

MS. WITTLA: How long would you say that the CPS worker was in the room, gathering up the children and their coats; that sort of thing; and then leaving again?

MS. COLEMAN: It was just a few minutes. It was in and out, and.....

MS. WITTLA: And how long before they left from the time that they originally entered the room?

MS. COLEMAN: I know, as soon as they barged in, they took the kids; it was probably, maybe five minutes, ten at the most, and you know, as soon as they got the kids out of the room, then they were kind of relaxed on letting us move around.

MS. WITTLA: How long after that until they cleared the scene; that they left with the children?

MS. COLEMAN: When we went downstairs,it was probably maybe ten minutes, fifteen minutes, something like that.

MS. WITTLA: So from beginning to end we're talking about twenty minutes of time?

MS. COLEMAN: Something like that, everything went so fast.

MS. WITTLA: So during that period of time, they came to the room, took the children out of the room, and went downstairs almost immediately?

MS. COLEMAN: Yes.

MS. WITTLA: Then they were downstairs for a while when you and Robert were saying your good-byes?

MS. COLEMAN: Yes.

MS. WITTLA: You stated that you begged the DHS worker to say a proper good-bye. Did she indicate to you that she wasn't going to let you say good-bye to your children?

MS. COLEMAN: Well, the kids were already being rushed off outside, so, you know, I wanted to hold them and she wouldn't let me, and I said can I at least say a proper good-bye?

MS. WITTLA: When they were rushed out of the room, did they walk under their own power or were they carried?

MS. COLEMAN: They were carried.

MS. WITTLA: Both of them?

MS. COLEMAN: I do believe so. I remember seeing the DHS worker carrying Ashley and I saw a police officer carrying Caitlyn.

MS. WITTLA: And your memory is clear on this. It's no fuzziness?

MS. COLEMAN: Yes.

MS. WITTLA: DHS worker, Ashley; police officer, Caitlyn?

MS. COLEMAN: Yes.

MS. WITTLA: I have nothing further.

THE COURT: Did you have anything Mr. Perhalla?

MR. PERHALLA: No, thanks your Honor.

THE COURT: And ma'am, you may step down. And your next witness is?

MS. WITTLA: My next witness will be Bonnie Huttunen.

Following the swearing in of Bonnie Huttunen, who was the DHS worker who came with police to the raid of our room, the testimony began:

MS. WITTLA: Would you please state your name for the record?

MS. HUTUNEN: Bonnie Huttunen, H-U-T-T-U-N-E-N.

MS. WITTLA: And your current occupation?

MS. HUTUNEN: I'm a children's services worker for the Michigan Department of Human Services.

MS. WITTLA: What county do you work out of?

MS. HUTUNEN: I work out of Baraga County.

MS. WITTLA: Is Baraga connected with Houghton, like a duel county type thing?

MS. HUTUNEN: We're a tri-county; Baraga, Houghton, Keweenaw.

MS. WITTLA: So on-call, you could end up in any one of those counties?

MS. HUTUNEN: Yes, when I'm on call, I'm on call for all three counties.

MS. WITTLA: How long have you worked in this field?

MS. HUTUNEN: Nine years, ten months.

MS. WITTLA: Do you know Caitlyn Brag and Ashley Coleman?

MS. HUTUNEN: I've had the opportunity to meet them, yes.

MS. WITTLA: Where did you first meet them?

MS. HUTUNEN: I met them on March 15th at approximately three o'clock in the morning, when the Houghton Sheriff's Department executed a warrant to obtain custody of the two children, at the Best Western Crown Hotel in Hancock, Michigan.

MS. WITTLA: Were you on-call that night?

MS. HUTUNEN: I was, yes.

MS. WITTLA: Now you just stated that this happened at the Best Western Copper Crown in Hancock. Did you meet up with law enforcement there before you saw the children?

MS. HUTUNEN: Yes I did. When I arrived at the hotel, I went into the door and the police were downstairs in the lobby, and they briefed me about the situation and we proceeded upstairs to the room.

MS. WITTLA: How many people proceeded upstairs to the room?

MS. HUTUNEN: There were eight police officers, myself, and a maintenance man from the hotel.

MS. WITTLA: Why the maintenance man?

MS. HUTUNEN: The maintenance man... the police had arranged ahead of time to have the maintenance man knock on the door, and he knocked on the door and said maintenance.

MS. WITTLA: So you were there when he did this?

MS. HUTUNEN: Yes.

MS. WITTLA: So when the maintenance man knocked on the door and said maintenance, was the door opened from the inside?

MS. HUTUNEN: A female, Janet Coleman, came to the door and Deputy Kowalski informed her of why they were there.

MS. WITTLA: But at this point in time the door is open?

MS. HUTUNEN: Yes, she answered the door.

MS. WITTLA: So when the maintenance man knocked on the door, Janet Coleman opened the door?

MS. HUTUNEN: Yes.

MS. WITTLA: The maintenance didn't open it?

MS. HUTUNEN: No.

MS. WITTLA: Door wasn't forced?

MS. HUTUNEN: No.

MS. WITTLA: After the deputy informs Janet Coleman why they're there, how many people would you say from your group of eight police officers, you, and a maintenance man, actually entered the room?

MS. HUTUNEN: At the most that entered the room, the maintenance man left; there was approximately four police officers that went into the room, and then I went into the room, so there was five of us total, at the most, in the room at one time.

MS. WITTLA: Do you know where the other officers went? Or were they just kind of hanging in the hall or?

MS. HUTUNEN: They were in the hallway, and then one did leave.

MS. WITTLA: When you first entered the room, where was Janet Coleman located?

MS. HUTUNEN: When I first entered the room, Janet was walking around, pacing, and she was, if you walk, she was at the end of the room from the door. She was back here, and there were two beds, side by side, like a typical motel room, and she was back over by the bed, towards the girls.

MS. WITTLA: At the far end of the room from where the door was?

MS. HUTUNEN: Yeah.

MS. WITTLA: And where was Robert Coleman?

MS. HUTUNEN: He was sitting in a chair by the first bed right when you walked in.

MS. WITTLA: Did he seem awake?

MS. HUTUNEN: Yeah, he was kind of groggy, but he was reading the paperwork that the police officers had given him, and Janet was pacing the room stating, "Call Pope."

MS. WITTLA: And where were Caitlyn and Ashley?

MS. HUTUNEN: Caitlyn and Ashley were laying on the bed sleeping, the one furthest away from the door, and Caitlyn was kind of waking up a little bit, and Ashley was sleeping.

MS. WITTLA: When you entered the room, did you ask for the parents' cooperation in collecting any of the children's personal belongings to take with you?

MS. HUTUNEN: Yes, we did. I asked—it was winter time—I asked if they could get the children's clothes together, favorite toy, something common that we ask when we have to remove children. And we were told that we were not taking any of that stuff.

MS. WITTLA: Who told you you're not taking anything?

MS. HUTUNEN: Janet Coleman.

MS. WITTLA: Did Robert Coleman have an opinion or—the question wasn't addressed to him?

MS. HUTUNEN: It wasn't addressed to him. He was reading. He was still sitting, talking to Dan Kowalski.

MS. WITTLA: What was Janet's demeanor when she said, "No, you can't take anything?"

MS. HUTUNEN: She was kind of emotional, I mean, she, she wasn't.... she was angry, mad, frantically walk-

ing around. She wasn't crying or anything, she was just worried about calling Pope.

MS. WITTLA: Would you describe her as being sad at that point?

MS. HUTUNEN: No.

MS. WITTLA: Okay, she was angry, mad?

MS. HUTUNEN: Yes.

MS. WITTLA: How long would you say you were in the room with the kids?

MS. HUTUNEN: In the room, probably only ten minutes, total.

MS. WITTLA: And from the time you entered that room until the time you left with the children, you left the Copper Crown, approximately how much time?

MS. HUTUNEN: Twenty, twenty-five minutes that I was there. It ended up being a little longer. Twenty-five.

MS. WITTLA: When you entered the hotel room, the kids were asleep. Who found or dressed the kids with winter items?

MS. HUTUNEN: The police officer and I when we could see that there were boots and jackets in the little closet. It was like a closet area where you hang clothes; typical motel room by the bathroom. The boots and the coats were there, so we got the boots and the coats and we put them on the children. I did ask again, and I kind of was told no, and kind of got the impression like you basically; you're taking them; you supply it and.....

MS. WITTLA: Wait one second. You asked what again?

MS. HUTUNEN: If we could take some of their clothes, shirts, pants, underwear, diapers. Ashley was a toddler in diapers. Bottles... and I was told no by Janet.

MS. WITTLA: Okay and then when you were told no by Janet you the impression, what?

MS. HUTUNEN: That, "Don't you have these things?" You're taking them, don't you have these things? She referred to that as when we had talked about getting a car seat, do you have Ashley's car seat, and well, don't you have it?

MS. WITTLA: So your impression from the little bit of conversation you had with her was that if you're taking the kids in your care, you supply what they need?

MS. HUTUNEN: Correct.

MS. WITTLA: Speaking of the car seat, did you get Ashley's car seat?

MS. HUTUNEN: Yes.

MS. WITTLA: How did you get Ashley's car seat?

MS. HUTUNEN: We went downstairs, and then, actually a police officer asked her to get the car seat, and she did go get it. At that point Mr. Coleman had come down and I had put the car seat in the car. We had a toddler seat for Caitlyn and she was put in that.

MS. WITTLA: So did you see Janet get the car seat out of their vehicle?

MS. HUTUNEN: Yes.

MS. WITTLA: And the toddler seat, I'm assuming like a booster chair for a bigger kid? For Caitlyn?

MS. HUTUNEN: Yes.

MS. WITTLA: After the kids have their coats, boots on, and you've made your second request to have some personal items for them, is that when you took them out of the room?

MS. HUTUNEN: Yeah. The deputy and I said we're going to leave now. They asked if they could say good-bye and I said of course. Caitlyn walked out of the room with me, holding my hand. I told her my name is Bonnie, and she said, "Oh, that's a pretty name." She was fine. Ashley was pretty clueless, tired, she was out of, just out kind of. We walked down the stairs and I buckled Caitlyn in, and I told Caitlyn that we're going for a ride; we're going to see my friend LaVerne, that was the foster home. Trying to make her feel really comfortable, and I said,

"Well, your parents have got to take care of something, it will be okay, it's not your fault."

MS. WITTLA: Now when you left the room, you said Caitlyn's holding your hand. Where is Ashley?

MS. HUTUNEN: The deputy was carrying Ashley; she was sleeping, kind of out.

MS. WITTLA: Okay, so she wasn't awake enough to go down the steps herself or anything?

MS. HUNUNEN: No.

MS. WITTLA: You indicated that you buckled Caitlyn in the car. Who buckled Ashley in?

MS. HUNUNEN: Mr. Coleman, Robert Coleman buckled her in. He was... it seemed like he was more concerned about Ashley, because he was crying, buckled her in, and then that's when he offered diapers and "Can I go get her bottle, her sippy cup, some diapers, her blanket?" And I'm like, "yeah", and so he never said anything to Caitlyn; he went upstairs and got stuff for Ashley.

MS. WITTLA: Did you see him again after he went upstairs?

MS. HUNUNEN: No, I didn't.

MS. WITTLA: Now I'm picturing a vehicle that has four doors in it. Is that....

MS. HUNUNEN: ... Correct, correct. It was a Ford Taurus, four door.

MS. WITTLA: So Caitlyn is on one side, Ashley is on the other, close to the doors?

MS. HUNUNEN: Correct.

MS. WITTLA: Did you see Robert Coleman go to the other side of the vehicle to talk to Caitlyn at all?

MS. HUNUNEN: No, he didn't.

MS. WITTLA: Were you within ear shot of these children the whole time?

MS. HUNUNEN: I was right by the car; right by the trunk area, yes. I was on the driver's side; Caitlyn was on the driver's side, behind the driver. Ashley was on the passenger side in the back seat, and he was over on that side.

MS. WITTLA: So you could hear him speaking to Ashley?

MS. HUNUNEN: Yes.

MS. WITTLA: And then he said to you, "I'll get these things for Ashley," and he left?

MS. HUNUNEN: Yes.

MS. WITTLA: Did Janet Coleman come down to say good-bye to the children?

MS. HUNUNEN: Yeah. She said good-bye to Caitlyn, and I was standing right next to her. And Caitlyn was fine when we got her buckled in, she was okay, and then when Janet came, Janet told her that "You're never going to see me again and you're going to live somewhere else." I immediately told her, I said, "Don't tell her that." And she goes, "That's the truth, you don't know how Gogebic works." And I said, "Well, you're upsetting her." Caitlyn just started crying, became visibly upset, and then State Trooper Rhoda went and got a teddy bear from his car, because now at this point she's crying, and we got a teddy bear for her to make her comfortable, and then another police officer got a blanket; so she had a blanket too. So she was upset after that point.

MS. WITTLA: Did anyone ever come back down with personal things for Caitlyn?

MS. HUNUNEN: No, and actually the police officer ended up going upstairs to get the items that Mr. Coleman was talking about; the diapers and the blanket, because Mr. Coleman ended up having a panic attack or something and an ambulance had to be called. And so he went upstairs and retrieved the blanket and the diapers and a sippy cup for Ashley.

MS. WITTLA: But it was only stuff for Ashley?

MS. HUNUNEN: Yes.

MS. WITTLA: The officer wasn't getting anything for Caitlyn?

MS. HUNUNEN: No.

MS. WITTLA: Were either Caitlyn or Ashley upset before Janet talked to Caitlyn?

MS. HUNUNEN: No. Caitlyn was fine. I said we were going to my friend's, she was awake and talking and I talked about where does she go to school and just some general things and told her about LaVerne was my friend, and she was fine. Ashley was pretty much out, clueless.

MS. WITTLA: Okay, so just talking about Caitlyn then; when you walked out of the room with her; went down the stairs, went out to the car, she's just having this chit-chat conversation with you about your friend LaVerne and where she goes to school and that sort of stuff?

MS. HUNUNEN: Yes.

MS. WITTLA: She didn't seem upset or crying or?

MS. HUNUNEN: No, she wasn't.

MS. WITTLA: She didn't seem scared to you?

MS. HUNUNEN: No, she was a very polite little girl and okay.

MS. WITTLA: So would you say she was shy or outgoing or?

MS. HUNUNEN: She wasn't shy, because she would be a little bit more of an outgoing girl, and considering at the time she was pretty talkative to me.

MS. WITTLA: When Janet Coleman was talking to Caitlyn about Caitlyn never seeing her again, what was Janet's demeanor?

MS. HUNUNEN: She still had this; she was very upset, you know. Just... an angry, she was angry.

MS. WITTLA: Did she stop when you asked her to?

MS. HUNUNEN: No. Well, she didn't say anything after that, but she did say, "You don't know how Gogebic County works."

Here is a place where the witness committed perjury! She had just been asked if, after she asked Janet to stop, if Janet stopped, and she said "No." And then she admits Janet did stop, but first had to fire off her rehearsed answer that Janet said, "You don't know how Gogebic County works." But I would remind readers that her first claim was that Janet made that remark before she reprimanded Janet. So now it comes after her reprimand? Of course not! First off, Janet never made such a remark, but even if she had, Ms. Hununen contradicted herself as to when the remark would have been made, and if, in fact, Janet didn't say anything after that, she perjured herself in saying "No" to Tracie's question.

MS. WITTLA: And how long was it before Caitlyn calmed down again and stopped crying?

MS. HUNUNEN: It was about fifteen minutes into the car ride when we left. I could hear her crying back there, and I was trying to comfort her. She named her teddy bear Cuddles at first, and then I asked her about what's your teddy bear's name again? And it was Grumpy. But she was sobbing a little bit in the back, I could hear crying. I told her it's going to be okay, and so tried to comfort her the best I could. And then she eventually fell asleep, probably twenty minutes into the car ride.

MS. WITTLA: Did you take the kids all the way to LaVerne's house?

MS. HUNUNEN: Yeah, it was arranged that I was just transporting them to the Sheriff's department to meet Gary Olkonen from Gogebic County Department of Human Services, but LaVerne's house was so close and I knew where it was. It didn't make sense to get the girls up and transport. I said I would drive over there with them and take them over there. I got them out of the car, Gary got Ashley out and I got Caitlyn up and she actually walked out and she was in that happy mood again, kind of how she was when I first met her, and I said, "Oh, this is my friend LaVerne," and she was, "Hi," and then, you know, she was saying hi to their dog and, you know, I said, "Well, do you want to see where you're sleeping?" Kind of acclimated her with the house; this is the bathroom and I didn't leave right away, I stayed to help her try to fit in, and so she did very well. When I was there and left, no distress at that point, with either girl. Ashley was actually walking around then too.

MS. WITTLA: She was more awake then?

MS. HUNUNEN: Uh-huh.

MS. WITTLA: Did you have any interviews with either Caitlyn or Ashley?

MS. HUNUNEN: No, I was just transporting them, and you know, I just talked general what's your name; where do you go to school; just no official interview of anything.

MS. WITTLA: Have you seen them since that day?

MS. HUNUNEN: No.

MS. WITTLA: Have you had anything at all to do with this case since the removal?

MS. HUNUNEN: I had to testify at a preliminary hearing.

MS. WITTLA: Aside from that, you haven't?

MS. HUNUNEN: No.

MS. WITTLA: You're not assigned to this case?

MS. HUNUNEN: No.

MS. WITTLA: You were just involved because you were on-call, and it was your county?

MS. HUNUNEN: I was on-call and they needed a transporter; that was my involvement.

MS. WITTLA: You've been doing this work for almost ten years, when you've had to remove kids from their homes and their caregivers in the last ten years, would you say that the parents who had been present at that time, typically reacted the way Robert and Janet did, or typically did not.

MS. HUNUNEN: Typically, they don't act like that. My experience has been that the parents are like, you know, "Well, you need to go; it's not your fault; kind of comforting, you know; it will be okay; you didn't do anything wrong; you know, explain to them where they are going, and I've never had anybody kind of "You'll never see me again, and you won't talk to me again," in my ten years.

MS. WITTLA: She's also said, "You won't talk to me again?"

MS. HUNUNEN: She said "You're going to go live somewhere else and you won't be able to talk to me," I believe, but it was....

MS. WITTLA: Did you do anything to try and comfort Caitlyn in that regard, about talking to her mom?

MS. HUNUNEN: I did. Actually I told Caitlyn, I told Janet, I said, "Well what's your cell phone number," and I said, "So Caitlyn can call you," and to kind of show Caitlyn that, no, you will talk to your mom again. And so Janet did give me her cell phone number, and I said, "Well I'm going to give this to LaVerne and then you can call in the morning when you wake up to make sure your mom knows you made it okay." And so I did take her number and tried to show Caitlyn that no, you're going to get to see her again, and you know, it's going to be okay; you kow this, that you'll get to talk to her, and I did get the number and I did give it to LaVerne and told her.

MS. WITTLA: Was that a number that you requested or that was offered to you?

MS. HUNUNEN: What was that?

MS. WITTLA: Did you have to request that number from Janet or did she say, "Here, take my number?"

MS. HUNUNEN: No, I requested it to show, you know, because just kind of show Caitlyn, no you.... that's not what's going to happen; that no, you will.... I wanted her to see that, no, that's not what's going to happen; you will get to talk to her. I asked for the number and she seen me write it down, and take it. And then she seen me give it to LaVerne too, and I even reiterate that at the foster home, that, you know, LaVerne's got your mom's cell phone number, that you can call her when you wake up, okay? So she knew about it and she was okay at the foster home, you know, to try to show that you will get to see your mom again, because it's traumatic, you know, if you say something like that.

MS. WITTLA: Did you see Janet interact with Ashley at all when they were out of the car?

MS. HUNUNEN: No, she was more attentive too, it was Caitlyn. Robert was more attentive to Ashley.

MS. WITTLA: Was Ashley, I think you described this already, but Ashley was pretty much asleep from the time she was removed from the hotel room, in the car, didn't really wake up much until she got to the foster home?

MS. HUNUNEN: That's correct.

MS. WITTLA: So whether or not her parents were talking to her, she may not have noticed?

MS. HUNUNEN: Yeah, she was pretty; she was just clueless, just... you know, because she was sleeping.

MS. WITTLA: Okay, just like a limp baby in the car seat?

MS. HUNUNEN: Yeah.

MS. WITTLA: Of the cases you have dealt with where there's been a removal, do most of those kids go home?

MS. HUNUNEN: I would say eighty-five to ninety percent of the children that we have removed because the goal of our agency is to reunite. That's our ultimate goal; eighty-five, ninety percent definitely do go home unless there's something very traumatic.

MS. WITTLA: Do you recall anything else that either Robert or Janet said to Caitlyn?

MS. HUNUNEN: No.

MS. WITTLA: Okay, fair enough. Thank you.

THE COURT: Mr. Perhalla?

MR. PERHALLA: Thanks your Honor. Just so we're clear on this, you get into the hotel room and you go to Caitlyn or, and the police officer goes to Ashley?

MS. HUNUNEN: Caitlyn was kind of up already and I was talking to her. Ashley was sleeping and yeah, I put on Caitlyn's boots and he was putting on Ashley's boots and jacket.

MR. PERHALLA: And she just took to conversing with you right away?

MS. HUNUNEN: Yeah.

MR. PERHALLA: Did she show any reluctance in leaving with you?

MS. HUNUNEN: No, not at all.

MR. PERHALLA: Okay, she just walked with you? I mean, it sounds like you had to go downstairs, this was an upper?

MS. HUNUNEN: Yeah, we were on the second floor.

MR. PERHALLA: Okay, so you go downstairs into the car and she's just chatting with you?

MS. HUNUNEN: Correct.

MR. PERHALLA: She's fully awake?

MS. HUNUNEN: Correct.

MR. PERHALLA: By that time, and she continues on with the chatty demeanor until her mother makes that statement to her?

MS. HUNUNEN: Correct.

MR. PERHALLA: And then when you get to LaVerne's house, she's back to her chatty self?

MS. HUNUNEN: Correct.

MR. PERHALLA: When you leave are they sleeping or just awake?

MS. HUNUNEN: At LaVerne's house?

MR. PERHALLA: Yes.

MS. HUNUNEN: They were just getting ready and getting tucked into bed and I could hear them talking in there actually.

MR. PERHALLA: So the entire time that you're at LaVerne's, Caitlyn is her usual chatty, talkative self?

MS. HUNUNEN: Correct, what I've seen of her.

MR. PERHALLA: That's all your Honor.

THE COURT: Mr. Findlay?

MR. FINDLAY: Thanks your Honor. (To Ms. Hununen): The Colemans were located at 12:30 a.m. that morning, weren't they?

MS. HUNUNEN: I'm not exactly sure what time they were located; I received a call at approximately, it was after two o'clock; and I live about forty minutes away from where they were located.

MR. FINDLAY: So if I told you though that they were located at, according to a DHS report itself, that they were located at 12:30 a.m., and staying in a hotel in, in a Best Western in Hougton, Michigan, would you disagree with that?

MS. HUNUNEN: I couldn't verify it; I don't know.

MR. FINDLAY: It it's....

MS. HUNUNEN: ... if it's in a report, I guess it's correct, yes.

MR. FINDLAY: And you were contacted at 1:15 a.m.?

MS. HUNUNEN: Oh! Okay.

MR. FINDLAY: Actually the call was made at 1:05 a.m. Houghton County DHS called service and asked for a Houghton County on-call worker to contact Gogebic County on-call worker. At 1:15 a.m., asked Bonnie to contact Houghton County as the assistance is needed; she was willing to transport to Ontonagon? Was it 1:15?

MS. HUNUNEN: It could be varied in time there. I thought it was closer to two actually, but....

MR. FINDLAY: Okay, well this says 1:15; do you think this is correct?

MS. WITTLA: Your Honor, I'd just ask the author of the report....

THE COURT: ... and just to clarify is it a Gogebic or an Ontonagon report because of the different time zones? I mean Gogebic or Houghton report because of different time zones?

MR. FINDLAY: This is an Ontonagon....

MS. HUNUNEN: That's the difference then, yeah. It would've been 2:15 my time; I'm on Eastern Standard time.

MR. FINDLAY: Okay, 2:15 your time?

MS. HUNUNEN: Yes.

MR. FINDLAY: So then you went directly from there to the hotel?

MS. HUNUNEN: Correct.

MR. FINDLAY: And this happened at 3:00 a.m. in the morning, correct?

MS. HUNUNEN: Correct.

MR. FINDLAY: And there were at least, were there eight officers? You say there were eight officers that showed up at the scene?

MS. HUNUNEN: There were.

MR. FINDLAY: These were all uniformed officers?

MS. HUNUNEN: Yes, two from the Sheriff's department; two from the state; two from Hancock City Police; and two from Houghton state police.

MR. FINDLAY: All uniformed? Guns, badges, the whole works?

MS. HUNUNEN: Yes.

MR. FINDLAY: Marked cars?

MS. HUNUNEN: Yes.

MR. FINDLAY: Three of four cars at least? Eight officers, there would be two per car?

MS. HUNUNEN: Five, I think.

MR. FINDLAY: Five, okay. And according to you, you were granted entry into the room. Correct?

MS. HUNUNEN: Yes.

MR. FINDLAY: You said that Janet Coleman opened the door?

MS. HUNUNEN: Yeah. I wasn't the one that knocked on the door; the maintenance man did, and then Dan, Officer Kowalski went into the home, but the.....

MR. FINDLAY: Okay, so you had the maintenance man; this wasn't a maintenance call though, was it?

MS. HUNUNEN: No.

MR. FINDLAY: So this was a little bit of deceit to get the Colemans to open the door, correct?

MS. HUNUNEN: It was set up ahead, before I got there, with the police.

MR. FINDLAY: And deceitful to get the Colemans to open up the door, correct?

MS. HUNUNEN: I guess it would appear that way, yes.

MR. FINDLAY: Well it would appear that way because it WASN'T a maintenance call, was it?

MS. HUNUNEN: Yes.

She lied. No maintenance was done. She perjured herself here.

MR. FINDLAY: Okay, so it was a little of a trick to get the Colemans to open the door?

MS. WITTLA: Objection, your Honor. Asked and answered.

THE COURT: Well, let's get to the final answer, so...

MR. FINDLAY: It was a bit of a trick to get the Colemans to open the door, correct?

MS. HUNUNEN: Yeah.

MR. FINDLAY: Okay, how are parents that are; their hotel room is barged into on, at 3:00 a.m.; were basically tricked into opening the door; how are they supposed to act?

MS. HUNUNEN: I, I don't know that. I've never had that happen.

MR. FINDLAY: So you would agree with me that; that it's pretty hard to predict how any given parent is going to act, react. Is that fair?

MS. HUNUNEN: Yeah.

MR. FINDLAY: Do you agree with me that it would be a pretty traumatic experience for anybody, wouldn't it?

MS. HUNUNEN: Yeah.

MR. FINDLAY: And not only just; and that's just the barging in at 3:00 a.m.; and you know, tricking somebody to get their door open, but then going in and taking their kids; do you think that would be a pretty traumatic incident for anybody?

MS. HUNUNEN: For anybody, yeah.

MR. FINDLAY: And the Colemans were, in fact, upset by this, weren't they?

MS. HUNUNEN: Yeah, Janet was pacing around; she appeared very angry and she wanted to call Pope, who apparently was their attorney.

MR. FINDLAY: I'd appreciate it if you would just answer my questions. I mean, if Ms. Wittla wants you to say something now, she can get up and, you know, let you fill it in. You think it's unreasonable or unusual for a parent to want to call their attorney when they're basically having their children taken away in the middle of the night, at 3:00 a.m.?

MS. HUNUNEN: Yeah, because I don't think an attorney would be available at that time.

MR. FINDLAY: I'm sorry?

MS. HUNUNEN: Yeah, because I don't think an attorney would be available at that time.

MR. FINDLAY: Well, do you KNOW whether somebody might be or not?

MS. HUNUNEN: I don't know, but....

MR. FINDLAY: ... you think it would be strange that a parent would want to talk to an attorney at that point, to know what their legal rights are?

MS. HUNUNEN: I guess not, if....

MR. FINDLAY: ... it doesn't seem unreasonable to you that they would want to call their attorney?

MS. HUNUNEN: ... I guess, under the circumstances.

MR. FINDLAY: Sorry?

MS. HUNUNEN: Under the circumstances, I guess.

MR. FINDLAY: Okay, so that's NOT an unreasonable thing to do. You want to call your attorney, is it?

MS. HUNUNEN: Yeah, I guess.

MR. FINDLAY: And it's my understanding and your testimony that you go into this room, you say there are four officers that went into the room. Correct?

MS. HUNUNEN: Yeah.

MR. FINDLAY: And they went over to the bed to make sure that Robert Coleman didn't get in the way?

MS. HUNUNEN: They what?

MR. FINDLAY: They went over to the bed that Robert Coleman was in to make sure that he didn't get in the way?

MS. WITTLA: Objection, your Honor. It's a mischaracterization of what this witness has testified to.

MR. FINDLAY: That's just cross examination, I can....

THE COURT: ... He is on cross, I guess we have a couple different versions out on the record, so....

MS. WITTLA: ... not from this witness though, your Honor; this witness has been sequestered and does not know what was previously testified to.

THE COURT: Well, but it's cross. He's got some latitude to phrase things how he wants, so, go ahead if you want to repeat the question.

MR. FINDLAY: Thank you.

THE COURT: But I will caution you, you're kind of doing what you objected to the Prosecutor doing, running over the witness before she answers.

MR. FINDLAY: I apologize for doing that.

THE COURT: Give her a minute to answer.

MR. FINDLAY: Four officers came into the room. Correct? According to you?

MS. HUNUNEN: Yes.

MR. FINDLAY: How many went over to the bed to make sure that Mr. Coleman didn't move around the room?

MS. HUNUNEN: There wasn't any, like surrounding him, like, for that reason.

MR. FINDLAY: I didn't say surrounding him. How many went over to the bed to make sure that he didn't get up?

MS. HUNUNEN: He wasn't in the bed. He was sitting in a chair.

MR. FINDLAY: How many went over to him to make sure that he didn't interfere or get involved in this?

MS. HUNUNEN: There was Dan, Officer Kowalski was talking to him and then there was one on the side, and then there were two... they were over on this end of the room, and the other two; there was one by the door and then one over by where I was.

MR. FINDLAY: Are you saying that there wasn't a concern in terms of what the reaction of the parents might be?

MS. HUNUNEN: I don't know what you're trying....

MR. FINDLAY: ... Wasn't there a concern in terms of what their reaction to parents were, having the kids taken away in the middle of the night would be?

MS. HUNUNEN: Well, I'm sure there would be a concern, but I didn't.... I didn't get the impression that they were guarding him like, you know, he was sitting down. He was reading the report, and....

MR. FINDLAY: ... They had, they had eight officers though. Correct?

MS. HUNUNEN: That's correct.

MR. FINDLAY: They had eight officers. Isn't that a reflection that going into somebody's hotel room at 3:00 a.m., in the middle of the night, taking their children, is a very potentially volatile situation?

MS. HUNUNEN: I would agree that there's potential for anybody.

MR. FINDLAY: And so it's a safety precaution against the potential, correct?

MS. HUNUNEN: Yes.

MR. FINDLAY: So I'm assuming that either people think it's a realistic potential, or maybe it's even happened before, that parents have reacted violently when having that done to them. Correct?

MS. HUNUNEN: I would imagine. I wouldn't know, though.

MR. FINDLAY: But in this case, the Colemans didn't react that way, did they?

MS. HUNUNEN: No.

MR. FINDLAY: In fact there was—you weren't fooled at all in carrying out what you went there to do, were you?

MS. HUNUNEN: Except for getting personal items.

MR. FINDLAY: But you did get the personal items, I thought you said.

MS. HUNUNEN: The deputy went up to get diapers and Mr. Coleman did offer diapers and a sippy cup and a blanket. No clothes, nothing else.

MR. FINDLAY: You did have clothes. You got their jackets?

MS. HUNUNEN: We had to take those from them.

MR. FINDLAY: Okay, so in other words you had to get them, when you barged into the room; the officers went straight for and looked for their jackets; they didn't ask anybody for them; they just went and got them?

MS. HUNUNEN: They didn't barge into the room, and the jackets, we did ask for the jackets, right from the get go, right away.

MR. FINDLAY: But you didn't ask anybody, but yet you went and got them?

MS. HUNUNEN: No. We asked Janet twice, and then we had seen them when we came in, and I said that—the officer said here's the— some boots, and then I said okay, then we grabbed the jackets and the boots.

MR. FINDLAY: Okay, so you went ahead and took the jackets?

MS. HUNUNEN: And the boots.

MR. FINDLAY: And boots, okay. So you did have; it's not true when you said that there wasn't, you didn't have any personal belongings; you did. You had jackets, you had boots, you a bottle, correct?

MS. HUNUNEN: A sippy cup.

MR. FINDLAY: Okay, the report again says a bottle; you had some blankets, correct?

MS. HUNUNEN: Yeah, for Caitlyn.

MR. FINDLAY: And some toys?

MS. HUNUNEN: And there was a toy for one of them, yes.

MR. FINDLAY: Okay, so they did have personal objects that you took with you, with them?

MS. HUNUNEN: That we took, and then the officer went and got the other items.

MR. FINDLAY: Okay, and in fact, even you say that Robert offered those things to you, Robert Coleman?

MS. HUNUNEN: Downstairs, yes, before we were leaving, for Ashley.

MR. FINDLAY: Okay, now are you aware that none of the police reports, at least that I've seen, that were filed regarding this incident, say ANYTHING about Janet Coleman, about what you say that she did to the kids?

MS. HUNUNEN: I haven't seen any other documents regarding this case.

MR. FINDLAY: Okay, but are, so you, you're not aware that they don't say that?

MS. HUNUNEN: No, no.

MR. FINDLAY: Would it surprise you if I told you that they didn't say that?

MS. HUNUNEN: No, because deputy Kowalski was the lead officer, and he's the one who did the report, and when those, when Janet conveyed the information down to Caitlyn when she made those statements, deputy Kowalski was not around when that took place.

MR. FINDLAY: Well, but there were other officers around though, weren't there?

MS. HUNUNEN: Trooper Rhoda was over behind the truck, and then they were really spread out down there, so they probably would not have heard.

MR. FINDLAY: So you would be the only one who heard this?

MS. HUNUNEN: Yes.

MR. FINDLAY: Oh. This was a traumatic experience for these little girls, wasn't it?

MS. HUNUNEN: A what?

MR. FINDLAY: A traumatic experience? These little girls?

MS. HUNUNEN: It didn't appear to be. They were, you know, they.... when the police... Ashley was clueless, she was sleeping; and she had no clue; Caitlyn, you know, she was looking around, she was fine and I told her who I was and you know, just said she's not in trouble, and she, she didn't cry at all until the car incident, and then....

MR. FINDLAY: .... You don't think that having eight uniformed police officers, four of which come into the room, remove you from your parents; your parents are obviously upset; Janet Coleman, you've testified was not happy about the situation; get driven away to some place else, with no indication of when they're going to see their parents again; you don't think that would be traumatic for children; a six year old and a two year old?

MS. HUNUNEN: They never, they never seen all the police officers; the most they would have seen were four.

MR. FINDLAY: Okay, four then?

MS. HUNUNEN: So, um....

MR. FINDLAY: You don't think that would be traumatic for children at three in the morning, get yanked out of their hotel room like that?

MS. HUNUNEN: I, it could be traumatic, but they were not traumatized; they were fine when we left, and then even when we got to the foster home. Usually if it's traumatizing, it's right from the get go; my experience, you know, children are crying, you know, clinging to their mom, their dad; there was none of this. Ashley was clueless, she was sleeping, and Caitlyn was, you know, looking around and talking, and the police officers, you know, she was talking to them, and it, well, it didn't appear to me to be traumatic compared to some other, you know, because I've done several removals, and they went willingly.

MR. FINDLAY: But you yourself said that Caitlyn was crying for at least, what, twenty minutes?

MS. HUNUNEN: That was after Janet told her she wasn't going to see her again, and talk to her.

MR. FINDLAY: That, the statement that only YOU heard? That Janet made the statement that only YOU heard?

MS. HUNUNEN: Yes, and that's when she started to cry.

MR. FINDLAY: Now isn't it true that the only time that you let anybody know that the girls were upset was because of what Janet had said; that it didn't find it's way into a document or a report, or testimony, until the 18th of March? Did it?

MS. HUNUNEN: That I told anybody?

MR. FINDLAY: Yeah.

MS. HUNUNEN: No. I told the on-call— I told Gary Olkonen about it; I told Trooper Rhoda about what she said and that's when he went and got, you know, the teddy bear. I told deputy Kowalski, because I talked to him later that evening.

MR. FINDLAY: Did you put it in a report anywhere?

MS. HUNUNEN: I believe I did. My contacts would be in the contact, the Gogebic County DHS, because we can go on line and tap into their system, and I just put my contact in there. And I believe it is in there; in fact, I know it's in there.

MR. FINDLAY: Caitlyn started crying when she was in the car, correct?

MS. HUNUNEN: Not immediately, no.

MR. FINDLAY: Okay, but it was in the car that she started crying, correct?

MS. HUNUNEN: After Janet made that comment.

MR. FINDLAY: Okay, and it's in the car, but that's the vehicle that's taking her away from her parents, correct?

MS. HUNUNEN: Yes, that was our car.

MR. FINDLAY: Don't you think it's possible that the reason she started crying then was because, the fact that she's being taken away from her parents has finally sunk in?

MS. HUNUNEN: No. I think the fact of the statements, a child being told you're never going to see—you're never coming home, you're never going to see me again.

MR. FINDLAY: That's if… IF they were told that, right?

MS. HUNUNEN: They were told that .

MR. FINDLAY: But obviously there's two sides to every story. You realize that Janet Coleman denies that she said that, don't you?

MS. HUNUNEN: I don't know any other testimony.

MR. FINDLAY: Well, if I told you that Janet Coleman denies that she said that…..

MS. HUNUNEN: I would say it's a lie.

MR. FINDLAY: But you don't think that the crying starts when she's in a vehicle being driven away from the parents? You don't think that's significant? That it starts when she's in a vehicle being driven away?

MS. HUNUNEN: No, she was in a car for a while before that, you know, before all that happened, she was fine, we were talking.

MR. FINDLAY: Okay, so it's your testimony that this was no big deal to the children at all until Janet Coleman said something?

MS. HUNUNEN: To Caitlyn, yes, because she became upset.

MR. FINDLAY: Nothing further.

THE COURT: Redirect.

MS. WITTLA: I believe you indicated that you could go on line and type on to reports?

MS. HUNUNEN: Yes.

MS. WITTLA: Tell me what that means.

MS. HUNUNEN: The Department of Human Services has a state wide computer program for Children Protective Services and foster care that any county, where you have a contact, you can go in to type in the name of a case; and there's an icon; it says social work contact; and that's where the....

MR. FINDLAY: ... Your Honor, I'm going to object as to what this has to do with cross-examination; I mean, to me, redirect is supposed to be going into things that were covered in cross, and I don't... maybe I missed it, but I don't know that has to do with cross-examination.

THE COURT: Yeah, well cross did come up, as a matter of fact it was your cross, that came up with the issue of her putting it in, in to her report, so now she's picking up on that point.

MR. FINDLAY: Okay, all right, that's what I, then I missed that. Go ahead.

MS. HUNUNEN: So I'm in Baraga County, I can access Gogebic County's, the case, the Coleman case; I went in and typed social work contacts and I can put in, and it says entered by me on the computer, and it has the date, the time, who I made contact with, and it goes into the computer and it becomes a Gogebic County record.

MS. WITTLA: Your Honor, may I approach the witness?

THE COURT: Sure.

MS. WITTLA:This is a document labeled CHILDREN'S PROTECTIVE SERVICES INVESTIGATION REPORT. Have you seen the report before?

MS. HUNUNEN: I haven't seen this specific report, but this is what our reports look like.

MS. WITTLA: You're familiar with the format?

MS. HUNUNEN: Yes.

MS. WITTLA: And, I'm sorry, I forgot to look the page, did you find a page that has your contact on it?

MS. HUNUNEN: Right here.

MS. WITTLA: Okay, when you looked at that page, did you put on there, that incident with Janet upsetting Caitlyn?

MS. HUNUNEN: Yes, it says Janet told Caitlyn that she is going to live someplace else and she wouldn't see her again. I told Janet not to say that, as Caitlyn was visibly upset; Janet told me that is the truth, that you don't know how Gogebic works.

MS. WITTLA: So did you put it in the report?

MS. HUNUNEN: I did.

MS. WITTLA: In your report do you also reference a reason why the Colemans were in Hancock to begin with?

MS. HUNUNEN: I overheard Janet telling a police officer that they were there visiting a friend.

MS. WITTLA: Regarding the question of contacting an attorney; when you have had to go and remove children from their caregivers, from their parents; is it usual that they want to contact attorneys when you are there?

MS. HUNUNEN: Not usually.

MS. WITTLA: You understand that they may want to do that?

MS. HUNUNEN: Yes.

MS. WITTLA: But they're not necessarily doing it when you're there?

MS. HUNUNEN: Correct.

MS. WITTLA: Have you ever had parents start saying I'm going to contact my attorney right now when you're still there with the children?

MS. HUNUNEN: No. That was the first time I've heard anybody say that.

MS. WITTLA: What is the focus of most parents while you are still there?

MS. HUNUNEN: Usually, their focus is, you know, they're getting their stuff together so, and telling them that it's not their fault; that it will be okay, that, you know, you have to— they're usually saying you have to go with Bonnie, it will be okay, and usually they will pack up some of their clothes, and you know, ask if they can bring their toys and blankets and stuff like that, and can certain people have contact with them, like grandma, grandpa, and you know, we talk about it there, an so.

MS. WITTLA: So would you say it's fair they're "kid focused?"

MS. HUNUNEN: Yes.

MS. WITTLA: Do you know how Caitlyn and Ashley ended up with toys with them?

MS. HUNUNEN: The police officer had went upstairs and got them.

MS. WITTLA: The police officer went upstairs and got toys for Caitlyn and Ashley; just Ashley, just Caitlyn?

MS. HUNUNEN: Just Ashley and I think the deputy that carried Ashley down to the Sheriff's department; he might have grabbed a toy because Caitlyn, I thought, had some kind of toy; unless she might have took it; it was a small My Little Pony or something; so I don't know if she had that from Ashley or?

MS. WITTLA: So when you left the room with Caitlyn, was she carrying anything?

MS. HUNUNEN: No, I don't think so because she was holding my hand when we were walking down the stairs so the police officer grabbed, must have, that's the only way she got that.

MS. WITTLA: Because when the other police officer came back with the blanket, sippy cup, diapers, there was nothing there for Caitlyn?

MS. HUNUNEN: No.

MS. WITTLA: Aside from the Michigan State Police who offered Caitlyn a teddy bear, were there any other agencies that offered her anything?

MS. HUNUNEN: The Houghton City Police gave her a blanket.

MS. WITTLA: Did anyone else offer her any comfort items?

MS. HUNUNEN: No, just the teddy bear from the State Police and the blanket.

MS. WITTLA: Okay, but nothing from the parents?

MS. HUNUNEN: No.

THE COURT: Mr. Perhalla?

MR. PERHALLA: Nothing, thanks your Honor.

THE COURT: Do you have any questions, based on the Prosecutor?

MR. FINDLAY: Yes, your Honor, just real briefly, may I approach the witness?

THE COURT: Sure.

MR. FINDLAY: I believe it's from the report that— would you read to me just what I've underlined there?

MS. HUNUNEN: Janet told Caitlyn that she is going to live someplace else, and she wouldn't see her again. I told Janet not to say that as Caitlyn was visibly upset.

MR. FINDLAY: And that's, that's what you entered?

MS. HUNUNEN: That's what I wrote, yes.

MR. FINDLAY: And so you entered that on the 15th?

MS. HUNUNEN: No, I probably entered that on the 17th.

MR. FINDLAY: 17th, okay....

MS. HUNUNEN: That's the date of the contact, that date. That's the date of the time when it happened.

MR. FINDLAY: The 15th was the day, was the time that it happened?

MS. HUNUNEN: Yeah, that Saturday, and Monday I put it on.

MR. FINDLAY: Okay, and that said, "I told Janet not to say that anymore as Caitlyn was visibly upset"... that's what you said then....

MS. HUNUNEN: That's what I, yes.

MR. FINDLAY: Okay, and then read the entry from the agency; the one I've got just out of....

MS. HUNUNEN: Read it out loud?

MR. FINDLAY: Yes.

MS. HUNUNEN: Bonnie called stated when she removed the kids they were fine leaving the hotel with her, and only became upset when, and crying when Janet came out to the car and told them they were being taken away and got them upset and crying.

MR. FINDLAY: So on the 17th, when you first wrote a note, it says don't say anything because they were upset, and then the next time when you talk to somebody, somebody else, you said that, well they were only crying because of what she had said.

MS. HUNUNEN: Well, she, it was... because she said that; they weren't crying until that, that was....

MR. FINDLAY: ... that's not the way you wrote it the first time?

MS. HUNUNEN: Well, the second one I just read is what Gary Olkonen ... because when I was leaving the hotel where I called him and told him so.

MR. FINDLAY: On the 18th?

MS. HUNUNEN: No, I called him, well, I guess I don't know who put that contact in, because that would only show on the computer.

MR. FINDLAY: Well, it says 12:43 successful phone contact, Bonnie Huttunen; and it's on the 18th at 12:43 p.m. or whatever—is that central or eastern, is then you're saying that they only got upset; that Janet is the one that got them upset?

MS. HUNUNEN: Yeah, and I'm, that is; I would say then that's a type-o on my part then on my contact that I put in because Caitlyn was not upset until Janet made that comment.

MR. FINDLAY: But that wasn't what you had written on the report?

MS. HUNUNEN: Um...

MR. FINDLAY: You reported what I, I told Janet not to say that as Caitlyn was visibly upset?

MS. HUNUNEN: Yeah, that's what I wrote.

MR. FINDLAY: Nothing further.

THE COURT: Okay, may the witness be excused?

MS. WITTLA: Yes, your Honor.

THE COURT: Okay, thank you Ms. Huttunen. You are free to go about your business.

MS. HUNUNEN: I'm done?

THE COURT: You're done, thank you for your testimony. I caution you not to discuss this with any other witnesses. (once she stepped down) And who is your next witness?

MS. WITTLA: Your Honor, I believe my next witness will be Sergeant Passuello. (Once sworn in, she begins her questioning.) Would you please state your name for the record?

MR. PASSUELLO: Rod Passuello.

MS. WITTLA: And your current occupation?

MR. PASSUELLO: I'm a detective with the Ironwood Public Safety Department.

MS. WITTLA: How long have you been employed with the IPSD?

MR. PASSUELLO: Just short of twenty years.

MS. WITTLA: Do you know Robert and Janet Coleman?

MR. PASSUELLO: Yes.

MS. WITTLA: What kind of contacts have you had with them?

MR. PASSUELLO: Because where I've responded if they've called in a complaint or complaints in their apartment building.

MS. WITTLA: Are you aware that the reason you're here today is because of an abuse and neglect case regarding their children?

MR. PASSUELLO: Yes.

MS. WITTLA: Have you done any direct investigation regarding this case?

MR. PASSUELLO: No.

MS. WITTLA: Have you interviewed Robert Coleman within the past three or four months?

MR. PASSUELLO: Yes.

MS. WITTLA: First, approximately how long ago did you talk to him?

MR. PASSUELLO: The beginning of March of this year; approximately the same time that this complain came.

MS. WITTLA: Of 2008?

MR. PASSUELLO: 2008, yes.

MS. WITTLA: When you spoke to him, did you ask him anything about Becky and Bobby Payne?

MR. PASSUELLO: Yes.

MS. WITTLA: How did he describe Becky Payne?

MR. PASSUELLO: That she was somewhat slow, and needed someone to watch over her finances. He said he was making sure that they ate nutritious food, basically that they needed someone to watch over them.

MS. WITTLA: Did he ever refer to them as children?

MR. PASSUELLO: He said they are like kids; like children; I don't know if he used the word children or kids, but....

MS. WITTLA: And when he referred to them as like kids or like children, that was in the context of needing someone to look after them?

MR. PASSUELLO: Yes.

MS. WITTLA: Did he give you any examples, if he wasn't the one there to look after them; like the kinds of stuff he thought they'd do?

MR. PASSUELLO: The ones that come to mind is that they couldn't manage their money very good without help; if someone wasn't there to see that they ate nutritiously, they would go and waste their money on junk food rather than eat a decent meal.

MS. WITTLA: How did he describe Bobby Payne?

MR. PASSUELLO: Basically pretty much the same, and that they had Bobby Payne's social security or disabil-

ity check; whatever it is, was tendered to them to disperse and take care of for them.

MS. WITTLA: So Becky and Bobby are pretty similar as far as slow, need someone to look after them, not good with money, and make bad choices with food?

MR. PASSUELLO: Yes.

MS. WITTLA: Did he describe them as impulsive the way children are?

MR. FINDLAY: Your Honor, I'm going to object to the leading of the witness.

MS. COURT: Sustained.

MS. WITTLA: Did he make any other observations as to how the Paynes were?

MR. PASSUELLO: Just that he called him dad and were more like his kids than renters at the apartment building.

MS. WITTLA: Did Mr. Coleman indicate whether any of his other tenants referred to him as dad?

MR. PASSUELLO: He didn't mention any to me.

MS. WITTLA: Did Mr. Coleman tell where Becky and Bobby lived?

MR. PASSUELLO: They were staying at that time in the basement of Mr. Coleman's apartment.

MS. WITTLA: Have you seen this basement?

MR. PASSUELLO: No I have not.

MS. WITTLA: Did Mr. Coleman tell you anything about it?

MR. PASSUELLO: That a part of it was being fixed up or remodeled, I believe, but other than that, no.

MS. WITTLA: Did you get the impression that they always lived in the basement?

MR. PASSUELLO: No, they did have their own apartment, and for some reason moved into the basement.

MS. WITTLA: Did he tell you what that reason was?

MR. PASSUELLO: I don't think he did.

MS. WITTLA: Did he tell you if the Paynes were still paying rent on that old apartment?

MR. FINDLAY: Leading again, your Honor!

THE COURT: Sustained.

MS. WITTLA: Did he tell you whether or not, if the Paynes abandoned their apartment? Did he tell you whether or not they were still under any lease obligations?

MR. PASSUELLO: I didn't talk about lease obligations with him.

MS. WITTLA: Did you talk to him about whether or not the Paynes could still live in that apartment?

MR. PASSUELLO: No. I knew myself that they were moving out prior to interviewing Mr. Coleman; so that subject of if they could stay or not did not come up.

MS. WITTLA: Were you aware if there was anyone else living there?

MR. PASSUELLO: In the basement, or?

MS. WITTLA: No, in the Payne's old apartment?

MR. PASSUELLO: Yes, there was another renter in that apartment.

MS. WITTLA: I believe that you stated that Robert Coleman said that the basement was in the process of getting fixed up?

MR. PASSUELLO: I believe he said one portion of it anyway was being remodeled of fixed up.

MS. WITTLA: Did Mr. Coleman mention whether or not he still considered the Paynes to be tenants?

MR. PASSUELLO: I took our conversation that he still believed they were tenants; he said they stayed there and he allowed them to use his kitchen. I asked about their living in the basement; how did they cook; was there a living area; living room, and Mr. Coleman said they had access to the living room and kitchen area upstairs, within their apartment, in his own apartment; that they ate with him and his wife and his children; they could watch TV; use his computer.

MS. WITTLA: Did they have access to any other parts of the Coleman's apartment?

MR. PASSUELLO: I know that specifically the bathroom, he said they did; other than that I don't know if they had access to the bedrooms or not.

MS. WITTLA: You just mentioned the bathroom. Did Mr. Coleman tell you that there was a bathroom in the basement?

MR. PASSUELLO: No.

MS. WITTLA: So the only bathroom would have been up in their apartment?

MR. PASSUELLO: Yes.

MS. WITTLA: Did you ever interview Robert or Janet Coleman about any allegations of child abuse for this case?

MR. PASSUELLO: No.

MS. WITTLA: Thank you.

THE COURT: Mr. Perhalla?

MR. PERHALLA: Nothing, thanks your Honor.

MR. FINDLAY: No questions.

THE COURT: May the witness be excused?

MS. WITTLA: Yes, your Honor.

THE COURT: Okay, detective, you are free to go. I caution you not to discuss your testimony with anybody else, we sequestered the witnesses; thank you. All right, we're going to take the mid afternoon recess until shortly after three, and you will have your next witness ready at that time?

MS. WITTLA: Yes.

THE COURT: And who is it going to be?

MS. WITTLA: I believe it will be Cheryl Saippa.

Thus, the court broke, and upon returning the prosecutor began her questioning of Ms. Saippa:

MS. WITTLA: Would you please state your name for the record?

MS. SAIPPA: Sheryl Saippa.

MS. WITTLA: You might want to move forward a little bit towards the microphone. And what agency do you work for?

MS. SAIPPA: Ironwood Public Safety, Ironwood, Michigan.

MS. WITTLA: How long have you worked there?

MS. SAIPPA: Since 2002.

MS. WITTLA: Have you met Robert and Janet Coleman before?

MS. SAIPPA: Yes, I have.

MS. WITTLA: So you recognize them? You know who they are?

MS. SAIPPA: Yes, I do.

MS. WITTLA: Were you involved with any investigations in March of 2008?

MS. SAIPPA: I was requested to stand-by from another agency while there was another investigation going on.

MS. WITTLA: Okay, so it wasn't your investigation?

MS. SAIPPA: No.

MS. WITTLA: Whose investigation was it?

MS. SAIPPA: DHS.

MS. WITTLA: And your capacity as standing by; what does that entail?

MS. SAIPPA: Standing by as a police officer to make sure everything stays peaceful.

MS. WITTLA: Do you recall what date that was when you were doing your stand-by?

MS. SAIPPA: I believe middle March, March 13th, not positive of the date.

MS. WITTLA: Somewhere early to mid-March?

MS. SAIPPA: Uh-huh.

MS. WITTLA: I'm sorry?

MS. SAIPPA: 2008.

MS. WITTLA: 2008. Would you have done any kind of a report on your stand-by?

MS. SAIPPA: There would be a call for service; a request from another agency; just a cover sheet.

MS. WITTLA: So that's a log saying where you were?

MS. SAIPPA: Yes.

MS. WITTLA: Did you type up anything about what happened?

MS. SAIPPA: No, I did not. I believe our administrative assistant typed a cover sheet.

MS. WITTLA: But you didn't interview Robert or Janet that day?

MS. SAIPPA: No, I did not.

MS. WITTLA: You didn't interview Caitlyn or Ashley that day?

MS. SAIPPA: No, I did not.

MS. WITTLA: So your function was basically just to make sure everything stayed calm?

MS. SAIPPA: Correct.

MS. WITTLA: While you were there, did you observe anyone interviewing Caitlyn?

MS. SAIPPA: I believe two DHS workers interviewed both girls.

MS. WITTLA: Do you know who the DHS workers were?

MS. SAIPPA: Elizabeth Fyle and Bob Ross.

MS. WITTLA: Were you present for that interview?

MS. SAIPPA: No, I was not.

MS. WITTLA: That took place....

MS. SAIPPA: I was in the building but not in the same room.

MS. WITTLA: So they were in a different room?

MS. SAIPPA: Correct.

MS. WITTLA: Was anyone else in that room?

MS. SAIPPA: I believe at one point, Janet Coleman came in the room with the workers. I don't remember which child was being interviewed at the time.

MS. WITTLA: Was there any point in time that you got involved in the interview?

MS. SAIPPA: No, there was not.

MS. WITTLA: Have you seen Caitlyn or Ashley since March of 2008?

MS. SAIPPA: No, I have not.

MS. WITTLA: Have you had contact with Robert Coleman regarding any incidences that he would have been reporting since March of 2008 till now?

MS. SAIPPA: I believe I was on two different calls. One, I stayed in the vehicle and Sergeant Carpenedo was the reporting officer; it was some nails in his driveway. And another time about a stolen ring.

MS. WITTLA: Did you do any interviews on either of these complaints?

MS. SAIPPA: I did not do the interviews; I stood by while Sergeant Carpenedo spoke with people involved on that one, on the ring, not on the nails.

MS. WITTLA: Okay, you were not present for the nails thing at all?

MS. SAIPPA: I was in the vehicle.

MS. WITTLA: So going back to the ring incident; were you present when Robert Coleman was being interviewed?

MS. SAIPPA: It wasn't an actual interview, it was his complaint; I stood in the same room with Mr. Coleman, Mrs. Coleman, Jamie Perlich, Sergeant Carpenedo and myself; while the questions and interview; I guess you would call it an interview but it was his complaint.

MS. WITTLA: What was Robert Coleman's complaint?

MS. SAIPPA: I believe it was a complaint about a stolen ring. He felt it had been stolen from him.

MS. WITTLA: Did he indicate who he thought....

MS. SAIPPA: ... He believed it to be Robert Payne.

MS. WITTLA: Robert Payne?

MS. SAIPPA: Payne.

MS. WITTLA: Were you aware of anything that happened after that complaint was taken to be a part of the investigation?

MS. SAIPPA: Well, I was working with Sergeant Carpenedo at the time when, at the same complaint, when Jamie Perlich stated that she believed she saw the same ring on Bobby....

MR. FINDLAY: ... Your honor, I'm going to object to that as being hearsay.

THE COURT: Okay, hold on. What is the objection?

MR. FINDLAY: Hearsay, indicating what Jamie Perlich said. She....

THE COURT: Response?

MS. WITTLA: I, I'll rephrase.

THE COURT: Sustained.

MS. WITTLA: I'm not asking you what anyone else told you aside from what Robert Coleman told you. What I'm asking is were you involved with the investigation after being with Sergeant Carpenedo the day that Robert made that complaint?

MS. SAIPPA: Not actually in the following up of it, no.

MS. WITTLA: Were there any statements that Janet Coleman made at that point in time?

MS. SAIPPA: What, in regards to?

MS. WITTLA: With the ring. That thing.

MS. SAIPPA: I don't remember Janet Coleman making any comments about the ring.

MS. WITTLA: Okay, so the only comments that you're aware of from Robert Coleman was that he believed that this ring was stolen by Bobby Payne?

MS. SAIPPA: Correct.

MS. WITTLA: Did you hear him describe anything else about it, or just that statement?

MS. SAIPPA: I don't know if he described the ring, but it was some type of a union ring. I don't remember exactly what the ring was.

MS. WITTLA: And after that day; fast forward to now. Did you have anything else to do with this ring investigation?

MS. SAIPPA: No.

MS. WITTLA: Thank you, I have nothing further.

THE COURT: Mr. Perhalla?

MR. PERHALLA: Thanks judge... you Honor. (To Saippa): In early to mid-March when you went to the Coleman's home to assist DHS in the interview, you did not go into the room where the interview happened. Correct?

MS. SAIPPA: Correct.

MR. PERHALLA: Where did you stay?

MS. SAIPPA: I stayed in the entry area; I guess it would be considered the living room.

MR. PERHALLA: Okay, so actually into the Coleman's apartment?

MS. SAIPPA: Correct.

MR. PERHALLA: And is it your understanding that that's the apartment that the Colemans actually reside in?

MS. SAIPPA: Correct.

MR. PERHALLA: Who stayed with you in that area, if anyone?

MS. SAIPPA: During the children's interview, Mr. and Mrs. Coleman were in the living room area.

MR. PERHALLA: Did you have a conversation with them while they were there?

MS. SAIPPA: I don't recall what we talked about.

MR. PERHALLA: When you arrived at the Coleman's residence that day, who actually went to the door? Was it yourself or was it DHS?

MS. SAIPPA: Both DHS workers and myself.

MR. PERHALLA: So someone knocked on the door and you were allowed in?

MS. SAIPPA: Correct.

MR. PERHALLA: Did the Colemans then freely allow the three of you into the house, the apartment?

MS. SAIPPA: Yes.

MR. PERHALLA: What was the purpose of going to their residence on that day?

MS. SAIPPA: My purpose?

MR. PERHALLA: Their, the group of you, the three of you.

MS. SAIPPA: I believe the purpose was to interview the Colemans and their children.

MR. PERHALLA: Okay, just for interviews, correct?

MS. SAIPPA: Correct.

MR. PERHALLA: As far as you knew.

MS. SAIPPA: Correct.

MR. PERHALLA: Which DHS worker started talking to the Colemans or was it both at once?

MS. SAIPPA: I don't recall which DHS worker.

MR. PERHALLA: How long were you there from start to finish if you even know?

MS. SAIPPA: Approximately an hour.

MR. PERHALLA: An hour. Was the majority of that hour then the actual interview of the children behind the door that you couldn't see, where you stayed out of?

MS. SAIPPA: I'd say about half and half.

MR. PERHALLA: Half and half. Were you present when DHS interviewed one or both of the Colemans then, Robert or Janet?

MS. SAIPPA: No.

MR. PERHALLA: Where did they interview the Colemans, Robert and Janet?

MS. SAIPPA: I believe it was one of the children's bedrooms.

MR. PERHALLA: So you just essentially stayed out in this living room open area?

MS. SAIPPA: Uh huh.

MR. PERHALLA: What time of day was this?

MS. SAIPPA: Afternoon, approximately three o'clock.

MR. PERHALLA: Still the daylight hours?

MS. SAIPPA: Correct.

MR. PERHALLA: Do you remember seeing both children, Ashley and Caitlyn, there?

MS. SAIPPA: Yes.

MR. PERHALLA: When they interviewed Caitlyn, did she just go right with them into the room?

MS. SAIPPA: Yes.

MR. PERHALLA: Okay, how did that happen? Did someone ask to interview her and they went in there or what can you recall?

MS. SAIPPA: I don't recall the exact words; all I know is that she went with them.

MR. PERHALLA: Freely with them?

MS. SAIPPA: Correct.

MR. PERHALLA: Was Caitlyn crying at all during the interview or the time you were there?

MS. SAIPPA: No, no.

MR. PERHALLA: Can you describe what kind of little girl she was that day?

MS. SAIPPA: Typical. Watching cartoons.

MR. PERHALLA: So the approximate hour that you were there you didn't see anything out of the ordinary with respect to Caitlyn?

MS. SAIPPA: No.

MR. PERHALLA: And I believe that was your only involvement in the case here today. Correct?

MS. SAIPPA: Correct.

MR. PERHALLA: Okay, thanks. That's it.

THE COURT: Mr. Findlay?

MR. FINDLAY: Thanks your Honor, just a couple. (To Ms. Saippa): These other times that you contacted Robert Coleman regarding rings and regarding nails. Is that correct?

MS. SAIPPA: Correct.

MR. FINDLAY: What were the dates of those, if you know?

MS. SAIPPA: I don't recall.

MR. FINDLAY: Were they after March 11th?

MS. SAIPPA: Yes.

MR. FINDLAY: How about before May 1st?

MS. SAIPPA: I don't recall.

MR. FINDLAY: The rings incident—that was in connection with Mr. Coleman reporting that he had some missing rings, or the rings were stolen?

MS. SAIPPA: Yes.

MR. FINDLAY: And the nails report would be regarding him reporting that somebody had thrown nails in the driveway?

MS. SAIPPA: Correct.

MR. FINDLAY: Who was he reporting had done that?

MS. SAIPPA: I don't know. He just said that there were nails scattered all over his driveway.

MR. FINDLAY: Were you there at the Colemans on the 11th? You said you were just there in a stand by mode?

MS. SAIPPA: Correct.

MR. FINDLAY: In fact, kind of, is that normal procedure?

MS. SAIPPA: Yes.

MR. FINDLAY: For DHS to call you?

MS. SAIPPA: Yes.

MR. FINDLAY: And was there anything that required you to do anything?

MS. SAIPPA: No.

MR. FINDLAY: You didn't collect any evidence or anything like that?

MS. SAIPPA: No.

MR. FINDLAY: Didn't conduct any interviews or anything?

MS. SAIPPA: Nope.

MR. FINDLAY: You were just there, and it went peacefully and without incident; is that correct?

MS. SAIPPA: Correct.

MR. FINDLAY: Nothing further.

THE COURT: Redirect?

MS. WITTLA: No, your Honor.

THE COURT: Okay, thank you officer, you are free to go. I will caution you do not discuss your testimony with any other potential witness. Thank you. Who is your next witness?

MS. WITTLA: Your Honor, if he has arrived, I'd like to briefly recall detective Passuello.

THE COURT: Okay, if not, then who?

MS. WITTLA: If not, it would be sergeant Carpenedo.

THE COURT: Who I saw in the hallway, right?

MS. WITTLA: Yes, I know he is here.

MR. FINDLAY: Who we recalling?

MS. WITTLA: Detective Passuelo.

THE COURT: Detective Passuelo. If you don't find Detective Passuello, then please send Sergeant Carpenedo in.

MR. FINDLAY: I thought we excused Detective Passuello, and I'm not sure why we are; I mean, I object to recalling him.

THE COURT: Okay, so why are we recalling him? I mean, we did excuse him for the day, but that doesn't mean he couldn't be re-subpoenaed.

MS. WITTLA: Your Honor, I contacted Detective Passuello on the break and I asked him to return and he is willing to do so. There were a couple of questions that I did not ask him that I should have.

MR. FINDLAY: Your Honor, that's...

MS. WITTLA: ... He's my witness. If the court would be happier for me to give him another subpoena, I can do so.

THE COURT: No, he was named as a witness; that's fine, the only thing I would ask is, he was not involved in anybody else's testimony was he, as part of this?

MS. WITTLA: I'm sorry?

THE COURT: Nobody talked to him about any other witness's testimony? It's not going to relate to what somebody else said and now he's filled in on something from a sequestered witness? That would be a problem.

Two things entered my mind here. Number one, why was the Prosecutor talking to him during the break? Isn't that against the rules as well, once he has testified and been dismissed? And secondly, was the court following proper procedure here? It seems to me the prosecutor should have been required to issue another subpoena. Was it because the judge wanted to finish this trial fast—within his self set time line—that he allowed this to go forward? After all, another subpoena would mean a little more time, wouldn't it? In any case, the biased judge did allow him to go back on the stand once they did locate him, and we pick it up where my lawyer objected to the procedure:

MR. FINDLAY: ... Your Honor, I apologize, but I'd just put the objection on the record again. I mean, this witness has been called, he's testified. It's just not proper for him to be recalled. He was her witness, she's called him to testify, and now because there's something that she didn't get out that she wanted, then to call him back? I mean, we can repeatedly call witnesses every time we remember a question we didn't ask. I mean, my objection is on the record, so....

THE COURT: And it's awkward, but it is in the court's discretion. I'm allowing it. I won't allow it for a whole bunch more witnesses, and I guess if it happens to you I would give you the same opportunity. So go ahead.

MS. WITTLA: Detective Passuello, when you testified earlier today, where did you go?

MR. PASSUELLO: Back to Ironwood.

MS. WITTLA: Did you talk to any other witnesses before you left?

MR. PASSUELLO: Not other than to say "hi" to Officer Carpenedo and Officer Saippa. As I was walking out, they were walking in, I said, "Hi."

And we are supposed to believe that? How do we know what they talked about, and he even admits he DID talk to other witnesses. We should have asked for dismissal right then and there.

MS. WITTLA: Thank you. Detective Passuello, you indicated that you had interviewed Robert Coleman in March. Do you recall that testimony?

MR. PASSUELLO: Yes.

MS. WITTLA: Did you have any conversations with Mr. Coleman by cell phone around that point in time?

MR. PASSUELLO: It was one. At one point I attempted to call him to see about talking to, I believe I needed to talk to him or, or give him some papers, and I called his cell phone to see where he was, because I went by his house, he wasn't there.

MS. WITTLA: Do you remember approximately when that was?

MR. PASSUELLO: Would have been Wednesday or Thursday, I believe, it would have been the 12th or 13th of the month.

MS. WITTLA: Did you get ahold of him on the cell phone?

MR. PASSUELLO: Yes.

MS. WITTLA: Did you ask him where he was?

MR. PASSUELLO: Yes.

MS. WITTLA: Where did he say he was?

MR. PASSUELLO: He said he was with his wife at a doctor's appointment in Marquette.

MS. WITTLA: Thank you, I have nothing further.

THE COURT: Any questions, based on that?

MR. PERHALLA: No, thank you your Honor.

THE COURT: Mr. Findlay?

MR. FINDLAY: No.

With that, Passuello was again excused, and they prepared to bring to the stand, Officer Carpenedo, and following a lengthy discussion over an original search warrant the prosecutor wanted dug out of the court file, Carpenedo was finally sworn in, and her questioning began:

MS. WITTLA: Would you please state your name for the record?

MR. CARPENEDO: Sergeant Ronald David Carpenedo.

MS. WITTLA: And what is your current occupation?

MR. CARPENEDO: Ironwood Public Safety Officer.

MS. WITTLA: How long have you been employed there?

MR. CARPENEDO: Since July 13th, 1990, approximately 18 years.

MS. WITTLA: Have you previously met Robert and Janet Coleman?

MR. CARPENEDO: Yes I have.

MS. WITTLA: We are here today on an abuse and neglect case. Have you interviewed anyone for this case?

MR. CARPENEDO: No, I have not.

MS. WITTLA: I handed you a document that was marked as Exhibit Number Four. I believe on the first page it says, AFFIDAVIT FOR SEARCH WARRANT?

MR. CARPENEDO: Yes.

MS. WITTLA: Is that a document you created?

MR. CARPENEDO: Yes.

MS. WITTLA: It is an accurate....

MR. CARPENEDO: ... It's an affidavit for a search warrant for locating where the cell phone useage of Mr. Coleman's phone was being used, in an attempt to assist DHS in locating the children because an order was issued to take the kids into custody. So I assisted the Department of Human Services in locating Mr. Coleman's phone by his usage for which towers it goes off of. We've used it in the past to locate people.

MS. WITTLA: Okay, I'm going to stop you right there for a second. So the document that you are holding contains the affidavit requesting the records from the cell carrier?

MR. CARPENEDO: Yes.

MS. WITTLA: And then it also contains the records that they sent?

MR. CARPENEDO: These records that it contains were sent to me by AT&T records department by email after a search warrant was served on them. These records consist of Mr. Coleman's telephone number, his cell phone number.

MS. WITTLA: So the number had all these calls going back and forth to it?

MR. CARPENEDO: Yes, and it shows what tower it's hitting.

MS. WITTLA: It shows what tower it's hitting?

MR. CARPENEDO: Yes. The reason you need to know which tower it's hitting is the tower locates where the phone is being used from.

MS. WITTLA: At the time that this search warrant was requested, did DHS know where Mr. Coleman was?

MR. CARPENEDO: The morning of.....

MR. FINDLAY: .... Objection! Objection! This officer can't testify to what DHS knows.

THE COURT: Sustained.

MS. WITTLA: Do you know why DHS contacted you for help?

MR. CARPENEDO: Yes, on the morning of the 14th, when I came to work, I learned that there was this order in place to locate these children; and from my past experience, I knew that cell phones can be located when they're being used, so I also learned from Detective Passuello that the subject, Mr. Coleman, had been using his phone the day prior and that he was supposed to have been in the Marquette area. I had also learned from social services that same day, couple hours later, that Mr. Coleman was to have been in the Marquette area. So I drafted a search warrant, and I knew that he was using it, at least twice that morning, to call Mr. Payne. He'd received two phone calls from Mr. Coleman, I believe at 8:30 a.m. and 11:02 a.m. So I knew at least two phone calls would show where he was calling from that day.

MS. WITTLA: The document that you are looking for where you say 8:30 and 11:02; where do you find the time on this?

MR. CARPENEDO: Those two phone numbers; Mr. Payne had reported to me that he received two phone calls that day; at approximately those times. It's in my affidavit in the last sentence of the affidavit for the search warrant. I knew Mr. Coleman had used his phone on that day, so I knew that we could locate him, at least where he was when he made those two phone calls on that day.

MS. WITTLA: If you look at the list of records that you received, from AT&T via email, do those calls show up?

MR. CARPENEDO: Yes they do. I remember viewing them, but I'd have to look for them now. I don't recall which, Mr. Payne's phone number, at that time I did know his phone number, and I could point out which phone numbers they were on here; but there was a call at 12:02 which would be 11:02 our time; these are eastern standard time phone numbers on here; and there's also one at 9:27 and 9:30. I'm not sure which one is which, but those were phone calls that were made by Mr.— ; that were either made by him or received by him, at, ah, those mornings of the 14th.

MS. WITTLA: Does the return show that the call was initiated or received, or just that the phone's in use?

MR. CARPENEDO: It showed what time the call was placed. It shows two phone numbers that were involved in the call, the number that he called; and the number that—um—it was a received call or placed a call; and it also shows that the tower, both towers that were used in the process, and in this case, in both of these calls it was Houghton, Michigan's tower and like I said, if I knew Mr. Payne's phone number, you would see both of them on here. I just don't recall his phone number. But you'll see that on the 14th, in the morning of the 14th, all the calls were placed from 12:11 a.m., that that would have been early that morning they started hitting the Houghton tower all the way thru the 14th until the end of the day of the 14th at 4:48 when I filed the search warrant. So every call that was placed by that cell phone was hitting a Houghton tower, and then on the 13th when I was under the belief that he was in Marquette; they were hitting the Calumet tower, which is right near Houghton.

MS. WITTLA: About ten miles away?

MR. CARPENEDO: Approximately, yes.

MS. WITTLA: Once you received these records; what did you do?

MR. CARPENEDO: I gave them to, along with the order that I had for pickup from Probate Court; I gave that order and a copy of the search warrant, the records, to Officer Colassaco, which was coming on the night shift.

MS. WITTLA: Did you ask Officer Colassaco to do anything with those records?

MR. CARPENEDO: I asked him to fax them to the Houghton County Sheriff's Department with information of what Mr. Coleman's vehicle looked like, which, ah, we had on file at our department, and his license plate, and that information was faxed to the Houghton County Sheriff's Department, I believe, by Mr. Colassaco; Officer Colassaco.

MS. WITTLA: You weren't there when he did that?

MR. CARPENEDO: No. I gave that all to him to do that; when I returned the next morning I was informed by Mr. Colassaco that he had done that, and that they had located Mr. Coleman.

MS. WITTLA: During this period of time when you received the cell phone records, you mentioned the 13th and the 14th that none of the calls originated from Marquette; are those the only two days covered here?

MR. CARPENEDO: No.

MS. WITTLA: There's a…

MR. CARPENEDO: … they covered a range from March 11th thru March 14th, and thru all of those days there was never a call that hit a Marquette tower, or, excuse me, there was one call on the 12th placed, from Mercer, I believe, to Marquette; and it did hit a tower in Marquette on 3-12 at 2:30 p.m. Otherwise I don't believe I saw any Marquette calls on here.

MS. WITTLA: So when you're referencing the call that hit the Marquette tower, it would have hit Marquette at the other end of the call?

MR. CARPENEDO: The way I read this, Mr. Coleman would have been— had his cell phone in that—hitting that Marquette tower on the 12th.

MS. WITTLA: And that's the only one that said Marquette?

MR. CARPENEDO: I'll have to find it again. Correct, but shortly later that same phone was off the Ironwood tower so, how that happened I'm not sure, unless that's the other end of the line, as there's, there's towers being used; one is Mercer and one is Marquette, and then minutes later there's one in Mercer and one in Ironwood. So whether he's in Mercer placing the call or vise versa, calling someone in Marquette, that, that could have been; because I don't know how he could get from Ironwood to Marquette in a matter of five minutes.

MS. WITTLA: Well as I'm looking at this report, at the first page of it, it says original SID and Bill SID and then Cell site, at the top, does yours say that?

MR. CARPENEDO: Yes.

MS. WITTLA: I'm sorry, go ahead.

MR. CARPENEDO: The second call would be the destination, so that's where he was calling to, was to Marquette. So he would have never been, he was in Mercer when he placed that call. That was where it originated.

MS. WITTLA: Okay and that clears, clarifies it better because you're right, it says origination and then destination and the duration.

MR. CARPENEDO: Yes.

MS. WITTLA: Your Honor, I would request entrance Exhibit Number Four.

THE COURT: Objections?

MR. FINDLAY: I'm tot— well, I didn't hear the request—it's hard to hear sometimes.

THE COURT: She wants, she wants it, it admitted as an Exhibit, yeah, it's part of the Court file; it's been identified; it's received. (At 3:43 p.m., Plaintiff's Exhibit Number 4 is received)

MS. WITTLA: Do you want me to give it to the clerk?

THE COURT: I'll put it back in the file and we're going to have to, as I said, piece it back together. Thank you.

MS. WITTLA: Seargent Carpenedo, from the time that you dealt with this search warrant issue up until now; have you responded to any other calls concerning Robert or Janet Coleman?

MR. CARPENENO: I was called once to his apartment building later on after that, I don't remember when it was, for someone had sprinkled nails in his driveway, and he was there, picking them up. And then I was also called to his apartment where I met with him, his wife, and a Jamie Perlich; and Robert explained to me, ah, he described to me how he had learned from Jamie Perlich that a ring; well, he explained to me first that a ring was stolen from him. I found out where it was; he said it was, he reported it stolen in Houghton, the Houghton Police Department when he was staying in Houghton in the past. He showed me what the ring, on a computer, what the ring looked like, and then he told me that Jamie Perlich….

MS. WITTLA: … But wait right there…

MR. CARPENEDO: … he told me this.

MS. WITTLA: I understand that, but did he say that Jamie Perlich was a witness to this theft?

MR. CARPENEDO: Yes, no, he said Jamie Perlich saw Robert Payne wearing this ring approximately a month ago, outside by the garages. And then I wanted to interview Jamie Perlich on my own, without Mr. Coleman present, because that's the way it would be done, and I attempted numerous times to get her in. Mr. Coleman attempted numerous times to get her in, ah, and trying to assist getting ahold of her for me, getting her in, tried to stay on a three way call, and have me interview that way. I told him that wasn't going to work that way; that I needed to speak to Jamie Perlich, ah, privately, referencing this. And I was also call—

MR. CARPENEDO: She, the first date she missed; I called her back, she declined to come in; and Houghton County Sheriff or Chief Of Police, Chief Donnelly was attempting for me to continue to interview her for them so that he could wrap up his case on his end. And finally, I did get Jamie Perlich to come in and….

MS. WITTLA: Okay, but I'm not going to ask you what she told you.

MR. CARPENEDO: No, but she did write out a statement for me which I don't have with me.

MS. WITTLA: She eventually wrote a statement regarding this situation?

MR. CARPENEDO: Yes.

MS. WITTLA: Would you say that it was difficult to get her to come in?

MR. CARPENEDO: Yes.

MS. WITTLA: How many times did you say you tried to get ahold of her?

MR. CARPENEDO: I tried approximately the day that we first met with her, a day that I called her on the telephone to have her come in, it for a Sunday afternoon, but she didn't show up, I tried one more time after that with the response that she didn't want to be involved. And then I tried the final time when I finally got her in, and then also Mr. Coleman attempted numerous times as he told me to get her to come in.

MS. WITTLA: I think I lost track in there, just say about eight times?

Again, this shows the exaggerations of this prosecutor (or should I call them direct lies). Go back to the statement Carpenedo just made and count:

(1) The day we first met with her

(2) A day I called her on the phone to have her come in

(3) A Sunday afternoon, but she didn't show up

(4) One more time after that with the response she didn't want to be involved

(5) A final time when I finally got her in

That is five times—not even close to eight—which this prosecutor exaggerated them to be. This was her pattern, to lie, to exaggerate, to present things as if they were factual statements, when in fact, they were not.

MR. CARPENEDO: Mr. Coleman kept calling me asking me if I had interviewed Jamie Perlich, and I told him the same story that I was having a hard time getting her to come in, and he attempted numerous times, in fact, he called her, got us on a three way call and tried to help getting a date for her to come in, and that was one of the dates that she missed.

MS. WITTLA: Do you recall when this was that this ring was reported stolen, approximately?

MR. CARPENEDO: No I don't. I did have the report from Houghton Police Department but it was a while back when Mr. Payne was living with Mr. Coleman, and I don't recall, and they were all staying at a motel in Houghton at the time, but I don't remember the date.

MS. WITTLA: So is your testimony that the ring was actually reported stolen in Houghton County?

MR. CARPENEDO: At the Houghton Police Department, yes; City Police Department.

MS. WITTLA: And then you were doing the follow up from this end?

MR. CARPENEDO: Yes, I received a call from Mr. Coleman originally stating that he had a witness that saw Mr. Payne with this ring, and I wanted to interview this witness alone, and that's how we went through all these stages, and then in the meantime also Chief Donnelly had called me to interview this same witness because Mr. Coleman had—I was informed by Chief Donnelly that Mr. Coleman called him saying that the same information that he gave me, that this Jamie Perlich was a witness. And the information that I was received from Mr. Coleman, on the day that Jamie Perlich was present did not make sense to me, that's why I wanted to interview Jamie Perlich alone because the timeline did not make sense, the timeline that Mr. Coleman said that Robert Payne was wearing this stolen ring, they were living together and it would not have made sense for him to wear a ring that he stole. If I was living with Mr. Coleman and I had stolen a ring, I would not be wearing it while I'm living with him. So it did not make sense that Mr. Payne would have worn this stolen ring in front of Mr. Coleman.

MS. WITTLA: And that is why you wanted to interview Jamie?

MR. CARPENEDO: Interview Jamie Perlich on the timeline and her timeline was not making any sense to me.

MS. WITTLA: Thank you, I have nothing further.

THE COURT: Mr. Perhalla?

MR. PERHALLA: Nothing, thanks your Honor.

THE COURT: Mr. Findlay?

MR. FINDLAY: Just briefly, thank you. Um, Seargent Carpenedo, the information on that, do you still have that affidavit with you?

MR. CARPENEDO: No I don't.

MR. FINDLAY: Can the court just give it to him, just to....

THE COURT: ... He needs to look at it. Okay, I just stuck it back together, hold on. There it is.

MR. FINDLAY: Thank you. The information under number three which is the fax that— isn't it true that, at least the— much of that information was, was on it, and that's just— there's nothing wrong with it; I'm not trying to attack the search warrant. It's legitimate, I'm not contesting that, but I'm not contesting that, but isn't much of that information upon information belief? I mean, it's been told to you by somebody else?

MR. CARPENEDO: Almost every search warrant is that way, but.....

MR. FINDLAY: ... I'm sorry?

MR. CARPENEDO: Almost every search warrant we do is on information and belief.

MR. FINDLAY: Well, no... I'm not trying to suggest that, I'm not attacking the search warrant... I just wanted you to clarify that, that the information you got in terms of, you know, the stuff in the Gogebic County Family Court Juvenile Division, somebody else told you that there was a, an order issued, and they have given you a copy of that order, correct?

MR. CARPENEDO: At that point in time I had a copy in my hand.

MR. FINDLAY: Okay, and you were... you're informed that Robert Coleman, according to the petition, abused children, right? So somebody else, somebody is telling— my point is that this isn't based on your personal information, personal knowledge?

MR. CARPENEDO: I'm reading that off of the order from Department of Social Service, or the order issued by Probate Court for pickup, and the allegations that were on it.

MR. FINDLAY: And again, the undersigned then furnished information by above referenced protective service workers that Coleman has left the area following the interview... when the children March 11th, that's.....

MR. CARPENEDO: I would have been furnished that information both by Liz Fyle from the Department of Human Services and by Detective Passuello. Separate occasions and I don't know if either one knew that the other one had told me the same story.

MR. FINDLAY: Okay, and also the bit about the essentially that he was seeking medical care for his wife in Marquette area and was to return last night; somebody else gave you that information, right?

MR. CARPENEDO: And that was also learned by those two people.

MR. FINDLAY: And so the only things that you've, I guess were your personal knowledge, were actually the numbers because you were involved in obtaining those, and the numbers and getting the echo records and reviewing them?

MR. CARPENEDO: Personal information was I knew there was an order for pickup; I knew Mr. Coleman's phone number; and at that time I knew Robert Payne's phone number; and I knew that two phone calls were placed to Robert Payne by Mr. Coleman's number because I viewed it on Mr. Payne's caller ID on his cell phone. There was a PPO in, out, and I was called to Mr. Payne's house to view the two calls, which he claimed were a violation of a PPO. I told him to file a show cause hearing, but he showed me those phone numbers; showing Mr. Coleman's calls at those two times; 8:30 a.m. and 11:02 a.m.

MR. FINDLAY: You've gone way beyond my question, but the gist of it is though is that the information in here was not personal knowledge, it was all told to you by somebody else?

MR. CARPENEDO: Not all of it, no.

MR. FINDLAY: Well the, you didn't write the order did you?

MR. CARPENEDO: No.

MR. FINDLAY: Okay, so that's something that somebody else put information on that order, when they gave you this order, right?

MR. CARPENEDO: Yes.

MR. FINDLAY: Okay, did you know the Coleman's phone number?

MR. CARPENEDO: Yes.

Let me stop right here to say something. If Mr. Carpenedo knew my phone number, why didn't he just call me and prevent a 3:00 a.m. raid and the scaring of our entire family half to death?

MR. FINDLAY: But you had no knowledge of what the Colemans had done, where they were, other than what the phone records showed you, correct?

MR. CARPENEDO: Correct.

MR. FINDLAY: You didn't. And as far as why this warrant was sought, that was to find, to—

MR. CARPENEDO: .... to locate the children.

MR. FINDLAY: Right, but you didn't know why they— why that was, other than that there is a court order saying that they, that they can take the children, correct?

MR. CARPENEDO: I knew that I needed to assist them in locating the children; I needed to assist social services in helping this court order be served.

Right. But did he even try to call me? I don't think so! Elizabeth Fyle, I am convinced, lied about that, because she was a liar from the get-go. But I wonder if Mr. Carpenedo ever even tried to call me? After all, he had wanted to see me go down for some time!

MR. FINDLAY: Right, and the court order....

MR. CARPENEDO: When a court order was issued to the police, we are, when it says you shall serve this, and that was my assistance to get it served, and I believe the police in Houghton were the ones that actually served it.

MR. FINDLAY: Okay, but like I said that was based on the information that was provided to you by protective service?

MR. CARPENEDO: Information that protective service had provided to the court, which provided to me, the court issued the order....

MR. FINDLAY: ... the order... second hand, it's third hand, and it went from protective services to the court, then to you?

MR. CARPENEDO: The (court) issues an order to me, and I carried it out.

MR. FINDLAY: I'm just trying to get the, the information was not your personal knowledge?

MR. CARPENEDO: Correct.

MR. FINDLAY: Thanks, nothing further.

THE COURT: Nothing further?

MR. FINDLAY: Pardon? Yeah. That's it.

THE COURT: Okay, may the witness be excused? All right, was there some redirect?

MS. WITTLA: No, your Honor, the witness may be excused.

THE COURT: Okay, thank you Seargent, you are excused and free to go; I would caution you that we have sequestered the witnesses. Do not discuss your testimony with any other potential witness. Thank you. And who is your next witness?

MS. WITTLA: Your Honor, my next witness would be Robert Ross.

With that, Robert Ross was sworn in, and the prosecutor began her questioning:

MS. WITTLA: Would you please state your name?

MR. ROSS: Robert Ross.

MS. WITTLA: And your current occupation?

MR. ROSS: I'm a foster care and child protective services worker.

MS. WITTLA: For the state of Michigan?

MR. ROSS: Yes, for the Michigan Department of Human Services.

MS. WITTLA: How long have you been employed in the field?

MR. ROSS: Eighteen months.

MS. WITTLA: Were you assigned to investigate a complaint of child abuse or neglect involving Caitlyn Brag and Ashley Coleman?

MR. ROSS: No, I was assigned to accompany Ms. Fyle, who was assigned the investigation.

MS. WITTLA: Do you recall when you accompanied her on her investigation?

MR. ROSS: Yes.

MS. WITTLA: When was that?

MR. ROSS: I believe it was March 11th of this year.

MS. WITTLA: Is it typical for more than one worker to go out for interviews?

MR. ROSS: Yes.

MS. WITTLA: Where did you go to interview Caitlyn and Ashley?

MR. ROSS: To the Coleman family residence.

MS. WITTLA: Which is located where?

MR. ROSS: Suffolk Street in Ironwood.

MS. WITTLA: Would you say that the, well, was anyone else there from law enforcement?

MR. ROSS: Officer Saippa was there from Ironwood Public Safety.

MS. WITTLA: Are you aware of her interviewing any witnesses in this case?

MR. ROSS: No, I'm not.

MS. WITTLA: What was her function there?

MR. ROSS: She was there to provide support to Ms. Fyle and myself.

MS. WITTLA: When you arrived at the house, were you present for the interview of the children?

MR. ROSS: Yes, I was.

MS. WITTLA: Was Ashley interviewed?

MR. ROSS: No. Ashley is two years old and normally two year olds don't, don't get interviewed due to their young age.

Hold on! This was an out and out lie. Go back to chapter four, and you will read where they took Ashley in following the interview with Caitlyn, for some five minutes. They even acknowledged they didn't get anything from her. But they did interview her, best they could, following Caitlyn's interview.

MS. WITTLA: Was Caitlyn interviewed?

MR. ROSS: Yes.

MS. WITTLA: What room was she interviewed in?

MR. ROSS: Caitlyn was interviewed in the bedroom of the two girls in the home.

MS. WITTLA: Who was present for her interview?

MR. ROSS: Myself and Ms. Fyle.

MS. WITTLA: And Caitlyn?

MR. ROSS: And Caitlyn, yes.

MS. WITTLA: No one else? Just the three of you?

MR. ROSS: Correct.

MS. WITTLA: Were you the one performing the interview or was Ms. Fyle?

MR. ROSS: Ms. Fyle was doing the interview.

MS. WITTLA: Did Caitlyn seem cooperative to go into her room to talk to you guys?

MR. ROSS: Yes.

MS. WITTLA: How would you describe her?

MR. ROSS: Energetic young child; very verbal for a six year old child that was in kindergarten at the time; she's a very articulate young lady. She spoke very well.

MS. WITTLA: Did she seem to have any problems answering questions?

MR. ROSS: No.

MS. WITTLA: Do you know what the Forensic Interview Protocol is?

MR. ROSS: Yes.

MS. WITTLA: Can you tell me briefly, I guess, what it is?

MR. ROSS: It's a method of interviewing small children or older children, even, to allow them to describe incidence in neglect and abuse without using leading questions, without using interrogation techniques. It allows a child to basically use their own words, use a free narrative to basically describe the situations that happen to them. You don't directly ask the children, you ask them to tell you a story.

Okay, so in chapter four, where Elizabeth asked Caitlyn, if her dad beats her on her tush, or if either of her parents beats her with a belt, it would seem to me she went against the protocol, as Mr. Ross describes it, as she asked those "leading" type of questions. So not only did Ms. Fyle lie about what was said, but also about her following this Forensic Interview Protocol.

MS. WITTLA: When you ask them to tell you a story, do you ask them anything about the truth in that story?

MR. ROSS: You set some ground rules initially with the child; you determine whether or not the child is able to determine the difference between a truth and a lie. You make sure the child, you play some word play with the child; you ask the child to tell you if they know the difference between the truth and a lie. You use some examples. Once you determine the child is capable of determining whether or not it's the truth or a lie, you move on to letting the child know that we only talk about the truth; you tell the child during the course of the interview process that if they don't answer to anything it's okay to tell you, "I don't know." You also tell the child that if we, if they give us an answer, we'll repeat the answer back to the child, and we say it wrong to them, it's okay for the child to tell us that we said something wrong, and to correct us so that we make sure that we get everything correct.

MS. WITTLA: Were you there for Caitlyn's entire interview?

MR. ROSS: Yes.

Again, this was a lie. When my wife entered the bedroom and interrupted the interview with Caitlyn, Ms. Fyle was left alone with Caitlyn while Bob Ross escorted her back out and explained to us why we could not be there, as our lawyer was then advising us. According to Caitlyn, that is when Ms. Fyle asked her if I beat her on her tush, etc.

MS. WITTLA: Were you there for the truth-lie bit of her interview?

MR. ROSS: Yes.

MS. WITTLA: Give me an example, generally speaking, like what's the kind of question that you would ask a kid to determine if they understood the difference between the truth and a lie.

MR. ROSS: If I had a shirt on that day that had a picture of a lion on it, I would ask the child is the picture on my shirt that of a monkey; if I told you the picture on the shirt was a monkey was the truth, if I told you the picture on the shirt was a monkey, is that a truth or a lie; the child would tell me no, it's a lie because that's a lion on your shirt. We use questions like that that they are able to answer and give us a direct answer. If it's a summer day and we ask the child is it snowing outside; they say no, they say no it's not snowing because it's summertime;

so those are the type of questions we use for to determine honesty or a truth or a lie.

MS. WITTLA: And you indicated that Caitlyn was in kindergarten?

MR. ROSS: Yes.

MS. WITTLA: Are you aware of how old she was?

MR. ROSS: She was six at the time.

MS. WITTLA: And I believe you stated that from your perspective she was fairly, I think you used the world articulate?

MR. ROSS: Yes, she spoke very well.

MS. WITTLA: When you do an interview with a child, are you allowed to have the parents present?

MR. ROSS: No. Child Protective Services Law in the State of Michigan tells us that we're not allowed to have children suspected of alleged abuse, alleged neglect and abuse interviewed in the presence of the alleged perpetrator of that neglect and abuse.

MS. WITTLA: So for this case, the alleged perpetrators of neglect and abuse would have been who?

MR. ROSS: Robert and Janet Coleman.

MS. WITTLA: So to follow that law, you could not interview these children in their presence?

MR. ROSS: Correct.

MS. WITTLA: Were they interviewed in their presence?

MR. ROSS: No.

MS. WITTLA: Were there any interruptions to the interview?

MR. ROSS: There was a time where we were in the— when Ms. Fyle was in the process of interviewing the parents, Mrs. Coleman came into the bedroom and said you need to stop the interview because my attorney, Michael Pope, said that you need to stop talking to our kids; and at that point Ms. Fyle stopped the interview. I went out back into the living room and I informed the parents that Ms. Fyle needed to continue the interview so we could, you know, find out what was going on, and I informed the parents that if they didn't consent to us allowing to continue the interview; that we may need to get a court order to finish the interview. The parents allowed us to go back in and finish the— allowed us to go back in, and then Ms. Fyle finished the interview.

MS. WITTLA: To your knowledge, while you were outside of the room, did Ms. Fyle continue to interview without you there, or was, were they like in a, in a timeout?

MR. ROSS: When I left the room, Ms. Fyle indicated that she was stopping the interview until I came back.

Well, we know now that did not happen. So either Ross lied, or was misinformed by Ms. Fyle, who lied. Because today, at age ten, Caitlyn told us what took place during that time, and not only did she continue, but she failed to follow the protocol, as we already pointed out.

MS. WITTLA: Were or was Robert Coleman with this discussion as far as the, you know, you can't be in the room for the interview or we're going to need to get a court order; was he involved in that discussion with you?

MR. ROSS: Both parents were sitting in the living room, or yeah, in the living room of the home, which was actually kind of a modified bedroom, because there was a big bed in the living room area as well. But both present when that was, when the discussion was going on.

MS. WITTLA: How big is the room?

MR. ROSS: I'm not quite sure, but there was a big screen TV, and a twin bed and some other furniture and some armoires and some dressers and stuff like that, so it's a relatively large room.

MS. WITTLA: Would you say your voice carries?

MR. ROSS: Yes.

MS. WITTLA: Would you say that anyone in the room probably would have heard you talking?

MR. ROSS: Yes.

MS. WITTLA: Okay, so it's not quite so big that they wouldn't have heard you?

MR. ROSS: No.

MS. WITTLA: Do you have to go through training to use the Forensic Interview Protocol?

MR. ROSS: Yes.

MS. WITTLA: Have you had this training?

MR. ROSS: Yes.

MS. WITTLA: Is it part of what you have to do when you first come on board for DHS?

MR. ROSS: It's part of foster care training; it's part of CPS training; and then there is a second advanced two-day Forensic Interviewing Protocol that everybody goes through when they are trained as a CPS worker.

MS. WITTLA: So for you, working at the department for eighteen months, how many Forensic Interview trainings have you been to?

MR. ROSS: Three.

MS. WITTLA: You described the Protocol as asking open-ended questions and letting the child tell their story; is that fair to say?

MR. ROSS: Yes.

MS. WITTLA: Who is in control about the interview? Is it the interviewer or is it the kid?

MR. ROSS: The child. The interviewer asks, starts to develop some rapport initially on, and the child starts telling a story and the interviewer basically tells the child or asks the child tell me more about that; or can you give me, can you tell me some more about that. And then the child continues their free narrative as far as what they needed; what they want to tell the investigator.

MS. WITTLA: Have you ever interviewed kids using the Forensic Protocol?

MR. ROSS: Yes.

MS. WITTLA: In the last eighteen months or so, can you give me like a ball park number, how many kids you would have interviewed?

MR. ROSS: Between 15 and 20.

MS. WITTLA: Fifteen to twenty, using this Protocol?

MR. ROSS: Yes.

MS. WITTLA: Have there been times when you used this Protocol and the child didn't tell you anything?

MR. ROSS: Absolutely.

MS. WITTLA: Have those interviews ended at that point?

MR. ROSS: Some.

MS. WITTLA: Is it possible to follow everything within the Forensic Interview Protocol, and the result is that the child has nothing that they can tell you?

MR. ROSS: Yes.

MS. WITTLA: Within the Protocol are you supposed to continue to interview the kid until they tell you what you want to talk about?

MR. ROSS: No.

MS. WITTLA: Have there been any times when you've used the Protocol and found out that nothing that would constitute abuse and neglect has happened?

MR. ROSS: Several.

MS. WITTLA: When you refer to the child telling their story, is this story like a made up story or is this a story like their version of the events?

MR. ROSS: On this, it's their version of the events of things that have happened to them; a child could tell you that they've been spanked or something has happened to them and you ask them to tell you more about that, and they go on and they tell you some more about what had happened to them.

MS. WITTLA: Okay, but just using the word story, doesn't mean that it's made up?

MR. ROSS: It's not a fairy tale, it's about things that have actually happened to them.

MS. WITTLA: While you were present for Caitlyn's interview, did she indicate whether or not she understood the difference between the truth and a lie?

MR. ROSS: Yes, she did.

MS. WITTLA: Did she promise to tell you the truth?

MR. ROSS: She did.

MS. WITTLA: Or Ms. Fyle, tell Ms. Fyle the truth?

MR. ROSS: Yes.

MS. WITTLA: Or did she promise you both, I guess?

MR. ROSS: No, she, Ms. Fyle did the interview, and I stood off to the side in the background, and just observed the interview. I didn't interact with the child at all during the interview.

MS. WITTLA: Okay, when you say you stood off to the side, to the back, if you're describing where everybody is, where was Ms. Fyle?

MR. ROSS: Ms. Fyle was in front of the child talking to the child and I stood off on the side of the room, kind of out of a direct line of sight of Caitlyn.

MS. WITTLA: To Caitlyn?

MR. ROSS: Yes.

MS. WITTLA: Would you say that, that followed the Protocol?

MR. ROSS: Yes. Support people are supposed to stay off to the side, and not interact with the child or interfere at any time with the interview.

MS. WITTLA: And why stay out of the line of sight?

MR. ROSS: Because we want the child to talk to the person that's doing the interview and not be looking around the room and trying to feel like they have to explain their story to other people that are in the room. They just want it one person, one on one.

MS. WITTLA: After Caitlyn got through the truth lie determination and promised to tell the truth, what's the next part of the protocol?

MR. ROSS: The next part of the protocol?

MS. WITTLA: Yes.

MR. ROSS: Is building rapport with the child.

MS. WITTLA: Did you observe any rapport building during this interview?

MR. ROSS: Yes. Ms. Fyle asked Caitlyn how she was doing in school and how she liked school, and what kind of fun things she was doing and basic small chit chat to build a little bit of a relationship so they could move forward with the interview. Caitlyn responded very well for that.

MS. WITTLA: And how long does rapport building typically take?

MR. ROSS: That depends on the child.

MS. WITTLA: For Caitlyn's case? Did it take a long time; a short time?

MR. ROSS: Relatively, I would say no more than five or ten minutes; it was, it moved rather quickly. Caitlyn felt very comfortable with Ms. Fyle rather quickly.

MS. WITTLA: After rapport building, what happens next?

MR. ROSS: They just start talking. They start talking about things, and they start talking about things that happen at home, and how things are going at home and....

MS. WITTLA: Is that where Caitlyn's interview went to next; as to how are things at home?

MR. ROSS: Uh-huh.

MS. WITTLA: So how did Caitlyn think things were going at home?

MR. ROSS: For the most part, Caitlyn said that things were going pretty well at home. Evasive about some things, but she, for the most part, was pretty happy and talked about the way things were going at home. Then the topic came up about her father getting mad, and she talked about how she... she talked about getting spanked and Ms. Fyle asked her about getting spanked with an open hand or with a belt; and Caitlyn went on to talk about sometimes with an open hand, sometimes, you know, it was a belt.

Right here, if this actually occurred as Ross described it, Ms. Fyle did not follow the protocol. She planted the idea of the belt, and Caitlyn, who had a very lively and vivid imagination, I'm sure picked up on that. Kids will do that, and do tend to make a story a bit bigger than it actually is if they are given the necessary tools.

MS. WITTLA: You mentioned that Caitlyn was evasive at some points in time. Were there any particular subjects that she became evasive about?

MR. ROSS: She didn't particularly want to talk about some of the things that happened with her father, as far as what happens when you get in trouble at your house; what happens when you don't follow the rules; those kind of things.

MS. WITTLA: So if you're talking about Caitlyn before that, if she was asked to talk about her day at school, was her response freer?

MR. ROSS: Yes, it was.

MS. WITTLA: Was she fairly descriptive?

MR. ROSS: We talked about school lunch, recess, most things a six year old talks about when they come home from school.

MS. WITTLA: So then when the subject of her father was brought up, Robert Coleman was brought up, how were her responses then?

MR. ROSS: Guarded. Kind of hesitant.

MS. WITTLA: What about talking about her mother?

MR. ROSS: She didn't say much about her mother.

MS. WITTLA: Going back to talking about her father, then, her step-father then, did she say how many times she had been spanked?

MR. ROSS: No.

MS. WITTLA: Did she say if it happened more than once?

MR. ROSS: She said it happened a lot.

MS. WITTLA: Did she mention any of the things that she would get in trouble for?

MR. ROSS: Um, not eating certain food items, she got in trouble for some physical stuff that she had done with her sister Ashley, some pushes, some shoves, some things like that.

MS. WITTLA: Did she indicate when these things happened?

MR. ROSS: No.

MS. WITTLA: When she described getting spanked, what words did she use to describe this?

MR. ROSS: What do you mean?

MS. WITTLA: Well, how did she describe getting spanked? Did she just say I get spanked or did she say something more than that?

MR. ROSS: She said she gets spanked, she said she gets spanked with a belt; she talked about times where she was held down by people when she was getting spanked; she talked about getting spanked and having to get put into a bath tub.

MS. WITTLA: Did she say why she's in a bath tub?

MR. ROSS: Because there was marks on her bottom, marks on her butt, is the way she talked about it.

MS. WITTLA: Did she say if anybody else was with her in the bathroom?

MR. ROSS: Becky was with her. Becky Payne.

Let me insert something here. I know for a fact this incident never occurred with me or my wife. There was, however, some discussion with the Paynes in which we all compared manners in which we were punished as kids growing up. There was some discussion of vinegar baths at that time, but no such incident ever occurred with our kids. Janet and I were both committed to the idea that none of the types of punishment we had to endure would ever be passed on to our children. It appears the Paynes might have taken note of the conversations however, in order to make up their false accusations against us. Caitlyn states even now, that Becky was a big liar. She describes Bobby as "dangerous." She admits now she was fearful of Bobby. And where the Fyle remarks followed nearly word for word every accusation the Paynes made, it would seem to me now that they may have been making up their story based on their own actions or experiences, and not ours. And even if you believe the story Fyle tells, and this testimony by Ross, why is it that, if indeed this did happen, that the Paynes were not also charged with child abuse? They did say, after all, that they helped us hold Caitlyn down while I was the one administering the beating. If I had done it, I should certainly have been charged with a crime, as should my wife, had she been involved. It leaves me wondering why we were not charged with crimes, and why, in fact, the prosecutors left the Paynes out of it entirely, if, indeed, they really did believe their story?

MS. WITTLA: She talk about anything else? Did she tell you anything else about being in the bathroom?

MR. ROSS: She said she was in there for a long time, I believe it was a couple of hours.

Whoa! Wait just a minute! There is no way Caitlyn could have said that! She had no concept of time at that age! Ross took that directly from the Payne list of accusations! So this, in itself, proves Ross was also lying!

MR. ROSS (continued): Um, she said when she got out of the bath tub that Becky said something about the marks, Becky said the marks were gone, but they were not really. The marks were not really gone.

MS. WITTLA: Did she tell you anything about what she did wrong the day that she ended up having to sit in the bath tub?

MR. ROSS: I don't recall.

MS. WITTLA: And when you're talking about she was spanked, was held down, that was the same day as the bath tub event?

MR. ROSS: I'm not sure.

Pardon me, here, but it seems to me that if she had made these statements, it would remain very clear in the minds of the interviewers. Yet Ross says he can't recall, and he's not sure. Maybe because it never was confirmed? Or even said?

MS. WITTLA: Did she indicate how she got the marks on her butt?

MR. ROSS: The marks on her butt were from getting struck with the belt.

MS. WITTLA: Did she tell you if she had clothes on or not?

MR. ROSS: No, she said most of the time when she got spanked, she got spanked on a bare butt.

MS. WITTLA: And when she got spanked on a bare butt, it was with?

MR. ROSS: The belt.

MS. WITTLA: The belt?

MR. ROSS: Yes.

MS. WITTLA: When she mentioned that someone held her down, did she say who that was?

MR. ROSS: She had indicated during the interview that she had been held down by Bobby Payne, by Becky Payne, and she had been held down at different times by her mother.

MS. WITTLA: Did she tell you anything else about interacting with her father, aside from being spanked?

MR. ROSS: There was some verbal stuff that I believe she, she mentioned, and she said that when she did things that weren't appropriate, she'd be told to go in the corner.

MS. WITTLA: So that was another form of punishment that she received, was going in the corner?

MR. ROSS: Yes.

MS. WITTLA: And I don't know if I was clear on this, but when we were talking about Caitlyn being held down, and someone hitting her with a belt, that someone would be?

MR. ROSS: Her father, Robert Coleman.

MS. WITTLA: Did she say if anyone else ever hit her with a belt?

MR. ROSS: No.

MS. WITTLA: After this conversation about being struck with a belt, time out being in a corner, did she describe anything else to you that she wasn't happy with in her home life?

MR. ROSS: No.

MS. WITTLA: After you have the interview, what's the last part of Forensic Interview Protocol?

MR. ROSS: You kind of get— you steer off of the subject that you talked about with the child. You kind of go back to the rapport building phase and you kind of talk about something off the subject; and then you thank the child for talking to you and you end your interview.

MS. WITTLA: When you go back to rapport building, then you go off the other subject, the reason you guys are there; why do you do that?

MR. ROSS: You don't want to walk out of the room from interviewing a child and leaving that impression that the last thing that you talked to that child about was something horrific that might have happened to them; you go back to something more neutral, some pleasant, something to leave that child feeling good about themselves and....

MS. WITTLA: Was that done with Caitlyn?

MR. ROSS: Yes.

MS. WITTLA: When you left the bedroom that the children had, what was her affect?

MR. ROSS: She was fine; she wanted to start playing again.

MS. WITTLA: After the interview with— something I forgot to ask you, um, did Caitlyn describe anything about where these belts were?

MR. ROSS: In a drawer, in the dresser or drawer someplace in the house; I believe it was a dresser in the house.

MS. WITTLA: Caitlyn knew that that's where they were?

MR. ROSS: Yes, and she kind of made specific reference to the orange, orange-ish, brown belt; she did make a specific reference to a certain belt.

MS. WITTLA: After your interview or after Ms. Fyle's interview with Caitlyn, was anyone else interviewed?

MR. ROSS: No.

No? Did he say no? Then what were the five minutes spent with Ashley in that same bedroom? They admitted in their report they took her in there, but that she had not much to say. Yet now, in court, they deny it? Something wrong here.....

MS. WITTLA: You didn't interview Robert Coleman or Janet Coleman?

MR. ROSS: No. Ms. Fyle spoke to the parents afterwards.

MS. WITTLA: You weren't present for that part of the interview?

MR. ROSS: I was present, but I merely observed.

MS. WITTLA: Okay you didn't; you observed Caitlyn's interview and you observed Robert and Janet's interview, but would you say you paid the same level of attention to all three interviews?

MR. ROSS: Mr. and Mrs. Coleman were kind of spoken to in the kitchen of the house, after everything was done. Ms. Fyle kind of talked to them about.....

MS. WITTLA: ... about what had been exposed by Caitlyn?

MR. ROSS: Uh-huh.

MS. WITTLA: Would you say that you were part of that discussion or were you just in the house?

MR. ROSS: I'm like, I made a few comments I believe.

MS. WITTLA: After you and Ms. Fyle and Officer Saippa left the house, did you have any other contacts with Robert Coleman?

MR. ROSS: The next day I called Mr. Coleman because, on behalf of Ms. Fyle, because Ms. Fyle wanted to go back and re-interview Caitlyn, we wanted to see if we could catch Caitlyn at school. And I called Mr. Coleman on his cell phone and he had indicated to me that he was in Marquette with his wife and two children because she had an appointment with a physician up in the Marquette area for her current pregnancy.

MS. WITTLA: Did you ask Mr. Coleman anything about when he would be back?

MR. ROSS: He indicated to me that he would be back later that afternoon, and that he would contact Ms. Fyle upon his return.

MS. WITTLA: At the beginning of your testimony, you indicated that March 11th was the day that this interview with Caitlyn took place?

MR. ROSS: Correct.

MS. WITTLA: What day was it when you had this conversation with Mr. Coleman? Was it the 12th—was it the 13th?

MR. ROSS: It was the 13th.

MS. WITTLA: It was the 13th. How do you know it was the 13th?

MR. ROSS: It was the 13th because the 12th we went to training in Escanaba for another, for DHS training and we came back on the 13th and we wanted to re-interview... Ms. Fyle wanted to re-interview Caitlyn.

MS. WITTLA: So that would have been Thursday; we had an all day training in Escanaba the day before? On Wednesday?

MR. ROSS: Yes.

MS. WITTLA: When you contacted Mr. Coleman, what time of day was that?

MR. ROSS: Late morning.

MS. WITTLA: On Thursday?

MR. ROSS: Yes.

MS. WITTLA: Did you try to contact him any more after that?

MR. ROSS: No, I believe Ms. Fyle tried to contact him afterwards.

MS. WITTLA: When was the next time you had any contact with Robert, Janet, Caitlyn or Ashley?

MR. ROSS: It would have been the following Monday when the two girls were in a shelter home in Ontonagon County.

MS. WITTLA: So if I'm doing my math right, that would have been on the 17th?

MR. ROSS: Correct.

MS. WITTLA: So on the 17th you had contact with Caitlyn and Ashley?

MR. ROSS: Yes. They were in a shelter home in Ontonagon. I accompanied Ms. Fyle to the shelter home because I had to start a foster care case on the children.

MS. WITTLA: Okay, so when this case began, Ms. Fyle was considered to be the investigator?

MR. ROSS: Yes, in the child protective services case.

MS. WITTLA: Okay, and you kind of hanging as the support for her?

MR. ROSS: Correct.

MS. WITTLA: You didn't have an open case yet?

MR. ROSS: No.

MS. WITTLA: And depending on how the interviews went you may not have had an open case?

MR. ROSS: Correct.

MS. WITTLA: But as of the 17th, since the children were placed out of their home, another case opens at DHS?

MR. ROSS: When children are removed from the parental home and placed into a shelter home or a foster home, a foster care case has to be opened up with the State with our agency.

MS. WITTLA: And that's what you did?

MR. ROSS: Yes.

MS. WITTLA: So as of the 17th, when you would have gone out to the shelter home, you would have had an open case as a foster care worker, would the other case have continued to be open?

MR. ROSS: Yes, until it reaches adjudication.

MS. WITTLA: And what is adjudication?

MR. ROSS: That's what we're doing today, we're deciding on whether or not the allegations in the petition are true or not.

MS. WITTLA: If the allegations in the petition are determined to be true, does Ms. Fyle's case go away?

MR. ROSS: Yes, and it would remain a foster care case.

MS. WITTLA: With you?

MR. ROSS: Yes.

MS. WITTLA: So then the kids would have one worker?

MR. ROSS: Correct.

MS. WITTLA: When you went up to the house on the 17th, did you interview Caitlyn and Ashley?

MR. ROSS: I didn't, no.

MS. WITTLA: Were you present when Ms. Fyle interviewed them?

MR. ROSS: Yes.

MS. WITTLA: When you first arrived, did you see the kids right away or were they somewhere else in the house?

MR. ROSS: The foster parent, LaVerne Pestka met us at the door, she let us in. We went through her, into her living area, when we got to her living area, Caitlyn and Ashley were playing on the floor in front of the television. Caitlyn got up and ran away and then she was running down the hallway, she says, "I'm not allowed to talk to you, my daddy says I'm not supposed to talk to you, you guys are the cops, I'm not supposed to talk to you about spanks" is what Caitlyn had said, on her way down the hallway.

MS. WITTLA: While Caitlyn was leaving, did Ashley do anything?

MR. ROSS: Continued to play and she kind of clutched on to the foster mom.

MS. WITTLA: Did Caitlyn come back?

MR. ROSS: Yes.

MS. WITTLA: And how did she come back?

MR. ROSS: Ms. Pestka went to the bedroom, got Caitlyn and asked her to come out and talk to us.

MS. WITTLA: How did Caitlyn appear when she came back into the room?

MR. ROSS: Guarded; a little hesitant; a little fearful.

MS. WITTLA: Did she seem different from the first time that you saw her on the 11th?

MR. ROSS: Yes, she wasn't as talkative; she seemed reluctant to talk to us.

MS. WITTLA: When she came back into the room, you indicated that Ms. Fyle had a conversation with her; interview?

MR. ROSS: Yes.

MS. WITTLA: And you were present for this?

MR. ROSS: I was present for some of it, and then a lot of my time was spent with the foster mom asking her if she needed things for the children; asking her if she needed things, you know, for herself or for the foster home or anything like that because I wanted to make sure that the foster mom had everything she needed for the children.

MS. WITTLA: While you were there, did you hear Caitlyn make any other statements?

MR. ROSS: Um….

MR. FINDLAY: … Your Honor, I'm objecting, lack of foundation for this. I didn't hear anything about Forensic Protocol Interview being followed for this, and I think that's only circumstance under which such hearsay can come in, but….

MS. WITTLA: Okay, I'll do a different question. Mr. Ross, on this particular date, are you aware of whether or not Ms. Fyle used the Forensic Interview Protocol when she spoke with Caitlyn?

MR. ROSS: I believe she did.

MS. WITTLA: Did she go through the same kinds of steps as previously that you described?

MR. ROSS: Yes.

MS. WITTLA: Do, "We're talking about truth lie, promise to tell the truth"; rapport building?

MR. ROSS: Yes.

MS. WITTLA: Were you present for that part?

MR. ROSS: I did hear that part, yes.

MS. WITTLA: Once they got to rapport building part, did Ms. Fyle go into an interview with Caitlyn?

MR. ROSS: She spoke to— yes, she did start an interview with Caitlyn.

MS. WITTLA: Would you say that interview was long, short?

MR. ROSS: We were not there very long; so it wasn't like—we were only there thirty minutes, tops; and I spent most—and we were kind of in and out. We were—I was on my way to a couple of court hearings in Ontonagon that day.

MS. WITTLA: So would you say it was a, it was an interview, but it was shorter than the first one?

MR. ROSS: Yes.

MS. WITTLA: Would you say that the Forensic Interview Protocol was followed as with the first one?

MR. ROSS: Yes.

MS. WITTLA: Did Caitlyn understand, well, did she seem to be responding like, "Oh yeah, I know this" because she had just been through it a week before?

MR. ROSS: No.

MS. WITTLA: Okay, so tell me what her response was like then?

MR. ROSS: Regarding?

MS. WITTLA: Regarding Ms. Fyle starting the interview with her.

MR. ROSS: She answered her questions, I mean, during the initial truth and lie, she answered her questions, just like in the initial interview.

MS. WITTLA: During that period of time would you say that, that she was guarded?

MR. ROSS: Yes.

MS. WITTLA: Did she warm up after a certain point?

MR. ROSS: From what I could see, yes, because I was, like I said, I was talking to the foster mom, but from what I could see they looked to be having a good conversation.

MS. WITTLA: At what point during this interview of Ms. Fyle's, the second interview of Ms. Fyle's, that at the foster home; would you say that you shifted your attention to the foster parent?

MR. ROSS: Almost immed— probably within the first five or ten minutes of us getting, when Ms. Fyle sat down and started talking to Caitlyn, I kind of walked through the rapport building process, they were having a conversation about how things were going at Ms. Pestka's house, and how they liked things there and, after that I kind of diverted my attention to take care of….

MS. WITTLA: … Go ahead, finish.

MR. ROSS: I diverted my attention to take care of whatever needed to, whatever the foster family required of me because I'm there to also support them as well as the children.

MS. WITTLA: How did Caitlyn describe being in foster care?

MR. ROSS: She liked it.

MS. WITTLA: Did she give any examples as to why?

MR. ROSS: I had heard Caitlyn say that she liked foster care because she didn't get spanked there.

MS. WITTLA: Did you hear anything else that Caitlyn said about being in foster care beyond that?

MR. ROSS: No.

MS. WITTLA: Was that approximately the point in time when you started talking mostly to Ms. Pestka?

MR. ROSS: Yes.

MS. WITTLA: Did you come back into any part of Ms. Fyle's interview with Caitlyn?

MR. ROSS: No. As I was wrapping up with Ms. Pestka, Ms. Fyle was wrapping up with Caitlyn and we had to excuse ourselves and get to court in Ontonagon.

MS. WITTLA: From that point forward in time, have you ever interviewed Caitlyn?

MR. ROSS: No.

MS. WITTLA: Have you seen her since then?

MR. ROSS: Several times.

MS. WITTLA: Where have you seen her?

MR. ROSS: We had set up parenting time appointments at my office initially, where the foster mom in Ontonagon would bring Caitlyn and Ashley to my office for parenting time with their parents in my office. And then on the 31st of March, due to conflicts at the shelter home we had to move Caitlyn and Ashley to another foster home in Marquette County, I'm sorry, moved the kids to Marquette County to another foster home.

MS. WITTLA: Is the DHS in favor of moving children?

MR. ROSS: No, moving children is never a good plan.

At this point, the judge interrupted the trial, so that court could adjourn for the day. So finally, after sitting through what seemed like endless time span, listening to lie after lie, day two was finally concluded!

—Chapter Twenty—

The Trial—Day Three

The first words out of the judge's mouth on this, day three of our trial, were indicative of the entire court case. It was a matter of hurry up, let's get them convicted and get on with more important cases I have to do. Not his exact words, of course, but definitely his assessment of this case and where it was going I think. In order to expedite the progress of the case, the judge would start the day with a new witness, holding the balance of testimony from Bob Ross until after the first witness was finished testifying. That first witness was Doctor Gary M. Pusateri, and once he was sworn in, the day's events began as our lawyer opened the questioning:

MR. FINDLAY: Would you state your full name for the record?

MR. PUSATERI: Sure. Gary Michael Pusateri.

MR. FINDLAY: And how are you employed?

MR. PUSATERI: I am a physician at the Lac View Desert Clinic in Watersmeet, Michigan.

MR. FINDLAY: And how long have you been a doctor?

MR. PUSATERI: I have been a physician for twenty years.

MR. FINDLAY: Do you have an area of ex—a specialty, or?

MR. PUSATERI: I've been in general practice for about, ah, this is my fourteenth year; I actually did emergency medicine for about six years; was the emergency room director here at Grand View in Ironwood for several years.

MR. FINDLAY: Right now you're family medicine?

MR. PUSATERI: Family medicine, yes.

MR. FINDLAY: Okay. Do you know the Colemans?

MR. PUSATERI: I do.

MR. FINDLAY: And have you treated their children?

MR. PUSATERI: Yes I have.

MR. FINDLAY: Okay, and by their children, I mean Ashley Brag or Coleman, and no, Ashley Coleman and Caitlyn Brag?

MR. PUSATERI: Correct.

MR. FINDLAY: How many times have you treated each of those kids?

MR. PUSATERI: Well, my office actually, has treated; I believe Caitlyn once and Ashley about five times.

MR. FINDLAY: And can you explain to me— is it possible you got their names mixed up because I just mixed them up too?

MR. PUSATERI: The younger one was treated once....

MR. FINDLAY: Okay.

MR. PUSATERI: The older one was treated about five times.

MR. FINDLAY: And you would agree that one is Caitlyn?

MR. PUSATERI: Yes.

MR. FINDLAY: And the younger is Ashley?

MR. PUSATERI: Yes.

MR. FINDLAY: What was Ashley treated for; what was the nature of her office visit?

MR. PUSATERI: I'm sorry, I'm reminded, Ashley is—

MR. FINDLAY: The two year old.

MR. PUSATERI: The two year old was, ah, I believe seen for a Well Child physical exam.

MR. FINDLAY: Okay, that would've been done by the Nurse Practitioner in your office?

MR. PUSATERI: Yes.

MR. FINDLAY: What's involved in a Well Child visit?

MR. PUSATERI: Basically you talk to the parents and see if there's any specific problems with the child, and then in addition to that, you do a physical examination.

MR. FINDLAY: How about Caitlyn, who is the older child?

MR. PUSATERI: Yes.

MR. FINDLAY: You said she had been seen five times?

MR. PUSATERI: I believe about five times, yes.

MR. FINDLAY: Explain the nature of those visits if you can.

MR. PUSATERI: One was a physical examination; that was also done by one of my Nurse Practitioners. Three, I believe— three of those visits were for a lesion on her lip. And one was for, ah, a cyst that was on her back and ultimately she was referred.

MR. FINDLAY: Okay, what was she referred for?

MR. PUSATERI: There was an inclusion cyst and we generally refer those out to a surgeon who does that type of surgical procedure more often.

MR. FINDLAY: Okay, and what is an inclusion cyst, just so we have an idea?

MR. PUSATERI: It's— it would be a cyst that would be just under the surface of the center, under the surface of the skin—or subcutaneous is what we would call it. It's a small space that would be filled with, um, tissue, small amounts of tissue. Most people would think of it, when they initially saw it, it would look like a big pimple.

MR. FINDLAY: Okay and this surgery treatment that is a small incision in removing it?

MR. PUSATERI: Yes, a complete excision of that,yes.

MR. FINDLAY: And that, but was that done in a different office?

MR. PUSATERI: That was done in a different office.

MR. FINDLAY: As a doctor, are you a mandatory reporter under Michigan's law?

MR. PUSATERI: Yes I am.

MR. FINDLAY: So can you explain to me what a mada— what you understand a mandatory reporter to be?

MR. PUSATERI: Okay, my understanding of a mandatory reporter is if I have any suspicion whatsoever of any type of abuse; I am obligated to report that abuse.

MR. FINDLAY: Did you ever have any suspicion regarding the Colemans' children?

MR. PUSATERI: Never.

MR. FINDLAY: Did you ever see— in whether your notations made in the medical records; or did you ever see any indications, physical marks or anything like that, that would make you think of abuse?

MR. PUSATERI: I've never seen anything that would indicate to me that there was any type of abuse, no. Just so that you're aware of it, in addition to seeing them, you know, I have seen the Colemans also when their children were present, so there, I've seen interaction between the Colemans and their children on a number of occasions.

MR. FINDLAY: Did observing any of that interaction give you any pause or any reason to suspect or...

MR. PUSATERI: ... None whatsoever.

MR. FINDLAY: And what treatment of, especially Caitlyn, the older child?

MR. PUSATERI: I believe she has been coming to our clinic for just about maybe a year and a half.

MR. FINDLAY: Okay, beginning when, if you, if you had the—

MR. PUSATERI:— I would say the Spring of '07.

MR. FINDLAY: Do you know the last time she was seen in your office?

MR. PUSATERI: I would say, I am aware of a visit in the Spring of this year.

MR. FINDLAY: Spring of this year?

MR. PUSATERI: Yes.

MR. FINDLAY: Would that be March?

MR. PUSATERI: I believe February or March, yes.

MR. FINDLAY: And again, during that visit, there was no signs of abuse or anything else?

MR. PUSATERI: No.

MR. FINDLAY: No further questions.

THE COURT: Ms. Wittla?

MS. WITTLA: Doctor, you referred to your office that was seeing Caitlyn and Ashley?

MR. PUSATERI: Yes.

MS. WITTLA: That means it wasn't you?

MR. PUSATERI: Well it was not me directly; I did see the older child once, yes.

MS. WITTLA: So you treated Caitlyn once?

MR. PUSATERI: Yes.

MS. WITTLA: You treated Ashley, never?

MR. PUSATERI: I have not personally treated her; however, you need to understand that my Nurse Practitioners work directly for me, so that I am ultimately responsible for whatever they do. Generally, they will discuss every single case with me.

MS. WITTLA: Do you have your case records with you?

MR. PUSATERI: I do not.

MS. WITTLA: Did you receive a request from the Department of Human Services to provide those records to the DHS?

MR. PUSATERI: My medical records person indicated to me yesterday that apparently they did, but there was no signature from the parents to release the records.

MS. WITTLA: Do you understand that the parents did not have to sign to release records?

MR. PUSATERI: No, I did not understand that, neither did my medical records person.

MS. WITTLA: So that's why the records were not sent?

MR. PUSATERI: Correct.

MS. WITTLA: So aside from your responsibility for your Nurse Practitioners; going back to how much interaction you, personally, have had with treating these children, you've never treated Ashley?

MR. PUSATERI: Correct, directly.

MS. WITTLA: And you saw, yes directly, do you understand doctor that I'm asking you for what you personally see?

MR. PUSATERI: I understand.

MS. WITTLA: I have an issue with you having access to records in your home office; I have what I believe are the records from your office here; they were faxed this morning. Actually, like two minutes ago, and as I'm looking at these, it would appear that Ashley was in your office sometime in December of 2007?

MR. PUSATERI: Yes, I believe so.

MS. WITTLA: And that was what you were referring to as the Well baby checkup?

MR. PUSATERI: I believe so.

MS. WITTLA: How often do children have Well Child checkups?

MR. PUSATERI: Generally, annually, and early on sometimes more frequently, they can be every six months in the first year or two.

MS. WITTLA: Do you know how old Ashley is?

MR. PUSATERI: Not off the top of my head no, I'm sorry.

MS. WITTLA: If I told you that she turned two in January; does that sound about right?

MR. PUSATERI: Sure.

MS. WITTLA: So if Ashley, and, well, if the Cole—well, let me ask you this, you indicated that Caitlyn first started seeing people in your office in the Spring of 2007?

MR. PUSATERI: I believe so, I'm sorry. I'm not real clear on the dates; I'd actually have to look at the records to tell you that; but I believe so.

MS. WITTLA: Did the Colemans come to see you before the children came to see you?

MR. PUSATERI: I think the very first person to see us was the youngest child; was that in '06?

MS. WITTLA: The youngest would be Ashley?

MR. PUSATERI: Ashley was there on August of '06, I very briefly reviewed the records yesterday.

MS. WITTLA: I'm looking at a document, looks like there's three pages including a cover sheet and it says Ashley Coleman, it gives her date of birth as January 24th of '06. It gives date of service of 12/12/07. Would you like to see it?

MR. PUSATERI: Oh, I believe you. Well, it would help to look at it, sure.

MS. WITTLA: Can you tell me if that's the record that you've reviewed?

MR. PUSATERI: That's it.

MS. WITTLA: Okay?

MR. PUSATERI: Yeah.

MS. WITTLA: Are there any other records for Ashley that we didn't get?

MR. PUSATERI: Not that I know of, no.

MS. WITTLA: That's the only one you remember looking at?

MR. PUSATERI: That's the only one I remember seeing, so that's when she— if that's the first time we saw her that would've been the first time that she would have been considered our patient.

MS. WITTLA: Now to the document with eight pages, including the first one, and I believe that these are records for Caitlyn.

MR. PUSATERI: Okay, thank you. Okay, it was Caitlyn what was seen in August of '06.

MS. WITTLA: Okay, so would Caitlyn, from your recollection, have been the first person that you saw from the Coleman family?

MR. PUSATERI: I believe so.

MS. WITTLA: Do the records that you're holding indicate how many times you've seen Caitlyn?

MR. PUSATERI: Yes.

MS. WITTLA: And how many times has that been?

MR. PUSATERI: Five.

MS. WITTLA: Could you give me the dates?

MR. PUSATERI: Sure. Initially was the August date, let's see here, that was 8-23-06; next visit was 12-12-07; then 3-13-07; 2-20-07; ah, actually this one is out of order, but it's 2-1-07.

MS. WITTLA: If the first time that Caitlyn saw you and became a patient of yours was in August of 2006; and Ashley was born in January of 2006; how old would Ashley have been at approximately that time?

MR. PUSATERI: This sounds like one of those questions they usually ask on a pre-med test; so if Caitlyn was....

MS. WITTLA: ... I'm thinking about seven months old.

MR. PUSATERI: Seven months old, okay.

MS. WITTLA: Does that sound right?

MR. PUSATERI: Yes.

MS. WITTLA: We're going from January to August?

MR. PUSATERI: Yes.

MS. WITTLA: Caitlyn's a little kid?

MR. PUSATERI: Yes.

MS. WITTLA: Ashley's just born—about seven months old?

MR. PUSATERI: Okay.

MS. WITTLA: But the first time that you ever saw Ashley was December of 2007?

MR. PUSATERI: That's correct.

MS. WITTLA: Three months before she... well, make it a month or so before she turns two years old?

MR. PUSATERI: Correct.

MS. WITTLA: It it's typical for kids to have an annual Well Baby checkup or maybe every six months under the age of two; you didn't see her at all before then?

MR. PUSATERI: I did not, no.

MS. WITTLA: You're not aware if she went somewhere else....

MR. PUSATERI: I'm not aware of that, no.

MS. WITTLA: You mentioned there was a cyst on Caitlyn's back that you referred out for surgery?

MR. PUSATERI: Yes, she was referred, I believe to, ah, more than likely would have been here in Ironwood, but let me.... if it's okay, I would just look at her note here. Okay, the note states that she was going to be referred to Houghton for an evaluation and possible removal.

MS. WITTLA: Do you know what time frame that was?

MR. PUSATERI: That was 12-12-07.

MS. WITTLA: And that's the last time that you saw Caitlyn?

MR. PUSATERI: That, I believe, is the last time I saw... um... yes.

MS. WITTLA: Did you ever receive any records back to determine whether or not the cyst was removed?

MR. PUSATERI: I don't have those. No, I don't believe so.

MS. WITTLA: You indicated it was on her back, can you give me some idea like where?

MR. PUSATERI: I can tell you. Right here, ah, the right back, near the, ah, scapula which would be the, ah, the wing bone back here.

MS. WITTLA: The wing bone?

MR. PUSATERI: The wing bone.

MS. WITTLA: Okay, like a shoulder blade?

MR. PUSATERI: In... shoulder blade, there's the, there's a better word.

MS. WITTLA: Okay, doctor, aside from seeing the Colemans at the clinic in Watersmeet; did you see them anywhere else?

MR. PUSATERI: Ah, no place other than the clinic.

MS. WITTLA: So you've never been to their house?

MR. PUSATERI: Nope.

MS. WITTLA: Hung out with them?

MR. PUSATERI: Never hung out.

MS. WITTLA: Okay, so including the time that you've seen Robert and Janet for perhaps their own appointments; how many times would you say that you personally have seen these kids?

MR. PUSATERI: I would say with the direct interaction here, and the times with the Colemans, probably six or seven times.

MS. WITTLA: Okay, and that's over the last?

MR. PUSATERI: Year and a half.

MS. WITTLA: Thank you.

THE COURT: Mr. Perhalla?

MR. PERHALLA: Thank you. I was just a little confused, of the five times that you saw Caitlyn, or your office saw Caitlyn, which date did you actually examine her?

MR. PUSATERI: Let's see here; I saw her on 2-20-07.

MR. PERHALLA: And that was an examination of her. Would that be the lip lesion?

MR. PUSATERI: Yes, actually, there was a small procedure that we do where we freeze the lesion.

MR. PERHALLA: And so how long were you with Caitlyn that day?

MR. PUSATERI: Oh that would take from the time, probably fifteen minutes.

MR. PERHALLA: She was accompanied by one or both parents?

MR. PUSATERI: Yes.

MR. PERHALLA: Both, or?

MR. PUSATERI: Both. I believe it was both parents.

MR. PERHALLA: All the visits were with both parents or you don't know the other four?

MR. PUSATERI: I can't tell you that for sure, but I can't recall a time that I did not— that I saw the Colemans' children that they weren't with both parents.

MR. PERHALLA: Were any of these visits with you an emergency nature, or were they just something scheduled?

MR. PUSATERI: ... Something scheduled, yes.

MR. PERHALLA: And the August 23rd, '06 visit with—ah—or exam with Caitlyn; that was just a physical exam? A checkup?

MR. PUSATERI: Yes, that's a Well Child exam.

MR. PERHALLA: And that was done by your Nurse Practitioner?

MR. PUSATERI: Yes.

MR. PERHALLA: So those other... those four times that your Nurse Practitioner saw Caitlyn; you would not be seeing the child?

MR. PUSATERI: To go into the direct exam, no.

MR. PERHALLA: Maybe in passing in the halls?

MR. PUSATERI: In passing, sure.

MR. PERHALLA: Do you know if there were any visits that were scheduled that were cancelled?

MR. PUSATERI: Not to my recollection.

MR. PERHALLA: And I'm not sure... the Well Child physical exam; actually that was done by you or the Nurse Practitioner?

MR. PUSATERI: Nurse Practitioner.

MR. PERHALLA: So the only time that you would have actually seen Ashley would be just in passing?

MR. PUSATERI: Yes, or the interaction that we'd have in the office when I was seeing one of the Colemans—her parents.

MR. PERHALLA: And these examinations of the parents; how long would they last?

MR. PUSATERI: Oh, anywhere from fifteen minutes to an hour.

At this point in the trial, a cell phone interrupted things. The judge asked whose it was, and it was Perhalla's. As you might recall, the judge strongly indicated there should be no cell phones as he talked to prospective jurors. Apparently, Perhalla was not listening, and you would expect a severe reprimand. Did he get it? No! The judge just commented, "Okay, yeah, well it happens." Imagine if it had been my cell phone! At any rate, the judge just let it go, and allowed Perhalla to continue on as if it was no big deal:

MR. PERHALLA: And you figured that out to be how many times?

MR. PUSATERI: When the kids were with them?

MR. PERHALLA: Correct.

MR. PUSATERI: Probably a half a dozen.

MR. PERHALLA: The children were always with them when they came for their exams too?

MR. PUSATERI: Yeah, um, until more recently, yes.

MR. PERHALLA: Thank you.

THE COURT: Redirect?

MR. FINDLAY: Just briefly. Just on the dates of the treatment Doctor. So there were no—were there any doctor appointments on February 16th of '08?

MR. PUSATERI: February 16th of '08. I don't see one listed here.

MR. FINDLAY: How about the 17th. February 17th of '08?

MR. PUSATERI: No, I'm sorry, I don't see that.

MR. FINDLAY: I'm not suggesting there should be. I'm just asking you about the... how about February 18th?

MR. PUSATERI: I don't see no.... I don't see any exams from '08 here.

MR. FINDLAY: Okay, are you familiar with all of the allegations in this case?

MR. PUSATERI: Yes.

MR. FINDLAY: Based on your dealings with the Colemans, do you believe them?

MS. WITTLA: Objection your Honor.

THE COURT: Sustained. I mean, he can't give his opinion as to the ultimate issue; that's for the jury.

MR. FINDLAY: Okay, no further questions.

THE COURT: Any based—narrowly on what he just asked?

MS. WITTLA: Yes. I need to borrow that—

MR. PUSATERI: ... You bet.

MS. WITTLA: Okay, Doctor, when I'm looking at this document, I can see the little notes from each visit that Caitlyn was seen for. If an appointment had been scheduled for this child and missed for any reason; would that be contained in the records that you reviewed here?

MR. PUSATERI: Ah, probably, and it looks to me like what my medical records person sent you would have been the visits rather than the face sheets; it is possible that an appointment could have been missed and they didn't send you a face sheet; so I can't tell you for sure whether or not there were appointments that were made and missed.

MS. WITTLA: Because this is the info on times that the little kids were at your office?

MR. PUSATERI: Right, correct.

MS. WITTLA: Okay, thanks.

THE COURT: Did you have any narrow?

MR. PERHALLA: No, thanks your Honor.

MR. FINDLAY: Can you get us those face sheets; could they be faxed here?

MR. PUSATERI: They could be, yeah.

MR. FINDLAY: Okay.

MR. PUSATERI: Do you want me to have them faxed?

MR. FINDLAY: Yes, please. Fax them to my office.

MR. PUSATERI: Okay.

THE COURT: As long as the doctor is here, are you, is anybody introducing the records or, or not, you don't have to, but?

MS. WITTLA: I wasn't going to your Honor.

THE COURT: Because he would be the only escorting witness, so; although what he said, it would be enough....

MR. FINDLAY: I guess I would ask for provisionally that the face sheets be—

THE COURT:— Just in case; oh, that the face sheets be admitted, um.

MR. FINDLAY: To accept that they confirm that there are no missed appointments in February of '08.

MS. WITTLA: Well, your Honor, unless this witness can identify these documents for the jury in court; I don't know how on earth they could be admitted.

THE COURT: Well, maybe they can be admitted through the Colemans' testify, I don't know.

MR. FINDLAY:— The ordinary—

THE COURT:— In any event, let me ask about what you just looked at; those were your regularly kept records of your office?

MR. PUSATERI: Correct.

MR. FINDLAY: Thank you, I was going to lay that foundation; I think they'd be admitted under that excep-

tion.

THE COURT: And you can later decide if you want to actually mark them and put them into evidence, and then the face sheets; we'll see, we'll cover that legal issue later, but possibly they are the Colemans records and they can introduce them.

MR. FINDLAY: Well, then can I ask one follow up question on the face sheets, are the face sheets something that would be regularly kept in the course of your business?

MR. PUSATERI: Yes.

MR. FINDLAY: All right, thank you.

With that, Doctor Pusateri was excused, and the prosecution then called Jamie Perlich, and we pick it up with her testimony:

MS. WITTLA: Would you please state your name into the record?

MS. PERLICH: Jamie Perlich.

MS. WITTLA: And where do you currently live?

MS. PERLICH: In Montreal, Wisconsin.

MS. WITTLA: How do you know Robert and Janet Coleman?

MS. PERLICH: I rented from them.

MS. WITTLA: And approximately what time frame was that?

MS. PERLICH: I rented last summer around August, September.

MS. WITTLA: August, September of 2007?

MS. PERLICH: Yes.

MS. WITTLA: Until when?

MS. PERLICH: March of this year.

MS. WITTLA: So did you stop renting from them approximately three months ago?

MS. PERLICH: Yes.

MS. WITTLA: Did you rent an apartment or a house?

MS. PERLICH: It was a house.

MS. WITTLA: Did you live there with anyone else?

MS. PERLICH: Yes.

MS. WITTLA: Who lived there with you?

MS. PERLICH: My boyfriend.

MS. WITTLA: And his name is?

MS. PERLICH: Eli Lipske.

MS. WITTLA: Eli Lipske. Have you ever rented an apartment or house from anyone other than the Colemans?

MS. PERLICH: Yes.

MS. WITTLA: Comparing the landlord-tenant relationship between the two different places....

MR. FINDLAY: ... Objection! How is that revelant? I mean, good grief!

THE COURT: Response?

MS. WITTLA: Your Honor, this is an attempt to show that Mr. Coleman's interactions with his tenants went far beyond a typical landlord-tenant relationship.

MR. FINDLAY: .... And how is that....

THE COURT: ... Well, I mean, if you have facts to that extent that bear on the petition, fine. But in general, it's a little too broad. So I'd sustain the objection, but if there is something you want to get at specifically that bears on the case, fine. But a generic statement like that is... does not appear to be relevant.

MS. WITTLA: Ms. Perlich, how often did you come in contact with Mr. Coleman?

MS. PERLICH: A lot.

MS. WITTLA: What does a lot mean?

MS. PERLICH: Um, I'd see him probably every day, every other day.

MS. WITTLA: Was your rent due every day or every other day?

This last question just illustrates more fully the sarcastic attitude of this prosecutor! Is it her business as to how often we might mingle? And just because we do, does it mean that the rent must be due? Of course not! I know a lot of tenants who are good friends with their landlords! This prosecutor wanted to make this sound as though it were a crime! Would it be better if all tenants hated their landlords? Get a grip! But to continue with Jamie's answer:

MS. PERLICH: No, every month.

MS. WITTLA: So you just saw him in passing?

MS. PERLICH: Yes.

MS. WITTLA: Did he ever seek you out to speak to you?

MS. PERLICH: A couple times when he would be working in the yard.

MS. WITTLA: So from the time that you started renting in August, September, 2007, until March 2008, you saw him a couple of times in passing?

See how Ms. Wittla tries to twist things and make it appear somebody said something they didn't say? The witness already told her it was a lot, not just a couple of times in passing.

MS. PERLICH: A lot.

MS. WITTLA: Okay, was there a point in time when you saw him more often?

MS. PERLICH: No.

Is it even possible for her to see me any more than every day? Good God, lady!

MS. WITTLA: Are you aware of where Ashley and Caitlyn are right now?

MS. PERLICH: Not really, no.

MS. WITTLA: Do you know if they live with their parents?

MS. PERLICH: That I know, they don't.

MS. WITTLA: How do you know they don't live with their parents?

MS. PERLICH: The Colemans had told me.

MS. WITTLA: And when did they tell you this?

MS. PERLICH: I think like a day or two after they were gone?

MS. WITTLA: Do you remember the time frame?

MS. PERLICH: No, I do not.

MS. WITTLA: Do you have any idea why? Is this just conversation or?

MS. PERLICH: What?

MS. WITTLA: Did you ask after the children, is that why they told you?

MS. PERLICH: Yes.

MS. WITTLA: After finding out that Ashley and Caitlyn did not live with the Colemans any more; did you have any more increased contact with Robert and Janet?

MS. PERLICH: Yes.

MS. WITTLA: How frequent did they contact you?

MS. PERLICH: Like once awhile, like maybe once a week.

MS. WITTLA: After their children were removed from their care?

MS. PERLICH: Yes.

MS. WITTLA: And why did they contact you?

MS. PERLICH: They needed somebody to talk to.

MS. WITTLA: Did you consider yourself to be friends with the Colemans?

MS. PERLICH: At a time, yes.

MS. WITTLA: Did you say at?

MS. PERLICH: At a time yes?

MS. WITTLA: At a time?

MS. PERLICH: Yes.

MS. WITTLA: At that time?

MS. PERLICH: Uh-huh.

MS. WITTLA: Do you still consider yourself to be friends with the Colemans?

MS. PERLICH: Yeah.

MS. WITTLA: Did Robert Coleman ever call you on his cell phone?

MS. PERLICH: Yes he did.

MS. WITTLA: After the kids were removed, how many times would you say he called you?

MS. PERLICH: Once, twice a week, once a week, twice a week.

MS. WITTLA: Was that for the same reason to have someone to talk to?

MS. PERLICH: That, and um, rent.

MS. WITTLA: Have you ever seen Robert Coleman strike Caitlyn or Ashley?

MS. PERLICH: No I have not.

MS. WITTLA: Have you ever observed Robert Coleman in a position where you believed he was going to strike someone?

MS. PERLICH: Once.

MS. WITTLA: When was that?

MS. PERLICH: Summertime. Last summer.

MS. WITTLA: Summer of 2007?

MS. PERLICH: Yes.

MS. WITTLA: Where were you in relation to him?

MS. PERLICH: I was in my house.

MS. WITTLA: And where was he?

MS. PERLICH: In, like the back. He was working on the garage, like, roof or staining the garage, one of the two.

MS. WITTLA: Who was with him?

MS. PERLICH: The Paynes, and one or two kids were outside, I believe.

MS. WITTLA: When you say the Paynes, do you mean Becky Payne?

MS. PERLICH: And Bobby.

MS. WITTLA: And Bobby Payne?

MS. PERLICH: Uh-huh.

MS. WITTLA: And you said the children also?

MS. PERLICH: Yes.

MS. WITTLA: And the children would be Ashley and Caitlyn?

MS. PERLICH: Yes.

MS. WITTLA: Who did you believe that Mr. Coleman was going to strike?

MS. PERLICH: At the time, I wasn't sure, um, there was the little one and then Bobby Payne was behind him and I just seen a, I didn't witness a slap or a hit, I did not see that, I just seen a arm go up.

MS. WITTLA: So were these people facing each other?

MS. PERLICH: Yes.

MS. WITTLA: So Robert Coleman is standing facing Bobby Payne and Ashley?

MS. PERLICH: Uh-huh.

MS. WITTLA: Is Ashley next to Bobby Payne, behind him?

MS. PERLICH: In front.

MS. WITTLA: In front; and you said you saw an arm go up, you crossed your arm across your chest, and put it by your shoulder, is that fair to say?

MS. PERLICH: Uh-huh, yes.

MS. WITTLA: Did you see any movement with that?

MS. PERLICH: Just… I just seen it swing a little.

MS. WITTLA: Okay, you saw a swing?

MS. PERLICH: Uh-huh.

MS. WITTLA: Was it swinging out, down?

MS. PERLICH: Um, like out.

MS. WITTLA: From your vantage point, who did it appear would have been in line of that?

MS. PERLICH: I—I did not know.

MS. WITTLA: Were you worried that it was Ashley?

MS. PERLICH: At the time, no.

MS. WITTLA: What did you do when you saw this happen?

MS. PERLICH: I went and grabbed my boyfriend.

MS. WITTLA: Why did you grab your boyfriend?

MS. PERLICH: For him to come and look.

MS. WITTLA: And why did you do that?

MS. PERLICH: I don't know.

MS. WITTLA: How often would you say you seen Caitlyn and Ashley?

MS. PERLICH: Once, once awhile, when I would go and pay rent.

MS. WITTLA: You've seen them in their apartment with their parents or something?

MS. PERLICH: Yes.

MS. WITTLA: When was the last time you saw the kids?

MS. PERLICH: Um, couple months ago.

MS. WITTLA: Has Robert Coleman ever been angry with you?

MR. FINDLAY: Objection, your Honor, as to relevance.

THE COURT: Well, I-I don't know. Maybe we'll find out—narrow it, I mean if it's—

MS. WITTLA: I'll be more specific. Ms. Perlich, has Robert Coleman ever asked you to do something that you did not do?

MS. PERLICH: Yes.

MS. WITTLA: What did he ask you to do that you didn't do?

MS. PERLICH: He wanted me to write statements for him.

MS. WITTLA: What kind of statements did he want you to write?

MS. PERLICH: Um, a statement about the kids.

MS. WITTLA: What did he want you to write about the kids?

MS. PERLICH: Um, that he has never hit his children.

MS. WITTLA: Anything else about the kids?

MS. PERLICH: Not that I recall, no.

MS. WITTLA: Why didn't you write those statements?

MS. PERLICH: Because I didn't want to be involved.

MS. WITTLA: Did he ask you one time or more than that?

MS. PERLICH: I think it was like twice.

MS. WITTLA: Was he just casually just asking or was he insisting?

MS. PERLICH: Casually asking.

MS. WITTLA: Did he seem okay with your response that you wouldn't do it?

MS. PERLICH: Yeah.

MS. WITTLA: Did he ever offer to give you anything?

MS. PERLICH: Yes.

MS. WITTLA: What did he offer to give you?

MS. PERLICH: He offered that he would knock money off our rent if we were to help him.

MS. WITTLA: And how were you going to help him?

MS. PERLICH: Um, write statements, I'm assuming, for him.

MS. WITTLA: Did he ever ask you to write any other kind of statements?

MS. PERLICH: Yes.

MS. WITTLA: What other kinds of statements?

MS. PERLICH: Um, a statement about a missing ring.

MS. WITTLA: What did he want you to write about the missing ring?

MS. PERLICH: Um, that I had seen it, and who it was with.

MS. WITTLA: And who was it with?

MS. PERLICH: Bobby Payne.

MS. WITTLA: Did he offer anything to you for writing statements about seeing the ring with Mr. Payne?

MS. PERLICH: That I can't remember.

MS. WITTLA: Was the request to write a statement about the ring, at the same time as the request to write statements about the children?

MS. PERLICH: I believe so.

MS. WITTLA: So maybe not the same day, but similar time frame?

MS. PERLICH: Yes.

MS. WITTLA: And they were not months apart?

MS. PERLICH: No.

MS. WITTLA: Did you tell Mr. Coleman that you wouldn't write statements regarding this ring?

MS. PERLICH: Yes.

MS. WITTLA: Was he okay with that response?

MS. PERLICH: He looked upset, but didn't really say much.

MS. WITTLA: How many times did he ask you to write statements about the ring?

MS. PERLICH: I believe just once.

MS. WITTLA: Did anyone else ask you to write statements about the ring?

MS. PERLICH: No.

MS. WITTLA: You were never contacted by the police?

MS. PERLICH: Oh, I'm sorry. Yes, um, the Houghton police I believe; the Houghton police.

MS. WITTLA: How about Sergeant Carpenedo?

MS. PERLICH: Yes.

MS. WITTLA: Were you ever on a three way call with Robert Coleman where he was trying to get you to go into Ironwood Public Safety to write a statement?

MS. PERLICH: I can't remember.

MS. WITTLA: Were you interviewed by Sergeant Carpenedo regarding this ring?

MS. PERLICH: Yes.

MS. WITTLA: Who else was there?

MS. PERLICH: At the police department?

MS. WITTLA: Well, I guess. How many times were you interviewed about this ring?

MR. FINDLAY: Your Honor, I'm going to object. I mean, I haven't said about this ring; I don't; it's not relevant.

THE COURT: It may be relevant as to the truthfulness we're kind of getting around, round about it, but can we kind of get to point or? I'm guessing if we're going to talk about the ring in general, it may not be relevant; the ring did come up on prior testimony without objection, but I'm surmising there is a point to it; and I'm asking that we get to it.

MS. WITTLA: Um, Ms. Perlich, if you had written a statement, that you were certain that you saw Bobby Payne with Mr. Coleman's missing ring, would that have been the truth?

MS. PERLICH: I wasn't; I had told him I wasn't sure if it was his or if it wasn't his; it looked like, like a class ring like you would get like in high school.

MS. WITTLA: Okay, but my question is, if you wrote a statement saying you were sure that that was it; would that have been the truth?

MS. PERLICH: No.

MS. WITTLA: And it is your testimony today that you're not sure if it was Mr. Coleman asking you to write statements about this ring or Mr. Coleman asking you to write statements about the children which he; which he; which one of those statements was willing to give you money off your rent for?

MS. PERLICH: I couldn't even remember.

MS. WITTLA: It was one of those?

MS. PERLICH: Yes.

MS. WITTLA: Okay, do you know how much money off your rent?

MS. PERLICH: No.

MS. WITTLA: Never... the conversation never got that far?

MS. PERLICH: No.

MS. WITTLA: Do you know who Bobby and Becky Payne are?

MS. PERLICH: Yes.

MS. WITTLA: Have you seen them more than once, twice?

MS. PERLICH: Yes.

MS. WITTLA: How often would you say you see them?

MS. PERLICH: Um, I probably seen them, when I lived there, every day.

MS. WITTLA: When you saw them, were they fighting all the time?

MS. PERLICH: Not from what I seen, no.

MS. WITTLA: Did you ever have conversations with them?

MS. PERLICH: Very short ones.

MS. WITTLA: So when you saw them, it wasn't like they were like across the complex or something?

MS. PERLICH: They would be like, like winter time they'd be like shoveling like our driveway or like a sidewalk way or in front of the Coleman's, um, like garages and stuff.

MS. WITTLA: Was it your understanding that that was one of their jobs?

MS. PERLICH: Yes.

MS. WITTLA: Were you ever shown the basement where they lived?

MS. PERLICH: Yes I was.

MS. WITTLA: Who did you go there with?

MS. PERLICH: My boyfriend, Eli.

MS. WITTLA: Anyone else?

MS. PERLICH: No, and Mr. Coleman.

MS. WITTLA: What was the basement like?

MS. PERLICH: It was really dark, we just had, um, Mr. Coleman had a flashlight. I couldn't really see, it was really dark. It was like a normal basement.

MS. WITTLA: Was it fixed up like an apartment?

MS. PERLICH: No.

MS. WITTLA: Was there any furniture down there?

MS. PERLICH: No. There was boxes, um, looked like clothes, and like personal property in like a corner of the Paynes'.

MS. WITTLA: Was this personal property ever identified to you?

MS. PERLICH: What was that?

MS. WITTLA: Did anyone tell you what, well, did Robert Coleman tell you whose boxes they were?

MS. PERLICH: Yes.

MS. WITTLA: Whose were they?

MS. PERLICH: Both of theirs. The Paynes'.

MS. WITTLA: Becky and Bobby Paynes'?

MS. PERLICH: Yes.

MS. WITTLA: Why did you end up going to the basement?

MS. PERLICH: I don't know.

MS. WITTLA: Did you ask to see the basement?

MS. PERLICH: No.

MS. WITTLA: Did Mr. Coleman ask you to see the basement?

MS. PERLICH: Yes.

MS. WITTLA: Did Mr. Coleman ask you to see the belongings that the Paynes' had left behind?

MS. PERLICH: He just walked down there and we just kind of followed.

MS. WITTLA: What did you do when you were in the basement?

MS. PERLICH: Stood there.

MS. WITTLA: Was there any conversation?

MS. PERLICH: Um, with him and Eli, yes.

MS. WITTLA: What did you hear Robert Coleman say when you were down there?

MS. PERLICH: Um, he was just looking through, he had found, um, jeans that were his down there.

MS. WITTLA: In his basement?

MS. PERLICH: Yes.

MS. WITTLA: Was this a concern to him?

MS. PERLICH: Yes, it's where Becky and Bobby were staying, sleeping.

MS. WITTLA: So he was concerned that his jeans were downstairs?

MS. PERLICH: Yes.

MS. WITTLA: Was he concerned about anything else?

MS. PERLICH: Not that I recall.

MS. WITTLA: Did he ask either you or Eli to look through the Paynes' boxes?

MS. PERLICH: Yes.

MS. WITTLA: Did you do it?

MS. PERLICH: No.

MS. WITTLA: Have you ever seen Robert Coleman interacting with Becky and Bobby Coleman— sorry, Becky and Bobby Payne?

MS. PERLICH: Just when they were working.

MS. WITTLA: When Becky and Bobby were working?

MS. PERLICH: Yes, they worked with him.

MS. WITTLA: Did you ever hear Robert Coleman swear at Bobby Payne?

MS. PERLICH: A couple times, yes. Both of them would yell back and forth at each other.

MS. WITTLA: Bobby and Robert Coleman would yell at each other?

MS. PERLICH: Yes.

MS. WITTLA: Did Robert Coleman call Bobby Payne any names?

MS. PERLICH: Not in front of me, no.

MS. WITTLA: Did Robert Coleman ever describe the Paynes to you?

MS. PERLICH: No.

MS. WITTLA: Have you ever heard Robert Coleman swearing about you?

MS. PERLICH: Yes.

MS. WITTLA: When was that?

MS. PERLICH: I'm not exact on the date, or the month, there was a time where he wanted us to move out, and we were at my boyfriend Eli's parents' house, and we had called, or he had called us, I can't remember what, what one; and he was threatening to evict us, so we had drove over there and we were going to go talk to him, and figure everything out, and we had heard him yelling saying how he wanted to evict us. And there was a couple of swear words in that line.

MS. WITTLA: Did he see you when he was saying these things?

MS. PERLICH: No.

MS. WITTLA: Okay, he didn't see you. Why?

MS. PERLICH: In the back of like his apartment, there's washer and dryers for the tenants; it's like by the—

MS. WITTLA:—In his apartment there is a washer and dryer for the tenants?

MS. PERLICH: Yes.

MS. WITTLA: Okay, and then what?

MS. PERLICH: It's like you walk thru like a garage door almost, and then on the side, you walk thru another one and there's a washer and dryer ; and then you go like down the hall and you turn and it's like where like living room and kitchen and everything else is. And they were in there and he was remodeling his apartment at the time so there was a big blanket over the door, so he did not see us.

MS. WITTLA: Okay, now I'm not, I'm not asking you to swear just to swear, but if you remember exactly what you heard Robert Coleman say, would you please tell us?

MS. PERLICH: He said he wants us the "F" out, and for his wife to call the "F-ing" cops.

MS. WITTLA: And that is in the context of wanting to evict you?

MS. PERLICH: Yes.

MS. WITTLA: Were there any other times that Robert Coleman said he wanted to evict you?

MS. PERLICH: Not to the term, but he said, he, um, he would like us to move out because we were behind on rent.

MS. WITTLA: Do you remember why you had a statement that you submitted to the Ironwood Public Safety Department?

MS. PERLICH: Yes.

MS. WITTLA: Do you remember writing a statement saying he has called my phone at all hours of the night asking about writing statements for him about getting his kids?

MS. PERLICH: Yes.

MS. WITTLA: Is that a true statement?

MS. PERLICH: Yes.

MS. WITTLA: He has sent people into our house without our knowing to peek around?

MS. PERLICH: That is what I was told.

MS. WITTLA: Okay, you don't know that that happened?

MS. PERLICH: No.

And that is because it did not happen, although I don't have to guess very hard to know who probably told her it did. This is a time when we need to break away from the trial questions, to explain this entire episode a little bit. I am going to show you the statement Jamie Perlich gave to the Ironwood Public Safety Department. I do not attempt to hide anything, so that is why I will not hesitate to show you this. But you will notice, from reading the testimony in court, that Jamie's frame of mind was quite different than what it was at the time she gave this statement. That is because, at the time she gave this statement, she had just been given her eviction notice. In court, Jamie states she still considers us friends, while in the heat of the moment when she wrote out this statement, she was very angry with me, describing me, for one thing, as creepy. Well, I don't know about you, but I don't have too many creepy friends! For me, it was just a business matter, because, at the time, as I've disclosed, we were under great stress due to a lot of revenue loss from bad tenants and lack of tenants. I was trying to survive, while at the same time taking on the state in a battle for my kids. So I was edgy, and of course I understand she was also, once presented with the eviction notice. And she was also being asked to testify, which she really did not wish to do. So what she said in the statement, I regard now as mostly anger at us over the eviction, and being called to testify in the court case. What she said in court, though, reflected a much different attitude, I thought, although she of course had to admit what she had written in the statement. So today, if she still considers us to be friends, we also would have that feeling regarding her. The statement, of course, gave this cut-throat prosecutor all she wanted from Jamie in order to try to cut down Robert Coleman, so she used it to the fullest. At any rate, here is what Jamie said, and I hope you can read between the lines, see it was mostly anger, and then reflect on her actual court testimony which reflected quite a different attitude:

I, Jamie M. Perlich, am not under arrest, nor am I being detained, for any criminal offenses concerning the events I am about to make known to the IRONWOOD PUBLIC SAFTEY DEPARTMENT. I volunteer the following facts and information of my own free will, for whatever purposes it may serve. My date of birth is 01/04/1986 and I live at 211 E. Vaughn St., in Ironwood, Michigan. On many occasions Robert Coleman has asked me and my boyfriend to write statements for him to knock off money for rent. He has called my phone at all hours of the night asking about writing statement for him about hitting his kids (which I have witnessed him do!) He has sent people into our house without our knowing to peek around. Every time I go pay him money for rent, somehow the money never comes off the bill. He begs us to help him out with stuff. He had told us the other night that we can move out on our own free will and he was going to terminate the contract and we would just have to pay him the money for the water bill. And as long as we cleaned the house when we move it would be no problem. He promised he wouldn't evict us, he would just let everything go. He says things to my friends & family when they come over. He is always walking around my house by my windows. He tries to get our help and if we don't help him he threatens to kick us out, now he's going to take us to court and everything. I want this creepy guy to just leave me alone. I'm sick of him threaten me about stuff and being a total nut case toward me and my boyfriend. Dated this 01 day of May 08. Signed Jamie M. Perlich.

There you have it. It was damaging to us, yes, but I accept now Jamie's anger and have been able to move on with my life too. It is my feeling she filed the statement out of her anger, and if my situation had been different, perhaps I would have decided to carry Jamie longer, but this entire fiasco had drained me both financially and emotionally. By now, decision making had gotten harder for me and my wife too. In any case, back to Ms. Wittla's questioning of Jamie:

MS. WITTLA: "Every time I go pay him money for rent, somehow the money never comes off the bill."

Is that accurate?

MS. PERLICH: Yes.

MS. WITTLA: He begs us to help him out with stuff; that's accurate?

MS. PERLICH: Yes.

MS. WITTLA: What, what was the stuff that he was begging you to help him out with?

MS. PERLICH: Like, the statement wise.

MS. WITTLA: The statements?

MS. PERLICH: Yes.

MS. WITTLA: So it wasn't just, ah, hey, will you do this for me? He was begging you?

MS. PERLICH: He would ask us a couple of times if we would.

MS. WITTLA: When he was calling you at all hours of the night, was that about the statements too?

MS. PERLICH: No, not all the time. Some of them were to, he, there was times where he was upset about the children being gone and him and his wife needed someone to talk to; so we were being nice and just thought we would talk to him and listen. And then there would be other times where he would want us to write, from our point of view, about the kids and I had told him I didn't want to, because I did not want to be involved.

MS. WITTLA: Is it fair to say you still don't want to be involved?

MS. PERLICH: Yes.

MS. WITTLA: Another statement you wrote says, "He had told us the other night that we can move out on our own free will; and he was going to terminate the contract, and we would just have to pay him the money for the water bill, and as long as we cleaned the house when we move, there would be no problem."

MS. PERLICH: Yes.

MS. WITTLA: He promised he wouldn't evict us, he would just let everything go?

MS. PERLICH: Uh-huh. Yes.

MS. WITTLA: So there were points in time when he was nice to you and said, "I won't evict you?"

MS. PERLICH: Yes.

MS. WITTLA: Would he renege on that deal?

MS. PERLICH: What was that?

MS. WITTLA: Did he change his mind?

MS. PERLICH: Yes.

MS. WITTLA: Did he go back and forth?

MS. PERLICH: Yes.

MS. WITTLA: Did he ever go back and forth in the same conversation with you where he's nice and then not nice, and then back to nice again?

MS. PERLICH: Um, I would say not nice, more like tone of his voice would change.

MS. WITTLA: How would it change?

MS. PERLICH: More like of in the yelling— not like a yelling loud; he would speak very loud.

MS. WITTLA: When he was upset?

MS. PERLICH: Yes.

MS. WITTLA: And when would he get upset with you?

MS. PERLICH: When I was behind on rent.

MS. WITTLA: When you were behind on rent?

MS. PERLICH: Yes.

MS. WITTLA: You said, "He says things to my friends and family when they come over; he is always walking around my house, by my windows; he tries to get our help, and if we don't help him he threatens to kick us out. Now he's going to take us to court and everything. Is that accurate?

MS. PERLICH: Yes.

MS. WITTLA: So aside from him wanting you to write statements for which he's knock money off your rent, the penalty for not writing the statements was that he was going to evict you?

MS. PERLICH: Yes, a couple of the Ironwood officers had told us when I got called down to the station.

MS. WITTLA: That Robert Coleman said he's going to evict you?

MS. PERLICH: He plans on evicting us and taking me to court.

MS. WITTLA: Is that still the status of the situation between you and Robert Coleman, as far as you know?

MS. PERLICH: I don't know, I haven't talked to him in a while.

MS. WITTLA: You haven't been served with papers yet?

MS. PERLICH: Eviction note?

MS. WITTLA: Right.

MS. PERLICH: No.

MS. WITTLA: You left on your own?

MS. PERLICH: Right.

MS. WITTLA: I have nothing further.

Ms. Wittla had nothing further, but my lawyer would. The court took a break at this juncture, but something should be noted here. Jamie either lied or stated incorrectly that she had not been served an eviction notice. It, in fact, happened on May 1st and was served by the police she referred to in her testimony. So following a short break, the court resumed with my lawyer's cross-examination of Jamie:

MR. FINDLAY: I, I just want to make sure I understood your testimony; that you testified that you never did see the Colemans hitting their children?

MS. PERLICH: No, I never have.

MR. FINDLAY: Okay, all right. Um, and were you, you were served with an eviction notice weren't you on May 1st?

MS. PERLICH: Yeah, I was um, yeah, we were.

MR. FINDLAY: Okay, and isn't it true that, um, Ron Carpenedo served that—may I approach the witness?

THE COURT: Sure.

MR. FINDLAY: Isn't it true that, this is a copy of it, isn't it true that Ron Carpenedo served that to you on the first?

MS. PERLICH: I don't know what officer it was, but yes.

MR. FINDLAY: Okay, so you did get an eviction notice on the first?

MS. PERLICH: Yes.

MR. FINDLAY: And that never— but it never had to go back to court; you left after that?

MS. PERLICH: Right.

MR. FINDLAY: And did you leave still owing the Colemans money?

MS. PERLICH: Yes.

MR. FINDLAY: And they haven't asked you for that, have they?

MS. PERLICH: Not yet, no. We had made an agreement that I'll pay him money when—

MR. FINDLAY:— When you can?

MS. PERLICH: When I can, yes.

MR. FINDLAY: That— I have nothing; thank you.

THE COURT: Is there redirect on that or?

MS. WITTLA: No your Honor.

THE COURT: Okay?

MR. PERHALLA: No.

THE COURT: All right, Ms. Perlich, you are excused and you're free to go. Thank you. Oh, ma'am, don't talk about your testimony with anybody else on the case because the witnesses are separated, so—

MS. PERLICH: Okay.

THE COURT: Um, next witness?

MS. WITTLA: My next witness would be Rebecca Payne.

With that, the court swore in Rebecca Payne, and the prosecutor began her questioning:

MS. WITTLA: Would you please state your name for the record?

MS. PAYNE: Rebecca Payne.

MS. WITTLA: And what city do you currently live in?

MS. PAYNE: Ironwood, Michigan.

MS. WITTLA: Ms. Payne, when you were in school, did you attend any special education classes?

MS. PAYNE: Yes.

MS. WITTLA: Was that through all of your school years?

MS. PAYNE: Yeah.

MS. WITTLA: Do you currently have help from the Department of Human Services?

MS. PAYNE: Yes.

MS. WITTLA: Do you have an adult human services worker?

MS. PAYNE: Yes.

MS. WITTLA: Do you know what her name is?

MS. PAYNE: I don't know at this moment.

MS. WITTLA: Do you know what your case worker helps you with?

MS. PAYNE: Um, she's helping us find a place.

MS. WITTLA: Housing?

MS. PAYNE: Yes.

MS. WITTLA: Anything else?

MS. PAYNE: Um, we are getting help by DHS too.

MS. WITTLA: You mean financial help?

MS. PAYNE: Yeah.

MS. WITTLA: Food stamps, that sort of thing, or the little card?

MS. PAYNE: Ah, that no, but we are getting help with, if we do find a place, we're going to be getting help with a security deposit.

MS. WITTLA: Ms. Payne, are you currently married?

MS. PAYNE: Yes.

MS. WITTLA: What's your husband's name?

MS. PAYNE: Robert Payne.

MS. WITTLA: Does he go by Bobby?

MS. PAYNE: Yeah.

MS. WITTLA: How do you know Robert and Janet Coleman?

MS. PAYNE: We—I moved up here in the middle of July of 2007.

MS. WITTLA: That's when you met them?

MS. PAYNE: Yes.

MS. WITTLA: And you moved up here from?

MS. PAYNE: California.

MS. WITTLA: Just you, by yourself?

MS. PAYNE: Me and my husband.

MS. WITTLA: You and Bobby?

MS. PAYNE: Yeah.

MS. WITTLA: When you moved here in July of 2007, did you start renting an apartment from Robert and Janet?

MS. PAYNE: Yes.

MS. WITTLA: Was this your own separate apartment that just you guys had?

MS. PAYNE: Yeah.

MS. WITTLA: How long were you in your own separate apartment?

MS. PAYNE: We were in our own separate apartment until February.

MS. WITTLA: February of this year?

MS. PAYNE: Yes.

MS. WITTLA: Where did you live after that?

MS. PAYNE: Down in Robert and Janet's basement.

MS. WITTLA: Why did you live in the basement?

MS. PAYNE: Because they wanted to get more money so they rented out our apartment, ah, furnished.

That was a direct lie, under oath—something we call perjury! They moved to the basement in order to try to save money for a move back to California, which they said they wanted to make.

MS. WITTLA: When you say they rented out your apartment furnished, did you leave your things behind?

MS. PAYNE: We had to leave some of it up there, except for our clothes and our food.

MS. WITTLA: Ms. Payne, from the time that you met Robert and Janet Coleman in July of 2007, how long was it before you had more than a landlord-tenant relationship with them?

MS. PAYNE: It wasn't that long.

MS. WITTLA: What kinds of things did you do with Robert and Janet?

MS. PAYNE: I, we helped them out with the kids; they had a, they had me changing, ah, Ashley's diaper; they had us helping them out with giving them a bath, and us helping out around the house once and awhile; and, um, Robert had us working with him out of the house too.

MS. WITTLA: So when we're talking about just you; how soon after you moved in in July of 2007 were you helping them with the kids?

MS. PAYNE: Um, about three days after we moved in.

MS. WITTLA: And three days after you moved in, what kinds of things would you do for them?

MS. PAYNE: Help them change Ashley's diaper.

MS. WITTLA: If you were around, were you always the one who changed her diaper?

MS. PAYNE: Not only me, Bobby changed it once in a while too.

MS. WITTLA: If you and Bobby were around, did you ever see Janet or Robert change Ashley?

MS. PAYNE: Ah, once in a while.

MS. WITTLA: You also mentioned working around the apartments?

MS. PAYNE: Yes.

MS. WITTLA: What kinds of stuff would you do for the apartments?

MS. PAYNE: Um, whenever a tenant moved out, they had me clean the apartments. Ah, they had us sweeping the sidewalks; picking up garbage; ah, making sure that everything was nice and clean for anyone that wanted to come and rent there.

MS. WITTLA: Did you get paid for this?

MS. PAYNE: No.

MS. WITTLA: Did you have money taken off your rent?

MS. PAYNE: Yes, we had a hundred dollars taken off.

MS. WITTLA: A hundred dollars on a monthly basis?

MS. PAYNE: Yes.

MS. WITTLA: How much time would you say that you spent doing these things for Robert and Janet Coleman, on a weekly basis?

MS. PAYNE: Um, all day.

More perjured testimony. They spent very little time doing it. They were far too lazy to spend much time on it, and Bobby spent most of his time playing video games in his apartment.

MS. WITTLA: So you spent your days doing things around the apartments?

MS. PAYNE: Yes.

MS. WITTLA: Did you also spend your days taking care of the kids?

MS. PAYNE: Yes.

MS. WITTLA: So it was both of those things back and forth?

MS. PAYNE: Yes.

MS. WITTLA: Was Bobby with you when you were doing these things?

MS. PAYNE: Off and on.

MS. WITTLA: Sometimes he was with you and sometimes he'd be somewhere else?

A nice leading question, which Ms. Wittla was good at doing. It helped her shape the case the way she wanted it to be— not as it actually was.

MS. PAYNE: Uh-huh.

MS. WITTLA: Did you ever work anywhere other than the apartments for Robert or Janet?

MS. PAYNE: Yeah, I started working at, ah, Gogebic Medical Specialties.

MS. WITTLA: And how much time did you put in there?

MS. PAYNE: Um, mostly every day after 4:30.

MS. WITTLA: From 4:30 until how long?

MS. PAYNE: It took about like an hour and a half for me to clean the clinic.

MS. WITTLA: So about 4:30 to 6?

MS. PAYNE: Sometimes.

MS. WITTLA: Did you get paid for that?

MS. PAYNE: Yes.

MS. WITTLA: Where did that money go?

MS. PAYNE: At first it was going towards our cigarettes and sometimes for whatever we need, and then afterwards, I had to give my money to Robert, because they needed help with bills and that.

MS. WITTLA: Did you have a, a food stamp card when you were living in those apartments?

MS. PAYNE: Yes.

MS. WITTLA: Did you keep that card?

MS. PAYNE: At first I did, and then I was told that I had to hand it over to Janet.

More perjury. Janet assisted Becky to shop because she spent money in such a reckless and wasteful manner. It was part of what Janet did to help them stretch what they did have. But she was never told to hand it over to Janet. All of what we did was to try to help this couple, but it was all turned into evil intent, assisted, I'm certain, by this prosecuting team.

MS. WITTLA: Did Janet buy food for you with that card?

MS. PAYNE: They helped us, ah, about two times with us, and then the last time I didn't see none of the money or food out of my last amount that I had.

MS. WITTLA: How much time would you say that you spent with Robert or Janet Coleman on a daily basis?

MS. PAYNE: It was mostly all day long that we spent with them.

Another perjured lie. I could not have stood it, had I been subjected to them day in and day out for the full day! Understand, they were kind of like stray dogs when you feed them. They just kind of hang around, and as long as you feed them, they keep coming back.

MS. WITTLA: Was that mostly Robert? Mostly Janet? Or both?

MS. PAYNE: Um, from morning till about five or six it was with Robert; and then at night time it was with Robert and Janet.

MS. WITTLA: So during your days with Robert, what kind of things would you do? Is that when you worked around the apartment and stuff?

Here was another time when the prosecutor was leading the witness.

MS. PAYNE: That was when we were working around apartments, and whenever had had a job with Coldwell Banker.

MS. WITTLA: And what is the job with Coldwell Banker?

MS. PAYNE: Ah, cleaning out the garbage out of houses.

MS. WITTLA: Is that when people moved out and they were going to re-rent them or?

MS. PAYNE: Yeah, it was when people moved out, and they left a whole bunch of stuff in there; we had to go in and clean it all out, make sure it was nice, and make sure all the garbage was out.

MS. WITTLA: Did he ask you to do these things as a favor to him?

MS. PAYNE: Um, he asked us if we could help him out with it, because he had other stuff on the side that he had to do; so he would actually sometimes drop me and Bobby off to do it, and then he would go off and do what he needed to do, and then come back to see how we were doing.

MS. WITTLA: So when you did this work for him, you thought you were being helpful?

MS. PAYNE: Yes.

MS. WITTLA: Did you expect to get paid for it?

MS. PAYNE: We expected to, but we never seen the money out of it.

MS. WITTLA: Did Robert tell you he was going to pay you?

MS. PAYNE: Sometimes he did, and sometimes he said that he would go buy us cigarettes for the work we have done.

MS. WITTLA: Are you a smoker?

MS. PAYNE: Yes.

MS. WITTLA: If you had to give your money from your job at Gogebic Medical Specialties to Robert and Janet, how did you buy your cigarettes?

MS. PAYNE: Ah, they used part of it out of that pay check to buy us cigarettes.

It should be noted here that we also used a lot of money from Bobby's money, which Janet managed, because they could not handle their own affairs, and even some of our own money was spent on their behalf, to buy them food, as well as other items they needed. Their money was never enough to cover it all. I guess the prosecutor forgot to ask her those questions, however.

MS. WITTLA: So when you'd get your pay check from Gogebic Medical Specialties, that's how you would buy your cigarettes?

MS. PAYNE: Yes.

MS. WITTLA: Was there ever a point in time that you didn't have any money to buy cigarettes?

MS. PAYNE: Sometimes there was.

MS. WITTLA: Was that because the money had already been given to Robert?

MS. PAYNE: Yes.

MS. WITTLA: From the time that you started living there, in July, 2007, until the time you left in March, did you always spend the same amount of time with Robert during the day and Janet in the evening?

MS. PAYNE: Yes.

Lie.

MS. WITTLA: What did you call Robert?

MS. PAYNE: I was supposed to call him dad.

MS. WITTLA: You were supposed to call him dad?

MS. PAYNE: Yes.

MS. WITTLA: And why were you supposed to call him dad?

MS. PAYNE: Because he had told me and Bobby that he loved us as his own kids.

MS. WITTLA: Did he ask you to call him dad?

MS. PAYNE: He asked us if we felt right to call him dad.

MS. WITTLA: Did he ever tell you that he wanted you to call him dad?

MS. PAYNE: He never told me, but he has told Bobby that.

MS. WITTLA: Okay, I'm not going to ask you what Bobby said. At any rate, that is what you called him, was dad?

MS. PAYNE: Yeah.

Okay. First of all, those last responses were totally fabricated to make it appear that I wanted these two to call me dad. I did not. They were the ones who always wanted to do that. From my perspective, it freaked me out! I surely never told Bobby what Becky indicated, so she lied again, but even at that, this should never have gone on record because it was hearsay pertaining to a third party's words.

MS. WITTLA: If Robert told you you had to do something, did you believe you needed to do it?

MS. PAYNE: No.

MS. WITTLA: Then why did you do it?

Who said she did do it Tracie Wittla? You?

MS. PAYNE: Because I was afraid.

Of what?

MS. WITTLA: Do you know who Caitlyn and Ashley are?

MS. PAYNE: Yes.

MS. WITTLA: Who are they?

MS. PAYNE: Caitlyn is Janet's biological daughter; and Ashley is both of their biological daughter.

MS. WITTLA: And how old is Caitlyn?

MS. PAYNE: Caitlyn is six years old.

MS. WITTLA: And how old is Ashley?

MS. PAYNE: Two.

MS. WITTLA: You've mentioned already that you were the one that changed Ashley's diaper?

Now there goes that prosecutor again! Twisting what was actually said and stating it as though it were indeed a fact. Even though Becky lied and said she did most of it, even she acknowledged that Janet and I did some of it too. Even Bobby. But this prosecutor was an expert at making a fact out of something that was not said, just as she does in this instance by saying Becky was the one who changed Ashley's diapers!

MS. PAYNE: Yes.

MS. WITTLA: Was Ashley home all day?

MS. PAYNE: Yes.

MS. WITTLA: As far as you know?

MS. PAYNE: Uh-huh.

MS. WITTLA: Was Caitlyn home all day?

MS. PAYNE: No, Caitlyn went to school from 8:00 a.m. to 11:45.

MS. WITTLA: Did you see Caitlyn after she'd come home from school?

MS. PAYNE: Sometimes.

MS. WITTLA: Did you ever eat at the Colemans' house?

MS. PAYNE: Yes.

MS. WITTLA: Was that once and awhile or fairly common?

MS. PAYNE: It was fairly common.

MS. WITTLA: Would you eat breakfast, lunch, dinner, or anything more than the other?

MS. PAYNE: Some dinner.

MS. WITTLA: Dinner. How often would you say you ate dinner with them?

MS. PAYNE: Mostly every night except for on Valentine's Day we didn't.

MS. WITTLA: Was there anything in particular that Caitlyn didn't like to eat?

MS. PAYNE: Um, she did not like to eat rice or green beans.

Um.... wrong again! As of this book writing, Caitlyn, at age ten, laughed when she heard such a claim was made. Her exact words to me when reviewing some of what the allegations were, including the so-called rice incident: "Daddy, that's crazy! I loved rice!"

MS. WITTLA: If she didn't eat her rice or the green beans, did she get in trouble?

MS. PAYNE: Yes.

MS. WITTLA: What happened when she wouldn't eat her rice or green beans?

MS. PAYNE: She got yelled at or she was put in the corner or she was told that if she doesn't eat it, she was going to get the belt.

MS. WITTLA: Who would tell her this?

MS. PAYNE: Robert.

MS. WITTLA: Did you ever see Ashley get the corner; I'm sorry, Caitlyn. Did you ever see Caitlyn put in the corner?

MS. PAYNE: Yes.

MS. WITTLA: Did you ever see Caitlyn get the belt?

MS. PAYNE: Yes.

MS. WITTLA: What did that mean to get the belt?

MS. PAYNE: Um, it meant that she's supposed to have listened and it was discipline for her.

MS. WITTLA: Was there an actual belt involved?

MS. PAYNE: Yes.

MS. WITTLA: Was Caitlyn hit with the belt?

MS. PAYNE: Yes.

MS. WITTLA: Who hit her?

MS. PAYNE: Robert.

MS. WITTLA: Was anyone else there when this would happen?

MS. PAYNE: Ah, Janet was there, um, when she mostly got the belt.

MS. WITTLA: You were there?

MS. PAYNE: Yes.

MS. WITTLA: Was Bobby there?

MS. PAYNE: Yes.

MS. WITTLA: So if Robert said that Caitlyn was going to get the belt, did anyone help him do this?

MS. PAYNE: Um, we were told to help him, and if we said no, we were scared that we were going to get hit because we didn't help out with it; and Janet helped him once and awhile.

MS. WITTLA: So what was your job if Robert was going to hit Caitlyn with a belt?

MS. PAYNE: I never, I've helped him once; by holding her on the bed while he hit her with the belt.

MS. WITTLA: How did you hold her on the bed?

MS. PAYNE: I had to hold her arms down.

MS. WITTLA: Was anyone helping to hold her down?

MS. PAYNE: No.

MS. WITTLA: Have you ever seen anyone else hold her down?

MS. PAYNE: I have seen Janet hold her arms while Robert was holding her legs and hitting her with his other hand with the belt.

MS. WITTLA: Did you ever see Bobby hold her?

MS. PAYNE: No.

MS. WITTLA: Who would go and get the belt?

MS. PAYNE: Ah, several times Bobby was told to go get the belt, to just scare Caitlyn with it.

MS. WITTLA: To scare her; was Bobby supposed to do something with the belt, or just getting it was the scary part?

MS. PAYNE: He is supposed to went to go get the belt to give to Robert to scare Caitlyn because she didn't want to eat her supper.

MS. WITTLA: Did Robert ever ask Caitlyn if she was scared?

MS. PAYNE: Yes.

MS. WITTLA: How many times did you see Caitlyn get struck with a belt?

MS. PAYNE: About two or three times a day.

Holy super belt, Batman! That is a lot, even for an evil creep like me! With me beating Caitlyn with a belt that many times daily, it would have been impossible for Caitlyn to ever walk! Of course none of this ever took place, but it made interesting ammunition for Ms. Elizabeth Fyle!

MS. WITTLA: Were there ever any marks left on Caitlyn's body after she was hit with a belt?

MS. PAYNE: Yes.

MS. WITTLA: Where were the marks?

MS. PAYNE: On her butt.

MS. WITTLA: And how did you see these marks?

MS. PAYNE: Because when Caitlyn got hit with the belt, she had to have— she had pants pulled down and she was hit by the belt bare butt.

MS. WITTLA: Did anyone ever tell Robert to, to stop hitting Caitlyn with a belt?

MS. PAYNE: No.

MS. WITTLA: Did you ever hear Janet say anything to Robert about hitting Caitlyn with a belt?

MS. PAYNE: Yes.

MS. WITTLA: What did she say?

MS. PAYNE: Janet told Robert not to hit her too hard with the belt because she had a doctor's appointment the next day so she didn't want any marks on Caitlyn.

MS. WITTLA: Were there marks on Caitlyn that particular day?

MS. PAYNE: Yes.

MS. WITTLA: What happened next after the marks were seen on Caitlyn?

MS. PAYNE: I was told by Robert to put Caitlyn in the bath tub and soak her in Vinegar water, so we could get the mark away.

MS. WITTLA: Did you go get the vinegar?

MS. PAYNE: No.

MS. WITTLA: Did somebody go get vinegar?

MS. PAYNE: Yes.

MS. WITTLA: Who did?

MS. PAYNE: Robert.

MS. WITTLA: Well what did he do with the vinegar?

MS. PAYNE: He brought it to the bathroom, and after I had the water set, he poured some vinegar in the water and told Caitlyn to get in and sit there for about two hours.

MS. WITTLA: Did you stay with Caitlyn while she was in the bath tub?

MS. PAYNE: For a part of the time, yes.

MS. WITTLA: Do you know how long Caitlyn was in the bath tub?

MS. PAYNE: I think she was in there for two and a half hours.

MS. WITTLA: When you said you were there for part of the time, did you leave and not return or did you leave and come back?

MS. PAYNE: I left and came back.

MS. WITTLA: Why did you leave?

MS. PAYNE: Because I was asked that I change Ashley.

MS. WITTLA: After you changed Ashley, what did you do?

MS. PAYNE: Then I went back into the bathroom to see how Caitlyn was doing.

MS. WITTLA: Did the red marks go away?

MS. PAYNE: A little bit, yes.

MS. WITTLA: Did you tell Robert that they had gone away?

MS. PAYNE: Yes.

MS. WITTLA: Was that true?

MS. PAYNE: No.

MS. WITTLA: Why did you tell him they were gone, if they weren't gone?

MS. PAYNE: Because he asked me if they were and I was afraid to tell him that they weren't.

Excuse me, but is this that poor, defenseless, abused woman making that last statement? If she had such a feeble mind, as the prosecutor and Ms. Fyle had been pretending all along, she would never have been so easily led by the prosecutor from the alleged bathroom incident (which never happened) to now going on to make me a monster, to be feared by all. They must have rehearsed for hours to figure out how to go from one topic to the next. If she were so mentally incapable, and the phony prosecutor was only asking about the so-called bathtub incident, the question and answer exchange, asking if the marks had indeed gone away would have been left at that. But to ask then, if it was true, was obviously set up so that Becky could first say no, and then get a follow up question as to why. That, of course, opens the door to start attacking me then as mean, and to be feared. You can't tell me they had not planned their questioning this way in advance.

MS. WITTLA: That they were what?

MS. PAYNE: That they weren't gone yet.

MS. WITTLA: That they weren't—sorry. Did you ever see Ashley punished this way?

MS. PAYNE: Not with the belt, but with a hand.

MS. WITTLA: Okay, and when you say she's punished with a hand, how did that happen?

MS. PAYNE: She always got hit with a hand on her butt for ripping off her pajamas and her diaper.

MS. WITTLA: Okay, so if I'm understanding you, she'd take her pajamas and diaper off, and she'd get hit with the hand?

MS. PAYNE: Yes.

MS. WITTLA: And that was where?

MS. PAYNE: On the butt.

MS. WITTLA: Was there any other time that you saw Ashley get hit?

MS. PAYNE: Um, the last time I seen her get hit was before we left. We were sitting in the living room while Bobby was on the computer, and Janet and Robert were laying on the bed, and Ashley came up to, and accidentally pounced on Janet's stomach, and Ashley was slapped in the face and pushed backwards down on the bed.

MS. WITTLA: And who did that?

MS. PAYNE: Robert did.

It gets tiresome explaining the truth as opposed to Becky Payne's lies. But the truth in this matter, is that a similar incident to the one she described here did occur, but none of the details in her story are correct, nor were they intended to be. But what did happen, is that Janet was pregnant with our youngest child, Brittney. Ashley did run in and jump on the bed, as kids will do, and landed right in the middle of Janet's stomach. As a dad and husband, naturally, this did concern me, for Janet's and the unborn baby's safety. So as she jumped, I did reach out and try to push her back a bit so she would not hurt Janet. Hardly what I would call a slap on the face to Ashley! And then, of course, I did scold her because she had to know that was not a good thing to do with her pregnant mom. That was the story. I don't know many fathers or husbands who would not have done the same in such an instance.

MS. WITTLA: Was this when Janet was pregnant?

MS. PAYNE: Yes.

Well what do you know? A straight question and a straight answer! Of course then, the prosecutor had to switch to another question because otherwise, I could never be painted as the bad guy they were attempting to paint me as.

MS. WITTLA: Do you remember the day when you left the Colemans?

MS. PAYNE: March 9th.

MS. WITTLA: Where were they when you left?

MS. PAYNE: They went to Walmart with the kids.

MS. WITTLA: Why did you leave when you did?

MS. PAYNE: Because we couldn't take it any more.

This was a total lie. They left because we had told them we wanted them to be gone by the time we got back.

MS. WITTLA: Did you want them to be home when you left?

MS. PAYNE: No.

MS. WITTLA: Did you take all of your things with you when you left?

MS. PAYNE: No, we only took what we could carry.

MS. WITTLA: Did you go back and get the rest of your stuff back?

MS. PAYNE: Yes.

MS. WITTLA: Where did you pick up your stuff?

MS. PAYNE: At the police station.

MS. WITTLA: You mentioned that you had to leave some things in the apartment so that it could be furnished; did you get those things back too?

MS. PAYNE: Not yet.

MS. WITTLA: And what kinds of things are still there?

MS. PAYNE: We have a dresser, a table, our dishes and pots, our toaster, ah, a coffee pot, our eighty dollar microwave that my mom had bought us and two couches.

MS. WITTLA: When you talk about being in the basement, what was down there?

MS. PAYNE: There was a mattress, a dresser, and our stuff.

MS. WITTLA: Did you have running water, bathroom?

MS. PAYNE: No.

MS. WITTLA: Did you have cable TV?

MS. PAYNE: No.

MS. WITTLA: Did you have a kitchen?

MS. PAYNE: No.

Ok, time once again for a truth check to go with her slanted lies. Understand, this basement arrangement had been made so this couple could save money to go to California. They had expressed they did not want to take the heavy furniture with them, as they could not take it all to California. So, after first saying no, following them simply moving in anyway, we agreed to let them stay in the basement without charge. And when Becky said she had no running water, no bathroom, no cable TV, no kitchen, it really paints a bad picture of what their vulgar landlord was doing to them, doesn't it? Which of course was the prosecutor's idea, and Becky's idea. But now, here is the truth: she did have all the running water she needed, a bathroom, cable TV, and a kitchen, all in our part of the apartment, which they did have access to. So they were denied none of those things!

MS. WITTLA: Did you want to live in the basement?

MS. PAYNE: Not really.

MS. WITTLA: Why did you live there then?

MS. PAYNE: Because they, Robert told us that he needed more money so he wanted to rent out our apartment instead.

I already told you why they were living there, the fact they said they wanted to save money to go to California. So instead of paying us rent, they could save it. So far as our part, she lied again when she said I had told her I needed more money. What I didn't need, was less money though, so naturally we went about renting the apartment to a paying customer. That was our business. There was never any question though, that if they wanted some of those bigger items back, they could certainly have them. It would be both cumbersome and expensive for me to store them! But they stated they did not want to take them to California, so we decided we could put them in the apartment until they did want them, so they would not need to be stored. Do the math!

MS. WITTLA: Becky, did you ever have a relationship with Robert Coleman?

MS. PAYNE: No.

No? No? Did I hear that right?

MS. WITTLA: Did you ever have sex with Robert Coleman?

MS. PAYNE: Yes.

Isn't that sort of like what you might call a relationship? I think I would have to call it that, and as I recall this numbered some three or more times, so that would be a relationship, even if not a love relationship perhaps. I do recall Becky proudly telling some of our acquaintances that she was more of a mother to our kids than was Janet. I wonder why she would make this comparison, when it was not a love relationship in her mind. Or was it?

MS. WITTLA: Were you in love with him?

MS. PAYNE: No.

MS. WITTLA: Did you like him a whole lot?

MS. PAYNE: Just as a friend.

MS. WITTLA: How many times would you say you had sex with him?

MS. PAYNE: I can't remember.

MS. WITTLA: Did you want to?

MS. PAYNE: No.

MS. WITTLA: Why did you do it?

MS. PAYNE: No.

MS. WITTLA: Why did you do it?

MS. PAYNE: Because I was forced to.

Oh? I wonder how I did that? Could it be that now Becky and the prosecutor wanted to make it out that I was a mad rapist? Well, my lawyer would handle that later, but this really angered me, to say the least, as it was all trash lies, for which she should be charged with perjury!

MS. WITTLA: Because he told you to or because he physically forced you?

MS. PAYNE: He physically forced me; he had told me that if I would have sex with him, he would go find a cigarette for me.

I see.... none of it true, but even if it were there is a contradiction of ideas in just that one statement. If what she said were true, I was either a mad rapist or she was a very easy prostitute! Either way, I would be regarded as a criminal, however, which was the prosecutor's intention. She would never follow through with that however, because first she had no real evidence of that, and second, it would mean I would get criminal trial, and her flimsy child abuse claims would also have to be proved at a higher standard. Tracie likes to win, at any cost, and she knew she could not with any kind of criminal trial.

MS. WITTLA: Was this at a point in time when you really wanted a cigarette?

MS. PAYNE: Yes.

MS. WITTLA: Did you have any of your own?

MS. PAYNE: No.

MS. WITTLA: When was the last time that you had sex with Robert Coleman?

MS. PAYNE: March 9th.

MS. WITTLA: Is that part of the reason that you left that day?

MS. PAYNE: No.

MS. WITTLA: What is the reason that you left that day?

MS. PAYNE: Because he was making us write sentences like little kids.

MS. WITTLA: What kind of sentences?

MS. PAYNE: Our lesson that we had to write sentences on March 9th was because Renee from Coldwell Banker came over and started yelling at him because the apartment on Pewabic Street was not cleaned.

MS. WITTLA: So why did you have to write sentences?

MS. PAYNE: Because he got yelled at for it, and he was making us clean that apartment.

MS. WITTLA: So he thought you guys did a bad job?

MS. PAYNE: Yes.

MS. WITTLA: And your punishment was to write sentences?

MS. PAYNE: Yes.

Ok, time to ask the readers a question. If you were working for me and were sent to clean an apartment, and the job were done badly, what action would be expected of me? Either I would reprimand you, or fire you, correct? But if I told you that you would have to write sentences, you would probably tell me to put it where the sun does not shine, or you might quit. Isn't that logical? Why would anybody go along with such a nutty concept as to write sentences? Well, of course, they would not, and no such request was made of Bobby and Becky either! If I would have done anything out of anger, I would have fired them immediately! But the prosecutor was happy to play this stupid concept out even more:

MS. WITTLA: How many sentences did he want you to write?

MS. PAYNE: Five hundred.

MS. WITTLA: What was the sentence you were supposed to write?

MS. PAYNE: I can't remember.

Now that is novel! They can remember how many times I insisted they write a sentence but can't recall what the sentence was! If I were asked to write a sentence five hundred times, I would have it very well memorized! This is not only insane, it is actually comical to conceive! But Ms. Wittla was still trying to convince people:

MS. WITTLA: You said it was the last time you were going to write sentences?

MS. PAYNE: Yes.

MS. WITTLA: Did you have to write sentences before that?

MS. PAYNE: Yes.

MS. WITTLA: How many times would you say that you had to write sentences?

MS. PAYNE: Whenever he said that we had to.

MS. WITTLA: Did it happen once or more than that?

MS. PAYNE: It was more than once.

MS. WITTLA: And why did you have to do that? What would have happened that made him want you to write sentences?

MS. PAYNE: Because we didn't do what he wanted done.

MS. WITTLA: Did you just write sentences or did Bobby too?

MS. PAYNE: Bobby too.

MS. WITTLA: You were together when you would write these sentences?

MS. PAYNE: Yes.

MS. WITTLA: How many times that you would usually write?

MS. PAYNE: Sometimes three hundred, sometimes a hundred, and sometimes five hundred.

Ok. That makes reams of sentences I would think. Where are they? Why are they not being produced in court? Oh! Becky and Ms. Wittla slipped up and forgot to manufacture some dummy sentences they could say I ordered written. But they rehearsed everything else pretty well, it seems!

MS. WITTLA: Did Robert yell at you?

MS. PAYNE: Yes.

MS. WITTLA: How often did he yell at you?

MS. PAYNE: Almost every day.

MS. WITTLA: Did he ever call you names?

MS. PAYNE: Yes.

MS. WITTLA: Did he ever call Bobby names when you were with him?

MS. PAYNE: Yes.

MS. WITTLA: He ever yell at Bobby?

MS. PAYNE: Yes.

MS. WITTLA: Do you like Robert Coleman?

MS. PAYNE: No.

MS. WITTLA: Are you still afraid of him?

MS. PAYNE: Yes.

MS. WITTLA: Thank you, I have nothing further.

THE COURT: Mr. Perhalla?

MR. PERHALLA: Thanks your Honor. Now you testified you moved into an apartment of Robert's last July, about a year ago?

MS. PAYNE: Yeah.

MR. PERHALLA: Did you get to know the Colemans close then or did it take some time to get to know them?

MS. PAYNE: It took us that night when it was pouring and they needed help sweeping water out of their new addition.

MR. PERHALLA: And when was this? In the summer or?

MS. PAYNE: Yes.

MR. PERHALLA: Last summer?

MS. PAYNE: Yes.

MR. PERHALLA: Okay, so that's when you got to know each other closer and became friends?

MS. PAYNE: Yes.

MR. PERHALLA: When did you start going into their apartment to eat with them?

MS. PAYNE: I can't remember at this moment.

MR. PERHALLA: Would it be fair to say it wasn't right away when you moved into the apartments?

MS. PAYNE: Yes.

MR. PERHALLA: It took some time?

MS. PAYNE: Yes.

MR. PERHALLA: When did you get to know Caitlyn and Ashley, right away or?

MS. PAYNE: It took some time after we had started hanging out down in their apartment with them.

MR. PERHALLA: Let's say around about Christmas of last year, were you hanging out with them more and more around that time or still not yet?

MS. PAYNE: We were hanging out with them a lot more.

MR. PERHALLA: By Christmas?

MS. PAYNE: Yes.

MR. PERHALLA: And is this when they had you live in the basement or are you still living in your own apartment?

MS. PAYNE: We were still living in our own apartment at that time.

MR. PERHALLA: Were you eating with them daily then, or were you doing some cooking in your own apartment?

MS. PAYNE: It was daily then, and then when we went up to our apartment, I went and cooked something like for a snack, when we were up there.

MR. PERHALLA: Do you recall when the first time was you would have seen Mr. Coleman hit Caitlyn with a belt?

MS. PAYNE: I can't remember when the first time was.

MR. PERHALLA: Was it after Christmas, before, or you just can't remember?

MS. PAYNE: It was before Christimas.

MR. PERHALLA: So for several months you observed Robert striking Ciatlyn with a belt, correct?

MS. PAYNE: Yes.

MR. PERHALLA: You had a— do you have— do you remember having a conversation with another lady on the telephone that was recorded?

MS. PAYNE: Yes.

MR. PERHALLA: And who was that with?

MS. PAYNE: I can't remember her name at this moment.

MR. PERHALLA: And in May the conversation was why didn't you report this earlier?

MS. PAYNE: Yes.

MR. PERHALLA: Why didn't you report this, say, around Christmas rather than later?

MS. PAYNE: Because we were told if we ever reported him for what he has done, and if he goes to jail and when he gets out he will come and find us and kill us.

MR. PERHALLA: And he, you're talking about Mr. Coleman?

MS. PAYNE: Yes.

MR. PERHALLA: So for several months you were living in some fear of him?

MS. PAYNE: Yes.

MR. PERHALLA: Would it be fair to say that the belt, that they were using the belt only on Caitlyn, right?

MS. PAYNE: Yes.

MR. PERHALLA: You never saw him use it on Ashley?

MS. PAYNE: No.

MR. PERHALLA: Did he treat her a little better?

MS. PAYNE: Yes.

MR. PERHALLA: Ashley?

MS. PAYNE: Yes.

MR. PERHALLA: What would Caitlyn say when the belt was coming out?

MS. PAYNE: She was scared to have the belt.

MR. PERHALLA: Did she cry?

MS. PAYNE: Yes.

MR. PERHALLA: Did she ever go to you when the belt was coming out to try to protect her?

MS. PAYNE: No, she always tried to hide from it.

MR. PERHALLA: Was she successful sometimes in hiding; she was able to get away?

MS. PAYNE: No.

MR. PERHALLA: No? Did you see any parent use anything else other than a belt on Caitlyn?

MS. PAYNE: No.

MS. PAYNE!!!! You forgot your lines!! Remember the brooms and the wooden spoons you had Ms. Fyle insert in her investigative findings report? Shame on you!!

MR. PERHALLA: So it was always the belts?

MS. PAYNE: Yes.

MR. PERHALLA: And where were they kept?

MS. PAYNE: Second drawer on Father Coleman's dresser.

Wow! For someone with a limited mind, as they've presented her, how did she recall so definitively where those belts were kept? I couldn't even remember myself when Ms. Fyle invaded our house! How did Becky know exactly which drawer? Was she always snooping through my drawers? Or did she, maybe, just maybe, plant them there?

MR. PERHALLA: Where was this dresser?

MS. PAYNE: It was in their living room.

MR. PERHALLA: Were you— you did not have to get the belts; someone usually got them?

MS. PAYNE: Yes.

MR. PERHALLA: I take it Caitlyn would cry then after the belting?

MS. PAYNE: Yes.

MR. PERHALLA: For how long?

MS. PAYNE: For a while until she finally calmed down.

MR. PERHALLA: Were these beltings, were they always real hard on the bare butt, or were some lighter?

MS. PAYNE: They were always hard.

MR. PERHALLA: So this was something that Caitlyn just knew that it would happen to her and?

MS. PAYNE: Yes.

MR. PERHALLA: That's all I have, thank you.

Finally, it was our turn to get some truth out of this chronic liar! Our lawyer now began his cross-examination:

MR. FINDLAY: You said you had sex with Robert Coleman for cigarettes?

MS. PAYNE: Yes.

MR. FINDLAY: You are aware what that word refers to usually, aren't you?

MS. PAYNE: No.

MR. FINDLAY: You wouldn't refer to it as prostitution?

MS. PAYNE: No.

MR. FINDLAY: And this abuse that you allegedly saw was going on for months and you never reported it, right?

MS. PAYNE: Yes.

MR. FINDLAY: In fact, you even participated in some of it, didn't you?

MS. PAYNE: Yes.

Then why on earth was this woman not sitting in front of this same court, charged with child abuse herself? Maybe we would now find out why:

MR. FINDLAY: And you haven't been charged with a crime have you?

MS. PAYNE: No.

MR. FINDLAY: Do you know why you haven't been charged with a crime?

MS. PAYNE: No.

MR. FINDLAY: Are you aware it would be very difficult to let them get you to testify here if you were charged with a crime?

MS. PAYNE: Yes.

MR. FINDLAY: Do you think that might have something to do with why you were not charged with a crime?

MS. WITTLA: Objection, your Honor, this is speculative.

THE COURT: Well it's cross, I mean, I— finish the question; it's questionable motivation of the witness, so go ahead.

MR. FINDLAY: Do you think the fact that it would be difficult for them to get you here as a witness is why they didn't charge you with a crime; think that might have something to do with it?

MS. PAYNE: Yes.

There was our case! This woman admitted on the stand that she traded her freedom from prosecution to come tell the story the prosecutor wanted her to tell! But wait! There is more! Much more, that we did not know about at the time of this testimony. I wish we had known, because if we had, we could clearly have ended this charade right then and there. But following the return of our kids, we had a private investigator research Becky's background, and it came to light via that investigation, and is a matter of public record, that at the time she was making this testimony, she was, in fact, charged with a warrant for a crime in Nebraska. It was on record by the LPD there as having involved stolen money or goods, and larceny of a building. So not only was she committing the current crime of perjury, but was wanted on an outstanding warrant at the same time as she was giving this testimony!

MR. FINDLAY: When you lived in the basement at the Colemans, you made it sound like it was a dungeon; but where did you go to the bathroom, in an out house?

MS. PAYNE: No.

MR. FINDLAY: In a bucket?

MS. PAYNE: No.

MR. FINDLAY: You used the bathroom upstairs, correct?

MS. PAYNE: They had us using to— they had us using the sump pump if we had to go Number 1, but if we had to go Number 2, we had to go upstairs to someone else's apartment to use their bathroom.

Would she have us believe she used another renter's bathroom? I don't think so! No renter would ever tolerate such as thing! Would you? Of course it was our bathroom they used! And the Number 1 and Number 2 gestures were just her lies to try to convince the jury she was a little child being abused! Not that this jury needed any convincing. They were already bought and sold! But had they been real jurors, all of her admissions would have won our case for us easily!

MR. FINDLAY: And how long did you live in this arrangement?

MS. PAYNE: Since Feb— since in February until March 9th when we left.

MR. FINDLAY: Um, Janet Coleman was your husband Bobby's representative payee wasn't she?

MS. PAYNE: Yes.

MR. FINDLAY: For his SSI?

MS. PAYNE: Yes.

MR. FINDLAY: And he needed that because he apparently wasn't able to handle money himself?

MS. PAYNE: Yes.

MR. FINDLAY: And that's a voluntary arrangement isn't it?

MS. PAYNE: Yes.

MR. FINDLAY: Nobody forced your husband to do that?

MS. PAYNE: No.

MR. FINDLAY: And in fact, you asked her for your husband, you and your husband asked Janet Coleman to do that for your husband, correct?

MS. PAYNE: Um, my husband did, but I didn't.

MR. FINDLAY: How many times have you, um, met with the Prosecutor regarding this case?

MS. PAYNE: Ah, the only time I met with her was on Monday.

Yeah. And I've got some ocean front property in South Dakota to sell you too!

MR. FINDLAY: This Monday of this week?

MS. PAYNE: Yes.

MR. FINDLAY: How about how many times did you talk with Ms. Fyle about it?

MS. PAYNE: Um, I've talked to her only on the phone and....

MR. FINDLAY: How many times?

MS. PAYNE: Not that many, only about once or twice about this.

But clearly, it was enough for her to be able to help you draft that large number of abuse allegations, wasn't it? Or did she just take whatever you wrote in your complaint and create them herself? Without the need to check them for accuracy!

MR. FINDLAY: When was the most recent time you talked to her?

MS. PAYNE: Ah, the most recent I met with Elizabeth was on Monday when we came in to meet with Tracie.

MR. FINDLAY: How about previous to that?

MS. PAYNE: Um, I called her to let her know that I was going to be in town.

MR. FINDLAY: Your husband has some, ah, mental health issues, doesn't he?

MS. PAYNE: Yes.

MR. FINDLAY: In fact, you had to call the police about him regarding suicide threats or him going missing?

MS. PAYNE: Ah, not me.

MR. FINDLAY: You never reported that to the police?

MS. PAYNE: No.

MR. FINDLAY: On February 11th, 2008, you didn't call the Ironwood Public Safety Department to report that your husband left your apartment, saying he was going to kill himself?

MS. PAYNE: I only called them to let them know that he was out, because he was mad; I didn't say anything that he was going to kill himself.

MR. FINDLAY: You didn't call and tell them your husband Robert left the apartment saying he was going to kill himself?

MS. PAYNE: No.

MR. FINDLAY: So this police report must be wrong?

MS. PAYNE: I only called them to let them know that he was out and I was afraid for him.

MR. FINDLAY: So, but, so you did make a report that he was missing then?

MS. PAYNE: That he was missing, yes.

MR. FINDLAY: And if the report says that you then told the police that you said he was going to kill himself, the police report is wrong?

MS. PAYNE: I was told to call to; I called them to let them know that he was missing, but I was pushed to tell him, to tell the police that he was going to kill himself; I was told by Robert Coleman.

Perjury.

MR. FINDLAY: So Robert Coleman made you do that?

MS. PAYNE: Yes.

MR. FINDLAY: So Robert Coleman makes you do everything, it sounds like?

MS. PAYNE: Yes he does.

MR. FINDLAY: Okay, does he make; you know who Christine Towne is, don't you?

MS. PAYNE: A little bit.

Perjury.

MR. FINDLAY: Okay, well, you've had a phone conversation with her, haven't you?

MS. PAYNE: Yes.

MR. FINDLAY: Did Robert Coleman make you call her?

MS. PAYNE: No.

MR. FINDLAY: Okay, and actually you talked with Christine Towne at least on two occasions about this haven't you?

MS. PAYNE: I only talked to her that once when it was that recording that was on You Tube.

MR. FINDLAY: Are you sure it was only once?

MS. PAYNE: Yes, it was only once that I talked to her.

MR. FINDLAY: Sure it's not two different phone calls?

MS. PAYNE: I know I talked to her about the, about what was happening with us that once, and ah, Bobby talked to her before.

MR. FINDLAY: Um, did Robert Coleman make you talk to her then?

MS. PAYNE: No, we weren't living at the apartments at that time.

MR. FINDLAY: Um, so in fact, when you talked to Christine Towne, you bragged about getting the Colemans kids taken away didn't you?

MS. PAYNE: Yes.

MR. FINDLAY: And you bragged you knew the judge, didn't you?

MS. PAYNE: Yes.

Hold it! Hold it! Hold it! Why, at this point did this judge just sit there like a bump on a log! Either what she said had merit, or he was sleeping on the bench, but he should have jumped right in there to confirm or deny if that was true! If it were indeed true, we should have been granted a mistrial right then and there! If not, she should have been charged with perjury right then and there. But this was not a question for the attorneys— this involved the judge! And he knew the answer to that question!

MR. FINDLAY: And you bragged that you put out bad word for Robert Coleman, didn't you?

MS. PAYNE: Yes, but not to everyone.

MR. FINDLAY: Well, obviously, enough; correct?

MS. PAYNE: Yeah.

MR. FINDLAY: They got their kids taken away from them? And you even bragged and told the police that he stole products from K-Mart and Steigers?

MS. PAYNE: Yes.

MR. FINDLAY: And you bragged that you had, "mostly screwed him over?"

MS. PAYNE: That's what we were feeling like we were doing.

MR. FINDLAY: And you bragged you got him fired at Coldwell Banker, correct?

MS. PAYNE: Not that, I know we didn't.

MR. FINDLAY: Well you bragged that you called Coldwell Banker and said you "screwed him over from that?"

MS. PAYNE: He told, he told me and Bobby that he was fired from Coldwell Banker because we didn't....

MR. FINDLAY: ... And then you bragged to Christine Towne.

MS. WITTLA: Objection your Honor. Would you please allow the witness to answer?

MR. FINDLAY: Well if the court would direct her to answer my question it would be....

THE COURT: Well everybody is running over everybody. Please take a breath, ask a question, allow her to answer, and then we'll go from there.

MR. FINDLAY: All right. Well, let's start over. You did write to Christine Towne that you got him fired from Coldwell Banker, right?

MS. PAYNE: Yes.

Oh? So now you did, where before you didn't? This means you are proving you perjured yourself in your first answer by denying it.

MR. FINDLAY: And you said you screwed him over from that, correct?

MS. PAYNE: No.

MR. FINDLAY: That's not your exact words? That you screwed him over from that? Referring to getting him fired from Coldwell Banker?

MS. PAYNE: No.

MR. FINDLAY: It's on tape; what would you say?

MS. PAYNE: I told her that we got him fired from Coldwell Banker because we didn't clean our apartment good enough.

MR. FINDLAY: And, ah, you bragged that you screwed him over for being able to get money, didn't you?

MS. PAYNE: Yes.

MR. FINDLAY: And you bragged that you told tenants not to rent from him, didn't you?

MS. PAYNE: Sorry, can you repeat that?

MR. FINDLAY: Yes, you bragged; you told tenants not to rent from them; the Colemans, didn't you?

MS. PAYNE: Yes.

MR. FINDLAY: And you bragged and called CPS on them didn't you? Children's Protective Services?

MS. PAYNE: Yes.

There you have it! She was the one who launched the complaint. This judge would later try to say that she was not the complainant in this case, but here she was, admitting to it in his court room! (See chapter 21 - day 4 of this trial and chapter 22 where the newspaper article quotes Elizabeth Fyle as saying Becky was not the complainant). If Becky, indeed, was not the complainant in this trial, then our constitutional rights were denied in that we were not allowed to face our accuser in a court of law. The judge, knowing who that complainant was, did not carry out the mandates of the constitution, and in that event, should be disbarred.

MR. FINDLAY: And you bragged that you had the kids taken away?

MS. PAYNE: Yes.

MR. FINDLAY: You bragged you took better care of the kids than the Colemans did, didn't you?

MS. PAYNE: Yes.

MR. FINDLAY: You bragged that you screwed Robert Coleman out of adopting Caitlyn as his own child didn't you?

MS. PAYNE: Yes, because we were told that before that he was trying to do it and someone else got him to not to.

MR. FINDLAY: So and this makes sure— and this makes he wouldn't be able to adopt her, right?

MS. PAYNE: Yes.

MR. FINDLAY: And you bragged that Caitlyn would never be coming home?

MS. PAYNE: Yes.

MR. FINDLAY: You even mocked Janet Coleman about going to the hospital for stress during her pregnancy when her kids were taken away didn't you?

MS. PAYNE: No.

MR. FINDLAY: You didn't? You said, "Boo-hoo, cry— bitch." You didn't say that?

MS. PAYNE: No.

MR. FINDLAY: Do you want to hear it on tape? You sure you didn't say it? Do I need, you want me to play it?

MS. PAYNE: I don't remember saying that about her.

MR. FINDLAY: Do you think it's possible?

MS. PAYNE: It might be, but I don't remember saying that.

MR. FINDLAY: Well if the tape says it, would you admit to that you said it?

MS. PAYNE: I guess.

As good as my lawyer did in some aspects of this trial, there were places I thought he blew it. And this was one. He should have played the tape right here. He did not.

MR. FINDLAY: You bragged that you'd be a lot better mother than Janet Coleman, didn't you?

MS. PAYNE: No.

MR. FINDLAY: Again, the tapes said that. Do you want to hear the tape?

MS. PAYNE: No.

MR. FINDLAY: Well the tape says that you said it, and your voice obviously saying it; what you're saying here now or what the tape says?

MS. PAYNE: I was told by someone that....

MR. FINDLAY: Your Honor, can you direct her....

This part is incredible! Read now, from the transcripts, how this judge then tried to defend Becky by playing the game the prosecution had brought forth about her lack of understanding!

THE COURT: Well, I don't know if she understands the question or not, you have to, you have to, you can't tell me what someone else said, but if you don't understand his question, say so.

MR. FINDLAY: Okay, it's pretty much a yes or no question. If the tape has you on there saying that you said you'd be a lot better mother than Janet Coleman, which is true? The tape of your testimony here?

MS. PAYNE: The tape.

MR. FINDLAY: And you also bragged that the cops believed you, didn't you?

MS. PAYNE: Yes.

MR. FINDLAY: And you bragged that you had every cop on your side?

MS. PAYNE: Yes.

MR. FINDLAY: You even went so far as to brag that an Officer Sterbrnz hates Coleman?

MS. PAYNE: That I did not say.

Why didn't this lawyer of mine, at that point, play the tape! He could state that he has her on tape, on several occasions, perjuring herself already, and based on that he could have asked for a dismissal.

MR. FINDLAY: In fact, the exact words that you used to describe what you did to the Colemans were, "So yeah, we screwed him." Isn't that true?

MS. PAYNE: Yes.

What more does a jury have to hear? But not this jury! Let's remember, they were all friends or relatives of cops!

MR. FINDLAY: Would you say, seeing what's happened here today, say you're successful?

MS. PAYNE: Yes.

MS. WITTLA: Objection your Honor, I don't believe that....

MR. FINDLAY: ... Withdrawn, I withdraw it.

THE COURT: Yeah, same objection you made before, please don't; all counsel, don't comment on the evidence. Just ask the questions and get your answers. Redirect.

Did anybody hear my lawyer say he was through yet? The transcripts don't show it!

MS. WITTLA: Ready? You've heard the tape that Mr. Findlay was referring to?

MS. PAYNE: Part of it.

MS. WITTLA: You mentioned that being on You Tube?

MS. PAYNE: Yes.

MS. WITTLA: Did you know you were being recorded when you were speaking to Christine Towne that day?

MS. PAYNE: No, because she told— when I spoke with her she said that she hadn't talked to him for a long time and that she was still in the town that she lived in.

MS. WITTLA: A different town from here?

MS. PAYNE: Yes.

MS. WITTLA: Did you think Christine Towne was your friend?

MS. PAYNE: No.

It is interesting to hear her answer no to that question, since she poured her entire heart out to her about what a devil Robert was and how she screwed him over. It is not like people who are not friends to place such confidence in them! And as for the recording, Tracie acted as though there is something wrong with recording. It is totally legal in Michigan, and if they do not know they are being recorded, they will reveal their true character. But of course Tracie wanted to continue to make it appear that Becky was a victim, even after caught in all her lies in court.

MS. WITTLA: When you spoke to her did you believe that your conversation was going to be repeated back to Robert Coleman?

MS. PAYNE: I asked, when I was speaking to her, I asked her if she was going to go back to Robert Coleman, and she said no to us.

MS. WITTLA: So she lied to you?

MS. PAYNE: Yes.

MS. WITTLA: Because obviously Robert Coleman has a tape of the conversation you had with Christine?

MS. PAYNE: Yes.

MS. WITTLA: Do you think Christine set you up?

MS. PAYNE: Yes.

MS. WITTLA: Were you mad at Robert Coleman when you were talking to Christine Towne?

MS. PAYNE: Yes.

MS. WITTLA: Are you still mad at him?

MS. PAYNE: Yes.

MS. WITTLA: Why are you mad at him?

MS. PAYNE: For what he has done to us, and what he has done to the two kids.

Another lie. She never had any interest in the kids and they totally dislike her, even to this day. Caitlyn, today, says she always lied. We've seen that in Becky's testimony. So a lie to Becky by Christine is simply justice.

MS. WITTLA: You know that Caitlyn and Ashley were taken out of his care, in part, because of the interviews you gave to DHS?

MS. PAYNE: Yes.

MS. WITTLA: Were you truthful in your interviews?

MS. PAYNE: Yes.

MS. WITTLA: Did you ever add stuff to make sure that the kids would be taken away that were not true?

MS. PAYNE: No.

PERJURY!

MS. WITTLA: Do you believe that you did take better care of Caitlyn and Ashley than Robert and Janet did?

MS. PAYNE: Yes.

MS. WITTLA: Why do you believe that?

MS. PAYNE: Because we were always down there helping out, giving them a bath, changing their diaper, I was, sometimes, getting their pajamas out, making sure they were dressed and ready for bed.

MS. WITTLA: Robert and Janet didn't do these things for their children?

MS. PAYNE: They did sometimes after Janet started yelling about it, that I was doing more for them than she was.

MS. WITTLA: You mentioned in the taped conversation he was fired from Coldwell, you mentioned that Robert Coleman was fired from working for Coldwell Banker. How did that happen?

MS. PAYNE: Because he dropped us off at the house as he had a job for; from Coldwell Banker, and he dropped us off and told us that we had to clean the house and make sure it was all ready for the new tenants to move in there.

MS. WITTLA: Is that the job that you were supposed to write the sentences about?

MS. PAYNE: Yes, after he got yelled at by Renee from Coldwell Banker.

MS. WITTLA: Did you purposely get him fired from Coldwell Banker?

MS. PAYNE: No.

MS. WITTLA: But it happened anyway?

MS. PAYNE: Yes.

MS. WITTLA: Are you worried about Caitlyn and Ashley?

MS. PAYNE: Yes.

MS. WITTLA: Why did you tell the Department of Human Services about what happened to them?

MS. PAYNE: Because we were afraid that they were still going to be treated the way that they were when we were there.

MS. WITTLA: Weren't you afraid that Robert would be mad at you if you told?

MS. PAYNE: Yes.

MS. WITTLA: Did it make it easier to tell you when you weren't living there?

Again, leading the witness. Ms. Payne wasn't about to come up with that on her own. But it was Ms. Wittla who wanted to see that stated. This entire part of the testimony was fabricated.

MS. PAYNE: Yes.

MS. WITTLA: When you told DHS what happened in that house, did Robert know where you live?

MS. PAYNE: Yes.

MS. WITTLA: Does he know where you live now?

MS. PAYNE: No.

MS. WITTLA: Do you want him to?

MS. PAYNE: No.

MS. WITTLA: Are you still afraid of him?

MS. PAYNE: Yes.

MS. WITTLA: At the beginning of this proceeding, the Judge asked you to tell the truth. Have you lied to me today?

MS. PAYNE: No.

A better way to describe it is that she lied for you, Ms. Wittla!

MS. WITTLA: Thank you.

THE COURT: Mr. Perhalla, anything?

MR. PERHALLA: Thanks your Honor. Those last few months that you lived with the Colemans, were you afraid on a daily basis?

MS. PAYNE: Yes.

MR. PERHALLA: Are you relieved now that you finally told people what's happened and you can get on with things?

How melodramatic! A nice act on the part of Perhalla, but again, leading the witness!

MS. PAYNE: A little bit.

MR. PERHALLA: You're still afraid of what he might do to you?

MS. PAYNE: Yes.

MR. PERHALLA: Are you relieved to no longer be around him?

MS. PAYNE: Yes.

MR. PERHALLA: Do you believe that Robert Coleman controlled you when you were living there?

MS. PAYNE: Yes.

MR. PERHALLA: Thank you.

THE COURT: Mr. Findlay?

MR. FINDLAY: Do you think the Colemans are glad they are no longer around you?

MS. PAYNE: I'm not sure at this moment?

MR. FINDLAY: I'm sorry?

MS. PAYNE: I'm not sure at this moment.

MR. FINDLAY: Nothing else.

With that, Becky was excused as a witness and the court took their noon break. When court resumed for the day, Bob Ross was called to complete his unfinished testimony:

MS. WITTLA: I think we ended with the children being moved from Ontonogon to Marquette, sounds right?

MR. ROSS: Correct.

MS. WITTLA: In case I didn't ask this question, why were the kids moved from Ontonagon to Marquette?

MR. ROSS: The shelter home family in Ontonagon, excuse me, had a conflict; they had some prior engagements; the shelter mom had a son who had a close friend of his pass away in an accident and, um, the timing of maintaining the kids in the home was not good.

MS. WITTLA: So is there a request that they be moved?

MR. ROSS: Correct.

MS. WITTLA: And how long were the children in a foster care home in Marquette?

MR. ROSS: From March 31st until, I believe, May 31st was the day they moved them again.

MS. WITTLA: During that period of time, are you aware of any investigations that were done of the foster home that the children lived in?

MR. ROSS: Yes, there was a foster home licensing investigation, and there was a CPS complaint directed at the foster parents.

MS. WITTLA: Are you aware of what the allegations were about?

MR. ROSS: Um, it's my understanding that there was a licensing complaint directed at Child and Family Services and their supervisor, and then there was some physical abuse allegations directed at the foster parents directed at the children, in regards to the two Coleman children.

MS. WITTLA: Ashley and Caitlyn?

MR. ROSS: Correct.

MS. WITTLA: Are you aware of any law enforcement investigations of these complaints?

MR. ROSS: Um, I believe the girls, Caitlyn in specific, was interviewed by a Trooper from the Negaunee State Police post.

MS. WITTLA: Are you aware whether or not these complaints are being pursued in any way?

MR. ROSS: No, they've all been unsubstantiated.

Unsubstantiated? What does that mean? What it meant was the police did not really wish to pursue it so no investigation took place. They went out to the house, looked around a few minutes, said hello to the girls, and left. No investigation. So if they don't want to do a real investigation, they call it unsubstantiated.

MS. WITTLA: The children were moved at the end of May to a foster placement in what county?

MR. ROSS: Delta.

MS. WITTLA: Is that where they remain?

MR. ROSS: Presently, yes.

MS. WITTLA: Are you aware of any complaints of abuse against the foster parents in Delta County?

MR. ROSS: Yes, there is a current complaint, but I'm not sure of the status of the investigation yet, but the allegations were made that there was some sexual abuse allegations directed at the foster parents regarding Caitlyn and Ashley again.

MS. WITTLA: How many days were the children in the Ontonagon foster care placement?

MR. ROSS: Were they, excuse me?

MS. WITTLA: Were they; Ontonagon? What, a few weeks? A few days?

MR. ROSS: Fourteen days; two weeks approximately.

MS. WITTLA: No complaints were filed there?

MR. ROSS: There was, I believe, there was a FOIA request looking for information on the foster parents in Ontonagon.

MS. WITTLA: Do you know who made that request?

MR. ROSS: Mr. and Mrs. Coleman.

MS. WITTLA: Mr. Ross, you were not the original investigator of this case, is that correct?

MR. ROSS: Correct.

MS. WITTLA: But you are the day to day guy?

MR. ROSS: Once the kids transition from a Child Protective Services case into foster care; it's my responsibility to oversee the day to day supervision of the children. Unless we contract out like we did in Marquette County with Child and Family Services through a purchase of services agreement, and then they monitor the day to day operations of the case.

MS. WITTLA: So for that period from March 31st to May 31st, that was a contracted out case?

MR. ROSS: Yes, I oversaw Child and Family Services' management of the case.

MS. WITTLA: What's known as a purchase of service agreement?

MR. ROSS: Yes, purchase of service agreement.

MS. WITTLA: Who was the caseworker there?

MR. ROSS: Angela Andriacchi.

MS. WITTLA: And it's her agency that the complaint was made against while the children were in Marquette County?

MR. ROSS: Correct.

MS. WITTLA: Are you aware of any complaints made against you?

MR. ROSS: Not yet.

MS. WITTLA: Are you aware of Robert or Janet Coleman contacting any of your supervisors at DHS to complain about you?

MR. ROSS: Yes, um, Mr. Coleman had a conversation with my supervisor, Ban Borth, um, made some comments about me and suggested to Mr. Borth that I be suspended or reprimanded or removed from the case due to the way I was monitoring the situation.

MS. WITTLA: Was the allegation that you weren't doing your job?

MR. ROSS: Yes.

MS. WITTLA: Do you tape Robert Coleman's phone calls?

MR. ROSS: No I don't.

MS. WITTLA: Why not?

MR. ROSS: Early on in the case I received a phone call from Mr. Coleman, um, who asked me questions about the case, um, the phone call later showed up on You Tube.com—and part of the conversation included Mr. Coleman telling me that I was going to be part of a law suit that he was filing against the State of Michigan. And rather than get into an argument with Mr. Coleman, I excused myself from the phone call, and elected to have any conversations regarding the care of the Colemans with Mr. Coleman's attorney, Mr. Findlay.

MS. WITTLA: Are you aware that you're being recorded today?

MR. ROSS: Yes, but I'm in court.

MS. WITTLA: Does that concern you that you're being recorded today?

MR. ROSS: No, the court proceeding is a matter of public record, and it's a controlled setting, so....

MS. WITTLA: Were you aware that you were being recorded the day you spoke to Mr. Coleman?

MR. ROSS: No.

MS. WITTLA: Are you aware of Mr. Coleman's claims that he has, I believe it was hours of tape on this case?

MR. ROSS: I've heard that, yes.

MS. WITTLA: Have you heard anything beyond your voice on You Tube?

MR. ROSS: My voice showed up on You Tube twice, and there's some other conversations with different workers that have showed up, and then there's been sound bites and different things from, things that Mr. Coleman has put together and put on You Tube.

MS. WITTLA: Do you want to be on You Tube?

MR. ROSS: No.

MS. WITTLA: I guess the obvious question, why not?

MR. ROSS: I signed on to work with the DHS to protect kids; I didn't sign on to make my work experiences and personal life and things like that a matter of public record. Um, the things that Mr. Coleman's put on You Tube are confidential case things that are going on, and if I put those things on the internet or talked about those publicly I'd be released from my job; so I guess it's okay for Mr. Coleman to put that stuff on the internet and publicly put out the confidential stuff of this case, but for me it's not. So I would prefer to stay off the internet, prefer to stay off You Tube.

MS. WITTLA: Were you part of the transport of the children from Marquette County to Delta County?

MR. ROSS: Yes I was.

MS. WITTLA: How did the children take the news?

MR. ROSS: It was difficult; it's difficult any time you have to move children from one foster home to the next foster home. It, ah, any stability that they had in the previous foster home is shot, and we have to build a new relationship of new foster parents; we have to build a new relationship with a new counselor if the child is seeing a counselor. So we've moved these children three times in the last three months, and we've had to re-establish foster parent relationships; we had to re-establish counseling relationships; and every time you move a kid it's more and more detrimental and more and more harmful to the child's well-being.

Well said. So if you had never moved them from their original home in the first place, based on the lies to two complete liars; one of them, if not both, mental cases; there would have been very limited damage. Then when you screw it up with your choices of bad foster parents, you compound the damage with every screwup. If you would only go after parents when they commit criminal acts, as it should be done, it would save a lot of kids and parents a lot of heartache and grief.

MS. WITTLA: From your perspective, did the false allegations against the foster parents play a part in the decision not to keep Caitlyn and Ashley in Marquette?

MR. ROSS: Yes.

In this last question and response we have two liars. First, Ms. Wittla calls them false allegations, which they were not. The word they use, when they have their own people do their phony limited check, in fact, is unsubstantiated. But as always, Ms. Wittla created her own set of so-called facts, and again, the court let her do it, calling them false allegations. And Ross, endorsing that, tells the same big lie.

MS. WITTLA: How many cases to you have, a caseload right now?

MR. ROSS: Three child protective services on-going cases; six investigations; and twenty foster care cases.

MS. WITTLA: Twenty-nine?

MR. ROSS: Twenty-nine total.

MS. WITTLA: Which one takes up most of your time?

MR. ROSS: This case does.

MS. WITTLA: What percent?

MR. ROSS: Of my time, of my time?

MS. WITTLA: Yeah.

MR. ROSS: Um, there's probably, out of an eight hour work day; there's probably at least an hour and a half to two hours; sometimes more of case staffings and meetings and Court hearings and dealing with service providers and dealing with complaints and comments from the family that it takes up a majority of my day, just one case.

MS. WITTLA: So if you're going to give me a percent; what, what's a majority of the day?

MR. ROSS: A third of my, a third of my day is probably tied up—is tied up doing this case.

You know I was not a great mathematician when I was in school, but even I can figure out that first, two hours a day out of an eight-hour day is twenty-five percent.

Not thirty-three and a third percent, which is a third of his day. So other than not doing his math very well, Mr. Ross should be told that even a third of his day is not the majority of his day. It would take fifty-one percent to accomplish that. You know— the same percentage required to prove a civil case!

MS. WITTLA: And the other two-thirds are left for the other twenty-eight cases you have?

MR. ROSS: Correct.

MS. WITTLA: Why does this case seem to be so time consuming?

MR. ROSS: There's no stability. We're always, we're constantly having to deal with complaints; we constantly have to—we're in court dealing with different proceedings; we're dealing with having to move kids; find new places for kids. Um, the move from Marquette County to Delta County took two days, because we didn't have a foster home in eight, eight or nine counties in the Western half of the U.P. to place these children. Um, fortunately we hooked up with a supervisor in Delta County who graciously gave us a bed; if that didn't work out, we were possibly looking at going Delta County possibly Chippewa County, or, I'm sorry, Luce County or Chippewa County, or even some place below the Mackinaw Bridge because there just aren't any homes.

Yeah! That's because you've got them all filled up with kidnapped kids!

MS. WITTLA: So when the kids had to be moved from Marquette County, is it your testimony that you checked with KeWeenaw, Houghton, Baraga; everybody at this end?

MR. ROSS: Yes.

MS. WITTLA: Okay, Gogebic, Ontonagon, Iron; nobody had a place for these kids that was closer than Delta?

MR. ROSS: They either didn't have a place or they were not going to take the case.

MS. WITTLA: Or were not going to take it?

MR. ROSS: Correct.

MS. WITTLA: Did they know how time consuming it was?

MR. ROSS: Yes.

MS. WITTLA: Subject of relative placement come up?

MR. ROSS: Correct.

MS. WITTLA: Have relatives been explored for these children?

MR. ROSS: Early on, early on in the case there was a request to possibly look at Mrs. Coleman's family in North Dakota. Um, that was withdrawn and Mr. Coleman suggested that we look into his brother, Randy, who is a police officer in the western Wayne County area. And a home study request was made of that to try to keep the children with some type of a, a relative rather than foster care.

MS. WITTLA: Did Mr. Coleman's brother accept?

MR. ROSS: No, Mr. Coleman's brother declined.

MS. WITTLA: Mr. Ross, do you have to have a home study done before you send kids to live with relatives?

MR. ROSS: Preferably we, we would like to, but it's not a requirement, we can get it done after the fact.

MS. WITTLA: In this case, are you going to send these kids anywhere before getting the reports?

MR. ROSS: I don't feel comfortable professionally or personally sending kids to a grandparent in North Dakota, several hundred miles away without getting, without at least getting a look at the situation in the home before we send a child that far away. Um, we know nothing about Mrs. Coleman's mother or parents, um, it's hours away; try to find somebody to courtesy supervise this case in North Dakota would be very difficult. Um, and it's, and it would be yet another move of the children. So until we got a home study done through North Dakota, I would not feel comfortable making that move.

Yes it would be difficult, because that would be asking you to do your job! And you would not feel comfortable making the move because they would go to somebody they know. And that is a horrible thought, isn't it Mr. Ross? I don't suppose, by any chance, your reasoning really had more to do with the fact the kids would no longer be under Michigan's supervision would it? Or that perhaps Michigan might lose the revenue to another state? Or that Michigan would lose control over our kids?

MS. WITTLA: Are Caitlyn and Ashley average kids?

MR. ROSS: They're not average kids.

MS. WITTLA: If we're going to talk about, um, there's a phrase in, at DHS, and I can't think of what it is, but I think it's difficulty of care?

MR. ROSS: Correct.

MS. WITTLA: They use a rating system. Tell me if I'm messing this up, where you rate how difficult it is to take care of a child?

MR. FINDLAY: Your Honor, I'm going to object, this is basically testimony by the Prosecutor, and it's a leading question.

MS. WITTLA: I can elicit it from him if you prefer; I just thought I'd make it faster.

Sure, Ms. Wittla. Never mind the rules, do it your way because this prejudiced judge will ride with you, irrespective of the rules anyway. And we must not forget, this is about you— isn't it Ms. Wittla?

THE COURT: If you have a lead into a question, that's fine. What you're doing is okay, but I mean, if you're going to make it leading with a yes or no at the end, then it's not fine, so go ahead as long as it's preliminary. Go ahead and describe it and we'll see if you have a leading question.

Oh! I get it! You can't have a yes or no at the end for Mr. Ross like you did all the way through Becky Payne's testimony, and it was okay then! And since you have this all rehearsed very well with Mr. Ross, who is a lot smarter than Becky, then you can get the answer if a form that is other than a yes or no. Sounds like a good judicial plan to me!

MS. WITTLA: There's a system, I believe it's zero, 1, 2, 3; zero being the least difficult level of care; 3 is the highest; I think you can get an administrative override for 4 or something higher. Are Ashley and Caitlyn listed on the difficulty of care scale?

MR. ROSS: When the children were placed in Marquette County, we did a determination of care through Child and Family Services; um, both children scored out at, what we call a DOC level 2, which is one level below having to go through a director's approval to pay for the rate of foster care. The foster parents are reimbursed at a rate of an extra ten dollars per day per child. And we scored the system out based on personal care, personal hygiene, behavior management, emotional needs, um, transportation needs, and we have a rating scale depending on the needs of the child to determine how much we have to, or how we feel it's necessary to reimburse the foster parents for the cost of the care. Both children, like I said, were level 2 kids because of the counseling needs, the transportation needs, the personal care needs, and those kind of things.

And every kidnapped kid has counseling needs, transportation needs, etc., because you will see to it that they do, right? And that can push the level up higher so that the state can hang onto them longer, right? I get it Bob!

MS. WITTLA: Were they scored higher because of their behaviors?

Careful now Bob! Remember, Ms. Hunenen said the kids were lovely, complying, lovely, delightful little angels, who willingly held her hand and gave nobody any trouble when they were kidnapped. Keep that in mind, and answer carefully, Bob:

MR. ROSS: Yes, um, behavior management was one of the first things we score, and ah, both girls in Marquette County commanded constant supervision because Ashley was physically aggressive towards the two year child of the, the natural child of the foster parents.

Damn! That blows Hununen's descriptions totally out of the water. But pardon me, Bob, isn't such behavior by a two-year old fairly ordinary? I think that's why we refer to this period of their lives as their terrible twos—isn't it? And I'd bet the natural child of the foster parents, also two, was probably aggressive as well. Or did you forget to look at that? Well, go on, Bob, let's hear more:

MR. ROSS (continuing): Um, there was some extreme behaviors in the home of, ah, smearing of faces, um, not being potty trained, um physical acting out, temper tantrums, and those type of behaviors, so that warranted the higher rate of care for the foster parents.

Hmmmm.... this is very serious! Let me ask any parent reading this book:

(1) Do any of you have a kid who might have been more than 2 before potty training was completed?

(2) Did your kids ever throw temper tantrums?

(3) Did your kids ever pretend and act out things?

I, as a parent, always thought all kids did those things. But for legal kidnapping purposes, I guess, these should be thought of as bad things that justify the state in the kidnapping game to keep children longer. (Maybe until they grow out of these normal patterns?)

MS. WITTLA: Because of their higher level of care, does that make them more difficult to place?

MR. ROSS: Yes.

Except of course, with willing relatives. But oh! I forgot! That makes you uncomfortable, doesn't it!

MS. WITTLA: Was that part of the reason it was so difficult to find a placement when the Marquette placement failed?

MR. ROSS: Partially, yes.

MS. WITTLA: What was the other part?

MR. ROSS: The other part is that this case is U.P. wide and statewide; has gathered a life of it's own. When people, when people ask you about kids and they find out that, you know, you tell them we're dealing with the Coleman kids; other DHS counties had basically told us, we're taking a hands off approach; we don't want to deal with it. They don't want to deal with the CPS complaints; they don't want to deal with false complaints directed at foster parents.

Yeah. All those darned things a caring parent, who loves their kids might do to keep you from kidnapping their kids for money—right? Oh—and again, Bob, get it right, will you? The word is unsubstantiated— not false.

MS. WITTLA: Are there enough foster parents in Gogebic County?

MR. ROSS: There's not enough foster parents in the U.P.— let alone Gogebic County. I would love to find a place relatively close to the parents to facilitate more and frequent, more frequent visitation with the family, but we don't have anything close.

How about my house Bob? That's where the kids should have been anyway!

MS. WITTLA: Is that because it's difficult to get foster parents up and licensed?

MR. ROSS: The laws have changed where they now need ten or twelve hours of training to become licensed. But there's just not a lot of people willing to step forward to become foster parents.

MS. WITTLA: So is it fair to say that part of it is the training requirements and part of it is just a lack of willingness on the general public?

MR. ROSS: Yes, and that's; and it's a tough job at fourteen dollars a day.

But that would be for kids who never have a tantrum, pretend, or need care, such as potty training. How much for those who do? And of course, each home has 4 or 5 kids, right? So yeah, it's hard to get someone to do this for $70-$80 a day minimum. But of course if you got over $14, which you try to do by touting how little you get, as you're doing here, you would take that money, keep more, and pay the parents about the same anyway. And then you'd go out and get more kids with the extra money you made, so you could keep telling this story and grabbing more and more kids.

MS. WITTLA: When you've dealt with other cases where children are in foster care; oh, let me start that; start over. Do foster parents expect to be involved in the case at a legal level?

MR. ROSS: No.

MS. WITTLA: What's their job?

MR. ROSS: Their job is to supply a safe place, and a safe and nurturing home for the children until they can be returned to their parents.

Until the state is done using the children for money you mean! And what is a safe and nurturing home? One where kids are dragged on carpets, up stairs? Or is it one where kids are locked in a dark basement? These are things that happened to my kids so they could protect them from my disciplinary spankings which were given to teach them right from wrong. But of course if the state endorses it with a phony license— it is okay!

MS. WITTLA: Is this case unusual then, because the foster parents seem to be drawn into the bulk of the case?

MR. ROSS: They're drawn into the case, yes, but they're drawn in because of complaints and different requests and a lot of unsubstantiated allegations that take away from the care of the children.

A lot of unsubstantiated allegations that take away from the care of the children. It sounds just like those unsubstantiated allegations that were made by Becky and Bobby about us, which also took away from the care of the children! The difference is this: Caitlyn today will tell you that while in foster care she was knocked out of her chair, dragged over rugs, sustaining rug burns, locked in a dark basement, and a few other sorted details. She will also tell you the state forced her to say some things for fear of never coming home if she did not say them. To me, that is a lot more substantiated than is a police visit to a home where they ask if they are abusing the kids, and when told no, they accept it at face value and the investigation is off!

MS. WITTLA: Do you think it scared them off?

MR. ROSS: Yes.

God, yes! The truth might come out!

MS. WITTLA: Do you think it's helped any that all of this stuff is on You Tube?

MR.ROSS: No.

It certainly didn't help you Bob— or you Ms. Wittla. But it does help inform the public as to what you and your criminal accomplices are doing!

MS.WITTLA: If the Delta County placement does not work out, what are you going to do?

MR. ROSS: If it doesn't work out, we'll ask, we'll start the process over and go county to county again, U.P. wide, and see if they can find a bed. There's Delta, there's Menominee, there's Luce, there's Chippewa.

MS. WITTLA: The last time you had to replace the children in the end of May, right?

MR. ROSS: Correct.

MS. WITTLA: Now we're here at the end of June?

MR. ROSS: Correct.

MS. WITTLA: Do you think it will have gotten easier in that period of time, to replace these kids?

MR. ROSS: It's never easier, the more you move kids, the more people ask why you're moving these kids so often.

MS. WITTLA: So the system itself becomes more difficult to work with?

MR. ROSS: Foster parents are less likely to take kids when they find out they've been moved so many times previously.

MS. WITTLA: Because they want to know why?

MR. ROSS: Exactly.

Exactly! You see, if they are a bad foster parent, they would not want to answer to some bozo like Robert Coleman might object to their own mistreatment of his kids! Remember, they don't want to be sized up by the legal system the same way that the parents are!

MS. WITTLA: Mr. Ross, have you offered any kind of financial reimbursement to the Colemans, for traveling to see their children?

MR. ROSS: Yes, I have. On March 31st when the children were first moved from Ontonagon County to Marquette County, I instructed the Colemans to enroll in a program called MAIN, which is on the State Department of Management and Budget website, and that's a mechanism to get them enrolled so I could turn in vouchers to get the parents reimbursed for their mileage to and from their parenting time appointments. Alls I needed was dates and times confirmed from the Colemans that they made their parenting time appointments and I would turn in those vouchers to reflect the dates that they went to Marquette to see their kids.

Bulletin! Here is something that the state should understand, that even a common member of society, such as myself, already understands: when you get in your car and drive, it takes gas to make the car go. It takes money to buy the gas. When you get where you are going, you need a place to stay, probably a motel. It takes money to get a motel room. Now, when the state puts your kids several hours drive away from you, in order to visit them, you need money! Not reimbursement. You need money— now; today! Not six weeks from now! Is anybody so stupid that they cannot figure that out? Other than government, of course?

MR. ROSS (continuing): Um, I haven't received any dates or confirmed any dates from the Colemans; I asked them for that; and when we had another court date at the end of May in which Mr. Coleman pulled me aside with his attorney present, and I was asked by Mr. Coleman about getting reimbursed. And I said, again, that I need to confirm those dates with the agency that you did your visits with; and since then I haven't received any dates to confirm as well.

Okay. Readers, bear with me on this: the state sets the dates, times, and places for your appointments to visit your kids. The visitation was either made, or not. If, in fact they are on a reimbursement program, why would they need vouchers to do it? There is a marvelous machine called the telephone, which even allows faxes to be sent on it. Email is also a marvelous invention. They can actually verify these visits took place, compare the record of the visit with the schedule, and have an answer as to if or not a check should be cut for reimbursement, within minutes. What do they need me for? Ok Ross, go on:

MR. ROSS (continuing): And then there was the day in June I stopped by Mr. Findlay's office, and I asked Mr. Findlay if he'd received any documents from his clients as far as the parenting time appointments, and Mr. Findlay said he either had them something on his email or he just doesn't have them, and I've been able to take care of that financially for them. So without the dates to confirm a child and family services, and to confirm them with my provider, I'm unable to pay them. I'd be—I'd like to pay them the money that they paid out to see their kids because it's very expensive.

Wow! He understands something!

MS. WITTLA: During these conversations you had with Mr. Coleman, was someone else always present or was it just you, you two, at one point in time or another?

MR. ROSS: On the 31st of March, it was done in my office; it was Mr. and Mrs. Coleman on a way to a visit. And then the time I had the conversation with Mr. Coleman in the courtroom, downstairs, Mr. Findlay stood by. And then the other time it was with Mr. Findlay in his office.

MS. WITTLA: Did you ever swear at Mr. Coleman during those exchanges?

MR. ROSS: You never swear in front of a client.

MS. WITTLA: Your answer implies that you, you do swear, but just not in your job?

Miss Witta! Please! You are making your good friend and partner in crime look like a hypocrite!

MR. ROSS: It's unprofessional to swear in front of clients; it's just something I don't do; I don't make a practice of using that language in front of clients.

MS. WITTLA: As we're sitting here today, have the Colemans been reimbursed for anything that you're aware of, as far as travel?

MR. ROSS: No.

MS. WITTLA: And the reason they haven't been is because the documents haven't been provided?

MR. ROSS: The documents haven't been provided and they've been staying in hotels in Escanaba to see their kids in Delta County, and I don't have any hotel receipts to add to the vouchers, so until I get those I can't pay them.

Flash! The state could pay the hotels directly and tell us where we are booked. No need for receipts if you do that! But that's too easy!

MS. WITTLA: And it's your testimony that you told him about the need for these receipts on at least two occasions?

MR. ROSS: Yes.

MS. WITTLA: Thank you.

No, thank you! Your long, drawn-out, b.s., questioning finally ended! As I listened to that last financial part, I was not sure if we were being tried for child abuse matters or for failing to register for reimbursement! I can't see where any of that financial b.s. had anything to do with whether or not I abused my kids!

THE COURT: Mr. Perhalla

MR. PERHALLA: When the children were placed, it was in Marquette County with the Children and Family Services, you did not no longer have the day to day contact with the children?

MR. ROSS: It's a purchase of services agreement and under— the way we do those things with the purchase of services agency is, they're responsible for coordinating the parenting time appointments; they're responsible for setting up services for the children; um, counseling appointments for Caitlyn; counseling appointments for Ashley; early on appointments; um, they would facilitate getting Caitlyn enrolled in school in the community that she lived in. Um, the day to day operations of the case would be done by them; they would also be responsible for doing an initial case service plan.

MR. PERHALLA: And what is Children and Family Services?

MR. ROSS: Child and Family Services is a private agency, contracted by the State of Michigan to provide; they license their own foster homes and then we borrow the beds from those foster homes, and they provide foster care services out to allow the specialized foster care if needed for children that need the care.

MR. PERHALLA: How long have they been in business, if you know?

MR. ROSS: I can't tell you. Many, many years.

MR. PERHALLA: So they're a private social working agency?

MR. ROSS: Correct.

MR. PERHALLA: And that's something that's normal in various parts of the state?

MR. ROSS: There's Child and Family Services all over the state, yes.

MR. PERHALLA: And other agencies similar to them?

MR. ROSS: Correct; like Teaching Family Homes; that's another agency we use.

MR. PERHALLA: And you relied upon them to provide the day to day care for these two girls while they were in Marquette?

MR. ROSS: Correct.

MR. PERHALLA: Did you see the girls at all, while they were in Marquette?

MR. ROSS: I personally delivered the girls to Marquette with Ms. Fyle. Um, I picked them up the day that we transitioned them to Delta County, and other than that, I don't believe I saw them while they were up there. Angela Andriacchi was the caseworker, and part of purchase of service agreement is that Angela make our required contacts for us; we're paying them to make our contacts for us; so there was no need for me to go to Marquette to physically see the kids.

MR. PERHALLA: Right, it would just be too far, that's why you hired them?

MR. ROSS: Correct.

But it sure as hell wasn't too far to expect us parents to go, with no money in our pockets, was it? Tell me what a hard life you live Ross!

MR. PERHALLA: Contracted with them. When you brought the girls to Marquette, ah, was it early in the day? Daylight hours? Later? What time was it?

MR. ROSS: It was daylight hours, because the parents had just completed a two hour visit in our office.

MR. PERHALLA: Did the girls behave on the trip to Delta County?

MR. ROSS: The girls were very good in the car. Both trips that I've been with the girls, they've been very good passengers.

MR. PERHALLA: So you had no problems or didn't see any behavioral problems at that time?

MR. ROSS: No.

But you said before they were monsters and scared the living hell out of every foster parent in the state! Mr. Ross, how can this be?

MR. PERHALLA: While they were in, or since they have been in Escanaba, have you been present during the visits or the Escanaba's DHS handles that?

MR. ROSS: Um, through the court we have contracted an individual in Marquette to act as a visitation supervisor; she picks up the children from the foster home, she takes the children to the visit at the Delta County DHS in Escanaba; she supervises the visit for two hours and then she takes the children back to the foster home. Um, I did have an opportunity, a few weeks ago, to stop in and see the girls in the foster home. I was on my— I went to Marquette to see some other children that I had, I went around to Escanaba and I spent about an hour and a half in the foster home, seeing the girls.

MR. PERHALLA: And how were the girls adjusting to the foster home at that time?

MR. ROSS: Um, there's some behavior issues; there's some acting out, some physical aggression. Um, Caitlyn seems to have a rivalry with the daughter of the foster parents right now, which is causing some difficulty.

MR. PERHALLA: And do— during these, ah, the driving from Marquette or from Ontonagon to Marquette, and Marequette to Escanaba, and this visit that you just saw with the girls, did the girls or did Caitlyn ever mention any of the abuse?

MR. ROSS: No.

We can assume Mr. Perhalla was asking about the girls making mention of the alleged abuse by me. But you can bet money he didn't want to address the real abuse— that was actually taking place at the foster home at that same time! Oh! I forgot. What happened there didn't happen, did it, because the state police said it was unsubstantiated.

MR. PERHALLA: But that wasn't you; you didn't use the Forensic Protocol, and that wasn't the purpose of those encounters anyway?

MR. ROSS: No, no.

In that case, if you didn't use the almighty Forensic Protocol, then the physical aggression by Caitlyn with the daughter of the foster parents didn't happen, did it?

MR. PERHALLA: The only two times, I believe, that you testified to yesterday that, um, they were interviewed, were in their home here in Ironwood, and then, ah, the second at the, in Ontonagon, correct?

MR. ROSS: Those are the two interviews I observed that Ms. Fyle had did, yes.

MR. PERHALLA: And you did not interview yourself personally, you said?

MR. ROSS: No.

MR. PERHALLA: And you're not aware of any other interviews, other than those two, correct?

MR. ROSS: Regarding the girls?

MR. PERHALLA: Right. Interviewing them pursuant to the Forensic Protocol policy?

MR. ROSS: The girls have been interviewed twice in Marquette, by Marquette County CPS on separate occasions for different allegations.

MR. PERHALLA: You were not present at those though?

MR. ROSS: No.

MR. PERHALLA: You're aware that the Colemans, Robert and Janet, had moved to the Houghton area. Houghton County?

MR. ROSS: Correct, I believe it's Calumet.

MR. PERHALLA: Were you—did you check to see if the girls could be moved there into a foster care?

MR. ROSS: I called Steve Stutz, who is the Program Manager up in Houghton County, Keweenaw County DHS, and Mr. Stutz told me that they had no beds available there. He referred me to Joe Mukka, who is the guy in charge of the foster homes through that same agency in Baraga County, and they don't have anything available either.

MR. PERHALLA: So those three counties had nothing?

MR. ROSS: No, and then Child and Family Services has got a worker in Houghton County, named Heather Gray, and Heather Gray indicated to me that she doesn't have any beds available in Houghton County. She's in the process of possibly licensing several more now.

MR. PERHALLA: When did you kow that the, ah, Robert and Janet Coleman moved to Houghton County?

MR. ROSS: I think they've been gone for a week or so from this area, and I think I discovered it through one of our financial workers, who told me that they had left.

MR. PERHALLA: Have you ever interviewed Robert Coleman about any of the abuse allegations?

MR. ROSS: No.

MR. PERHALLA: How about Janet Coleman? Have you ever interviewed her?

MR. ROSS: No.

The question here would be, "Why not?" Has it ever occurred to any of the lamebrains in Michigan state that perhaps we had our side of the story—and that just maybe our side would dispell the phony lies of Bobby and Becky Payne?

MR. PERHALLA: You've met with both of them though, you?

MR. ROSS: Yes.

MR. PERHALLA: Are there any other relative placements that you can think of that have been suggested to you other than the two that have been, that you testified to?

MR. ROSS: Um, I was contacted by a woman from Ohio, who is Mr. Coleman's sister, and Mr. Coleman's sister indicated to me that she does not know Caitlyn Brag, who was Mr. Coleman's step daughter; therefore, we couldn't use her home as a placement because it doesn't meet the criteria fictive kin. For the criteria to meet, to be, to be fictive kin she would have to at least have some type of realtionship with Caitlyn, and that's never been established.

MR. PERHALLA: Other than a blood relation, some relationship with one another; know each other at least?

MR. ROSS: Correct.

What this means, folks, is that it is better to be placed with a total stranger than with a relative of yours who hasn't met your kid. Go figure!

MR. PERHALLA: So North Dakota was the closest relative placement she could have found?

MR. ROSS: Um, if they wish, if they wanted that angle pursued, yes. Aside from the brother in Detroit that declined the placement.

You haven't mentioned why he declined it Mr. Ross. I'm sure you'd like people to believe it was because my brother and I did not see eye to eye on things. Wrong! I'll have to tell the readers, since you won't. It was because Mr. Ross kept screwing around and not getting anything done on the home study effort, so Randy (my brother) finally got fed up with messing around with it. Ross did that in every home study he supposedly was making in this case, including that of Caitlyn's biological father, John Wade.

MR. PERHALLA: Had Caitlyn, first of all, with respect to, ah, the relatives in North Dakota, had Caitlyn had any type of a relationship with them that you're aware of?

MR. ROSS: That's unknown. When they requested that we not pursue Mrs. Coleman's family in North Dakota, we didn't make any contact or even discuss that issue with the children.

MR. PERHALLA: And how about the brother in Wayne County?

MR. ROSS: Um, Mr. Coleman's brother indicated to me that he'd spoken to the girls several times on the phone, and there had been photos and different things like that exchanged between the families.

MR. PERHALLA: When you were present in the home, to interview when, when Ms. Fyle interviewed Caitlyn, did you look around the apartment too?

MR. ROSS: Just for what I could see by eyesight. I didn't walk around the, I didn't walk around the home, and open drawers or look through anything, I just kind of glanced around the home.

MR. PERHALLA: Were you present when anyone looked for the belts?

MR. ROSS: I was present when the drawers were opened and the belts were pulled out of the drawer.

MR. PERHALLA: And there, there was consent given by either Robert or Janet that they could look around?

MR. ROSS: Mr. Coleman pulled the belts out of the drawer himself.

Yeah, I did. You see, I didn't know it was a crime to own belts! Even if I rarely ever used one, and was not even sure which drawer they'd be in. But Becky and Bobby sure knew! And strangely enough, so did Elizabeth Fyle! Wow! What a coincidence!

MR. PERHALLA: So did you see the belts yourself?

MR. ROSS: Yes.

MR. PERHALLA: How many were in there?

MR. ROSS: There was handful, probably four or five, maybe more.

MR. PERHALLA: All in one drawer?

MR. ROSS: Correct.

MR. PERHALLA: That's all I have your Honor.

So now, as my lawyer, Mr. Findlay was about to question Bob Ross, the question crossed my mind: "I wonder if Mr. Perhalla and Mr. Ross own any belts? More importantly, are they all kept in one drawer?" This was becoming very intense! So now my lawyer began:

MR. FINDLAY: Mr. Ross, why are you make— trying to make it sound like that you were actually trying to place them with the family?

MR. ROSS: Because your client asked for a relative home study to be conducted.

MR. FINDLAY: Okay, but you didn't; you didn't go to, I mean, you never told Randy Coleman that the kids would be placed with him, did you?

MR. ROSS: When the children were initially placed, I asked you....

MR. FINDLAY: ...Just answer my question, please, you didn't tell....

THE COURT: ... now just, counsel, he, he has the right to answer a question fully. He can't be limited to a yes or no. If you want to re-ask your question, go ahead.

Oh! So the COURT now found it necessary to PROTECT the state's witness! The prosecutor could not object— it is the COURT who must now intercede! You see? That's what this case was all about!

MR. FINDLAY: Well, it's a yes or now answer... did you tell....

THE COURT: .... Well, no! Counsel, in THIS court, no witness is limited to a yes or no answer; this isn't' TV, they can fully explain their answers, so don't limit anybody to a yes or no answer. Proceed.

Take it easy judge!!! Your bias is showing!!!

MR. FINDLAY: Well go ahead and testify to what you want then.

What else can a decent lawyer say at this point? Without getting hit with contempt of court that is! He should be able to say, "I can ask any question I want to ask, and require a simple yes or no if I want to! You can't tell me how I have to ask my questions!" But that is not the law is it? The law is not about arriving at the truth. It is, rather, about playing the game the way the court wants it played! So go ahead, Ross, give your rehearsed answer since this judge obviously doesn't want you pinned down to the simple truth:

MR. ROSS: Um, when the children were, were, were originally placed into care; I'd ask about relatives being considered for placement of the children. And Mr. Coleman indicated something about his brother, and I indicated the quickest way to get his brother possibly looked at for a relative placement for— would be for his brother to go to the DHS office closest to his home in Wayne County, and say, "Hey, I've got a brother in a situation in Gogebic County. Could you please contact such and such a worker in the U.P. to see what we can do about speeding up the home study process." That was never accomplished; I sent a letter down to Wayne County, which for some reason, got messed up in their mail room; and was sent back to me and I faxed it back down there, and I, ah, re-sent it, and then started the home study with the brother.

Now wait! Wait! Wait! First you said my brother declined to accept my kids. Now you are saying you and your system screwed up the process, which is what my brother told me too. So how about the truth? You say you started the home study. You did not ever start it, just as you never started home studies for anyone, including Caitlyn's biological father, Janet's parents, or any other relative of ours. Go on though Bob, your lies are fascinating!

MR. ROSS (continued): If the brother would have panned out, we would have considered that for a placement, but the goal in this case has always been reunification, and it would have been difficult to facilitate parenting time for two parents in Ironwood, Michigan or now in Calumet, Michigan to go down and have meaningful parenting with their children in Detroit. So in order to facilitate reunification and the family counseling and things that needed to be done; to put the children back together with their parents, to me, it doesn't make a lot of sense to send the kids to Detroit.

MR. FINDLAY: You're telling me that you had an intention at some point in time to send the kids to Detroit?

MR. ROSS: Do I?

MR. FINDLAY: Yes.

MR. ROSS: No, I've got an intention— when we opened this case, was in reunifying these kids with their parents.

MR. FINDLAY: I'm sorry. Say again. Your, your intention was to, to return them to the parents?

MR. ROSS: Yes.

MR. FINDLAY: But they'd have to admit what the allegations in the petition are, right?

MR. ROSS: Correct.

MR. FINDLAY: So they're not going to get returned until they admit what they did?

MR. ROSS: Correct.

There you have it! Whether you did or did not do anything, you are blackmailed by the state to say you did it. And Ross admitted they would keep the kids until you did say what they want you to say!

MR. FINDLAY: Admit to what you say they did?

MR. ROSS: I didn't write the petition. Ms. Fyle wrote the petitition.

MR. FINDLAY: Okay, but they're not going to, until they, until they give the court jurisdiction, you're not going to return the kids?

MR. ROSS: Correct.

He just pled guilty to kidnapping. They have no court basis yet to keep the kids, but they plan to keep them forever, even without court permission to do so. That, my friends, is kidnapping!

MR. FINDLAY: Okay, so it's not, you don't have any, you're not looking forward to returning the kids; I mean, it's if they admit they did something that you say they did, then you'd return the kids.

MR. ROSS: Correct. After, after we provide services for the family.....

But just what if the family does not need those services because, God forbid, the family is innocent of the contrived allegations? But of course, in Michigan, that's not how it works, is it? Instead, the state first kidnaps the kids, holds them without a court determination of guilt on the part of the parents, until a court decides if the parents are guilty or not guilty. And then, the state selects their own jury, all of whom are friends of the court or the law enforcement teams that go around doing the kidnapping, so that their case can stand up once it does go to trial. That's why you can do all your foster care placements as you want, when you want, with who you want, and you can take kids to doctors you choose, without parental permission, get them to say what you want in court, etc. Not that it matters what they say, as your hand selected jury will have their verdict prepared before the trial ever starts, and if that were not enough, the biased judge will make sure nothing gets entered on the record that may prove damaging to the kidnapping team. It's quite a business enterprise, to say the least.

MR. FINDLAY: All right. Um, back on, I'm just.... you had an intention of placing the children with Randy Coleman?

MR. ROSS: I had an intention.... I, I explored the possibility to using Randy Coleman for a relative placement.

MR. FINDLAY: How realistic was that possibility?

MR. ROSS: If Mr. Coleman would have accepted the children for placement?

MR. FINDLAY: Yeah, I mean, did.... answer however you want.

My lawyer was remembering he could not pin Ross down to a yes or no answer, under the rules of the judge!

MR. ROSS: Mr. Coleman was given the opportunity to take the children.

MR. FINDLAY: When was that?

MR. ROSS: Not, let me explain myself. I talked to Mr. Coleman on the phone, what....

MR. FINDLAY: ... Are you talking to Randy Coleman?

MR. ROSS: Randy Coleman, yes, to do a relative home study. Um, I contacted a supervisor in Wayne County about doing a home study; his name is Joe McDermott. Um, the DHS office in Wayne County was supposed to do a walk thru of Mr. Coleman's home in Wayne County to make sure it's suitable. In the process of doing that, Mr. Coleman's brother got into a conversation with the DHS worker down there; and discovered that it would cause a financial hardship for him to take the children because Mr. Coleman, Randy Coleman, and wife both work, and their income levels don't meet the criteria to get reimbursement from the State for the cost of their day care; so Mr. Coleman declined. Randy Coleman declined.

You mean he had to decline because of the state's own rules for relative placement of kidnapped kids! So if you refuse to reimburse a relative, as you would any other foster parent, you can prevent relatives from taking custody of kids, can't you? It's quite a plan! Good work Michigan! But at least Ross was now forced to say why it happened, instead of making it look like nobody liked Robert Coleman, as they slyly were trying to show prior to this testimony!

MR. FINDLAY: Is, is there any possibility that prior to trial that the children were going to be placed with family; prior to this trial happening?

MR. ROSS: Any possibility?

MR. FINDLAY: Yes.

MR. ROSS: Not without a home study.

Which, of course, Ross would never do when asked, or if he initiated one, you would find state rules, such as in the case of my brother, which would prevent meeting the state criteria.

MR. FINDLAY: What else would have been needed?

MR. ROSS: What else would have been needed?

MR. FINDLAY: Yeah. To place the children with the family?

MR. ROSS: Acceptance by the family.

MR. FINDLAY: What's your email address?

MR. ROSS: My email address is Ross....

MR. FINDLAY: ... Well, I won't ask you, but do I have your email address?

MR. ROSS: Yes.

MR. FINDLAY: Um, do you remember sending me an email that said no, that I, my inquiry was about whether that I'd gotten a call and did you tell somebody that, that the kids were going to be placed with Randy Coleman?

Your response with me is, "No, that is not true. I recall the judge saying he didn't want the kids in Wayne County till after the trial."

MR. ROSS: That's correct.

This part of the testimony is interesting because, at this point, the court did not have jurisdiction over the kids. That was the purpose of this trial. To determine if they would be given jurisdiction, or if, in fact, the kids would be returned to us. So what gives the judge the right, before such jurisdiction is determined, to decide who the foster parents might or might not be?

MR. FINDLAY: So isn't it true that the kids were not going to family anywhere, out of state, until after this trial, unless the judge changed his mind?

MR. ROSS: The judge told us on the record that he didn't want the kids in Detroit until after the trial, yes.

MR. FINDLAY: Okay, so there was no possibility before trial they would be placed with Randy Coleman, regardless of whether, what the status of the, of the....

MR. ROSS: ... by a court order.

MR. FINDLAY: Okay, but so when you make it sound like that you were looking to place them with family, that really wasn't true because that couldn't happen because the judge said it couldn't happen, correct?

Once again, a question that could be answered with a simple yes or now, is dodged by Mr. Ross, knowing the judge would not require him to answer directly:

MR. ROSS: Based on the fact that we had to move these kids several times, due to complaints and foster parents not willing to keep these kids because of the CPS complaints and false allegations presented agains them; if I needed a place to place these kids prior to the trial, I would have asked to come back into court and have the judge reconsider placing the children with Randy Coleman. Fortunately, I found a bed in Delta County.

Convenient, Mr. Ross, and we are so glad you did find a bed. And of course we do believe you would have come back to court too. Oh, I still have that ocean front property for sale in South Dakota. Anyone? Oh, and by the way, you forgot to answer the question my lawyer asked you.....

MR. FINDLAY: When did you learn from Randy Coleman that, ah, he didn't think he'd be able to take the kids?

MR. ROSS: June 13th.

MR. FINDLAY: And this, the kids were moved what, on March 15th, right?

MR. ROSS: The kids the first time were moved on March....

MR. FINDLAY: No. Removed from the Colemans on March 15th?

MR. ROSS: That's when they were removed from....

MR. FINDLAY: ... the Colemans in Hancock?

MR. ROSS: Yes.

MR. FINDLAY: These behavior issues, um, those weren't happening in Ontonagon, were they?

MR. ROSS: No, they weren't there long enough for those behaviors to manifest.

MR. FINDLAY: Um, you don't think these behavior issues might have something to do with the fact that the children had been removed from their parents?

MR. ROSS: Removed from their parents?

MR. FINDLAY: Yes.

MR. ROSS: Sometimes when kids are removed from their parents, there's definitely a possibility of behavior issues.

MR. FINDLAY: And am I understanding you correctly that you're saying that other counties, other DHS offices, and counties wouldn't take the case?

MR. ROSS: Correct.

MR. FINDLAY: Against the Colemans?

MR. ROSS: Correct.

MR. FINDLAY: So were you, in essence, telling us that they're basically prioritizing their convenience and ease of dealing with a family over the children's safety?

MR. ROSS: No, I didn't say that. I'm telling you that other counties called me and told me that they had no beds available.

MR. FINDLAY: But you also said that they also told you they didn't want it; they wouldn't take the case. They didn't want it filed; they didn't want to deal with the Colemans?

MR. ROSS: Marquette County refused to open any of their homes to us, yes.

Oh! Now it is only Marquette County? Not the whole world, as you made it sound in your previous testimony? God, and just when I thought I was becoming famous!

MR. FINDLAY: When you went there, the first time to the Colemans' home, um, on March 11th, you saw the children; um, there was no visible evidence of any injury on these children was there?

MR. ROSS: I didn't see any, no.

MR. FINDLAY: Was there any examination made of them at that time?

MR. ROSS: No.

MR. FINDLAY: You indicated that the Forensic Protocol was followed?

MR. ROSS: Correct.

MR. FINDLAY: When you interviewed the children?

MR. ROSS: Correct.

Oops! You forgot your lines Bob! This is when you are supposed to pass the buck to Ms. Fyle and say you didn't interview the kids. She did. You really have to work harder at memorizing your lines Bob!

MR. FINDLAY: Okay, are you familiar with the Forensic Protocol? Forensic Protocol?

MR. ROSS: Yes.

MR. FINDLAY: Okay, so what's the establishing the ground rules phase?

MR. ROSS: That's where you determine a child's ability to determine between the truth and a lie.

MR. FINDLAY: So how would you do that?

MR. ROSS: You ask the child questions; you, you provide an example and you ask the child to tell you…

MR. FINDLAY: … I mean, I'm not trying to object, what did you say? I didn't… finish your answer.. or are you finished?

MR. ROSS: You ask the child if they can tell you the difference between a truth and a lie.

MR. FINDLAY: Okay, I just wanted to make sure I wasn't cutting you off. Is that where you ask like, ah, do you know, if I was told I was wearing a green tie, would that be the truth or a lie?

MR. ROSS: Correct. You try to avoid colors in case the child is color blind.

MR. FINDLAY: I'm sorry?

MR. ROSS: You try to avoid colors in case the child is color blind.

MR. FINDLAY: But you're saying that's the establishing the ground rules part, where you are trying to get the difference between the truth and a lie?

MR. ROSS: Correct.

MR. FINDLAY: Um, I'm looking at, is the Forensic Interview Protocol book? May I approach the witness please?

THE COURT: Sure.

MR. ROSS: Um, it's an old copy, yes.

MR. FINDLAY: Isn't that the one that; isn't that just like the one you gave me?

MR. ROSS: No, I think I gave you a pink copy, that is probably updated.

MR. FINDLAY: Well if I told you, you didn't; and I bring in a copy that you gave me that was scuffed in the front, and I remarked about it, would that refresh your memory?

MR. ROSS: Maybe, but I don't; I, I didn't give you a yellow copy of it.

MR. FINDLAY: You don't recall being in the Prosecutor's office and giving me a yellow copy that had scuff marks on it and it just kind of looked like it had been?

MR. ROSS: No.

MR. FINDLAY: Anyways, un, now this I'm looking at here— legal, it says establishing the ground rules is basically, well let me rephrase that; strike that. That; the bit about telling the difference between a truth and a lie in on the legal competency portion of it. I mean that, they break it down into a staged interview; preparing the interview environment, introduction, legal competency, establishing grounds; legal competency is where they talk about using the examples of so if my shoes are black, is that a truth or a lie. So, not under the establishing ground rules, is it?

MR. ROSS: Establishing ground rules?

MR. FINDLAY: Yes.

MR. ROSS: You kind of roll everything into one thing. If there's; it's, it's not necessarily a step by step process; some, some of the, some of the process is the initial part of the interview overlapping—

MR. FINDLAY: Okay, is it, maybe this outdated book, I guess, they don't have this in the, the manual, new manual anymore. Most— protocols advise interviewers to proceed through a series of distinct interviewing stages with each stage accomplishing a specific purpose; so that, you're telling me, that's not true, you kind of mix them all up together?

MR. ROSS: The newest part of the Forensic Interviewing Protocol said you don't even have to go through the truth and the lie procedure anymore.

Well what do you know? This distinction between a lie and a truth that the state had been making such a monster deal about, didn't really matter any more! So now it isn't important if Caitlyn lied or told the truth, right? And what about the interviewer? Does it really matter if they lied or told the truth? As in Elizabeth Fyle?

MR. FINDLAY: So that you don't even have to do it, but you went ahead and did it anyways?

MR. ROSS: Ms. Fyle did that, I didn't do that.

That's better Bob! Now you're playing the game right and passing the buck like you are told to do!

MR. FINDLAY: Okay, um, but that's not part of establishing ground rules though, is it?

MR. ROSS: As I stated....

MR. FINDLAY: ... Here is the exception of ground rules? I mean, look them up! Tell me where there are, the,

the truth and the lie part is in?

MR. ROSS: According to the book, it says, establishing ground rules is part of the truth and the lie part; but like I said it's prior; many of these steps overlap.

MR. FINDLAY: Okay, but the, what, where is the.... what's the heading for the truth and the lie part?

MR. ROSS: Legal competency.

MR. FINDLAY: Not establishing the ground rules, correct?

MR. ROSS: Correct.

MR. FINDLAY: Now when, and they also changed the protocol to, um, basically say that, ah, interviewing children in their own bedroom is a good idea?

MR. ROSS: You try not to interview the children in the presence of the alleged perpetrators; you try to find a neutral setting, but our county isn't blessed with an area that we can take a child to that's a neutral setting to interview the children in an environment that would make them safe. Um, rather than make a quick decision and take the children to Ironwood Public Safety and interview the children about the allegations at a police department; Ms. Fyle decided it was best to interview the children in the comfort of her own; to interview Caitlyn in the comfort of her own bedroom.

Oh, please! You are not going to let that slide, are you? Of course Gogebic County has places where the children could have been taken! How about a quiet restaurant somewhere? Or are you afraid someone might overhear you—a witness if you will—who might see what you really say to scare the kids into submission during your kidnapping schemes? Well, then, a school? Your protocol book even concurs that would be all right. They do have schools, believe it or not, in Ironwood! So, this being true, are you going to tell me that Gogebic County is still the only county in the world without any facitilites! We understand you don't want parents or lawyers as witnesses because it might tend to incriminate you, hence, your use of your own state approved Forensic Interview Protocol!

MR. FINDLAY: Um, don't they also recommend you shouldn't have toys and other things that might be distracting around?

MR. ROSS: Caitlyn didn't play with toys while she was there.

MR. FINDLAY: That's not what I asked; don't they recommend they shouldn't be around?

MR. ROSS: Yes.

MR. FINDLAY: And they were around, because they; you were in a bedroom, correct?

MR. ROSS: Correct.

MR. FINDLAY: You indicated when you were being, um, questioned by Ms. Wittla, something about focusing the interview with a child. Isn't that getting them to talk about what you want to talk about?

MR. ROSS: Would you repeat that please?

MR. FINDLAY: You mentioned, um, that you need to focus the interview during the interview of a child; that you— when she was asking you the, the protocol. And I'm asking you, doesn't focusing the interview; doesn't that mean getting the child to talk about what you want them to talk about?

MR. ROSS: No, it's a matter of getting the child to talk about what they want to talk about.

Right! Sure! I'm certain that when you asked Caitlyn how school was, that she came right out and said, "I don't want to talk about that! I want to talk about how my daddy abuses me!" Stop lying Ross!

MR. FINDLAY: So then who is focusing the interview?

MR. ROSS: The interviewer.

MR. FINDLAY: The six year old? Or, or the, the interviewer?

MR. ROSS: Ms. Fyle did the interview.

Good! Passing the buck nicely now! You're getting it now, Ross!

MR. FINDLAY: Okay, so who is focusing the interview?

MR. ROSS: Ms. Fyle is focusing the interview, but it's a free narrative interview, so you let the child basically talk about what they want to talk about, and you work your way into the, the subjects of the neglect or the abuse.

Right! The things you want the child to talk about, you let them talk about, after your first program them by planting the idea of what you want them to talk about. Got it! But you never scare her, do you, by telling her if she doesn't say that Daddy spanks me, she will be taken away? Right? Not like what Caitlyn told us later? Oh, but I didn't have any witnesses to that, did I? I should have used the Forensic Interview Protocol, damn it! Then I wouldn't need any witnesses! And Caitlyn's so-called statements were so believable when Fyle was writing them down from the Becky and Bobby playbook. But later, after we had our kids back and complained about foster care abuses, the officials all said she was just a little liar! Guess if it goes against the state, she is, but if it goes against us, in testimony nobody else even heard, it is acceptable.

MR. FINDLAY: But you need to focus the child and right, and focus the interview?

MR. ROSS: Yes.

MR. FINDLAY: Okay, I mean, you go into these interviews with, ah, if not conclusion, at least knowing what you're looking for, don't you? I mean you have— I'm sorry.

MR. ROSS: You can't have a conclusion until you talk to the child.

MR. FINDLAY: That's what I said, if not a conclusion, at least knowing what you're looking for, correct?

MR. ROSS: You're listening.

MR. FINDLAY: Yeah. You have the allegations from the, all the stuff from what the Paynes had said, you had that ahead of time, didn't you?

MR. ROSS: Yes.

MR. FINDLAY: Okay, so you don't go in with a blank slate.

MR. ROSS: No.

MR. FINDLAY: Was there, this interview with, ah, Caitlyn; it wasn't recorded was it?

MR. ROSS: No.

MR. FINDLAY: And that's not prohibited by the, ah, protocol is it?

MR. ROSS: No, in fact it's recommended if you can find a neutral setting, and it's a place that has the type of equipment available.

What do you need Ross? A recording studio? For goodness sake, there are great quality hand-held recording devices that would work fine for this! All you need is a quiet background!

MR. FINDLAY: And why is that recommended?

MR. ROSS: To preserve the interview.

MR. FINDLAY: Okay, isn't it also recommended because then we don't question who said what? And what questions were asked and whether the protocol was actually followed or not?

MR. ROSS: Correct, but we don't have those facilities available.

MR. FINDLAY: You don't? You can't get, I mean, what does pocket recorders cost? Thirty, forthy bucks, you can't get one of those? I mean they're digital recorders, you can get them at Walmart for thirty, forty bucks. You don't use those to record the interview?

MR. ROSS: No.

MR. FINDLAY: It would certainly help us now, wouldn't it, if we had that?

MR. ROSS: Yes.

MR. FINDLAY: You characterized, I think you did, and correct me if I'm wrong. Um, didn't you characterize the alleged abuse in the petition as being horrific when you were being questioned by Ms. Wittla?

MR. ROSS: When I think of a young child alleged to have welts raised on her buttocks; I think of that as pretty horrific.

MR. FINDLAY: Okay, so might the answer be yes to my question?

MR. ROSS: Yes.

MR. FINDLAY: Not horrific enough though to follow up on this investigation on the 12th of March though, correct?

MR. ROSS: Ms. Fyle is the investigator, not me.

All right! You have passing the buck down pat now, Mr. Ross!

MR. FINDLAY: Well, but you didn't do anything on it on the 12th then, and that's because you had training, right?

MR. ROSS: Yes.

MR. FINDLAY: Okay, so as horrific as this alleged abuse was, according to you; it wasn't horrific enough, well, the training was a higher priority than, than protecting these children, correct?

MR. ROSS: No.

MR. FINDLAY: Well you went to the training instead of following up on the interview or conducting further investigation about it didn't you?

MR. ROSS: It wasn't my interview.

Right, we got that part.

MR. FINDLAY: Did; you thought it was horrific; did you do anything independently then? I mean, did you have an opinion that, geez, I can't believe Ms. Fyle isn't following up on this thing; I'm skipping the training and I'm going to go and protect these kids; you didn't do that did you?

MR. ROSS: Supervisor assigned me to go to the training that day, and not to follow up on the investigation.

MR. FINDLAY: Um, I guess going back to the general recording issue, um, I get it that DHS doesn't like being recorded. Is that a fair statement?

MR. ROSS: Yes.

MR. FINDLAY: Wouldn't you agree that recording, we would avoid a lot of these difficulties if, if either conversations, ah, interviews with the kids, um, interviews with the Colemans, interviews with who— witnesses; if these things were recorded, don't you think that would solve a lot of problems?

MR. ROSS: Sure, if both parties knew they were being recorded.

MR. FINDLAY: Why? Why would that matter?

MR. ROSS: Um....

MR. FINDLAY: Well, let.... I'm sorry, I'll let you answer that. I didn't mean to interrupt you, go ahead.

MR. ROSS: A one party recording gives the other party an opportunity to edit, author, provide sound bites, do whatever they want to do with that recording.

MR. FINDLAY: Um, and do you think Mr. Coleman is fair, if they believe that children are taken and put into foster care because, ah; for money reasons?

MR. ROSS: I'm not qualified to answer; attest to Mr. Coleman's state of mind.

MR. FINDLAY: Okay, um, do you think it's paranoid to assume that people are going to edit, manipulate, and you know, manufacture tape recordings?

MR. ROSS: I can't tell you that.

MR. FINDLAY: But that's the reason why you don't want to be recorded?

MR. ROSS: I don't want to be recorded because I don't want to have my conversations or my private life or everything else exposed on the internet.

MR. FINDLAY: Why you, you talk about your private life with the Colemans?

MR. ROSS: Not my private life. My conversations.

MR. FINDLAY: Isn't your conversation work related and what's wrong with that? With that being open to the public? I mean, you're, aren't you a government employee?

MR. ROSS: Mr. Coleman's got the opportunity to take my conversation and edit it and alter it any way he wants to, and broadcast it for everybody to see in cyber space.

MR. FINDLAY: You're a government employee aren't you?

MR. ROSS: Yes.

MR. FINDLAY: So why shouldn't your conversatiions about work be open to the public? Unless it's dealing with something, you know, extremely confidential and sensitive?

MR. ROSS: The entire matter of this case is confidential; I can't disclose it to the public. If Mr. Coleman wants to disclose it to the public, I guess that's okay.

MR. FINDLAY: So it is okay that he records?

MR. ROSS: Fine.

MR. FINDLAY: Well, but then, then how come visits were stopped when he wanted to record them?

MR. ROSS: I didn't stop visits. Child and Family Services did.

Man, he's got this passing the buck thing right down to a natural science, hasn't he?

MR. FINDLAY: Yeah, but they're contracting with DHS?

MR. ROSS: They're a private agency.

MR. FINDLAY: So you don't take any responsibility to the visits being stopped. Or, or....

MR. ROSS: The supervisor at Child and Family Services felt it was a worker safey issue, with the Colemans bringing in videotaping equipment, taping and showing workers, physical and images on the internet.

MR. FINDLAY: What about audio taping?

MR. ROSS: Same. They're out in cyber space.

MR. FINDLAY: It, it sounds like the DHS wants to be able to operate with impunity, is that fair?

MR. ROSS: No.

No? Did he say no? Well, maybe Mr. Ross didn't feel it was fair to DHS, but it is certainly fair to parents, whose kids they are trying to steal! And if in his view it was not fair for my lawyer to make that statement, it would still be accurate! Why else would they not invest in a thirty or forty dollar tape recorder? And thus, allow us to actually hear our daughter telling them the things they say she said, and seeing how she said it, under what kind of questioning!

MR. FINDLAY: Well, you certainly don't want what you do exposed! I mean, what do you have to hide that you don't want, I mean, I, I understand that you don't want your... on it; I don't want a picture on it because

I'm overweight. Frankly, I, I don't photograph that well. I understand that part of it, but, you know what? I don't mind if they put me on camera here doing my job. I mean, I'm embarrassed about the way I look, but I, I— it's part of the job. Why shouldn't that be part of your job?

Actually having; it had a recording of what's going on, so we don't know, so we're not in the dark about what actually happened in this interview; what actually hap— what did the Colemans actually say? Who is right in characterizing how the Colemans acted? We don't know that, we only have your word for it. Isn't that correct?

MR. ROSS: I don't have a problem being recorded, as long as I know I'm being recorded.

MR. FINDLAY: So the only thing, was so if the Colemans had said to you, hey Bob, we're recording this conversation with you, you would have been all right with that?

MR. ROSS: Certainly.

MR. FINDLAY: Ah, it sounds like from your testimony, um, that this has been a rather difficult case, is that fair?

MR. ROSS: That's fair.

MR. FINDLAY: Okay, and that you've done more work on this one than many of your other cases?

MR. ROSS: Correct.

MR. FINDLAY: All your other cases; or, I mean, is this the most you've ever done on any of your cases?

MR. ROSS: This has been the most time consuming case I've had.

MR. FINDLAY: All right, um, and how many cases have you done, would you say?

MR. ROSS: I've got twenty-nine currently.

MR. FINDLAY: How many are going to trial?

MR. ROSS: Um, two or three.

MR. FINDLAY: So not many of these go to trial to the adjudicated phase, do they?

MR. ROSS: No.

MR. FINDLAY: So is it fair to say in your experience, you've never come across parents who have fought this thing as much as the Colemans have?

MR. ROSS: Yes.

MR. FINDLAY: You don't think they have a right to basically do whatever it takes; I mean as far as they're concerned, to get their kids back; when they're not violating the law?

MR. ROSS: Everybody's got a right to their day in court.

MR. FINDLAY: You don't think they have a right if they're concerned about how their children are being treated in foster care, to raise those concerns?

MR. ROSS: They have every right to.

MR. FINDLAY: You don't think they had a right to, to know; in fact, you know, that their children are in a safe place?

MR. ROSS: They have a right to know their children are in a safe place, yes.

MR. FINDLAY: And who do they have to rely on to— for that information? The safety? DHS?

MR. ROSS: Correct.

Okay, if we truly had those rights, we were not given those rights. We were punished by these people every time we raised an issue. Our actions were described as false allegations by several people in the system, when in fact, they were never really fully investigated!

MR. FINDLAY: Okay, so they're just supposed to take and trust DHS, the same group of people that, that, you know, came and put forth this, these allegations from the interview with a, their child, without their presence on March 11th; the same organization that, you know, tracks them down by cell phone; the same organization that comes to Houghton with eight officers, three or four cars, and barges in a, a hotel room at three in the morning. They're supposed to trust you that, that the children are in a safe spot?

MR. ROSS: I've never had a problem with any other client doing this.

MR. FINDLAY: How many, how many times has that happened to other clients? How many other cases have you had where they've gone, traced cell phone records, and gone and busted into somebody's door at 3 a.m. in the morning in a hotel?

MR. ROSS: Um, to my knowledge, we've never had a client abscond from, abscond from an investigation.

MR. FINDLAY: How many other; I'll ask it again, how many other cases have you had where they have gone to their hotel room at three in the morning and removed the children, after tracking them down by cell phone?

MR. ROSS: None of my cases.

MR. FINDLAY: And abscond is the way you characterize it, correct? That's your characterization of it, correct?

MR. ROSS: Yes.

MR. FINDLAY: Yet you're aware that Mr. Coleman maintains that he didn't tell you that he was in Marquette?

MR. ROSS: Okay.

MR. FINDLAY: Okay and there—you would agree that there are two sides of every story?

MR. ROSS: Correct.

MR. FINDLAY: And, but apparently, we're just to take your side as the truth? And I—I'm not accusing you of lying, I, isn't it possible that you misunderstood what he said?

MR. ROSS: No.

MR. FINDLAY: Is it possible that he said we headed to Marquette, ah, it's now Houghton, her, her doctor used to be in Marquette, but now it's in Houghton?

MR. ROSS: No.

MR. FINDLAY: So the only— so according to you then, the only alternative is one of you is lying?

MR. ROSS: If that's the way you want to interpret it, yes.

MR. FINDLAY: Well, is it possible that one of you is mistaken?

MR. ROSS: I know what I heard Mr. Findlay.

MR. FINDLAY: And I'm sure Mr. Coleman would say he knows what he said, so where does that leave us? Isn't it true that as difficult as this has been, I mean in terms of the way this has gone, this case; that is part of your job?

MR. ROSS: Certainly.

MR. FINDLAY: Fair to say that you kind of resent the Colemans for making it this difficult?

MR. ROSS: No.

MR. FINDLAY: Well, is it fair to say that you understand some of the reactions to this happening to them?

MR. ROSS: Yes.

MR. FINDLAY: Um, you were involved—how many of the visits were you directly involved in? The child, parent time visits? Weren't you at the first couple? You were at least for one, or more than one?

MR. ROSS: The ones here in our office?

MR. FINDLAY: Yes.

MR. ROSS: Ms. Fyle supervised the first one. I supervised two additional ones.

MR. FINDLAY: Two. Okay, um, so you were there when; and when you say supervised that means that you're in the room at the DHS office, um, and you're in the room while they're meeting with their kids?

MR. ROSS: Yes.

MR. FINDLAY: Isn't it true that those visits went, I mean, as well as can be expected in given those circumstances; at least the ones that you witnessed?

MR. ROSS: Yes.

MR. FINDLAY: Isn't it true that, ah, the children were excited to see their parents?

MR. ROSS: Very much so.

MR. FINDLAY: And isn't it true that there were, you know, hugs and kisses all around?

MR. ROSS: Yes.

Hmmmm.... that sure sounds like some terrified kids, unable to deal with all of thehorrific events of home— doesn't it?

MR. FINDLAY: And isn't it true that the children were, were reluctant, I don't think that's putting it mildly; they were reluctant to see their parents leave?

MR. ROSS: The end of the visits were difficult. Um, we had to stifle some of the end of the visits because rather than saying good-bye, making a clean break; there were comments made by the parents at the end that caused the children to cry, and additional, unnecessary comments, in my opinion, that didn't need to be made to....

MR. FINDLAY: ... Okay, that; that's the first I've heard of these. Is that—if you— I know Ms. Andriacchi has or Ms. Huttunen has alleged that; but that's the first—you haven't; you put that in a report anywhere before?

MR. ROSS: I haven't had to do a report in this case yet.

Are you kidding me? How long do you wait before you do a report Bob? God, no wonder home studies never get done!

MR. FINDLAY: Have you brought it up in Court any time before?

MR. ROSS: No.

MR. FINDLAY: So this is the first time, when I asked you about it, that you came up with that?

MR. ROSS: Yes.

MR. FINDLAY: Nothing further.

THE COURT: Redirect?

MS. WITTLA: Yes. Mr. Ross, when you were talking about visits that were supervised; how many did you personally supervise?

MR. ROSS: Here in Gogebic County— two.

MS. WITTLA: Did you make any notations regarding those supervised visits?

MR. ROSS: Um, just some brief contact notes in my, in my contact log, yes.

MS. WITTLA: Okay, so when you referenced not having written a report yet, you haven't done a foster care report yet?

MR. ROSS: When the case was transferred to Child and Family Services, they're required to do an initial service plan on the case. When the case came back to me at the end of May, I'm required to do an updated service plan on the case. And I went through all my case contacts in the report.

MS. WITTLA: So it's not that no one did a report, it's just that when it was a contract case with Child and Family Services, they would have been doing that?

MR. ROSS: Right. The purchasing service agency is responsible for the initial service plan in the case.

MS. WITTLA: Okay, so knowing the squeak of the wheel, there's paperwork being done.

MR. ROSS: Yes.

Nice try Tracie! And you are so clever with words! Even if the jury had been paying attention, they would have never followed your squeak of the wheel jargon. In their sleep, they probably missed it anyway. But now about the paperwork. When you do paperwork folks, do you think it is normal to wait until a month later to recall what took place prior? If you were going to do that, you would maintain some kind of log for your own office, wouldn't you? So you would know you had the details right? And especially if you are handling some thirty cases at one time! And tell me, if you wait that long to write anything down, can you really call that an update? In my thinking, it is more like a review.

MS. WITTLA: When Mr. Findlay talked about, ah, whether recording things that DHS does would have been helpful, I believe you indicated that, that the answer to that would be yes, potentially?

MR. ROSS: Yes.

MS. WITTLA: Does DHS have many forms to fill out?

MR. ROSS: Yes.

MS. WITTLA: Would you say you have to do a lot of paperwork on these cases?

MR. ROSS: Yes. There's probably forty or fifty different forms in a foster care case.

All designed to protect the state and make it possible for them to continue to hold your kids for ransom!

MS. WITTLA: Are those forms designed to just give people like the overview of a case or detail a lot of information?

MR. ROSS: It's a detailed description of every step of the case from treatment plans, to programming, to preparing treatment agreements, to financial documentation, to medical records, to dental records, to anything involving every child in the family involved with the case.

MS. WITTLA: When you received the initial service plan from Child and Family Services, did they use the State of Michigan forms?

MR. ROSS: It's a standard form.

MS. WITTLA: Same like you would have used?

MR. ROSS: Yes.

MS. WITTLA: Approximately how long was that report?

MR. ROSS: Twenty four or twenty five pages.

MS. WITTLA: Are those reports available to the parents?

MR. ROSS: They are actually sent to the parents, and they're supposed to be signed by the parents.

MS. WITTLA: Is that so that the parents know what's going on in a case?

MR. ROSS: Yes.

MS. WITTLA: Does it help to, I guess, get them involved in the case?

Flash! News bulletin! For Tracie Wittla, this is a wake up call! Parents are involved in a case the moment the state raids them and kidnaps their kids!

MR. ROSS: It outlines their specific responsibilities as far as what they need to do to get their children back in their care.

MS. WITTLA: Are parents involved in coming up with those objectives?

MR. ROSS: As a part of the parent agency treatment plan, yes.

MS. WITTLA: So they're consulted when this stuff is drafted?

MR. ROSS: It's done jointly between the agency and the parents.

MS. WITTLA: Mr. Ross, you indicated that if you knew you were being recorded, you would have been okay with it?

MR. ROSS: Yes.

MS. WITTLA: So you wouldn't have wanted any other provisions regarding those recordings?

MR. ROSS: As long as I know I was being recorded, I mean, I mean I don't have a problem with that.

MS. WITTLA: You wouldn't have wanted a copy?

MR. ROSS: Well certainly.

MS. WITTLA: Mr. Findlay asked you whether or not the children would be returned until the parents admitted the petition; do the parents have to admit to the petition for the children to be returned?

MR. ROSS: No. That's, that's being decided here at trial.

But in the meanwhile, your kids are not returned unless you admit to their crazy accusations! So you are some time without your children even with a trial, which is already set up for you to lose in any case via the jury selection process.

MS. WITTLA: What do the parents usually need to do for children to be returned?

MR. ROSS: Upon adjudication of the petition whether or not it's decided by the judge or an admission of the parents or it's decided by court, um, we have a parenting treatment plan, we have a list of goals, what the parents and the children need to be reunified. Once these goals are met or there's significant progress made towards completion of these goals, we would then consider returning the children to the family.

Okay, you have rested my case! What you have just said is that you already have the programs and plans all laid out, you need only to get the guilty verdict in court… no matter how that occurs, be it a parent admission, a judge's decision, or a verdict by the jury. So the only way it could not take place is if the parents are found innocent in court! And since you stack your jury, that is likely to occur maybe once in every one hundred years, when an unbiased jury somehow sneaks through the cracks of your system! Fat chance!

MS. WITTLA: Is it your understanding, then, that once issues, problems are identified, then, until those things are dealt with, the children don't return home?

MR. ROSS: Correct.

MS. WITTLA: So if we put a stop to this whole thing today and Janet and Robert said, "Heck, yeah, we admit to everything in the petition," that would not get those kids home today, would it?

MR. ROSS: No.

Can anybody see now, why a parent might to choose to fight? Under this system of law, you are guilty until proven innocent! Isn't that in itself contradictory to our own constitution which says you are innocent until proven guilty? Also you are to be given a fair and speedy trial by a jury of your piers. It doesn't say by a jury of the prosecution's choosing. Yet that is what you have in child abuse cases. I don't even know you, but if you have kids, I could go out tomorrow and charge you with child abuse simply because I don't like you. You would have to prove you are not guilty if you had a liar from the state come out and talk to your kids and say they said something bad about you. How would you do it? You have no recordings, which you should have. And even if you won, you'd go months without your kids in the process of waiting for your court hearing.

MS. WITTLA: Mr. Findlay asked you if you'd ever come across any parents who fought this process as much as the Colemans, and I'm sorry, I don't quite recall your response?

You are a liar Ms. Wittla. You fully recall the response. You should be charged with perjury for lying to this court.

MR. ROSS: My response was no.

MS. WITTLA: Do you think that it's okay that they object to this proceeding?

MR. ROSS: That's their right.

MS. WITTLA: Is it okay if they want to have this proceeding, they want to go through trial, and all that sort of thing?

MR. ROSS: That's well within their rights.

MS. WITTLA: Would you say it's fair that as long as they're not violating the law, they can stand up for what they believe in?

MR. ROSS: Yes.

Then it must also follow, that it is fair for me to have a tape recording of everything so everyone can see, without question, what is said, and by who!

MS. WITTLA: Is it a violation of the law to file a false report of child abuse?

MR. ROSS: Yes, it is.

But it is not against the law to file a true one, which is what we did. And nobody, other than the prosecution, ever labled it is false. That is an out and out lie that should result in the revocation of the license of Tracie Wittla. The only thing any of the officials ever said was that our charges were unsubstantiated. Even then, they might have substantiated them had they bothered to take the time to investigate them thoroughly. To this day, they have not done that. But even if they did do it, and they did not agree with our claims, they could not be labled as false, unless they could prove, in court, that I lied about it. And since I did not, and since they cannot produce any evidence that I did, they cannot call these reports false. If I had filed a truly false report, I would agree, it would be against the law. Just as it should be for a prosecutor to falsely claim my report was indeed, false.

MS. WITTLA: In your opinion, do you think they violated the law?

MR. ROSS: Yes.

MR. FINDLAY: Your Honor, no....

THE COURT: ... Did you object?

MR. FINDLAY: Yeah! I objected! I'd ask that be stricken, that calls for a conclusion, he's not a judge, jury, or....

THE COURT: ... Sustained because he can't and shouldn't voice his opinion as the whether it's in violation of the law, pretty much as Mr. Findlay stated. Sustained.

Try exactly as Mr. Findlay stated, judge! Even though it is obvious you don't like his objection! And Ross should lose his license to practice also, as he also cited this as a false report, by citing his yes response indicating I broke the law.

MS. WITTLA: Are you aware of false allegations of child abuse being made in this case?

MR. ROSS: Yes.

A lie. Unsubstantiated is the proper term.

MS. WITTLA: Do you believe that those came from.....

MR. FINDLAY: ... I'm going to object, to just a conclusionary nature of the statement, ah, I mean, "false." I mean, who has decided that they're false? I mean, I... that's a legal conclusion that I don't know that's been....

THE COURT: I guess we can move on to the point. We understand his opinion, we, we don't have an adjudication or a court finding that somebody was false or true, so go ahead and ask another question.

MS. WITTLA: Are you aware of your agency actively pursuing any abuse complaints against; that were; are you aware of your agency purusing any child abuse complaints involving Caitlyn and Ashley?

MR. ROSS: There's an active investigation in Marquette, I'm sorry, in Delta County regarding allegations of sexual abuse on the part of the foster parents regarding Caitlyn and Ashley.

MS. WITTLA: Regarding the foster parents?

MR. ROSS: Yes, the allegations are directed at the foster parents.

MS. WITTLA: That they themselves did something wrong or somebody in their house?

MR. ROSS: Somebody accused the; somebody accused the foster parents of abuse, including sexual abuse at Caitlyn and Ashley. Um, they were investigated and the allegations were found not to be true. The investigation just hasn't been closed yet.

Somebody? Somebody? Come on Ross, point the finger at me! Because it was me you moron! And of course I filed a complaint! Your own state, after we had fought them about taking our kids to doctors without our endorsement, went ahead and did this anyway, with the hope of finding a criminal case against Robert Coleman, derived from a doctor's findings! They almost got away with it. Their bought-off doctors did produce a report that said it appeared Caitlyn's hymen had been broken. What they did not know however, is that she had already been checked after the state took possession of the kids, and that no such evidence existed! So what that meant to me, is that if this report were true, the foster home was at fault, not us! Thus, my complaint! What parent would not do this under the same circumstances? Secondly, that complaint was for Caitlyn, not Ashley, so again Ross lied and committed perjury here. As for the investigation, it was never explained to me how they got around the doctor's incorrect report in order to conclude the allegations were not true. But I was relieved to find out they were not true. False allegation? No. Unsubstantiated? Apparently so. But we had cause to believe they were true, since the state made it an issue.

MS. WITTLA: That's an internal DHS thing?

MR. ROSS: Yes.

MS. WITTLA: Not a law enforcement thing?

MR. ROSS: No.

MS. WITTLA: The same thing; did the same thing happen in Marquette County?

MR. ROSS: Yes.

A total lie. What happened in Marquette had nothing to do with sexual abuse. It had everything to do with other forms of abuse.

MS. WITTLA: Allegations of child abuse were made against the foster care provider in Marquette County?

MR. ROSS: Correct.

MS. WITTLA: And DHS determined internally that those were unsubstantiated?

MR. ROSS: Unsubstantiated complaint.

Naturally. The state policeman sent out to investigate spent about a half hour in the home. Some investigation!

MS. WITTLA: Mr. Ross, Mr. Findlay asked you some questions about the Forensic Interview Protocol, and where certain things take place, under which heading, so to speak. Is that fair to say?

MR. ROSS: Yes.

MS. WITTLA: And I think there was some dispute about whether or not you're supposed to ask the kid about the difference between a truth and a lie in establishing ground rules?

MR. ROSS: Yes.

MS. WITTLA: Your Honor, may I approach the witness?

THE COURT: Sure, and since we've got different colors, would you specify what date or what.....

MR. FINDLAY: I'm just using the one the Prosecutor gave me, so....

THE COURT: Is that, is that the yellow one?

MR. FINDLAY: If they gave me outdated copies, I....

THE COURT: Is there a date on it though?

MR. FINDLAY: I looked for a date and I couldn't find one.

MS. FYLE: On, on the back.

MR. FINDLAY: Is it 08-'98 I got; is that the date?

MS. FYLE: Could be.

MR. FINDLAY: 08-98.

MS. WITTLA: Mr. Ross, on the copy that you have, if you open it to the cover pages, did the back cover page print?

MR. ROSS: The back cover page?

MS. WITTLA: Well, what's the date on that one?

MR. ROSS: 10-2007.

MS. WITTLA: Okay, so that one is more recent than the yellow copy?

MR. ROSS: Correct.

THE COURT: Go ahead with your question. Everybody should understand that we're talking about two different editions of the same thing, of the same document, but probably with some changes.

MS. WITTLA: I think I have it opened up to pages 9-10. 10-11. Something like that?

MR. ROSS: 10-11?

MS. WITTLA: What's the heading on that first page?

MR. ROSS: On the first page, Establishing Ground Rules.

MS. WITTLA: And if you flip it over, is that a continuation of Establishing Ground Rules?

MR. ROSS: Correct.

MS. WITTLA: And I made a little asterisk in the corner there; that line straight across from there. Could you read that to me?

MR. ROSS: I'm going to say some things, I need you to tell me whether they are true or not true, and in parenthesis it says a lie.

MS. WITTLA: So when you; keep that document for a minute; so when you testified that the truth/lie, setting up ground rules, overlap?

MR. ROSS: Correct.

MS. WITTLA: That document is using the truth and lie determination within establishing the ground rules?

MR. ROSS: Correct.

MS. WITTLA: So it is, I guess, accurate, to say that they overlap to some extent? They talk about all of it sort of at the beginning?

MR. ROSS: Yes.

MS. WITTLA: When we were talking about focusing the interview, is there a point in time when you introduced the topic?

MR. ROSS: Yes.

MS. WITTLA: What does that mean?

MR. ROSS: Introduce the topic?

MS. WITTLA: Yes.

MR. ROSS: You talk about things that happened in the home, you talk about, you may introduce a topic by talking about what happens in your house when you get into trouble.

MS. WITTLA: Okay, I'm talking about the question before that; what is the topic?

MR. ROSS: The topic is child abuse and neglect.

MS. WITTLA: Okay, is it fair to say the topic was the reason you were sent out in the first place?

MR. ROSS: Correct.

MS. WITTLA: So once you go through the beginning statements of the interview, where you set the ground rules, truth/lie, the rapport building, at some point in time the interviewer introduces the topic?

MR. ROSS: Yes.

MS. WITTLA: Have you had interviews where you've introduced the topic and the child has not said anything at all about the topic?

MR. ROSS: Absolutely.

MS. WITTLA: Is that the way Caitlyn's interview went?

MR. ROSS: No.

MS. WITTLA: Once the topic was introduced for Caitlyn's interview, did she lead the interview from that point?

MR. ROSS: It was an open narrative, and she talked freely and openly about being spanked and the way she was disciplined in her home.

Sure. No pressure. No leading questions by Ms. Fyle. No threats that unless she produced the right answer about spanking that she would be taken away. WHERE IS THE TAPE? Oh! I forgot! You didn't have a recording studio handy!

MS. WITTLA: So she wasn't answering yes, no questions for Ms. Fyle?

MR. ROSS: No.

MS. WITTLA: Was she asked leading questions by Ms. Fyle?

MR. ROSS: No.

Oh? Then tell me, how was she able to articulate all of Bobby and Becky's play list questions, without missing a beat? If I had a tape, I'd bet my life on the fact there were a lot of yes or no questions. Caitlyn tells me today that one of the questions she was asked by Fyle was if she was chased with a broom or a wooden spoon? And there was the question she asked when Ross went out of the room, something about does your daddy spank you on the tush? Since we didn't even own a wooden spoon, and since that was in Bobby and Becky's play book, we know she did not recite that without a lead!

MS. WITTLA: Was there a point in the interview where she seemed like she didn't want to talk about that subject any more?

MR. ROSS: Yes.

MS. WITTLA: How soon after that point did the interview end?

MR. ROSS: Within a matter of minutes, when she, when she said she didn't want to talk about it any more; um, you could tell that she basically wanted to stop talking about the things, and Ms. Fyle reverted to something more neutral, more pleasant, and ended the interview.

MS. WITTLA: And I believe your prior testimony was you referred to something neutral, more pleasant, so that the last thing you talk to them about is this potentially negative experience?

MR. ROSS: Correct.

MS. WITTLA: Mr. Findlay asked you about whether or not there were toys in the room; were there toys in Caitlyn's bedroom?

MR. ROSS: It's a bedroom. Two, two small children live in bed— sleep in the bedroom; there's toys and games and all kinds of things like that in a, in the bedroom.

MS. WITTLA: Did Caitlyn seem distracted by all that stuff?

MR. ROSS: No.

No, of course not Ross! That's probably why when they write the book you are supposed to follow, they tell you not to do interviews in a bedroom!

MS. WITTLA: Thank you.

THE COURT: Mr. Perhalla, any redirect or recross?

MR. PERHALLA: Thank you your Honor, just a couple. The Forensic Interview Protocol. It's on the internet, correct? The document?

MR. ROSS: I believe so.

MR. PERHALLA: So if someone wanted to get the most recent copy, they should probably go to the internet and get it, shouldn't they?

MR. ROSS: Yes.

Yes? Yes? Mr. Ross! You just said you believed it was on the internet! You are not even sure, yet you answer yes with such conviction? And why would you, when you assume that what the prosecutor gives you is the most recent copy? It would seem a better question would be, Why is the prosecutor handing the defense team an outdated copy of this book? Motives, it would seem, are very suspect, to say the least!

MR. PERHALLA: Thank you.

THE COURT: Mr. Findlay?

MR. FINDLAY: Yeah. Um, regarding the mileage question, we've established that I had your correct email address, right?

MR. ROSS: Yes.

MR. FINDLAY: Okay, didn't I send you an email with the visit dates and times on June 12th?

MR. ROSS: No.

Perjury! A lie! We have email printouts to prove it!

MR. FINDLAY: I'm; was your email down at the government at, on June 12th; do you know, at the DHS office?

MR. ROSS: I don't believe so....

MR. FINDLAY: ... I'm looking right here, from Mike Findlay to Robert Ross, Coleman visits mileage, and then it lists it March 20th Bessemer, left from Ironwood, March 24th, left from; and sent, I sent it on June 12, 2008 at 3:55, and it's to your; the same email address that everything else I got on is, so you, you're saying you never got that?

MR. ROSS: Correct.

And this is the guy who is going to write updates on a month-long case? He can't even remember his emails! He really does need to keep notes in a log book!

MR. FINDLAY: On the forms that, um, the Prosecutor was asking about; the DHS has; what are these forms?

MR. ROSS: There's different, each form that goes into a foster care case file has got a number to it. There's initial service plan forms, updated service plan forms; medical forms, dental forms, funding forms, payment forms.

MR. FINDLAY: And the forms regarding visits as well?

MR. ROSS: There's not a visitation form in a DHS file.

MR. FINDLAY: Okay, but these forms, these are, ah, these are DHS's version of the case, right?

MR. ROSS: Yes.

MR. FINDLAY: Okay, um, did I hear you correctly say something about there's reports prepared, that are given to parents?

MR. ROSS: The initial service plan and all that information is distributed to the parents.

MR. FINDLAY: Okay, well isn't it true that, that the initial service plan wasn't given till; to the parents until, I mean, not that long ago, isn't that correct? I mean, it was— when was it given to the parents?

MR. ROSS: I can't tell you that. Child and Family Services prepared the report.

MR. FINDLAY: You don't... you don't know when?

MR. ROSS: I don't... I don't know when they distributed it to the parents, no. I don't have my copy here to tell you when I got my copy either, so....

MR. FINDLAY: Okay, isn't DHS supposed to oversee that? I mean, the copy I've got, I mean, isn't DHS supposed to oversee that?

MR. ROSS: Yes.

Take note businesses! It may be a good idea not to make Bob Ross your next CEO!

Doesn't seem like the delegation effort is working too well!

MR. FINDLAY: Copy I've got here is dated April 30th. I didn't; don't you normally give this to attorneys as well?

MR. ROSS: I'm assume; normally it prints it on the distribution list of the....

MR. FINDLAY: ... I'm sorry! Say again.

MR. ROSS: Normally all the attorneys involved with the case are on the distribution list of the plan.

MR. FINDLAY: Okay, could you explain why I didn't get this until sometime in June?

MR. ROSS: No.

MR. FINDLAY: Would you dispute that?

MR. ROSS: I have no reason to dispute you; you know, you got it when you got it.

MR. FINDLAY: Ms. Wittla was asking about what the Colemans could do to get the, um, children back. What could they do prior to this trial to get the children back?

MR. ROSS: Prior to this trial?

MR. FINDLAY: Yeah. What would they have to do?

MR. ROSS: They could have admitted to the petition.

MR. FINDLAY: Okay, all right. So there's, I mean that, the rest of it, I mean, we don't even get there if they're not admitting to the petition, do we?

MR. ROSS: Until we have adjudication in this matter, the parents aren't required to comply with any service plans.

MR. FINDLAY: And in order, right, so, so the fact they hadn't done that, you can't hold that against them because they're just exercising rights, correct?

MR. ROSS: Correct.

So then what right do you have to be holding my kids for ransom, Mr. Ross?

MR. FINDLAY: But we agree that the only way they can get their children back, up until this date, until it's in the jury's hands, and they make their decision, is to admit to something in the petition?

MR. ROSS: That's the only way possible to provide services and....

MR. FINDLAY: Okay, um, back on this recording thing. You said you don't have a problem with recording if you know it's being recorded. Isn't it true that when the children were moved to Delta County, um, court ordered that two visits a week, that you drafted the visitation rules for that, and don't those visitation rules say no recording?

MR. ROSS: Yes.

MR. FINDLAY: So it's not true that you're okay with recording as long as you know about it; because you put it in the visitation rules?

MR. ROSS: No, I didn't want any more pictures of the children or the visitation supervisor or anybody else involved with the case in Delta County subject to having their images put back up on the internet.

Oh! What you really mean, Mr. Ross, is that you did not want us to be taking photos or recording anything that might uncover the abuse taking place by the foster parents in Delta County! In other words, you wanted to cover it up!

MR. FINDLAY: So....

MR. ROSS: ... the Judge ordered not to have any recording during the visits as well.

How very convenient! Can anybody see yet how one party to the kidnapping ring works with the other to assure their success as the process unfolds? How can you go wrong when you have the judge, the jury, the cops, the agencies, all working with one another, making up their own rules as they go along, and getting the court to reinforce their steps when they need to so they can continue on with their little game!

MR. FINDLAY: Okay, didn't he leave that in your discretion? He left that in your discretion, that, that whatever DHS says is fine, and that's what we got to live with, isn't that correct?

MR. ROSS: And I elected to do it then.

MR. FINDLAY: Okay, so but, so don't, I mean, it wasn't the judge that ordered it; it was your decision not to allow the recording?

MR. ROSS: Okay.

Thank you for that admission Mr. Ross! It's about time!

MR. FINDLAY: Isn't it true that, um, well, on the lines of the, the things that Ms. Wittla was asking you that, um, in terms of the goal being reunification, but isn't it true that taking the jurisdiction or having the parents admit the contents edition, the first thing, the first step towards termination of parental rights?

MS. WITTLA: Objection your Honor.

THE COURT: Calling for a legal conclusion, sustained. You know, I, I guess you can explore the concept of if that's his plan; but you know you can't have him legally determine whether that's going to happen or whether this is the proper procedure, whatever.

MS. WITTLA: Your Honor, I would renew my objection based on the fact that the jury is here to determine whether or not these allegations occurred and they're not to determine what happens after, after adjudication.

THE COURT: And that is true, and I would so instruct the jury that you are not to concern yourself with what happens if there is an adjudication, but I, I guess he still has the ability to ask, you know, what the plan of the DHS is, and what the goal is. I mean, that's already been put on the record that the goal was reunification, so if you want to ask in that general parameter, go ahead.

MR. FINDLAY: But um, and I, I guess I'm not trying to ask you for a legal conclusion, but a termination of parental rights doesn't occur unless jurisdiction is taken first, correct? I mean it can't, it can't occur?

MR. ROSS: Right.

MR. FINDLAY: So in, just in that sense, taking jurisdiction is the first step in the process?

MR. ROSS: Yes, but that's never been part of the plan.

MR. FINDLAY: Um, about these, the reports of abuse that have been filed by the Colemans, or the alleged allegations, um, and now again, I'm not asking for a legal conclusion, I'm just asking the facts. The Colemans have never been charged with filing a false police report, have they?

MR. ROSS: No.

MR. FINDLAY: And do you, well, are you aware that, that the standard or the, the burden for charging a crime is, is the lowest it gets in the legal system; it's only probable cause?

MR. ROSS: I'm not familiar with charging somebody in the legal system.

MR. FINDLAY: Um, Forensic Protocol, so if I, now I find out it has been modified, correct?

MR. ROSS: Yes.

MR. FINDLAY: Why did they modify it?

MR. ROSS: Because the steps in the.... I'm not qualified to tell why it was modified, I didn't write the protocol, I've just been training how to use it.

MR. FINDLAY: Okay, but it's been, it's been changed?

MR. ROSS: Yes.

MR. FINDLAY: Any reason to believe it won't change again?

MR. ROSS: I can't tell you that, I don't work for the Prosecutor's Association.

MR. FINDLAY: Fine. Isn't it fair to say that if it's, the reason it was changed is because things were not right the first time?

MR. ROSS: I can't tell you that.

MR. FINDLAY: But obviously somebody thought it needed to be changed, even if you didn't; weren't aware of it. Somebody thought it needed to be changed because it wasn't doing the job the first time?

MR. ROSS: If it was changed, it would have been done prior to me coming to work for the agency.

MR. FINDLAY: Can you tell me where that would've come from? I mean, have you seen those; the yellow copy?

MR. ROSS: I've never seen the yellow copy.

No. Those are reserved for the prosecutor to hand out to unsuspecting parents, so she can confuse the parents' lawyers in court. The prosecutor has them, and she knows full well they are outdated. This type of practice should get her disbarred!

MR. FINDLAY: Never seen the yellow copy?

MR. ROSS: No.

MR. FINDLAY: If I told you it came directly from the Prosecutor's office, would you dispute that?

MR. ROSS: You got it from the Prosecutor's office?

MR. FINDLAY: Yes.

MR. ROSS: Possible.

MR. FINDLAY: Would you dispute that? You wouldn't dispute that?

MR. ROSS: No.

MR. FINDLAY: Nothing further.

THE COURT: Okay, I'd like to cut it off without any redirect, we need to move the case along; was there any major redirect; I shouldn't have qualified it with major.

MS. WITTLA: Can I just have, honestly, like two questions?

THE COURT: Two.

MS. WITTLA: I won't even go over there. Mr. Ross, are you okay with yourself being recorded as long as you get a copy of the tape?

MR. ROSS: Yes.

MS. WITTLA: Are you not okay with the kids and the visitation supervisor being recorded?

MR. ROSS: Yes.

MS. WITTLA: That's it.

THE COURT: Did you have any follow upon that point?

MR. PERHALLA: On that point, no your Honor.

MR. FINDLAY: No.

THE COURT: All right Mr. Ross, you may step down and are excused or may stay as you see fit, but you're completed as a witness. Um, we're going to take, now you got a follow up call on the; on your witness issue, what time are they coming in?

MR. FINDLAY: Three, because that would coincide perfect, if the court allowed that. It would coincide...

THE COURT: We're going to take the mid-afternoon recess till approximately 10, 5 or 10 after 3, and we'll discuss the witnesses then; we're in recess.

Following the break, the judge allowed our attorney to lead off witness questioning, in order to accommodate time schedules of the witnesses Mr. Findlay had, so it was our lawyer who led off the questioning with Renee Anderson.

MR. FINDLAY: Please state your full name for the record please?

MS. ANDERSON: Renee Toni Anderson.

MR. FINDLAY: And where do you live?

MS. ANDERSON: 229 East Vaughn Street, Ironwood, Michigan.

MR. FINDLAY: Do you know Robert and Janet Coleman?

MS. ANDERSON: Yes I do.

MR. FINDLAY: How do you know them?

MS. ANDERSON: I met him five years ago when I was a housing agent for MSHDA.

MR. FINDLAY: How would you characterize your relationship with them?

MS. ANDERSON: Very good.

MR. FINDLAY: Friends?

MS. ANDERSON: Very good friends, uh-huh.

MR. FINDLAY: Um, do you know their children?

MS. ANDERSON: Yes I do.

MR. FINDLAY: Do you know their names?

MS. ANDERSON: Caitlyn Brag and Ashley Coleman.

MR. FINDLAY: Do you know their ages?

MS. ANDERSON: I don't know their ages, no; I think it's like five and two.

MR. FINDLAY: Okay, so if I told you six and two; for Caitlyn; six for Caitlyn, and two for Ashley, does that sound right?

MS. ANDERSON: That sounds right.

MR. FINDLAY: You; when you said you were friends with the Colemans, does that mean you socialize with them?

MS. ANDERSON: I see them on occasion; I don't really socialize with them or go out with them.

MR. FINDLAY: Um, have you seen them with their children?

MS. ANDERSON: Yes I have.

MR. FINDLAY: And how often is that?

MS. ANDERSON: At least once a month.

MR. FINDLAY: Um, what are the circumstances of when you see them?

MS. ANDERSON: When I first started seeing them it was just Caitlyn. Um, and he would come in because he was one of my landlords, and then he would bring Caitlyn in and stuff during, after school and stuff because she wanted to show me books and different things like that. And then when Ashley was born, he called me and let me know she was born and brought her into my office.

MR. FINDLAY: How was Robert Coleman with Caitlyn the times that you saw him?

MS. ANDERSON: Excellent. Very understanding.

MR. FINDLAY: Um, did you ever have any occasion to see, you know, discipline incidents or things....

MS. ANDERSON: Yes, I did.

MR. FINDLAY: And can you describe for us?

MS. ANDERSON: The discipline that I witnessed, well like if he was in my office and he was trying to sign papers um, and she would act up, he would give her a timeout, and after the timeout she would say I'm sorry, and that was about it.

MR. FINDLAY: She? That was referring to Caitlyn?

MS. ANDERSON: Pardon me?

MR. FINDLAY: Was that referring to Caitlyn, the older child?

MS. ANDERSON: Yes.

MR. FINDLAY: When did you see um, Ashley for the first time?

MS. ANDERSON: Oh, just when she was like three days old.

MR. FINDLAY: Okay, and how? Explain...

MS. ANDERSON: I went to the apartment with a gift.

MR. FINDLAY: Okay, and how was that?

MS. ANDERSON: Very good. He was a very proud papa, very proud.

MR. FINDLAY: And was Caitlyn there too?

MS. ANDERSON: Yes she was.

MR. FINDLAY: Just describe the, I mean, hopefully, just go ahead and give us a little taste of what that was like. I mean, was it a happy scene?

MS. ANDERSON: It was, it was to see a family. It was very nice.

MR. FINDLAY: Was Caitlyn being slurred out because....

MS. ANDERSON: Not at all. A matter of fact I bought a gift for her and just about everybody that stopped there bought a gift for Caitlyn and for Ashley; and she seemed to welcome....

MR. FINDLAY: How about the parents, like not paying attention to Caitlyn?

MS. ANDERSON: Oh no, oh no! As a matter of fact when I left, Caitlyn was holding Ashley.

MR. FINDLAY: Um, have you ever seen either of the Colemans do anything you'd characterize as abusing their children?

MS. ANDERSON: Never.

MR. FINDLAY: Have you ever had any concerns that way?

MS. ANDERSON: Never.

MR. FINDLAY: Have you ever seen any incidents where it appears that Caitlyn's afraid of Mr. Coleman?

MS. ANDERSON: Only when she did something wrong and she knew a timeout was coming.

MR. FINDLAY: And is that the, the extent of the discipline?

MS. ANDERSON: That was the only discipline I ever witnessed.

MR. FINDLAY: Now you said that you worked with him; he's one of your landlords?

MS. ANDERSON: He was a; at that time, I was a landlord for MSHDA and now I work in the rental business, so where I help landlords find tenants.

MR. FINDLAY: Um, and how is that relationship?

MS. ANDERSON: Very good. If I need a place to find, you know, find a nice rental; I would call them.

MR. FINDLAY: Was he an easy landlord for you to work with?

MS. ANDERSON: Very easy.

MR. FINDLAY: Um, do you know Rebecca or Becky Payne?

MS. ANDERSON: Yes I do.

MR. FINDLAY: How do you know her?

MS. ANDERSON: We, um, I just got to know them when I just recently started this other job I have, and we had to hire the Colemans for cleaning, and that was part of the cleaning crew.

MR. FINDLAY: And where was this new job?

MS. ANDERSON: My job is at Coleman, ah, Coldwell Banker, the Real Estate store.

MR. FINDLAY: Okay, so you were involved in having the Colemans cleaning properties that were vacated?

MS. ANDERSON: Correct. Correct, and do maintenance.

MR. FINDLAY: And, um, the Paynes were involved in that, as far as you knew or?

MS. ANDERSON: In the very last job, yes.

MR. FINDLAY: What was your experience like with the Paynes?

MS. ANDERSON: Very difficult.

MR. FINDLAY: And describe why that was?

MS. ANDERSON: They weren't doing what they were supposed to do and resulting in the Colemans getting fired from the job.

MR. FINDLAY: Okay, how did that happen? What?

MS. ANDERSON: Um, how did we handle it?

MR. FINDLAY: Well, we have to explain cirumstances. What, what was supposed to be done?

MS. ANDERSON: We had hired them because we had new people moving into an apartment; they had three days to clean before the new tenant moved in; I checked on them daily, sometimes twice, three times a day, and I couldn't figure out what the heck they were doing, and at that time, um, Janet had to go to the doctors so Robert wasn't available, and then the second day I had to call Robert to go check on them and there was nothing being done. We eventually, I ended cleaning the apartment myself.

MR. FINDLAY: And did you have an actual contract with the Paynes?

MS. ANDERSON: Yes I did.

MR. FINDLAY: Um, describe that.

MS. ANDERSON: Um, after they were fired, um, and I don't know exactly what the dates were because I knew the new tenant moved in on March 8th; so about two weeks after that I got a call from Rebecca, um, stating she needed an apartment and I said well, what do you need an apartment for .....

MS. WITTLA: Objection, your Honor. I believe that the response she will giving will be hearsay, a statement from Becky Payne.

THE COURT: Unless it's a prior and consistent statement of a witness, is that what we are looking for here, or I mean, I guess we have a full....

MR. FINDLAY: I, I'll rephrase to try to get around it. Um, based on that contact, did you form an opinion about Ms. Payne?

MS. ANDERSON: Yes I did.

MR. FINDLAY: And what was that opinion?

MS. ANDERSON: A very vindictive.

MR. FINDLAY: Who was vindictive?

MS. ANDERSON: Rebecca.

MR. FINDLAY: And why did, without telling me what she said, and why did you form that opinion?

MS. ANDERSON: Because what, what she told me was actually very false; she was lying to me.

MR. FINDLAY: Nothing further your Honor.

THE COURT: Ms. Wittla?

MS. WITTLA: Ms. Anderson, you indicated that you saw them on occasion, approximately once a month?

MS. ANDERSON: Approximately once a month, yeah, I would see them outside there because I'm three doors down from them, on the same street.

MS. WITTLA: Once a month over what period of time?

MS. ANDERSON: Oh, my goodness. Over the last several years.

MS. WITTLA: I think you said five years at one point in time?

MS. ANDERSON: Yeah, I, yeah it was before Ashley was born. He had come to my office almost two times, three times a week even for paperwork.

MS. WITTLA: So you saw them more than once a month?

MS. ANDERSON: Sometimes, uh-huh, it depended.

MS. WITTLA: What would be the— I'm looking for a ballpark figure here, like on a monthly basis or maybe over a couple of months period of time, what was the average number of times you saw Caitlyn and Ashley?

MS. ANDERSON: If it was on a yearly average, once a month; some months I would not see them as often and other times I would see them weekly, depending on paperwork.

MS. WITTLA: Just so we're on the same page, once a month was about twelve times a year?

For God's sake! What part of once a month can you not understand? It does not take a rocket scientist to figure out that an average of once a month is the same as an average of twelve times a year! This woman could spend more time asking the same unimportant question repeatedly than any lawyer I ever saw in any court! Talk about wasting the time of the court!

MS. ANDERSON: At least.

MS. WITTLA: Okay.

MS. ANDERSON: I never thought to count.

MS. WITTLA: Okay, Ms. Anderson, would you have considered yourself to have been Robert Coleman's employer?

MS. ANDERSON: Never.

MS. WITTLA: Didn't he make money from having this association with you?

That does not set the criteria for being an employer stupid! If she were my employer, she would be paying payroll taxes for me, making sure I paid SSI, etc., etc. We were business partners, and as business partners we are both entitled to make money. I can't believe anybody could be so stupid!

MS. ANDERSON: From Coldwell Banker, he got paid, but not from me. I'm an independent contractor with them; I'm self-employed.

MS. WITTLA: So what is it that you did then?

MS. ANDERSON: I would call people and have them connect with Janice to get jobs.

MS. WITTLA: Janice?

MS. ANDERSON: Uh-huh, the owner.

MS. WITTLA: The owner of what?

MS. ANDERSON: Coldwell Banker.

MS. WITTLA: And then what would happen?

MS. ANDERSON: I would check up on them to make sure the job was going to be done, because I needed to place tenants into units in certain amounts of time.

MS. WITTLA: So if we're talking about the cleaning of the—

MS. ANDERSON: Cleaning, maintenance, you name it, we hired them. Lawn mowing. Anything we needed done.

MS. WITTLA: And Robert Coleman got paid for this?

MS. ANDERSON: From Coldwell Banker, yes.

MS. WITTLA: Okay, you also indicated you were a housing agent with MSHDA?

MS. ANDERSON: Correct.

MS. WITTLA: How did that work as far as your relationship with Mr. Coleman?

MS. ANDERSON: He was a landlord; it's Michigan State Housing Authority, which is HUD money, and when we needed good places for people to rent, when their names come off the waiting list, if he had vacancies, I would call him and tell him such and such is looking for an apartment, and I would send them their way, and then we'd have to do an inspection, etc.

MS. WITTLA: So he made....

MS. ANDERSON: ... and the state would pay him, not me.

MS. WITTLA: Okay, but he made his money off of....

MS. ANDERSON: .... MSHDA.

MS. WITTLA: ... you sending people to his apartments?

MS. ANDERSON: Correct.

MS. WITTLA: And MSHDA paid him?

MS. ANDERSON: MSHDA paid him, yes.

Tracie, you make everything so hard! Just compare it to your own business—the business of kidnapping kids! You kidnap the kids, get federal money to take care of them via channeling the money to your state, and you are paid by your state to go about prosecuting the parents to justify your kidnapping! It's not hard to figure out Tracie! So why do you prolong all this?

MS. WITTLA: And when you're talking about good places to stay, you're talking about places that were MSHDA approved?

MS. ANDERSON: MSHDA approved, quality, clean, um, would pass our inspections.

MS. WITTLA: No lead paint?

MS. ANDERSON: No lead paint, correct.

MS. WITTLA: Okay, windows aren't painted shut, that kind of stuff?

MS. ANDERSON: Yeah, all that. We have to check everything, yeah.

And as disappointing as this no doubt was to you, Ms. Wittla, the Colemans' properties did pass!

MS. WITTLA: If you only saw Mr. and Mrs. Coleman and their children once a month, how would you describe your relationship with them?

MS. ANDERSON: I'd consider a friend; friends to me.

MS. WITTLA: Close friends?

MS. ANDERSON: We call if we had problems or if I had problems, or I wanted to talk to them about different things; we developed a friendship.

MS. WITTLA: So you'd know about Robert Coleman's affair with....

MS. ANDERSON: Yes, I did.

MS. WITTLA: Affair with Becky Payne?

MS. ANDERSON: Yes, I do.

MS. WITTLA: Who told you about it?

MS. ANDERSON: Robert did.

MS. WITTLA: When did you find out about it?

MS. ANDERSON: I found out about it on March 7th, it was a Thursday evening.

MS. WITTLA: When did the Paynes stop living with the Colemans?

MS. ANDERSON: I'm not sure. It was sometime between March 8th and the end of the month. They were look-

ing for a unit by April 1st.

MS. WITTLA: Did you want to deal with them?

MS. ANDERSON: Um, not really.

MS. WITTLA: Did you?

MS. ANDERSON: No we didn't.

MS. WITTLA: Is it because of your friendship with the Colemans?

MS. ANDERSON: No, the unit we had available, they didn't like.

MS. WITTLA: So the way that you knew that they weren't living with the Colemans any more was because they hit the radar with your business when they were looking for a place to stay?

MS. ANDERSON: She called and was looking for a place to stay, yes.

MS. WITTLA: You didn't hear that from Robert and Janet then?

MS. ANDERSON: No, I did not.

MS. WITTLA: So your once a month contact for March would have been the 7th?

MS. ANDERSON: No, I probably— I didn't really at that time, um, we had a grave illness in our family, and so certain things I did not deal with, and he respected my time that I needed, and he knew I was very stressed.

MS. WITTLA: When you dealt with Robert and Janet Coleman, and you would, ah, send people to, to them, was it your understanding that Robert and Janet was in charge of the financial stuff?

MS. ANDERSON: I believe, the only one that signed for our MSHDA paperwork ever was Robert. But as far as, I don't know which one deal, dealt with the financial; I was never told.

MS. WITTLA: Were you involved when the Paynes moved into Coleman Estates?

MS. ANDERSON: No, I was not.

MS. WITTLA: They were not MSHDA people?

MS. ANDERSON: No, they were not.

MS. WITTLA: Are you aware of when they moved into Coleman Estates?

MS. ANDERSON: No, I'm not.

MS. WITTLA: Are you aware that they lived in the basement of Coleman Estates?

MS. ANDERSON: No, I was not aware of that.

MS. WITTLA: I have nothing more.

THE COURT: Mr. Perhalla?

MR. PERHALLA: Thanks your Honor. Is it fair to say that your primary involvement with Robert Coleman is business related?

MS. ANDERSON: At the current time, no.

MR. PERHALLA: Since knowing that, isn't it true that your primary involvement with the Colemans has been business related?

MS. ANDERSON: Previously yes, that's how I got to meet them.

MR. PERHALLA: It sounds like you just live a few doors down from them?

MS. ANDERSON: From their actual apartment, we're the fifth house down, right on the corner.

MR. PERHALLA: Absent the business relationship, is it possible you may never have gotten to know them?

MS. ANDERSON: It's quite poss—I probably would never have got to meet them.

MR. PERHALLA: Now going to their home, you stated you went there when Ashley was born. Since then, have you been there regularly?

MS. ANDERSON: Yes, actually quite often and um, oh, just about, I know I would be there when I would drop off their check, ah, the Real Estate store.

MR. PERHALLA: Okay, so just stopping there and...

MS. ANDERSON: ... yeah, I'd stop in or I'd see them playing outside, and I'd yell down to them.

MR. PERHALLA: In the last year, have you seen the Paynes there too?

MS. ANDERSON: I didn't exactly know what car they were driving, so I didn't know if they were there or not.

MR. PERHALLA: You didn't see them in the house, the apartment?

MS. ANDERSON: One time when I stopped there, Bobby, I think his name is, was there.

MR. PERHALLA: You stated that you didn't know that they were living in the basement, correct?

MS. ANDERSON: No, I didn't.

MR. PERHALLA: Had you ever been in the basement?

MS. ANDERSON: No, I haven't.

MR. PERHALLA: You stated that when Robert brought Caitlyn, well this when you were at MSHDA, sometimes she'd have to be disciplined when, um, papers had to be signed?

MS. ANDERSON: Correct.

MR. PERHALLA: Okay, was this regularly or?

MS. ANDERSON: Um, at my office, when I had my own private office, probably about once, once a week when he has a new tenant, because there's quite a bit of paperwork.

MR. PERHALLA: So once a week he would bring Caitlyn there and she'd be acting up?

MS. ANDERSON: She'd be acting up, yes.

MR. PERHALLA: So she sounds like she acted up on a regular basis?

MS. ANDERSON: Just if she wanted to get his attention.

MR. PERHALLA: And these meetings with Robert to do paperwork, how long would they take?

MS. ANDERSON: Sometimes upwards of an hour.

MR. PERHALLA: Incidentally, when did you leave MSHDA?

MS. ANDERSON: Ah, was May of last year.

MR. PERHALLA: These, this would be paperwork when new tenants would move, is that what...

MS. ANDERSON: Correct. Or move out, or inspections or anything like that.

MR. PERHALLA: So one hour, once per week, approximately?

MS. ANDERSON: Some, yeah, sometimes if there was new tenants moving in, yes.

MR. PERHALLA: Part of MSHDA, working in MSHDA, the Colemans' apartments were always somewhere you could put people if you needed to?

MS. ANDERSON: Correct.

MR. PERHALLA: At that was true, at least, up until you left MSHDA?

MS. ANDERSON: Yes.

MR. PERHALLA: Do you still have any contact with MSHDA or?

MS. ANDERSON: No, I don't.

MR. PERHALLA: Wouldn't he bring Ashley into the apart— or when he— you'd come visit—

MS. ANDERSON: Right after Ashley was born, sometimes if he was picking Caitlyn up from school, he would bring her in, in her car seat or carrier, I guess you call it.

MR. PERHALLA: But it was primarily Ashley, I mean, primarily Caitlyn?

MS. ANDERSON: Primarily Caitlyn because Ashley would be home with mom.

MR. PERHALLA: Okay, thank you.

THE COURT: Redirect?

MR. FINDLAY: No. No, thank you.

With that, Ms. Anderson was excused, and Mr. Findlay then called Kristen Semo:

MR. FINDLAY: Okay, would you state your name for the record?

MS. SEMO: My name is Kristen Mueller Semo.

MR. FINDLAY: Semo. Is that how you pronounce it?

MS. SEMO: Yes.

MR. FINDLAY: Okay, I'm making sure I'm saying it right. What is your occupation?

MS. SEMO: I'm a teacher.

MR. FINDLAY: Where at?

MS. SEMO: I teach kindergaten at Sleight School in Ironwood.

MR. FINDLAY: And was Caitlyn Brag—

MS. SEMO: I knew her as Caitlyn Coleman.

MR. FINDLAY: Caitlyn Coleman—was she your student?

MS. SEMO: Yes, she was this year.

MR. FINDLAY: And for how long was she your student?

MS. SEMO: Beginning of the school year, which was what, September?

MR. FINDLAY: Okay.

MS. SEMO: Till March 13th. Probably was when she started being absent.

MR. FINDLAY: Um, can you describe her as a child?

MS. SEMO: Um, Caitlyn was a really nice, normal kid. She, ah, wasn't too quiet, she wasn't too loud, um, she just was, just a real nice and happy kid.

Just the kind that should be separated from her family, right?

MR. FINDLAY: Happy child with any behavior issues?

MS. SEMO: No. No, just normal. No.

MR. FINDLAY: How did she do in school?

MS. SEMO: At, at our first parent-teacher conference, kindergarten is harder than it used to be; and at first, first parent-teacher conference she, like we really concentrated on letters and sounds and stuff, and um, she needed a little bit extra help at home, and the parents said they do that with her, so she was an average student who maybe needed a little extra help, but pretty average.

MR. FINDLAY: Did, from your knowledge, did she get that extra help at home?

MS. SEMO: I assume so. They came in a couple times and it seemed like they were doing things with her; I don't have any proof of anything.

MR. FINDLAY: Um, but it wasn't a situation where you were concerned that the child went home and not getting any involvement from the parents or help from the parents with school?

MS. SEMO: I don't know what they do at home; they don't have, you know, if there was homework, we rarely have homework, but she was barely ever sick. Um, you know, the kids have homework if they're sick, and I as-

sume she— they returned it, yeah, I know they did.

MR. FINDLAY: Did you have any contact with the parents?

MS. SEMO: Um, I don't know if I ever initiated contact with them. Sometimes mom stopped in to pick her up or something, and we just kind of say how things are doing. Mr. Coleman came in on our first field trip, when we went to the Fire Department, and the Police station. Um, he came, that was in October; another day he came in and just kind of hung out with the kids. I can't remember when that was, um, he spent part of the day with us, once or twice they came and just said how are things going, or, it was kind of informal.

MR. FINDLAY: Okay, um, now it's true as a teacher, are you considered a, a mandatory reporter for child abuse?

MS. SEMO: Yes.

MR. FINDLAY: Did you ever see anything with Caitlyn that gave you a suspicion or a reason for reporting it?

MS. SEMO: No, no.

MR. FINDLAY: Um, if you had seen something, would you have reported it?

MS. SEMO: Yes.

MR. FINDLAY: Thank you.

THE COURT: Ms. Wittla?

MR. FINDLAY: Wait, your Honor, I have more. I'm sorry, how often— did you see her basically on a daily basis during the school year?

MS. SEMO: Yes.

MR. FINDLAY: So what was—

MS. SEMO: Kindergarten. She was in my morning, I saw her every morning.

MR. FINDLAY: Half a day?

MS. SEMO: Half a day.

MR. FINDLAY: Thank you.

MS. WITTLA: Do you recall being interviewed by Elizabeth Fyle from DHS?

MS. SEMO: Yes, wait, yeah.

MS. WITTLA: Do you remember what day that was?

MS. SEMO: No, I have no clue.

MS. WITTLA: Do you know what month?

MS. SEMO: (Laughing): No.

MS. WITTLA: Do you remember why she came to see you?

MS. SEMO: She had questions about Caitlyn, right? I, I really don't remember much, because I didn't have anything specific to say.

MS. WITTLA: Well, that's interesting, because today you said specifically that she was a real nice, happy kid, and had no behavior problems; that's your testimony today, right?

Wow! Does this prosecutor really show her snide, sarcastic attitude when the response to her question is not as she would like it to be?

MS. SEMO: Can— overall, yeah.

MS. WITTLA: Do you recall telling Ms. Fyle when she came to see you that you really didn't have much to say about Caitlyn because you had twenty-eight kids in your class?

MS. SEMO: Um, I had twenty-three kids in my class, and it's very busy. We don't sit down one on one and say,

"How's it going Caitlyn, how's it going going Susie, tell me about your day at home." It's very busy. Um, there is certain children that are, obviously, have behavior problems; there are certain children that are very, very quiet, when you kind of try to bring them out.

MS. WITTLA: So to be clear then, Caitlyn wasn't one of the really, really quiet kids you had to bring out?

MS. SEMO: No, she was not.

MS. WITTLA: And she wasn't one of those obvious behavior problems?

MS. SEMO: She wasn't a behavior problem, no. She was not too quiet, she was just kind of, you know, if she had something to say, she'd say it; if another child was bothering her, she would, you know, she would stand up for herself. Um, she was, yeah.

MS. WITTLA: Average kid?

MS. SEMO: Yeah, as far as average can be. Every child is just so different, every child is unique.

MS. WITTLA: So going from what you just stated, um, you had a lot of kids in your class?

MS. SEMO: Uh-huh.

MS. WITTLA: And aside from knowing that she wasn't, um, a big behavior problem or a behavior problem at all actually, she was just an average kid in your class?

MS. SEMO: You know, define average, are you trying to trap me here? I don't know what you're trying to get at.

From my observation, Ms. Semo, Ms. Wittla is always trying to trap witnesses who don't say what she wants them to say. It is her personality to be dishonest, conniving, sarcastic, and rude. I've seen a lot of prosecutors, and they all have some of that built in, but I've never seen a prosecutor who enjoyed so much being vindictive, as this one does! Oh! And I forgot, defensive, and on the attack, as you see in her next comment:

MS. WITTLA: Well, actually, you're the one who used the word average— so I just asked—

MS. SEMO: Oh! Okay, yes.

MS. WITTLA: Do you know why you're here today?

MS. SEMO: Yes.

MS. WITTLA: Tell me.

MS. SEMO: Um, well, no, from what I understand, is Caitlyn went to foster care, and a parent was charged with abusing her, physically, that's all I know.

MS. WITTLA: Do you know the status of Ashley?

MS. SEMO: No.

MS. WITTLA: Do you know Caitlyn has a younger sibling named Ashley?

MS. SEMO: Yes, I guess I do know that Ashley was also taken away.

MS. WITTLA: I believe that Mr. Findlay already asked you this question to some extent, you are not aware of what Caitlyn's home life was like?

MS. SEMO: No.

MS. WITTLA: You didn't go to their house?

MS. SEMO: No.

MS. WITTLA: On the other hand, Caitlyn didn't tell you it's terrible?

MS. SEMO: No.

That's probably because it wasn't terrible! That was Bobby and Becky's version of it, designed because they wanted to retaliate against us!

MS. WITTLA: Do you know why she was absent on March 13th?

MS. SEMO: No.

MS. WITTLA: Was there a point in time when, when you were ever told....

MS. SEMO: Oh, on March 13th, um, I was thinking of um, I do't what day the police officers came in to talk to me; I think it was that day. I had been gone for a week because I had a death in my family, and it was the day I had returned, and so she was absent that day and you know, and kids are absent every now and then, um, and I can't remember when the two police officers came, if it was that day or shortly after that day, and asked me questions.

MS. WITTLA: Did the police officers come on their own or were they with Ms. Fyle or do you recall?

MS. SEMO: I think it was just the two police officers.

MS. WITTLA: And they were asking you about Caitlyn?

MS. SEMO: Uh-huh.

MS. WITTLA: Now this is a while ago, and no, I'm not trying to trap you, but do you recall if you knew when the police officers came and talked to you, why Caitlyn wasn't there?

MS. SEMO: No, I didn't know at the time; they, they told me.

MS. WITTLA: They told you?

MS. SEMO: No. They— from the questions they asked me, perhaps I had assumed. They were asking me questions if I had ever seen abuse of Caitlyn?

Now here we go again! What business do the police have asking those questions. It was their purpose to see if Caitlyn was in school, allegedly, although they already knew she was not, but in order to solidify Elizabeth Fyle's contrived version of why they were not there, they had to play the game. If they didn't, Elizabeth could never get a court order to remove our kids, which is what she wanted. And if I were to bet, I would bet that one of those police officers was Ron Carpenedo. Any takers?

MS. WITTLA: And your response then would have been the same as now?

MS. SEMO: Yeah. I said not, nothing that I specifically noticed. And actually, I didn't know that Caitlyn was going to be gone at that point because every day she was absent, and then I don't sure— when I found out for sure that she was coming back.

MS. WITTLA: So from your perspective, it wasn't a pre-arranged hey, I'm going to be out of town for a few days kind of thing?

MS. SEMO: No, but also I was, I was on a funeral leave for a week; I was not there, so the timing was kind of odd; so I don't know when this specifically happened; I don't know anything other than that the police came to talk to me, and I didn't know of anything; and then Caitlyn was absent for a couple more days, and I'm not sure who told me that she was in foster care; I don't remember who told me that.

MS. WITTLA: Do you recall when Spring break was for Ironwood schools this year? What I mean by saying that, is you, you just said you came back to work on the 13th?

MS. SEMO: Yes.

MS. WITTLA: And you had been gone the previous week?

MS. SEMO: Um, my mother-in-law died on Thursday of the previous week.

MS. WITTLA: When you were gone the previous week, was that the Spring break part?

MS. SEMO: No.

MS. WITTLA: When you came back, was that Spring break?

MS. SEMO: No.

MS. WITTLA: It was coming up? Still hadn't happened yet?

MS. SEMO: I don't remember when Spring break was; (laughing) I really don't; it wasn't the same week, no. I was going to check that before I came; you'd think something that important I would remember, you know.

Yeah. But why? This is very accessible information. All you have to do is call the school secretary, which was already done by the prosecutor, I'm sure. So she didn't have to play the dramatic role here, all she had to do was to confirm the dates, and that she'd check them, and then get on with the pertinent questions. But not Tracie! She would rather play the role, and waste a lot of time in court.

MS. WITTLA: But it wasn't the week before and it wasn't that week when you were talking to the police officers, because you were at work?

MS. SEMO: I was at work, right; Spring break started on a Friday. I don't know if it was that following Friday. Um, it could have been actually that, that following Friday.

MS.WITTLA: The 14th?

MS. SEMO: I don't know. I don't know when Spring break was. Yeah. It was probably after—it could have been the following week.

MS. WITTLA: But the one thing we are clear on is that when you were interviewed, you were interviewed at school?

MS. SEMO: I was interviewed at school.

MS. WITTLA: And you'd be at school because you work?

MS. SEMO: Yup.

MS. WITTLA: Okay, that's all I have.

MS. SEMO: It was the day after the funeral, so....

THE COURT: Mr. Perhalla?

MR. PERHALLA: Thank you. Um, the twenty-three kids, that's how many you had in the morning?

MS. SEMO: Yes.

MR. PERHALLA: And there's more in the afternoon?

MS. SEMO: Yes.

MR. PERHALLA: And how many were in the afternoon?

MS. SEMO: Twenty two; actually, by March, I was probably down to twenty one in the morning class.

MR. PERHALLA: In the morning; so you had forty some kids between the two to keep track of?

MS. SEMO: Uh-huh.

MR. PERHALLA: That's all, thank you your Honor.

THE COURT: Redirect?

MR. FINDLAY: On the Spring break issue, if you remember, you said the, the Spring break started on a Friday. Do they have the Friday off as part of the Spring break? So they have the Friday and then the following week off for Spring break, is that correct?

MS. SEMO: Yes. I'm sorry I didn't look at my calendar, because sometimes we have the, the week and then the following Monday, depending when Easter was; I didn't look at my calendar.

MR. FINDLAY: If, if I told you that, that the Spring break, the week they had off was that week from the 17th, March 17th, thru whatever—to the 24th, would that sound right?

MS. SEMO: When was Easter? When was Easter this year?

MR. FINDLAY: 23rd. So they had that, that week off up thru the 24th, that which was the Monday following Easter?

MS. SEMO: We get the Monday off after Easter.

MR. FINDLAY: Would they have gotten the Friday off prior to that week?

MS. SEMO: No.

MR.FINDLAY: Okay, that's all.

THE COURT: Any questions, based on the one calendar issue?

MS. WITTLA: No.

With that, Ms. Semo was excused as a witness, and it was now time for Ms. Wittla to call her witnesses once more. And her next witness was Elizabeth Fyle:

MS. WITTLA: Would you please state your name for the record?

MS. FYLE: Elizabeth Fyle.

MS. WITTLA: And your current occupation?

MS. FYLE: I'm a Children's worker for the state of Michigan for the Gogebic County Department of Human Services.

(That's a long version for state authorized child kidnapper)

MS. WITTLA: How long have you worked there?

MS. FYLE: Almost nine years.

MS. WITTLA: You're been here throughout the testimony in this case?

MS. FYLE: Yes I have.

A point and admission well made! If you recall, witnesses for this trial were supposed to be sequestered! Why was this one witness exempted from that? It should have resulted in dismissal of this case!

MS. WITTLA: Were you assigned to investigate a complaint of child abuse or neglect regarding Caitlyn and Ashley?

MS. FYLE: Yes I was.

MS. WITTLA: Do you remember when that happened?

MS. FYLE: March 11th of 2008.

MS. WITTLA: We've already heard testimony from Bob Ross; how is your function different than his?

MS. FYLE: I was the primary investigator of this case, um, and he currently is the ongoing foster care worker, since the children have been placed in foster care.

MS. WITTLA: So as of right now, in this case, what are your responsibilities?

MS. FYLE: My responsibilities are to see this petition through until jurisdiction or not is established.

MS. WITTLA: At which point your case closes?

MS. FYLE: Yes.

MS. WITTLA: When you're assigned an investigation for child abuse or neglect, what's the first thing that you do?

MS. FYLE: Well you try to get some cursory details and try to set up a; formulate a plan of what you're going to do next. Details as far as the family, where they live, is the child in school, um, just trying to figure out, like I said, what, what's going to happen next; where am I going to start; you know, go from there.

MS. WITTLA: When you were first given information on this case, who was identified as the suspect for child abuse or neglect?

MS. FYLE: Robert and Janet both.

MS. WITTLA: Did anyone else accompany you on your investigation?

MS. FYLE: Yes, Mr. Ross did.

MS. WITTLA: Anyone from law enforcement?

MS. FYLE: When we went to the home, Officer Sheryl Saippa came with us as well.

MS. WITTLA: Was she basically there doing a stand by thing?

MS. FYLE: Yes.

MS. WITTLA: Have you been trained in the use of the Forensic Interview Protocol?

MS. FYLE: Yes I have.

MS. WITTLA: How many trainings have you gone to?

MS. FYLE: I would say, minimum of four, but there's probably been more than that; but I would say minimum of four.

MS. WITTLA: Did you use the Forensic Interview Protocol when you interviewed Caitlyn?

MS. FYLE: Yes I did.

MS. WITTLA: Where was that interview?

MS. FYLE: Caitlyn's first interview was in her bedroom at their home; at the Colemans home.

MS. WITTLA: And who else was there?

MS. FYLE: Um, the interview was with myself and Caitlyn, and then Mr. Ross, um, was also in the room out of Caitlyn's eyesight.

MS. WITTLA: Okay, when you say he was out of her eyesight, was he next to her or behind her or?

MS. FYLE: I was seated on the bed, Caitlyn was seated like next to me, and then Mr. Ross kind of stood, like, several feet away, I would say 6, 8 feet away, kind of off to the side; so Caitlyn was focused on me sitting here, and he was back there.

MS. WITTLA: When you began your interview, did Caitlyn seem concerned or afraid to be in a room with you and Mr. Ross?

MS. FYLE: No she was; she was fine.

MS. WITTLA: And how; how would you describe her demeanor?

MS. FYLE: Pretty talkative. Um, pretty, very friendly, um, pretty sweet girl.

MS. WITTLA: How old is she?

MS. FYLE: Six.

MS.WITTLA: Were Janet and Robert Coleman allowed to be present during the interview?

MS. FYLE: No, they were not.

MS. WITTLA: Why not?

MS. FYLE: Because it's against the Child Protection Law that children are not allowed to be interviewed in the presence of the alleged perpetrators; so that we were, they're able to tell our story without fear of retribution, I guess, if the parent sits right there; as well as children, I guess are, the ability of them getting the evil eye from a parent if they say whatever a parent perceives them to be as the wrong thing, um, is minimized. The kids are able just to tell us, because nobody else was in the room that, you know, potentially would be bad for them to hear this information.

But it's not against the Child Protection Law for you to record the interview, is it? Ross admitted that. So why did Ms. Wittla not ask you why you did not record this interview? Had you done so, you could prove Caitlyn said the things you say she said, and you could prove you didn't use leading questions in violation of the protocol. But again, maybe you knew that, and that is why you did not want to record the session, right?

MS. WITTLA: No one's judging them?

MS. FYLE: Right.

MS. WITTLA: We've heard a lot of testimony from Mr. Ross regarding the protocol, so I'm not going to take you through that again; was there anything he described in the protocol that you would have said that's not right?

MS. FYLE: No, he was accurate in his description of the protocol.

MS. WITTLA: How did your interview with Caitlyn begin?

MS. FYLE: I told her who I was, um, and that I come out and talk to kids sometimes, um, we talked a little bit about, you know, who she was and how would school go that day; that kind of thing. Um, I went through the, the truth lie, does she, you know, can she tell, promise to tell me the truth. Um, went through; as Mr. Ross described, you know, through the if I ask you a question; if you don't know the answer to it, I don't want you to guess and answer; I want you to tell me I don't know. A typical question that I asked in that is, you know, so if I asked you, you know, what's my dog's name, you know, and then well I don't know; so that's a typical question that I would ask, just to make sure that they know that it's okay if I don't know an answer. I don't want them to guess; I want them to say I, I don't know. And then I went through, if she tells me something and if I repeat it back to her incorrectly; I call her the wrong name, um, I say something that's wrong, that it's okay for me, for her to correct me and not to be afraid. Sometimes children are nervous if they correct an adult that, you know, the adult is going to be ticked off, that, you know, that the kid, I guess, corrected them or whatever, messed with them, um, so I want to make sure that she can tell me whatever, whatever it is. Correct me if I'm wrong, that kind of thing. So I got to know her, established some rapport with her, um, she told me a little bit about, about some of the toys that she had in her room;

Oh! You mean those toys that didn't distract her that Ross was so quick to point out did not play into this interview at all? Are those the toys she talked to you about, Ms. Fyle?

MS. FYLE (continuing): and then I asked her, I said, do you know why, why we're here today, and she said no, not really, and um, I explained, I said, well you know, I'm here becauseI said, I'm here because there's something; I heard something is going on here, and I said, what, what, tell me what happens when you're in trouble. And she said, well, I go in the corner; and I said okay, I said could anything else happen? She goes, or I get the belt. I said, well, tell me about the belt. What do you mean about the belt? Well, he smacks me. I said, well who smacks you; my, my daddy; I said oh, and I just basically kept; continued going on through the interview, um, and she explained how she do; struck, um, many times. Um, that typically she would get one or two swats with the belt, um, or smacks with the belt; that's another part of the protocol is that if the children uses a word, um, that you basically try to continue that word throughout the conversation so I—I'm sure that I probably used it she—her word was smacked; my daddy smacks me; and so tell me, about those smacks and like I said solicited the information.

MS. WITTLA: Stop for a second. So when you're having this interview with Caitlyn, do you ask her yes and no questions?

MS. FYLE: Not usually. I mean, can it happen, yes, but not usually, no. It's....

MS. WITTLA: When you were talking to Caitlyn, did you ask her, I guess, leading questions?

MS. FYLE: I would not say they were leading, no.

A better word for it, according to Caitlyn at the writing of this book, is they were frightening questions, or as Caitlyn puts it, scary questions. You should have recorded them, Ms. Fyle, so we could know if they were leading, threatening, or just what?

MS. WITTLA: What kind of questions would you typically ask?

MS. FYLE: Um, as I stated earlier, when she said, you know, well he smacks me; then I'll ask well who, who smacks you, and then she would, she said my daddy. And I said well, tell me about that or tell me more about that, and then what happened, and basically just let her tell me what happened.

MS. WITTLA: So is it fair to say that when she made the statement, if she continued to speak, you'd let her speak until she stopped?

MS. FYLE: Yes.

MS. WITTLA: And then you'd say something to her?

MS. FYLE: Right.

MS. WITTLA: When she mentioned getting struck with the belt, did she tell you anything about the belt?

MS. FYLE: She, she told me that it was an orange belt. Um, I asked her, I said where, where is this belt, and she said in my daddy's drawer. Um, I can't remember if she told me other details about the belt, other than that's what she got smacked with.

MS. WITTLA: And that it was in the drawer?

MS. FYLE: Yes.

MS. WITTLA: I believe you said; you testified that she got smacked one or two times with the belt; did she give you any indication as to how many incidents there were?

MS. FYLE: Many incidents.

MS. WITTLA: She didn't give it a number?

MS. FYLE: No. She said many times, I believe, were the exact words that she used.

Do you want to get out Bobby and Becky's allegations list so you can be sure Elizabeth? I think it is all written down there, and it was, after all, what you used to put the words in Caitlyn's mouth I believe.

MS. WITTLA: Did she say who else was present when this happened?

MS. FYLE: Ah, she said her mom, um, obviously her dad, um, and then Bobby and Becky.

On every one of those many times cases? Bobby and Becky didn't stay with us that long! Careful, Elizabeth, it is becoming more obvious that your information came from the Bobby and Becky playbook!

MS. WITTLA: Did she say that anyone else had ever hit her with the belt?

MS. FYLE: No, only her dad.

MS. WITTLA: Did Caitlyn tell you why she got in trouble to get the belt?

MS. FYLE: Um, she said she could get the belt if she, um, for instance, was directed to go to her room, to clean her room, and if she went to her room, but was caught playing instead of cleaning as she was supposed to be doing; um, she would get the belt. Um, she mentioned the occasion with, with not eating her rice; and she got the belt for that. She talked about a time that she was apparently playing in a crib and she was told to get out of the crib, and she did not. I, I don't know if she did get out of the crib and she got back in, um, but ultimately she, she continued on in the crib and apparently the crib broke. And she described an incident that she got smacked in the eye with a belt on that occasion.

MS. WITTLA: When Caitlyn would get in trouble and get the belt, what were, well, what was Janet doing then?

MS. FYLE: I, I know on one occasion, Caitlyn stated that her mom held her legs, while her dad held her arms above her head and that, ah, her dad pulled her pants down, and that he hit her with the belt.

MS. WITTLA: Did she tell you where Bobby Payne was?

MS. FYLE: On that occasion, I, I don't recall me asking her to clarify that.

MS. WITTLA: Did she tell you anything about Bobby Payne being involved with her getting the belt?

MS. FYLE: She, she; I asked her, I said did,did anybody else, you know, ever hold you, and she had said that sometimes mom, sometimes Bobby, and sometimes Becky.

If that's true… why were Becky and Bobby also not charged with child abuse in this case? Can you answer that Tracie? This is either a case of selective prosecution or just a complete lie. Either way, Tracie and Ms. Fyle are guity as hell.

MS. WITTLA: Did she talk about whether or not she was afraid?

MS. FYLE: I don't recall. I recall her telling me that her dad would ask her, are you scared as he was coming towards her to hit her with the belt.

MS. WITTLA: Did Caitlyn tell you anything about her mother trying to stop her from getting hit?

MS. FYLE: No.

MS. WITTLA: Caitlyn tell you anything about her mother saying anything about her being hit?

MS. FYLE: I don't believe so, or not that I can recall.

You blew it Ms. Fyle! Don't you remember the part in Bobby and Becky's play book where my wife is supposed to have reminded me we had a doctor's appointment the next day and we had to put her in the tub to sabbotage the evidence? You need to study the allegation book more fully, Ms. Fyle. You did manage to get that into you allegations list when you made it up. How could you now forget it in court? But it's ok, the prosecutor will help you out with her next question:

MS. WITTLA: Caitlyn tell you what happened after she got hit with the belt?

MS. FYLE: On one occasion she described that she had to go into the bath tub and to sit for a really long time. Um, she didn't know specifically what vinegar was, and, but she said something got put in the tub, and I said, well, I said, did it smell kind of funny; was there anything different about it?

THAT is not a leading question? It got those words repeated by Caitlyn, according to you:

MS. FYLE (continuing): And she said it smelled funny, that she had to sit there for a really long time. Um, I asked her, I said, well who had to watch you while you were in the tub, and she said that Bobby, Becky, and her dad had to watch her. I then asked her if, um, I said, well did anybody say anything or whatever and, she said that, that; or did anybody what or; let me think.

Yes, THAT would be refreshing!

MS. FYLE (continuing): I asked her if— who checked on her and if anybody said anything, and she said that Becky had checked on her, and that Becky hollered out, um, of the bathroom and said, Daddy, it's all gone. But Caitlyn said, but, but Becky lied because she said it wasn't. She said the marks were still there.

MS. WITTLA: After this interview that you had with Caitlyn, what— regarding the interview with Caitlyn, did Caitlyn say that anyone else had struck her with anything?

MS. FYLE: She talked about sometimes that her mom would use a wooden spoon, and she also brought up that, um, that sometimes she's be struck with a broom, the belt, or a yellow or green plastic spoon.

This is where we were sure Elizabeth got this all from Bobby and Becky, and not from Caitlyn. We had never even owned a wooden spoon, nor and yellow or green plastic one. Yet there it was in Bobby and Becky's allegation play book, big as light!

So if we didn't own them, how could Caitlyn have come up with that? But it was pretty clear where Ms. Fyle came up with it, after we saw the list of allegations!

MS. WITTLA: After your interview with Caitlyn, did you talk to Robert or Janet Coleman?

MS. FYLE: Yes, at the end of my interview with Caitlyn, um, she asked me to not, you know, don't, don't talk, I don't know if she said my daddy or my parents, but basically she said don't talk to my parents about what I told you, um, and I didn't confirm one way or the other with that, I would or would not communicate this, um, I guess I didn't want to, I didn't want to freak her out, but yet I knew the reality was I had to talk with her parents about the allegations and what she had told me. So I didn't confirm one way or the other; we went out into the living room then, into that living area. Um, I attempted to interview Ashley and she was too young to be interviewed. Um, then at this point in time, Caitlyn had gone out into the living room area where the— Robert and Janet's bed was, and Caitlyn was sitting on the bed watching cartoons, and so I asked Robert and Janet to come in the kitchen so we could discuss the allegations and, and what I'd just been told. I, I told Robert and Janet, um, what the allegations were and that there was concern about physical abuse. Um, they stated that they do not beat their children, but they do discipline their children.

MS. WITTLA: Hold on one second; when you say they, they both said the same thing to you?

MS. FYLE: I believe that was Robert who told me that, they both were standing there, and they both kind of confirmed what each other was saying, so I don't, I don't know if I, I can differentiate everything that was said from each person, but both of them, like I said were there, and both of them confirmed what the other was saying essentially, if that makes sense.

Actually, no, Ms. Fyle, is doesn't make sense! How do you "kind of confirm" something? You either do or you don't. And if you can't remember if I talked or Janet did, it seems your recall isn't too good either. The only thing you seem to recall real well are the allegations in the Bobby and Becky play book.

MS. WITTLA: But, so the gist of it was, you know, we don't hit our kids.

MS. FYLE: We don't beat our kids, but we do discipline them.

MS. WITTLA: Did they describe what the discipline was?

MS. FYLE: Um, they described that they used corner, um, they used timeouts in a corner, um, I asked them if they ever have used a belt for discipline, and I believe Rob said that he has used a belt on Caitlyn in the past.

That was a total lie! I said no such thing!

MS. FYLE (continuing): I then asked him, I said do you, do you own any belts, and he showed me, he says, well the one I have on, and he kind of lifted up his sweatshirt and showed that he had a black normal man's belt, approximately two, I guess about two inches wide. I asked, I said, do you own any other belts, um, and he said, ah, I don't know, Janet do I own any other belts, well if I did, he said they would be in my armoire, and so we went over into their, the kitchen was— Caitlyn's bedroom was off the kitchen, and then the kitchen was essentially next to that, and there was almost like a, maybe potentially a dining room area, and then their living room was next. And so, like I said Caitlyn was in the living room, and so the armoire would have kind of been in the dining room area, the next room over. Um, he opened up that and he said, well if I had any, they'd be by my suits, and so he opened up this armoire and he began to kind of dig through there, and I, I don't know, I don't know if I have any belts in here. Um, from talking to Caitlyn and also from interviewing the Paynes, um, they both confirmed that the belts were kept in a drawer, and so I asked Rob, I said, do you have any in your drawers, and so we went over to his dresser which was in the living room, and as Rob was opening up drawers, um, he opened up, I want to say it was like the third or fourth drawer down first, as he's opening up drawers, Caitlyn was sitting on the bed, and she kind of caught my eye, and she goes, I told you not to say nothing.

Another total lie! And if that had happened, why was it not in her report? She made this up for the court!

MS. FYLE (continuing): And then Rob continued to open up the drawers and I directed him to open up his, I thought it was the third drawer. I was told by the Paynes it would be in the third drawer down.

There you have it! She admitted in court what we already suspected! It came from the Paynes, not Caitlyn! And it happened that way because the Paynes had planted the belts, probably while we were at Walmart after asking them to leave! That is the kind of people we were dealing with. The Paynes were sneaky, dishonest, liars, and totally vindictive!

MS. FYLE (continuing): Um, the top level of his dresser had two drawers on it, and the next drawer down was a full drawer; anyways, so it turned out to be in the second drawer down; the second level down was the drawer that he opened up. I noticed that there were socks on the side that was closest to me, and there was like a mess of belts that was in the middle, and I didn't see what other clothing was on the other side of the drawer. Um, he acted surprised and he had no knowledge of how these belts got in here; he pulled them out and included in there was a belt, again it was about two inches wide, had a large silver buckle on it, oval shaped buckle, um, that was, at one pint it was probably brown, it had, it had kind of like faded from, from wear and whatever; it was kind of orangeish, rusty colored brown. Um, he stated to Janet, he said, well Janet, he says, well Becky's been doing our laundry, and you know, apparently we're going to have to search our home because, apparently she's been, you know, this has been planted here.

Now, let me break here for just a moment and bring something to the attention of you, as a reader. If I had actually been guilty of beating my kid with a belt, would I have voluntarily lifted my shirt to show the one belt I did wear, when I did wear one? I had no clue they were seeking a particular belt, so if I were to be charged with abuse with a belt, I could just as well have used the one I wore. So what would it matter where my belts were kept? Nobody had told me they were looking for any particular belt! I could have used any belt. The only reason they could be looking for a specific one, is if the Paynes themselves had put it where the belts were found, so as to make their story seem more credible. This whole belt thing was a farce that any good investigator could have seen through. But we were unfortunate to have Elizabeth Fyle as opposed to a good investigator.

MS. WITTLA: Was there any other discussion regarding the belt after the belts were located in the second drawer?

MS. FYLE: Um, well then we went back into the kitchen; we left there, we went back into the kitchen area and at that point both Rob and Janet confirmed that they had been beaten with belts as children, and that they would never do such a thing to their children.

MS. WITTLA: Did you take that belt into custody as evidence?

MS. FYLE: I did not.

Why not, if you were telling the truth about what Caitlyn said? You should have! The fact of the matter is, Caitlyn didn't say it. You lied. The Paynes said it, so you felt you needed no such planted evidence! Had you taken a belt as evidence, though, it would most likely have been laughed out of court, because the display of a belt hardly proves it was used to abuse anyone. But again, maybe in this court..... ah, who needs it? You already have the stacked jury!

MS. WITTLA: Is that part of your function to collect physical evidence when you're out on an investigation?

MS. FYLE: It, it's not, no.

MS. WITTLA: Do you think you could be mistaken and you really didn't see the belts in that drawer that day?

MS. FYLE: No, it was pretty obvious there had to have been, I would guess six or eight belts of varying sizes, some thinner, dress belts; some, you know, thicker ones, and like I said, I guess, I was, I wouldn't say shocked, but I guess, I, I felt all the pieces of the puzzle were kind of coming together, especially when this belt, that's been described is located and, you know, and Bobby and Becky stated it was a brown or black belt, and Caitlyn stated it was an orange belt, and like I said, out comes this rusty, orange colored brown belt; I was kind of shocked; you know, whoa, there it is you know.

Can we review what this woman just said? This is contradiction upon contradiction! First, Fyle says Bobby and Becky described it as brown. Caitlyn, if you were to believe this lie, said it was orange. And she, herself describes it as rusty!

And then she says, "Whoa, there it is?" The black belt I was wearing could match the description given by Bobby and Becky. There was no all orange belt, by Fyle's own admission, so her lie about an orange belt described by Caitlyn is apparent. And it is her interpretation that the rusty belt she saw was the same referred to by all of them! Hell, if I had used a belt on my step daughter, which I didn't, it could have been any belt, and Fyle's so-called "discovery" is the biggest "fraud" in this entire case! Caitlyn today, still denies she was ever beaten with a belt! But she does say the state threatned her with never coming home if she didn't say she was!

MS. WITTLA: After the discovery of these belts and the statement that they were struck with belts as children, they wouldn't do that; what did you do next?

MS. FYLE: I explained to Robert and Janet that we had some more investigating to do, we had some more interviews to complete. Um, you know, I didn't really know where this, where this was headed. Um, I made them give me the verbal promise that they would not use physical discipline with their children at all until after we had communicated again, and we'd just kind of sorted some other details out. Um, and then we left shortly after that.

MS. WITTLA: Did they mention to you that they were going out of town for a few days?

MS. FYLE: No.

MS. WITTLA: Did you ask them?

MS. FYLE: No, I didn't ask them, you know, we said that we would be following up with them shortly, but I didn't ask them if they were leaving town; I had no knowledge or I guess no reason to ask them that.

Then why the pretense about panic, when you found out we did leave for a short time? And the over reaction you displayed in making others believe we were on the run? What crap! First, if it had been our intention to run, we would have been far away immediately! We would not have waited. And her court filing came two days later, after she took a day off for training! Doesn't reality tell you we could have been much farther away by this time if we were truly intending to run? How stupid! But she could sure manufacture it well, which is exactly what she did! And the prosecutor and the police were right there with her, all the way!

MS. WITTLA: It's been testified to previously that, by Mr. Ross, that you attended a training the next day, is that accurate?

MS. FYLE: We did.

MS. WITTLA: You guys both there?

MS. FYLE: Yes.

MS. WITTLA: When did you make the decision that you wanted to re-interview Caitlyn?

MS. FYLE: I knew that I wanted to re-interview Caitlyn before we even left their home.

MS. WITTLA: Why did you know that you wanted to re-interview Caitlyn before you left?

MS. FYLE: Because in the middle of Caitlyn's, well, for one, the interview was in her home; um, it was in her bedroom, um, I took the opportunity to interview her right then and there because I had an opportunity and I wasn't certain that I was going to get another opportunity again. But I knew it wasn't my first choice for a loca-

tion of the interview.

Then why did you not wait until a better time, when you could have a better choice? That was another straight out lie! The truth is, you and the police chief and Ms. Wittla, among others, all wanted to fry Robert Coleman! Why don't you just admit it? This was a chance to do it, and you didn't want to wait another day! There was no urgency, it could have waited another week! And don't tell me that you do not have places in Gogebic County—you have done multiple interviews there, outside of parents' homes! So that portion of your response was a total lie. But go ahead, lie on:

MS. FYLE (continuing): Um, during my interview with Caitlyn, Janet Coleman had popped open the door and walked in and stood at the, stood in the entry of the, of the bedroom with her arms kind of folded, and I asked her, can I help you with something? Well, we talked with our attorney she said, and he said that I should be present here in the interview. Um, I didn't want Caitlyn to, I guess, pick up as, as little as she could that this was a, a problem, I guess, um, and I asked Mr. Ross if he would go out and speak with the parents about the need for me to interview her alone. Um, he left the room with Janet, and then Caitlyn and I, I didn't speak at all about the topic of, you know, abuse or neglect while there, or during that time. Um, we chit chatted about her stuffed animals that on, had on her bed; she told me the names that she had for some of, some of her stuffed animals. Um, then after several minutes, Mr. Ross came back into the room and, and stated that, that we were okay, that the parents said it was okay, and I should continue the interview. And then I did.

MS. WITTLA: Did anything else happen during the interview that made you wonder if someone was going to come back in the room?

MS. FYLE: Several minutes after that, um, I was doing the interview and we heard some kind of a thump or a bump or something that sounded just outside of the bedroom door, um, and so I kind of paused, not certain if the door was going to pop open a second time or not, um, and then I continued. But it was kind of a, a disruption, I guess, kind of an interruption of, you know, of a, I guess of a; well, I was trying to make as comfortable a setting as I could, given the nature of the topics that we were discussing.

MS. WITTLA: Did Caitlyn notice it?

MS. FYLE: I don't recall.

Could that be because it was you who was uncomfortable, knowing we might be listening? We were not guilty of that, of course, as we had a cop watching us the whole time, but to a paranoid, Ms. Fyle, I can see where there might be doubts, and that could make somebody uncomfortable.

MS. WITTLA: So when you left on, on the 11th, was when you knew you wanted to re-interview her?

MS. FYLE: Yes.

MS. WITTLA: You were at training on the 12th?

MS. FYLE: Yes.

MS. WITTLA: When did you plan on re-interviewing her?

MS. FYLE: On the, on the morning of the 13th when we came back; when I was back at work.

Did you tell Janet and I that? No! No! No! So how were we supposed to know what your plans were, Ms. Fyle?

MS. WITTLA: Where were you going to interview her?

MS. FYLE: At school.

Oh? So there is another place in Gogebic County where you can interview kids! It's called a school! Imagine that!

MS. WITTLA: When did you find out that Caitlyn was not in school?

MS. FYLE: When I went to the school; I went, I went to the school and I went to the office, and, and informed them who I was, and that I needed to interview Caitlyn. Um, they said that she wasn't in school that day, that she— they didn't know why she wasn't there; she was absent that day.

We had told the school. Perhaps they didn't relay the message, but we told them. Either there was some confusion, or Ms. Fyle was lying again.

MS. WITTLA: Did you have any conversations with either of the Colemans regarding where they were on the, on the 13th?

MS. FYLE: Um, I, I did not; I was seated right next to Mr. Ross when he made the phone call. I was, I was driving and he was the passenger in the car, and he made the phone call to them.

MS. WITTLA: So you didn't talk?

MS. FYLE: I did not.

MS. WITTLA: Did you believe the Colemans were coming back on Thursday?

MS. FYLE: Yes, yes. Um, I didn't talk to them the first phone call, um, I was I was under the impression they were coming back later that evening, and I was the on-call worker, um, and so it worked out, I guess well because, I was, you know, I was on call worker and I would have more than likely be called out to complete this interview that night or that evening. Um, so I was under the impression they were coming back later that afternoon, um.....

MS. WITTLA: Sorry, go ahead.

MS. FYLE: That they, that they had been in Marquette and that they were returning that evening. And that they, that they were going to be calling and having me paged, um, upon their return.

MS. WITTLA: Did anyone try to contact them later on in the evening?

MS. FYLE: At six o'clock I had not heard from them yet, and so I placed a call to Mr. Coleman's phone number, um, left a message saying this is Elizabeth Fyle, um, I do need to complete a re-interview of Caitlyn, um, please call me as soon as you guys return to town. Um, I never received a return call, so at seven thirty I called to the Ironwood Public Safety Department and asked them to call on my behalf, um, as I had, had not had any luck. Um, I called them again at nine to ask them if they had heard anything back; if this interview would in fact, take place, um, and was told that they had not returned a call to them either, and that Ironwood Public Safety Department was going to be, I guess, keeping tabs on their, on their home. Um, they would notify me if they, in fact, had returned.

So is that what all this panic was supposedly about? That you might not get your interview on the time schedule you set up without notifying us? As it was, we did not get any messages, perhaps the phones were not receiving properly, I don't know. But that is why no return calls were made. But with all of that, it doesn't warrant this kind of panic!

MS. WITTLA: When did you draft the petition in this case?

MS. FYLE: On Friday morning.

MS. WITTLA: The 14th?

MS. FYLE: Would have been the 14th— yes.

MS. WITTLA: So approximately three days after your interview with Caitlyn?

MS. FYLE: Right.

Let's see now. In three days, I could have driven at least 1500 miles quite easily. If I were on the run. They located us in state. No doubt, a real flight risk! Right?

MS. WITTLA: Did you check to see if she was in school on the 14th?

MS. FYLE: Yes, I did, she was not in school, and again they didn't know why she was not in school.

MS. WITTLA: Were you involved with the search warrant to request cell phone records?

MS. FYLE: I had, I had called and requested assistance from Ironwood Public Safety Department. Um, let me think, I believe I had called up there and had stated that we were trying to locate, you know, we didn't know where the Colemans were, and Ironwood Public Safety Department was notified from the previous day that I was interested in knowing their locations and trying to, you know, trying to find them so I could do another interview with the kids. Um, I got a call back later and said, and was told that, um, that the Paynes' cell phone had received several calls from the Coleman cell phone, um, I then was talking with Sergeant Carpenedo and he had mentioned that in previous cases he has used, um, has, has been able to, you know, seek or search out a search warrant, um, to be able to figure out what tower the Colemans' phone was bouncing off of to determine their location.

So there we go! There is the proof that my dear policeman friend, who constantly badgered me throughout this case, was indeed the driving force behind the raid at our motel. He was the one tracking us, and no doubt who made other enforcement people believe we were so terribly dangerous that they needed what amounted to a swat team to raid our hotel at 3 in the morning! Even had I not heard Elizabeth make this statement, I would have suspected as much! After all, he was the heavy for the police chief, who hated me as much as Carpenedo, himself, did!

MS. FYLE (continuing): Um, so he stated that he'd be working on drafting a search warrant and he did; um, I got a call back at 3:30 that afternoon, stating they had gotten the records and that, in fact, the Colemans were believed to be, um, in the Houghton, Michigan area.

MS. WITTLA: Once you knew that they were in the Houghton, Michigan area, were you aware of what efforts were being made to recover the children?

MS. FYLE: I was told that the, um, police departments or the Ironwood Public Saftey Department had, um, put out a BOL, which I guess is a Be On The Lookout for, for the Colemans' vehicle in that area, because that's where they believed they were because of their cell phone records.

MS. WITTLA: When was the next time you knew, I guess, anything about this case, from the point on Friday when you knew that the cell phone records had shown they were in Houghton; when was the next contact you had with the case?

MS. FYLE: The next call that I got was at 12:30 a.m., on Saturday morning, um, from Ironwood Public Safety Department, notifying me that their vehicle had been located at a hotel up in Hancock.

MS. WITTLA: And when we're talking about 12:30, we're talking about 12:30 Central?

MS. FYLE: Yes.

MS. WITTLA: Did anyone tell you then, what the plan was as far as retrieving the kids or they just said hey, they've been located and?

MS. FYLE: Um, I believe the next call that I had gotten was from, let me think. I believe the next call I had gotten was from Gary Olkonen, who was, that the then on-call worker, and he, um, he stated that they were requesting that, that the DHS basically go there to help arrange for the kids' placement. Um, and he,um, I, I knew that he was basically enroute then to, to Ontonagon, and that he had communicated with Bonnie Huttunen, as far as she was going to be with them since that's where she was located, and then they were going to be coordinating between the two of them for the placement of the children that night.

MS. WITTLA: When was the next time you saw Caitlyn and Ashley?

MS. FYLE: I would have seen them that, that next Monday morning, which would have been the 17th, 17th , 18th, whatever that next Monday morning would have been.

MS. WITTLA: Where did you see them?

MS. FYLE: At the shelter home up in Ontogagon.

MS. WITTLA: When you arrived at the shelter home in Ontonagon, were Caitlyn and Ashley in a common area of the house?

MS. FYLE: They were in the living room.

MS. WITTLA: What was Caitlyn's response to seeing you guys?

MS. FYLE: She smiled and then she proceeded to run down the hallway towards her bedroom, um, saying you know, I, I can't talk to them, I don't recall her exact words, but, um, I can't talk to them, they're the cops, and my daddy says I can't, I can't talk about spanks with them.

MS. WITTLA: Did you follow her down the hall?

MS. FYLE: I didn't, I stayed in the living room and her, and then LaVerne, the shelter foster mom walked down and said, you know, Caitlyn what are you doing and, and she kind of brought her back into the living room area. Um, Caitlyn was playing with a puzzle at the time, on the living room floor, so I just kind of plopped down with her and I started kind of building this puzzle, um, just trying to get her again, comfortable with me. Um, and then Caitlyn asked me if, if I wanted to see her bedroom, and I said sure, so we walked back down the hallway, um, which is, I don't know, maybe a ten foot, twelve foot long hallway, um, to her bedroom. Um, ans she showed me her room and that kind of a thing and then, um, and then I began the Forensic Interviewing Protocol because I wanted to know what had gone on; like what, you know. And so I wanted to make sure that she told me her story, so I began again about make sure you tell me the truth, um, like I said, all the steps of the Forensic Interviewing Protocol. Um, I asked her, I said well, I said what, what's happened since our, you know, what happened since we saw you last, and she, um, told me that her dad was very mad at her, um, that her dad told me that told her she should not speak with me because I'm the cops, and I will try to trick her, and I will take her away.

MS. WITTLA: Did she have any comments about how things were going at the foster home?

MS. FYLE: I asked her, I said, well, I said, tell me so how are things going here? And she said, huh, really good; and I said really, I said, well tell me about that, what, what's really good? And she says, well, here she says, if I get in trouble, she said I just have to go and sit for a timeout in a chair. I said, well how is that different from before; she said at home, she said I have to stand in the corner for a really long time, or I get the belt.

MS. WITTLA: When you stated really good, your voice reflection changed. Was that to mimic Caitlyn's voice?

MS. FYLE: That's how she said it. It was really good. I mean she was.

MS. WITTLA: After speaking to Caitlyn, on the 17th, were there any other times when you interviewed her?

MS. FYLE: About the allegations of the petition, no.

MS. WITTLA: You've seen her since then?

MS. FYLE: Yes.

MS. WITTLA: Have you had contact with Robert and Janet Coleman since your interview on the 17th?

MS. FYLE: Yes, I supervised their first, their first parenting time, that was arranged for them at my office.

MS. WITTLA: Do you recall what date that was?

MS. FYLE: Not off the top of my head. It wasn't long after the 17th, but I don't recall the exact date.

MS. WITTLA: I'm looking at a report, it says Children's Protective Services Investigation Report?

MS. FYLE: Yes.

MS. WITTLA: Yes, Investigation Report. And the complaint date was 3-11-08?

MS. FYLE: Yes.

MS. WITTLA: That would have been your report?

MS. FYLE: Yes.

MS. WITTLA: If it states in here that 3-20-2008 @ 9 a.m., successful face-to-face contact, Robert, Ashley, Cait-

lyn, Janet, would that have been the date? Yes?

MS. FYLE: Yes, that would have been the date.

MS. WITTLA: How long was the visit that you supervised?

MS. FYLE: I believe it was scheduled for an hour.

MS. WITTLA: Did it last that long?

MS. FYLE: It lasted for over an hour.

MS. WITTLA: At the beginning of the visit, what was the children's reaction when their parents arrived?

MS. FYLE: Um, Caitlyn saw them and she was glad to see them, happy to see them; um, she ran and gave her mom a hug and Ashley went to her dad, gave her dad a hug, um, Robert then put Ashley down and gave Caitlyn a hug, and Ashley kid of looked over at her mom, and then she ran over to me and she put her hands up, like pick me up, pick me up; you know, she didn't say that, but I mean it was like the, like pick me up and I tried to turn, I said now Ashley, go and see your mom, and she just kind of like got insistent, and so I picked her up and she kind of hugged me around my neck, you know, almost like a little monkey.

Who is the woman trying to kid? Someone the kids have seen maybe twice in their life, and they are going to refuse their mother to cling to her? That takes a lot of gall, and not only is she a liar, but the lowest of low life to even tell such a story in court! Anything to win a court case! My daughter Ashley loves her mother, and would never in a hundred years prefer the hugs of this lying pig over her mother!

MS. FYLE (continued): I mean she like didn't want to let go, like a death grip around my neck and I, um, I tried to, you know, get her engaged with her mom, I tried to pick up some toys, hey do you want to show your mom and dad, look at the this, you know, this car. Um, and she just basically, you know, clung to my neck. Um, I tried to sit, I was, you know, could hopefully try to, I guess, uncling her from me so she could be with her parents, um, and like I said, she wouldn't let go, and then, um, Robert came over by the couch, there's two couches that essentially face each other in our visitation room. I was in between there and then Robert came over and he sat on the, the couch that was opposite of where I was, um, and said, well, can I, can I hold my kid or something to that affect, and I said absolutely and then he just basically took, you know, took her off my neck, like pulled her off and she was fine with that at that point. Um, she went to her dad and the visit continued.

You could have made your lie more dramatic, Ms. Fyle, if you had told the court I took her dragging and screaming from your tender arms! Of course my daughter came to me willingly and of course she was fine! Both of them always came running— excited and willingly— at every visit we made. That was even confirmed by DHS. Why, in her visitation, as she tells it, is it different? Because she lied!

MS. WITTLA: Were the kids fine interacting with their parents, from that point forward in that visit?

MS. FYLE: Um, yeah, they were fine for a while, um, after I don't even know exactly how many minutes, but after a while, um, Caitlyn was sitting in Robert's lap and Robert said something to the affect of, you know, I, I, I miss you or something and Caitlyn said I'm sorry daddy, I won't tell them again, and buried her head in Rob's neck and I couldn't hear what else she had to say. Rob responded something to the effect of you know, something to the effect anyways of no matter what I'll always love you. Um, and then the visit kind of proceeded and things kind of calmed down for a bit. Um, and then at the very end of the visit, is when things kind of, I guess I would say, kind of went south.

MS. WITTLA: Well, okay, before we get to that, did Caitlyn seem sad when she was with Rob or happy or mad or?

MS. FYLE: She, she was fine up until, up until the, up until the point that she apologized for, for telling. I mean, she was fine interacting.

MS. WITTLA: And then, well then what was she like at that point?

MS. FYLE: Um, like I said, she, she kind of pulled it together and they kind of, you know, played and did a few other activities for a while.

MS. WITTLA: The rest of the visit was fine as far as interacting, everybody was getting along?

MS. FYLE: Uh-huh, no problems.

MS. WITTLA: Was there anything notable that happened at the end of the visit?

MS. FYLE: Towards the end of the visit, I believe about three minutes before the visit was to be about ending, um, I just quietly let the parents know, you know, the visit, you know, we just have a few minutes left here, um, just so they were aware and Rob I think, asked you know, has, has it been an hour, and I said yes it has been. Um, and typically, I guess, what, what, um, we like parents to kind of wrap up the visit on their own; um, it's less traumatic for the kids, if they say, you know, we'll be seeing you later, that kind of thing vrs. um, I guess, it's just, it's just, it's just better if the parents end the visit; but so, we, um, they proceeded to hug the kids, um, and they were crying and, and, Caitlyn was crying. I, I don't think Ashley, I guess, quite understood the concept, I guess of, of what was going on, but Caitlyn began to cry, um, and then Rob began to make comments to Caitlyn, um, as far as, you know, you know these people that; you know, you know the people that did this to you and; that they're going to pay. Um, he made the comment that, um, that, you know, once they get the kids back, this is never ever going to happen to them again. He asked Caitlyn, he said, Caitlyn do you remember meeting the Governor? And Caitlyn, um, kind of looked like, I don't know, you know, kind of like that, ah, me kind of look on her face and he says well you know— no, no before that Rob had said something about how Caitlyn, I've got lots of people working on this, lots. And then later on, like I said, shortly thereafter, he made a comment to Caitlyn do you remember the Governor, um, and when she kind of looked, like I said, kind of like maybe I do, maybe I don't, I don't know; he says, well he's working on this for us too. And I kind of though it was kind of odd because our governor is a she, so I thought, I remember that specifically because I thought, well that's kind of weird, but like I said, it proceeded on to, like I said the kids were crying; Robin— Rob and Janet were crying, and a couple of times I had to kind of remind them to, you know, kind of wrap it up, like I said because it was just, I felt it was, it was not beneficial to the children to continue the, the goodbye as, as long; I mean, longer than what it was.

MS. WITTLA: Could you understand why the kids, or Caitlyn, would have been sad saying goodbye?

MS. FYLE: Oh, sure.

MS. WITTLA: During the visit, was there anything that, I guess, that caught your attention, aside from the kids interacting with Robert and Janet?

MS. FYLE: At one point in time, um, they brought in like a, a diaper bag or like, yeah, like a big bag anyways with them, and all of sudden there was like some type of electronic weird noises talking, something I know that I couldn't make what was being said, and Rob made some kind of, oh, you know, cell phone, something to that effect, and kind of reached in the bag and did something, and I didn't really pay much attention to it, um, other than I thought that I don't think that was a cell phone; it wasn't a cell phone sound.

MS. WITTLA: After the visit, when the parents left, did you talk to Caitlyn at all?

MS. FYLE: I did. I brought her back in my office, um, and I talked with her and her foster mother was there, and I just, you know, got down on her level, and I said Caitlyn, I said, you know, I, you know I heard you, you talk with your dad, or mention to your dad that you know, that you wouldn't tell or you're sorry that you're sorry that you told. And I reminded her, I said, Caitlyn, I said you always need to tell the truth and that it's okay to tell the truth. And I told her, I said, I said, do you know why you're in foster care because I felt at that point in time she felt it was because she told; that that was why, you know, why she was in foster care. Um, that she was taking responsibility for it. And I said Caitlyn, I said that you know, I said do you remember when we talked about, you know, your daddy, you know, spanking you, and that, and that he left marks on your butt, and she said yeah, and I said you know, that's not okay for that to be happening; and that's, and that's why you're in foster care right now. Just like, I said, because I didn't feel it was her responsibility to feel it was her, her fault.

MS. WITTLA: Did you supervise any other visits between the Colemans and Caitlyn and Ashley?

MS. FYLE: I think that was the only one that I can recall.

MS. WITTLA: Have you had contact with the Colemans since that point in time?

MS. FYLE: Just in court hearings, not beyond that.

MS. WITTLA: Have you had contact with Caitlyn and Ashley aside from— well, I guess, have you had contact with Caitlyn and Ashley since the 20th?

MS. FYLE: Yes.

MS. WITTLA: And where did you see them?

MS. FYLE: Um, I was, I had gone with, with Mr. Ross when we moved the children from the Ontonagon shelter home to their placement in Marquette, um, and then again from their placement in Marquette to their placement in Delta County.

MS. WITTLA: Aside from those contacts, have you seen them?

MS. FYLE: I don't think so.

MS. WITTLA: Is it fair to say that the most of the day to day stuff from this case is Mr. Ross's responsibility at this point?

MS. FYLE: Yes.

MS. WITTLA: I have nothing further.

THE COURT: Okay, we're getting to the usual closing time, did you have many questions Mr. Perhalla, or I mean, I, I'm trying to decide whether we should stay through, examine her now, or, or wait till the morning, if you can wrap it today, that's one more out of the way to make sure we finish tomorrow.

Yeah, that's right! We sure want to move this unimportant matter along so you can meet your desired agenda, don't wc judgc?

MR. PERHALLA: I don't think I have—

THE COURT:— Okay, I'm going to, I'm going to have you examine then, and does anybody have a problem with staying over a little more so we can make sure the case fits tomorrow, and then we will break before Mr. Findlay, he'll start in the morning then.

MS. WITTLA: Your Honor, you mentioned staying longer until?

THE COURT: Beg your pardon?

MS. WITTLA: How, how long are you speaking of?

THE COURT: You'd have to ask—

MS. WITTLA:— I have a commitment at five o'clock that I have to get to.

Oh! Well God forbid anybody take up any of your time Tracie! But you sure haven't had any problem repeating your same stupid, unessential questions multiple times on the time schedule of everybody else, have you?

THE COURT: Right, and I'm hoping Mr. Perhalla will be through well before that.

MR. PERHALLA: The interview that you had with Caitlyn in her home, she had no problem going and sitting down and talking with you?

MS. FYLE: No.

MR. PERHALLA: Did, was anyone resistant to her talking to you? Her parents or?

MS. FYLE: Um, I guess I kind of picked up that they were less than thrilled that we were there; um, but they allowed us to do the interview.

MR. PERHALLA: Prior to this time, had you spoken with anyone else? Becky, Bobby, or anyone else?

MS. FYLE: Um, the first interviews that I did, were with Bobby and Becky, um, because I had heard that they had just recently been in the home, and I wanted to know if they had any information to tell me, um, about what had gone on in the home.

You are such a hypocrite! You interviewed them because your police friends could not wait for you to go after Robert Coleman when Becky and Bobby went running to the police to seek revenge! What are you all hiding? The judge pretends the complaint was not filed by Bobby and Becky. You make it sound like it wasn't. Is it just a total lie on your part, or is it that a corrupt official actually made the complaint to get the ball rolling to go after Robert Coleman. Tell us—who did file the complaint if it wasn't Bobby and Becky? The world would like to know!

MR. PERHALLA: So after receiving the complaint of child abuse, would it be fair to say that you first went to the, to— Bobby and Becky?

MS. FYLE: Yes.

MR. PERHALLA: And got your initial information?

MS. FYLE: They were the first interviews that I did, yes.

MR. PERHALLA: Where did you interview them?

MS. FYLE: Um, at the home that they had moved into that they were staying at temporarily.

MR. PERHALLA: And they freely spoke with you?

MS. FYLE: Yes.

MR. PERHALLA: Had you met them before?

MS. FYLE: Um, I had never met Bobby before, I had, I had met Becky before.

MR. PERHALLA: The next step then was to interview the child?

MS. FYLE: Yes.

MR. PERHALLA: Caitlyn? Did, you didn't talk to the parents in between Becky and Bobby and, and Caitlyn?

MS. FYLE: Other than to explain why we were there and that I was there, and I needed to interview their child, no.

MR. PERHALLA: Right. No independent seeing them first somewhere else?

MS. FYLE: No.

MR. PERHALLA: Okay, when you spoke with Caitlyn, did she talk about her sister getting hit or struck at all?

MS. FYLE: I, don't if she—

MR. FINDLAY: Your Honor, I'm going to object; I thought that— what we'd go into in terms of Caitlyn's out of court statements, um, at a motion that we had was pretty limited in terms of what we could do and this would be hearsay.

THE COURT: I think that's accurate; unless you would remind me that that topic has been covered before, I would sustain the objection.

MR. PERHALLA: And she didn't give you an idea of how many times he struck her with a belt?

MS. FYLE: She said that, that, um, many times as far as occasions of getting struck, and that on each occasion she was struck one or two times with the belt.

MR. PERHALLA: When—did she use the term many times?

MS. FYLE: Yes.

MR. PERHALLA: And you; did you inquire further as to what many times meant, or?

MS. FYLE: I, I didn't.

MR. PERHALLA: That's a term that could mean different things to different children?

MS. FYLE: It could be four, it could be ninety-two, it could be two thousand, I, I didn't, I didn't clarify.

MR. PERHALLA: How did you bring up the topic of, of child abuse?

MS. FYLE: I asked her, I said, what happens at home here when you get in trouble, and she says, you know, I, I have to, you know, I get the cor— I have to stand in the corner. I said well what else could happen, and she said I get the belt. And then I asked her, with a belt, what did that mean, and then she explained it, that then her next words were he smacks me. I said well who smacks you, and she says my daddy.

MR. PERHALLA: Was she reluctant at all to talk about the, once, once the topic was brought up?

MS. FYLE: No, no she, I mean, she,she just kept explaining and then, I guess, I asked some clarifying questions as far as well, where is this belt, and that kind of thing, and she told me where it was and what color it was and.....

MR. PERHALLA: Sort of matter of fact, she was just talking about it?

MS. FYLE: Uh-huh.

MR. PERHALLA: Did you get the impression that getting hit with the belt was something she was accepting?

MS. FYLE: I guess we never really got into that kind of a topic. That's what happened to her, I mean, that's what happened when she got in trouble, but I guess, we— I never really asked her if she accepted, I guess, or....

MR. PERHALLA: And other than the many times you had no idea when it might been— it may have started? Like at what age?

MS. FYLE: No.

MR. PERHALLA: That would be difficult to find out?

MS. FYLE: Right.

MR. PERHALLA: How long when Janet came into the room during the interview, how long was she in there?

MS. FYLE: Well, when she walked in, I mean, I stopped asking because I was like, whoa, I mean, like what's, you know, what's going on and um, I said, can I help you with something, because I didn't know, I mean, maybe she did come in and get a diaper, you know, I didn't know if she was planning on staying or just had to come and get something; I didn't know. I said can I help you and I said, and she said, well, you know, my attorney said that, you know, that I need to be present here and I need to be here. I said well that's, you know, we don't really allow that and then I said Mr. Ross, I said, could you, you know, please, you know, talk with the parents and explain what's going on, and like I said, then they left, and then Caitlyn and I just chit chatted about her toys and what not.

MR. PERHALLA: And this; Janet coming in; I take it, it was fairly short she was in there?

MS. FYLE: I would guess she was in there for maybe, and like I said, she walked in and I stopped and I would say from a few— back and forth until Bob left with her, I would say is probably thirty seconds, a minute.

MR. PERHALLA: In any event, it didn't seem like Caitlyn thought her mom was putting her nose into the interview?

MS. FYLE: I, I don't know what she thought, I guess I wanted to get Janet back out of the room before it, before Caitlyn, I guess, comprehended that it was something that she needed to be concerned about.

MR. PERHALLA: In any event, it was very short?

MS. FYLE: Right.

MR. PERHALLA: In and out type of thing; did you, in looking around the home then that, that day, did you look for spoons too, or just focus on the belts?

MS. FYLE: We did look for spoons too, um, the Colemans stated that they don't even have a yellow or a green spoon, um, they brought me in the kitchen, they pulled open multiple drawers that they've had, and I did not locate a yellow or green spoon, um, in their kitchen.

MR. PERHALLA: But they chose the drawers what to open and show you?

MS. FYLE: They, they showed me many of them, I mean it, I didn't see one and like I said the multiple drawers that they did open.

And that just broke Ms. Fyle's heart, I'm sure! I guess Bobby and Becky screwed up and forgot to plant those! But you still had those belts, right? As the prosecutors have brought up again and again— oh hell! Let's do it again:

MR. PERHALLA: The orange belt though, was it very close orange or was it?

MS. FYLE: I, I could see certainly where a child could perceive that it was orange, like I said it was a, it was like a rusty, orangey brown.

MR.PERHALLA: And you decided; you didn't think it was right for you to keep the belt or take it or seize it, right?

MS. FYLE: DHS doesn't seize property as a general rule.

What difference would it make anyway? There would be no absolute proof of it being the one belt used to torture my daughter with! Unless of course you ask Bobby or Becky to identify it, and they would identify a green one, if you picked out a green one! Liars are liars.

MR. PERHALLA: Did you go into the bathroom at all?

MS. FYLE: No. I believe I, I saw it like in passing because the bathroom kind of goes off to the left as you kind of walk towards the, the girls room and the kitchen.

Yes, Virginia, there is a bathroom! Maybe that was where those damn spoons were! Or worse yet— a bath tub!

MR. PERHALLA: Okay, did you see a bath tub in there?

MS. FYLE: Yes, I believe I did.

Uh-oh? We're screwed now! All they need now is to find vinegar in our home and they will know we are child abusers! I mean, what kind of normal American would have belts, bath tubs, AND vinegar— all in the same house!

MR. PERHALLA: Because the room does, the, the apartment sounds like it was somewhat being remodeled in parts?

MS. FYLE: Right. Yeah, the Colemans' bedroom was essentially in their living room, like when you walked into the entrance that I walked into, off to the left, like I said, their, their bed and there was a big screen TV, and like you kind of turn the right and there was the dining room area which, like I said, looked kind of like an office dining room area type space and then the bathroom would have been off to left, but there was some kind of construction or sheeting or something like that up; and there was a bathroom and then you walked down and you kind of jog around a little bit, and then off to the right would have been the girls' bedroom, on like that end of the house.

MR. PERHALLA: And then it sounds like the next interview with the, or strike that, when you left then did you feel confident that the Colemans would not engage in any more physical abuse of their children?

MS. FYLE: I guess I was, I was, I was, um, I guess.....

Come on Elizabeth, spit it out! The judge and Ms. Wittla only have so much time!

MS. FYLE (continuing to start): I felt we had an agreement that they would not until after we sorted things and had spoken further.

Oh! Okay, and under the terms of your perceived agreement, which we never endorsed because we never abused our kids to start with, we would agree not to beat them until we sorted things out and had spoken further—right? But after that, it would be Okay, right?

MR. PERHALLA: And Ashley, I'm sorry, Caitlyn, ah, she'd been described as a happy type of child, so you didn't see an immediate fear of Robert at least when them two were together?

MS. FYLE: When we first walked in?

MR. PERHALLA: Right.

MS. FYLE: Ah, no. I didn't notice anything immediately out of order, no.

MR. PERHALLA: Then you interviewed her at, um, or your next contact with her again is in Ontonagon, right?

MS. FYLE: Yes.

MR. PERHALLA: And again it sounds like she gave you the same test or same incidences of being struck with a belt, right?

MS. FYLE: Right. She talked about, about the spanks again.

MR. PERHALLA: And this had been how many days in between?

MS. FYLE: I first spoke with her on a Tuesday, and then I would have talked with her on a Monday, so six days.

MR. PERHALLA: And you believed you were getting the same consistent information from her?

MS. FYLE: Yes.

MR. PERHALLA: Finally, then, when you see her at, um, the DHS office here, you take her aside after the interview?

MS. FYLE: Yes, I did.

MR. PERHALLA: What was her— was she really afraid that she had, when she, let me start over;

Good idea Rudy! Just relax, take a deep breath, and get all the previous lies straight in your mind! Then you can finish this with what might sound like an intelligent question:

MR. PERHALLA (continuing to start): You were concerned because she told dad it's her fault, she told her dad it's her fault?

MS. FYLE: Right. She said, I'm sorry daddy, I won't, I won't tell them again or something to that effect, and then like I said she buried her head in her dad's neck, shoulder area, and I couldn't hear what else she had said, but I felt she was taking responsibility for why she was in foster care.

MR. PERHALLA: And when you're now aside— in the back room and the parents are done talking to her about that, is she still taking responsibility?

MS. FYLE: I, I think she understood when I explained to her that they were in foster care because of the spanks and because of the, because of the, you know, the welts that were left on her, ah, those aren't the terms I used with her but, um, because of that, you know, that's, that's the reason why she was in foster care, it wasn't because she told and I reminded her that it's always important to tell the truth.

MR. PERHALLA: And that comforted her not to worry about it?

MS. FYLE: It, it appeared so.

MR. PERHALLA: You did draft a report?

MS. FYLE: Yes I did.

MR. PERHALLA: I'm going to show you what's been marked as Exhibit #5. Can you identify that document?

MS. FYLE: Yeah this is my, um, my initial investigation report from this incident, from March 11th of '08.

MR. PERHALLA: And that's your work?

MS. FYLE: Yes.

MR. PERHALLA: Other than what I believe Ms. Huttunen, Ms. Huttunen said she added to?

MS. FYLE: Yes. Some of the contacts were done by my co-worker Gary Olkonen, because he was the one that was on-clal; and then went basically from her to Ontonagon and then Ms. Huttunen, some of the contacts are from her and her involvement from, from Hancock to Ontonagon.

MR. PERHALLA: And that's a document you prepared and reports your business with DHS.

MS. FYLE: Yes. We prepare these after every investigation that we do.

MR. PERHALLA: Your Honor, I'd move to admit it.

MR. FINDLAY: I'd object your Honor.

THE COURT: On the basis of?

MR. FINDLAY: Hearsay, the same way the police report doesn't, didn't admit it into evidence, because full of hearsay, this is the same thing.

THE COURT: What; what's the number on that by the way; five?

COURT REPORTER: Five.

THE COURT: Response?

MR. PERHALLA: That's a business record. She kept it in there.

THE COURT: But I mean there, what we just heard, I don't know what's in it, I didn't read it, but if we just heard there may be levels of hearsay of Mr. Olkonen's situation, maybe in there, I'm not, I'm not going to allow the admission at this time. Counsel wants to bring it up again tomorrow morning before we get into Court with some authority for the exception, then we'll deal with it then.

MR. PERHALLA: Yes, thanks your Honor.

THE COURT: And again, the jury should not concern itself with my legal rulings on what comes in or out. You'll be given the things that are appropriate.

MR. PERHALLA: That's all I have your Honor.

And with that, the court recessed for the day. Thank God, day three was over!

—Chapter Twenty-One—

The Trial—Day Four

At long last, we had reached day four, in what we knew would be the final day of this trial. After all, this judge had predetermined that, and emphasized strongly each and every day the importance of wrapping this up in this time frame, so he would be able to attend to his more important matters.

Knowing this to be the case, and knowing the type of jurors we had listening to our case, it seemed pointless to be going through all the charades of this trial. But we were to have one redeeming experience on this day, watching Elizabeth Fyle squirm under the questioning of our lawyer. After some discussion of procedures to be legally implemented for the day, it was time for Ms. Fyle to face the music under questioning by our lawyer:

MR. FINDLAY: Ms. Fyle, isn't it true that you either have, or do refer to yourself, as the terminator?

MS. FYLE: That's not true.

MR. FINDLAY: Didn't you admit to Naomi Kauppi on a previous court hearing you used that term?

MS. FYLE: I did not. I did not use that term.

MR. FINDLAY: Do other people use it about you?

MS. FYLE: It is, it has been used in black humor, yes.

MS. WITTLA: Objection your Honor, the relevancy of this line of questioning, this is not a termination case.

MR. FINDLAY: If it applies to the witness—

THE COURT:— true, but it does look biased, so, and I think we've gotten through it.

MR. FINDLAY: Um, you said it's been used as black humor?

MS. FYLE: Yes.

MR. FINDLAY: Do you think that termination of parental rights is a humorous topic?

MS. FYLE: No, I believe it's a black humorous topic; it's a topic that is so awful to think of that someone is going to lose their parental rights that you have to almost make light of it because of the awfulness of it.

Wow! Can you believe what this woman just said? If something is that awful, the last thing in the world you would ever want to do is make light of it! So it seemed very apparent to me, at this point, that she truly enjoyed the title she had been given, and that kidnapping for the state was a sheer joy for her!

MR. FINDLAY: So you think it's something that should be made light of?

MS. FYLE: I don't think it's something that should be made light of.

MR. FINDLAY: But it has been made light of?

MS. FYLE: In a black—

MR. FINDLAY:— When you say black, it's still, it's still humor, right?

MS. FYLE: I don't find it humorous.

At least when you are under fire in this court room, right? I'd love to have heard your remarks at your victory celebration later, however!

MR. FINDLAY: Um, is there anything wrong with a parent not wanting a child to be interviewed by CPS outside of their presence?

MS. FYLE: Is there anything wrong with it?

MR. FINDLAY: Yes.

MS. FYLE: I guess, I, I don't, I don't understand what you're asking?

MR. FINDLAY: Is there anything wrong with a parent not wanting their child to be interviewed by CPS, Child Protective Services, you, and other workers, outside of the parents' presence?

MS. FYLE: I don't know why they would have a problem with it.

You don't? You don't? What kind of lie is that? Here we are, fighting for our lives to keep our children because you invent things and you don't know why a parent would have a problem with it! That is total and complete bull! I can give you case after case, excluding my own, what has happened to parents because they let CPS in the door without their lawyer present! The first thing I tell people now is if CPS ever comes smiling to your door— don't let them in! Their favorite trick, once inside, is to observe your house and write down any small thing they see to insert into their report! Never, I repeat never, let them in your house!

MR. FINDLAY: So you think that any parent should have no problem with their child being interviewed by government agents without them being there to see what happens?

MS. FYLE: Yes.

MR. FINDLAY: So if you wanted to come talk to my kids, I mean, my daughter's not very far from here, she's eleven years old, you want to go talk to her about something, somebody doesn't like me, said something about me, you think you— it's— I'm, I'm in the wrong if I don't let you go talk to her without me there?

MS. FYLE: I could see where you— maybe somebody would not like the fact that the child is interviewed; but do I think that their child should be able to be interviewed? Yes, I do.

Right! So there you have it parents! CPS 101, which says the state— not you— owns your children!

MR. FINDLAY: So you think that unfair access to people's children (is ok), correct? Any time you hear something, you should have unfair access to go talk to their children without them intervening, without them objecting, basically the door should be open and you should be able to—

MS. FYLE:— I believe if allegations of abuse or neglect have been made, um, I believe that is my job to go and interview children outside of the presence of the alleged perpetrators to ensure that child's safety, to see, in fact, if what has been alleged did or did not happen.

MR. FINDLAY: I understand what you believe your job is. That's not what I'm asking. You understand, I'm not asking that?

MS. FYLE: Okay.

MR. FINDLAY: I'm asking, from your perspective, on, on how a parent reacts to you doing your job?

MS. FYLE: I guess I can't respond for every parent.

MR. FINDLAY: Um, is it true that the court taking jurisdiction is the first step in a termination proceeding— correct?

MS. FYLE: It's also the first step in reunification.

MR. FINDLAY: But nobody's rights are terminated until that there's been— a jurisdiction has been obtained, correct?

MS. FYLE: That is the first step, yes.

MR. FINDLAY: I guess I'm, from your testimony previously, it appears to me, and correct me if I'm wrong, that you don't truly, you don't understand the difference between DHS's policy and family's rights, do you?

MS. FYLE: I don't understand what you're asking.

MR. FINDLAY: Well there's a difference between your policy that says that you have to go interview children without their parents being present, and what the law is, isn't there?

MS. FYLE: I don't know specifically what are you matching up? I don't know what you're matching up; I mean, which, which policy and which law?

MR. FINDLAY: Well if a parent objects to you interviewing a child without their being present, what do you have to do?

MS. FYLE: If a parent is suspected as a perpetrator of child abuse and neglect; the law says that we must interview children outside of their presence. And so, if the parents will not allow us to do so, then we would request a court order to have the child interviewed outside their parents' presence.

You know, here is a point that was never brought up in any of the court hearings we went through, nor in this trial: Why does this interview need to be done immediately, without taking the time to first acquire a suitable site for it, then contacting the parents to see if they wish to have representation and/or a recorded verification of such an interview (meaning a taped verification, not some dumb bimbo's notes)? You can't tell me the danger is any more imminent, because you can have it all set up ahead of time, before bringing parents in on it. And why does this need to be done in such haste, before ever taking the time to look into the backgrounds or possible motives of those making the accusations?

MR. FINDLAY: Right, so that parents have a right to refuse that you're interviewing the child outside of their presence; and then you have to go to court to get a judge or a magistrate or somebody, hopefully independent to, to make a decision and look at the allegation and say, "You know what, I can allow this to happen; or no, I'm not going to allow this to happen." There's oversight?

MS. FYLE: Correct.

MR. FINDLAY: And so parents in general—oversight— aren't they— or do you not think they should—they don't (deserve) some oversight?

MS. FYLE: I guess what; what oversight; as far as have a judge make the decision?

MR. FINDLAY: Yeah.

MS. FYLE: I think that's fine.

MR. FINDLAY: But in fact you told the Colemans if they didn't let you interview Caitlyn alone, you'd get a court order to take away their children, didn't you?

MS. FYLE: I did not tell them that; that discussion happened outside of the room with, with Mr. Ross and them.

Oh? Not as I remember it Ms. Fyle! And incidentally, how would you know what we talked about outside the room. You were not even there!

MR. FINDLAY: The discussion that they would have their parents taken away if they didn't want them to be interviewed happened outside of the room?

MS. FYLE: No. The discussion that we would be requesting a court order to interview the children; if they fact— they did not allow it.

MR. FINDLAY: (You) tell a lot of people that if (they) don't cooperate with (you) that you will take their children away?

MS. FYLE: No, it's not true at all.

MR. FINDLAY: Well, all reports I hear of you saying that are false?

MS. FYLE: They must be.

MR. FINDLAY: All right. Bobby and Becky Payne. Um, they were the people who reported these allegations in the petition to you, weren't they?

MS. FYLE: No.

MR. FINDLAY: Who reported them to you?

MS. FYLE: I can't disclose the referral source.

MR. FINDLAY: So that's a secret that nobody else gets to know?

MS. FYLE: The judge can order me to disclose it, but I, by law, I can't disclose the referral source.

MR. FINDLAY: The petition doesn't say there was a disclosure by anybody else, does it? Does it? It doesn't say un-named source came in and told us?

MS. FYLE: No, the petition does not say that.

MR. FINDLAY: Okay, the petition actually says, um, on 3-11-08, DHS received a referral of physical abuse to the children by Robert and Janet Coleman; Robby or Bobby, Robert and Bobby, ah, Robert or Bobby and Rebecca were interviewed in regard to these allegations as they recently lived in the home.

MS. FYLE: Yes, I knew they recently lived in the home and I—

MR. FINDLAY:— So you're saying it wasn't Bobby and Becky that reported these allegations?

MS. FYLE: Correct.

MR. FINDLAY: But you can't tell us who it was?

MS. FYLE: Correct, unless I'm court ordered to do so.

MR. FINDLAY (to the judge): Will you order her to tell us who reported this?

THE COURT: Let's reserve that issue till the close of the—when we're at the end of her testimony—and then if counsel want to bring it up, we'll talk about it, out of sight of the presence, because it's a legal issue.

There you have it! I had just been denied my constitutional rights by this judge! I should have been given this information, so that I could face my accuser, before this trial ever began! And now, asked point blankly to name my accuser, he still refused! And who was it he did not want this to be heard in the presence of? The jury? They, after all, have the right to know also who the real accuser is! So they selectively kept this from the jury, which again, violates my basic rights!

MR. FINDLAY: So you can start these things on anonymous tips, right?

MS. FYLE: Yes.

MR. FINDLAY: You don't have a problem with that?

MS. FYLE: No I don't.

Of course not! She loves her nickname of the terminator and the money-hungry state loves an employee like her! The only time she would have a problem with this type of activity is if somebody did it to her! Well, I don't know about you, but I am a big believer in this thing called karma, and I fully believe that she, as well as all of these state workers, will see their day in court as well.

MR. FINDLAY: You're the heck out of me that you think it's okay!

MS. WITTLA: Objection! Counsel is commenting.....

MR. FINDLAY: I withdraw the question....

MS. WITTLA: ... commenting on the evidence again.

THE COURT: Yeah, now that— actually, both sides have objected to that and both sides have commented.

Please don't comment on the evidence, just ask the questions.

MR. FINDLAY: All right, so (you) interviewed, um, Bobby and Becky Payne together—correct?

MS. FYLE: Yes I did.

MR. FINDLAY: So that way they keep their stories straight, correct?

MS. FYLE: I would not agree with that.

Of course you would not! And you also would not agree that, since you too, are a witness, Ms. Fyle, you should not be sitting with the prosecution this entire trial either, right? And it would seem, likewise, to keep your story straight. Why is it you could do this, where no other witness could?

MR. FINDLAY: You didn't do any kind of checking to see what, what kind of people they were, did you?

MS. FYLE: At that point in time, no, I did not.

There you have it! No matter what kind of character they might or might not be, this state jumps at the opportunity to go after someone, based solely on accusations. As a defendant, you are automatically guilty until proven innocent— in a complete reversal of what the constitution and the bill of rights allegedly provide! And in so doing this, the state hides the name of the person who files the complaint in the first place, using second-hand information from the un-named complainant to make up a petition. And then, this same person wants us to believe what she says is true because that is her job! Seems to me her job is to bring false cases against parents, using baseless information as her means of propelling a case into something much larger than what is in fact, reality!

MR. FINDLAY: And actually, you basically believed everything they told you and then set out trying to get evidence to support that conclusion didn't you?

MS. FYLE: I took their information, as information they provided and I set forth to see, as I testified yesterday, if I could put the pieces of the puzzle together, did everything coincide with what I was— with what I was originally told in the allegations.

Or maybe you simply didn't believe them, but found the allegations fit for pursuing another state kidnapping, even if they were not true?

MR. FINDLAY: You didn't go to Caitlyn's school first, did you?

MS. FYLE: No, because I, I had previously found out that she attended morning kindergarten and this would have been in the early afternoon; so I knew she would not be at school.

In that case, Ms. Fyle, why the urgency? Why not wait until morning? You used the lame excuse that you used my daughter's bedroom because you had no place private to do the interview, but being the hypocrite you are, suggested in the same breath that the school is private enough. You could still have done your surprise interview without having to confront us, as parents. Obviously, you didn't place a high priority on this, having shown your training classes were more important. The interview could have waited. You could have met all your own standards, not having to use my daughter's bedroom with all of it's distractions, without parental confrontation by simply waiting to do this interview the next morning.

MR. FINDLAY: Okay, and, and you didn't; so you had time to— the allegations were first reported to you on the 11th—right?

MS. FYLE: Correct.

MR. FINDLAY: The same date you did the interview?

MS. FYLE: Correct.

MR. FINDLAY: And what time was the interview?

MS. FYLE: I don't recall at the top of my head— with, with you, Caitlyn, or Bobby and Becky?

MR. FINDLAY: Caitlyn.

MS. FYLE: It was in the early afternoon, I don't recall exactly the time.

MR. FINDLAY: And you had an interview with Bobby and Becky Payne?

MS. FYLE: Previous to that.

MR. FINDLAY: That morning?

MS. FYLE: I don't recall the time.

MR. FINDLAY: But it's that day?

MS. FYLE: It was on the 11th, yes.

MR. FINDLAY: So other than Bobby and Becky Payne, you didn't do any investigation before going to interview Caitlyn, did you?

MS. FYLE: As, as—

MR. FINDLAY: You didn't have time to—

MS. FYLE: ... as far as what are you asking now, what did I do, I mean, I found out Caitlyn was in morning kindergarten.

MR. FINDLAY: Okay, I'm talking about on the allegations that were made in the petition you didn't do any investigation other than talking to Bobby and Becky Payne, correct?

MS. FYLE: That was, that was the first thing that you said I did, you.

MR. FINDLAY: And then you went directly to interview Caitlyn outside of the presence of her parents?

MS. FYLE: Correct.

MR. FINDLAY: You didn't call the Colemans at first to have them come in and talk to you, did you?

MS. FYLE: No, I did not.

MR. FINDLAY: I mean, you wrote the petition, you wrote this— right?

MS. FYLE: Yes I did.

MR. FINDLAY: So in other words, it's, it's your version or your claim of what happened— correct?

MS. FYLE: That is the information that was presented to me.

MR. FINDLAY: Okay, that's what you claim is, I mean, these are your; your clients, right?

MS. FYLE: They are the allegations to the petition. I mean, they were what was told to me and then I, I wrote it out in, in allegation form.

MR. FINDLAY: Can you explain to us what an allegation is?

MS. FYLE: An allegation is information provided of a situation.

MR. FINDLAY: Anybody (can) allege anything, can't they?

MS. FYLE: Sure.

MR. FINDLAY: And you have no personal knowledge of the underlying allegations, do you?

MS. FYLE: What do you mean?

MR. FINDLAY: I mean you didn't see any of these incidents happen, did you?

MS. FYLE: No I didn't.

MR. FINDLAY: These alleged incidents; I mean, you didn't see, you'd never seen, have you ever seen other than until this case started; have you seen the Colemans discipline their children?

MS. FYLE: No, I did not. Me, myself, no I did not.

MR. FINDLAY: Did you have; now do understand the word you. Why do you say me, myself, and I. I'm asking if you had that personal information?

MS. FYLE: I responded no I had not.

MR. FINDLAY: Okay but then you tried to slip in the me, myself, and I, implying that there is somebody else that has.

MS. FYLE: There have been previous allegations that other people have witnessed such things.

Who, Ms. Fyle? When? Where? Name them? You can't do it! Unless it is your mystery complainant, who probably does not exist in the first place! I challenge you now, Ms. Fyle—years after this case was closed— tell us who!

MR. FINDLAY: Would you agree that children are susceptible to the power of suggestion; especially young children?

MS. FYLE: Depends on the circumstance.

MR. FINDLAY: Would you agree that children can be very suggest— very susceptible to the power of suggestion?

MS. FYLE: Depends on the circumstance; depends on the child. I, I wouldn't say that it is a general rule.

Well I would! Any parent will tell you they are very susceptible to this! I don't know a child that isn't!

MR. FINDLAY: Why do they have the Forensic Protocol Interview if that's not true? If, if children are not susceptible to the power of suggestion; or being led or being encouraged, or being coached or whatever; why have a Forensic Protocol Interview; what's the point of it?

MS. FYLE: I believe the point of it is to ensure that children are allowed to tell their story; that they're not asked leading questions; that they're not asked or— questions; that they're not—

MR. FINDLAY: ... And why not ask those?

MS. FYLE: Because you want the children to be able to tell their information without, you know, a yes or no question, without a, you know, and then this happened right, ah-ha.

Pardon my ignorance, Ms. Fyle— what does "ah-ha" mean?

MR. FINDLAY: Right, exactly, so, so they are susceptible to the power of suggestion; you can get a child to say and this happened didn't it? And it's more likely that a young child that they're going to yes or tell you what you want to hear than an adult, isn't it?

MS. FYLE: Again it depends on the child, depends on the adult.

MR. FINDLAY: But why do they have this? If that, if that's not a recent— about children, why not the Protocol Interview if they're not susceptible to suggestion?

MS. FYLE: Again, because you want the children to be able to tell you all their information open-ended and give you their free narrative about what's going on.

MR. FINDLAY: And would you agree that many young children do have a tendency to tell an adult what they want to hear?

MS. FYLE: It can happen, that's why we use the Forensic Interviewing Protocol

MR. FINDLAY: But in this interview, you; you introduced the subject of discipline, didn't you?

MS. FYLE: I, I asked Caitlyn, tell me what happens when you get in trouble.

MR. FINDLAY: Right, so you introduced the topic of discipline; you didn't— okay, Caitlyn didn't bring it up by herself, you introduced it? And so in fact, you were in control of this interview, correct?

MS. FYLE: I wouldn't agree with that, I would say Caitlyn was in control of telling me what she wanted to.

MR. FINDLAY: And when you say, I remember on direct— her when well, whatever direct it was, um, you said that it wasn't a topic that you didn't— that you wanted to cover. I, I forget what the topic, but you indicated that it wasn't a topic that I, you know, intended to cover, do you remember saying that on direct?

MS. FYLE: Not, not specific, you have to give me; I'd have to listen to it.

MR. FINDLAY: I don't have to listen to it, I assume that the record has it, at a point when you were testifying, I believe on Ms. Wittla's questions, when she asked if you asked about something else, and you said that was not a topic that I wanted to cover, or something about you didn't choose the idea topic…

MS. FYLE: …. I, I'd have to hear what the questions were and the response; I don't know.

MR. FINDLAY: The point is though, you controlled the topics, correct?

MS. FYLE: Well, I, I guess per the Forensic Interviewing Protocol, we introduce the topic from what the allegations, I mean, what the allegations are; we kind of open up the door; can you tell me about this and we allow the child to tell what they do or don't want to tell us.

MR. FINDLAY: So the adult introduces the topics to the child, correct?

MS. FYLE: Right in a general open-ended, can you tell about whatever.

MR. FINDLAY: And then in, when you asked her that the first time, you know, what happens when you get in trouble, um, she only answered that she goes to the corner?

MS. FYLE: Correct.

MR. FINDLAY: That wasn't enough to make your case though, was it? I mean you, you wouldn't be in here if that's all that she had told you, you wouldn't be in here would you?

MS. FYLE: Correct.

MR. FINDLAY: So the corner wasn't the right answer, was it?

MS. FYLE: It was the right answer; that is a form of discipline that she had been used or been; had been used with her.

MR. FINDLAY: But you communicated to Caitlyn it wasn't the right answer, didn't you?

MS. FYLE: I would not agree with that; I asked her if anything could happen when she's in trouble.

MR. FINDLAY: Right. Doesn't that suggest to a child that you took, I asked you what happened when you get in trouble; I, I'm a child, you asked me what do I, you know, what happens when you get in trouble; I say I go in the corner. And then you respond with another question to me saying well, what else happens; even to myself I think obviously that's not the answer that she's looking for….

MS. FYLE: Uh-huh; I didn't ask….

MR. FINDLAY: She… she wants more.

MS. FYLE: Okay, I didn't ask her did anything else happen, I said could anything else happen when you are in trouble; and some, I, I— suggest that she could have said no, I just go to the corner. If that was all that happened, that's all she would have told me.

MR. FINDLAY: But you asked the question, what else happens when you get in trouble, correct?

MS. FYLE: Not specifically that question, no.

MR. FINDLAY: Well what question did you ask? Do you have it written down somewhere so we could see what you asked?

MS. FYLE: I don't know if I wrote the exact question, but I wouldn't have asked her specifically, what else happens; I would've asked her could, could something else happen.

Ok, stop right here! There is a big difference between could something else happen and did something else happen. Ms. Fyle just admitted she asked could something else happen. Now since Bobby and Becky were always talking about giving her the belt, but it never happened, in her mind, if asked could it happen, her response could quite easily be that it could—but not that it did! Ms. Fyle, it would appear, took it upon herself to interpret that type of response to mean it did— and that would have come directly from Bobby and Becky, not from Caitlyn! Caitlyn will tell you today that it did not happen, which is the truth. But when an investigator wants to bring a charge, let not the truth stand in the way!

MR. FINDLAY: Let's go off on that question. There is no record of this interview is there? Other than what you're testifying to right here?

MS. FYLE: What? What do you mean? Record a tape?

MR. FINDLAY: I mean it wasn't recorded.

MS. FYLE: It was not recorded.

MR. FINDLAY: It wasn't transcribed. Nobody was there taking notes and writing down the questions and answers?

MS. FYLE: I, I wrote down the information that Caitlyn told me as she told me it, and then I transcribed that into my report.

MR. FINDLAY: You wrote it down verbatim?

MS. FYLE: I used quotes, and then I, and then ....

MR. FINDLAY: And what?

Go ahead, Ms. Fyle, you can tell him! You edited it! Tell him!

MS. FYLE: So the quoted information that's in the petition, those are specifically quotes from Caitlyn.

MR. FINDLAY: But the quote information is stuff that you put in your own words, right? Like when you say that Caitlyn confirmed something, that's; she didn't—

MS. FYLE: ... that's my word, right.

MR. FINDLAY: Caitlyn didn't say that word, right?

MS. FYLE: Right.

MR. FINDLAY: You wouldn't agree that when you would say to a child, if you asked one question and they give you an answer, you disagree that if you ask them another on the same topic, you're not communicating to that child that the answer they gave wasn't what you wanted to hear?

MS. FYLE: I would disagree with, with that.

MR. FINDLAY: But then that wasn't all done, when you also said tell me more about that?

MS. FYLE: Uh-huh.

MR. FINDLAY: Wouldn't you agree that that communicated to Caitlyn that the belt stuff was the right answer? You didn't say tell me more about the corner; tell me more about the belt, right?

MS. FYLE: I, I didn't specifically say tell me more about the belt.

MR. FINDLAY: After she told you about the belt.

MS. FYLE: Yeah.

MR. FINDLAY: And you said she told you about the belt, right?

MS. FYLE: Yeah. I didn't limit it to the belt; I said tell me more about that, and then what happens.

Wait! Ms. Fyle! Ms. Fyle! You just contradicted yourself again! You just said you asked her "what could happen"—and now you are going back to your desired version of "what happens". Let's get it right!

MR. FINDLAY: You're dealing with a six year old.

MS. FYLE: Uh-huh.

MR. FINDLAY: I, again, you asked the first question what happens when you get in trouble; she tells nothing, that would be abusive; you say well, what else happens, and then she tells you something, you claim she tells you something that is abusive; then you tell me more about that, what does the child think that you're asking about except the previous question, the previous answer?

MS. FYLE: I don't know. I would, I would guess she was thinking; was, would be thinking I'm asking her about she's already previously told me.

MR. FINDLAY: About the belt, right?

MS. FYLE: Or the corner.

You would guess? Guess? But it really doesn't matter, does it Ms. Fyle, because you will incorporate it all into your report to match what you allegedly heard with the lies and distortions of Bobby and Becky, won't you? It makes a much better case that way!

MR. FINDLAY: Okay, we turned a little bit. But in (allegation) 53, you said Caitlyn also confirmed the story being smacked for not eating her rice.

MS. FYLE: Yes.

MR. FINDLAY: You don't have the quotes about that, do you?

MS. FYLE: I don't believe they're quoted, I must....

MR. FINDLAY: ... and that's not her answer to that, or that's not written down anywhere is it?

MS. FYLE: What do you mean?

MR. FINDLAY: What she said that made you, that you turned into Caitlyn also confirmed the story of being smacked for not eating the rice; I mean, that's not written, that response didn't get written down here; you don't know what the response was, do you?

MS. FYLE: Verbatim, no.

There you go! And that coincides with what Caitlyn says today about that! She laughed when she heard that claim was made, saying to me, "Daddy, I loved rice!" And as I said earlier, at six years of age, she had never used or heard the word smacked. That came directly from Bobby and Becky.

MR. FINDLAY: Right. Wouldn't you think that would be helpful to have that verbatim? We wouldn't— I, I, I, we'd have, I wouldn't be asking you these questions if you had a record of what was said; there wouldn't be any question whether you, we'd all get to listen to it and say, you know what, here's what the kid said.

MS. FYLE: I do have a—

MR. FINDLAY: But you set this up in a situation where we have no alternative but to either believe you or disbelieve you, right?

MS. FYLE: I did; I do have a record and the record is my report and the petition, and that is what Caitlyn said.

Because you say so? Why are you so afraid of using a tape recorder, Ms. Fyle? I did it! Oh! But damn me! The state has to put a stop to that, don't they? I might edit something! But you wouldn't— would you Ms. Fyle? I have learned that the best way to know when someone in the government is lying, is when they say trust me!

MR. FINDLAY: She said, how did she say, she say, well, I confirm your story of, of the story of getting smacked for not eating rice, she said that?

MS. FYLE: No.

MR. FINDLAY: Um, Bobby and Becky Payne are the ones that told you about the belts, right?

MS. FYLE: They did tell me that— about the belts, yes they did.

MR. FINDLAY: So when you went in to interview Caitlyn, you were looking for confirmation of what you already decided what happened, weren't you?

MS. FYLE: No. I was looking for other puzzle pieces to see if in fact, what I already had been told was truthful or not.

MR. FINDLAY: Exact. I, you said it for me, you referred to it as pieces of a puzzle; so to use your analogy you had a puzzle to complete, right?

MS. FYLE: Or not.

MR. FINDLAY: And a puzzle, you have, you get the box and it shows you what the picture is, so you know what the outcome is; you just got to find the right pieces to make that picture, right? Isn't (that) a puzzle?

MS. FYLE: It is, but I, um, in many cases we get— we (are) presented with allegations, and we go out and the puzzle never (is) built because whatever's been alleged doesn't fall into place; it doesn't; it's, it either has never happened, it's not happened the way it's been reported, etc., etc. So there are many cases where it just doesn't come together.

MR. FINDLAY: You'd agree this isn't the preferred way of doing a Forensic Protocol Interview?

MS. FYLE: Which way?

MR. FINDLAY: The way you did it.

MS. FYLE: Which way? In Caitlyn's bedroom?

MR. FINDLAY: Yeah.

MS. FYLE: I guess I, I was comfortable if that was the, my best option at the time—

It wasn't. Your best option was the school, which could have waited until morning. Except, of course, you were so anxious and excited to go after Robert Coleman that it would not wait until morning, would it Ms. Fyle?

MR. FINDLAY: It's not the—

MS. WITTLA: Objection your Honor, would the attorney please allow the witness to answer the questions?

Oh, what's the matter Ms. Wittla? Are we getting a little too close to the truth? And is that making you and your assassination team a little uncomfortable? Try and help them out here, judge!

THE COURT: Yeah. We're getting a little close to that overlapping of the question and please, please give her a chance to answer and go ahead with the next question.

MR. FINDLAY: It's not the preferred way according to the— the Protocol— is it?

MS. FYLE: To interview a child in their bedroom?

MR. FINDLAY: Right.

MS. FYLE: You know the, the Protocol, um, how do I; could explain this; I would say the Protocol has flexibility based off of the circumstances that you're presented with. Um, is it the preferred way? Probably not, um, they do recommend that if, if you have a Forensic Interviewing Center, for instance, that that be used if possible. We don't have such a thing here.

But you do have a school, don't you? (smile)

MR. FINDLAY: Under now who knows what version I have, but I, um, if there's a change, feel free—let me know, um, under the physical site, the best environment for conducting the Forensic Interviews, the center is typically equipped for this purpose, correct?

MS. FYLE: Correct. And we don't have one.

But you do have a school! Oh! But frying Robert won't wait until morning, will it?

MR. FINDLAY: So, so an interview in a child's bathroom— bedroom— is not the way to conduct a Forensic Protocol Interview, right?

MS. FYLE: I would agree.

MR. FINDLAY: So you, a stranger to Caitlyn; Bob Ross, a stranger to Caitlyn; a uniformed police officer who I'm—I'm assuming is a stranger to Caitlyn; show up at their house and separate her from her parents; um, is that the preferred fair way of making a child comfortable with an interview?

MS. FYLE: I believe we introduced ourselves when we were there, and I said, Caitlyn, I'm Elizabeth, can you come and talk to me for a little bit? And I said, and then, I don't remember who I asked, but eventually we were able to figure it out anyways that we would be able to use her bedroom as a, as a quiet and separate place in the home.

MR. FINDLAY: That, that wasn't my question, was it? Was that the preferred way of making a child comfortable?

MS. FYLE: Is, it what the preferred way?

Are you sure you ever graduated from college Ms. Fyle? Or even grade school? Even Caitlyn would be able to understand this question from my lawyer!

MR. FINDLAY: What I— two strangers and a uniformed police officer showing up at the house, separating a child from her parents in a bedroom in the house and then questioning her? Is that the preferred way of making a child comfortable?

MS. FYLE: I believe I did make her comfortable.

MR. FINDLAY: If somebody did that to your child would you think that would be a good way to make them comfortable?

MS. FYLE: It would depend on what they chose to do; if they introduced themselves and were friendly to them, then maybe my child would be comfortable with talking with somebody; I don't know.

MR. FINDLAY: This doesn't qualify as a neutral location, does it?

MS. FYLE: It was a separate and private location in the home; what do you mean by neutral, I guess?

MR. FINDLAY: You don't— you don't know what neutral means?

Let me see if I can help her out here Mr. Findlay. Using Webster's Standard Dictionary, the word neutral is defined as not supporting either position in a controversy; unbiased or disinterested. Caitlyn understands the meaning of that word Ms. Fyle! What grade did you actually make it through?

MS. FYLE: It, I guess I don't know specifically what—

MR. FINDLAY: I thought you guys were familiar with the Forensic Protocol Interview; that's where I got the word that— so you don't know what that means, in your own Protocol?

MS. FYLE: I guess I'm not; I don't know what you mean by neutral?

MR. FINDLAY: Well, how does it mean in the, in the Forensic Protocol Interview?

MS. FYLE: I would say a neutral location is a, is a neutral location that is comfortable for the child, that is away from alleged perpetrators.

And comfortable, using your definition, is pulled away from her parents with two strangers and a cop with a gun— right?

MR. FINDLAY: There's not supposed to be noise and disruption, is there?

MS. FYLE: No.

MR. FINDLAY: And, in fact, there was for this one, right?

MS. FYLE: There was.

MR. FINDLAY: Also, aren't you supposed to avoid playrooms or other locations with visible toys and books that distract children?

MS. FYLE: If you can, yes.

MR. FINDLAY: And you were in her bedroom?

MS. FYLE: Yes.

MR. FINDLAY: That's not been qualified as that, does it?

MS. FYLE: There were toys in her bedroom.

MR. FINDLAY: And actually it says, interviews should not be conducted in a child's home.

MS. FYLE: If you can help it, yes, they should not be.

You could have helped it— by waiting until morning and going to her school. Oh! Damn! I keep forgetting! You can't fry Robert so soon if you do that though! I must get my (or your) priorities straight!

MS. WITTLA: Could you tell me what page you're on?

Oh! Yeah, that's right! Ms. Wittla gave you the wrong book on purpose Mr. Findlay, so now she can't track with you as you go through the pages of the book she gave you!

MR. FINDLAY: Well you gave me the book; five, page five.....

Judge! Judge! Help! Help!

THE COURT: .... But you are reading from it, so please give her the reference.

MR. FINDLAY: Pardon me?

THE COURT: You are reading from it, so it's not unreasonable to ask for the page reference. Maybe it matches what she has.

Then again, maybe it doesn't! In fact, it probably doesn't, which would explain why she is passing out old versions of the protocol book to defense lawyers when new ones are used by her and have been available for years! It gives her an advantage if she needs to use it in court! It's the type of corrupt activity that should also get her disbarred.

MR. FINDLAY: (To the judge) Well, I thought she was supposed to address you. That's fine. Page five of this— this book that I have. (Continuing then with Ms. Fyle) Doesn't it also say, now I realize that she's, that she wasn't near you, but doesn't it say you should avoid the wearing of uniforms or having—it's on page six of the interview guidelines, having guns visible during the interview?

MS. FYLE: There were no guns visible to Caitlyn during the interview; the officer stayed out in the living room area, and we went into Caitlyn's bedroom; Mr. Ross and myself.

Whew! Well that's got to make a kid feel better, knowing that the guns are in the next room! They have, of course, already seen them!

MR. FINDLAY: The uniformed officer showed up and she was wearing a gun I'm presuming?

MS. FYLE: She was, right. She's not part of the interview.

Did you tell Caitlyn that? It would seem to me she would be thinking if she did not provide the correct answers that you might shoot her parents!

MR. FINDLAY: Why didn't you record this interview?

MS. FYLE: I didn't have a recorder with me at the time.

Yeah. There was no time to stop and get one because she was in the process of launching her invasion of our home, so she could more quickly go after me! Keep in mind this attack (I mean interview) could not wait until morning! Aside from the fact that those damned taped recorders can be used to reveal the truth!

MR. FINDLAY: Why is it DHS is apparently opposed to getting contact with being recorded?

MS. FYLE: I guess my, my personal concerns about recording, um, made without my knowledge would be, again, that they can be edited, sunbathed, altered.

MR. FINDLAY: If you go ahead, I didn't mean to interrupt you.

MS. FYLE: So that would be my personal concern, unless I'm aware that I'm being recorded and that I'm going to be provided with an accurate copy of the recording that has been made of me; that would be my concern.

Hmmmm... then since you would have been the one making the recording in this instance, one might think you would have been assured you got a fair copy, right? I fail to understand how you could conduct a raid (I mean interview) without bringing along your recorder, so you would have proof of what was actually said— unless, maybe you don't want that proof!

MR. FINDLAY: Um, there's been a little bit of the You Tube stuff?

MS. FYLE: Yes.

MR. FINDLAY: There is absolutely no evidence that these recordings had been— I mean they're been put up in a place you don't like and that kind of stuff; I, I have yet to hear a claim, if you're aware of them, that somebody's voice has been altered, changed; they, you know, been made to say something they didn't say; that hasn't happened has it?

MS. FYLE: I don't believe the entire conversations of every, every portion of every conversation has been played on You Tube, so I believe that certain parts have been chopped off. I believe only what the Colemans have wanted people to hear over You Tube has been presented.

Not correct. Granted it can't all be on there. Any idiot understands that. But as to our fear of someone hearing the rest? No fear. We make it available to anyone who wants to listen to it all. It's on the links to my website. So Fyle again, has tried to invent something that is a total lie and fabrication, but I've got her here, as it is available to anyone wanting to hear it all.

MR. FINDLAY: But you have all of it now don't you?

MS. FYLE: I don't personally know.

No, you don't know! And since you don't, you should keep your big trap shut! Talk about only matters you do know about or understand!

MR. FINDLAY: Are you aware the state of Florida gives parents a right to record interviews, visits and any other contact with—

MS. WITTLA: Objection your Honor, the relevancy of the state of Florida's practices.

THE COURT: Yeah, this isn't the state of Florida, but I guess as a general concept, just ask, if you could answer that question.

MS. FYLE: I have no clue of Florida's rules and regulations are.

MR. FINDLAY: Um, are you aware that GM in a different court in Michigan had recommended that parents be allowed to record such things?

MS. FYLE: I have no knowledge of that.

MR. FINDLAY: You aware that they did that precisely because there were different perceptions of the events coming out?

MS. FYLE: I, I don't know about that.

MR. FINDLAY: Don't you think it would be a good idea to have recordings of these things so we would; so everybody else besides the people there could decide, it's not a matter of they, they said, they said; wouldn't that be helpful?

MS. FYLE: I could see where at times it could be helpful, if, like I said, if everybody's provided with an accurate copy and a complete copy, and everybody's aware that they are being recorded at the time.

MR. FINDLAY: Did you, didn't you say that the petition, or you said the petition had everything in it that Caitlyn said?

MS. FYLE: It had, it had all the allegations that were of concern to this case; it doesn't have everything this and or the that she said no. It is not a transcript of her interview.

MR. FINDLAY: So in other words, you edited; you edited it, right?

MS. FYLE: I put the allegations of the petition, in the petition.

MR. FINDLAY: You... and that would be a form of editing, wouldn't it? She's told you something, and you decided what to put in the petition?

MS. FYLE: I could see where you would say that, yes.

MR. FINDLAY: Okay, so aren't you kind of, ah, guilty is the wrong word, but aren't you, done saying a thing if you (are) accusing and afraid of what the Colemans are going to do to you?

MS. FYLE: I could see where you might say that, yes.

MR. FINDLAY: And you didn't put it in the claim, your claim, like when Caitlyn said don't tell my parents about what I said, did you?

MS. FYLE: That's in my report.

MR. FINDLAY: But it wasn't in the petition?

MS. FYLE: I don't, I don't recall if it was in the petition or not; if you say— you've got (it) in front of you and said it's not, it's not. It is in my report.

MR. FINDLAY: You don't; you're saying you don't recall what's in the petition?

MS. FYLE: I don't recall if every single statement that Caitlyn told me, there are some additional information that is in the report, that did not make it into the petition.

You forgot to mention that a lot of what is in the petition were not things Caitlyn told you! There wasn't enough time, in the short time you had for that interview, for Caitlyn to have told you all that was in the petition. But there was certainly ample time for you to manufacture and fabricate it in, using the allegations given to police by Bobby and Becky. It's amazing how many of those things did find their way into the petition!

MR. FINDLAY: What, um, what are the plans for the Colemans' unborn baby?

MS. WITTLA: Objection your Honor!

What is your objection based on Ms. Wittla? Are they now exposing your plans?

THE COURT: Sustained, the jury should not concern itself with anything further than this proceeding.

Oh! Then that means the character assassination against me, the case the prosecution is trying to insert as to our taking advantage of the Paynes, our reports of abuse by foster parents, among other things— none of that should be considered by them judge? Or the phony charges of manipulation that both you, judge, and the prosecutor cooked up against me, when in fact it was the system doing all of that manipulation? None of that should be considered? Okay, in that case, we would really have a child abuse case, and since all of that was based on the lies of two people, and their allegations have no substance, this case should be dismissed then, right judge?

MR. FINDLAY: It— I wasn't clear; your direct; were you planning on moving the children after the initial interview of Caitlyn?

MS. FYLE: At that point and time, when I walked out of the door, no, I was not.

MR. FINDLAY: And you didn't schedule any follow up interviews with the Colemans, did you?

MS. FYLE: I did not schedule them, no, and not at that point in time.

No, because you had to first manufacture a better story as to why you should take the kids away, right? Let's see, maybe you can pretend you are afraid we are flight risks and you can tell the judge that story. That might work.

MR. FINDLAY: Wouldn't that have been helpful? Wouldn't that have avoided this claim that they fled and, and you may have one way or the other; you, you had a second interview and said, no, we need to see Caitlyn, ah, we have training on the 12th, so it's not important for us to do it then, um, how about the 13th at two o'clock; wouldn't that have helped?

MS. FYLE: It could have.

MR. FINDLAY: And you wouldn't have this allegation that they somehow went on the lamb, would you?

MS. FYLE: I believe they did.

He didn't ask you what you believe stupid! He asked you an easy question! But you don't want to answer it do you, because you know your claim of us having fled was bogus! Try again Mr. Findlay, maybe she will answer your question this time.

MR. FINDLAY: You wouldn't have the allegation that they went on the lamb if you scheduled something, would you?

MS. FYLE: I don't know if they would have participated in it or not.

Oh! You don't know if we would have participated, so instead of scheduling something to find out, you make up a phony story instead. That is, once you followed your own plan not to schedule something. Is that how it works Ms. Fyle?

MR. FINDLAY: I'm sorry; go ahead if you want....

MS. FYLE: ... I don't know that they would have participated in another interview or not; I don't know that at this point in time, it's after the fact.

MR. FINDLAY: Right, we don't know that.

MS. FYLE: Right.

MR. FINDLAY: So you didn't give them the opportunity to do that, did you?

MS. FYLE: I did not schedule an interview with them, no I did not.

MR. FINDLAY: And actually, it would cut both ways wouldn't it; just like the recording thing, it would cut both ways; it would have been, ah, there would have been no question about the interpretation of the Colemans' actions; it would be we had an interview scheduled for this time; they didn't show up for it, right?

MS. FYLE: We did speak with the Colemans that we would be back on that, we needed to do some follow up interviews, and I was specific....

MR. FINDLAY: ... you told them that...

MS. FYLE: you're, you're correct they did not have a specific time, but they were aware that it was not; the issue was not resolved and fully complete.

MR. FINDLAY: You are not suggesting that parents have to keep you informed of their whereabouts or keep abreast of all their clients are you?

MS. FYLE: No, I'm suggesting when they've been asked where they are going to be, and they, and they misrepresent where they are; that's a concern for me.

MR. FINDLAY: Okay, you didn't talk to them, did you?

MS. FYLE: I was right next to Mr. Ross when he made the call.

MR. FINDLAY: Was it on a speaker phone?

MS. FYLE: No.

MR. FINDLAY: So you didn't talk to them, did you?

MS. FYLE: I did not talk to them. On that first conversation, I did try to call them that evening, I requested IPSD to call them a second time, and I was involved with IPSD to check out and see if they actually returned to the house.

MR. FINDLAY: So just to be straight, you didn't talk to them, correct?

MS. FYLE: When they said they were in Marquette, no, I did not have that call.

MR. FINDLAY: Okay, um, so you only know that based on what Bob Ross was telling you?

MS. FYLE: Right. He held up the phone and that's how I knew.

MR. FINDLAY: And, and, are you suggesting that, that parents have an obligation to always pick up the phone or be near a phone so they'd always get your call, your phone calls?

MS. FYLE: No, I'm suggesting that if a parent is aware that there's a current CPS investigation going on with their family, and they are aware that CPS is, is going to re-contacting them that they provide accurate information as to where they are, and that they voluntarily participate in that.

MR. FINDLAY: Did you leave messages for them?

MS. FYLE: Yes I did.

MR. FINDLAY: Did, in any of those messages, did you tell them if you don't call us we'll be getting an order to removed your children?

MS. FYLE: I did not. I, I wasn't aware if the judge would grant it or not.

MR. FINDLAY: Did you tell him that you were going to be trying to get the judge to grant it?

MS. FYLE: I did not.

MR. FINDLAY: Don't you think that might have been helpful? Maybe that would have avoided all of this?

MS. FYLE: I couldn't tell you.

Why not Ms. Fyle? Maybe because it was always your plan for this to be a surprise to the judge as well— an emergency case which would make it difficult for him to say no? In my opinion, you wanted these kids removed because your entire ring wanted them removed in order to punish Robert Coleman! So why not invent a phony story about flight, and use your phone attempts as your committed effort to try to save the kids, who were in imminent danger! God, I wonder how Caitlyn ever lived to be six years old if that danger were so imminent!

MR. FINDLAY: Well, don't you think a, a reasonable, well, would you, if you were told that, would you then say no, we better get down there, I don't want to have my kids removed?

MS. FYLE: I probably would have called back the first time.

MR. FINDLAY: That's not what I asked. If you were told that, that if you don't get in touch with us by "X" time, we're going to seek an order to removed your children. Wouldn't you, wouldn't you then respond?

MS. FYLE: Would, would that have upped the ante? Certainly.

MR. FINDLAY: But it would, it would, ah, destroy the element of surprise though, wouldn't it?

MS. FYLE: I guess I wasn't looking to surprise them.

MR. FINDLAY: Three A.M. in the morning. That's not surprising somebody?

MS. FYLE: The fact that they were located when they were was out of my control and how that, how that removal went down; that was out of my control.

How about if we just say YOU were out of control Ms. Fyle?

MR. FINDLAY: They're, they're at a hotel in Houghton, um, car parked outside, in front of the hotel, license plate identifying them, um, you know, would you think it's a pretty lousy way to hide?

MS. FYLE: If people thought that I was in Marquette and I, in fact, wasn't, it might be a pretty okay way to hide.

For you, maybe Ms. Fyle, but I'm not that stupid! If I were truly on the run, I'd have been in Canada before you could have ever done any of this, and I'd have gone directly from my home to Canada with no stops in between. But I was not on the run, and you already knew that Ms. Fyle. But you wanted those kids immediately… not later!

MR. FINDLAY: Um, why couldn't it have waited until the morning out, like 9 AM?

MS. FYLE: That wasn't my call to make, I don't know.

MR. FINDLAY: Whose call was it to make?

MS. FYLE: I believe it was the, the police officers up there. Had the court order and felt that it needed to be enforced, and they were the ones that went ahead and removed the children.

MR. FINDLAY: So if you, but you were in contact, you were in contact with Bonnie Huttunen, weren't you?

MS. FYLE: I was not; I did not, I did not speak to Bonnie until Monday, after the children were removed.

MR. FINDLAY: You couldn't have communicated to anybody and, and you don't think they would have, at least, taken what you had to say, say this, you know, this is not something you needed to, ah, a, you know, a raid type event on, um, but, you know, have a, have the police and a car there about nine in the morning or at least watching them to make sure they don't take off? Wouldn't that have a far more, have a less aggressive; of doing this?

The point is though, this is how they wanted it to go down because they were so eager to punish Robert Coleman and they so much wanted to illustrate how dangerous they wanted to paint him!

MS. FYLE: You know, I guess, again, I, I can't comment on how that went down; that was not my decision to make.

MR. FINDLAY: But you didn't try and stop that from happening that way, did you?

MS. FYLE: It was not my decision to make.

MR. FINDLAY: So you don't have any responsibility for it; that what you're trying to do?

MS. FYLE: Correct. I, I didn't decide when they were going to go to the hotel room or anything, no.

No, Ms. Fyle, but you damn sure made certain that the judge and law enforcement saw this as a flight attempt, didn't you? You put it all in their mind that we were doing that, and that was purely lies and deceit. You were responsible for all of it!

MR. FINDLAY: This is your petition. Um, you were making the allegations; you did the interview; um, you're the one that went and got the order to get the children removed, right?

MS. FYLE: Uh-huh.

MR. FINDLAY: But there, your responsibility ended, that what you're saying?

MS. FYLE: No, my responsibility continues until this day.

MR. FINDLAY: Okay, so you only don't have responsibility the fact they did it at three in the morning; that's, that's where....

MS. FYLE: ... the timing that when the Colemans' vehicle in the parking lot and the timing of when the police arranged to go into the room, and to, to remove the children; that I do not have responsibility for; I was out of that, that's not my....

MR. FINDLAY: So from a single phone call, you assumed that the Colemans were fleeing, correct?

MS. FYLE: No, I would say from three phone calls, and from them not returning to their home when they said they were going to be.

MR. FINDLAY: From a single phone call, and you, you said it all along, and now you're changing that. You're trying to add more on to it, you said it's this call they, they allegedly told Bob Ross they were in Marquette; that's not where they were?

MS. FYLE: Right.

MR. FINDLAY: That was what you based on the fact that they were lying to you and they were fleeing, correct?

MS. FYLE: No. The fact that I called them again at six o'clock, the fact that IPSD called them again at seven thirty, the fact that they did not return the whole night of Thursday night and/or Friday, Caitlyn was not in school on Friday morning, and the fact that we did request the court order. The court order was granted, they did pick up the search warrant. They did locate, in fact, that they were in Hancock, Michigan, that is what I based it all on fleeing.

MR. FINDLAY: Aren't you putting the cart before the horse? You said the fact that you got the court order was part— how can that be part of your thinking, the fact you got the court order, and can you be part thinking that you needed to get a court order; no— you say a need a court order, so they fled?

MS. FYLE: Right.

MR. FINDLAY: Okay, so, so it's not, because the court order has nothing to do with it, does it?

MS. FYLE: To do with what?

MR. FINDLAY: You believing they fled?

MS. FYLE: No, I believed they fled before I got the court order.

Yes! It's about time you said that. Of course you wanted people to believe we fled, but I sincerely doubt you really thought so Ms. Fyle. But you sure wanted others to think so, so this became your story. But this was in your mind, to present such a phony case, before you ever thought of seeing the judge!

MR. FINDLAY: Right. And you think they fled based on the one phone call from Bob Ross that they made to

Bob Ross (clerical error—should have said Robert Coleman in this transcript)— where he said they told him they were in Marquette.

MS. FYLE: And the two phone calls that were placed subsequent—subsequently after that, and the fact they did not return, as they had, they had told Bob Ross that they would.

OK. Fact check. What we really told him is we would be back on Monday, and would bring our attorney to see Ms. Fyle for an interview with Caitlyn when we got back. We informed him we had an attorney, which is probably what prompted Ms. Fyle to invent the fleeing story. She wanted to interview Caitlyn before we could do it with an attorney, so she had to do something quick! Oh, and to add good measure to her trumped up effort, she places two calls, within an hour and a half, at times when any family would most likely be out to dinner or otherwise enjoying themselves if they are on vacation. Which, of course, we were doing. Ask yourself why she didn't try calling at 11:30 that night?

MR. FINDLAY: So they get; so parents do have an obligation to keep the government informed of their whereabouts, um, and return at certain times from vacations or from trips, is that what you are saying?

MS. FYLE: I had the expectation that if somebody is going to say yes we'll be back and we'll contact you; we'll set up the next interview; not a problem, and then they don't show up and they don't respond to multiple phone calls: that is greatly concerning for me.

MR. FINDLAY: Well is it possible maybe they didn't prioritize it?

MS. FYLE: I would not put this low on my priority list if I was a parent.

MR. FINDLAY: But you did just that. You went to a training on, on Tuesday, as opposed to following up on this case, didn't you?

MS. FYLE: I would not say that I put (it) at lower on my priority list. This, this case lower on my priority list, no I did not.

Then please tell us all why you chose to go to the training class? You are caught in another lie here Ms. Fyle!

MR. FINDLAY: Did you follow up on the case on the Tuesday, the 12th?

THE COURT: Thursday, I believe.

MR. FINDLAY: No, no, I think Wednesday, Wednesday....

MS. FYLE: Wednesday, the 12th?

MR. FINDLAY: Wednesday, the 12th?

MS. FYLE: Did I, did I follow up on the case?

MR. FINDLAY: On the 12th?

MS. FYLE: As far as what?

MR. FINDLAY: Did you follow up on the case on the 12th?

MS. FYLE: I, I discussed the case, yes I did.

MR. FINDLAY: Did you follow up with the Colemans on the 12th?

MS. FYLE: No I did not.

MR. FINDLAY: Did you go to your training on the 12th?

MS. FYLE: Yes I did.

MR. FINDLAY: And, and you, I won't be argumentative, um, you're still, I mean, is it your testimony that you didn't prioritize the training about following up with the Colemans?

MS. FYLE: That is correct.

MR. FINDLAY: Um, it's true that the, the absences from school were excused, isn't it?

MS. FYLE: Absences from school can be excused after the fact of a child missing school.

MR. FINDLAY: It's true that absences from school were excused, isn't it?

MS. FYLE: They were not excused as of the dates that I went there, on Thursday and Friday.

MR. FINDLAY: It's; I'll ask it one more time. It's true that they were excused, isn't it?

MS. FYLE: I believe the school records reflect they have been excused, they were not excused as of Thursday or Friday.

MR. FINDLAY: Did you have the school records from that day?

MS. FYLE: I spoke to the office on those days.

MR. FINDLAY: Do you have the school records from that day?

MS. FYLE: I do not.

MR. FINDLAY: I do. It says they're excused.

MS. FYLE: Okay, and again, my, my response is that the school, you can excuse an absence after the fact.

But we should believe you, Ms. Fyle, because you say the school said that. Even though their records for those days, which my lawyer had, stated it differently. Not after the fact, but records from those days! Gee, a trend that seems consistent in the way you do things. You should have recorded the school too. Just as you should have recorded Caitlyn. As it is, we are all supposed to just believe you, in both cases? Just because you say it is so?

MR. FINDLAY: Can I have, can I have this marked as an exhibit?

THE COURT: It is number....

MR. FINDLAY: It would be Respondent's 1.

THE COURT: Well sometimes...

MR. FINDLAY: ... or how you do it.

COURT REPORTER: Six.

THE COURT: Yeah, we just mark— it's Exhibit Number 6; it's the school record....

MR. FINDLAY: Caitlyn's attendance at school.

MR. FINDLAY: Would you dispute that that shows the Thursday and Friday as excused absences?

MS. FYLE: I, I do not dispute that, no.

MR. FINDLAY: I'm going to ask it to be admitted.

THE COURT: Objections?

MR. PERHALLA: Your Honor, I'd object to foundations.

THE COURT: Well there... there's a problem with foundation there. I'm, I'm assuming, I will allow the Colemans to testify that it is her record of their child; you really should have a school person here to make it proper, but I'm going to, I'll admit it. There's no dispute about the issue.

MR. FINDLAY: I mean, I can wait until the Colemans are....

THE COURT: No. I don't want to have to bring a school secretary to say it's a real record.

Gosh no! A secretary testifying to it would simply emphasize again what a big liar Elizabeth Fyle is!

MR. FINDLAY: It's admitted? (Then back to his questioning): And you're aware that the Monday after the week was the beginning of school for the Spring break too, aren't you?

MS. FYLE: I don't know when Ironwood's spring break was this year.

MR. FINDLAY: Where do you live?

MS. FYLE: Bessemer.

MR. FINDLAY: Would you disagree if I told you that the, ah, spring break was on the 17th?

MS. FYLE: I couldn't confirm it or deny it; I don't know when their spring break was.

MR. FINDLAY: Do you have reason to doubt it?

MR. PERHALLA: Objection. Asked and answered; it's like the third time.

THE COURT: Well yeah, it is for the third time so, she doesn't know. So that's the answer.

What? What? The judge now determines what a witness's answer is? Not in any court of law I know about! She should have to answer yes, no, or I don't know— but it is not for the judge to provide answers for the witness! This guy should be removed from the bench!

MR. FINDLAY: Did you bother trying to find out? Apparently not?

MS. FYLE: I didn't have any reason to know why Ironwood spring break; when the Ironwood spring break was.

MR. FINDLAY: Well, but the Colemans claimed that they were on a family vacation. You're aware of that, aren't you?

MS. FYLE: They've said that after the fact, yes, they have.

Liar! We said that before the fact— not after the fact! Stop manufacturing things, Ms. Fyle!

MR. FINDLAY: Wouldn't finding out whether spring break was that following week, wouldn't that, ah, I mean, shed some light on whether that was a true or false claim?

MS. FYLE: I, families can choose to take vacations whenever they choose to; it doesn't have to be during spring break.

MR. FINDLAY: Well, but apparently they can't cause your....

MS. FYLE: ... they, well they were not on, their— Caitlyn's school was not on spring break that Thursday and Friday she was absent, so.

MR. FINDLAY: I didn't suggest; I didn't suggest that they were, but the following week was, so it's not, it's not unheard of for parents to take their children out of school early to begin a vacation, is it?

MS. FYLE: Again, parents can choose to take vacations whenever they choose to, but school was in session those days.

How many times does this make that you failed to answer the question put to you, Ms. Fyle. People don't do that unless they are trying to hide the truth.

MR. FINDLAY: But, um, incidentally, how much school did Caitlyn miss in relative to, um, her being removed from her home and parents?

MS. FYLE: I don't know.

MR. FINDLAY: Wasn't it true that she didn't get back into school until after getting into Marquette, then a new term or a new semester started?

MS. FYLE: I don't know.

The answer is more than a month! And of course you don't know, Ms. Fyle, because you don't care. Your only goal in life is serving to terminate parental rights and assist with the kidnapping of kids for the state. You apparently don't know much else!

MR. FINDLAY: I want to, um, turn your attention back to what you claimed that Caitlyn said on that, it was the first visit that you were present at?

MS. FYLE: Yes.

MR. FINDLAY: And you claim that Caitlyn said, I'm really sorry for what I did to you— or something along those lines— I'm sorry that I told—

MS. FYLE: The quote is in my report; I don't recall exactly the quote, if you want me to quote it, I have to refer to my report.

MR. FINDLAY: But she was apologizing?

MS. FYLE: I'm so— something to the effect of I'm sorry Daddy, I won't tell any more or something to that effect.

MR. FINDLAY: Okay, um, and you claim that she was taking responsibility for the incident?

MS. FYLE: I felt she was.

MR. FINDLAY: Isn't it true that what she really said was I really wanted to be; I really want to be with you Daddy?

MS. FYLE: No.

MR. FINDLAY: Should we listen? Do you want to listen to the tape of the interview, of, of that visit?

MS. FYLE: Sure, if you'd like to play it; although I don't know who taped that, so if it's been edited or changed or anything.

MS. WITTLA: Your Honor, is counsel suggesting we're going to listen to an entire....

MR. FINDLAY: ... we can listen to how much you want; I'll just, you can play the whole visit or you can play what Caitlyn said.

THE COURT: You asked a specific question, you should play back the part, that part you're talking about.

MR. FINDLAY: Play back as much or as little as possible?

THE COURT: As little as....

MR. FINDLAY: That, that's what my intention was now...

MR. PERHALLA: I'm, I'm going to object to anything being played here until there's a foundation bill. We have no idea where this came from.

Nice try Mr. Perhalla! You've showed your true colors here when you no longer care what Caitlyn has to say! After all, you are supposed to be representing her! Why would you ever object in hearing what she wanted to say? Unless, of course, you are actually serving as a second prosecutor, while disguised as her protector!

THE COURT: Well, yes, yes we do! I'm assuming he will connect it up later, you are correct in an evidentiary, but why, we're not going to call the Colemans to the stand, have people step down, I'm assuming you can connect it later.

MR. FINDLAY: You're aware that the Colemans recorded just about every visit and contact aren't you?

MS. FYLE: That's what they testified to.

MR. FINDLAY: Okay and you actually, you have copies of those, or the government has copies of those recordings, don't they?

MS. FYLE: I believe, they're, they have been provided with copies from the Colemans, yes.

THE COURT: Have you been able to find that one?

MR. FINDLAY: Yeah.

THE COURT: The; that place?

MR. FINDLAY: It's queued up?

(CAITLYN BRAG ON TAPE RECORDED BY THE COLEMANS)

CAITLYN: I miss you too, Dad.... (inaudible to the court recorder).

MR. FINDLAY: Didn't she say I really want to be with you and she said it twice?

MS. FYLE: I couldn't; I couldn't; she, she did say that during the visit, yes, she did, but the quote I put is, is that, is what she said during another part of this.

MR. FINDLAY: Where was that in the visit?

MS. FYLE: I don't recall specifically.

MR. FINDLAY: Okay, well if I gave you this recording and we took a break and let you go through it, could you find it for me?

MS. FYLE: I could try, but that's; it's very difficult to hear; I could certainly try though.

(RECORDING BEING PLAYED AGAIN, BUT INADUDIBLE TO THIS (COURT) RECORDER)

MS. FYLE: I don't dispute that she said I miss you too.

MR. FINDLAY: Play again?

MS. FYLE: No, I don't dispute that she says I missed you too during that part of it.

MR. FINDLAY: Okay, if so, you don't see that?

MS. FYLE: No.

MR. FINDLAY: And you're saying you can't hear it on there?

MS. FYLE: I, I heard it that time. When it was closer to me.

MR. FINDLAY: So the tape that recorded the visit would be close enough, it would be intelligible enough to, to find out whether in fact she said that during that visit, wouldn't it?

MS. FYLE: The, the quote that I said she said?

MR. FINDLAY: Yes.

MS. FYLE: You know I, I don't know. Um, as I testified to earlier Caitlyn's—Caitlyn was sitting in mom's lap and he said, he said I missed you and Caitlyn buried his; buried her head by her, his neck, and said Daddy I'm sorry I told them, whatever exactly the quote was, and then she buried her head in his neck, so I don't know if that would....

MR. FINDLAY: Well you heard it right here, he says Daddy misses you and it's after that, she said I really want to be with you. (now addressing the judge) Your Honor, I make a motion that we take a break and let Ms. Fyle....

THE COURT: ... No, we're not going to do that. Let's continue with your cross-examination.

What? Say, WHAT JUDGE? This judge had just denied my lawyer the right to lay out his case! This woman, who had already been caught lying, was now claiming that what she heard was not what we just heard on the tape— and that, in fact, what she heard was now on another part of the tape. And the judge is going to let her get away with this, without even listening to the tape in its entirety! He must have had a hot date that night, because he was more concerned about his time factor, than he was about the fairness of how this case could be laid out! I wonder what any lawyer in the land thinks about his refusal to allow my attorney to defend me!

MR. FINDLAY (to MS. FYLE): So your, your testimony is still that after Mr. Coleman says Daddy misses you; she says, I'm really sorry or takes responsibility somehow for, for this, this incident?

MS. FYLE: Yes, that is still my testimony.

What gall she has! She has just been caught in a bold, red-faced lie, and still denies the tape said what we all heard it say!

MR. FINDLAY: In, in spite of what we just heard on the recording, where it says Daddy I really want to be with you; she said that, twice?

MS. FYLE: She said both during, during the course of the visit.

MR. FINDLAY: But you don't know where in the visit she said that— excuse, um, I'm sorry you do know where, if she said, you testified that she said, right after Robert Coleman says Daddy misses you, and then she buries her head in his shoulder and says; isn't that the spot we played on the, the tape?

MS. FYLE: I don't have a clue.

That last sentence she muttered was the only true thing I heard Ms. Fyle say during this entire case!

MR. FINDLAY: You heard it— say Daddy misses you?

MS. FYLE: He did.

MR. FINDLAY: Okay, then according to you she says that right after he said that. We hear on the recording she doesn't say that, she says I really want to be with you...

MS. FYLE: Mr. Coleman said Honey I've missed you more than one time during the visit.

MR. FINDLAY: Do you want an opportunity to go through the tape recording?

MS. FYLE: Not really. I mean I certainly could, but I was present at the visit, so....

So WHAT Ms. Fyle? Because you were present, we are AGAIN required to take only YOUR WORD? Your pattern is becoming apparent my dear!

MR. FINDLAY: So if it's not on the recording, what does that tell us?

MS. FYLE: It could tell us many things.

MR. FINDLAY: Either that you have really super hearing or that you're not being honest about what was said at that visit, right?

MS. FYLE: Or that it's been edited out of that visit.

I'm so HAPPY you said that Ms. Fyle! Even though it got by your prejudiced judge and a jury already knowing what their verdict would be before this trial ever began, it does give me the opportunity to disclose something that would show again what a liar and con-person you are! I CHALLENGE YOU to let me have an expert go over this tape NOW—years after the case is over, because, yes, I still have the tape! They can determine if something has been edited out! In your case, you did a LOT of editing, using only YOUR WORD to support your editing IN of facts you wanted to make up. No way to check on you. But let's PROVE right now, that you are a total liar by having this expert check my tape, and SEE if it runs consistently without editing! It would PROVE you make this stuff up as you go along!

MR. FINDLAY: Of course.

MR. PERHALLA: Objection! Move to strike! Argumentative. This whole line of questioning is becoming....

HELP JUDGE! HELP JUDGE! THEY ALL NEED YOUR HELP!

THE COURT: Yeah, let's, you know, frankly counsel in preparation everybody here could have decided what they are going to do on securing that tape; what they're going to put in; we're not going to sit and consume everybody's time with reanalyzing the whole tape; let's move on.

Yeah! Because the judge obviously has a hot date or something, and we would not want to waste our time getting at the truth!

MR. FINDLAY (to the judge): Well, your Honor, the only problem with that is that, that there's a suggestion that the Colemans have edited that.

THE COURT: Let's move on.... Suggest....

MR. FINDLAY (to Ms. Fyle): Do you have any evidence that the Colemans have edited that?

MS. FYLE: I do not.

MR. FINDLAY: Um, in your second interview with Caitlyn, and you stated it took place at the, ah, foster care home?

MS. FYLE: Yes.

Was that because she once again could not find a school or more suitable place?

MR. FINDLAY: Didn't you also claim that Caitlyn said that you would trick me?

MS. FYLE: Caitlyn told me that's what her father told her; my daddy said that you're the cops; that I can't talk to you about spanks and that you're going to trick me and take me away.

MR. FINDLAY: And that, and she said then you would take her away?

MS. FYLE: That's what her daddy told her.

MR. FINDLAY: That you claim she told you, right?

MS. FYLE: That's what she told me her daddy told her.

MR. FINDLAY: And that turned out to be true didn't it?

MS. FYLE: What turned out to be true?

MR. FINDLAY: You took her away?

MS. FYLE: That she's removed; yes, she was removed from her home.

MR. FINDLAY: Nothing further.

At this point the judge called for a break, and once the jury was cleared from the court room, he picked up with some discussion with counsel:

THE COURT: They all out? Okay. The question popped up about the reporting, original source, what's your position? What are you asking for?

MR. FINDLAY: It terms of what? I didn't ask any question about reporting; she... her response was something that wasn't what I asked her, I just asked her something Caitlyn said. I didn't ask her....

THE COURT: No, no, no, I'm way back, I'm way back at—

MS. WITTLA: There was a; there was a foundation issue.

THE COURT: No, no, no, I'm back at the reporting, the original reporter, you asked me if I would—

MR. FINDLAY: Oh, I'm sorry. I, I—

THE COURT: You asked me if I would order, order her to answer, and I said we'll put it off till the end.

A lot of good it does now judge! Because the jury should be hearing this also. We had asked that Ms. Fyle be required to divulge the name of our accuser! Obviously, you did not want to share that information!

MR. FINDLAY: I mean, I, I think the, well, for the record, um, given that parents had a liberty interest in the, the, their children and their family, um,— Supreme Court, um, I think that they have also a right of confrontation to— and it is not quite as well defined or as broadened as it would be in a criminal case. Um, accordingly, I would say that, that under that right of confrontation, um, even if it is more limited than in a criminal case, I'm not, granting that, but even for the sake of argument it is, um, that they should have the right to know who is reporting this. I mean, you get anonymous tips, um, and I think that that needs to be known.

THE COURT: Any response?

MS. WITTLA: Your Honor, the only response to be that if the court rules that reporters, the source of the reporters is disclosed, that Mr. Findlay ask this witness in front of the jury and that it's disclosed; it's not disclosed right here.

MR. FINDLAY: (Laughing) I would get surprised by it! (Laughing) Good grief!

THE COURT: I, I have to tell you....

MS. WITTLA: Well that's the way he wanted to ask her the question, and I think that's the way it should be presented to the jury. It's their decision.

First, Ms. Wittla, wait your turn! The judge was talking. You don't interrupt the judge! Second, stupid, it is the way it was presented, and my lawyer asked the judge to order her to answer in front of the jury. She refused!

THE COURT: Okay, I mean that's kind of strange though, is what I'm saying, saying, if we're talking confidentiality issues.

MS. WITTLA: Well what's the point in knowing it right now and then not actually giving them the answer, if he decides he doesn't like the answer.

Okay stupid! Let's figure it out! First, it is a thing called disclosure— and when you have information as a prosecutor, you are supposed to share that information with the defense in court. He has a right to know. He doesn't have to like the answer, but he does have the right to have his question answered.

MR. FINDLAY: So I can, I am presuming you let me ask the question?

THE COURT: What we'll do from here, and I suppose some day I'll find out why we had this confusing type of— it's confusing to me, and I'm sure you have your reason for it. Um, Mr. Perhalla, I, I didn't ask you for your input, but would— anything you want to say?

MR. PERHALLA: Well, should have asked for it months ago, I mean this could have been, this could have been a motion, I mean it's—

Okay more stupid! My lawyer only learned it was not the Paynes who brought the complaint when he was questioning a state witness. In reality, you are a prosecutor too, in this case, so why did you not reveal this information to my lawyer as you should have done? And so far as it being done months ago— we were always led to believe it was Bobby and Becky who brought the complaint. So how would we have been able to file a motion on something we didn't know was out there? You are even more stupid than the other prosecutor!

THE COURT: Okay, there you go and that's part of it. Okay, Sandusky vrs. Cramer, the Maryland case you talked about; In Re. Brock, the parents have a liberty interest in the ability to parent their child. Brock especially has tailored that; it's different than a criminal issue, and that is why, um, the cases and the court rules have done things like allowed child hearsay under limited circumstances. So it's not exactly like a criminal case, but clearly it is a constitutional right, and I quote that over and over and over until the, till the, ah, petitioner's side rolls, tends to roll their eyes.

Note what the judge just said. He said "Clearly it is a constitutional right." But he is now about to overrule the constitution with what else he manufactured and used as his means to defy the constitution:

THE COURT: Um, but it's true, um, however, this is a narrow issue, I couldn't find any quick authority on it, the only authority I find is that a, that, that ah, the court can order disclosure in an, there was a divorce case where the judge determined that it was a, ah, ah, important to the determination of the issues in the case. The actual issue, that was whether or not somebody should have been prosecuted for disclosing it, and whether the judge should have ordered it to be disclosed, and they said he could. Um, I don't find anything else specific to what's happening here, ah, and I'm going to rule that even though, under Brock all, ah, and under the statute all privileges are abrogated; there still is a public policy of protecting the reporters; had the issue come up prior to trial in a motion, I would have had to gone through it and analyzed it. Um, parties have exchanged witness lists, parties have exchanged what discovery they could, no such issues came up, and to bring it up now in the middle of the trial; I'm not going to allow it, balancing those interest; so, we'll just move on with the redirect of Ms. Fyle.

Okay, so what the judge just said in this last paragraph is that the prosecution is not required to divulge what they knew to the defense when they exchange witness lists and discovery. Never mind the fact the defense had no information that there was another party initiating this complaint. We were never told that, but we should have known anyway? What the hell kind of ruling is this? And to then go on and say you won't allow it to be brought up in trial? Remember, it was divulged first by a state witness under the questioning of my lawyer! Once done, we had all the right in the world to question further—and receive answers for—statements of the hostile witness. This judge screwed up. Pure and simple.

AT THIS POINT, THE JUDGE TOOK A BREAK, INDICATING THE REDIRECT WOULD FOLLOW THE BREAK, AND THAT IS WHERE WE NOW PICK IT UP:

MS. WITTLA (to Ms. Fyle): Ms. Fyle, determining jurisdiction in this case is the first step towards what?

MS. FYLE: Determining jurisdiction in this case is the first step towards, I would say, making progress towards returning the children home or, or, I guess I perceive jurisdiction as it is, what's the word I want to use; um...

How about kidnapping?

MS. FYLE (continuing): ... that the judge basically takes control of the case and ensures that steps are made towards making sure that there are changes that have been identified as issues in the family to ensure the child safety in the future.

MS. WITTLA: So by filing this petition, what are you asking this court for?

MS. FYLE: I'm asking this court for an order to ensure compliance with services so that the children will be protected in the future.

MS. WITTLA: You're not asking to take the kids away forever?

MS. FYLE: No.

But you damn sure tried your best to keep them after the trial, didn't you, Ms. Fyle?

And Ms. Wittla? Another lie, as readers will see as they read the chapters following this one.

MS. WITTLA: You're not asking to terminate parental rights?

MS. FYLE: No.

MS. WITTLA: Mr. Findlay asked you what record exists of the interview that you had with Caitlyn. I believe one of your, part of your response was that you had your report?

MS. FYLE: Right.

MS. WITTLA: In your opinion does the petition represent a record of your interview?

MS. FYLE: Yes.

I can interview Ms. Fyle and talk about the weather, then write a report too, which might say Elizabeth Fyle beat her father with a baseball bat. It doesn't mean such a report would be true, does it? However, I could say it is my opinion that my report represented my interview with Ms.

Fyle. With this court, that is called evidence.

MS. WITTLA: Does your testimony represent a record of your interview?

MS. FYLE: Yes.

MS. WITTLA: Does Mr. Ross's testimony represent a record of the interview?

MS. FYLE: Yes.

Let's see now.... that would be the testimony that Ms. Fyle heard when she was supposed to be sequestered, right? In any real court she would not be able to say yes, because she would not know how Mr. Ross testified, but then, with a setup, as this was, a question like that can be asked by the prosecutor and gotten by with.

MS. WITTLA: Mr. Findlay also asked you about the physical setting for the interview, and I believe your response was that the best environment would be a Forensic Interview Center type of place to go to?

MS. FYLE: That's what the protocol recommends is like, the best option.

MS. WITTLA: Do you know where the closest one is from here?

MS. FYLE: I don't believe there is one in the U.P.; um, I'm not certain; I, for sure, I know there's not one locally or in the near proximity to here.

Ok, first off, what makes one of these centers any better than a simple neutral location, such as a school? Do these centers have brainwashing machines? Or some other unknown to science device that can be used to elicit responses desired by the kidnapping rings? What makes them so special?

MS. WITTLA: So if I'm looking at page five of the Forensic Interview Protocol which talks about a first, select the most neutral location possible?

MS. FYLE: Right.

MS. WITTLA: Second, select locations that are away from traffic, most distractions?

MS. FYLE: Right.

MS. WITTLA: And third, interview room should be simple?

MS. FYLE: Right.

MS. WITTLA: Given the location you were at, what turned out to be what fit those three things?

MS. FYLE: Caitlyn's bedroom.

Very nice rehearsed answer, Ms. Fyle. One problem. It's a lie. The school would have easily been a much better choice, but damn me! I keep forgetting it can't wait until morning! Ok, forgive me, go ahead with your lies and deceit:

MS. WITTLA: Because you believed that Caitlyn's bedroom was a neutral location?

MS. FYLE: Right. It was a comfortable space for her to be in.

MS. WITTLA: And it was away from other noise?

MS. FYLE: Should have been; I mean, the, the location of it in her home, it should have been.

MS. WITTLA: Why wasn't it?

Ms. Wittla! She hasn't had a chance to produce her rehearsed answer that it wasn't yet! You have to let her say that first, before you interject that it wasn't comfortable! But go on you two, it gets funnier:

MS. FYLE: Because of Janet's disruptions; disruption; and then whatever thump or bump we heard outside, I don't know where that came from.

Hmmmm... well let me give you a clue. It's called another kid, most likely. This was a house Ms. Fyle, and despite what Bobby and Becky might have told you, I do not keep my kids on a leash! So if Ashley was playing, she would probably produce a thump or a bump. God, do you think maybe the school might have been a better choice?

MS. WITTLA: And as far as the living room being ah, simple and uncluttered?

MS. FYLE: It was her, it was her bedroom, like I said it certainly had a lot of toys in it, um, but Caitlyn was not distracted by the toys; we did play with the toys during the, the time that Mr. Ross was speaking with the Colemans. Um, but she was not distracted while we were discussing or while I was doing the interview.

Oh? I think I know my daughter. If you played with toys, as you have also denied having done, I'm sure you got her to just drop them so she could pay full attention to you! This whole thing was a game to her, Ms. Fyle—don't you get that yet? Her chance to show off— which, if you knew anything about kids, you would know they love to do as much as to play with toys! What do you really know about kids, Ms. Fyle, other than how to kidnap them?

MS. WITTLA: So when you were talking with her, or she was describing something that happened at school; she wasn't just looking off at toys and putting puzzles together or anything like that?

MS. FYLE: No.

No. Ms. Fyle was the one doing that— playing with puzzles!

MS. WITTLA: Your Honor, may I approach the witness?

THE COURT: Sure.

MS. WITTLA: I opened that internet copy of the Forensic Interview Protocol's page five; does it say anywhere on that page you cannot interview children in their bedrooms?

MS. FYLE: No.

MS. WITTLA: And I underlined a sentence on there; would you read me that sentence?

MS. FYLE: If the interview must be conducted in the home, child is preschool age or on school break, select a private location away from parents or siblings that appears to be the most neutral spot.

MS. WITTLA: From your perspective, Caitlyn's bedroom fit the bill?

MS. FYLE: Yes.

Ok, but how about from a normal person's perspective? Even the sentence Ms. Fyle quoted said "if the interview must be conducted in the home". The protocol book is still suggesting the school is a much better choice! It could have waited until morning!

MS. WITTLA: The petition doesn't contain everything that you talked about with Caitlyn that day does it?

MS. FYLE: No.

No. But a recording would have.

MS.WITTLA: You didn't include the rapport building discussions that you had in the petition?

MS. FYLE: No.

MS. WITTLA: Is the petition considered to be a legal document?

MS. FYLE: Yes.

Hmmm.... interesting. Don't most legal documents require notary stamps? And witnesses?

MS. WITTLA: Is there any reason why you would put everything you talked about with Caitlyn in this document?

MS. FYLE: No.

Yes there is! It would allow my lawyer and us, as defendants, to know how and why everything was said. It would prove who is telling the truth. Tape recordings do that, and she could have made a tape recording, dubbed it in our presence, and given us a copy, and both sides of this issue would know how it all really went down.

But you can't act in corrupt ways if the truth keeps surfacing, now can you, Ms. Fyle?

MS. WITTLA: Do you dispute that, ah, Caitlyn talked about other things with you that day, aside from getting things out?

Who is she going to dispute that with, Ms. Wittla? We never made that an issue! Is it you she would have such a dispute with?

MS. FYLE: Do I dispute that? No, she did talk about other things.

MS. WITTLA: I believe you made a statement that goes something like this; when they misrepresent where they are—

MS. FYLE: Yes.

MS. WITTLA: And I believe the "they" was the parents?

MS. FYLE: Yes.

MS. WITTLA: Why was that a concern that they said that they were in Marquette, and the belief was that they were in Houghton; Hancock?

Go ahead, make up a good story and lie to us some more Ms. Fyle, since we never told you we were in Marquette, as Ms. Wittla tried to sneak in here as if it were a fact in her last question:

MS. FYLE: Because I guess, I had;

Yes, think carefully now; this is being recorded after all:

MS. FYLE (continuing): I guess I had no knowledge; I was very concerned, fearful even, um, that I didn't know what was happening with those children. I didn't know if they were being harmed further. Um, at that point in time, I didn't, I didn't know if they were being coached;

Oh! Now it comes out! Your biggest fear is that we might advise them what sinister people your kidnapping ring consisted of! Well that's why I'm writing this book! So the people can see for themselves how your state officials go about their business!

MS. FYLE (continuing): I didn't know, I had, I had no knowledge of what was going on, and I had no knowledge of even where they were, um, so it was very concerning to me because I, I didn't know what was happening.

MS. WITTLA: As of Tuesday night, March 11th, after you interviewed Caitlyn, did you believe at that point that she was being truthful with you?

MS. FYLE: Yes I did.

But not later, when after she was returned to us from foster care she began to tell what foster parents and people in the system had done to her, right? Your state then dismissed it all as she is just a little liar— right again? Well, brace yourself Ms. Fyle— at age ten she still says it and it might come back to haunt you when you are made to defend yourself against a lawsuit in court!

MS. WITTLA: At that point do you believe that there was a problem as far as discipline?

MS. FYLE: Yes I did.

MS. WITTLA: Did it become more concerning to you, knowing that when you couldn't locate them 36 hours later?

MS. FYLE: Absolutely.

MS. WITTLA: It was suggested that you based their fleeing on the single phone call?

MS. FYLE: That's... that's what Mr. Findlay said, yes.

No. That is what you said first—before you changed your testimony and made it go up to three calls, not all made by you. You really must do something to memorize your lines a little better Ms. Fyle!

MS. WITTLA: When, when, I guess, Mr. Ross was made aware of, ah, Mr. Coleman making the statement he was in Marquette or however that came about; at what point in time did it seem that, that statement may not have been true?

MS. FYLE: Um, well, I was expecting them back, um, in the early afternoon, like later afternoon, somewhere in that range. Um, I believe Mr. Ross made the call sometime in the later morning, like ten-ish, eleven-ish. I'm thinking, um, off of memory. So I would have thought that they were coming back from Marquette, had a doctor's appointment, I was expecting to be back like three-ish, four-ish maybe. When I didn't; did not receive a call, that's when I placed my call to them at six. Um, so I was concerned as of, before I made my call. I was kind of concerned, wondering what's going on.

But not so concerned as to try as late as 11 pm, or so, when normal people would either be back at their hotel after a day's outing, or on their way home if they were driving late. Right? But I understand. Sleep was your priority, because you would have another big kidnapping plan to undertake the next day perhaps. Priorities. Kind of like the priority of going to a training session instead of an interview before.

Because you were so concerned about the kids! Know what? I've stayed up with them because they were sick and had no sleep at all when I did have to work the next day! That's the concern I have for my kids. Your concern stops at the end of your eight hour day!

MS. FYLE (continuing): Again, I called at six, left a message on their phone, I believe it was a cell phone, um, explaining, you know that his was Elizabeth Fyle, um, I need to; still need to interview Caitlyn this evening. Um, please have me paged through the Ironwood Public Saftey Department when you've returned to town. Again, I, my concern heightened at 7:30. I called Ironwood Public Safety, hoping that they would have a better response. Um, again I got no call back, I was more concerned at nine when I call Ironwood Public Safety and said, have you seen them, are they around, did you hear from them? They said they didn't, my concern greatened again to the following day, um, when they had not returned throughout the entire night. Again, no call, no knowledge of where they were, um, Caitlyn was not in school. School didn't know why she was not in school; um, like I said, my concern continued to grow.

MS. WITTLA: Is it fair to say that when you first were informed that they were out of town and expected to return that you weren't concerned at that point in time?

MS. FYLE: Not that I expected they had to report to me their every move. But I kind of thought, oh, like I would have thought that they would have maybe said something, knowing that we needed to discuss further, I guess. I would have thought maybe they would have said well, we got a doctor's appointment on Thursday, you know, I would have; I guess I thought maybe they would have told me that, but I thought, well, all right, they'll be back this afternoon so, I thought, well, we'll see. And like I said, then when they didn't call that's when my concern began; so I was a little bit, I guess, maybe a little, ah, I don't know what the word is that I want to use;

How about paranoid?

MS. FYLE (continuing): or maybe a little ticked off, something maybe wasn't quite right, just because I thought it was a little odd, but like I said wasn't overly freaking out yet.

MS. WITTLA: Is it fair to say that nobody— any kind of an alarm, ah, lunch time on Thursday?

MS. FYLE: No.

MS. WITTLA: Would you say to the wait and see attitude?

MS. FYLE: Yes, I guess I, I guess I was expecting that maybe any moment a call might come in, hey, we're home; you know, we had car trouble something, and I never received that call. Or hey, we're out of town, we're not coming back till Monday, we're doing a family vacation, we'll see you then.

Liar. That message had already been delivered. And even if Fyle knew that, it would not be good enough for her and she would have gone to the court to try to get our kids removed anyway, because that is what she planned to do as soon as she found out Robert Coleman had been accused. After all, as you recall, she lost her bid to fry Robert the first time around. This time she wanted the kids before my lawyer could successfully defend me!

MS. WITTLA: But instead of getting more information about them being back or changing their plans, you didn't have any contact with them at all?

MS. FYLE: Right. I heard nothing, after repeated attempts to get ahold of them.

MS. WITTLA: So you already know the allegations or statements that Caitlyn made to you on the 11th?

MS. FYLE: Right.

MS. WITTLA: Thursday has gone by, they're not showing up, Friday gone, they're not back, at what point in time did you decide that you were going to request a, an order for pick up of the children?

MS. FYLE: After Caitlyn wasn't in school, and I had not received a return call. Um, it might have been just shy of 24 hours and not having any knowledge of where they were.

MS. WITTLA: So that would have been on Friday?

MS. FYLE: Friday, hm, late morning, mid morning; well, yeah, mid, late morning.

MS. WITTLA: So after, you made the decision to ask for a, a pick up order?

MS. FYLE: Uh-huh.

MS. WITTLA: You received that order?

MS. FYLE: Right.

MS. WITTLA: And somewhere in that time frame, the subject comes up with looking for them through cell phone records?

MS. FYLE: I believe the next call that I got was from Ironwood Public Safety Department because they knew; I mean, they were assisting me, and I guess monitoring to see if in fact they returned to their home.

Oh, come on Fyle! Tell the truth! You started to say "assisting me" which would be correct, because they were, in truth, conspirators with you in going after me in the first place! Ron Carpenedo was there every step of the way during this entire process, and it was he who joined you in your failed effort to trap me earlier. So when the name Robert Coleman pops up in a bogus charge of child abuse, both you and he cannot wait to make a second attempt! I'm sure you both conspired to go about putting out a phony need for a search warrant to "find" us, and it would also explain the 3 a.m. raid! He exaggerated everything in his report the first time around, so why would he not exaggerate the seriousness of this to the Houghton police, who would then be asked to make the "raid" on our hotel? But go on, tell them about the next call you got… you know, the one where you "forget" to mention it was Carpenedo:

MS. FYLE (continued): And the next call that I got was "Hey, they're making calls, you know. Bobby Payne's received a couple of calls"; which at the time, they (meaning Carpendo) thought may have been against the PPO's, or PPO, whichever. Um, and so, I guess at least I knew that somebody was out there, and that was the next call that I had gotten.

MS. WITTLA: When you say that at least you knew somebody was out there; what do you mean when you say that?

MS. FYLE: I had no knowledge, um, I guess worse case scenario could be that the entire family, um, was a homicide-suicide, I didn't know; that's absolutely worse case scenario, I had no knowledge, good, bad, or otherwise where they were, just that they were gone, and they were not responding to my calls.

And we all know you come first before anything else, like previous plans, current activities we might be engaged in, all of the things we were doing on our trip. The only exception to you being first, might be Tracie Wittla being first. And when you say you had no knowledge, you could say you still have no knowledge, and we could leave it at that. Anyone with knowledge would not have concerned themselves until the weekend played out, or they would have listened more carefully to find out we did in fact tell the school and Mr. Ross that our intent was not to be home until Monday. At which time we would have a lawyer with us. But again, maybe you did listen to that part, which might explain your real reason for the haste you showed in having our kids removed!

MS. WITTLA: So once the cell phone records were retrieved, were you made aware of the fact that they were in Hancock, Houghton area?

MS. FYLE: Yes.

MS. WITTLA: To your knowledge, does the cell phone; do the cell phone records indicate a specific point on the map where someone is?

Wait! Wait! Ms. Wittla, I'm ashamed of you! Did you forget Ms. Fyle just said she had no knowledge? Oh, go ahead! Answer anyway!

MS. FYLE: Not um, not specifically; I believe they can locate them, I mean, to be honest with you, I don't have any idea other than I know that cell phones, they register off of whatever tower they happen to connect off of, when you place or receive a call; whichever one you're, you're nearest to, but I believe is how they connect. So you get a general, I mean, within a, I mean, obviously if you're in Florida it's not going to register that your cell phone pinged off of Ironwood's tower. I mean it's going to give you generally that you're in the Ironwood area.

So now you've become a cell phone expert, right? You made a pretty good attempt to repeat Carpenedo's lines, but you really should have spent more time with him in practicing those lines, because even from your response it is still clear you know nothing about cell phones or how they operate. But as you were in communication constantly with him then, and got to sit and listen to others testify in this case, which you should not have been allowed to do, you did pick up a little, even if some is quite wrong. And Florida? You forgot my lawyer got reamed for making comparisons with Florida, so you should refrain from doing it also.

MS. WITTLA: So wherever the service area is for that cell phone tower?

MS. FYLE: Right.

MS. WITTLA: So when it was discovered that they were in Hancock-Houghton, nobody knew at that point in time specifically where as far as you know.

MS. FYLE: Correct, correct. Just that they were in that area and their cell phone was registering off of that tower.

MS. WITTLA: And then at some point you were made aware of the fact that local law enforcement was going to be on the look out.

MS. FYLE: Yes.

MS. WITTLA: I believe that you testified that you received a call at 12:30 a.m., Saturday, the 15th?

MS. FYLE: Yes.

MS. WITTLA: That they had been located at a specific hotel?

MS. FYLE: Right.

MS. WITTLA: And I believe you also testified that Gary Olkonen was the on-call worker for that period of time?

MS. FYLE: Yes.

MS. WITTLA: Because your; you go by weeks at a time?

MS. FYLE: Yes.

MS. WITTLA: And your shift had ended; his had begun?

MS. FYLE: Yes, I believe that's how it worked.

MS. WITTLA: When law enforcement decided to pick up the children in Hancock, did they consult you for how you wanted it done?

MS. FYLE: No.

MS. WITTLA: Would you have expected them to?

MS. FYLE: No, not really.

MS. WITTLA: Did you believe that you should have told them how to do it?

MS. FYLE: No, that's their, that's their job, that's, I mean they, they, you know, they, they had the court order; they decided that they needed to carry it out and that, that— how they did it, that's up to them to decide how they best want to do it. I knew everybody was concerned because of the; what was believed that they had fled, um, that they needed to maybe strike while they could; if that's, I mean, you know what I mean, if they knew where they were, they may not have another opportunity to remove the children. And for officers' safety, I believe that it, you know, to do it under the element of surprise has been earlier talked about or brought up; I mean that was the best.

MS. WITTLA: To make it....

MS. FYLE: ... maybe...

MS. WITTLA: Were you here for Ms. Coleman's testimony?

MS. FYLE: Yes I was.

MS. WITTLA: Would it have been possible for you to tell law enforcement how they should have done it?

MS. FYLE: I probably could have offered my suggestion; it's ultimately up to them to decide what, how they do it, and when they do it and all the details.

MS. WITTLA: So, so we're talking about this not like, I guess, the impression was made earlier that, you know, you just don't care about how they did it?

MS. FYLE: Right, that was the impression that was given or brought up by Mr. Findlay.

Oh! So now these two co-conspirators want to try to show that all of a sudden Ms. Fyle developed a big heart, and that in truth, she really cared about how this went down? I've got more beach front property in South Dakota. Anybody want some?

MS. WITTLA: Does it concern you how this went down, or?

MS. FYLE: Um, hum.... Could it have been a traumatic situation? Absolutely. Um, do I feel that the kids actually came out of it fairly well; absolutely they did, um, from Ms. Huttenen's testimony you know.

Let's talk about how well the kids came out of it. Today, at the writing of this book, Caitlyn is ten years old and Ashley is six. Both of them still have continual nightmares about people coming to get them in the middle of the night. This is four years after this event occurred. Does that sound to you like they came out it fairly well? And not only that. The girls both now continue to talk about how much they hated being in foster care. So I would say the entire experience was extremely damaging, and is far worse than a spanking with the bare hand on the butt for disciplinary purposes. The state of Michigan has scarred my kids for life, and if I am a bit bothered by that, perhaps it is because I am a parent. That kind of comes with trying to protect your kids. If I were the only victim of this state, it would be bad. But check the record. Michigan, as a state, was the subject of a class action lawsuit that they lost in that same period of time! It is time to do something about CPS, but the only thing we can do is write a book to try to expose them and their methods. People have to rally to get Congress and the government to do away with CPS and let local officials handle the abuse matters, and in fact, criminalize them in doing so if they wish. That would be better, because then, they would have to prove more fully any case they bring, it will cost them more to do it, and they won't do it unless they really have a serious case in that event. Too many kids get hurt under this current system, and it is just plain wrong.

MS. WITTLA: Well, what about from your experience, when you, ah, talked to the kids, you saw them on the 17th?

MS. FYLE: Right.

MS. WITTLA: Two days after this happened?

MS. FYLE: Right.

MS. WITTLA: Now I'm not going to ask you any direct quotes about what they said, but did the subject come up about how they were taken out of the hotel room?

MS. FYLE: No.

MS. WITTLA: It's also been suggested that this case really wasn't that important to you because after all you went to training on the 12th instead of looking after Caitlyn and Ashley?

MS. FYLE: Right.

MS. WITTLA: What provisions did you make before you left that house on the 11th to insure their safety?

MS. FYLE: I made provisions, um, based on a promise from Robert and Janet Coleman that they would not use any further physical means of discipline with their children, and that I would be back.

Now that is real protection! Put yourself in a position of being a protector of a flock of chickens. You have two red foxes constantly posing a danger to your chickens. You tell the foxes not to eat the chickens while you tend to other business. What do you think the foxes will do when you leave? They will eat the chickens. Ms. Fyle, in this case, is supposedly the protector. Janet and I, the red foxes. If, as Janet and I were painted by Ms. Fyle to be, we were really the dangerous couple that might act violently with our children and must be raided at 3 in the morning, does it seem likely she would just say, "be nice to the children" and then go about her business? No. If we were so dangerous, she would have taken the kids right then and there. So she didn't take any provisions at all.

MS. WITTLA: Did you ask them not to talk about the case?

MS. FYLE: I probably did, but I, I, I'm not sure, but I believe that I, I remember discussing that, you know, we kind of need to keep things calm, we need to, you know, figure out a few more details, a few more interviews to do, you know, made the arrangements that they promised to not, you know, use physical discipline with the children. Um, and that we'd be, that I'd be contacting them to— further.

MS. WITTLA: Did you believe that they would do as you asked?

MS. FYLE: At that point in time, I, I did.

MS. WITTLA: Can you imagine the situation where you wouldn't leave a message on someone's cell phone, where you don't know where they are, and saying something like, well if you don't respond, then we're going to need to get a court order to take the children into custody?

MS. FYLE: Probaby very unwise.

MS. WITTLA: Why do you think it would be really unwise?

Get out the paint brush for this part Ms. Fyle. You need some dangerous villains:

MS. FYLE: Because any number of things, again, it could turn into a homicide-suicide; they're taking my— and you know they're not taking my kids, you know, I'll kill them myself and my children before I do. Um, they could have fled for further; they could have gone into hiding deeper, um, any number of things could have happened.

Could have? Gee, that is sure solid testimony. Well let's see what I can dream up in this case, using the scenario of what could have happened with Ms. Fyle using the methods she did use. First, when she came knocking at my door, if were real dangerous, I could have shot it out with the police as soon as I saw them. Or, I could have refused their entry, made them get a court order to come in the house to interview Caitlyn, meanwhile getting a lawyer to sit in on all of this, and gone from there. (Probably that would have been best). Or, I could have done what I did do, and that is, say to my wife that we need a break from all this, and since we had a doctor appointment anyway, combined a couple of days for a mini-vacation for the family, to included Easter, and try to put this in the back of our minds until the time came for us to do the followup interview Ms. Fyle spoke about. As no indication was given that it needed to be done immediately, I was not all that focused on it. I was much more concerned about our own family problems at that time, and needed to try to give us all a few days or rest and relaxation.

MS. WITTLA: Just to quantify this for my own purposes, I guess, at the time that you left the house on March 11th, on a scale of 1 to 10, where 10 is the most concerned, and 1 is not concerned, where would you peg your level of concern for the safety for Caitlyn and Ashley?

Notice she says for her own purposes. But she didn't tell the jury not to listen… and it's a real cute way to get her witness to continue to paint us as dangerous people.

MS. FYLE: I'd say about a 6 or a 7.

MS. WITTLA: Thursday morning, when they were out of town, where was that level?

MS. FYLE: Thursday morning when I just heard that they were out of town, a firm 7.

MS. WITTLA: Thursday night?

MS. FYLE: Probably an 8.

MS. WITTLA: Friday morning?

MS. FYLE: Nine.

MS. WITTLA: Friday afternoon?

MS. FYLE: I guess by the time I filed the peition, I was at a 10, and remained a 10 until after I knew that the children were safe and were, were in foster care.

Truthfully now, didn't you think that last part was well rehearsed? I mean, the number thing? No doubt, right off the cuff! (Choke!)

MS. WITTLA: Thank you.

THE COURT: Mr. Perhalla?

MR. PERHALLA: When you received this CPS claim, by law you're required to go interview the children?

MS. FYLE: Yes.

MR. PERHALLA: And do you interview the children or are there cases where you do not?

MS. FYLE: Um, we have to interview all suspected victims in a, in a case, and if there are children that are in the home, but are not considered the victims, we have to see them, confirm their well being, we don't actually have to do a complete, full interview of them; but we could, depending on, you know, depending on what that sibling, who may have been uninvolved in the actual abuse and neglect may have seen or heard or what not.

MR. PERHALLA: And I believe you testified previously that, after interviewing the children many times the complaint of abuse that your office received or complaint of neglect is unsubstantiated after interviewing the child, if it's not true, correct?

MS. FYLE: Had I many times interviewed children and come up with no preponderance, yes, absolutely.

MR. PERHALLA: That's all, thank you your Honor.

THE COURT: Mr. Findlay?

MR. FINDLAY: Just, just a couple. Um, you characterized, um, Janet Coleman's coming into the room while you were interviewing Caitlyn as, ah, disruption?

MS. FYLE: Absolutely.

MR. FINDLAY: And is it fair to say you were irritated with her doing that?

MS. FYLE: I was surprised that she did, I don't know that I was irritated.

MR. FINDLAY: You were surprised that she would check on a child and see what's happening?

MS. FYLE: I was surprised that she would pop open the door and walk in, and stand there with her arms closed, staring at us. I was, I was taken aback by that.

MR. FINDLAY: You were in the Colemans' home, accusing them of child abuse, on the words of a mentally challenged and a lying and vindictive woman, and then you separate them from their children and you ask, can I help you, when she comes in the room? Whose house was it?

MS. FYLE: Well, first off, Bobby Payne does have some, some, he's on SSI for a reason; I do not believe that Becky Payne is a lying and vindictive woman, um....

MR. FINDLAY: You've heard her testimony?

MS. FYLE: What?

MR. FINDLAY: You've heard her testimony?

MS. FYLE: I did.

Yes she did, because she was the only sequestered witness who was not sequestered.

MR. FINDLAY: Um, I would, I was pretty sure that yesterday both you and Bob Ross said that, um, she wasn't playing, Caitlyn wasn't playing with toys during your interview, where you just said on redirect, um, that Caitlyn was playing with toys during the interview. Which is true?

MS. FYLE: She was not playing with toys during the interview of the allegations, she played with toys during the time that Mr. Ross brought Janet Coleman out to speak with the parents about continuing the interview. Because I didn't want to continue the interview at the parents' request, until I'd been given permission again, so like I said we chit chatted, talked about her stuffed animals, what their names were,

that kind of a thing.

MR. FINDLAY: Didn't; didn't both of you say yesterday that she wasn't playing with toys at all?

MS. FYLE: Not during the interview she was not.

MR. FINDLAY: What?

MS. FYLE: Not during the interview of the allegations, she was not.

MR. FINDLAY: Okay, but now you're saying she was playing with toys, although you're clarifying it as saying, well....

MS. FYLE: She, she, she did play with toys during the tiem that Mr. Ross was out and spoke with Mr. Coleman.

MR. FINDLAY: But yesterday you were here; you said— he said she didn't?

MS. FYLE: He was not in the room during that time; he wouldn't know if she did play with the toys during that time.

MR. FINDLAY: How long did the interviewe last; wasn't it five, ten minutes?

MS. FYLE: I don't recall how long it took.

MR. FINDLAY: This bit about the flight and everything, um, is it fair to say that you didn't believe the children were in eminent danger, absent this flight allegation?

MS. FYLE: I, I was concerned for their safety in their, their family's home.

MR. FINDLAY: Is it fair to say that didn't believe they were in any eminent danger, absent your claim that they fled, took flight?

MS. FYLE: I guess I don't know if I could answer that.

MR. FINDLAY: Did you think they were in eminent danger after you left the house on the 11th?

MS. FYLE: I was— no, I was concerned for them. I was concerned for the safety of their children, but I— of the children, but I felt that I had made a safety plan with the Colemans and I took them at their word at that point in time, and felt that I had made an appropriate safety plan for the children when I left.

MR. FINDLAY: Okay, so you didn't feel there was an eminent danger until these allegations about flight?

MS. FYLE: Correct.

MR. FINDLAY: Why didn't you just answer it that way when I asked the first time?

MS. FYLE: Because I guess I didn't understand your question as you were asking it.

MR. FINDLAY: No other questions.

THE COURT: Okay, I'm going to.....

MS. WITTLA: You Honor, I do want to ask another question about that.

THE COURT: One.

MS. WITTLA: Okay, I shouldn't have said one, I should have said two.

THE COURT: Because they, they have been compounded into more questions by everybody, so one please.

MS. WITTLA: Um, Ms. Fyle, when the flight became apparent to you, what did that tell you about whether or not you could trust the Colemans' word?

MS. FYLE: It proved to me that I could not, that they were not, that they were not going to be compliant with me, that they were not, um, I guess interested in, in not the word, I want to use peacefully but in rectifying the concerns that had been brought to their attention; um, that they had no intentions on, on working with me any longer.

MS. WITTLA: Thank you.

THE COURT: Mr. Perhalla? One?

MR. PERHALLA: Nothing, thank you.

THE COURT: Mr. Findlay?

MR. FINDLAY: No, nothing.

THE COURT: Thank you ma'am. Have a seat, I know you're going to remain for the trial. Um, we're, Ms. Wittla, any more witnesses?

MS. WITTLA: No your Honor.

THE COURT: Mr. Perhalla, you are not calling any independent witnesses?

MR. PERHALLA: That's correct, thank you.

THE COURT: Mr. Findlay, do you have one of your witnesses available?

MR. FINDLAY: Yes I do, I hope they're out there.

THE COURT: And who are you calling?

MR. FINDLAY: Christine Towne, I'm sorry.

At that point, Christine Towne was called to stand and sworn in, and my lawyer began his questioning:

MR. FINDLAY: State your name for the record please.

MS. TOWNE: Christine Lynn Towne.

MR. FINDLAY: And where do you live?

MS. TOWNE: In the basement of my parents' house at 4170 Westwood Drive, Eagle River, Wisconsin.

MR. FINDLAY: So you, ah, live in the basement?

MS. TOWNE: Yes.

MR. FINDLAY: You comfortable down there?

MS. TOWNE: Yes.

MS. WITTLA: Objection your Honor, the relevancy in this.

THE COURT: It's preliminary; let's move on to the issues.

MR. FINDLAY: I guess...

THE COURT: I know the basement is an issue but her basement is not an issue; let's keep on going.

MR. FINDLAY: Um, do you know the Colemans?

MS. TOWNE: Yes I do.

MR. FINDLAY: How well do you know them?

MS. TOWNE: Quite well.

MR. FINDLAY: And how do you know them?

MS. TOWNE: I met Janet and Robert, um, I met Rob and a friend of his I was dating, and became family friends with them.

MR. FINDLAY: How long have you known them?

MS. TOWNE: Probably a year and a half.

MR. FINDLAY: Um, do you know their children?

MS. TOWNE: Yes I do.

MR. FINDLAY: And you've been with them when they're with their children?

MS. TOWNE: Yes I have.

MR. FINDLAY: Have you ever seen anything in their care that rises to abuse of the Colemans to their children?

MS. TOWNE: No, I have not.

MR. FINDLAY: Can you describe, at least, what you've observed of their relationship?

MS. TOWNE: A very loving, caring family. Um, we've had picnics and whatever together and always playful, and....

MR. FINDLAY: What is, um, your job over in Wisconsin?

MS. TOWNE: Home health.

MR. FINDLAY: Are you a mandatory reporter in Wisconsin?

MS. TOWNE: Yes, I have to report any kind of abuse.

MR. FINDLAY: So if you'd seen anything, do you think you, you'd have an obligation to report it?

MS. TOWNE: Yes.

MR. FINDLAY: Do you know, ah, Bobby or, and/or Becky Payne?

MS. TOWNE: Yes I do.

MR. FINDLAY: How do you know them?

MS. TOWNE: I knew Beck, um, through the Colemans; um, they were renting from the Colemans.

MR. FINDLAY: How would you characterize your relationship with them?

MS. TOWNE: I was somewhat friends, um, I mean, I wouldn't just ignore them or whatever, but I did talk to them.

MR. FINDLAY: And is it true that you, ah, tape recordeda couple of conversations between you and Becky Payne?

MS. TOWNE: Yes it is.

MR. FINDLAY: Why did you do that?

MS. TOWNE: Because during one of the text messages, um, Becky threatened to kill Janet.

MS. WITTLA: Objection, your honor, this is hearsay.

THE COURT: Well, it may or may not be. I mean, is this a prior inconsistent statement, or?

MR. FINDLAY: (not audible to the court reporter)

MS. WITTLA: I have no idea where this is coming from.

So what? Is every witness supposed to check in at your office and tell you what they are going to say on the stand? Too bad when you get a surprise, Ms. Wittla, but it is certainly ok for you to surprise others!

THE COURT: Well you, you know that there was conversation, you know it was taped, there was testimony by Ms. Payne on that, but, I guess the question is, is this somehow inconsistent....

MR. FINDLAY: ... And it is not hearsay, your Honor, it doesn't go, it doesn't go to the truth of the matter; I'm just asking of why she recorded it, I'm not into any detail about that; I just want to know why she recorded?

MS. WITTLA: And she responded?

MS. TOWNE: Because of the threatening.

THE COURT: Hold, hold it, ma'am... ma'am... you, you got to lean back here while we make a legal determination, and you were in the middle of something Ms. Wittla?

That's right judge! Protect your prosecutor!

MS. WITTLA: She's referencing some sort of text message that's never come up before, I've never seen it, I think it would be hearsay.

MR. FINDLAY: And I'm saying it's not hearsay if it's not offered to prove the truth of the matter asserted. The assertion is what she said, I won't repeat it, I'm not offering to prove that; I'm offering it— I'm asking her why she would record it.

THE COURT: Well, okay, and the answer has come out for now. I, I'll let it stand. Let's, let's move into whether you have prior inconsistent statements or not.

MR. FINDLAY: How many, were there just two conversations you recorded?

MS. TOWNE: Yes.

MR. FINDLAY: Based on your relationship with Becky Payne, how would you characterize her?

MS. TOWNE: Very vindictive and jealous.

MR. FINDLAY: And why do you say that?

MS. TOWNE: Because when you say you're going to be a better mother and that you're going to screw over the Colemans and whatever, yeah, that's jealousy and vindictiveness.

MR. FINDLAY: When was the last time you seen the Colemans with their children?

MS. TOWNE: It was in January.

MR. FINDLAY: And just to finish up, and you've never seen any abuse or anything?

MS. TOWNE: None whatsoever.

MR. FINDLAY: Thank you.

THE COURT: Ms. Wittla?

MS. WITTLA: When did you tell Becky you were recording your conversation?

MS. TOWNE: I did not tell Becky that I was recording it.

MS. WITTLA: And when did you tell Robert Coleman?

MS. TOWNE: Shortly after I recorded it.

MS. WITTLA: Isn't it true Ms. Towne, that you set up Becky to get some juicy bits of information on a tape you always intended to give to Robert Coleman?

MS. TOWNE: No, it is not true; when somebody threatens somebody's wife or....

MS. WITTLA: ... I'm not asking you about threats...

MR. FINDLAY: Your Honor, the....

THE COURT: Well, ah, just like with Mr. Findlay, please don't run over the witness's answer.

MS. WITTLA: Well, your Honor, I would object to her answer as being prejudicial and not relevant, in an attempt to taint the jury.

You OBJECT to an answer on a question YOU ASKED???

THE COURT: Yeah, but you asked the question, I mean, let's....

MS. WITTLA: ... well that's not responsive as well....

And now you are INTERRUPTING THE JUDGE??? Does this case belong to YOU, Ms. Wittla— or to the COURT?

THE COURT: Well, but when you ask the question, ma'am, let's not go into the text message that we've already all heard, and we're not going to go into those details, but answers the question, and then I'll ask the proscutor, since we had this little discussion to proceed with your questioning. She, she got to pick up, because I'm sure you don't remember in between my talking what was asked. Go ahead.

MS. WITTLA: Ms. Towne, isn't it true that you always intended to turn over the tapes to Robert Coleman?

MS. TOWNE: No.

MS. WITTLA: Isn't it true that Robert Coleman wanted you to get Becky on this tape?

MS. TOWNE: No it is not.

MS. WITTLA: Was he happy when you gave him the tapes?

MS. TOWNE: No. He didn't really know what was on the tapes until they listened to them.

MS. WITTLA: Whose equipment did you use to make these tapes and how did you give them to Mr. Coleman?

MS. TOWNE: I have....

MS. WITTLA: And where do you live again?

Ms. Wittla! Again, you ran over the witness and did not allow her to answer! After YOU asked a question? But I'll provide an answer to what you were trying to establish! It was NOT Robert Coleman's equipment. That's what you wanted to put over to jury, wasn't it? Believe it or not, many people own recording devices these days! A lot of people!

MS. TOWNE: Eagle River, Wisconsin.

MS. WITTLA: Does Eagle River, Wisconsin, or Wisconsin, the state, allow participant recording?

MS. TOWNE: I have no idea.

Now here folks is another example of the hypocrisy of this woman. You might recall that earlier my lawyer talked about laws in Florida and this woman fought the idea of that, saying Florida had nothing to do with Michigan. Then why is she now introducing a question talking about Wisconsin? It would seem the same to me, Wisconsin also has nothing to do with Michigan!

MS. WITTLA: Why didn't you tell Becky that you were recording the conversation?

MS. TOWNE: I didn't see a purpose of telling her.

MS. WITTLA: Ms. Towne, isn't it true that if you told Becky that you recorded a conversation that she wouldn't have said those things to you?

MS. TOWNE: I don't know.

MS. WITTLA: Ms. Towne, did you ever tell Becky that you weren't going to tell Robert Coleman about what you guys talked about?

MS. TOWNE: I don't remember.

MS. WITTLA: It was in the tape that you said you weren't going to tell Becky what was talked about, would that be true?

MS. TOWNE: What Becky was talking about?

MS. WITTLA: Yeah. As you are talking to her, if you said, you know, oh well, I'm not going to tell Rob about this or something to that effect?

MS. TOWNE: Yeah.

MS. WITTLA: You lied to her?

MS. TOWNE: Not necessarily, because it comes back to the text messaging.

MS. WITTLA: How long after you made the recording, let's say, did you turn it over to Robert?

MS. TOWNE: I would say within four or five days.

MS. WITTLA: How long after that till you saw it on You Tube?

MS. TOWNE: I didn't see You Tube.

MS. WITTLA: Are you aware that it was posted on You Tube?

MS. TOWNE: No I did not.

MS. WITTLA: You indicated the last time you saw the Colemans with their kids was in January of this year?

MS. TOWNE: Yes.

MS. WITTLA: Before that, how many times did you see them?

MS. TOWNE: Twice, three times a month.

MS. WITTLA: How long at these visits?

MS. TOWNE: Oh, we would spend the day together.

MS. WITTLA: And I believe you indicated that you knew them for about a year and a half?

MS. TOWNE: Yes.

MS. WITTLA: And that you knew them quite well?

MS. TOWNE: Yes.

MS. WITTLA: So you're aware about Robert Coleman's affair with Becky Payne?

MS. TOWNE: Yes.

MS. WITTLA: When did you find out about it?

MS. TOWNE: When this all came about.

MS. WITTLA: Do you remember when that was?

MS. TOWNE: No I don't.

MS. WITTLA: Who told you?

MS. TOWNE: Janet told me.

MS. WITTLA: Would you consider yourself a better friend of Janet or Robert?

MS. TOWNE: I would say probably equal because I am a family friend.

MS. WITTLA: So of the approximately eighteen months that you've known the Colemans and their children, would you say it was consistent that you saw them two or three times a month?

MS. TOWNE: During the summer it was more.

MS. WITTLA: How much more?

MS. TOWNE: I would spend weekends up there; I would come up on a Friday, leave on a Monday. Um, so I have spent the nights up there, and that was like every weekend.

MS. WITTLA: So a matter of three to four days a month or....

MS. TOWNE: Pardon?

MS. WITTLA: Three or four days a month?

MS. TOWNE: No, a week.

You will have to forgive Ms. Wittla! Her math is not too good. The only question with her math is if it is really that bad, or accidentally-on-purpose that bad.

MS. WITTLA: Okay, so...

MS. TOWNE: I would come on a Friday night and leave on Monday morning.

MS. WITTLA: Every weekend?

MS. TOWNE: Yes.

MS. WITTLA: So during the summer you'd probably see the Colemans and their children twelve days in a month?

MS. TOWNE: Probably sixteen.

MS. WITTLA: And non-summer time, two to three times a month? I have nothing further.

THE COURT: Mr. Perhalla?

MR. PERHALLA: Thank you, your Honor. (To Ms. Towne): You, when you were visiting with the Colemans overnight, were you also with the Paynes?

MS. TOWNE: Yes, not on every occasion that I would stay.

MR. PERHALLA: You testified you last saw the children in January?

MS. TOWNE: Yes.

MR. PERHALLA: Would that have been the last time you had been there with the Paynes?

MS. TOWNE: I believe so.

MR. PERHALLA: Prior to that, were you up there regularly when the Paynes were there?

MS. TOWNE: Not... they were not present every time I was there.

MR. PERHALLA: What were the Paynes doing with respect to the Colemans; what did you see happening?

MS. TOWNE: I had seen Bobby and Becky argue and have their marital problems or arguing and whatever.

MR. PERHALLA: Okay, with respect to the Colemans, did you see anything there?

MS. TOWNE: No I did not.

MR. PERHALLA: Okay, the Colemans, were the Colemans having Becky and Bobby work for them?

MS. TOWNE: Not that I'm aware of.

Oh, but Mr. Perhalla, you would love to continue to put us on trial for abuse of the poor Payne couple, wouldn't you? I thought this case was about if or not I abused my kids! And YOU are supposed to be worried about my KIDS—not the Paynes! But then, rather than a GAL, you are actually another PROSECUTOR, aren't you?

MR. PERHALLA: Were the, were the— Becky and Bobby eating with the Colemans?

MS. TOWNE: When I was there and they were around, yes, they would come and then eat, um, with us.

MR. PERHALLA: Were they helping around the house? The Paynes?

MS. TOWNE: Becky was. Um, she took it upon herself to do certain things in the house.

Ooops! Not the answer you wanted was it Mr. Perhalla? Because it confirms what Janet had said all along in her testimony, that Becky was attempting to take over.

MR. PERHALLA: Now the telephone conversation that you recorded of Becky, isn't it true that she told you that she had seen physical abuse?

MS. TOWNE: Yes.

MR. PERHALLA: And what did you say to her?

MS. TOWNE: I don't remember my exact words, but I do remember one part where I said, well, I would have reported it right away, and she said, well I'm afraid of him, I couldn't, and whatever. And I'm like, well I would have stood up to Rob and Janet and told them I was reporting them and left.

MR. PERHALLA: And you know Becky Payne, do you not?

MS. TOWNE: Yes.

MR. PERHALLA: And isn't it true that she finally stood up to him and left?

MS. TOWNE: Well, she left.

MR. PERHALLA: Nothing further.

THE COURT: Redirect?

MR. FINDLAY: No.

With that, Christine Towne was excused and Mr. Findlay called his next witness, and Mr. Don Layman was sworn in:

MR. FINDLAY: Please state your name for the record.

MR. LAYMAN: Donald Layman.

MR. FINDLAY: And where do you presently live?

MR. LAYMAN: Ah, Coleman estates.

MR. FINDLAY: And where is that located?

MR. LAYMAN: Ah, in Ironwood.

MR. FINDLAY: How long have you lived there?

MR. LAYMAN: Two years.

MR. FINDLAY: During that time, um, where was your residence in relation to the Colemans' residence?

MR. LAYMAN: Um, I'm upstairs, probably above the kitchen.

MR. FINDLAY: So you're in an apartment?

MR. LAYMAN: Yeah, an apartment.

MR. FINDLAY: And you, for a period of time, you were upstairs above their apartment?

MR. LAYMAN: Yes, the, the kitchen area mostly and the laundry room.

MR. FINDLAY: How well do you know the Colemans?

MR. LAYMAN: Ah, pretty good; I have babysat for them a few times.

MR. FINDLAY: Would you characterize them as friends?

MR. LAYMAN: Yeah.

MR. FINDLAY: Have you been around them and their children a fair amount?

MR. LAYMAN: Yes.

MR. FINDLAY: How often?

MR. LAYMAN: Oh, once a month and we, I go for help them when they needed a ride, they had to go somewhere, they had to.... I watched the kids in the truck for her.

MR. FINDLAY: Did you ever witness the Colemans interacting with their children during the time you lived there?

MR. LAYMAN: Ah, what do you mean by that?

MR. FINDLAY: Did you ever see them with their children?

MR. LAYMAN: Yeah.

MR. FINDLAY: Sorry about that, um, how often do you say you saw them?

MR. LAYMAN: Practically every day.

MR. FINDLAY: Did you ever see any signs of abuse?

MR. LAYMAN: No.

MR. FINDLAY: How would you describe the way the Colemans acted with their children?

MR. LAYMAN: Very good.

MR. FINDLAY: How; did the children seem to be happy?

MR. LAYMAN: Yes.

MR. FINDLAY: Do you know, ah, Bobby and Becky Payne?

MR. LAYMAN: Yeah.

MR. FINDLAY: How do you know them?

MR. LAYMAN: Ah, they rented an apartment from Robert Coleman.

MR. FINDLAY: How much contact have you had with them?

MR. LAYMAN: Um, every so often I'd see them.

MR. FINDLAY: What was your impression of either one, Bobby or Becky?

MR. LAYMAN: My; they're very good people.

MR. FINDLAY: I'm sorry?

MR. LAYMAN: Good, good people.

MR. FINDLAY: Were they; did you know if Bobby and Becky Payne were living with the Colemans when you were there?

MR. LAYMAN: Yeah.

MR. FINDLAY: How; for how long?

MR. LAYMAN: Ah, I figured maybe a month or two.

MR. FINDLAY: Did you ever hear any interaction?

MR. LAYMAN: No.

MR. FINDLAY: Hear any interaction between the Colemans and the Paynes?

MR. LAYMAN: No.

MR. FINDLAY: Did you ever hear, um, any yelling or screaming, anything like that?

MR. LAYMAN: No, no.

MR. FINDLAY: Nothing further, thank you.

THE COURT: Ms. Wittla?

MS. WITTLA: Mr. Layman, is Robert Coleman still your landlord?

MR. LAYMAN: Yeah.

MS. WITTLA: Thank you, I have nothing further.

THE COURT: Mr. Perhalla?

MR. PERHALLA: Nothing, thanks your Honor.

THE COURT: Redirect? (Nothing said) Okay, Mr. Layman, that's it. Thank you for your testimony. You are free to go or come if you want; come or go or stay, sorry.

MR. LAYMAN: Okay.

THE COURT: Um, and I'm indicating, now other than the part, other than the parties you weren't going to call, any other witnesses, right?

MR. FINDLAY: I'm sorry?

THE COURT: Other, so I don't know that it's necessary to caution Mr. Layman or anybody else.

MR. FINDLAY: No.

THE COURT: Because we are getting to that point. All right, who is your next witness?

MR. FINDLAY: I call Robert Coleman.

At this point I was called to retake the stand, and once seated, Mr. Findlay began his questioning of me:

MR. FINDLAY: Your name is Robert Coleman, right?

MR. COLEMAN: Yes sir, it is.

MR. FINDLAY: Okay, um, how did you meet Janet Coleman?

MR. COLEMAN: I met her in the mall.

MR. FINDLAY: When was that?

MR. COLEMAN: It was back in 2002, I'm pretty sure. I'm sorry, it was 2004.

MR. FINDLAY: When did the two of you end up getting married?

MR. COLEMAN: We got married on July 12th, the—that following— that year.

MR. FINDLAY: So at that time was, ah, did Janet have Caitlyn?

MR. COLEMAN: Ah, yes she did.

MR. FINDLAY: And what was your impression of Caitlyn as a child, at that time?

MR. COLEMAN: She was just a good, sweet little girl.

MR. FINDLAY: When you married Janet, what were your intentions regarding Caitlyn?

MR. COLEMAN: To be her father.

MR. FINDLAY: And during the time of your marriage to Caitlyn—married to Janet— have you acted like Caitlyn's father?

MR. COLEMAN: Yes I did.

MR. FINDLAY: When was Ashley born?

MR. COLEMAN: She was born in 2006.

MR. FINDLAY: So there, you had a year and a half of marriage, with just Caitlyn, before Ashley was born?

MR. COLEMAN: That's correct.

MR. FINDLAY: Can you describe some of the activities that you'd do? The three of you together?

MR. COLEMAN: We'd go hiking and just go walking a lot and fly kites; we built this little bird feeder for her for school.

MR. FINDLAY: Did you do things at her school?

MR. COLEMAN: Yes I did.

MR. FINDLAY: Was she in preschool at that time?

MR. COLEMAN: She was in pre-kinde—pre—pre-school at the time.

MR. FINDLAY: Did Ashley's arrival change things much?

MR. COLEMAN: It did for Caitlyn because we spent a lot of time with Caitlyn and then the new one came, and so we had to even it out.

MR. FINDLAY: How did you even it out?

MR. COLEMAN: Just, put as much time with both of them as I could.

MR. FINDLAY: When did you meet Bobby and Becky Payne?

MR. COLEMAN: Janet set up a lease through her mother over the internet or something they have, we have a website, and ah, then they came out and they rented and that's how I met them.

MR. FINDLAY: How, how long did they rent from you that, that apartment?

MR. COLEMAN: They've rented two of them; they wanted to move so we moved them over to our building.

MR. FINDLAY: Can you explain the circumstances under which they, um, moved into your basement?

MR. COLEMAN: Bobby and me went to go do some work and stuff, and we came back and this is just shortly after I had slept with Becky; she just took all of her stuff and put it down in the basement, move out, in there, and said for us to rent out her apartment.

MR. FINDLAY: Did you tell them they had to move into the basement?

MR. COLEMAN: I didn't want them to move into the basement.

MR. FINDLAY: Did you ever get them out of the basement?

MR. COLEMAN: Yes.

MR. FINDLAY: And when was that?

MR. COLEMAN: That was the fight that they had. Bobby had smashed their marriage license, and I got in between the middle of those two, and I, he pushed and Caitlyn cut her foot; I just decided that was enough.

MR. FINDLAY: Do you remember what the date of that was?

MR. COLEMAN: That was on the 11th.

MR. FINDLAY: You sure it, it was not before the 11th?

MR. COLEMAN: I'm... I'm sorry, it probably was the 10th.

MR. FINDLAY: The 11th is when DHS showed up at the house, correct?

MR. COLEMAN: That's correct. They came the next day after they left.

MR. FINDLAY: What were you doing when, um, DHS showed up at the house?

MR. COLEMAN: I was just in the house discussing to Janet about, I mean, we, we just got hit with everything.

MR. FINDLAY: You say it was everything; what do you mean?

MR. COLEMAN: Xcel called, they accused us of stealing power; Bobby called Xcel Energy and told us we stole power.

MS. WITTLA: Objection your Honor, this is hearsay.

THE COURT: Okay that was hearsay, proceed with your questions, ah, sustained.

MR. FINDLAY: Um, without telling what anybody said, what was, what was going on? You said everything came at that time. What?

MR. COLEMAN: Just utility companies, anything that we could get hit with we were getting all day. We were just getting audited for everything.

MR. FINDLAY: And did you believe this was the result of what the Paynes had done?

MR. COLEMAN: Yes, I do.

MR. FINDLAY: You indicated that you had, um, slept with Becky Payne?

MR. COLEMAN: Yes I did.

MR. FINDLAY: When did you tell Janet about the relationship?

MR. COLEMAN: I wanted to tell her sooner, but I told her that day.

MR. FINDLAY: What did; strike that; who came to the door first, um, on the 11th, when DHS came in?

MR. COLEMAN: I'm sorry, I don't understand.

MR. FINDLAY: Who came to the door first? Was it the police knock on the door, did Ms. Fyle....

MR. COLEMAN: All three of them.

MR. FINDLAY: Okay.

MR. COLEMAN: Elizabeth Fyle, Bob Ross, and—

MR. FINDLAY:—and who answered the door?

MR. COLEMAN: I did.

MR. FINDLAY: How did they get into the house?

MR. COLEMAN: They said they wanted to talk to Caitlyn.

MR. FINDLAY: Did you let them in the house?

MR. COLEMAN: I just opened the door and let them in.

MR. FINDLAY: Did they tell you what they wanted to talk to her about?

MR. COLEMAN: They wouldn't say.

MR. FINDLAY: How long were they there before they took Caitlyn into the bedroom?

MR. COLEMAN: They just pretty much proceeded and wanted to pull Caitlyn aside and take her to the bedroom.

MR. FINDLAY: What was she doing when they got there?

MR. COLEMAN: She was watching TV in the living room.

MR. FINDLAY: Did they tell you— did anytime— time before they took Caitlyn to her bedroom, did they tell you what they wanted to talk to her about?

MR. COLEMAN: Not that we knew of; they just, they had to talk to Caitlyn.

MR. FINDLAY: Did you ask them what it was about?

MR. COLEMAN: Yes.

MR. FINDLAY: And what did they tell you?

MR. COLEMAN: They said that, that they had an allegation or something and they needed to talk to her and discuss things before they could....

MR. FINDLAY: Did you object to them talking to Caitlyn?

MR. COLEMAN: No.

MR. FINDLAY: Did Janet object to them talking to Caitlyn?

MR. COLEMAN: No.

MR. FINDLAY: At some point Janet entered the room where she was being interviewed?

MR. COLEMAN: Yes she did.

MR. FINDLAY: Do you know why she did that?

MR. COLEMAN: Because I called my attorney.

MR. FINDLAY: And what did you tell Janet as a result of that phone call?

MR. COLEMAN: I said that the attorney advises that we should have a witness in there with Caitlyn during the interview.

MR. FINDLAY: How did Janet go into that room?

MR. COLEMAN: An officer was in the dining room and she just walked over and walked and just opened the door and just went in there.

MR. FINDLAY: I mean, did the door get barged open, was she flying in there or did she walk in?

MR. COLEMAN: The door was already open ajar, I, it wasn't shut all the way.

MR. FINDLAY: How long was she in there?

MR. COLEMAN: She was in there for just two minutes or just to, I, I mean things just went fast and I heard her say well, we're going to get a court order to take your children.

MR. FINDLAY: Who did you hear say that?

MR. COLEMAN: I heard Elizabeth Fyle say that.

MR. FINDLAY: Where was she when she said it?

MR. COLEMAN: She was in the bedroom with Janet.

MR. FINDLAY: How, after Janet came out of the room; um, anybody come out with her?

MR. COLEMAN: Yes, Bob Ross did.

MR. FINDLAY: How long was Caitlyn in the room with Elizabeth Fyle after that?

MR. COLEMAN: I would say about three or four minutes.

MR. FINDLAY: Did, ah, Bob Ross go back into the room with Caitlyn and Ms. Fyle?

MR. COLEMAN: No sir, he did not.

MR. FINDLAY: He stayed out in the living area with you?

MR. COLEMAN: In the foyer. We were talking in the foyer.

MR. FINDLAY: How long total would you say that, ah, they were in the house?

MR. COLEMAN: I would say the whole thing lasted about twenty minutes.

MR. FINDLAY: What did they tell you when they left?

MR. COLEMAN: They just left.

MR. FINDLAY: Did they at any time tell you why they had come to interview Caitlyn?

MR. COLEMAN: After they talked to Caitlyn.

MR. FINDLAY: Okay, and what did they tell you?

MR. COLEMAN: They; I invited them in to the kitchen to sit down. They didn't want to, but me and Janet did, and they started, ah, talking about what supposedly had happened.

MR. FINDLAY: Do you remember what they told you; what had happened?

MR. COLEMAN: Elizabeth Fyle said that in the room Caitlyn said that I hit her with a belt.

MR. FINDLAY: What was your reaction to that?

MR. COLEMAN: Well I looked her right in the eyes and I says ma'am I don't believe that.

MR. FINDLAY: What else did they tell you?

MR. COLEMAN: Well they, they told us that, um, you know, um, about spoons and things like that and I got up and I pulled out the drawers and searched through every drawer. I, I wanted to find these spoons.

MR. FINDLAY: Did you ever indicate to Ms. Fyle or Mr. Ross or anybody there that you had used a belt on Caitlyn?

MR. COLEMAN: No sir.

MR. FINDLAY: When asked if you used a belt on Caitlyn, what was your answer?

MR. COLEMAN: I told her she was a liar.

MR. FINDLAY: How do you discipline your children Mr. Coleman?

MR. COLEMAN: I just put them in the corner; I like to talk to Caitlyn and try to explain to her that she's got to be good and if she doesn't she'll go in the corner, and just stand there for a minute until she calms down and usually I'm working during the day and stuff, so I want to spend as much time with my kids as possible.

MR. FINDLAY: Um, did you ever spank Caitlyn?

MR. COLEMAN: Yes sir, I have.

MR. FINDLAY: And when I, what do you mean when say, when you hear the word spank, what are you referring to, what, what does that mean?

MR. COLEMAN: I just say a swat on the butt with an open hand.

MR. FINDLAY: Have you ever done anything further than that in terms of disciplining Caitlyn?

MR. COLEMAN: I've put her in the corner.

MR. FINDLAY: I mean, anything further physically in discipline?

MR. COLEMAN: No sir.

MR. FINDLAY: How about Ashley? How do you discipline Ashley?

MR. COLEMAN: She's just small, I just redirect her, the kids are fighting over a toy, I'd try to get Caitlyn to get her to understand that Caitlyn, that Ashley doesn't know any better, and, ah, give them a different toy or distract them.

MR. FINDLAY: Did you ever spank Ashley?

MR. COLEMAN: Never.

MR. FINDLAY: Would, would you stand up for a second? How tall are you?

MR. COLEMAN: I'm six foot four.

MR. FINDLAY: How much do you weigh?

MR. COLEMAN: I weigh 240 pounds.

MR. FINDLAY: How tall is Caitlyn?

MR. COLEMAN: Caitlyn is about three feet.

MR. FINDLAY: Do you know how much she weighs?

MR. COLEMAN: And she weighs; I don't know, she's been gone for three months.

MR. FINDLAY: What did she weigh when she left?

MR. COLEMAN: She weighed 56 pounds.

MR. FINDLAY: What do you think would happen to a, a little girl that size if a six foot four, 240 pound man would hit her with a belt?

MR. COLEMAN: I could probably kill her if I hit her with a belt.

MR. FINDLAY: You may sit down. Did they make; also tell you they had— there was an allegation that you, something, something happened and you had pushed Ashley by the face?

MR. COLEMAN: Yes sir, they did.

MR. FINDLAY: Do you remember what they told you?

MR. COLEMAN: As far as the allegation?

MR. FINDLAY: Yes.

MR. COLEMAN: They said that I, I don't even want to think about it; I just, I guess she had jumped on Janet and I pushed her off it.

MR. FINDLAY: Did that ever happen?

MR. COLEMAN: No, that would never happen.

MR. FINDLAY: Did they ever tell you anything about they make— no new allegation regarding something in the crib?

MR. COLEMAN: Yes.

MR. FINDLAY: Do you remember what they told you?

MR. COLEMAN: The allegation said that Caitlyn had broke the crib and I hit her in the eye with a belt.

MR. FINDLAY: Did that ever happen?

MR. COLEMAN: No.

MR. FINDLAY: Did the crib ever break?

MR. COLEMAN: Yes it did.

MR. FINDLAY: What happened?

MR. COLEMAN: Ashley and Caitlyn were playing in the crib jumping up and down and we just heard a crash and we went in there and I got them out of the crib.

MR. FINDLAY: What happened to the crib?

MR. COLEMAN: My wife called Michigan State and they recalled the cribs.

MR. FINDLAY: So the crib was defective?

MR. COLEMAN: Yes it was.

MR. FINDLAY: When they left, ah, on the 11th, I know if I say the, I'm referring to DHS, um, what did they tell you?

MR. COLEMAN: I'm sorry, what?

MR. FINDLAY:— what they tell you? Did they tell you that they wanted to interview you again? Did they tell, you know, what did they tell you to do, or what did they tell they were going to do?

MR. COLEMAN: Exact words was Bob Ross said this will just be wrapped here in two days and they left. I said goodbye and I shut the door.

MR. FINDLAY: Did they tell you that they wanted to re-interview Caitlyn at some point?

MR. COLEMAN: No they did not.

MR. FINDLAY: Um, Janet is obviously pregnant, um, where is her gynecologist, OB-GYN doctor? Where is he located?

MR. COLEMAN: It's in Houghton.

MR. FINDLAY: Um, so after the 11th, at any time during that week; well, strike that. Let me back up, what did you on the 12th, and the 12th is the day after, what did you do on the 12th?

MR. COLEMAN: Caitlyn just went to school and Janet and me went about our business, and was just pretty much prepared for going out of town.

So you see? Again, Elizabeth Fyle could have done her second sneak interview, had she wanted to do on the morning of the 12th, while were still in town! Her priority, however, was her training session!

MR. FINDLAY: Okay, so you did go; why did you go to Houghton?

MR. COLEMAN: Because Janet and I had an appointment.

MR. FINDLAY: And what was the day of the appointment?

MR. COLEMAN: That appointment was on Wednesday, Thursday.

MR. FINDLAY: Thursday, and was that a pre-scheduled appointment? Was it scheduled previously?

MR. COLEMAN: It's been scheduled for quite awhile.

MR. FINDLAY: What were your intentions when you, well, when you left for Houghton?

MR. COLEMAN: We had packed andwe planned on staying up there for the weekend and....

MR. FINDLAY: And where were you going to stay?

MR. COLEMAN: We were going to stay in a motel.

MR. FINDLAY: Did you know which motel?

MR. COLEMAN: The Best Western.

MR. FINDLAY: How was that room reserved?

MR. COLEMAN: It was reserved when, um, well we had called to make sure that they had availability and then we had to come in and pay for it then, and get it right then and there.

MR. FINDLAY: Did Janet's mother ever pay for it?

MR. COLEMAN: Yes sir, she did.

MR. FINDLAY: How did that, how did that, how did that work?

MR. COLEMAN: They just called with a credit card number and they paid for the room.

MR. FINDLAY: Ah, and how many nights were you staying there?

MR. COLEMAN: We were going to stay there for four; at least till Monday.

MR. FINDLAY: Did Caitlyn have school the following week?

MR. COLEMAN: No, she was off for spring break, it was Easter time.

MR. FINDLAY: You, you said it was the Best Western in Houghton?

MR. COLEMAN: Yes.

MR. FINDLAY: Why did you choose that hotel?

MR. COLEMAN: Because it was close to the hospital.

MR. FINDLAY: Anything there for the kids to do?

MR. COLEMAN: Yeah, there was a swimming pool there.

MR. FINDLAY: Did the kids go swimming?

MR. COLEMAN: Yes they did.

MR. FINDLAY: So which nights were you there? Thursday night, then Friday night?

MR. COLEMAN: That's correct.

MR. FINDLAY: Did you ever receive a, a telephone call from Bob Ross?

MR. COLEMAN: Yes I did.

MR. FINDLAY: When was that?

MR. COLEMAN: It was on Thursday.

MR. FINDLAY: What time?

MR. COLEMAN: It was at six o'clock.

MR. FINDLAY: What was he asking you or telling you?

MR. COLEMAN: Well, we were in that magic shop in the store, and that's all I remember, and the phone rang and I answered it and he told me that they wanted to talk to the kids. And I explained to him that we have an attorney and that we will be back on Monday.

MR. FINDLAY: Did you ever tell him that you were in Marquette when he called?

MR. COLEMAN: No sir, I did not.

MR. FINDLAY: Did you tell him you'd be back later that day or that; the immediate following day?

MR. COLEMAN: No sir, I did not.

MR. FINDLAY: And you said you told him that you would be back on Monday?

MR. COLEMAN: That's correct.

MR. FINDLAY: What was his reaction?

MR. COLEMAN: He seemed satisfied with that.

MR. FINDLAY: Um, were there any other calls placed to your phone? Did you receive any other calls from anybody?

MR. COLEMAN: I did not receive any more calls after that.

MR. FINDLAY: How about any messages?

MR. COLEMAN: I didn't receive any messages.

MR. FINDLAY: When you heard from Mr. Ross they wanted to talk to Caitlyn and; Caitlyn again, what was your intentions at that time? What did you plan on doing?

MR. COLEMAN: After I talked to Mr. Ross?

MR. FINDLAY: Yes, after he told you that they wanted to interview Caitlyn again, what was your intention, what were you going to do?

MR. COLEMAN: Well, Monday, I was going to go back into town and have my lawyer present.

MR. FINDLAY: Where was your room in the, the Best Western?

MR. COLEMAN: It was upstairs.

MR. FINDLAY: On the second floor?

MR. COLEMAN: Yes.

MR. FINDLAY: It it, to the inside, I mean, some— or to the outside— inside to the hotel?

MR. COLEMAN: There's a parking lot underneath, and we parked up in the front, and we had to walk down the stairway to get to the— underneath parking.

MR. FINDLAY: Is it, um, it, it's not a room that's facing outside; it's— you go in past the lobby, and then through the hotel, to go to your room?

MR. COLEMAN: You have to walk up through the lobby, and then walk all the way down the hall, it was a walk.

MR. FINDLAY: Where did you park the car— or your vehicle?

MR. COLEMAN: I parked my car in the front.

MR. FINDLAY: Were you, did you have any intention at that time to hide from DHS or the authorities, anything like that?

MR. COLEMAN: No I did not.

MR. FINDLAY: When you went to Houghton was it your intention to flee from them?

MR. COLEMAN: No I did not.

MR. FINDLAY: And in fact, you said that it was your intention on Monday to come back and get with your lawyer?

MR. COLEMAN: That's correct. You know, it's a funny thing too because Best Western has an indoor garage, that you can actually park your car in and hide it perfectly. I— they put snowmobiles in there, and....

MR. FINDLAY: (Inaudible to this court transcriber)

MR. COLEMAN: No, I just had it out front.

MR. FINDLAY: Do you remember what happened at 3 a.m., the morning of the 15th?

MR. COLEMAN: Yes I do.

MR. FINDLAY: What were you doing?

MR. COLEMAN: I was sleeping.

MR. FINDLAY: What happened?

MR. COLEMAN: Well, I got woke up by the noise of a chain hitting the door, and pushing on it trying to bang it open, and Janet got out of bed and answered the door. Then, these police just rushed in and just went right for the bed with Caitlyn and they grabbed the children and put their coats on and I wasn't allowed to get out of bed; I was laying there.

MR. FINDLAY: How many police officers did you think were in the room?

MR. COLEMAN: I thought there were at least five or six.

MR. FINDLAY: This is a, a pretty standard room with two double beds; the room that we're talking about; a standard hotel room with two double beds, and the TV and that kind of thing?

MR. COLEMAN: The TV is across from the beds, and they had a table in there.

MR. FINDLAY: This wasn't a suite, was it?

MR. COLEMAN: No sir, it wasn't.

MR. FINDLAY: Was not— we're not talking a big room?

MR. COLEMAN: No.

MR. FINDLAY: I mean five adults, well more than that, but was it pretty crowded in there?

MR. COLEMAN: I don't think it was more than two feet between the bed and the dresser from the TV.

MR. FINDLAY: The police officers were wearing uniforms?

MR. COLEMAN: Yes they were.

MR. FINDLAY: With guns?

MR. COLEMAN: Yes.

MR. FINDLAY: What did they say to you?

MR. COLEMAN: They told me not to get out of bed.

MR. FINDLAY: What were they saying to Janet?

MS. WITTLA: Objection, your Honor. Hearsay.

THE COURT: Well, I guess what the officer said is hearsay too, sustained.

Wrong again judge! Hearsay is when you put words into what was said to somebody else! So it would be hearsay to answer the last of his questions, the part that pertained to what they said to Janet. But the officer was speaking to ME, and that is not hearsay! Go read a law book sometime!

MR. FINDLAY: All right. What was Janet doing?

MR. COLEMAN: Janet was just wondering what they were doing in the room, and why they were taking our children. The police officers, they said just stay in bed, we'll have them back Monday; we just want to check the kids out, want to make sure they're safe.

You know I never really thought about when it was happening, but I wonder why the police officers said we'd have them back on Monday? That was never going to happen, but it makes me realize they did have information that we would be back in town on Monday, as I told Ross. But Fyle kept saying we didn't tell him that. If we had not, how would these police officers have formed that opinion?

MR. FINDLAY: Were you ever told why they were taking them?

MR. COLEMAN: They didn't say anything other than the fact they were just taking the kids.

MR. FINDLAY: What did they do to take the kids? I mean, how did that proceed?

MR. COLEMAN: They just came in and they grabbed their coats and grabbed whatever; the kids were out of the room really quick; they were just picked up and out they went.

MR. FINDLAY: Okay, at some time, were you finally able, allowed to get out, out of bed?

MR. COLEMAN: I sat up, after the children left, and then I wanted to sit in the chair, and the officer told me no, and it was a back and forth thing; and two police officers were standing at the end of my bed and there's only about a foot in between there and there was two chairs to the, to the side of my bed, and I, they wouldn't let me up.

MR. FINDLAY: How were you dressed at this time?

MR. COLEMAN: I was in my pajamas.

MR. FINDLAY: Did eventually they tell you what was going on?

MR. COLEMAN: After our kids were removed and everything, the officer had given Janet some paperwork and said that they had a warrant to enter the motel room.

MR. FINDLAY: Did you provide the, the police or anybody else there with any, um, personal items for the girls?

MR. COLEMAN: I was more wanting to go see my girls; I wanted to see where they were going.

MR. FINDLAY: Did you have— did they end up taking personal items of the girls?

MR. COLEMAN: Yes, they— they just came in and they took what they wanted, they just went through and....

MR. FINDLAY: ... did you end up providing them with the blankets and a bottle and those type of things?

MR. COLEMAN: I tried. I couldn't get to them.

MR. FINDLAY: Well, I mean, not the girls, the, the— did you give them to the officers?

MR. COLEMAN: Not at that point. I—the officers did get them. I gave them to them.

MR. FINDLAY: Was there also, ah, somebody from DHS there?

MR. COLEMAN: Yes there was.

MR. FINDLAY: Do you recall her name?

MR. COLEMAN: I, I know what her name is now, but I didn't at the time.

MR. FINDLAY: Um, what was she doing at the time?

MR. COLEMAN: I didn't really see her until I came down the stairs.

MR. FINDLAY: Did you hear your wife during this; while this was going on, were you able to hear your wife?

MR. COLEMAN: Yes.

MR. FINDLAY: Did she ever say that, to the girls, I'll never see you again?

MR. COLEMAN: She'd never say that.

MR. FINDLAY: What did she say to the girls?

MS. WITTLA: Objection your Honor. Hearsay.

MR. FINDLAY: She's a respondent to the party.

MS. WITTLA: She's not an adverse party.

THE COURT: She's not an opponent, but, I don't know, there's prior state—

MR. FINDLAY:—and it would— like I said, evidence too, I believe.

THE COURT: Well, and there's prior statements on the record, go ahead.

MR. FINDLAY: What did she say?

MR. COLEMAN: When we got downstairs, she said that because I got Ashley, I wanted to hold her so bad and we just pleaded with them— I actually grasped the police officer and I was hugging them and I said please let me see my children, and so they, they handed me Ashley and I held her so tight, and I told her I loved her and Caitlyn was in the car and she was saying about the Easter Bunny and the Easter Bunny will wait, because she was worried and she just said, mama why are they taking me? Why are they taking me?

MR. FINDLAY: Have you, have you ever been through anything like this before in your life?

MR. COLEMAN: No, it was just terrible.

MR. FINDLAY: Do you recall what was going on through your mind while that was happening?

MR. COLEMAN: The kids were really scared. I was more worried about them, than myself.

MR. FINDLAY: How many times have you seen the girls, if you recall, since they were taken?

MR. COLEMAN: I remember every minute— total of 24 hours.

MR. FINDLAY: Do you recall the first visit?

MR. COLEMAN: Yes I do.

MR. FINDLAY: Did you record that?

MR. COLEMAN: Yes I did.

MR. FINDLAY: Why did you record the visits?

MR. COLEMAN: Because I don't trust the government. The way they did everything, the way they just came in and took our children; the way we got this piece of paper thrown in our face; in exchange for our children; I don't trust them.

MR. FINDLAY: Were you in court on or about, um, was it March 18th at the emergency removal hearing?

MR. COLEMAN: Yes I was.

MR. FINDLAY: Do you recall the testimony of Bonnie Huttunen at that time?

MR. COLEMAN: I recall it.

MR. FINDLAY: Do you recall the, the claim that Janet had upset the kids by saying I'm never going to see you again? You're aware that's what DHS claimed at that time, and did that, it's your; well, you're telling us that's never happened, correct?

MR. COLEMAN: That's correct.

MR. FINDLAY: Did that have anything to do with why you wanted to record the visits and contact with DHS?

MR. COLEMAN: They told us they wanted their birth certificates, original social security cars, shot records, we're done; and they wanted us to take pictures, done.

MR. FINDLAY: But is that why, the fact that they said something they— you knew wasn't true, is that why you wanted to record future contacts with DHS?

MR. COLEMAN: That's correct. They just added to it.

MR. FINDLAY: Have you, the recordings that you've made, have you in any way changed what somebody said, edited them or anything like that?

MR. COLEMAN: No I haven't.

MR. FINDLAY: Would you even know how to do that?

MR. COLEMAN: I, I can't figure how it would be done.

MR. FINDLAY: So the recordings you've made; those accurately reflect the… what was said?

MR. COLEMAN: They reflect the truth.

MR. FINDLAY: Including the one of the first visit?

MR. COLEMAN: Everything.

MR. FINDLAY: Did Ashley ever say to you during that visit, I'm sorry, or take responsibility or, you know, blame herself for, you know, telling DHS that you had spanked them or anything like that?

MR. COLEMAN: Caitlyn?

MR. FINDLAY: Caitlyn, I'm sorry.

MR. COLEMAN: She'd never say that, she missed me so much.

MR. FINDLAY: Just to finish up, have you ever hit either of your children with a belt?

MR. COLEMAN: I never would.

MR. FINDLAY: Have you ever hit them with a spoon?

MR. COLEMAN: No.

MR. FINDLAY: Have you ever hit them with any object?

MR. COLEMAN: No.

MR. FINDLAY: Have you ever abused either of your children?

MR. COLEMAN: No.

MR. FINDLAY: How does it feel to be accused of that when you didn't do it?

MR. COLEMAN: It hurts me bad, I love them so much.

MR. FINDLAY: Thank you.

THE COURT: Mr. Coleman, do you need some water? I think considering what's happening?

MR. FINDLAY: Can we take a break?

THE COURT: Well, I was going to commence the cross for time purposes, but considering what's going on what we will do is, we will reconvene, we will break early, we'll reconvene right at one o'clock. Ladies and gentlemen, I think we've made enough progress in the case that it's going to get to you today, and then the process will go on. It may be that you're not through here right at 4:30 as we have been, so you may need to inform your families or make, make whatever arrangements to try to conclude the case today. We would stay beyond normal hours if deliberations were going on, and how long depends on, on how things go.

Why don't you try to put a little pressure on this jury, Judge? Do your best to hurry up and surrender their preconceived guilty verdict so you can get on with the important things in your life!

THE COURT (continuing): I mean, I can't predict, I'm not going to keep you here, obviously, till midnight but, but, ah, we may go beyond regular hours; so if you need to make arrangements you should do so; if there's a family problem, a real issue, you need to communicate to the bailiff why you couldn't be here somewhat longer. It may, and that, we may not, that may not happen; all depends on the rest of case, for now we are in recess. Counsel if you want to come on into chambers please.

(COUNSEL & JUDGE MET OFF THE RECORD IN CHAMBERS. FOLLOWING THIS, COURT RESUMED):

THE COURT: Be seated. Thank you again for being prompt and we're back on the record. Um, Mr. Coleman, you would resume the stand please; and be seated, I'll remind you that you are under oath, and Ms. Wittla, you are about to cross examine.

MS. WITTLA: Mr. Coleman, I think when Mr. Findlay was asking you questions, I believe you responded at one point, I wanted to tell her sooner, but I told her that day. I believe that was in reference to telling your wife about the affair you had with Becky, sound familiar?

MR. COLEMAN: Yes, I recall that.

MS. WITTLA: What day was that day that you told her?

MR. COLEMAN: Ma'am I don't know.

MS. WITTLA: You don't know what day you told your wife about having sex with Becky Payne?

MR. COLEMAN: I told my wife the day that this whole event had occurred.

MS. WITTLA: What, what day are you referencing, the day that CPS came to your house, the 11th?

MR. COLEMAN: I told my wife the day on the 11th or yes.

MS. WITTLA: The 11th, that's what you just said?

MR. COLEMAN: That's correct.

MS. WITTLA: Any idea why you would have told Renee Anderson on the 7th?

MR. COLEMAN: Because she's a friend of mine.

MS. WITTLA: You told Renee Anderson that you had an affair with Becky Payne on the 7th, four days before you decided to talk to tell your wife?

MR. COLEMAN: Ma'am what does this have to do with me spanking my children?

Help! Help! Help her judge! Don't make her do her own work!

THE COURT: Okay if you just answer the question sir. You're not here to ask questions, if there's an objectionable issue, one of the lawyers will raise it, and I'll address it, but….

That of course applied while I was on the stand. But when Ms. Fyle or Mr. Ross or any of the state witnesses were questioned, they were allowed to wander off in any direction they wanted without responding directly to the questions. They were even told once they did not have to answer a direct yes or no— recall?

MS. WITTLA: Did you understand the question?

MR. COLEMAN: Yes I do.

MS. WITTLA: Could you respond to the question?

MR. COLEMAN: I don't know.

MS. WITTLA: Were you here for Rebecca Payne's testimony?

MR. COLEMAN: Yes I was.

MS. WITTLA: Did you hear her say that the last time you had sex with her was on March 9th?

MR. COLEMAN: I, I don't recall.

MS. WITTLA: From your memory when was the last time you had sex with Becky Payne?

MR. COLEMAN: I, I don't recall. I had sex with her, it was, I, I would need a calendar ma'am so I could look at that and I can give you some exact dates.

MS. WITTLA: I believe in prior testimony, you indicated that you had had sex with her more than once, is that accurate?

MR. COLEMAN: That's correct.

MS. WITTLA: So if Becky Payne describes the sex between the two of you not as an affair, but from her perspective as rape, is she telling the truth?

MR. FINDLAY: Your Honor I don't think that word was ever used, she said she did it for cigarettes, but I don't think that's rape, but I don't think the word was used.

Oh, but this sneaky prosecutor would want it to be rape, wouldn't she? I have no doubt this prosecutor was, among other things, a women's libber who hates all men! She would give anything to be able to bring criminal charges against me! Well, all I can say, is that after her actions in our case, I'd love to be able to do the same and bring criminal charges against her! In my mind, she is the real criminal! It would be interesting to find out if she ever brought one case in which she dealt with real facts— and not manufactured ones!

THE COURT: In any event, the, the legal classification of, of that is not for the jury to consider, so, if you want to rephrase it in some manner without using the legal term, rape, which really isn't a legal term any more, but is classically such.

MS. WITTLA: Okay if Becky Payne describes that the sex that occurred between the two of you was forced, is she being truthful?

MR. COLEMAN: No she's not.

MS. WITTLA: So Becky lied.

MR. COLEMAN: That's correct.

MS. WITTLA: You've stated that Elizabeth Fyle told your wife, while she was still in the bedroom interviewing Caitlyn that we're going to get a court order to take your children?

MR. COLEMAN: That's correct.

MS. WITTLA: You were here for Ms. Fyle's testimony?

MR. COLEMAN: Yes I was.

MS. WITTLA: So if, if Ms. Fyle's testimony was that you—was that she never said that at all; that was a conversation that Mr. Ross had with Janet, is Elizabeth Fyle lying?

MR. COLEMAN: I'm sorry, could you please rephrase again?

MS. WITTLA: If Elizabeth Fyle's testimony is that she never had a conversation about getting a court order regarding interviews with Caitlyn, because that's the conversation that Bob Ross had, is she telling the truth?

MR. COLEMAN: I heard Ms. Fyle say that.

MS. WITTLA: Is it truthful?

MR. COLEMAN: Is it truthful that Ms. Fyle said that? Yes.

MS. WITTLA: Is, is that what happened?

MR. COLEMAN: Yes.

MS. WITTLA: If Bob Ross had that conversation with Janet?

MR. COLEMAN: After she had said that, Bob Ross had came out of the room and then talked with us in the foyer.

MS. WITTLA: So your testimony is that she also said that?

MR. FINDLAY: Your Honor, this has been asked and answered, I mean, she keeps asking a different way, but what—

MS. WITTLA: I'm sorry your Honor, I'm just not clear; if he is saying that both of them said the same statement.

She is such a liar! It should be clear from the way she asked the questions, she was trying to confuse the issue! She knew exactly what my answer was, but was trying to confuse me!

THE COURT: Can you repeat the question?

MS. WITTLA: Mr. Coleman, is it your testimony that both Elizabeth Fyle and Robert Ross made a statement to you or your wife that they were going to get court orders to remove your children if you did not cooperate?

THE COURT: Okay, if you can answer that, we won't ask it any more. But go ahead and answer.

MR. COLEMAN: I heard Ms. Fyle say that ma'am.

MS. WITTLA: And Mr. Ross say that?

MR. COLEMAN: I, I don't recall. I, I heard her say that.

MS. WITTLA: You indicated that the length of time that Elizabeth Fyle, Robert Ross, and Cheryl Saippa were at your house was approximately twenty minutes?

MR. COLEMAN: That's correct.

MS. WITTLA: How long was the interview with you?

MR. COLEMAN: We had an interview in the kitchen for about ten minutes.

MS. WITTLA: And how long would it take to find the belts in your dresser?

MR. COLEMAN: They told me that they wanted to see my belts, so I took them over to my armoire and I went to show them.

MS. WITTLA: That there were belts in your armoire?

MR. COLEMAN: That's correct, that's where I keep them.

MS. WITTLA: And that's where they were found that day?

MR. COLEMAN: No, ma'am they weren't there.

MS. WITTLA: Where were they found?

MR. COLEMAN: They were found in the dresser, where she had directed me to go to.

MS. WITTLA: How long did that process take?

MR. COLEMAN: I, I don't know.

MS. WITTLA: Do you have problems with memory, Mr. Coleman?

MR. COLEMAN: Ma'am, I am stressed out, okay? I am very stressed out, so yes, at this time I am very stressed; I'm sorry I can't answer these questions for you, but they have been asked again and again, and I am sorry, but I am very stressed out.

MS. WITTLA: So the question is, do you have memory problems Mr. Coleman?

This is the way this prosecutor gets her jollies! She loves to insult, or try to scare or intimidate people, and she will ask the same stupid questions, which have nothing whatsoever to do with anything, just to feel the sense of her power. Today I have no problem whatsoever with my memory Ms. Wittla, and I remember very well you used the lies of Becky and Bobby Payne to manufacture a case, and you did that with several other accomplices, including Elizabeth Fyle, Bob Ross, Ron Carpenedo and several others who all fit into your corrupt little kidnapping ring. Exposing you here may return some of the intimidation, because now you have to explain why it is you base your cases on false information.

MR. COLEMAN: Under enormous amounts of stress, with the social worker being ordered to watch over my baby and they're going to take it if we lose, yes, I am very stressed out.

MS. WITTLA: Mr. Coleman, if you were to strike Caitlyn with a belt, why would it kill her?

MR. COLEMAN: Ma'am, I've never hit my child with a belt.

MS. WITTLA: Your statement earlier was that if you did, it would kill her.

Yes, and if I shot you between the eyes with a gun, it would kill you too! But I have not done that, have I Ms. Wittla?

MR. COLEMAN: I'm a very large man. If I struck a child like that, I would injure her dramatically; I, it's just common sense. That's why you don't do those things.

Quick! You are in trouble with my last answer! Invent something! Invent something!

MS. WITTLA: Mr. Coleman, is it your testimony that if you were going to hit someone with a belt, that you'd only be able to do it one way, full force?

No, that wasn't my testimony, Ms. Wittla, and you know it. That was your invented hypothesis!

MR. COLEMAN: If I was going to hit someone with a belt?

MS. WITTLA: Yes.

MR. COLEMAN: You know, ma'am, up until this court, I've never really had the idea to ever strike anybody with a belt.

MS. WITTLA: Mr. Coleman, your testimony earlier today was that if you hit Caitlyn with a belt, with a belt, it would probably kill her. All I'm asking is if the only way that you could ever hit someone with a belt is full force, to cause that much damage?

MR. COLEMAN: Well ma'am, I've never had practice to find out, so I guess we'll never know. I'm sorry.

MS. WITTLA: Mr. Coleman, you indicated that you're a six foot four, two hundred and forty pounds, and that when the officers came to the motel room in Hancock, that they refused to let you get up out of bed?

MR. COLEMAN: That's correct.

MS. WITTLA: Were handcuffs used?

MR. COLEMAN: Should there be? They were armed with tasers and guns.

MS. WITTLA: The question Mr. Coleman, was whether or not handcuffs were used on you?

MR. COLEMAN: I did not do anything that they told me not to do, so I don't see why they would want to use them.

MS. WITTLA: So, just so we're clear, you are stating that you were sitting on the bed, in a hotel room, with four or five police officers in the room, and their preference was for you to stay in that bed instead of getting up?

MR. COLEMAN: I was lying in bed when they had came in, I'm still lying in the bed. I wanted to sit up, they would not let me get up.

MS. WITTLA: And they didn't try to secure you in any way with handcuffs?

Duh! What part of they didn't need to are you having problems understanding here, Ms. Wittla? Ms. Wittla, do you have a memory problem?

MR. COLEMAN: Gee, I would think two officers armed with guns and tasers would be enough. Wouldn't you think so? Especially when you woke up and you're in your pajamas?

MS. WITTLA: Well, Mr. Coleman, wouldn't it be more typical that they would want to get you out of the bed, away from those blankets and pillows so that they knew that you didn't have anything in your hands?

Actually, Ms. Wittla, no, it would not be more typical in such a case. These are police officers, doing their duty, and their first concern is removing the children. In doing so, they will observe me very closely, and if I make a move, shoot me dead. But their first concern, is getting the kids out. So if they make me lie still, not moving, I cannot do anything, whereas if I'm standing I might fight them, resulting in somebody getting hurt. The way they did it was technically right, because the only one who could be hurt would be me, if I were the villain you have tried to paint me up to be. But of course I'm not, so therefore your complete fabrication is way off base again.

MR. FINDLAY: Objection your Honor. I don't know how Mr. Coleman is supposed to know what the police were to do.

THE COURT: Yeah, you're speculating what the officers would have thought. Sustained.

MS. WITTLA: Mr. Coleman, you do understand that the DHS caseworker, Bonnie Huttunen had said that the way that they gained access to your room, was through a rouse with the maintenance man? You heard her testimony?

MR. COLEMAN: Yes I did.

MS. WITTLA: Was that accurate?

MR. COLEMAN: I was asleep. I didn't hear a maintenance man; I heard a door pounding with the chain, and the officer had the key in his hand. He had the key card in his hand after he came in and they were in the room.

MS. WITTLA: So are you saying that your earlier testimony that the door was pushed open and the chain was still latched—

MR. COLEMAN:— yes, my wife got up to take the chain off.

MS. WITTLA: So you saw that door pushed open, that chain still latched?

MR. COLEMAN: I could hear it. You can hear a chain, bang, bang, bang. I—I know what that sounds like, it's not a very good thing to wake up to, okay? It's horrible; it was horrible.

MS. WITTLA: My question to you Mr. Coleman is whether or not you saw it?

MR. COLEMAN: No, I didn't see the chain on the door being opened.

MS. WITTLA: Isn't that because when they banged on the door, Janet voluntarily went and opened that door and took the chain off?

MR. COLEMAN: No, that's because they would have kicked the door in if Janet didn't take the chain off the door, that why it's because.

MS.WITTLA: You can see into the future and you would've known that that's what they would have done?

Let's ask the readers! What do you think that police on a raid would have done if we had refused to take the chain off the door? Isn't it a bit ridiculous to say you can see into the future in such an instance? Of course they would have broken the door down if they had to! But people who don't know anything but how to lie, like Ms. Wittla, would never be privy to actual life situations!

MR. COLEMAN: I could know that CPS is on a power trip, and I know that they were trying to force their way into our apartment; or into our motel room.

MS. WITTLA: You knew that CPS was on a power trip and trying to force their way into the hotel room that night?

MR. COLEMAN: After that ma'am, I did.

MS. WITTLA: Mr. Coleman, how many times did Bob Ross call you?

MR. COLEMAN: He called me once.

MS. WITTLA: When was that?

MR. COLEMAN: Six o'clock on Thursday.

MS. WITTLA: AM or PM?

MR. COLEMAN: It was PM.

MS. WITTLA: So your testimony to this court is that Mr. Ross called you at 6 PM eastern time?

MR. COLEMAN: It was 6 PM on my phone. I, I just remember that because we were in a magic shop. I was going to buy my daughter one of those little pens to go through some, some stuff and he had called me, and I had answered the phone. I had explained to him that we have an attorney and I, I mean, ma'am, I could try to go word for word what he has said, and he said that he wanted to interview Caitlyn. I explained to him that we have an attorney and I explained to him that we are out of town, and he had said then, why are you calling from a 932 phone number? And I had said that it was ported; it's a ported phone number. And I told him that my wife had an attorney and my children, I says, my children have rights and I said that I'll be in Monday and we can deal with this then. I didn't feel that it was necessary to take my children all the way back; I was looking for the best interest of my children.

MS. WITTLA: How many times did Ironwood Safety call you?

MR. COLEMAN: None.

MS. WITTLA: Does your phone show the numbers that call you?

MR. COLEMAN: Sometimes.

MS. WITTLA: Mr. Coleman, if I told you that in the return for the search warrant, it appears that the phone number 932-1234 was contacted on the 13th of March at 11:45 AM, would you recall that call?

MR. COLEMAN: No ma'am, I wouldn't.

MS. WITTLA: Do you recall having a conversation with Sergeant, I'm sorry, Detective Passuello about being interviewed?

MR. COLEMAN: I'm sorry? About being interviewed?

MS. WITTLA: Uh-huh. Detective Passuello wanted to interview you on, on an open complaint that he had. Remember talking to him on the 13th?

MR. COLEMAN: I'm sorry. What date was the 13th?

MS. WITTLA: Thursday.

MR. COLEMAN: I did not talk to Officer Passuello or any officer on the 13th in regards to an open complaint.

MS. WITTLA: Do you recall Detective Passuello testifying that you told him you were in Marquette on the 13th?

MR. COLEMAN: Ma'am, I don't recall. I, I don't know.

MS. WITTLA: You don't know if you told Detective Passuello you were in Marquette?

MR. COLEMAN: I don't recall talking to a police officer on the phone about Marquette. I, I don't know, it was three months ago, it's—

MS. WITTLA:— any reason you can think of why Detective Passuello would state that you told him that you were in Marquette on, on Thursday?

MR. FINDLAY: Objection, that's out of the scope of Mr. Coleman's knowledge—

THE COURT:— yeah, for his state of mind, um, sustained.

MS. WITTLA: If the, if the return of the search warrant also indicates that you had two different calls come into your phone later on the 13th at 12:17 and 12:20 that originated from Ironwood, I have 906-364-3042 number, do you know who that is?

MR. COLEMAN: I'm sorry ma'am, a number for what?

MS. WITTLA: Do you know anyone with the phone number of 364-3042?

MR. COLEMAN: No ma'am, I don't recall.

MS. WITTLA: How about 932-4011?

MR. COLEMAN: Ma'am, I, I'd have to call it to find out.

MS. WITTLA: Mr. Coleman, do you believe that anyone that I've put on for, for this case, has testified truthfully about you?

MR. COLEMAN: That you have put on for me?

MS. WITTLA: Yes, witnesses I've called. Have they been truthful about you?

MR. COLEMAN: Well ma'am, I, I know I've heard a lot of lies in this courtroom from the State, so I, I would not believe that there would be a lot of truth.

MS. WITTLA: Do you recall hearing testimony from Bonnie Huttunen about your reason for being in Houghton/Hancock?

MR. COLEMAN: On what occasion?

MS. WITTLA: Let me ask it a different way. Why were you up in Houghton/Hancock?

MR. COLEMAN: Because we had an appointment for Janet and for myself.

MS. WITTLA: Doctors appointments?

MR. COLEMAN: That's correct.

MS. WITTLA: But haven't you also stated that the reason you were there was for a family vacation?

MR. COLEMAN: We are a family; we were having a vacation.

MS. WITTLA: And did you refer to your vacation as spring break?

MR. COLEMAN: Oh, ma'am, I don't know because the police took my children before we were really allowed to have a vacation.

MS. WITTLA: But wasn't your testimony that you always planned on coming back on Monday?

MR. COLEMAN: Yes, we would come back on Monday.

MS. WITTLA: Well, wasn't the Monday the start of the spring break?

MR. COLEMAN: That's correct; does CPS work on Mondays? We were going to come back on Monday.

MS. WITTLA: And it's your testimony that you told everyone involved that, that's, that was your plan?

MR. COLEMAN: I'm sorry, I, everyone....

MS. WITTLA:— it's your testimony that you told Mr. Ross that that was your plan, and he was okay with it?

MR. COLEMAN: I told Mr. Ross that we would be back, I have an attorney and we would deal with it then. Mr. Ross never indicated to me that they were going to have a search party out looking for me if I didn't show up. And if I would have been in Marquette, would you have not raided our motel room with SWAT? I mean I don't see what difference it would matter if we were in Marquette or Houghton; we were in Houghton. Clearly you knew that. You found us.

MS. WITTLA: I have nothing further.

THE COURT: Mr. Perhalla?

MR. PERHALLA: Nothing. Thanks your Honor.

THE COURT: I'm trying to decide where we are at here, did you have redirect?

MR. FINDLAY: We have redirect and we, I don't have anything, no we're all set.

THE COURT: Okay, thank you Mr. Coleman, you may step down. Your next witness?

MR. FINDLAY: Janet Coleman.

At this point Janet took the stand, was sworn in, and Mr. Findlay began his questioning of her:

MR. FINDLAY: State your name for the record, Janet?

MS. COLEMAN: Janet Coleman.

MR. FINDLAY: Um, what are your kids' names?

MS. COLEMAN: Caitlyn; Caitlyn Brag and Ashley Coleman.

MR. FINDLAY: Can you tell me up to you, ah, your educational background?

MS. COLEMAN: Um, well after high school, I went on to, ah, a college in, ah, North Dakota; I studied early childhood and elementary ed, and then I went on to, a few years later, right when Caitlyn was born, I went back to college in, ah, Duluth, Minnesota, and there I got a degree in graphic design media.

MR. FINDLAY: How many, how many years did you go to college for that?

MS. COLEMAN: Five; five and a half.

MR. FINDLAY: Did you get a degree?

MS. COLEMAN: I've got a degree in, an associates ah, applied science.

MR. FINDLAY: How about your past employment?

MS. COLEMAN: Um, let's see, I've worked at various daycares, um, I volunteered at, ah, YMCA in Minnesota; I've also managed motels, I've done a variety of, you know, most recent, I, ah, before I met Rob I was working at Headstart.

MR. FINDLAY: What were you doing at Headstart?

MS. COLEMAN: I was the, ah, um, assistant.

MR. FINDLAY: Did that; would that be a mandatory reporter?

MS. COLEMAN: Yes.

MR. FINDLAY: So you had a legal obligation to report abuse and such?

MS. COLEMAN: Yes.

MR. FINDLAY: When they came, when, and when I speak, refer to they, I mean DHS, um, on the 11th, do you recall what you were doing when they arrived?

MS. COLEMAN: I was, um, sitting on the couch and was just— it's going to be about maybe a hundred feet away, fifty maybe, and right before then me and Rob were discussing our personal issues; what had happened that day.

MR. FINDLAY: And when you say personal issues, what are those?

MS. COLEMAN: The, all the allegations, the affair, the, you know, everything that was confronted that day.

MR. FINDLAY: Um, and what time do you recall that DHS arrived?

MS. COLEMAN: I think it was in the afternoon, maybe around two-ish, something like that.

MR. FINDLAY: Did they tell you why they were there?

MS. COLEMAN: Not at first. At first they just said they wanted to talk to Caitlyn.

MR. FINDLAY: And just to explain to me how that proceeded, they arrived, you unlocked the door, who let them in?

MS. COLEMAN: Ah, Robert.

MR. FINDLAY: And then what happened?

MS. COLEMAN: Um, I think, ah, Rob or for some reason they had something that, you know, CPS is here, they want to talk to the kids and Rob let them in, and then I remember asking well, what for, and they wouldn't tell me. Only thing they would say is that they needed to talk to Caitlyn.

MR. FINDLAY: And did they get Caitlyn into the bedroom?

MS. COLEMAN: I think, ah, if, I believe that's when I got up and I kinda directed where her bedroom was.

MR. FINDLAY: Why did you direct them to the bedroom?

MS. COLEMAN: That's where they, I think, said that they wanted to talk to Caitlyn at.

MR. FINDLAY: How long were they in the bedroom before you entered the room?

MS. COLEMAN: It was just a couple of minutes.

MR. FINDLAY: And why did you enter the room?

MS. COLEMAN: Well, right after, um, they had come in, Rob had called our attorney, and then Rob had told me that, you know, the attorney had said that I can, I should, needed to be in there.

MR. FINDLAY: So you entered the room on your attorney's, at that time, advice, right?

MS. COLEMAN: Yes.

MR. FINDLAY: Who was your attorney at that time?

MS. COLEMAN: Michael Pope.

MR. FINDLAY: How did you enter the room?

MS. COLEMAN: I just, the, the door wasn't completely closed or latched; I just pushed it open and walked in.

MR. FINDLAY: Did you say anything?

MS. COLEMAN: I had said that our, I, we just talked to our attorney and he advised me to be present.

MR. FINDLAY: And what did, ah; Ms. Fyle and Bob Ross were in there, right?

MS. COLEMAN: Yes.

MR. FINDLAY: What did they say to you?

MS. COLEMAN: Um, they said that if you don't allow us to talk to Caitlyn, we're going to get a court order and take your kids.

MR. FINDLAY: Now did, there's some question brought up, do you know that they both said that, or just one of them said that?

MS. COLEMAN: It was Ms. Fyle that said that.

MR. FINDLAY: Did at any time; did you recall Bob Ross saying that to you?

MS. COLEMAN: I don't believe so.

MR. FINDLAY: How long did the interview go on? Or did the, them being in the room with Caitlyn go on after— well— how long were you in the room when you went in?

MS. COLEMAN: Oh, just thirty seconds—maybe a minute at the most.

MR. FINDLAY: How long did the interview go on after you stepped back out?

MS. COLEMAN: I would say maybe five, ten minutes.

MR. FINDLAY: Did, did you ever do anything to obstruct DHS from talking to Caitlyn or even in entering your home or that?

MS. COLEMAN: Only thing is, um, I said I wanted to be present; I didn't prevent it; I didn't stop it; I just said I wanted to be present.

MR. FINDLAY: As far as you're concerned, were you cooperating with them?

MS. COLEMAN: Yes.

MR. FINDLAY: How would; what was told to you when they left?

MS. COLEMAN: Um, they said that, ah, we'll keep in touch.

MR. FINDLAY: Did they give you an appointment date or a specific time about when?

MS. COLEMAN: No.

MR. FINDLAY: Did they tell you that—

MS. COLEMAN: I did, I did overhear Bob Ross explaining to Rob that this should be over in a couple of days, but he was directing that to Robert.

MR. FINDLAY: Did; were you ever told that, ah, they needed to re-interview Catilyn?

MS. COLEMAN: No.

MR. FINDLAY: The, ah; what did you go to Houghton that weekend for?

MS. COLEMAN: That Thursday morning I had a, an appointment and as well as Robert; and we had plans that we were just going to stay there for the weekend.

MR. FINDLAY: How long had these plans been made?

MS. COLEMAN: Um, I know the doctor's appointment was probably a couple of weeks in advance, and then that, ah, I know that Tuesday night me and Rob had discussed staying there, but then Wednesday afternoon I had to call the school and left a message with the secretary that Caitlyn was going to be gone, and that's kind of when we decided that we were going to stay there that, the weekend.

MR. FINDLAY: So when did you tell the school?

MS. COLEMAN: Wednesday afternoon.

MR. FINDLAY: On the 13th?

MS. COLEMAN: Yes.

MR. FINDLAY: And what was your doctor's appointment for?

MS. COLEMAN: It was, um, during my pregnancy, I was having some back problems, so she referred me to a physical therapist.

MR. FINDLAY: You said who; who referred you?

MS. COLEMAN: My, ah, OB doctor in Houghton.

MR. FINDLAY: So your OB doctor is in Houghton too?

MS. COLEMAN: Yes.

MR. FINDLAY: Um, Rob had testified that the kids go swimming up, when you're up at the motel?

MS. COLEMAN: Yes.

MR. FINDLAY: Did either of you go swim with them?

MS. COLEMAN: Yeah, we both went swimming.

MR. FINDLAY: What had you done, ah, during the day Friday?

MS. COLEMAN: Well we were, well, swimming, we just kind of drove around town, you know, looked at the—be tourists and did some shopping, just enjoyed the day together.

MR. FINDLAY: Do you recall the time when you got back in the room?

MS. COLEMAN: Around dinner time. Five, six, seven-ish, something like that.

MR. FINDLAY: What time did you turn off the lights then?

MS. COLEMAN: Probably about ten, eleven that night.

MR. FINDLAY: Was everybody in bed?

MS. COLEMAN: Yes.

MR. FINDLAY: Did everybody go to sleep around then or soon thereafter?

MS. COLEMAN: Yeah, um, we were watching the news, Caitlyn and Ashley were coloring pictures, we were playing games with them, and then, you know, around ten o'clock when the news or eleven o'clock when the news started, I noticed Caitlyn and Ashley were asleep, and I just turned the lights off and Robert was sleeping and so I went to bed.

MR. FINDLAY: Where was; you know, in the motel room, you were in the two beds, were you in the bed closest to the door or further from the door?

MS. COLEMAN: Closest.

MR. FINDLAY: Is that where Rob was too?

MS. COLEMAN: Yes.

MR. FINDLAY: Um, so what happened at 3 AM?

MS. COLEMAN: Um, I heard some loud banging on the door, and I, you know, I tried to wake up Rob, but I got up, I went to the door.

MR. FINDLAY: Did you open the handle of the door yourself?

MS. COLEMAN: No, the door was already open, there's just the chain was holding it.

MR. FINDLAY: That's the little chain....

MS. COLEMAN: ... yeah, the security chain.

MR. FINDLAY: Was the chain, was there any slack in the chain when you went to the door?

MS. COLEMAN: They kept pushing it, so it was back and forth, and I, I had said hold on, hold on, and then the door was shut so I can undo the chain and that's when it opened.

MR. FINDLAY: Had they identified themselves at that point?

MS. COLEMAN: No, I didn't know who or what was going on.

MR. FINDLAY: Um, what happened then?

MS. COLEMAN: Then the door flew open and cops barged in.

MR. FINDLAY: What did they do when they got into the room?

MS. COLEMAN: They flipped the lights on and went directly to Caitlyn and, ah, I know two officers were putting boots and coats on her.

MR. FINDLAY: And to shorten it up, at any time when they were there, did you go over and say to either of your daughters that you weren't going to see them again?

MS. COLEMAN: No.

MR. FINDLAY: What, if anything, did you say to your daughters?

MS. COLEMAN: They wouldn't let me talk to them until I got to the car. Um, I know as I was leaving myself to go outside, I pleaded with the DHS worker, Bonnie, to, you know, please can I at least say a proper goodbye to them. But I didn't say anything to them until both, both children were in their car buckled in.

MR. FINDLAY: Um, and then when was the next time you saw your children after that?

MS. COLEMAN: Was, ah, March 20th.

MR. FINDLAY: So they took them the morning of the 15th, and you saw them the 20th?

MS. COLEMAN: Yes.

MR. FINDLAY: Were you allowed to call them?

MS. COLEMAN: No, we didn't know where anything, what, where they were, how they were doing, nothing.

MR. FINDLAY: Have you ever yourself hit either of your children with an object?

MS. COLEMAN: No.

MR. FINDLAY: Have you ever seen Robert Coleman do that?

MS. COLEMAN: No.

MR. FINDLAY: Have you ever held either one of your children while Robert Coleman was hitting them?

MS. COLEMAN: No.

MR. FINDLAY: Have you ever done anything abusive to your children?

MS. COLEMAN: No.

MR. FINDLAY: How have you felt through this whole proceeding?

MS. COLEMAN: Just horrified that something like this could possibly happen.

MR. FINDLAY: Do you have; are you worried about what's going to happen next?

MS. COLEMAN: I'm basically; this is the scariest day of my life. You know, my life, my children's life is in the hands of seven people right now.

MR. FINDLAY: When is your baby due?

MS. WITTLA: Objection your Honor, relevancy of this.

THE COURT: Yeah, sustained. We already cut it off before that anything subsequent to today is not for the jury to concern themselves with.

MR. FINDLAY: What have you learned from all of this?

MS. COLEMAN: Um, basically, um, savor every possible moment I have with my children, because it might be my last.

MR. FINDLAY: Is there anything you would have done differently?

MS. COLEMAN: I think that, ah, the times that Caitlyn and Ashley have come up to me asking will you read this book or will you play this game or can we do this, I think if I could turn back time, if I would have said, you know, well later, later, and that later never happened, I wish I would have stopped what I was doing and, and spent that time with them.

MR. FINDLAY: Can you think of anything worse that could happen to you than have your children taken away?

MS. COLEMAN: No, no really.

MR. FINDLAY: Thanks.

THE COURT: Ms. Wittla?

Now it was time for more heavy handed lies, as Ms. Witta began her questioning of Janet:

MS. WITTLA: Ms. Coleman, you testified today, and I believe the other day that the door was open in the hotel room when you got up to remove the chain?

MS. COLEMAN: Yes.

MS. WITTLA: And you just testified that when you opened the door you didn't know who was there?

MS. COLEMAN: No I didn't.

Yes Ms. Wittla. It isn't really that hard. The chain was holding what they had already opened, and unless you are superman, you can't see through doors! As they lied about who they were, it is a little difficult for someone not expecting visitors to ascertain who is on the other side! Even you, Ms. Wittla, can't be that stupid!

MS. WITTLA: You're telling us that you opened the door, in a hotel room, at 3 AM, to people who you did not know and who were already trying to access your, your room?

MS. COLEMAN: Yes, I, I guess. Well, I assumed that if they would have kept kicking the door open they would have eventually broken the chain, so...

MS. WITTLA: So now we're kicking the door?

We? Were you there Ms. Wittla?

MS. COLEMAN: They were pushing it very hard, so....

MS. WITTLA: Do you believe they were trying to break the chain?

MS. COLEMAN: Yes.

MS. WITTLA: So to prevent that, you got in front of that door?

MS. COLEMAN: I undid the chain, and the door flew open.

MS. WITTLA: And these people who were trying to break down your door, allowed that door to get closed again?

MS. COLEMAN: That was the only way to undo the chain.

MS. WITTLA: Mr. Findlay asked you what you would have done differently; would you have chosen not to record your kids and taken that visit?

Are you kidding? After all the lies this state told, we would record a lot more than we did! What we would have done differently, knowing now what we know, is never move to Michigan! And never meet Bobby and Becky Payne!

MS. COLEMAN: No, I, I believe that, ah, after, ah, knowing what actually happened in those visits and then reading transcripts of what other people had written, were two different stories, so I felt that we needed to protect ourselves and my children.

MS. WITTLA: So despite the fact that you would have spent more time with the kids; in a home, home setting, reading to them or playing games, you wouldn't go back and change your actions on that day in Marquette and take that visit with the kids?

What kind of bull is that? No matter what, you were going to fight to keep our kids, even after this trial was over! Recording is the one way to expose you and your state vultures who kidnap kids and manufacture stories, evidence, and so-called facts along the way! You rely on the fact people won't fight back, and we just happen to be one couple who did! And we did it for our kids, as much as we did for ourselves! The best thing that could ever happen in this country would be if people forced the abolishment of Child Protective Services, who fund criminals such as those in the state of Michigan.

MS. COLEMAN: No, I, I would have continued to record. I felt I had no choice.

MS. WITTLA: Thank you, I have nothing further.

THE COURT: Mr. Perhalla?

MR. PERHALLA: Nothing, thanks your Honor.

THE COURT: Any redirect?

MR. FINDLAY: Just briefly. Why did you feel you had to record?

MS. COLEMAN: I felt that, well, our first, ah, when Bonnie Huttunen had stated in a previous court that I said goodbye, farewell, I'll never see you again, I, I felt I would, you know, that the state or, you know, they were lying, so I wanted to make sure that I had the proof of what I was saying, what was going on. I wanted to protect ourselves.

MR. FINDLAY: So, so you already had some experience with somebody reporting something that wasn't true?

MS. COLEMAN: Yes.

MR. FINDLAY: No further questions.

THE COURT: Recross on that?

MS. WITTLA: When was it that Bonnie Huttunen made those statements?

MS. COLEMAN: I believe there was a hearing. I'm not sure exactly what date it was.

MS. WITTLA: Sometime in March?

MS. COLEMAN; Yes.

MS. WITTLA; Are there any visits that you've had with the children that you haven't recorded?

MS. COLEMAN: Um, no, I don't believe so.

MS. WITTLA: Thank you.

THE COURT: Mr. Perhalla?

MR. PERHALLA: No.

MR. FINDLAY: I just have one question. Did Bonnie Huttunen say that before any visits took place?

MS. COLEMAN: Can't remember if she was at the emergency hearing or not.

MR. FINDLAY: Do you recall her testifying by phone; saying that at the emergency hearing?

MS. COLEMAN: Um, I, I know she said that at one point so that was the, the main reason that we started recording.

MR. FINDLAY: Do you know that, do you recall the date of that emergency hearing?

MS. COLEMAN: That was the Monday, the 17th.

MR. FINDLAY: And then your first visit was on?

MS. COLEMAN: The 20th of March.

MR. FINDLAY: Thank you.

THE COURT: I guess the recross would get the last question, but I see you're looking for something Ms. Wittla, so was there some clarification on that, times and dates and whatever?

MS. WITTLA: If I told you that that date was April 7th, does that sound about right that Bonnie testified in court?

MS. COLEMAN: I, I don't know.

MS. WITTLA: Do you recall her stating that you told her you're not going to see me again, you don't know how Gogebic County works?

MS. COLEMAN: No.

MS. WITTLA: She didn't say that at that court hearing?

MS. COLEMAN: She said that, but that's not what I had stated to her.

MS. WITTLA: Okay, I, I understand that part but, but she said that at that court hearing weeks ago or a couple months ago or something like that?

MS. COLEMAN: Yes.

MS. WITTLA: And that's what set you off and said, hey, we got to record all these visits?

MS. COLEMAN: Yes.

MS. WITTLA: I have nothing further.

THE COURT: Okay, you may step down ma'am. Mr. Findlay, I undestand that is your last witness?

MR. FINDLAY: That was my last witness. Yes, yes it was.

THE COURT: Do you rest?

MR. FINDLAY: Yes.

THE COURT: Was there a rebuttal?

MS. WITTLA: No.

THE COURT: Okay, all right then the proofs, sorry, it looked like you were going to say something?

MR. FINDLAY: No.

So the testimony was finished. And now all that remained was the closing arguments and the deliberation of the jury. Before all that, the court took a break here, and listened to arguments as to what could be given to the jury and what could not, for all the good that that would do with a jury comprised of people who sided with the state in any case, and had already made up their minds. In any case, the court went through the motions, and we will pick it up with the beginning of the closing arguments, and Ms. Wittla:

MS. WITTLA: Good afternoon, this took a lot longer than we thought it would, and now we are on Day four. I will have the opportunity to speak to you twice; it's my burden to carry, and I have to essentially prove to you that the allegations in the petition are truthful and that they have met the statutory grounds the judge is going to read to you. That being said, you be wondering at some point during the last four days what is this case about? Because you've heard testimony about all kinds of stuff; stolen rings, affairs, forced sex, whether the parents are being punished, ah, whether it's a termination of parental rights case; unborn children, the internet, texts, criminal charges, all kinds of stuff. And unfortunately, the reason you needed to hear that is because the witnesses to what happened to Caitlyn and Ashley are not perfect people. Before, during, after they've done some stuff that if I had my way, they wouldn't have done. Becky Payne getting on the phone and talking to Ms. Townsend about feeling happy, glad, ah, to use Mr. Findlay's word, bragging, about all the things that she accomplished by finally telling her story, telling what happened to the children is not something I would have wished she would have done, because there's no doubt it can impact your credibility.

You mean if this were not a pro-state jury, as it was via the corrupt manner of choosing jurors? But since it was, it would have no impact on credibility. The fact that Becky lied about her allegations as well as all else she pretended we were doing to her, and the fact the state supported and acted upon her lies, (in many cases it was demonstrated) would have no effect on this jury, and we all knew it.

MS. WITTLA (continuing): But the thing you have to remember is that especially with Becky Payne, that she

was a person who was living under Robert and Janet's thumb for months; months and months of time.

No, actually she was more like a leach, as was Bobby, her useless husband. It was a case of us trying to help out helpless people, who could not handle money, could not make any move without grabbing on to someone for assistance. We did it because they asked us to— not because we were taking advantage of them, as the state did their best to portray.

MS. WITTLA (continuing): For this case began last July when she and Becky; sorry; she and Bobby moved into Coleman Estates, and you heard her testimony that within just a few days they are, they are helping them; they are taking care of the kids, ah, she was always the one to change the diapers, if she was around for Ashley.

Were you there Ms. Wittla? First, she only said that was the case. In reality, Janet had always done that, continued to do that, and only submitted to her requests to do that, when Becky decided she wanted to run the house. Janet knew what it was to change diapers, she'd been doing it for years before with Caitlyn. We sure didn't need Becky to do it!

MS. WITTLA (continuing): They started working on the house, ah, within a couple of months they had moved to a different apartment, and the arrangement was made; the arrangement to have a percent off their rent if they would work for the Colemans.

An arrangement we made to help them out because they were having difficulty making the rent. But it was not a night and day requirement, as the state falsely portrayed. And in reality, Bobby, especially, did a lot more sitting and playing his computer games than he ever did working.

MS. WITTLA (continuing): Well that work turned out to be all day;

Were you there Ms. Wittla?

MS. WITTLA (continuing): So for the paltry sum of a hundred bucks Becky and Bobby Payne worked for Robert and Janet Coleman; either in the house or around the apartments, or going off to Coldwell Banker to clean the, and they clean houses that, that Mr. Payne; sorry; Mr. Coleman was hired to clean. And worse than that, the, the money that Becky earned by going to work for the Gogebic Medical facility was also taken by Robert Coleman.

A direct lie.

The food stamp card that they received from the state of Michigan; controlled by Robert and Janet Coleman.

Lie. As Janet explained Becky was too stupid to know how to use it. So when we did our shopping, Janet assisted Becky to use it. But Becky carried it. Becky used it. The state supported her lie by making this their lie.

MS. WITTLA (continuing): Their food, their money, their housing, all this stuff is wrapped up, part and parcel, with Robert and Janet Coleman.

Yes, we were sinners. We helped and assisted to weak human beings who asked for our help. We did not make money on them. In fact, they took up a lot of our valuable time, which we could have used more of.

MS. WITTLA (continuing): They're treated like children; they're told to call him dad; they write sentences when they don't do what Robert Coleman wants them to do, and incredibly they do it.

This prosecutor did not care what she said! In the first two instances, she has it totally backward. They acted like children, we didn't treat them as such. Becky and Bobby were the ones who wanted to call me dad, and as I testified, it freaked me out! And the sentence writing never did happen! That was complete fabrication, which the prosecution presented as facts. Why didn't they show the court samples of this letter writing? Why? Because there wasn't any!

MS. WITTLA (continuing): Now most of us would not do that, most of us would say hey man, we are not going to be subjected to this kind of behavior; but you met Becky and she testified about how she's been in special ed classes, and she's more susceptible to be influenced than others.

Yeah, sure! A real helpless case, isn't she? Poor, poor thing, no mind at all. But she was smart enough to figure out how to con a prosecutor and a jury, wasn't she? That is, unless Elizabeth Fyle and the prosecutor helped her to manufacture such a phony case as this one! But the Becky I knew was not that stupid, but she sure put it across in court, didn't she?

MS. WITTLA (continuing): There's been a lot of talk about whether or not kids are susceptible, the Forensic Interview Protocol and that sort of stuff. From my perspective, I put Becky in that class with those kids; that she doesn't really believe, or didn't at the time, that she was living at Coleman Estates; she would not believe that she had the right to tell Robert Coleman, no, I'm not doing it. I'll not write those sentences, because he controlled all these things in her life, and in her husband's life.

Isn't it amazing the power I possess over people! Then why is it that both of them were subjected to my powers when nobody else in this world is! If I told anybody to do those things they would tell me to take a flying leap! Only this prosecutor is able to dream up such a scenario as for me to control every aspect of both of their lives! Boy, she really laid it on thick with those statements! Even a prejudiced jury should be able to see through that! If, of course, they really cared, which they didn't.

MS. WITTLA (continuing): And it was like a light switch, like they moved in on July 15th and the 16th everything went like this, it was progressively over time.

Yeah, like a light switch. I can just switch it off and on, right? Actually, Ms. Wittla, I have a mind control machine in my basement, that is why I had Becky and Bobby stay down there, because they were not responding to my commands as well as I wanted them to. I also still have ocean property in South Dakota for sale. Want some?

MS. WITTLA (continuing): They started working for them, the money goes to them; Janet Coleman becomes her husband's rep payee so now she really controls all the money; her paychecks are going there; their food stamps are going there; everything is going there. They can't leave, they have nothing; they don't have anything.

Actually? No, we didn't pay any money, only gave a rent credit, so that didn't go to us. Janet was Bobby's payee so he would have something left at the end of the month, as he was not accomplishing that prior to her taking over in that effort; we never had anything to do with Becky's paychecks, except we provided transportation for her to the bank; the food stamp card was used by Becky, not us, although she did ask us to go to the store with her to help pick out foods because she felt incompetent to do so; and I haven't been able as yet to define what Ms. Wittla meant by everything. But from what I've just explained, I don't see any money in our pockets! They could leave any time they wanted, we were not holding them as prisoners. They don't have anything because they are too stupid to hold on to anything, and that is why we tried to help them. We will never try to help anyone in the future though, this case has taught us we should not.

MS. WITTLA (continuing): They were told that the Colemans needed the money because they had extra bills.

No they were not. That is a direct lie, supported by the prosecutor, who is taking that lie from the Paynes.

MS. WITTLA (continuing): They were told that they had to move in the basement so that the Colemans can make some extra cash off of their apartment.

No they were not. That is a manufactured lie. Whose? The Paynes or the prosecutor? I'm not sure, but it was supported by the prosecutor if nothing else. In fact, what happened was they said they wanted to go back to California, and wanted to move into the basement so they would not have to pay rent and could save for their move. We told them no, but they did it anyway. When they moved out, they did not want the stuff from the apartment, so we just left it in the apartment, which we were renting in any case, as we always would, but agreed to keep the stuff there since they had nowhere to put it. It was theirs to claim whenever they wanted it, but in the meanwhile, yes, we used it to rent the apartment as furnished somewhat. We should have made them move the stuff into a storage unit, where they would have to pay for the storage as well as for the moving. But being the cruel people we were, we did not make them do that.

MS. WITTLA (continuing): They didn't move into the basement because they wanted to.

No. We forced them to do it, which is why they did it when we were not looking. They chose to do so, even though we said no.

MS. WITTLA (continuing): And worse than that, they had to leave their stuff behind so this apartment could be rented out furnished. Do you think Becky Payne wanted to leave her mother's $80 microwave in that apartment? I think she sounded a little upset about it.

Isn't that how you told her to sound Ms. Wittla? And as for the first part of that question, maybe she didn't want to, but she chose to. We certainly did not require them to do it! We would continue to rent our apartments— furnished or unfurnished, regardless of what she chose to do.

MS. WITTLA (continuing): So as all of this is going on, they start eating with the Colemans; well, they have to because that's where all the food is.

Also because Janet is a good cook. Becky did not do that for Janet.

MS. WITTLA (continuing): When they are living in their basement apartment, they use a sump pump for a bathroom.

I'm betting this one was manufactured by the prosecutor. I don't think Becky even knew what a sump pump was, and they didn't use one either. They had total access to our bathroom upstairs in our apartment, and they used that.

MS. WITTLA (continuing): And during this time they discover, the Paynes discover, that Robert and Janet Coleman are not really that good of parents, because they are beating on Caitlyn, and they help them. And they have— Becky and Bobby help them, because they're told to and they do what they are told, because they're afraid.

Yeah, my criminal background probably scares them. I never had as much as a fight in all my school days, yet they are scared to death! Funny, Caitlyn remembers no such thing today, and laughs when someone suggests her mother ever held her while I beat her. That was a complete lie that Elizabeth Fyle and this prosecutor could not wait to run with!

MS. WITTLA (continuing): I believe during Ms. Townsend's testimony, she indicated that Becky said on the phone to her that she was afraid of them, when she asked Becky why don't you report this? And her response was, well I'm afraid, or I was afraid.

And for once, she was probably telling the truth, and we do know she said that, as we have that conversation on tape. But if you are telling a lie about accusations of child abuse, you might be afraid of how the parents might respond too, when they find out they are accused of something they did not do.

MS. WITTLA (continuing): And I believe she was because even after all these other things that happened, the financial exploitation, the control of their lives, using them as indentured servants; having to shovel people out, fetch and carried, I mean, everything they possibly could; then Robert Coleman decides to go a step further; and have a sexual relationship with a woman who calls him dad. Do you really think it was by her choice?

The answer of course to that last question is yes. And Ms. Wittla, you believe she was forced because that was how you wanted it to be. None of those things were true, of course, but that is beside the point when you are a prosecutor with no moral principles. And as for her calling me dad, that was her choice—not mine, as I said before, and it made me sick! But Tracie, you wanted so badly to pin a rape charge on me, didn't you? Why didn't you? Because you knew it was all a lie!

MS. WITTLA (continuing): In the end this case isn't about the safety of two little kids; all the rest of it is just to explain why the witnesses to this behavior have acted the way they have, and you needed to know that, to some extent, because honestly, it's kind of an amazing story. From my perspective, it's a true story, there's lots of twists and turns; it's not just a straight, simple case—

Oh, my God! That's enough! I'll let my lawyer offer his rebuttal this time:

MR. FINDLAY: Your Honor, I'm going to object. She just vouched for her witnesses; that's improper for the Prosecutor to do. She said that "from my perspective" it's a true story. That's improper for a Prosecutor to do.

THE COURT: Okay then.

MS. WITTLA: I'm arguing it based on the evidence your Honor.

You mean your manufactured evidence don't you?

THE COURT: Well, but you did use the word "my" and, and it is improper. In a criminal case, and this is a Prosecutor, even though this is not a criminal case, um, to vouch for the credibility of the witnesses, you should judge that on your own, and I would just caution the Prosecutor not to personalize the, whether she believes or not that, that is inappropriate, for all the lawyers actually. Proceed.

MS. WITTLA: Your Honor, is it acceptable for me to say that I believe the evidence shows this to be true?

You mean the manufactured evidence don't you?

THE COURT: That's probably a safe step, but it's—

MR. FINDLAY: I couldn't hear all that she said.

THE COURT: She asked is it appropriate to say I believe the evidence shows this is true. I mean, you are arguing that the evidence is— we're kind of getting into the—

MR. FINDLAY: I, I still think it's vouching, but I don't think the Prosecutor is supposed to vouch at all.

THE COURT: In any event, it is inappropriate for the Prosecutor to vouch for and indicate the truth, and ah, you should try to— your words in other terms, because of the objection, I'm not going to penalize you for this last two minutes, proceed.

Oh? You are going to reward her for improper procedure?

THE COURT (continued): Oh, ah, Ms. Wittla, could you tip the microphone your way, because the reporter is having a hard time.

Yes, it would make your lies easier to hear. But not to digest!

MS. WITTLA: It's true you have to determine the credibility of the witnesses before you; you have to decide if you're going to believe Robert and Janet Coleman or if you're going to believe the rest of the people who testified essentially. Because you have to remember that in order for Robert and Janet's version of events to be true, Elizabeth Fyle is a liar; Robert Ross is a liar; Bonnie Huttunen is a liar; Sergeant Passuello is a liar; Jamie Perlich is a liar; and Rebacca Payne is a liar.

You forgot yourself and Ron Carpenedo. And yes, you would have to believe that, as in any criminal kidnapping ring, there must be a lot of liars. Most do it for the sake of money, which is why there are so many liars working directly with Child Protective Services (CPS). DHS, of course, is their local syndicate in Ironwood, and they do the dirty work there, backed up by a corrupt court and a handful of lawyers and law enforcement people who work with the state. So yes, you are right. They would have to believe they are all liars. And they are.

MS. WITTLA (continuing): It's the only way for their version of events to be true, because there are too many discrepancies; it's not a question of shades of gray, it's the door was partially open, and the chain was there holding them— holding it closed or it's a rouse by the mainteance man to get into that hotel room in Hancock.

Yes, you are right again. It is not a question of shades of gray. There is no question the raid was conducted at 3 AM. I have no criminal record, so why was a swat team necessary? There is no question the state lied when questioned about the claim of maintenance, and they had to admit it when confronted with the fact that they raid team lied about who they were. So, yes, there are many instances where there is no gray, and it is pretty easy to see to pretentiousness of the state in this case.

MS. WITTLA (continuing): There are no shades of gray in this case; but the other thing that you need to be aware of in this case is that this is not a case where the state is trying to permanently remove these kids.

Another lie, as you will see as you read on in ensuing chapters of their efforts to do just that.

MS. WITTLA (continuing): This case, which you are determining today, is whether or not this court is involved with these kids' lives at all. If your decision today is that there is no jurisdiction, we will all go away; kids go back to Robert and Janet; and whatever happens, happens.

Here is this sneaky prosecutor at work once again, trying to instill fear and guilt into the jurors if they don't find us guilty, because the dangerous Colemans will more than likely beat the crap out of the kids if they are returned to them! Somehow, though, Caitlyn had managed already to make it to age six, without a death blow, or even amazingly any marks on her body, and today, at age ten, she still knows how to smile! Fascinating, isn't it? After her bad experiences with the government, however, I would not blame her if she did not ever smile!

MS. WITTLA (continuing): If your decision is that jurisdiction is the decision and this court gets involved, then this judge determines what happens next—

THE COURT: I'm going to, I'm going to cut you off— go ahead.

MR. FINDLAY:—the, I'm really, I don't usually like interrupting closing arguments, but I, disposition is something for the court to decide and she went into all of it; I, if the court wants to let me go into disposition; I don't have an objection to it, but my understanding is we were not supposed to.

THE COURT: Well, and counsel, you did actually raise the issue of termination before anybody else did, but you were also prevented from doing so; I'm just going to indicate to the jury which there is going to be an instruction coming that tells you don't concern yourself with anything from this day forward. And I'll also caution the Prosecutor not to talk about anything beyond the jury's verdict. And again, I won't penalize you because of the legal issue.

What? Again you reward her because she violated procedure? That's twice now, judge!

MS. WITTLA: Your Honor, am I allowed to quote the jury instructions?

THE COURT: Sure, because I'll be reading those.

MS. WITTLA: You'll hear from the judge that if the court has jurisdiction of the children, the court will then decide at the later time what to do about them and their family. There are many options available to the court. So again, what are we here for? What happened? Back in March of this year there was a report of abuse to the Child Protective Service Agency in our state, which is the Department of Human Services, and Elizabeth Fyle went out and did an investigation to determine whether or not that allegation was true. She did not know ahead of time whether it was, and because of that she had to do some interviews. So she spoke to Becky and Bobby Payne. She spoke to Caitlyn, she spoke to Robert and Janet, and she made a decision that because of the lack of privacy during that interview with Caitlyn, that she wanted to talk to her again on another day. And in order to preserve Caitlyn and Ashley's safety, she made an agreement with Robert and Janet and said, look don't use physical punishment on the kids; this is still an open investigation, you know, we'll; we're going to have to do some more interviews in the future.

An agreement? Their idea of an agreement is that we do whatever they say! First of all, there was no need for the request for no physical punishment, because we did not do what the Paynes said we did. So that was her one-sided request over something that was not factual. Secondly, they told us they would want to do more in the future, but did not specify when that might be. Certainly they did not tell us it would be in the next day or two! So we went about our business as usual, that being our doctor visits that had been scheduled for some time, and then deciding to try to make it a fun weekend as well. Was that next interview of so much importance that it could not wait until we returned on the next Monday? Only if it was a problem for them that we mentioned we would have a lawyer there! So in any case, her agreement was only for that which she drew up in her head, but did not bother to tell us about!

MS. WITTLA (continuing): And unfortunately, she took them at their word; she believed that they would do these things; because what happened 36 hours later proved that, that they were not a good risk because 36 hours later, they were gone.

No we weren't! 36 hours later we were on our vacation, and we were not hiding from anybody! Like Fyle's imaginary agreement, she also imagined we were trying to flee, which can easily be reputed, because we were not doing anything that one would be doing if they were indeed trying to flee! Why stop in Houghton? Why not, on day one, head directly for Canada or some other state where they could never trace us? We had plenty of time to do that, if that had been our thoughts. But those thoughts belonged only to Elizabeth Fyle! Gone? Hardly!

MS. WITTLA (continuing): And when Robert Ross was trying to get ahold of them to find out where they were to set up this interview because they already know Caitlyn is not in school; Robert Coleman's on the phone saying, Oh, we're in Marquette for an OB visit, knowing darn well that he was in Houghton. If you've ever been to one or the other, you know which city you are in.

Yes, you do know which city you are in. And Janet heard me tell Bob Ross where we were, and nobody told him we were in Marquette. All you have to do is check out our doctor's appointments for that time, and you would see we had already scheduled them in Houghton. Likewise, we had already booked our hotel there. It was either very bad memory on the part of Bob Ross or he purposely lied about it, but he never heard anybody say we were in Marquette. And Fyle was made to admit she never heard it under questioning of my lawyer. Besides, what difference does it make where we were if we were coming back Monday. And at that point, we had no idea they were searching for us because they indicated our plan to come on Monday was fine. Without them telling us they were searching for us, what would be the reason for us to flee? Elizabeth Fyle's imagination got the best of her—it was that simple!

MS. WITTLA (continued): So after that fabrication, he makes another and says we'll be back later today, which essentially buys him some time.

Good Lord, woman! Buys me time for what? To go swimming with my kids? Had I been paranoid, imagining a sneak attack, I'd have hit the hills at that moment, if that was my purpose! But first, we felt no need for that, we had a lawyer who would represent us upon our return. And secondly, nobody told them we would be back that day. And nobody fabricates better than this prosecutor. She is a master of that, and this was one total fabrication on her part!

MS. WITTLA (continued): CPS is not going to worry about the, the return of those children until that night, because they believe they're coming back; they don't have to worry yet.

Are you nuts woman? Who would ever think like that? We were worried when CPS showed up at the door. So why would we not worry now? But if we were going to run, we'd have done it already! How stupid!

MS. WITTLA (continued): But as Elizabeth Fyle testified to when she left that night on the 11th, her concern level for those kids was between a 6 and a 7; and the following morning with Cait— and two days later when Caitlyn was not available in school it bumped up to a 7. When they didn't return that night it went up to an 8. During that period of time Detective Passuello also called Robert Coleman, and said hey, where are you I need to talk to you, need to interview you; and again gets the same response,

Oh I'm in Marquette; you really think that both Detective Passuello and Robert Ross got that wrong? Neither one of them know the difference between Marquette and Houghton?

The only problem with that story, Ms. Wittla, is it never happened. I never talked to Detective Passuello period. So how could I tell him either Houghton or Marquette? And I love Ms. Fyle's little invented tracking posture, putting it all on sliding scales of concern! What total poppycock that is! And the only one with any concern, frankly, was her, and that is because she wanted the court to hear how she was so concerned so they would grant her a removal order before we were able to get a lawyer upon our true scheduled return date, which we had told Ross already was Monday.

MS. WITTLA (continued): So now we're at Friday and Caitlyn's not there; and now the level of concern from Ms. Fyle is bumped up to a 9; and worse case scenario is playing in her head and she decides that she's going to ask for a pickup order which is granted from the court.

Let's change the wording a little bit to reflect what this would have been, had it been truly Ms. Fyle's intent. Instead of calling it a concern level measurement, let's go by the more scientific name for it: paranoia. This woman was totally delusional if she really felt this, because nobody else gave this any thought, until she pushed for it. I happen to believe she never did feel this, that in fact, she simply wanted to grab the kids for her own personal reasons, so this was a nice, fake little scenario she could play out with the court to accomplish this. What remains a mystery to me though, is who she was in fact doing this for, and who, in fact, wanted this child kidnapping to happen in the first place, and what their motive was for doing it. If I knew who it was who filed the original complaint, I am quite certain it would match up as the same person. I have my suspicion, because I had been bumping heads with that one person from the day I first arrived in Ironwood, Michigan. But since we have a court protecting his identity, we can never prove the identity. The court says only it was not Bobby and Becky. I will continue to try to find out, and maybe if I sue all of them, one will divulge that information in exchange for clemency.

MS. WITTLA (continued): And around the same time there's a discovery that the cell phone conversations are taking place with Robert Coleman's cell phone. And Sergeant Carpenedo gets involved to help find Robert and Janet Coleman; whether they be in Marquette, Houghton, dark side of the moon, wherever.

Ain't that cute? Dark side of the moon. Funny you should mention Carpenedo though, because, interestingly enough, he was the one who pulled me over my first day in Ironwood, the one who followed up with hard questions after pulling me over for plates right after the raid incident, and more or less gave me the third degree for having asked questions about my stolen wallet, which I suggested Bobby took. He seems to have been involved in every aspect of this case. And go back a few years, he was even the way who tried start a child abuse case against me after John Cain had complained, following Caitlyn's injury over the ball in Cain's house. That was the complaint they did not win, and he's been with me every step of the way since then. Coincidence? Can policemen themselves file cases of child abuse under a cloak of secrecy, as to their identity? Would a court protect him if he did? All good questions. Don't you think? And someone helped Bobby and Becky organize their complaints. They could barely write their own names, much less do anything like that. Maybe Ms. Fyle and Mr. Carpenedo could shed some light on that. The judge, who has the answer, would not. But please, Ms. Wittla, go on with your fairy tale.

MS. WITTLA (continued): And those cell phone records come in and say, you know what, they're not in Marquette; they're in Hancock/Houghton area.

Big discovery! Especially big since we told them in the first place where we had to go for our doctor's appointments, and never told anyone it was Marquette. But it sure supports your phony story to insist somebody was told that.

MS. WITTLA (continued): So the paperwork gets sent to Houghton County for them to be on the lookout for the Colemans, and why would they park that vehicle where they did?

Maybe because we had nothing to hide, and did not feel anybody would be searching for us! But go ahead, give us your opinion, Ms. Wittla. After all it was your story that had to be sold to the jury:

MS. WITTLA (continued): Because they already threw everybody off the trail. Everyone, to their way of thinking should have been looking for them 100 miles away in Marquette. There's no need to hide that vehicle, because they think that anyone who is looking for them is way off the trail by now.

Ms. Wittla, please! You can certainly manufacture something better than that! You are either a paranoid, like Ms. Fyle, or you are simply doing your best job to sell her paranoia! Hard to believe you could both actually believe such nonsense as this!

MS. WITTLA (continued): So the vehicle is located, and a plan is formulated by police and the rouse is set up as far as using the maintenance man, and Bonnie arrives on the scene.

Such intrigue! Exciting, ain't it? A better plan of course would have been a single knock on the door, just announcing who they are and why they were there. And at a reasonable hour. We would have opened the door with no problem. I mean, what else would we do? You don't have a back entrance to a hotel room; you can't go through the roof? Of course we would open the door and all the swat sillyness is not needed. But then, neither was there a need to remove our kids. It excites the state to play these kind of stupid games!

MS. WITTLA (continued): And together they all go up to the room to secure these children.

You mean steal them!

MS. WITTLA (continued): Maintenance man knocks on the door; Janet opens the door; for the maintenance man; not for a bunch of crazy strangers trying to bust down the door, because frankly that just doesn't make any sense at all; a pregnant woman at three o'clock in the morning is going to open a door that's already been opened and someone is trying to kick it in? For people she doesn't even know? Or did she open that door for the maintenance man rouse; which one do you think is more truthful?

It is obvious our version makes a lot more sense than the crap you are speeling out! I think what you would have desired would be if I had got a gun (which I don't have) and started a shoot-out with police. Then you could have had something real exciting! But tell me, talking about common sense, why not put your police at the door and have the hotel manager just call the room, explain to them who is outside, and just ask us to open the door. Why the lies and deceit, other than it is just your way of doing business?

MS. WITTLA (continued): So CPS and the police officers go into the room and Robert's up.

No, Robert is not up. You lied again Ms. Wittla. Robert is told by police not to get up. Had I tried, I'd have certainly been maced, clubbed, or shot! Oh! Again, that is what you would probably have desired!

MS. WITTLA (continued): And his biggest concern is reading the documentation involving the case because he knows he has his legal rights.

If that were how it happened, it would be one thing. But it wasn't. And yes, Ms. Wittla, it bothers you immensely to think someone might be given their rights, does it not? Why follow the law? Or why follow court procedures? You never did, in the course of this trial, did you?

MS. WITTLA (continued): He's not concerned where Caitlyn and Ashley are; he's not getting stuff together for them; he's not worried about saying goodbye to them yet; he's making sure the I's are dotted and the T's are crossed in the paperwork he is provided. Janet's yelling call Pope.

Yeah, well, NEWS FLASH! When I was allowed to see the paperwork, once allowed to get up, I would be checking to see if your raid was legal. You can call it dotting I's and crossing T's, but in fact, what I would be checking is to see if you had a valid court order for the county we were in. I doubt you did. And since we were not expecting visitors, and planned to have Pope with us to defend us against your vicious people on Monday, Janet wanted him to know what was going down at that very moment! That is called concern for your kids! Trying to protect them against kidnappers!

MS. WITTLA (continued): So Bonnie Huttunen is trying to find the things the kids need because it is March and it's cold. It's the U.P.; and she gets coats, boots, gets them bundled up; heads out the door; walking out the door, mind you, holding Caitlyn's hand, talking to her. Not carrying her; and no one is crying.

It is quite interesting that you bring that up, because today, at age ten, my daughter Caitlyn tells a far different story. She says she never even went with her. A police officer took her. And she says she was scared out of her wits, trying to figure out what was going on. So Bonnie lied through her teeth, in her story about the demeanor of Caitlyn. Caitlyn has already said, at 18, when she is of legal age to do so, she plans to sue these people for all the lies they told in the courts. So you better run now, all of you corrupt people, because it's only eight short years away. We are not forgetting this, or all the corruptness that went with it.

MS. WITTLA (continued): They get outside, Janet gets the car seat from the vehicle that they had and puts it into the DHS vehicle. There was not a raid, they didn't rifle through the entire room, they didn't swipe up the car keys and run out like maniacs to rifle through their vehicle and take the car seat. Janet got the car seat, she put it in the car; Bonnie hooked it up in the car, but Janet go the car seat.

You know a lot for someone who was not there, don't you Ms. Wittla? Small problem. Caitlyn says none of this is true. And the raid has been admitted, so who are you trying to fool Ms. Wittla?

MS. WITTLA (continued): So now we're outside and Robert comes down, and now he's upset because he realizes the truth of what's happening here.

Gee, that's funny! I don't recall anybody's testimony that said that! You even make up your own facts when you summarize a case, don't you Ms. Wittla? Maybe you should at least use some testimony as the basis for your lies! But this one is not even supported by testimony!

MS. WITTLA (continued): They've been found; he can't stop this right now; and he's upset, and who does he go to see? Caitlyn? No, Ashley, his kid, he goes to see Ashley, hugs Ashley, buckles Ashley into her car seat, offers to go and get a sippy cup, a blanket, toys, diapers for Ashley; nothing about Caitlyn; nothing.

Here is a life lesson for Ms. Wittla, who probably doesn't understand family life, as she is too busy trying to separate families to ever understand what keeps them together. I went to Ashley for several reasons. First, Janet was already with Caitlyn, so I was very confident she was being attended to. Second, noone was with Ashley. So if I go to Caitlyn, as Ms. Wittla thinks I should have, it leaves noone with Ashley. Does that make sense to you? Finally, Ashley was only two years old. I wanted to be certain she had what she needed first, before moving on to Caitlyn, who I knew was already being comforted by her mother. You see, that is what parents do. They work as a team. I know Ms. Wittla knows about teamwork, on a much larger scale. Kidnapping teamwork. But a marriage is based on a lot more, and at stressful times your marriage is tested as it cannot ever be during peaceful moments. We, as you might guess, were under terrific stress, yet still working together for our kids. We would continue to do that as we fought this corrupt government, and all the sick people who make it up, including a vicious prosecutor who knows nothing more than to try to frame people for what they are not.

MS. WITTLA (continued): But Janet has her chance to say goodbye and what does she say? You're never going to see me again; they're going to take you away and you're going to live somewhere else, and Caitlyn, at that point, starts to cry, because those were the parting words from her mother because she's mad at what the system is doing; that's her parting shot to her daughter.

Caitlyn today says her mother never said that. In fact, she says they talked about the Easter Bunny and how much her mother loved her. So tell me how Bonnie got her quote out of that. And Caitlyn absolutely says that was a lie. As for the crying, Caitlyn says it began during the room raid, as they were being taken away, and did not stop during their entire ride, until they fell asleep.

MS. WITTLA (continued): So the caseworker has to drive away the crying kid, ha, ha, I got back at the system. Doesn't matter if I used my own kid to do it; I still got back at them, because they're driving off with a crying kid. They got to deal with her now.

How sick is this prosecutor? Never mind, it was not the truth! The last thing on Janet's mind at that moment was to get back at anybody! The only thing she wanted to get back was her kids! And then for this sick puppy to insert a "ha-ha" into her sick lies, just shows how truly sick this woman really is! I mean, who would ever stoop to such a low level?

MS. WITTLA (continued): So who, so who is there for Caitlyn? Bonnie Huttunen and the police officers are there, because they're the ones that gave her the Teddy bear and the blanket for the ride to Ontonagon.

Wow! That's really being there for someone, isn't it??? I mean, it's like, "Here, kid, just forget we are totally scaring the hell out of you by raiding your room, and forget about the fact we are totally tearing your life apart by stealing you from your parents! Here is a blanket and a Teddy bear!" That makes life perfect! And of course, any parent knows that works perfectly! How idiotic can it get?

THE COURT: Fif—fifteen.

MS. WITTLA (continued): Thank you. So they make it over to Ontonagon, children are, are settled in, and a couple of days later Elizabeth Fyle goes over to ask her how things are going, how, ask Caitlyn how things are going. And Caitlyn's response, contrary to what people would expect is, really good. She's been removed in the middle of the night from the only family she's known, her mother and her step-father, and her response to Elizabeth Fyle is really good.

A good analogy to draw right here is this: imagine, you, as an adult, have just been kidnapped by terrorists in a country that hates the United States. What you fear is what these terrorists are going to do to you. How do you think most adults, under such circumstances would reply if these kidnappers said to them, "I will ask you one question. What do you think of the United States?" Answer honestly to yourself, and remember, so far as you know your life is dependent upon your answer. It is no different for a six year old, who has been kidnapped by people she does not know. And her capability to answer is going to be less than that of an adult. She is going to give them the answer she thinks they want, because she fears she can never go home if she does not. Not so unlike what even an adult might do. I doubt a very high percentage of adults would speak up and say, "it is the greatest country in the world" if they were in such circumstances. If a person says they would, they have never been in such a situation. So think about that, and then see if you can maybe understand why Caitlyn's answer might have been as it was!

MS. WITTLA (continued): Why is it really good? Because here when I get in trouble, I get a timeout. That was her focus. That's what made her life better.

I sincerely doubt it, Ms. Wittla. But she knew it was what you wanted to hear. What would make her life better would be to go home, and she'll tell you that today.

MS. WITTLA (continued): This case is about these kids. It's not about punishing the parents; it's not about the worst day of Janet Coleman and Robert Coleman's life being today. It's not about them. It's about Caitlyn and Ashley.

So what you are saying, Ms. Wittla, is that it is about punishing Caitlyn and Ashley!

That is child abuse madam!

MS. WITTLA (continued): I want you to remember that when you're deliberating because Mr. Findlay used a line in his opening statement that you're the last line of defense, and I can't say I agree with a heck of a lot about what he said, but that rings true; because you are, because if you decide that this court is going to be involved in these children's lives; that can make a difference to them.

And it truly did make a difference. It meant they were subjected to the torture of living in foster homes for almost a year! It meant a lot of physical and other types of abuse at the hands to the state, which made even our charged abuse seem small. The difference? Their abuse actually happened. Ours didn't. At least not in the sense of the invented belt use, which was the basis of the state's case. So yes, it did make a difference, but today the kids are happy to be home, feel safe, and no longer have to endure the punishment inflicted on them by the state of Michigan. I'd like to say anger management made me a better person, and for that reason that experience was a good one for us. But that would be a total lie. Nothing could ever lessen the anger that I feel, or that my wife feels, for the corruption that is Michigan.

In essence, not one element of this entire fiasco changed anything in our family. It might have allowed us to gain some strength, just knowing there are bad people out there just waiting to tear us apart, but we are, as we were before, a strong family, and living once again as we used to live before the state of Michigan literally tore us apart.

MS. WITTLA (continued): That can help them change what's going on in their family so that they can be safe; and that's what I'm asking for you to do today.

They already were safe, Ms. Wittla. The state did not make them that way. What you were asking for was to punish the kids for a crime they did not commit; in fact, for a crime which we did not commit either. The only change today, that is surely a positive one, is that we got rid of Bobby and Becky, who were the only disruption to our family in the first place. The ones you have made the vicitims in this case. You seem to have lost sight of the fact that the real victims here were our children, and you made them the victims by accepting what two incompetent people said was true.

MS. WITTLA (continuing): I'm asking for you to bring back a verdict of jurisdiction; bring back a verdict that says you believe these witnesses; that you believe these petition allegations were proven; and that you believe statutory grounds exist for these kids to have the protection of this court. At the beginning of this case I've noticed there's a lady up there holding a scale and that scale was dead even when we started, and my hope is that after listening to all the witnesses that we've presented, that you understand or believe that we have proven our case way beyond the 51 percent mark, which is where I have to get to, and that you believe that his court should have jurisdiction over these children. Thank you.

Thank God! She was done! Now we just had to sit through Rudy Perhalla, and one more round of Ms. Wittla, and we could quit listening to all of these fairy tale stories of the prosecution! Perhalla was next, and of course was equally as willing to spill the falseness of the Payne list of manufactured allegations.

THE COURT: You're within your time, then, including what you reserve. Mr. Perhalla?

MR. PERHALLA: Thanks your Honor. Ladies and gentlemen, again, I thank you for your service here these past four days. And as I told you in my opening that there are statutory grounds and you've heard about the statutory grounds. And when you get the petition, the paper that has the allegations on it, the first two paragraphs will be the statutory grounds. In two of the statutory; the first paragraph has two, ah, statutory grounds contained in it, and the second paragraph has another statutory ground; so there's actually three statutory grounds you will be looking at. So when you look at the petition, just remember those first two paragraphs under allegations are the statutory grounds. Factually, ladies and gentlemen, the bottom line in the evidence before you is that Robert Coleman has smacked, as Caitlyn calls it, has smacked Caitlyn with a belt on more than one occasion.

Factually incorrect. Smacked is a term Caitlyn did not even know, but it was one Bobby Payne knew very well. And the association of the belt came in the same list of allegations Bobby and Becky Payne presented to Elizabeth Fyle, and the truth is, it never happened. Since you are quoting Caitlyn, let's quote her today. She says it never happened with a belt.

MR. PERHALLA (continued): That allegation which now, when I had an opening was an allegation; that allegation now is proven.

God, did I miss something? Did I fall asleep? When did the jury come in with it's verdict? I thought to be proven, the jury had to say it was so! Unless I slept through my lawyers arguments and the verdict was rendered, that allegation has not been proven!

MR. PERHALLA (continued): There is evidence before you that that, in fact, did happen. And when you look at that one fact and look at the statutory grounds, it can fit into any one of those statutory grounds. I believe it most properly fits into the third one, and that one talks about cruelty to a child, and I firmly feel that that is where you will find jurisdiction, and that's where I'm going to ask you to find jurisdiction; that it is definitely cruel to hit a child with a belt; a six year old child with a belt on her bare butt.

I'm so glad he finally made it clear what had been proven. The belt thing. Ok, and the so-called evidence of that was Ms. Fyle, taking Bobby's lies, and telling the court that Caitlyn said it happened. Trouble is, Caitlyn says today she didn't. She did say she gets a spanking, but never with a belt. Like most kids. But Fyle, working so hard as she did to make it Bobby's version, forgot she used his allegations to make up the allegation list, and not actually Caitlyn's comments. Of course she conveniently forgot to record her session, so there was no way to go back and check. Or, the other scenario, is, that she didn't forget what she was doing; rather, she did it on purpose. Who is going to drag a six year old into court and make her testify? Even Robert Coleman is not that low. So it is easy for someone in her position to create and manufacture evidence as Mr. Perhalla conveniently calls it.

MR. PERHALLA (continued): Ladies and gentlemen, let's look further at some of the testimony though. This is a case where the Michigan Department of Human Services receives a complaint of child abuse.

From WHO Rudy? Can YOU tell me? Nobody else will! I challenge any state ring member to tell me who this mystery person indeed was!

MR. PERHALLA (continued): And the law states they must go and investigate any— any complaints of child abuse. Thus, Liz Fyle has a job to do, and in doing her job, she interviews Caitlyn. During this interview is when we hear the disclosure of the child abuse; of the smacking, and the beating with a belt.

Yes, the Elizabeth Fyle self-created lies that you call evidence. Recall, though, you are hearing all this from Elizabeth Fyle— not from Caitlyn. Tell us more of what we heard from Ms. Fyle:

MR. PERHALLA (continued): We hear that it is her father that is smacking her with a belt; we all agreed in the beginning of this trial that we would not ask the six year old girl to come up here and testify. So to find out what she says, this is how we do it; the Department of Human Services conducts an interview, follows a procedure to conduct that interview, and then testifies here at this, on the stand, what the child says.

Rather than to record it, as should be done. Go ahead:

MR. PERHALLA (continued): Liz Fyle works for the Department of Human Services; she's worked with them for nine years; she's interviewed many, many children.

Yes, I'm sure she has made a lot of money for the state of Michigan over that time. Oh, and by the way, Rudy, was it you who gave her the nickname of the terminator?

Or was it one of the other kidnap ring members? She didn't get that nickname for no reason, and the many, many children you refer to had to contribute a great deal toward that reputed nickname!

MR. PERHALLA (continued): She knows the Michigan— the Forensic Protocol, how to use it, she's had training.

No dispute on that from here. After all, her training was a priority to interviewing my daughter on a day she could have done so before we left to visit our doctors.

MR. PERHALLA (continued): She's not— and in the nine years of experience, she's testified that there have been incidences where you— she hasn't even had to bring a petition— its— there's been no preponderance, is what she's testified to.

How many? One? Two? She didn't earn her nickname for nothing!

MR. PERHALLA (continued): So I believe there's sufficient evidence here on the record, ladies and gentlemen, that Ms. Fyle knows what she was doing when she interviewed Caitlyn.

Boy did you get THAT PART right! But not the next part. Go ahead Rudy:

MR. PERHALLA (continued): And again, during that interview, Caitlyn disclosed that her father, on more than one occasion, smacked her with a belt.

Bobby's words. Not Caitlyn's. Where is that darned tape, Ms. Fyle?

MR. PERHALLA (continued): That statement, ladies and gentlemen, is evidence; that is what I am asking you to decide this case upon.

In that case, Mr. Perhalla, we should be vindicated, because it, in fact, is not evidence, it is merely a claim that Ms. Fyle is making. Where is the tape? Where is the actual evidence? Caitlyn denies it!

MR. PERHALLA (continued): But let's look at a few other witnesses in this case.

Oh! We do have others! Okay, let's look at them.

MR. PERHALLA (continued): You had a doctor testify and it's nothing against doctors, they can come up her and testiy, but I believe in the total amount of time that he was with the child, was about fifteen minutes on one occasion, he actually examined her; it was usually the staff.

Yes, that would be a staff of other medical professionals who are also quite competent in their field.

MR. PERAHALLA (continued): The parents control when they brought the child in, what does this show? It shows a doctor, what he saw upon one time.

Yes, and what his well trained staff saw on further occasions. Very unreliable. Not as good as the word of a prosecutor, who never spent a minute with the child, right? Of Elizabeth Fyle who studied harder the playbook of Bobby and Becky than she did to engage my daughter in the few minutes she actually spent with her. But go on Rudy, you're doing fine:

MR. PERHALLA (continued): Let's talk about, ah, I believe Renee Anderson, obviously she has a business relationship with Mr. Coleman, with both of the Colemans. She's the MSHDA person, the person who makes sure he gets paid for rent. She still is working with him in another job, though it still has to do with the landlord and tenant work.

So what is your point Rudy? That she is not a good witness because she knows us? I would grant you that, but knowing us is a much better indicator of whether or not we are child abusers than not knowing us would indicate. What bothers you is she said we were not. But you forgot that, didn't you? You need someone who knows us better, like maybe Elizabeth Fyle, right? Or Bob Ross? Or someone in your gang who in combination haven't spent as much time as this one witness did observing me and Janet with our kids. Or you could go for someone like Bobby, who we haven't known nearly as long as we have known Renee Anderson. You may have to go to a mental hospital to get him to testify though—you'll notice he didn't make it to this trial.

MR. PERHALLA (continued): Let's look at Mrs. Semo, the, the teacher. She testified she didn't see anything but she has 40, 40 some kids. In the course of the day, forty and some 5 and 6 year olds, running around all day long.

And did you know, Mr. Perhalla, that makes her a great candidate to detect real child abuse, because in a crowd like that, an abused kid stands out like red on a white milk carton! It is obvious to a well-trained teacher. Oh, and let's not forget she only spent the entire year with Caitlyn and the other kids! Again, though, Rudy, what is your point? You didn't make one!

MR. PERAHALLA (continued): Let's talk about Mr. Layman. Mr. Layman was a pretty nice guy, pretty happy guy, he said nothing wrong with the Paynes. Nothing wrong with the Colemans. Struck me as a very nice guy, a guy who probably wouldn't say one thing about anyone bad.

Yeah. That makes him a real jerk, doesn't it Mr. Perhalla? He even likes me!

MR. PERHALLA (continued): Let's talk about Jamie Perlich. Do you remember she testified that Robert Coleman offered to reduce her rent if she wrote statements; ladies and gentlemen, this is a bribe, pure and simple. And I ask you to keep that in mind when you listen and talk and deliberate about what Mr. Coleman had to say on the stand.

No, a bribe would be if I were telling her what to write. I was not. I was merely trying to get help explaining to DHS that I had never had anyone witness me hit my kids, so I could explain that to them. And if enough people came forward to show I did not do such a thing, it would blow a hole in the accusations by the Paynes that I had done such things! There's a big difference between defending yourself against lies and phony charges and offering a bribe. I was looking for any help I could get from anybody who knew me, to contradict what Elizabeth Fyle couldn't wait to try to charge me with! I think any parent, falsely accused, would do the same.

MR. PERHALLA (continued): Becky Payne, I believe the Prosecutor talked a bit about her, but actually, I think we should be grateful for her because she's finally the one who brought this all to our attention. Did the Colemans control her?

No. And if you examine her testimony there can be no mistake that her motive in this entire bogus case was to seek revenge on me. Bobby joined her, because, after all, she did control him, he had always been at her mercy! And while she pretended to be a little uneducated, defenseless misfit that I so unmercifully took advantage of, just listen yourself to her taped conversation with Christine Towne and I don't have to say a word. You can see she is vindictive, cunning, plotting, and just about anything else you might want to apply to her—but certainly not defenseless! And even in her court testimony, she openly admitted she was happy to screw Robert Coleman. So yeah, Rudy, defend her, and try to make a case that she is believable!

MR. PERHALLA (continued): I'm asking you to look at that control. What did they do to her? And obviously, the Prosecutor summed it up some. But Janet Coleman was a representative payee, controlled the— the social security money that was coming into the Paynes' family.

Uh— is this another trial? Or are we here to consider if I abused my children? If Janet and I are to be charged with abusing Becky, let's get on with it! It really has no bearing on child abuse however, as Becky is not a child... nor is she defenseless. But go on Rudy:

MR. PERHALLA (continued): They took control of her food card; shopped for her; controlled the food; went grocery shopping for her.

Count with me folks. He just said the same thing four different times, but all meant the same thing. Kind of like Bobby's allegations. One allegation, but stated a lot of different ways to make it sound like there's more. And like Bobby's allegations, dead wrong. We helped her shop, she kept her card. How many times do we have to say we were helping her, not stealing her money?

MR. PERHALLA (continued): Obviously there was a relationship between Mr. Coleman and her. She states she did it because she was offered cigarettes.

As my lawer stated, if that were true, it makes her a pretty cheap prostitute, doesn't it? No, she was happy to take her clothes off. But she did like to smoke. I won't deny that. It kind of hurts me though to think that she only cared about me because of my cigarettes!

MR. PERHALLA (continued): The Colemans make her, make both of them, write statements.

Whoa! Hold it there Rudy! Let's get your drummed up charges right, if you are going to review them! Remember, they said it was ROBERT who made them write the statements. Nothing was said about JANET. Yet you are now accusing BOTH OF US of this horrendous act! Holy cow man! If you can't get the facts right, at least get the charge right before you pop off!

MR. PERHALLA (continued): The Colemans reduce their rent by a hundred dollars, and, and basically make them their two full time servants; hundred dollars a month to work around the house, to work at other places.

But as the realtor could confirm, they never did any work! My expectations must not have been too high! And if you recall, we did that so they could pay less rent, as they had wanted to pay less rent. Again, we were finding a way to help these people. Not abuse them. But a scorned woman can fast change the facts to reflect what she would like people to believe. Unfortunately you also have dimwitted state workers who listen to this kind of garbage before they check out her motives.

MR. PERHALLA (continued): And when they wanted even more money they put them down in the basement; an unfinished room in the basement and told them to live there.

You are a liar Mr. Perhalla. Elizabeth Fyle is a liar. And Tracie Wittla is a liar. You all tell the same lie on this one. WE did not PUT THEM in the basement. WE told them NO when they ASKED US to go there so THEY could save money for their planned move to California. But despite our telling them NO, Becky took it upon herself to move her things in there anyway. My only mistake was in not ordering her out as soon as we discovered they had done it. And I should never, ever, have allowed them to stay in their apartment if they could not pay the rent. I should never have given them the opportunity to lower their rent so they could pay it. I should never have helped them in any way. But because I am such a low life jerk, I did try to help. For that, my life, and that of my family, was torn apart.

MR. PERHALLA (continued): Ladies and gentlemen, the Colemans, for a few months there, did control the Paynes; but Becky Payne finally had enough. She got out; she left there and when she left, as I said, thankfully she told others and the abuse of Caitlyn then was brought to light.

Yes, I'm sure the state was very thankful for the business this brought, the result of Becky's lies to others. After all, these false claims all help Michigan state's budget. But you guys can't even all tell the same story! According to the judge and the prosecutor, someone first filed a charge of child abuse, and only then were the Paynes interviewed. Now, you say she told others first, and only at that time was this brought to light. Which is it?

MR. PERHALLA (continued): Let us look at Mr. Coleman, Robert Coleman. If you remember he admits that he does have a temper, but he doesn't lose his temper with his daughter, he's able to control it. Well, nonetheless, ladies and gentlemen, there's an admission, there's testimony here that he does have a temper. His stories, his

stories about the state, I think they are a, they're a little bit far fetched ladies and gentlemen.

So because I have a temper, that makes me an abuser? Then you'd better round up the millions of others who have kids, because they have a temper too! As far as I know, it is no crime to have a temper, so long as it is checked and no abuse results. It would even appear to be a normal, human trait. Heck, Mr. Perhalla, I'll bet even you have a temper! As far as my stories about the state, mine is just one story. If it were not fact, why is it in the same year, at the same time this trial was going on, the state of Michigan came under a class action lawsuit for their abuse of parents in the state. And Michigan lost! Far fetched?

MR. PERHALLA (continued): The story about having to go undercover because he's a Latter Day Saint; the story of the state being broke; where, where are the facts to support any of this? That's all it is ladies and gentlemen, it's just merely stories; smoke.

Go to my website. Follow the link to the Latter Day Saints story. So that is where it is at Rudy. Sorry to bust your bubble, but you really should check it out before you shoot off your mouth!

MR. PERHALLA (continued): Again ladies and gentlemen there is no evidence on this record other than Liz fyle did her job.

And that is because Ms. Fyle did not record anything, as she should have, and because the court is accepting as evidence her word only, and we've proven she lied on many occasions. If her testimony is the only testimony that matters, because of a position she holds with the state, and they call that evidence, she could get away with a lot of lies, could she not?

MR. PERHALLA (continued): As I stated she received a child protective services complaint; she talked to the Paynes and she followed the Michigan, ah, Forensics Interview Protocol.

You stated that one time, but you stated it differently just moments ago. And how do we know she followed anything? Because she said so? Or because Bob Ross (who spent half his time out of the room) said so? Caitlyn's stories differ.

MR. PERHALLA (continued): And that protocol; it sets forth the guidelines, what you're supposed to do when you interview children.

Something we know now she did not do in at least one instance, when she chose to interview Caitlyn in her bedroom. The protocol states strongly it is a bad idea, but she did it.

MR. PERHALLA (continued): And she testified that she first established the ground rules; the ground rules in interviewing a child; that she built rapport with the child;

Something she did in less than five minutes! I won't believe anyone can establish any kind of rapport in such a short time. That's just bogus, made up propoganda, nothing else.

MR. PERHALLA (continued): That she asked open-ended questions of the child;

Oh yeah, we really believe that! You mean questions like Caitlyn quoted back to us in Chapter 13 of this book. Questions like, "Does your dad chase you with a broom?" "Does he touch you in your private?" Those, I suppose, are just total free narrative, without being labeled as "leading questions?"

MR. PERHALLA (continued): And that she, she closed with some more rapport building, so to comfort the child. She testified that Caitlyn was a little girl, a little girl who warmed up to her; that started talking with her. Ms. Fyle properly filed this protocol— followed this protocol, and when she followed the protocol ladies and gentlemen, she gathered some very disturbing evidence. And it's in the; it is in the petition, the two pieces, well it's

act—that the allegation part of the petition is in three pages; you will get a couple more I believe. But I believe the evidence on the record clearly establishes the following: that Caitlyn stated when she's in trouble she has to go in the corner; it established that Caitlyn says she also gets the belt; it establishes when asked about a belt Caitlyn states, "he smacks me" and said that it was her daddy that does it. It supports that Caitlyn states— said she is struck one, two times most often; it supports that Caitlyn said getting smacked with a belt has happened many times; and then it goes on. You have evidence ladies and gentlemen, clear evidence.

Clear? By that you mean Elizabeth Fyle's word? Isn't very clear to me. She did not record it to prove what she says. That to me is no evidence at all that Caitlyn said any of those things. I don't believe she did, and I told her that on the spot. I told her she was a liar then, and still maintain that is true today. If she were not a liar, she would not fear putting her conversations on tape. In fact, she would make it a policy to do so.

MR. PERHALLA (continued): Clear evidence that this child was hit with a belt; that is something the laws of this state do not tolerate; that we should not tolerate, and for that reason, your Honor, I—ladeis and gentlemen, I'm asking you to give this court jurisdiction.

Forgot who you were telling your lies to, did you Mr. Perhalla? Remember, it is the jury you are talking to, even though most of them, like you, are fast asleep and don't care what the truth is. You are in summary, not addressing the judge, sir!

MR. PERHALLA (continued): I'm asking that there's a statutory ground that this is cruel, and based upon that, that the others possibly, but definitely the cruelty that this little girl was hit and to grant this jurisdiction. Thank you.

Thank God! The two prosecutors have completed telling their lies! Now we can go on and hear an argument that makes sense:

THE COURT: Thank you. Okay, Mr. Findlay; you want to be warned at fifteen or twenty, or?

MR. FINDLAY: Um, about twenty. I'd just ask you to observe one thing in terms of evaluating all this is that who's talking— Mr. Perhalla? Um, you sit at the Prosecution table; I say you basically acted like another Prosecutor in this case, and I also point out to you that he never, until the day of this trial, he never asked the Colemans a single question. Never came to talk to them about it to make an independent evaluation of what they had to say; he basically bought DHS's and the Prosecutor's story, hook, line, and sinker from the get go. I've been asking myself as this trial been going on, what is this trial about? I said in the beginning it's about a family, and the Prosecutor wants to separate, literally and figuratively, the children from the family. So this is about the family unit; about the children and the parents, for a family unit. What did the Proscutor try to make this about? Ah, to me, it sounded like character assassination; the state has done everything the can to paint the Colemans as bad people you should not like. Whether it's the stuff about his views on government; whether it's the stuff he's a lousy landlord; whether it's, his, his, ah, religion, the Latter Day Saints thing; couple of points on that. If you are a parent and your children are taken at 3 AM on a Saturday morning, a raid by officers and DHS, wouldn't you try and figure out why that happened? I mean, maybe you don't agree with his explanations for it, but isn't it human nature to want to try and figure out what it is and why this happened to you? Their children had been gone from them since 3 AM on Saturday morning, March 15th; where are we now? June 28th? Well, let's look at that actual evidence; what the Prosecution is claiming is evidence. I'd submit to you that, um, and I think she testified to it, in fact, that Elizabeth Fyle's mind was made up about this case before she even got to their house on the 11th. She went there looking to have the pieces of her puzzle fit in, to confirm her story; she bought the Paynes' story, hook, line and sinker and went there basically to, to confirm that.

Not only is Mr. Findlay correct in that, but we should note again that Ms. Fyle had a long forgotten score to settle with me for having defeated her and Ron Carpenedo some years prior when they attempted to do this at that time, over the Cain incident. So there is little doubt she wanted us to be guilty and was prepared to do all in her power to see that we were found guilty this time. And note also, throughout this ordeal, Carpenedo was also fully engaged, taking part at every interval of the case's progress.

MR. FINDLAY (continuing): What is the evidence of abuse? The Paynes, actually, only one Payne wasn't it? And I, I point that out to you. The petition contains quite a bit of information; a number of allegations where Bobby said this and Bobby said that; did Bobby testify here in this proceeding? The answer is obvious; don't you think that he was going to say the same thing as Becky Payne if they would have called her— called him? You know, in the, in the criminal law, and law in general, there's a proposition that the fact that a— the people trying, the plaintiff doesn't call the witness—

MS. WITTLA: Objection your Honor. I believe this is a criminal reference he's making.

THE COURT: Yeah, sustained. This is, that law is not applicable to this proceeding but you may certainly argue the absence, but it's, there's not the same presumption; go ahead.

MR. FINDLAY: The absence of him being called here should communicate volumes to you. He obviously wasn't enough of a reliable witness for them in court; for you he wasn't reliable, of course, he's reliable enough for Ms. Fyle to basically buy this story and, and go forward on it; but it wasn't reliable enough to put him before you. So you have Becky Payne; I, I know they tried to paint the Colemans as, you know, whether it's a Svengali or monster or something that controlled them, um, but you heard her testimony. She bragged about getting the kids taken away; she admitted that; she bragged that she knew the judge. I'm guessing that was probably a surprise to the judge. She bragged that she put out a bad word for the Colemans. I'd say she certainly did that. She bragged that they had mostly screwed them over, that too. Bragged she got him fired from Coldwell Banker, screwed him over from that. Bragged they screwed him over from able to getting money. Bragged that they told tenants not to rent from them. She even bragged she called CPS on him; bragged that she took better care of those kids than the Colemans; bragged they had screwed Robert Coleman from adopting Caitlyn as his own child; bragged that Caitlyn would never become a Coleman; even went so far as to mock Janet Coleman for going to the hospital during the stress of all this; during her pregnancy. She bragged that all the cops believe her; she bragged every cop was on her side, and her words out of her own mouth that she admitted saying were, "so yeah, we screwed them." And that's who the government wants to hang their hat on! That's the word that they want you to take. That's the, the, the kind of person that they started this whole thing with, and put together this petition; and put together this whole case; and are basing and putting before you as reliable evidence that the Colemans have abused their children. I sure hope not, that, that's; that you are not buying that when you are evaluating and looking at this witness in that light. The only other thing they have, the only other evidence they have, are the alleged, and there's that word again, because I'm, I'm alleging, I think it's an allegation that she made those statements and it is an allegation in the petition that Caitlyn made these statements. And I'd submit to you that on cross-examination, it was evident that Elizabeth Fyle was dishonest about what Caitlyn had said. You heard the tape yourself. She heard it. Said no, it doesn't say it there. I offered, do you want me to play the whole thing? Oh, no, no, because the Colemans just would have changed it anyways. At the same time, the exact location where it said that Robert Coleman has said, "daddy misses you" and then Caitlyn buried her face in Mr. Coleman's shoulder, then she supposedly apologized on the tape. What Caitlyn said was "I sure want to be, I miss you, I want to be with you daddy." She said that twice. We have that tape recorded, the government doesn't want to play it, because that statement that Elizabeth Fyle said Caitlyn made isn't on there. But she wants you to believe that this Forensic Protocol Interview was followed and that everything that she says Caitlyn said, well that's true. Let's look at the Protocol, this is what she's supposed to have done. She controlled the interview; she introduced the topic; she basically communicated to a six year old child that, that going to the corner is, that's not enough. I want some more, tell me something else, tell me more about the bath, you know, the purpose of that, that protocol is to eliminate those type of influences on a child and what a child is going to say. And I'm submitting to you that Caitlyn didn't say those things, and I, I think that's verified by her dishonesty in terms of that visit. She demonstrated that she's willing to tell you something that Caitlyn said; that Caitlyn; there is no evidence that Caitlyn said, and it could by easy to prove one way or the other. What, what, let's look at the other absence of that and what there wasn't evidence of. No physical evidence of abuse, no pictures, no medi-

cal records, you don't think that if a six foot four, two hundred and forty pound man were beating a child with a belt, there wouldn't be some evidence of an injury? The GAL just pointed out the; he's been losing his temper, so are we saying he was all calm and collected when he did this beating and that's why he had control and so he didn't hit her as hard? There's basically, the GAL, basically saying it's okay so he lost his temper and beat his child to death. Six foot four, I mean, the size of the guy, I mean, I have to look up to him and I'm a big guy; you think he'd beat his child with a belt, and there wouldn't be an injury? You don't think Kristen Semo, who saw this child every, or five days a week for the whole school year wouldn't have some evidence of that? You don't think Christine Towne, Renee Anderson, Donald Layman, the other people you heard from, even Jamie Perlich, who was there to witness and they're trying to say— points out that Robert Coleman is lying, said he— she never witnessed him hit his children. In fact, no other witness; no other witness has ever seen the Colemans abuse their children; in fact, just the opposite. The people that you heard from said it was a loving family, happy kids, and even DHS through Elizabeth Fyle and Bob Ross had to admit that about the visits; that they appeared to be happy kids; the acted appropriate; they didn't act afraid of Robert Coleman. It's true that they're not charge with a crime, the Colemans aren't, and I would point out to you who also isn't charged with a crime; I think I did it before, but the Paynes are not charged with a crime. And again, I will remind why they are not charged with the crimes is because then they wouldn't be a witness. If you're charged with a crime, you have a fifth amendment right not to say incriminating things about yourself. She certainly incriminated herself here; I mean, she said that I participated in it. I mean, if that were really true, wouldn't she, and shouldn't she be charged with a crime? Shouldn't, if the things that they said that Bobby Payne said, which they didn't bother to have him say here were true; shouldn't he be charged with a crime? And if the Colemans had done these things, shouldn't they be charged with a crime? And I told you one reason why they wouldn't be charged with a crime is because it's a lower burden of proof; in a crime, if this was a criminal trial, they had to prove that beyond a reasonable doubt, and the Prosecution knows they could not do that. That they could not do, no, they know, that all this lack of evidence, and the flimsy evidence they had produced would not be enough to get a conviction of twelve other members of this community for child abuse. The other reason they've done this is because the rights of confrontation which is a constitutional right, are much higher in a criminal case. Meaning that they would not be able to use these statements from Caitlyn the way they've used them. That's why they chose to pursue it here, they can get by with flimsier evidence, they can get in stuff that in a criminal trial, would never get, would pass— in terms of being evidentiary liable. The reason those things: one, that such hearsay is excluded in a criminal trial—

MS. WITTLA: Objection, your Honor. Are we going to con— consider criminal trials constantly? This is not a criminal trial.

THE COURT: Yeah, well I didn't hear the whole sentence, but if you're saying a criminal trial, what, what did you say? This is not a criminal trial; and you will be instructed on that—

MR. FINDLAY: I'm talking about the differences.

THE COURT: And if you pick that up, go ahead, and I'll, ah, I'll stop you if it's objectionable. You have a lot of, a lot of leeway on it; lawyers have a lot of leeway on argument.

MR. FINDLAY: In a criminal trial, both those things, hearsay and not being reliable and not being able to admit it is not considered liable that's based on, you know, somebody's liberty sake. Well, I this, this isn't a criminal trial, I'm not trying to tell you it is, but I am telling you that the Supreme Court in this country has also said, that families have a, a liberty interest in their family right; in their family unit; in having rights to family, being together— so why do they get to use such flimsy evidence and expect you to do what they want is beyond me. Well, I, I know why they're doing it, but it seems the height of unfairness. And as I said in the opening also, I think, in my personal opinion the stakes are higher here for than that in a criminal case. You could lock me up for something I didn't do, and I'd fight it, I'd appeal it, I'd proclaim my innocence from the roof tops; I'd, you know, do whatever I could, but you take my kids away from me, and you've destroyed me. I don't know what I'd do if somebody came and took my kids for something I didn't do. These are high stakes, here folks, and I want to point out something too, and I'm telling you right now, I don't know what I"d do in that situation. But have you heard one shred of evidence, one allegation, one iota of information that leads you to believe that the Colemans have done anything threatening, illegal, or even intimidating, unless of course, you want to use the recording of, of calls or visits and that type of thing as, as being intimidating? And I; it's apparent that that does intimidate the DHS. They don't like having their words and what they have to say being exposed, they don't want somebody to, you know, have an independent record, a true record, like we seen of what was exactly said. They want to be able to just present their version, and nobody else can challenge that. And why wouldn't somebody want to record your contact with DHS both to, to preserve a record and also be able to tell others what you're going through and what's being done at the hand of DHS. DHS doesn't like recordings, and, and they don't like their stuff being put out in public, and apparently they don't like the First Amendment. It, it strikes me, you know, that the way they think they have a right to our children and do whatever they want if they deem it appropriate, if they deem it appropriate, seems to me that they've forgotten a little bit about, we the people. That they work for us, we're not their vassals, their, their people to order around; their children aren't theirs, our children are not theirs. And, and, you know, getting back a little bit to what I think this case is about, I think, I think some of it, a lot of it has been about how difficult that the Colemans have been for DHS to deal with. They seem to make a big point of that; this is the hardest case that, you know, Robert Ross has had to deal with. Apparenlty, DHS expects people to, to roll over and give up when faced with false allegations. You even heard evidence in statements that, you know, well if DHS said yes, and we could be offered service and we try to reunite them; of course, they got to admit what DHS says they did. It's a, to me, and I'm hoping I'm not alone, maybe I am, but to me a disturbing view of what parents' rights are, have emerged in this trial. Parents are not supposed to be upset that CPS workers demand to interview their children, out of their presence; and that's not supposed to upset you; oh, I wouldn't have a problem with that for my child. I, I, maybe they are so entrenched in the system or something that they have become such part of the system, and institutionalized, they think that everything that they want to do should be just hunky dory and that we should all be okay with that. I can tell you again, me, you come to my door and ask to interview my kids, you better get a court order and you better get a police officer telling me that this court order is valid before I'm going to let you interview my kids without someone being there; without me being there. Or, I'm going to say I want this done in a location where there's going to be an independent witness, or, here's a tape recorder, record the thing, do something so that I know that you're not making this stuff up. Parents, DHS also maintains, parents shouldn't be upset about a 3 AM raid on their hotel room to take their children away. If Bonnie Huttunen and I, and I may be paraphrasing a little of this, but my memory is that she even said that it wasn't, she didn't think it was a big deal; it shouldn't have been seen as a big deal. I mean, how credible are people that believe that? Have we gone that far that we let them do this to us without any kind of resistance? Without saying no, wait a minute, I have rights too, my kids have rights too! It's apparent to me that, that CPS thinks it is above the law. They don't think that they are subject to it, and they want to be able to act with impunity. They want unfair access to your children and you should not mind. One false allegation, somebody out there could say something about me that I don't like, that's enough. Somebody who doesn't like me can say something false, make something up, and that's enough. This information in the petition; I mean, you're going to get the whole thing; and I'm going to remind you that until you say otherwise, regardless what the GAL tells you, until you say otherwise, these are still allegations. And at least one, two, three, four, five, six, seven, eight, nine of the multitude of them they split stuff up and to trump this thing up. You'll have to deal with, with Bobby saying something, and they don't even bother to have him testify here. I do believe that you are the last line of defense, at least for the Colemans in this instance; somebody has got to, I hope, bring some reason to this and say, you know, well, it's enough, and that they, that being— to have your children taken away from you for this long—that's enough. On this evidence, is that, know that our community standards say that's; that's not what's going to happen. And just the, the, there's much been made of the instruction that you're going to hear about in the disposition.

THE COURT: You're at twenty.

MR. FINDLAY: Twenty. Thank you. If the court has jurisdiction, does that not necessarily mean that they would be removed from their home? Well, all we know is that's already been done. I'm not sure what else I can say to convince you. I mean, there was, you know, the pages of notes of, on the evidence and I, I venture to say we've all been here more than long enough, and I apologize for that, we've been stuck here. Um, I hope that you do the right thing; I hope you know what I think the right thing is at this point. Um, it's in your hands, and, ah, thank you very much.

THE COURT: Ms. Wittla, you have ten for rebuttal.

MS. WITTLA: It's true that Bobby Payne did not testify, does that mean that he would have been this horrible and unreliable witness for us, or that we feel we've proven our case with the witnesses we gave you? Darlene Antcliff, Jim Albert, Rod Stockhaus, and Rouse didn't testify either; those people were listed on the respondent parents' witness list; where are they? Were they so darn unreliable that they could not be hauled in either because they would have messed up their case? Is that what you're supposed to believe about witnesses that aren't here?

MR. FINDLAY: Your Honor, I'm going to object. I hope the Prosecutor knows the difference between the people and the respondent and the difference, she bears the burden of proof and those types of things that I'm objecting to that—

THE COURT:— again we're splitting hairs on criminal cases and this is a civil case, so just proceed.

Uh— time out! It should be very apparent, even to the most ignorant juror, that there is a huge difference between a witness who might be called to cite their opinions about observations they might have made, and a witness who basically created the case, as Bobby Payne did. He makes all these accusations, and then does not have the guts to show his face. Or his prosecutor does not have the guts to let him come in and make a fool out of himself and the prosecution!

MS. WITTLA: When you talk about character assassination, whose character has been assassinated in this case?

Duh! What kind of criminal did you NOT infer I might be Ms. Wittla? Let's see, I was a sexual abuser of my daughter, I was a rapist of Becky, I was a child abuser, I was a mind control freak.... to cite just a few of your assassination efforts!

MS. WITTLA (continued): The evidence shows that Robert Coleman has beat his step daughter, Caitlyn, with a belt, it's not character assassination; it's what happened. But the character assassination part is a curious thing to talk about because there have been a number of people who had their character assassinated. Elizabeth Fyle is a big liar. Jamie Perlich is a disgruntled tenant, who Robert Coleman threatened to evict when he couldn't get what he wanted out of her, to bribe testimony; the written statements. Bobby Payne is painted as a violent person; Becky Payne, well, she's just this woman scorned so you can't believe anything she'd say. But remember, when she was taped in that conversation with Ms. Towne, and she believed that her conversation was just between the two of them, she was venting, and she was mad because of all the crap that she had to put up with by Robert Coleman; up to including being sexually assaulted.

This is the way this prosecutor sneaks her dirty little lies in as though they were fact. The fact is, Becky loved to flirt, loved to have sex, and was assaulted by nobody. It was her choice. If it were not, she would not have done it several times! So excuse me if nobody swallows your lies here, Ms. Wittla, my lawyer is right about what a woman who sells her body for cigarettes would normally be considered to be. And please don't try to excuse her because she was mad. The state certainly used that against us, when we challenged their authority, didn't they? And they went after both me and Janet on that score! Remember Bonnie Huttunen's attack on Janet, saying she made a statement she didn't make because she was supposedly mad? It all depends on if the ball is in your court or the other court, doesn't it Ms. Wittla?

MS. WITTLA (continued): She was still mad when she was here, she was also scared; is it really that unreasonable to think that she'd be on the phone carrying on about a bunch of stuff and taking responsibility for all these things that happened?

PLEASE! Just tell me what is it she had to be scared of Ms. Wittla. Check my criminal background! Look it up! I have never committed an assault on anybody! But you have done your best, Ms. Wittla, to make me a dangerous man, with nothing at all to back that up! And you don't call THAT character assassination? The only thing Becky had to be afraid of is getting charged with perjury for all her lies in court! Or somebody discovering that at the time this case was being heard, there was a warrant out on her! (We discovered that later) She certainly had nothing to fear from me, and Ms. Wittla knew it. But what is this about responsibility? That is a joke! Becky never did understand anything about responsibility, and it sure was not going to start here!

MS. WITTLA (continued): She made a whole bunch of statements in there, she knows the judge, blah, blah, blah, all of a sudden, stop; half of that stuff wasn't accurate; she was venting to somebody she perceived to be a friend of hers at that point in time. I can't deny that she said it because she did, but she also stated that everything that she told Elizabeth Fyle and told you was the truth. I asked her, did you lie to me today, and she said no.

Well, that certainly makes us all believe her, doesn't it? Remember the foxes guarding the hen house? Why should we believe she would not lie to the prosecutor? After hearing Becky on the stand, do you really believe that it would be beneath her dignity to lie to the prosecutor? Or anybody else? The prosecutor would have known Becky had lied to her, when Becky said she had no criminal record, if she had simply done a background check on her. But she was much more interested in frying Robert Coleman than she was in seeking the truth. And by the way, Ms. Wittla, what does blah, blah, blah mean? I don't recall hearing that on that tape.

MS. WITTLA (continued): It was hard for her to be here, it was darn hard for her to sit in that chair and talk about her personal life; her sex life, with a bunch of strangers; but she did it; and she did it because she wanted to help those kids.

Come on now! The kids? Well, if that is true, rest easy Becky, and you too, Ms. Wittla! Today they are back where they belong! They have been for 4 years, and they are happy as hell! Don't you hate that Ms. Wittla? Oh, and Becky, Caitlyn thinks you are a slut! Still want to help her?

MS. WITTLA (continued): Elizabeth Fyle never said don't play the tape; someone said she was ambivalent, played it, don't play it; kind of waiting for, I think, me or the judge to give her some direction in that regard.

Another lie Ms. Wittla! God, how many is that? When asked she said NO. Go back and read the testimony. I think my lawyer asked her more than once, and she kept saying it was not necessary. She wasn't waiting on anyone, except maybe the judge, because the judge has assisted the prosecutor's efforts all through this trial. But don't say she did not say not to play the tape. She said no repeatedly.

MS. WITTLA (continued): But Bob Ross also testified as to what Caitlyn said during that interview; and that first interview when both Bob Ross and Elizabeth Fyle heard Caitlyn talk about the belt marks and being hit by her father is what this case is really about. And aside from the pretty picture over there that could be on a Christmas card; that's not how life was like for Caitlyn.

She was referring to a family photo with these last snide remarks. What is it Ms. Wittla? You don't like Christmas either? I knew you were hateful, but you should really think about being married to Scrooge! Same thinking.

MS. WITTLA (continued): Those two little kids on there, their names are on this case; it's not the Robert and Janet case; it's not the Coleman family case; it's Caitlyn Brag and Ashley Coleman. Those are your concern, those are the kids that have been petitioned into this court, those are the kids this state is trying to protect.

You mean trying to kidnap!

MS. WITTLA (continued): Robert Coleman is six four, two hundred forty pounds. He doesn't need to be protected; Janet Coleman, an adult woman, she doesn't need to be protected; Caitlyn and Ashley do.

In other words, folks, if you are grown and you are a parent, the state owns your kids. Nobody has any right to challenge the state or protect the parents from their kidnapping activities. She's telling a jury that even parents do not have that right. But the truth is, if the people do not put a stop to this state and other states making money via the kidnapping of kids from parents who are capable of handling things, if left alone, there will be thousands more kids hurt like mine were by the state! Not by parents! The scars this left on my daughters will be with them for the rest of their lives. They are happy at home now, but still have nightmares about foster care and the state. Why is it they don't have nightmares of me trying to beat them? If I had done that. Interesting, I would say. Until we take away federal funding for Child Protective Services (CPS) and make the states have to pay for their efforts to, as Wittla puts it, protect kids, this entire kidnapping saga will continue. Stop the funding, you will see a sudden dramatic reduction in child abuse cases. I guarantee it. Because then, the states will be required to be certain they actually have abuse cases or go broke!

MS. WITTLA (continued): Why aren't there marks on these kids? Why wasn't there any marks on Caitlyn? Well, you already know the answer to that; she was forced to sit in a vinegar bath for two hours so she didn't have any marks; because Robert Coleman is a smart cookie.

You know what? The internet is a marvelous tool! We are so fortunate to have a wealth of information at our finger tips in this day and age, and nothing can expose a liar faster, or better, than the internet, because you have experts in all fields contributing to it every day. And as smart of Ms. Wittla thinks she is, telling sinister stories like this bath incident to win a case, the information available on the internet, if someone cares to look it up, will shoot her right out of her saddle! I decided to do research on welts and the use of vinegar to get rid of them. And what I found reveals that even had I done the abuse the state lies say I did, it would have been impossible for me to hide it in the short time span scenario they were presenting— that is, the next day, when we were supposed to be going in for a doctor's visit, according to the lies of Bobby and Becky Payne. Here is what I found in my research of the matter: (1) Welts are actually fluid buildups beneath the skin, so taking care of them will take time! One treatment— even of a longer endurance— would not do it. (2) While some remedies to get rid of welts are available in your home, and vinegar is one, you will have to use it several times a day, because you treat first, the symptoms, and only time will get rid of them. You will recall, we had no time according to the Becky and Bobby lie, because we had to see the doctor the next day! The research we did also indicates that a little more study of home remedies would reveal you may find several other things that compliment your skin as well, if not better than the use of vinegar. So for this prosecutor to pretend that we initiated a 2-hour bath, as Becky and Bobby were claiming, is totally fabricated, and the medical facts all support that.

MS. WITTLA (continued): He wants his abuse to remain a family secret. He wants it to continue to happen behind closed doors. It doesn't happen over at other people's houses; it doesn't happen in public; it doesn't happen when he's out contracting business throughout the day; child abuse doesn't happen all over the place; it happens in controlled environments, where parents can hide their behavior, because they know that if it was put to scrutiny of you or the community they'd be in a lot of trouble.

Very impressive. Your made-up facts never cease to amaze me. Let me ask you when you were given the key to my mind though, Ms. Wittla. How do you know what goes on inside of my head? How do you know what family secrets I may or may not have? How do you know what I want? You are basing that on your biased opinions, just as I must admit I base some of my disgust with you on my biased opinions! But there are undisputed facts too. And my bias, or yours, cannot alter those. You and your witnesses have been caught in many factual errors already, and it is obvious you took the word of two very unreliable people to try to bring and win this case. That is fact. My feelings of disgust for you may be challenged as simply opinion, but I dare say, there will be a lot of readers, after seeing your methods in court via the transcripts here, who will share my opinion. And you cannot alter the transcripts, to try to lie about the type of methods you use.

MS. WITTLA (continued): When was Elizabeth Fyle's ah-ha moment? She kind of testified to that, she kind of pointed it out because she said no, when we saw those belts in that drawer, there's that orange belt; that rusty orange belt, I mean, who has an orange belt? Robert Coleman does; he hit Caitlyn with it.

Damn! Everybody get rid of your belts quickly! If Elizabeth Fyle comes there, and sees a color she doesn't think you should own— you are guilty of hitting somebody with it! On the same level of thinking, if they find a gun in my gun cabinet, does that mean I shot somebody? Of course I don't own guns. But I didn't own all those belts either. But even if I did, I think quite a few men probably have a number of belts in their wardrobe. Are they all guilty of child abuse? Or only if it is Bobby and Becky who are mad at them and have the opportunity to plant their ficticious evidence and then find lame-brains like Elizabeth Fyle to side with them?

MS. WITTLA (continued): Becky's not charged because she would not testify? There are no secret deals, I didn't buy her testimony, didn't promise her a darn thing.

And nobody said you did. Are you feeling guilty about past cases here, Ms. Wittla? It is true Becky was not on trial at this time, but she should have been. Had there been a marshall there who knew she had a warrant out on her at the time, she would have been arrested right there in court. But of course this prosecutor did not check her background, so she did not know. And Becky needed no incentive. She wanted to be there so she could fry me. She was mad at me and was doing all she could to see that I paid for not accepting her in my life. Sorry, that is factual, Ms. Wittla.

MS. WITTLA (continued): The only person in this case that tried to buy testimony is Robert Coleman when he was telling Jamie Perlich hey, you write out this statement, I'll knock some money off your rent. She had the guts to tell him no.

My effort was to try to show there were people out there who knew I did not abuse my kids. My mistake was in trying to be nice to her at the same time, which I see now was a mistake. But I was not trying to buy testimony. I was trying to line up a few character witnesses, and until I had to evict Jamie for non-payment of rent, we had been good friends, as she testified. She was very mad over the eviction, and that is when she wrote the letter Ms. Wittla worked from. I think she regretted having done that, because that got her hauled into court by Ms. Wittla. And that was the one thing she wanted to avoid. I'm sure she blamed me for that, and once in court, she could not deny what she had written, and with the presence of the letter that would contradict what she might say in court, if she were to recant any of it. It was incumbent upon her to acknowledge what she wrote. Who knows what she might have said in the absence of that letter, but I for one, believe it would have been different. I forgive Jamie, and still consider her a friend. I just wish I could have handled her eviction differently.

MS. WITTLA (continued): The stakes are higher here. Absolutely. I can't deny that the stakes are high here. The stakes are high, but for Caitlyn and Ashley, they're really high.

THE COURT: Three minutes.

MS. WITTLA: And what kind of intimidating actions have the Colemans been up to since this case started? How about the secret recordings that ended up on the Web?

Yeah, how about those? It's just terrible when your state people are caught doing and saying things they do every day, isn't it? It's terrible when you don't let them make up lies and phony stories to cover their real actions!

MS. WITTLA (continued): How about recording every visit according to Janet Coleman's testimony today? Despite the fact that you heard Robert Ross say that he set out parenting guidelines that said you can't record visits, she said we've recorded them all, against Robert Ross's guidelines.

Yeah, how about that? That damn wife of mine! Why would she insist on following the law. A question though.... is Robert Ross above the law? Because in setting those guidelines he breaks the law. We have a constitutional right to record, so we do it. You are a prosecutor Ms. Wittla. Do you not have an obligation to prosecute when someone breaks the law? When are you going to charge Bob Ross for breaking the law here? Or when is someone going to prosecute you, Ms. Wittla, for turning your head and pretending you don't see a violation when it occurs?

MS. WITTLA (continued): And what about the false reports of abuse made against the foster care placements? That's not intimidating anybody? That wouldn't scare anybody off?

Sure, it would intimidate any foster parent who does it. And it would scare them off if they do it. If they did not do these things themselves, it would not bother them at all. But let's set the facts straight again, as you continue to lie to people about it Ms. Wittla: these were not false reports. They were labled unsubstantiated by your own ring of crooks. They didn't even go so far as to label them as false. If they had labeled them as such, I would have been charged with a crime. The fact I was not charged indicates they knew they were not false, but had to find a way to lessen the impact of their importance. Your people did nothing about it, after their own so-called investigations. Since your people are in total control of all that, it is not too surprising they would come up with nothing. But if they were false allegations, as you lie and say they are, I should have been charged with a crime. You are the prosecutor, Ms. Wittla. Why did you not do your duty, and charge me with a crime, if what you say is true?

MS. WITTLA (continued): Bonnie Huttunen didn't say that taking those kids out of that hotel was not a big deal; what she said is that it didn't seem to be a big deal to Caitlyn.

I showed this part of your argument to Caitlyn today. Caitlyn says Bonnie is a liar, Ms. Wittla.

MS. WITTLA (continued): Caitlyn wasn't upset by it, until her mother upset her.

Caitlyn today says you are a liar, Ms. Wittla.

MS. WITTLA (continued): It's not a good thing to have to take kids away from their families, but they did it in the quietest, calmest way that they could, and because of that Caitlyn wasn't upset about it.

Caitlyn says you are a liar Ms. Wittla. She says she cried the entire time. Oh, and the calmest, quietest way to do this is to raid a hotel room at 3 in the morning? Not in my book! That scared the bejesus out of everyone! I'm sure there is a much more reasonable way to do that, but they probably don't involve punishing Robert Coleman as much. And that, in reality, was Ms. Fyle's purpose. Flexing muscles and dictating power, and nailing that damn Robert Coleman! Remember, she hasn't forgotten how she and Carpendo failed in their effort years prior to do just that.

MS. WITTLA (continued): And Caitlyn didn't talk about it to Elizabeth Fyle. She talked to Elizabeth Fyle about how good, foster— the foster home was.

Funny! Caitlyn says today she hated all of the foster homes. Do you think, just maybe— she might have tried to say what Fyle wanted to hear so she could come home? Or, again, it's quite possible she said nothing. We don't know because Fyle won't record her interviews. She would rather sneak them in, present her version, and question why anyone would not simply believe her. She was caught in several lies already in this case, so it is kind of hard to figure why someone might not believe here, isn't it?

MS. WITTLA (continued): Mr. Findlay made a statement that false reports are not for kids to, for kids to be taken away essentially; false reports, it's enough to start this whole case. But you know that's not true because the false reports made by Robert Coleman would deny it. They didn't go anywhere. False reports don't go anywhere ladies and gentlemen; the truth does.

Does it? Then why didn't you charge me with a crime for filing false reports Wittla? Because they were not false reports—they were unsubstantiated— and your criminal element, known now to readers as your kidnapping ring, are the ones in control of all that. And truth? You could care less about the truth! You did no checking on Bobby and Becky or their false report could have gone nowhere, if you were not the criminal element that you are. My attorney was right. False reports started this whole case. Oh! But you said it wasn't Bobby and Becky who filed the case, didn't you? Then WHO WAS IT MS. WITTLA? Who was it that filed the false report, and why won't you and this court divulge that to people?

MS. WITTLA (continued): And that's why we're here. And that's why the kids need to be in care of this court, because the truth is, is that Robert Coleman beat Caitlyn with a belt and her mother didn't do a darn thing to stop it. Thanks.

And with that, thank God, we had heard the last lies we were going to hear from this prosecutor during this trial! It was all over but the verdict now, and following the jury instructions which we won't go into, but which you can read on the links to my website if you wish, the verdict would come in. Prior to their retirement, however, one of the jurors would be considered the alternate, and would not decide on the outcome. There were seven, recall, but only six would deliberate. So the court chose to excuse juror number 17, Dean Struble, the one juror we felt might take our side in the case. Of course, it was mere coincidence. Sure. Anyway, we waited and at 5:15 PM, the verdict was read, announcing that this jury had found that one or more of the statutory grounds alleged in the petition had been proven. So, as we knew they would find, even before trial began, we had lost our case. It was not a great surprise for me and Janet, because we knew at the time of the raid what the state's intent was, and that was to keep our kids forever. That is why we went to trial, to show them we would fight. And the fight would not stop now. We were willing to take every step necessary to reign in this criminal element, so now it was only a matter of where we would go from here.

The judge, who had already showed his true colors during trial and in other hearings we had to suffer through, would again do that in his after trial remarks, once the jury had exited the court room. Here were his remarks:

THE COURT: Okay, be seated. Based upon the verdict of the jury in this case, I take jurisdiction of these children. Um, only a couple points I want to make. I want to make it very clear, um, I'm glad that Mr. Borth is here as supervisor, there are occasional statutory requirements or policy requirements the DHS must follow. Ms. Coleman is expecting another baby; I want to make it very clear, I will not entertain an emergency petition to take custody of that child upon birth. Based on the record here, I will elaborate on it further in disposition, ah, but I do not find an immediate threat to that child, and I balance that with the, um, trauma and, ah, potential threat based upon removal of child. We have done that, we have done that on a number of occasions, in cases where it is more clear that the parents are tragically incompetent of basic care or have serious mental deficiencies or things like that. Ah, I don't see that in this case. I intend to communicate this to Houghton County so that there are no efforts within that county overlapping to do that; I have jurisdiction of these two children; I have prior jurisdiction of the family and, again, I'm going to communicate that up there, so I want to take that

tension off of everybody in the room. Um, that being said, maybe we should have the family picture back up again, because that's the goal of everybody here, believe it or not, DHS has stated the goal of reunification, that is what the law requires them to do. The law also requires Mr. and Mrs. Coleman, you, to cooperate within the process; nobody asks you not to have your opinions; nobody asks you to agree or even like the government; but the evidence in this case in terms of, ah, ridiculous theories about the seizure of LDS children and things taken to extreme, absolutely are baseless. They are not proven because you stick it on the internet; it is not the case; it is not the truth. And this court is not going to be dealing with fantasy in this effort.

Go to my website links regarding the judge's description of so-called fantasy. Read the real life suffering LDS members suffered in real terms at the hands of the government. In his court, he may regard it as fantasy. But losing your kids to the government is no fantasy to the real life LDS parents who actually lost them, and they have many real life stories to reveal about that. I didn't post those stories. Others did. Real people. Unfortunately, this judge's fantasy is somebody else's reality! But in his hidden little world, the judge could determine his own reality level.

THE COURT (continued): The other issue is it's very clear the two of you, and especially you, Mr. Coleman; have sought to manipulate the system. I have no quarrel with your fighting the system, but I believe that the record is clear that there have been unfounded complaints against personnel of the DHS, against foster families, if foster families indeed were getting rich on stealing children, we would not have the problem we have in this county and this state in finding suitable care.

This judge was not only biased, he also apparently didn't hear too well. Or else he was sleeping. Nobody said the foster parents got rich on stealing children. We never said that. We said the states get rich, and they do. They prey on federal funding to exploit their own corrupt activities, which they choose to carry out in more and more numbers every year. And their efforts to return children is not a priority. If they can keep them until they are 18, they make every effort to do so. At 18, they can't wait to dump them on the streets, without a concern in the world over their welfare. Read the links on my website for more true stories of that. Please listen to the talk show hosts I've invited you to listen to, and read the true life stories of abuse by CPS. I didn't manufacture these stories. And if to manipulate the system means you will fight it, I am GUILTY, GUILTY, GUILTY! So are all the parents who won the class action lawsuit against Michigan. And many others in other states who have had their fill with the abuse of CPS all across the country!

THE COURT (continued): And while things do happen, in foster care to children, terrible things sometimes, in cases in this court and every court in this state, ah, because of overcrowding, because of the difficult nature of, ah, of those families, ah, I don't find it happening in this case. I find you purposely trying to manipulate the system. That is not going to help get your children back.

Why not just say it the way you mean it judge? Knuckle under or we'll keep your kids forever!

THE COURT (continuing): Again, you need to demonstrate that your goal is not to bring down the government of this state in the United States, but to get your children back.

Ok, judge, this is four years later. I have my kids back now. NOW can I bring down the state of Michigan? Do I have your permission to do it NOW?

THE COURT (continuing): The DHS has already stated that was the goal; that is their goal, it has to be their goal and I push them in that direction. That's what is required by law. So let's all take the family portrait, take a good look at it, and see if we can't reach that goal sometime in the near future. As of today, I am continuing all current orders in place, at a dispositional hearing to be set in the near future. After consulting with, ah, counsel next week, um, we'll start to work out a plan and hopefully that plan will include expansion of parenting time and, and those kinds of issues. For today, we are in recess.

—Chapter Twenty-Two—

The Trial Aftermath

The trial was over. The state had prevailed via the use of lies, a stacked jury, corrupt court and law enforcement officials, in what goes down as just another *legal kidnapping* in the state of Michigan. So now, we were truly at the mercy of the state.

It would be one thing if it were just the case of Robert and Janet Coleman vrs. the state. The local Ironwood, Michigan newspaper, *Your Daily Globe,* could not wait to report the results of the trial, of course, because they were in bed with all of the corrupt law enforcement officials and other Ironwood officials, and would not dream of doing any honest reporting. They did a hideous job of pre-trial coverage, with their slant always totally in line with what prosecutors wanted to see reported. I had made requests to make my views public, but it all fell on deaf ears. So when a verdict favoring the officials was rendered by a jury that was either related to the prosecuting side or friends of same, they jumped at the opportunity to report it. But outside of Ironwood, and outside of the corrupt courts in Ironwood, newspapers who did not take direction from corrupt authorities were reporting on cases such as ours with a different perspective. As a matter of fact, during our trial, on June 25, 2008, the South Bend Tribune exposed the corruption of the state very openly in an article that read as follows:

MICHIGAN IS LETTING DOWN ITS FOSTER KIDS

The breakdown last month of settlement talks in a federal class-action lawsuit against Michigan's foster care system is unacceptable.

It's past time for Michigan, with the country's seventh largest population of children in foster care and a spectacularly bad track record for serving them, to enact meaningful reform. Michigan's Department Of Human Services is responsible for protecting about 19,000 abused or neglected children each year. This is the second time negotiations have reached an impasse. They broke down last year when the DHS said it had no money to fix the system.

Among the six plaintiffs is "Lisa J." Lisa first entered the legal custody of Berrien County's Department Of Human Services in December, 2002 as a normal 9-year-old girl, according to court documents.

"Within her first 12 months in foster care, Lisa's emotional health spiraled perilously downward as she was moved among five different foster homes, sexually abused by a foster father, and left unsupervised to engage in inappropriate behavior with one of her older brothers. Lisa is now 13 and is not getting the services she desperately needs," the suit says.

And independent study, ordered by the U.S. District Court, found Michigan's system is so understaffed and riddled with failures that many children don't get routine medical and dental care.

Worse, Sara Bartosz, an attorney with Children's Rights, a New York-based advocacy group that in 2006 sued the state on behalf of thousands of children, said in an Associated Press story in February, "The system is so fundamentally broken that children are dying." The system has been under particular scrutiny since the murder of a 7-year-old Lansing area boy, Ricky Holland. In 2006, Ricky's adoptive parents, who first served as his state-licensed foster parents, were convicted of the crime. The DHS admitted to mistakes.

However, a lack of face-to-face visits with children by caseworkers, a lack of background checks before placing children with relatives and delays in adoption referrals continue, according to a court-ordered review.

Michigan children abused and neglected in their families are likely to be no safer in foster care, concluded John Goad, who reviewed the deaths of five foster children. Goad, former director of child protective services in Illinois, said in the February AP story that he found serious shortcomings in how DHS is structured and managed.

Only a helpless constituency would tolerate this deplorable performance.

This budget year, Michigan hired nearly 200 more foster care workers and boosted pay to private agencies that care for abused, neglected and delinquent children. Gov. Jennifer Granholm proposes to extend the increased funding next year. If the state loses the lawsuit and the foster care system is placed under federal oversight, the cost to taxpayers could be as much as $400 million dollars, according to some estimates. A negotiated solution likely would be much less costly than loss at trial and just as meaningful in improving the lot of Michigan's foster children. The latest hang-up appears to be Attorney General Mike Cox's concern that the proposed consent decree could take control of the system away from the Governor and DHS in violation of the state's constitution.

The Michigan Department Of Human Services' current and former directors in April launched the Michigan Child Welfare Improvement Task Force with a goal of radically reforming the state's child welfare programs.

The 60-member child welfare task force is a good sign that Michigan's leadership is serious about reform. The state should settle the class action lawsuit quickly and follow the task force's recommendations.

Whatever the cost, it will be small compared to the price of continuing to fail foster children.

Nice article. But of course you have to understand, the state of Michigan, and apparently many other states across the country, don't really *want* to reform any of this. This is a money maker for them, at the expense of the Federal Government who finds it easier to just hand out money to take care of such things, rather than to attack the problem at its roots. And the feds, apparently, would rather turn their backs to the children in our society, as well as their families, than to become engaged in a true effort to assist needy children and families. They leave it to the states, offering them big federal money for each child they can bring into the system. This of course entices the states to find more and more children, to where, now, you have child kidnapping cultivating across the land so that states can pad their pockets with big federal money.

Janet and I, of course, were just one more victim. Corruption is rampant across the country, and the leaders of our country could care less – – just as they could care less that the banks are screwing us, the insurance industry is ripping us off and forcing us to buy their products, and the medical establishment is gouging us with out of control prices for their services. It would be nice (if you were a crook) to be able to get the middle man price for aspirin you would expect to get in dealing with hospitals. When a hospital can charge $100 for an aspirin, the normal middle man could then get $50 or more of that. One bottle of aspirin (100 pills) would amount then to $5,000, which leaves a pretty nifty profit after you buy it at the retail store for about $4 or $5. Of course the hospitals do better, because they don't pay their middle men like that.

So all around us, we find corruption. Oil prices inflate on a yearly schedule, when it is time to claim "shortages" are driving up prices. Why at the same time each year, I wonder?

It is also amazing to me how the Congress and Senate people can make only six figures a year while they serve, but collectively amass fortunes in the millions. How is that possible?

I think it is all made possible in the same way. Get the corrupt politicians to support the two or three percent rich in this country, and make it legal for the rich to invent their own laws (using these corrupt politicians). Then fund the activities with the public paying the cost. Whether it is a bank bail out or CPS child kidnapping, the premise is the same. Use federal dollars, supplied by all Americans, to fund what would ordinarily be illegal activities.

In any case, my website has story after story of those abused by Child Protective Services in this country. Check out Doc Bean and his story about Sarah Sandy. Or the CD by Nancy Schaefer, who exposed the CPS Child Kidnapping rings in a big way – – and was killed for it, with the government then attempting to frame her husband for having killed her in a murder-suicide case. Subsequent investigations seem to suggest they were both killed in a government attempt to conceal their killing of her and silencing of him. When you hear her story, it leaves very little doubt just how far governments will go to hide what they do, while allegedly *protecting* your children. Another absolutely great web site to go to for finding out the severity of the child kidnapping rings across the country, go to the following site and read about DCFS MONSTERS! It goes into sorted detail as to how the rings operate, and what you can do to protect yourself against them. The web address for this site is:

http://www.jesus-is-savior.com/Family/dcfs_monsters.htm

Type that entire address into either your google or yahoo search box and the site selection option will come up. You need only click onto that selection and you can read for hours! So please, check out my website.

In any case, there we were, our case decided. And the spineless little newspaper report of what happened, leaving out, of course, the details not reported, which would have exonerated us easily, had they been heard by an unbiased jury, with an honest court. (There is no such thing as that in smaller communities such as Ironwood of course.) But for the sake of those who want to see what this cheesy little paper reported, here is the article they wrote:

JURY REACHES VERDICT IN CHILD CUSTODY CASE

It took a six-person jury just over an hour to award jurisdiction of the two daughters of former Ironwood residents Robert and Janet Coleman to the courts.

Now that jurisdiction has unanimously been given to the courts, a hearing to decide what will happen next will be scheduled, said Gogebic County Assistant Prosecuting Attorney Tracie Wittla.

The Colemans' daughters, ages 6 and 2, were placed in protective custody by the Gogebic County Department of Human Services on March 15 and remain there today.

Ironwood attorney Rudy Perhalla represented the children.

Evidence presented during the trial indicated that on several occasions Robert Coleman struck his 6-year-old daughter with a belt. It was those allegations that led to the investigation by Child Protective Services, fol-

lowed by the girls' placement into protective custody.

Following three days of testimony in Gogebic County Circuit Court – Family Division, the case went to the four men, two women jury just after 4 pm Friday.

"I am glad to know the kids are going to be safe," Wittla said after the verdict was returned.

"We will appeal the decision," both Robert, 39, and Janet, 30, said. "I have lost faith in the judicial system," Robert said. "This is a waste of taxpayers dollars. The prosecutors failed to prove their claim on the original offense."

The issue of the police removing the two children from the Colemans' custody at 3 am on March 15 from a motel room in Houghton came under scrutiny as petitioner Elizabeth Fyle from the DHS testified.

Fyle said after a couple of days of searching for the Colemans, she filed the petition seeking jurisdiction over the kids, and also obtained a court order to have the children picked up.

Fyle initially interviewed the 6-year-old at her home on March 11 after a complaint had been filed with her office alleging that Robert Coleman had used a belt to spank Caitlyn many times.

Bessemer attorney Michael Findlay, who represented the Colemans, made several references during the trial to Bobby and Rebecca Payne, former tenants of the Colemans, filing the initial complaint of abuse with the DHS.

Fyle testified that the Paynes had not filed the complaint. She was then asked by Findlay to reveal the complainant's name, however, probate judge Joel Massie ruled that the name would remain confidential.

Why? If this newspaper story was correct, who was the judge trying to protect, if not the Paynes? We even have recordings that reveal Rebecca admitting proudly that she was able to nail us. If it was another person who filed after consulting with Rebecca, a defendant is entitled to face his accuser. We were not given that right, and obviously, the judge was biased. Continuing:

After Fyle's initial interview with the 6-year-old, Fyle said she was concerned for the children's safety, and so, before leaving the home "The Colemans promised they would not use any type of physical punishment on their children. I believed they were sincere," she said.

Ranking from one to 10, Fyle said her level of concern was between 6 and 7 at that time.

On March 12, social worker Robert Ross called Coleman to schedule a second interview, Fyle said. Coleman told Ross the family was in Marquette and would be back later that day, she said, nothing that her level of concern was now at 7.

Again, why? Why would her concern level rise when we talked with Bob Ross? If we were going to run, as she and her co-conspirators set out to paint in a picture of the awful Coleman parents, we would never have answered the phone or talked to Bob Ross. We would instead have just fled to Canada, a short few hours away. So this was all lies, to try to sell a jury on how threatening we were to our own children. Unfortunately, it worked. And the acquaintance I had interview Caitlyn later, in his transcripts, says she indicated strongly she was *never* afraid of us, but was deathly afraid of the state officials and police. So continuing on with the biased *Daily Globe* article, they continued to repeat the state version of things:

Fyle said she called Coleman at 6 pm that day with no response. She said she left a message. During his testimony, Coleman said Fyle did not call him, nor did she leave any messages. Fyle said she called the Ironwood Public Safety Department at 7:30 pm and expressed her concerns. She said her level of concern was now at 8.

Nice, cute little trick. You wait and call the police agency (IPSD), expressing your dismay at your inability to get someone on the phone, when in fact, you made no calls. That way they can corroborate your *efforts* and your *terrible concern* you expressed when the situation did not, in fact, necessitate that at all. A great way to force the issue and get a court to issue an order that should have never been issued. Continuing her and the newspaper account's version:

On Friday, March 13, her level of concern had reached 9, and by Friday night, when she filed the petition for court jurisdiction over the children, her level of concern had reached 10, she said. "It stayed at 10 until I knew the children were safe and in foster care," she testified.

After the pickup order had been obtained, the IPSD put out a "be on the lookout alert" for the Coleman vehicle that was later discovered at the Best Western motel in Houghton.

Now. First of all, had we been "on the run" as Fyle so dramatically insinuated, why would we check in to the motel, using our own name, and then park our vehicle in the front of the motel? Her story was totally invented, to make it appear we were trying to kidnap our own kids. We didn't have to. They were already ours. They had no jurisdiction over our children, although as you can readily see, to gain such jurisdiction was their intent. After all, this was a two-in-one state income, since we had two children, who were obviously in severe peril. Right? If that were so, why is it that the state did not take our newborn, who was born the same night the court decision came down? No such court action was ordered, although there was an effort by the prosecution to do this. If failed, but it leaves me wondering, why, if we were dangerous to our other two girls, would we surely not be a danger to our newest – – especially in light of what had happened? Let's listen to rest of the b.s. the newspaper reported:

Asked about law enforcement picking the children up at 3 am, Fyle said, "That's their job. They had a court order and it was up to them to decide how they wanted to do it."

Both Fyle and Rebecca Payne testified to Robert Coleman spanking the 6-year-old.

Interesting, isn't it. Fyle had never seen it personally, so what gave her the authority to testify to such a thing? And remember Payne? She was the one who never filed a complaint to start this case. So how did she get on the witness list? And what about the unnamed individual who, according to the judge, *did* file the complaint? Doesn't it seem logical that person would also have testified in this case? Why such protection measures, because if I were the dangerous person they tried to paint me up to be, I would surely have gone after *all of them*— not just the complainant. It seems to me all of their very lives would be in danger. But maybe because it was all invented to paint me as *dangerous,* the rest, who in fact know I am not dangerous, were without fear. Continuing the so-called *coverage:*

Fyle said she told the girl to "Tell me what happens when you get into trouble." She said the daughter said she either has to "go to the corner or I get the belt. He smacks me." When asked who "smacks" her, the girl responded, "my daddy." Fyle said the girl told her she got struck many times, but typically one or two "smacks."

This is real interesting, because it would appear Elizabeth Fyle is the only one who ever heard that from Caitlyn. The others have all indicated, she would not talk to them about home issues. How is it that this woman managed to elicit so much on her first conversation with Caitlyn, when she totally shut down to other strangers. And most interestingly, even to this date, Caitlyn denies she ever said any such thing. Here's more:

Fyle said the 6-year-old told her that her dad used an orange belt (later found in a drawer with other belts). Asked if anyone held her down, the girl responded, "sometimes mom, sometimes Bobby, sometimes Becky," Fyle said.

Why then, does Caitlyn, at age ten, deny all this? And why is she now in fear of the state taking her away from us "abusive parents" again? She even laughed at her latest interview when asked if her mom ever held her down. "She would never do that," she indicated.

"She (oldest daughter) described sitting in a bathtub for a long time. She said something got put in the tub. She said it smelled funny," Fyle said. Payne earlier testified that Robert Coleman hit his daughter with a belt, leaving welts on her butt. She said Coleman instructed her to place the girl into the bathtub, with vinegar. She said the girl remained in the bathtub for over two hours.

Great journalism, right? Except there wasn't an ounce of truth to anything they quoted the unquestionable Ms. Fyle about. Isn't it odd that the daughter told only Ms. Fyle about the "funny smell"—while Rebecca Payne was totally "fabricating" her story about being instructed to put my daughter in the bathtub with vinegar. If I wanted that done, either Janet or I would have done it. Why would I ask a former tenant to do it? She was a tenant, and a bad affair I unfortunately chose to get myself into. When she was not getting what she wanted with me, she chose to go after me and invent a story that would make me pay. Her husband, who it was proven needed mental help, supported her efforts. That is the long and short of it. I have recorded proof that such was her intent. If the court were fair, it would have listened to that, threw it all out of court, and the verdict would have been ours. But that is not profitable for the state.

So now, it was on to the next step, as we found ourselves totally at the mercy of the state. It was only a question of how, now, we would ever get our kids back.

—Chapter Twenty-Three—

Revelations Of A One-Sided Judge

We already knew we had a one-sided judge in our case, as he favored and worked so hard to adhere to every aspect of the prosecutor's requests in hearings prior to the trial. Denials were the common answer to any of our claims or requests. It was a case built on lies, starting with the initial complainant, one which any judge could clearly see was incompetent to bring legitimate charges. But in his comments on our first hearing following the trial, his one-sidedness was finally expressed in his words as he firmly stated that instead of us being victims of the complainant's lies, it was we who abused the lying complainant. It was infuriating to hear his one-sided opinions, of course, but we were at the mercy of the state and they were holding our kids hostage. So we knew we had to bite the bullet and at least pretend to submit to their requests.

While the entire hearing on July 17, 2008, reflected his one-sided views, there were some, particularly, that sparked rage and made it clear he had already decided on this case before it ever went to trial. The fact he would not even consider the truthfulness of the complainants, and accepted everything the complainant said, so long as it was presented by the state co-conspirators in our case was totally prejudicial. There was no effort whatsoever to investigate what the complainant and a lying state investigator (Elizabeth Fyle) charged. Fyle merely relayed the complainants words and brought them forward in the form of allegations. She had no "proof" of any belt use, for instance, and I know that because it did not happen. My daughter, Caitlyn, even to this day, still acknowledges that was a lie. And that was the basis for this case. Yet, still, because this judge allowed these lies to be admitted as "evidence", we were convicted of a crime we did not commit. Clearly, it was case of a rejected lover and her mental case of a husband, seeking revenge against us because of the breakdown of their status with us as landlords, and because we did not want to make them permanent house guests in our home. But to cast us as *using them,* as the judge did in that hearing is idiotic at best. We gave them a place to live and a job when Bobby Payne was incapable of finding one. In retrospect, as a landlord and business person, I should have simply cast them out in the cold from the very beginning, and as I stated prior in this book, my affair with the wife, Rebecca, was the biggest mistake of my life. But villains for helping them?

Give me a break!

In this hearing, the judge started by concurring with the state co-conspirators that the reason for all the movement of the children was because of my wife and myself. He accepted their lie that we made false allegations against the foster parents who were abusing our children. The sham *investigations* of these charges amounted to nothing more than a house visit, in which the law enforcement authorities did only what they had to do to write a report. It's like the wolf guarding the hen house. The authority comes up, asks the wolf if the hens are OK, and the wolf says, "Sure" — just before he eats them. The prosecution made a big deal out of asking a Mormon Church member if he would be willing to take our kids into his home as a foster parent. After the bad experiences my kids had already gone through, why would I *not* seek out people I felt were qualified to treat my kids in a humane way? What kind of parent am I if I just said, "Oh, it's OK if you beat my kids, sexually abuse them, or anything else you want." Yet that is precisely what the state wanted, for us to just concur with everything they said, and they made it perfectly clear in this hearing. So of course the prosecutor challenged us for having done this.

The next thing they brought up was the money that was sent to my wife for child support for the children. They wanted it. Even though her ex had never bothered to ask anything about his kids during our marriage, it now became an issue. He had made the child support payments, but since the state had taken control of our children, they now wanted that money. Several questions about this:

(1) Why, when the state removes our children without our approval, are they now entitled to this money? In particular "back" money?

(2) Why, when the state had still never reimbursed us for travel and other various things they were supposed to pay for, do they think this money should go to them, especially when we are still using it for our kids? We still have to maintain their house, for a time when the state would reunite us with them, and of course we had many added costs in our efforts to concur with all the state requests, including our travel, hotel stays, etc.

(3) Why do they even *need* this money when, in fact, they are already making a killing from the federal government for stealing our kids? (It is pretty obvious that the state is only in this for *the money).*

Then came the attack from the Guardian Ad Litem, Rudy Perhalla, in which he said he would not call them *false accusations,* but ranted on as though they were. The complete transcript of this and every other hearing we've discussed in this book are available on my website, so if you want it all, you can read it there, as I have only so much space in my book. Just look it up under *transcripts* on my web pages. In any case, Rudy inserted into his comments this paragraph, which I found to be most intriguing:

"I'm just going to put the parents on notice if there are unfounded allegations again, brought against Menominee County somehow; I would, now that we have jurisdiction, I would ask, I would bring a show cause petition against these parents, and do whatever we can to, to stop them from engaging in this type of behavior."

Does that sound a *threat* to you? In essence, it means if we, as parents, do not play ball and unquestionably allow the state to treat our children as they wish to treat them, even if abusive, we would be met with retribution from the state. Under a pretense of reunification, the state in fact, was violating the laws of their own state by indicating we, as parents, could not use the tools that are in place to protect our own children. And I might add, Rudy claimed he had jurisdiction. He did not. His place was supposedly to represent the interests of my kids. But jurisdiction remained with the *court* — not with Rudy Perhalla.

Our own lawyer then attempted to make the biased judge understand that we, as parents, had not fairly had our concerns addressed, and he insisted that allegations we had made were not, in fact, false. Unsubstantiated, yes, because nobody *wanted* to really investigate the complaints. It is much easier to make a short house visit and write it off as "unsubstantiated" because you don't find a hangman's noose with blood on it, or anything that obvious in the living room. My lawyer worded it best when he made the following statement to the court:

"Unfortunately I guess I can't focus on the children; I mean, we've got to deal with this foster care stuff.

Apparently they're forgetting that, I think it was July 3rd of this year; the state of Michigan just settled a large lawsuit against foster care and some of the allegations that have existed against foster care are pretty chilling. I did a little bit of research on it after the trial because I know that nobody bought anything the Colemans were saying and dismissed their concerns about how their children were being treated. They blew them off and they've been accused here of making false allegations. I'm yet to be aware of any false police report or charges being filed against them. So I don't think that it's necessarily true. They've raised concerns about their children the first time they see bruises that were, at the time, being used to demonstrate that THEY had abused their children. And they report that. Are they not supposed to raise concerns about bruises on their kids? On another occasion Caitlyn says something to Mr. Coleman that is very strange. I think it would get any parent concern, so they raised concerns about that, and now it's that they're accused of making false allegations. Based on my research, in the state of Michigan, and I'll put it bluntly, that the foster care system in Michigan sucks. I mean there are obviously good foster parents within the system, but there are also serious problems, and for this to be turned around, pointing a finger at the Colemans for raising concerns about the safety of their children and what's going on with foster care, I think is just unfair. It kind of turns the focus away from what I was hoping we were going to be doing here today.

My lawyer went on to plead our case from a humane basis, but to no avail to this judge, who was obviously siding with the prosecution and the co-conspirators all the way. Mr. Findlay even suggested giving the children back to us, but of course, that was not even given consideration. What *was* under consideration, I found out, was removal of our newborn infant, who was born the last night of our trial. The judge did negate that, but it was the only thing he did that was favorable to us. But I wondered, if we were good enough parents to parent our newborn, why were we not good enough to bring our other kids home?

Then came the discussion about "why" our children were removed from our home in the first place. This was a total lie, from start to finish. According to Ms. Fyle, she was not planning on removing the children and it was the *flight allegations* that had made her decide on it. But they had already decided to do that, because they were already tracking us. It was only a matter of opportunity, and building their false case. As our lawyer correctly pointed out, if it were truly a flight situation, it was a lousy job of it. He pointed out, as I said, that if we were so inclined, there was an international border not far away (Canada), and also other places to go. Our lawyer pointed out that we had a teacher testify she had no evidence of anything abnormal or out of the ordinary for a child. We had a doctor testify to it. All of this had no impact on the judge, who frankly, did not want to hear any of it, as the state had prevailed and it was now in his hands legally.

Now, it was time for the judge to make his irrational comments. To try to "justify" the decision of the jury, which as we already pointed out, was rigged with friends and family of the court and the state. His comments included:

Let me make something absolutely, perfectly clear. This case was hotly contested before a jury; and all counsel in terms of an objective view of performance did your jobs. And you all did a good job, vigorously advocated for the positions that you represented. That is now concluded, by a jury verdict, which determined that based on some broad definitions under the Michigan Child Protection Law, for some reason the jury concluded that these children were in need of protection. The language being on, at least, part of the instructions that the home was an unfit place for these children to live. That's the conclusion of the jury. It took an hour or less for the jury to conclude that. The evidence presented in this case was not one of a close call on an over spanking. The evidence was that there was discipline with a belt, and the jury may very well have concluded that that was true.

What "evidence"? You mean a mental case statement and a lie by the investigator who said there was belt use when there wasn't? Caitlyn never said it, and denies it to this day. Only Ms. Fyle, who was obviously *fed* this information from a mental case, made such a statement. Is that, in fact, *evidence?* To a corrupt jury it would be. So again, review who the jurors were and who they were either friends with or related to. Continuing on:

The evidence was of a home situation involving a prime witness who was a developmentally disabled individual who worked basically with her husband on almost a slave basis for the Colemans here, at a drastically reduced payment of some sort of reduction of rent.

What a crock! A *prime witness?* A witness caught admitting her motives on the stand! The judge described Rebecca as developmentally disabled. And she was married to her husband who was a bonafide mental case! We have proof of that via his visits to mental facilties, which are outlined again on my web pages, giving places who treated him, etc. So, even by the judge's admission, they needed help! And *slave* employment? It was more like compassion employment for someone totally incapable of finding a job! We only allowed them to work off what they could not pay, and I don't believe that is criminal. We could have just cast them out into the cold. The judge totally bought the reversal established by the deceit and lies of the co-conspirators in this case. Or perhaps it was his *plan* all along to *buy it* as a member of their team. But that wasn't all, as the judge continued:

There was a relatively sorted situation described involving personal interaction with the wife there, in terms of a sexual relationship. All of which painted a picture that the jury made a determination and jurisdiction on it. And had I been trying it as the Court, I would have made the same conclusion as the jury. It was not a close call.

Right on, judge! The truth is you *were* trying it as the Court, when you allowed the testimony of unreliable witnesses to begin with, not allowing their credibility to be challenged. The judge then voiced his opinion that we had interacted, disrupted, and manipulated the system. *How dare us!!!* So far as I can see, that was our biggest crime, that we refused to allow the system to do as they chose, including the abuse of our children! We were framed from start to finish, and the judge was a good part of it! The rest you can read for yourself by accessing this manuscript in in chapter 21, and reading his comments after the verdict was rendered. But the comments of this judge were so ridiculous, in light of the way the co-conspirators lied and exaggerated everything from the start, so as make most courts *laugh* at such a court action. And you want to talk about manipulation? Just read the court transcripts and you see it from start to finish by the corrupted state prosecutor!

So, with the instructions now given for the coming times, my wife and I had to begin preparations for how we could best reunite with our children.

Meanwhile, the local *rag* newspaper, *The Daily Globe,* quoted just what the judge and the prosecution wanted the public to hear, one-siding it as usual. They quoted the judge as saying that he would have made the same call the six-person jury made when it awarded jurisdiction of my kids to the court. Yes, I do believe he would have, and that he and the system's hand-picked jury all think alike and had me and my wife already convicted before the trial had even begun, just as my lawyer indicated before the trial started. It is convenient to believe, so the state can go about their illegal kidnapping of kids, a worthless newspaper can continue to write their fiction and retain their ads from sponsors who would be offended if they printed the truth. Yes, they will all side with the state every time. No parent really has a chance. Had they had any parents on the jury, who were not related to someone in social work or law enforcement, we may have stood a chance — and would surely have prevailed had it been a court of law that stood for something, such as is supposedly true in a criminal proceeding. At this time the law still allows manipulative system figures to run amuck and do as they please. The comical part (had it not been so disgusting) was to read what this rag printed about Rudy Perhalla's assessment:

Ironwood attorney Rudy Perhalla, representing the two girls, said the frequent moves from one foster home to another are preventing "rapport building" between DHS workers and the children. Each time the children are moved, rapport building must begin all over again.

What a joke! In the entire process from removal of our kids to our getting them home, this idiot (Perhalla) didn't visit my kids more than twice that I know of! So how is he to know how "rapport building" was going?

In any case, the decision had been made, and it was our effort now to try to regain our children.

—Chapter Twenty–Four—

The "Turning Point"

It was now on to the resumption of visitations and the implementation of the various "treatment programs" the state wanted Janet and myself to undergo. I was to take anger management classes, and both of us were counseled at Bell Behavioral Services, a part of the Bell Hospital in Marquette. Janet had actually been having a bit of counseling since April, but for me it was a new experience. I can't say it was a bad experience, in and of itself, but I haven't changed my views as a parent as to how we relate in a family setting. Now, as it was then, we don't spank with belts or engage in any of the other ficticious allegations that made this entire bad dream a reality. I do think the turning point of this whole affair, however, came with meeting and working with Sherry Benson, a parent aide and visitation supervisor we began now to deal with. From the time we started making visitations with her making the reports, we actually got honest appraisals of how things were going. Her summary of visits from the day after our disgusting hearing of July 17, to the end of August are to the point, honest, and accurate. And that, in itself, was refreshing!

Here are her reports, as delivered to Bob Ross on September 4, 2008:

SUMMARY OF VISITS:

July 18, 2008

Visit was at DHS in Menominee, Mi. Held from 8-11. First visit with the family. Ashley, Caitlyn, Brittany, Robert, and Janet were present for the entire visit. The parents brought along snacks and drinks for the children. They also brought an array of items to use in playing with their children, bubbles, crayons and coloring books, computer games, etc. Kids were very active and the parents did a good job of entertaining them. They attended to all their needs and when the bathroom was necessary, Mom took them across the hallway (visible from the room) and stood in the doorway till they were done. We discussed future visits and the parents wanted to spend more time and outside. We decided on parks and a one day long time slot as opposed to a 2 day small time slots. I told them I would get an okay from Bob Ross and let them know if this was okay. We exchanged phone numbers and email. I called Bob and cleared this with him. Spoke to the parents and set a time and place. Overall it was a good visit. Only concern was that Robert tended to give the kids everything they wanted... didn't see any parenting skills at the visit.

July 25, 2008

Visit was at parks today. We first went to Watertower Park. Observed much play between parents and children. Equal amounts given to all. Brought along some sandwiches to eat for the kids. Caitlyn did get stung by a bee when we first arrive and dad was able to give her some first aid and a little tlc. Reported the sting to the foster home when we returned. Went to Walmart after a call to Jennifer Savage to see if I could take them into Wisconsin. She okayed it as long as I was comfortable with taking them there. Kids got a new toy, a new outfit and we then headed back to Henes Park. Kids played and swam at the park. Concern again was the lack of discipline. Caitlyn was testing both mom and dad. Mom was more able to state NO, but then dad would give in to her. Overall good visit. Much interaction, fed the kids appropriate foods and less snacks today!

August 1, 2008

Went to Perkins to eat breakfast and then over to the park for awhile. Dad and mom were both attentive to the girls. They had brought along some toys and bikes for the kids. They played on the bikes, played baseball for awhile with the girls, fed the kids sandwiches and juice. Kids were again testing mom and dad and they seem to have the skills, I am just not seeing a whole lot. I get the impression that they are trying too hard to please the kids... or makeup for not being there during the week. I called Bob Ross this week to ask about what he needs from me as far a report goes and if I am to be offering parenting advice on the visits. He told me to give them all the advice that I felt they needed. Overall good visit. No concerns other than those listed above.

August 8, 2008

Watertower Park today after a muffin and juice at Perkins. Played baseball, golf and jump rope with the kids. Kids had their bikes along to ride in the circle. Played on the swings. Ate a barbecued lunch of hot dogs, cheese and juice. Talked to them about how they needed to follow through with parenting and gave them a few examples of what they did on the last two visits and how they would need to change that. Dad asked a lot of questions and at one poin the did discipline his daughter Caitlyn. Half way through the discipline he asked for some advice on how to connect with his daughter and get her to comply. I talked him through the incident and then we talked a bit afterwards about consistency and structure. He admits to giving into her a lot (which is accurate) and how he hates to spend his time with her disciplining her. I talked about how she needs to know about the rules everywhere she goes and in every time in her life. We talked about how he needs to have consistency with her in the visits... how it will look when she gets back home if he isn't consistent with her now, etc. Both parents were very engaged with the concepts. Overall good visit. Did a nice job of following through with consequences when necessary.

August 15, 2008

Went to Perkins for muffins and drinks (coffee and juice). Caitlyn has a nasty habit of burping a lot to gain attention. I worked with mom and dad at Perkins on giving choices to her and allowing her one of the choices to be what they wanted and the other choice to be something they thought she wouldn't like. They did this and Caitlyn chose to go without snacks for the rest of the visit! I reminded them both that now that she had made her choice, everyone would have to follow through with that choice. Went to the park. Caitlyn asked several times for snacks and dad was good about reminding her about her choice. Towards the end of the visit, dad left to go and get ice cream while the rest of us stayed at the park. When he returned he had ice cream for all. Mom was quick to remind him about the choice Caitlyn made. He started to give in and argue the point. I remained silent to see what he was going to do. Mom stated again that he needs to be consistent. He then told Caitlyn that because of her behavior at Perkins and the choice she made that she could not have the ice cream. (Hurray!) Caitlyn was very calm about it and congratulated him and he admitted that it was very hard for him to do. But he was glad that he did. GOOD visit overall. Nice parenting skills today!

August 22, 2008

Visit at the park. Barbecue today for lunch. Lots of playing and activity with the girls. Some down time spent talking and listening to the girls tell them about their days. They don't ask any questions about the foster home or the names of others in the home. They have been very good about this. The girls only refer to the foster parents as MOM and DAD... their other mom and dad... and don't even mention the names of the other children, just that there are other children there. Lots of good follow through with parenting today from both parents. I see a more united front from when I first started working with them. They asked me some questions about how to get compliance, gave some suggestions and had some rehearsals of how to enact the methods. Good visit... lots of fun.... good discipline.... good discussions.

August 27, 2008

Dad is now working and so we have had to change the visit days to meet his schedule and fit into mine. Today we have an afternoon early evening visit. At the start of the visit I called to speak with Bob Ross about the parents attending open house with Caitlyn. He was not available and so I spoke with his supervisor Dan Borth. He told me if I was OK with this and made sure the FP were not going it was fine with him. I called the FP and told them what Dan had stated and she would call the school to make them aware of who was going to attend the open house. Went to the Open House and both parents thanked me for allowing this opportunity to meet the teacher and see the school. I told them to thank Dan as I had nothing to do with it. We then went to Henes Park so that the girls could go swimming. Had a good time at the beach. Both parents told me that they had spoken with Len Welling at Menominee DHS about what else they could be doing to get their children back into their home and asked me about the Family to Family Meeting. I told them a little about the program and stated that they should talk to someone in their county about this program. They stated that they would do that. Dad spent time with the girls in the water and building in the sand. Kids really do enjoy the time with their parents. Nice job of discipline today and the girls have actually been less of a problem since both parents have started working with the discipline. They still ask if they get "stuck" in a situation and are not quite sure what to do, but for the most part they are showing some nice skills. They asked me about unsupervised for next week while Caitlyn has to be picked up… I told them I would email Bob Ross about the issue. I stated that I would let them know next week when I see them with the kids. Meeting set for September 4 at 2 pm CST with just Ashley till Caitlyn gets out of school at 3 pm. Good visit.

Things couldn't be going any better at this point. We finally had a visitation supervisor who seemed interested in working with us and not against us. And on August 29, 2008 we received an in home visit from Steve Pelli, a DHS worker from Houghton. Following his visit, he sent a very nice message to Bob Ross regarding his visit. It read as follows:

On 8/29/08 (12:25 pm) a scheduled visit was made with Mr. & Mrs. Coleman and their daughter, Britney, as their residence in Calumet.

They reported the following regarding their participation with services: Each week they attend approximately 5-6 hours of counseling and parenting classes through the LVD Tribe in Watersmeet. This has included individual counseling to address anger management and marriage counseling. Mr. & Mrs. Coleman expect to complete the parenting classes within the next two weeks, although the completion date will depend on how well they are developing. They reported having an additional caseworker in Watersmeet who is helping with Britney's needs. Mr. & Mrs. Coleman reported that they had completed their psychological evaluations on 8/28/08 at Bell Hospital and the assessor could not think of any additional services to offer them.

They reported that the supervised parenting time visits are going well and they hope to move towards unsupervised visits soon. Both parents were pleased with being able to meet Caitlyn's teacher during the 8/27/08 visit. Mr. & Mrs. Coleman are hoping that the children will be returned home following the next review hearing on 10/9/08. By this time they anticipate that they will have completed all of the required programs/services.

Mr. Coleman reported that he is now employed part-time (30-40 hours/week) with KBIC Tribal Security in Baraga. He anticipates that the hours will increase to fulltime with benefits when the children return home.

When asked how they felt the reunification efforts were going, both indicated that things have been going good and Mr. Coleman stated that the parenting time visit this week was the most productive one to date. They were asked if any additional services were needed, which have not yet been offered. They mentioned financial reimbursement (e.g. travel expenses) in a more timely manner and more time with the children. They are concerned about potential travel issues if the children are still in care this winter. Mr. & Mrs. Coleman both reiterated that they are willing to do whatever it takes to get the children back and will continue to cooperate with services and DHS visits when this occurs.

A tour of the home was provided and the conditions were observed to be clean, well organized, and free of any apparent child safety hazards. Bedrooms have been set up for the girls.

Next came a letter to our attorney from the Lac Vieux Desert Band of Lake Superior Chippewa Indians. This report related to the anger management counseling I was required to undergo. Here is their letter:

October 1, 2008
Attorney Michael Findlay
Bessemer, Michigan
Re: Robert Coleman (Anger Management Counseling)

Dear Mr. Findlay:

The following is a summary of the services provided for Robert Coleman in regards to Anger Management Counseling, as requested by Robert to work towards the goal of family reunification. I have signed consent, from Robert Coleman, to release information regarding attendance, participation, and internalization of concepts.

Robert's attendance was above average, in that he never missed a session. Initially, Robert was quick to interrupt in order to feel as though his side of the story was being heard. However, in later sessions, Robert was more able to focus on self-reflection and the redirection of his emotions. Robert was able to verbalize the sources of his current and past frustrations. Robert was able to identify behaviors and characteristics such as: voice volume, height, and intensity, which are some times interpreted as aggressive, even if the intent is to express his emotions. Areas that were covered include: Identifying Causes Of Anger, Learned Anger Responses, Appropriate and Inappropriate Anger, Assertion v. Aggression, Relaxation Techniques, Problem Solving, and Conflict Resolution.

In summary, Robert was a willing participant in Anger Management Counseling. His requirements, as our program is concerned, have been satisfactorily completed based on attendance and progress. His completion date was September 30, 2008. Should you need any additional information, please feel free to contact our agency at the number above.

Sincerely,

Charissa Jeske, LLMSW

In September, Bell Behavioral Services released their assessments of both myself and my wife. As I am a bit more contentious than my wife, as you might expect, the assessment of me left some doubt, but certainly left room for the possibility that what I've been claiming throughout this book were indeed the facts. In the case of my wife Janet, it clearly vindicates her, in my judgement, and only goes to prove more fully that our claims were indeed valid and correct. The full reports are on my website once again, as I have nothing to hide, but here were the final assessments of the clinical judgements as they wrote them:

ROBERT COLEMAN

Robert Coleman is a 40-year-old married native American male who is seen for a mental health assessment and anger management assessment. Collateral information for this assessment was also obtained from Bob Ross of DHS and service providers from the mental health agency where Robert and Janet are receiving service. Robert was cooperative with the intake process and the interview. He appeared mildly agitated. He presented as tearful and distraught over his childrens' removal. Robert views himself and Janet as innocent victims of the system. He vehemently denies ever abusing his children and believes it was the spurned woman, Becky, who created this situation as a way to get back at Robert. This is in contrast to Mr. Ross' indication that physical abuse allegations were substantiated with evidence that included his step-daughter's testimony. Robert was quite verbal throughout the interview. His answers to questions appeared vague and perhaps evasive at times, while at other points he appeared quite candid. This left the impression of an overall inconsistency with this gentleman's presentation.

With regard to mental health, Robert was given a symptom checklist to complete as part of the assessment. Robert identified no slight, moderate, serious, or extreme problems on the written portion of the assessment. This fact appears quite inconsistent with both the current situation and the verbal portion of the interview. For a person to have their children wrongly removed and be fighting child abuse allegations, it seems highly likely that they would at least have some slight or moderate symptoms. Robert indicated in the written portion that he was taking Lexapro. When asked why he was taking Lexapro, he admits to a history of depression over the past few years. He has been treated by his Family Doctor, Dr. Pusateri for this. He denies any current depression and indicates the medication is working. At another point in the interview, he indicates that he cries all the time about his babies and at times hyperventilates with anxiety. Robert indicates that he was also diagnosed with ADHD as a child though does not take any medication for this. At a minimum, it appears that Robert is struggling to cope and adjust with the recent ongoing events, the legal process, and the removal of his children from the home.

An additional mental health component is that Robert presented himself as someone who potentially struggles with paranoid thoughts, perhaps more so when under stress. This was also seen by his counselor Karissa who works with him at the tribal mental health center. Robert indicated that the jury in his trial was against him because they knew or were related to people he had evicted in the past. Robert also reportedly verbalized in court that there was conspiracy to remove Mormon children from their parents and that was what was happening in their case. Others report that Robert had alluded to the judge keeping some money. These instances all appear to have a paranoid flavor and this aspect may need further exploration for accurate assessment.

With regards to anger management issues, clearly a substantiated physical abuse incident would alone warrant a need for anger management intervention and hence he is currently in counseling for this. It is worthwhile to note, however, that Mr. Coleman denies in this interview any history of anger problems as well as any history of being a victim or perpetrator of abuse. Robert notes he has no history legal or otherwise of any type of violence. He was not in any fights as a child. His previous relationships were not reportedly abusive. His parents were not abusive to the children or to each other. It is the undersigned's impression that Robert could come across as physically intimidating based on his size and voice. He can appear somewhat agitated or angry when discussing the perceived wrongs he has endured. These factors contrast with verbal report of no difficulties either current or past with anger.

It is recommended that Robert complete a psychological evaluation based on the lack of clear findings and numerous inconsistencies in his assessment. It is believed that his may help shed light on further understanding of this individual. Mr. Coleman should also continue his previously assigned anger management and parenting classes.

Identified strengths in this individual appear to be a strong faith, good physical health, and a strong desire to maintain an intact family.

So yes, I will admit I am an individual who is not easily put into a box that says, "This is

Robert Coleman." I don't think any individual can be typecast in such a fashion. But despite the parts I may disagree with, there are some things in this assessment that leave quite an impression regarding this case.

(1) The fact that Bob Ross contributed to it. Their lies created the fabrications of abuse that made this a case in the first place, and he did nothing to verify the facts of the accusations of Elizabeth Fyle, particularly where it came to my step daughter. To this day, my step daughter states that Ms. Fyle's claims were untrue.

(2) Paranoid thoughts. What are they? Could it be they consist of truths that others do not wish to recognize. Why is it so hard to believe that people in the system lie. It happens at the federal level as well. Just look at how many have been prosecuted at all levels for criminal actions based on lies. And why, when you have a state with the record of Michigan on child care problems, would you believe they don't kidnap kids, using any means to do so, when it means money to them?

(3) Regarding anger management. Yes, if indeed I had done what they say, and used a belt on my daughter, it would warrant anger management. I didn't. And Caitlyn, to this day (at age 10) will tell you I did not.

Here is a test I'd like for every reader of this book to take: Put yourself in my shoes for a moment, and ask now, if it were you and:

(1) You were falsely accused of abusing your child by a mental case;

(2) You nearly lost your marriage due to an affair, even though it was your fault;

(3) Your lost your children to the state;

(4) You lost your business because of the financial difficulties arising from a fight

to get your children back;

WOULD YOU THEN HAVE SHOWN ANY STRESS, ANXIETY, OR ANGER AT AN INTERVIEW YOU WERE FORCED TO UNDERGO TO TRY TO DEFEND YOURSELF, WHEN IT IS THE SAME STATE SYSTEM THAT SETS UP THE INTERVIEW?

Yet that is what these people use to render opinions when they see such symptoms displayed, be they demonstrative or simple indicators.

Now, here is the rest of the story. Even if you don't agree with my responses to all this, let's look at the clinical judgement given to my wife, who supports everything I say. Is she also a paranoid? Here was her clinical evaluation:

In the undersigned's clinical judgement, Mrs. Coleman's attitudes and behaviors make sense as either the result of a conscious and deliberate effort to escape responsibility for abuse of young defenseless children and an implied attitude of dedication to continuing to do that—OR—the resolute efforts of a parent who has been falsely accused and traumatically victimized by a child protective system run amok and who will not stand by meekly and let this happen to herself and her family. From a clinical point of view it should be one or the other, and not something mixed or in between.

Well, I can tell you it is the latter part of that statement that holds true. Anyone who knows Janet can verify that.

So with everything having been said, and with us complying and doing well with our forced compliance issues, everything should work out well and our kids would be returned. Right? Wrong!

—Chapter Twenty–Five—

A "Paranoid" Michigan State

Up until now Robert Coleman was the only *paranoid* according to all the state efforts to make it so. But following the release of the Bell Hospital papers as they related to Janet and myself, the October 14, 2008 hearing by the court resulted in a massive display of paranoia by the state itself. It came as somewhat of a surprise in that the state had always taken the high road so far as their righteousness in this case. Suddenly, though, the result of just a few words on paper, they displayed a totally different look... a *defensive* look if you will that had everyone at the hearing taken aback, I think. And it seemed the effort to keep Robert Coleman's kids away from him now took a fever pitch. It seems the state was *resolute* to show that they had *not* falsely accused us of child abuse, a scenario that could be interpreted if the second set of facts proved to be correct from the statement issued in regards to Janet's assessment. And their effort to *fight* such a possible thought was intense and organized in this October 14th hearing. The resistance occurred from all of the co-conspirators, including Bob Ross, Tracie Wittla, and Rudy Perhalla - all of whom seemed anxious to reestablish their position of dominance in the matter, and even the judge seemed to go out of his way to defend his own position, which came as no great surprise.

The hearing started with the judge announcing they had Mr. John Wade (Caitlyn's biological father) on a speaker phone. Wade could hardly hear, and stated such, at the beginning of the speaker phone conversation. But rather than get to him right away, the court began discussing the other things they were intent on discussing, as a defensive effort was mounted to establish the parts of the assessments they wished to establish. So while poor Mr. Wade waited, the judge and the co-conspirators got down to work.

The judge began on a light note, indicating he had the Bell Behavioral assessments, as well as reports from Lax Vieux Desert Behavioral Health Programs, indicating the anger management counseling had taken place, as well as parenting issues having been addressed. He had received these reports, other than the Bell assessments from our attorney just prior to court. He wasted no time in asking Mr. Ross, first, what the agency's position on the matter was.

After what must have been very humiliating to Ross, admitting that positive things were coming from all of this, particularly Sheri Benson's reports, he slyly began his attack:

Um, the only area that I'm confused about, is the Bell Behavioral Assessments. Where there's a lot of confusion and according to the Bell Assessments, from what I can read and I understand, the Colemans at the assessment are still feeling persecuted. They're still taking no responsibility for their role in the children being placed into foster care. We may never get to that point, and I'm not sure how to address it. They may never take responsibility for what they did, so until we can come to some conclusion how we're going to address that, I'm unclear how we are going to move forward.

So in other words, he would like to keep the kids in captivity forever, unless I were willing to concede I committed an offense I did not commit? Right? Continuing:

The other thing in the Bell assessments, it looks like they recommend psychiatric or psychological assessments for both parents, and if that's something that the Prosecutor and the GAL and the bench would like me to arrange, I will do that.

Here again, the state was trying to put forth a concept not expressed in that manner in the Bell assessments. And that is something the prosecutor and the GAL should have nothing to do with. The bench had custody of our children, not the GAL or the prosecutor. So if the bench felt this might be necessary, they would be the ones to instruct such a thing; but not at the whim of the state, the GAL, or the prosecutor. If, in fact, you read the Bell assessments, it indicates that *further* assessments *might* be done to reach other conclusions. But it was *not* in any way, a *recommendation* as Bob Ross lied about and tried to conclude with the judge. But Ross went on with his attack:

We're still doing the parenting time, one time a week, and I'd like to continue that at least for now in a supervised basis.

Why? His own supervisor from Marinette (Sheri Benson) had already been moving with us towards unsupervised visits. We had plenty of opportunity to do something rash if we were going to do it during our visits she did supervise, but left us alone at times, or in open parks, etc. So why did Ross suddenly view this as a big deal? At this point the judge turned to the GAL, Rudy Perhalla, who intensified the attack:

THE COURT: OK, Mr. Perhalla, what do you recommend?

MR. PERHALLA: Your Honor, I'm recommending that the children stay in the foster care placement and that the parenting time be supervised, and I'm going to ask that it remain strictly, completely supervised. My understanding right now is that the parents do receive somewhat unsupervised parenting time; the parent aide does leave for short periods of time, and comes back. I believe it should be supervised at all times. If we remember early in this case, your Honor, there was statements from the child that she was not to talk to social workers, and this was at a point after the initial investigation and before the child got to the first foster care home. So I do not want there to be any opportunity for these parents to influence the child, especially since the child hasn't even started counseling yet here in Menominee County.

Back it up a minute! No one even ordered such counseling for Caitlyn, this was strictly the idea of the state! So now, because we were making progress, something the state did not want to see, the counseling we undertook was not good enough, and we should remain away from our kids so that the kids could now undergo counseling? And so far as opportunity, we already had that many times, and the state paranoia about *flight,* which was strictly *their* idea, and not ours, created this mess in the first place! We could have flown the coop when we were at the motel, but it was never in our minds! So who is the paranoid here? But more on Perhalla's mad ranting:

MR. PERHALLA: She (Caitlyn) did start it, and this is entirely at the fault of the parents. The child started counseling in Marquette County. We could be long past the rapport building with the counselor up there, had the parents not acted in the way they did in Marquette County and likewise in Dickinson County.

WRONG! Not our fault. Your foster parents were at fault, and the state, for having chosen them. And *Rapport building?* Didn't he *really* mean *brainwashing* and trying to extract a few statements they could use against us in the future, even if they were *not* Caitlyn's original thoughts? That is the way Michigan goes about keeping kids indefinitely, at least until they turn eighteen, at which time they can legally speak for themselves. And if you research it, you will see they have kicked kids out of their programs as soon as they reached that age because the feds no longer fund them under their programs. But we, as parents, are supposed to role over, play dead, and say nothing about it as they first kidnap, then brainwash your kids, and finally put false ideas in their head that they can extract what is, in fact, their own statements, under pressure. This is what you call *rapport building.* In fact, what it amounts to is the attempt to turn the children away from their parents in favor of building a false trust with the social workers. Perhalla's attack continued:

MR. PERHALLA: Until we do get that counseling for Caitlyn going, and now even Ashley at this time, I don't think anybody can feel comfortable allowing these children to have unsupervised visitation.

And now Mr. Perhalla got to *meat* of the state's paranoia, and why they all lined up to attack us at this point of our so-called *re-unification effort:*

MR. PERHALLA: I just want to read the one, one sentence that just jumps out at me. Obviously, they denied everything, and the assessments seem to indicate it cannot be one — it has to be one or the other. Either they are telling the truth, and we, the system, have completely done everything; we're wrong and didn't do our jobs.

DO YOU THINK?

MR. PERHALLA: I don't believe that whatsoever, so the other alternative is that they did abuse their children, and they will not admit it. The statement I have a problem with, your Honor, is the one that I believe is in Janet's statement, close to the end of it where it states: "It is possible that the Colemans are in fact too weak as adults to parent without abusively terrorizing their children. Abusively terrorizing is the language that this assessor put in there, that's some pretty strong words. And I do not want to take one chance, whatsoever, in a case which had abuse to the level that it was set forth before the jury.

Wow! You talk about exaggerating the facts, and in fact, what was said in the Bell assessment! This guy took it *all* out of proportion to try to influence the judge! (Who of course was already in their pockets) But let's look at what Perhalla said. First, "It is *possible.*" The report did not say *probable,* and the word *possible* falls right in line with the real statement, which scared him to death to begin with. And that is that perhaps Janet was telling the truth, and the state *did not* do their job. The Bell assessment did not take a side on this, they only set the stage for debate, and if that scared somebody so much, it is probably because they were aware of their own guilt. We were not fearful of the other scenario, so why were they? Is it because we had the *truth* on our side? And I love how he played on the word *terrorize!* That word never came up during the entire trial, and now the state's supposed charges of spanking with a belt have suddenly elevated to *terrorism?* I have to laugh at that. If my kids were so *terrorized* as Perhalla obviously lied about, why is it that when we made a visitation the kids came running, hugging and saying they miss us so much? And why did they have so much *fun* with us? If I am truly *terrorized* by someone, I don't want to be near them. How about you? It is a joke for this man to even make this evaluation, and it is obvious he was only interested in covering his own mistakes. Let's hear more of what he said:

MR. PERHALLA: Here, six months later, there's no admission by their part. They're not dealing with the problem whatsoever.

Whose fault is that? The kids should never have been taken, and we were not the ones keeping them there six months later — it was the state, because of stupidity like Perhalla's. Continuing:

MR. PERHALLA: In my opinion, your Honor, no progress (has been made) whatsoever. I'm very concerned with us taking a chance of sending children back to parents who have already been written on paper as possibly abusively terrorizing.

Okay, I understand. And I would certainly be very concerned with us taking a chance of keeping our president in office because someone wrote on paper that he is possibly going to turn the country over to the Russians as well. (Of course because somebody wrote that, it does not mean he is going to do it, but if you follow with the thought process of Perhalla, it would result in a paranoia of this kind). So now it was the prosecutor's turn to take aim at us. But she would use the old "shock and awe" approach:

THE COURT: Ms. Wittla?

MS. WITTLA: Your honor, I was shocked to find out that these children were having unsupervised contact of any kind with their parents. And I'm horrified at that prospect because of the fact that we know through the testimony that came out at the jury trial that during that brief period of time between the first interview with Caitlyn and the second interview with Caitlyn for approximately one week in time, that Robert Coleman went to Caitlyn and said don't talk to the social workers. Don't talk to the police, you know, they're going to trick you, they're going to take you away, and it's not speculation that he's going to do this, we already know it happened.

Yeah… I understand her complete horror over this. After all, *her* job is to see that we never have contact with our kids again! And it is pretty shocking to think somebody might interfere with your own scheme to keep kidnapped kids. Let's hear more:

MS. WITTLA: So now we're in a position where this little child does not have a counselor, where she can go and talk and spill her guts and confide in, and yet we're putting her in a position with the same man who tried to brainwash her before. I think it's ridiculous in the extreme that this ever, ever took place.

Hmmmm…. Why? Because she might know the truth about the state of Michigan? It seems that the state's *brainwashing* of the *little child who wants to spill her guts out to some stranger* is okay though. Okay, then why is it she only says she wants to go home on visitations? Please, Ms. Wittla! Get real! Let's see what else she was *horrified* about:

MS. WITTLA: I'm horrified at the sort of standstill that we've come to and all these little comments here and there. Well, they are doing well in counseling here, they're doing well in counseling there. They have been able to present themselves very wonderfully to any number of people in the community, but that's not who they really are, because when you finally send them through an exam, it comes back saying you know what, this doesn't make sense. They're saying no symptomology of anything at all, but they have this huge problem where the system is systematically trying to destroy them emotionally, psychologically, financially. Everything that's ever gone wrong in their lives is being lumped into this case and saying DHS, the system, has ruined us. It's ridiculous, but yet they say they have no symptoms.

Hmmmm…. I guess because we don't curl up in a little ball and require a straight jacket, it really bothers her, huh? Sure, things can be wrong, but it doesn't mean you have to go crazy over it to be normal. But try explaining that to a crazy person. Let's see how she continued to view the Bell reports:

MS. WITTLA: When you go through these Bell reports, what they screen to me is that they're playing the game, they're still trying to present a certain way and try to find the magic answer to give to these assessors. And with a number of people they've been pretty darn successful, all these glowing letters from Watersmeet. Well, Ok, fine, but what about the assessment? What about the fact that these two assessors who assessed them individually said we don't know what's going on with them because they're not giving us the straight story, nothing is matching up, from a clinical point of view.

What about it, she says? Well, try this. First, the report says "from a clinical point of view." And that means, ordinarily, in a case where there are definite problems, a reaction would be expected to be of a certain kind. But in our case, they were not getting that reaction. So what does this mean? Either one of two things. We were damn clever (which we weren't) — or, God forbid — we were telling the truth. But of course, Tracie, whose vindictiveness knows no bounds, had to try to interpret all of this in a villain oriented manner, so that we could be the perpetrators she wanted us to be. It is pretty clear that this woman's outlook on life is that all people who go into a courtroom are guilty until proven innocent. Let's look at more of what her sorted interpretation of the report consisted of:

MS. WITTLA: When you look at Mrs. Coleman's assessment, these pages are not numbered, but it's towards the end, we're still at this particular sentence; this leaves DHS and the Court without a viable avenue of parental family reunification, and problem resolution that would facilitate reunification of Caitlyn and Ashley with their parents, and thus frustrates every involved party ultimately including the Colemans themselves. That's where we are; that's where we still are, after March, after June, after September. We're still there. We haven't gotten anywhere.

Where did you *think* we would be considering your bogus charges in the first place? After all, this is your ticket to keep my kids forever, right? You should be happy! Oh, and now on to her defense of the poor, defenseless children:

MS. WITTLA: It's pathetic that Caitlyn does not have a counselor. I'm not laying it at Mr. Ross's feet. I know there have been problems trying to get that set up. But she needs to have that first, so that she has someone that is there for her before we reintroduce her to unsupervised parenting time with her mother and father.

Oh, so now Ms. Wittla's expertise includes psychology, does it? She is forgetting that Caitlyn already *had* two *some ones* to be there for her.... her father and mother; and her pleading throughout this ordeal was to go *home*... not to have someone to talk to. That was strictly a state idea. From there on, it was Ms. Wittla's idea to have a home study done on the biological father, and she asked the court for that at this juncture. Why? He had expressed no interest in Caitlyn up until now, and did not reply when people tried to contact him. Why now? Tracie seemed to go to extraordinary efforts to bring him into this case, when he had *never* expressed any interest in Caitlyn during her entire 6-year life! It was clear that her intent in doing this was to get Caitlyn permanently removed from us, no matter who she went to! There could be other purpose for doing this, except perhaps, pure spite. In any case, that concluded her part of the attack, except for answering a couple of questions from the judge, questions which asked who would do further evaluations, and of course, she could not answer that, but still expressed her desire to see it happen. From there, the court turned to our lawyer for his input:

THE COURT: All right, Mr. Findlay?

MR. FINDLAY: Thank you your Honor. If everybody knew how much I've been trying to convince these parents that the purpose was not to terminate their children and take their children away, I wish I really knew how hard that was. And how the comments I'm hearing from the Prosecutor and the GAL here basically makes every fear and suspicion — I know everybody else thinks its paranoia - but you know the concern of the parents certainly legitimates it. Me, listening to the stuff that's been spewed here in court today. You have something as simple as the Guadian Ad Litem not even to be able to read correctly the report. It didn't say it... ...

MR. PERHALLA (interrupting the defense).... I object to that characterization your Honor, if somebody is going to get personal....

Yes, I imagine you do object! I objected to your personal attacks too, Mr. Perhalla! But the truth, once expressed about you in court hurts, doesn't it?

THE COURT: Let's get to the bottom of it now, okay?

MR. FINDLAY: I will get to the bottom of it, but it says is it possible he has two — whoever asks two separate questions. He doesn't suggest that it is a possibility, he's pointing it out that there are two opposed questions, and so to read it that way is such a bias against these parents that I'd just ask that we get another GAL.

THE COURT: Wait… wait now. You're not speaking English. I don't understand what you're saying.

MR. FINDLAY: It's right here in the thing, it says, " is it possible that the Colemans are in fact, too weak; is it possible the system…."

THE COURT: Okay, okay.

MR. FINDLAY: It asks two questions that it doesn't say it is possible they are; there's a huge difference in terms of semantics and what those questions mean.

THE COURT: You would say in the legal parlance query?

MR. FINDLAY: Yes, I mean it's just it is throwing it out there, if not raising spectra, at a huge difference for the GAL to propose that as a specter, just shows bias. I make a motion here that you remove this GAL and have a different one who has a perspective and isn't so biased against these parents. I….

THE COURT: … okay, denied. Get to the point.

You see? I think he *made* the point. This GAL was biased and was never going to let us have our kids back if he had his way, despite the fact he was inventing facts to insert into the situation. My lawyer continued, despite the bias of the judge as well:

MR. FINDLAY: OK, on every level these parents have done what the Court has asked them to do. They've completed parenting classes; they've completed anger management; they've gone to counseling sessions; they've done everything they're supposed to. Visits have gone — I have the copies of this — the summaries of the visits from the caseworker Sheri Benson — glowing, for the most part. Glowing reports other than the initial thing that Robert Coleman wasn't just putting enough in at that point. I would submit, understandably so, even accused of abusing, so he doesn't want to do anything that makes it appear that way. This is about the children. I mean these kids have gone seven months now. Caitlyn is having a hard time in school, which we heard. You know if you want to bring up the trial and keep looking back at the past, we also heard testimony from Ms. Semo in court that she was a very good student. A pleasant child, a happy, joyful child. It certainly isn't that now, I submit, that the separation for seven months from their parents has a lot to do with that. They don't, we don't see no counseling for Caitlyn, that they're asking for that still again. The Bell assessments were supposed to be psychological assessments in the first place, and now to delay this again because they want to have another assessment is just such an unfair burden to place on the parents — and to keep these children separated. The home studies that have been done of their home by the other worker up in the Copper country are good; everything is appropriate. They're doing on an objective level, everything they're supposed to. The only thing they won't do that won't make Ms. Wittla and the GAL happy is come and say, "Oh, we did this all wrong, please forgive us." You know, that probably isn't going to happen in this case, I'll be straight with everybody here. I think everybody knows that's probably not going to happen. Does that mean they never get their kids back, because of that? I certainly hope that's not the injustice that's going to be done here, simply because they won't cow tow and admit. They maintain that they didn't do it, there's people that maintain that they didn't do things all the time. They do concede that the jury found what it did, and that's where we're at, so they're living with that situation now. I would ask that the children be returned home. I realize that's going nowhere, I'm still asking for the record, but in alternative, at least we have some unsupervised visits. The reports from the visits are good, very good, not just so-so, but excellent. These children deserve to have some time, you know, either a weekend and extended times when they can go to a hotel and spend the day at a pool and that type of thing. And the parents desire to have some kind of unsupervised time with their children. I'd ask for that, and then thirdly, as an alternative, Mrs. Coleman's parents are here today, and we would also request that a home study be done on them, in terms of placement with the girls there, if this is going to keep going this way. I mean, they are family members. True, they are far away, but they traveled here to Court to show they're willing to do it. I ask that as soon as possible, a home study be done on them, so these children can be at least placed with family, as opposed to strangers. In terms of either report, there are reports that they're talking to the children and telling them to say certain things or coaching them. There's no reports that they're doing any surveillance. Are they checking out on the foster parents? None of this. They have been doing everything the court has asked them to do since disposition. And it just seems extremely unfair to not acknowledge that and to still try and characterize this as that these people are horrible people and should never have their children back. And that's, frankly, what both the GAL and the prosecutor are characterizing. You know, if the Court has to do psychological assessments, I object to doing it now. Because they were already supposed to have been done. But that shouldn't be a delay in terms of moving this case forward. At least, going to unsupervised visits or extended visits over weekends and times like that. I'd just ask the Court to at least grant, acknowledge what's been happening and what the Colemans have done... and reward the children, at least, for that. Mrs. Coleman has gone and done further things, gone to further counseling and even gotten advanced stuff with Watersmeet. That's all I have your Honor, I'd like the Court to at least make unsupervised visits or extended visits over weekends and also order a home study of Janet Coleman's parents.

THE COURT: And you folks are from the Dakotas or from where?

MR. BRAG (Janet's father): Finley, North Dakota.

THE COURT: Finley, North Dakota, ok.

The court then turned to Mr. Wade, the biological father of Caitlyn:

THE COURT: I guess I'm asking you where you stand on it and what you got to say?

MR. WADE: I have had very little contact with Mrs. Coleman, I've had no contact with Mr. Coleman and (with) regards to my daughter (or)otherwise. My attempts have been futile with the state of Wisconsin in trying to obtain pictures, updates of my daughter so on and so forth. But I have already requested and received a copy of the case file in regards to Caitlyn and her separation from her parents, and I am patiently awaiting an interview from Child Protective Services. I am petitioning the state of Wisconsin, who I have been paying my child support through, with the intention of acquiring full physical and legal custody of Caitlyn Brag.

THE COURT: Ok, thank you. Just to fill you in, and I can't give you legal advice, but, as long as this case exists, this case is the one that controls where the kids are and that sort of thing. Now if this case ends, which is always the goal, then it goes back to whatever prior jurisdiction there was and if that is in Wisconsin, then that is the court that will take it up, so I only encourage you to keep in touch with Mr. Ross, because I encourage all parents to do that, especially if they reflect and interest in their child,

because all children need all their parents. And that's all I'll say, that's on a blank slate of not knowing any of the facts of the relationship, the history, or anything else.

MR. WADE: I'm just going through the paperwork circus right now. I'm just starting it and I've had contact with Mr. Ross, and I've requested pictures of my daughter and an update on how she's doing, and he's emailed me once in reply. I haven't gotten any pictures yet, and I've sent her some toys. I'm just patiently waiting to have the ball rolling.

It would be interesting to see that email, and to know what type of *encouragement* to try to get custody of Caitlyn might have been *planted* by Mr. Ross. We were, of course, not aware of his contact with Caitlyn's father. But now the judge had to answer my lawyer, and his answer, of course, was to scold him for defending us as clients:

THE COURT: Ok, just let me say this. Obviously, this case remains hotly contested, and frankly, Mr. Findlay, your raging against the machine is no more helpful than the other side of the table's. As you pretty accurately state, pointing to them as horrible people. So what's interesting is Mr. Ross very carefully taking a somewhat of a middle line on the thing, after he's been subjected to personal attacks as part of the whole thing. Make no mistake here, whatever happened with the spanking incident, which I believe and the jury believed occurred, there was a description of a very sorted household there. It was not good; it was an unfit place for these children to live. There's not even a 50% plus 1, talking about the jury, it is an 80/20 or 90/10 overwhelming situation that did not take a jury very long to sort out. It would not have taken me very long either.

For sure. Especially since the jury was *stacked* and the judge very biased. Continuing:

THE COURT: Ok, that being said, we got jurisdiction; that was the point of that step. Now the point becomes not necessarily condemnation as to how to help the family and have these children a permanent home. And to some degree we have to put away our swords and our armor and work towards that. Now, I do acknowledge and have to acknowledge the indications that the Colemans have taken necessary steps; they have gone through counseling sessions; they have gone through anger management issues; there are good reports on those. The Bell Memorial report points out some concerns and I agree that the gentlemen, Mr. Maas put in a sense as I would like a legal opinion, query, you know.... are we at one end of the spectrum or the other? As I said, he didn't help me by telling me what he suspects. To some degree the other lady did by at least reaching a diagnosis before her final thing. So I am concerned because of the history here that the Colemans would manipulate the system beyond their surface, but, you know, as I've said all along on this case, while serious and while I've called the situation as extreme as sorted, it is not the most incurable, worse situation that we have ever encountered in this court. And if the parties can try to work together, I think the reunification is and has to be the goal. I'm going to order counseling for Caitlyn forthwith and indicate that I want the agency to go with that immediately, like this week or next week. Get counseling set up. After Caitlyn has had a session, I am going to have it supervised until that point, until a counselor is contacted. While I know it takes time to build rapport with a counselor, if something has been working, if the Colemans have been doing enough to not clearly manipulate the system, which was pretty clearly being done in every single foster home before; if it's working to some degree, I don't want to upset that apple cart either if we are making progress. So if the agency decides that they're going to proceed with these and if the supervisor and everybody else are comfortable with the sessions expanding to unsupervised, then that will be up to the agency. As I always do by default, I'll leave it in their hands, but first I at least want that counseling contact made, because I do agree that Caitlyn needs to get in that place. I'll order the follow up psychologicals, because they're recommended, but as I said, based on the first assessment here, which in a lot of cases gets us everything we need, I don't know that any other steps are going to give us a whole lot more, but I guess we'll see. I'm also going to ask Mr. Ross, we've got the whole world asking for home studies here, so what is the agency's intentions on Mr. Wade, the grandparents.... I mean....

MR. ROSS: We'll get them done. We'll put them out there.

THE COURT: I mean in the initial plan it is to go back to the parents, you know, so I mean, why are we going from North Dakota, Wisconsin, etc.? Mr. Wade does have the right, you know, to fight for his child at that level, but why are we looking to bounce these kids around if.....

MR. ROSS: ... I'm not looking to bounce anybody around. I'm, if people are asking for home studies, we'll put the home study requests out, but....

MR. FINDLAY: ... and your Honor, we're not asking that the children be bounced around either. It's just that if there's no light at the end of the tunnel, I guess our position is that we would like that the children be with family. I will try to ratchet it down, but from listening to the Prosecutor and the GAL, it gives me the perspective that from their perspective there's no light at the end of the tunnel. And if so, then at least have to go down the road of getting a home study, so at least the home study is done.

THE COURT: Yeah, they certainly appear slanted that way, and to some degree, as I said, it's because of the drawn battle lines. But don't forget the DHS, a lot of times, when those cases are going that way.

MR. FINDLAY: Yeah, and I acknowledge that 100%, I mean, that's why I'm specifying who I'm talking about, I didn't include the DHS in that.

THE COURT: All right. In any event, implement the current service plan, keep the current placement in place, recommended. We would indicate ordering counseling for Caitlyn. Follow up psychologicals and supervised until a counseling session is completed for Caitlyn. And then, up to the DHS in terms of how they work this step by step because, like it or not, I'm not saying the strong position of the Prosecutor and the GAL aren't justified. But I have to base it on evidence, and some of the evidence I'm getting is that they're doing the do. There are nothing but glowing reports from the LVD people anyway. You look like you are going to say something.

MS. WITTLA: I don't have the glowing reports from the LVD people, so I just....

THE COURT: .... Just handed them in today.

MS. WITTLA: I guess I'd ask for copies of those at some point.

MR. FINDLAY: I'm happy to make a copy, I didn't make enough copies.

THE COURT: Or we can do it too.

MR. FINDLAY: Makes no difference.

MR. ROSS: I've got one more thing and it's more of a legal problem or a situation that we need to resolve because it's going to have to deal with the way we legally handle the case. In Mr. Coleman's mental health and anger assessment, he identifies himself as a Native American. There's never been anything in anything that we've ever found that he's a member of a Native American tribe or eligible for enrollment in any Native American tribe. But this could be problematic if we're dealing with a Native American child in Ashley and we don't have it documented the right way, so I need to know.

THE COURT: Mr. Coleman, are you a member of a tribe or eligible?

MR. COLEMAN: What I told her your Honor, is that we are researching it right now.

THE COURT: Oh, all right. Well, you should consult with your lawyer, it is an issue. It's more of an issue if termination happened; that's not happening right here, but it's clearly a legal issue that the tribe is entitled to notice.

MR. FINDLAY: I understand that and it is my understanding there was question mark on some of the genealogy. If that became a real issue, I would certainly bring it to the Court's attention.

THE COURT: Can you tell me what tribe, do we know?

MR. FINDLAY: No.

THE COURT: We've had some experience from transfer out to Midwest, but the bottom line on it is the tribe makes the call, if there's a question.

MR. FINDLAY: Right.

With that, the court set the next hearing for January 7th, and then recessed the hearing.

—Chapter Twenty–Six—

Renewal Of The "War"

Even had the October 14th hearing not been marred by the vicious personal attacks of the GAL and the Prosecutor, we would have still viewed the process as somewhat of an uphill battle, since our children were not yet returned to us. But now, the war was rekindled, and our lawyer was as disgusted with the whole conspiracy team as we were. Apparently, the DHS was also becoming disenchanted with the prosecutor and the GAL, as was made clear in the motion filed by the pair on November 18, 2008. The NOTICE OF HEARING stated the following:

PLEASE TAKE NOTICE that the above referenced case is set for a Family Court hearing on a MOTION TO ORDER HOME STUDY ON CAITLYN'S FATHER AND PREVENT UNSUPERVISED VISITS in the Family Courtroom in the Gogebic County Courthouse, Bessemer, Michigan, on TUESDAY, NOVEMBER 25, 2008 at 9:30 AM or as soon thereafter as counsel may be heard.

Inside, the revealing *reasons* for the requested hearing were given. We draw your attention particularly to items 7 thru 14, which outlined the apparent falling out of the GAL and the Prosecutor with the DHS. (Also #16 and #21) But here were all 28 of the points this vindictive pair conjured up:

1) That Ashley Coleman, age two, and Caitlyn Brag, age six, have been placed with the Department of Human Services since March 15, 2008.

2) That after these children were placed with the DHS there was a trial during the last week of June, 2008 to establish jurisdiction over Ashley & Caitlyn.

3) That after the jury awarded this Court jurisdiction, Robert Ross became the caseworker for these children.

4) That approximately three weeks later a dispositional hearing was held in July, 2008.

5) That just after the dispositional hearing, the Prosecutor's Office located Caitlyn Brag's father, John Wade.

6) That Mr. Wade was completely in the dark regarding the abuse perpetrated upon his daughter Caitlyn by Janet and Robert Coleman.

7) That Mr. Wade spoke with Robert Ross in July, 2008 and told him of his interest in being part of Caitlyn's life and expressed an interest in seeing her and Mr. Ross informed him of the possibility of having a home study done on his residence. Mr. Wade requested a home study be done.

8) That Mr. Wade subsequently contacted the DHS and requested a copy of his daughter's entire CPS file.

9) That Robert Ross indicated in his parent agency treatment plan fourteen times that he would fill in information for John Wade WHEN INTERSTATE HOME STUDY HAS BEEN COM-

PLETED.

10) That Ms. Wittla emailed Robert Ross in September asking about the progress on getting the home study done on Mr. Wade.

11) That Mr. Ross stated during several conversations he had with Ms. Wittla between August and October 2008 that he would get the home study done on John Wade as soon as he found time to do so.

12) That at the review hearing on October 14, 2008, Ms. Wittla again asked about the home study regarding John Wade and requested it be done as soon as possible.

13) That John Wade also appeared at the October 14th hearing by telephone and stated he had been "waiting patiently" to hear from the DHS to get the home study done and further stated his interest in petitioning Wisconsin for full custody of Caitlyn.

14) That Mr. Perhalla spoke with Mr. Ross the week of November 10th and found out that Mr. Ross does not intend to ever do a home study for Caitlyn's father despite the request made by John Wade.

15) That there is a lengthy history of both Robert and Janet Coleman essentially creating an alternate reality where they are the true victims in this case being persecuted by a system run amok.

16) That Ms. Wittla had spoken with Mr. Ross several times between June and October, 2008 about not moving too fast on this case and making sure he communicated changes in the case to her before they occurred.

17) That Robert Coleman's Mental Health/Anger Management Assessment came back stating, "It is recommended that Robert complete a psychological evaluation based on the lack of clear findings and numerous inconsistencies in his assessment."

18) That Janet Coleman's Mental Health/Anger Management Assessment came back stating, "Instead, it is suggested that further assessment via psychological evaluations including testing, interviews, and inclusion of as much collateral information as possible (Ms. Eltmann, Dr. Puseteri, Mr. Ross, etc.) would be desirable as a clarifying next step."

19) That the assessor's obvious intent in making these statements is to try to get to the truth of what is going on with Robert and Janet Coleman since they could NOT get it from the clients themselves.

20) That the Colemans presented through their assessments as victims of the system and took zero responsibility for the removal of their children, nor did they acknowledge that any abuse ever occurred.

21) That despite the results of these mental health assessments and despite no therapy being provided to Ashley and Caitlyn, unsupervised contact was authorized by Robert Ross between the Colemans and the children.

22) That at the October 14th review hearing, Ms. Wittla was surprised with the news that Robert and Janet Coleman have been having unsupervised contact with Caitlyn and Ashley.

23) That the Court ordered that no further unsupervised contact occur until a counselor was obtained for the children.

24) That the Court order reads that the visitation between the Colemans and the children is supervised by the Department of Human Services.

25) That the parent agency treatment plan for Ashley and Caitlyn's case shows several needs for Robert and Janet.

26) That as of today neither Robert nor Janet have completed parenting classes nor have they completed a psychological evaluation the depth of their mental health issues.

27) That the most recent progress evaluation shows the Colemans as having a range of refused services to partial progress.

28) That the unsupervised visits would be premature at this time since there are several outstanding unresolved issues that directly affect the safety of these two young children.

So there you have it. That was their motion. Needless to say, it had a lot of holes in it, which I shall point out of few of now. First, on point number 16, Tracie Wittla makes our case. It clearly demonstrates her intent to keep our children as long as she could, even to the point of asking openly for a "slowdown" on DHS activity to allow for such. On point number 19, once again Tracie forgot she is a prosecutor, not a mind reader. How does she know what the assessor's *intent* was? It may have been obvious to her, but not to anyone else. On point number 21, she got her facts wrong, as was pointed out by my lawyer in his response letter (see the next paragraph). It was clear that what she *thought* was a Ross decision to allow unsupervised contact really ticked her off. But of course she was wrong about everything in this case, her first mistake listening to a mental case issuing bogus charges. And finally, on point number 26, she is again, forgetting she is a prosecutor and not a psychologist. Who gave *her* the power to determine what the *depth* of what our mental health issues were? And secondly, she was dead wrong again about our completion issues, as my lawyer adequately pointed out in his response to this crock of a motion in his letter that followed the notification of the motion. Here now is my lawyer's letter to the court:

RESPONSE TO GAL'S and PROSECUTOR'S PLEADING

Up to this point in time John Wade has expressed no interest in his daughter Caitlyn Brag. Pushing to have him involved in this case creates the appearance that the Assistant Prosecutor and GAL, (the "Prosecution"), are willing to seek any option that doesn't involve the return of these children to the Colemans.

The parents have completed parenting classes and proof of that was provided on October 14, 2008 and acknowledged by the court in open court, on the record, with both members of the Prosecution being present. Also acknowledged by the Court was the fact that the parents in this case have done everything that has been asked of them by the court and/or DHS. Ignoring these facts reveals a disturbing bias and personal animus that the Prosecution has against the parents in this case.

The Prosecution's pleading also reveals their ignorance of the status of the case and the fact that both girls were assessed on November 12, 2008 and that an Initial Plan of Service Meeting (IPOS) occurred on November 18, 2008. Upon information and belief individual counseling for Caitlyn has not been deemed necessary and the reommendation is that both girls receive community support services.

Further, DHS has arranged and allowed telephone contact between the parents and the girls at the foster care home on a twice a weekly basis and that such contact has gone well with no complaints from anybody. The par-

ents have also been involved in the girls' schooling and communicating with Caitlyn's teachers, which communications has resulted in the improvement of Caitlyn's academic and social behavior in school. By all accounts Caitlyn and Ashley miss their parents terribly and want to return home. While a child's wishes are not, and should not, always be determinative the question is raised as the whether the GAL even talked to the children before filing this pleading.

Unfortunately, the Prosecution's pleading only serves to further fuel the suspicion that from day one the Prosecution's intent in this case has been the termination of the parents' parental rights. One would hope that all involved in this case understand, even if they don't like it, that the cooperation and participation of the parents is necessary for the successful reunification of this family, and that unnecessarily fueling these parents' suspicions is counter productive.

The timing of this motion is also suspect, coming right before Thanksgiving, a traditional family holiday. Arrangements were being made for the parents to spend time and have Thanksgiving dinner with Caitlyn and Ashley.

Ironically, one thing that the Prosecution did get right in their pleading was that the Court did order that DHS supervise visitation. That is what the DHS worker has been doing in this case. Thankfully, he doesn't share the Prosecution's animus towards these parents and is doing what he, as the case worker actually involved with the parents, children, services, etc., believes to be appropriate to reach the law's stated goal of family reunification.

WHEREFORE, the parents, through counsel, request this court to deny the Prosecution's motion and allow this case to continue progressing towards the reunification of Caitlyn Brag and Ashley Coleman with the only individuals that these girls have known as their parents.

So now the fight was on again. And it would next pick up at the scheduled hearing on November 25, 2008.

—Chapter Twenty–Seven—

The Repetition Fight For Rights

So here we were again, back in court because a belligerent prosecutor wanted to put a stop to the progress we were making with the DHS. It seemed it had become a personal vendetta on her part, as it had for the GAL, both of whom simply wanted to see anybody but the Colemans have custody of what is rightfully ours - our kids!

It started, as it always did, with the lies and deceit of the prosecutor:

MS. WITTLA: Your honor, I spoke to John Wade this morning, and he confirmed that he is still very interested in being a part of Caitlyn's life. Before that, obviously last week when I filed this motion, I was still under that impression. Today's conversation just really confirms what I already knew. The other thing that I already know is that the DHS, for whatever reason, has not taken an interest in pursuing any kind of contact with Mr. Wade. This is unusual to say the least because the DHS is usually looking for families, parents specifically, to be actively involved in their childrens' lives.

"Their children?" Ms. Wittla, please, the children still belong to the parents! The acting parents! Mr. Wade disappeared 6 years ago, and had no interest in Caitlyn, and Janet is still her biological mother. Is Ms. Wittla's interpretation that Janet is not a parent? And Ashley is biologically Janet's and mine! Not Wade's! So if this prosecutor really cared about this, she would desire to see the kids go to the home where she is truly wanted, and truly has blood lines— with us!

MS. WITTLA: I may never request that Caitlyn be relocated to Durango, Colorado (where Wade was living), but I've certainly always been under the expectation that a home study would be done for this man, who requestedit back in July. For that reason, I'm requesting that this Court order it to be done. That may be somewhat of an unusual move on my part, but I have made the request several times for the agency to get this done. I was told repeatedly that it would be done, and it isn't done. So I'm afraid that unless the Court actually orders this step to be taken that we will never get past. We know what John Wade's name, address, and phone number are; and we need to know that because he has a right to have access to Caitlyn during the pendency of this case, if at no other time. We know that Robert Coleman has been abusive to Caitlyn;

Let's clarify something right here! Elizabeth Fyle admitted earlier, if you recall, that they went after us for what they interpreted as our attempt at flight. A jury found us guilty of child abuse, based on lies. But to say you know I was abusive is only her opinion, based on the conviction she got. She didn't know anything! She said she knew John Wade's status earlier too, but could only confirm it with the later phone call? Why do you have to confirm what you knew already? What she meant to say is she suspected. But suspecting something is true, or even using a later phone call to verify it is not proof! Continuing her lies:

We know that Caitlyn has a biological and legal father out there—and I don't understand why we're not trying to perceive some kind of a relationship, so that Caitlyn's not left with the only male figure in her life, being the abusive Robert Coleman.

So I guess that's why Caitlyn always ran up and hugged me, said "I love you", and asked when she could come home when we saw her at visitations— right? But there is a bigger reason: she has a mother, Janet! What about the female figure? Janet is her biological mother. Would this prosecutor have her removed from her daughter's life? Would that be a solution for this prosecutor? Or would Ms. Wittla like to set up a divorce procedure for Janet at the same time they turn custody over to Mr. Wade? Do you think Janet and Wade want to get together to solve this problem? Not likely! This nonsense could only be conjured up in the mind of an uncaring, unthinking prosecutor! Continuing:

It has been suggested to this Court through the glowing letters from LVD (Tracie must have HATED THOSE) that Robert Coleman is perfectly fine, a wonderful upstanding citizen, at this point in time; and that I am the one who is in the dark, in a defensive position, still fighting the battle lines that have been drawn back in June of 2008. But nothing can be further from the truth, because, from my perspective, I am the one who is saying that all this stuff still matters because it hasn't been resolved. All that stuff came out at trial and through the Bell assessments and still matter. These things have not been resolved, and we're still stuck with parents, Robert and Janet Coleman, that refuse to take any kind of responsibility for what happened.

What you mean is we would not get on our hands and knees and apologize to the state for fighting their kidnapping of our kids. And why would we take any kind of responsibility for something that never happened?

Do I expect them to come into this Court and genuflect and say we are terrible people, we completely screwed up, and it's never going to happen again? (Yes) No, I think Mr. Findlay made it clear at the review that that's never going to happen. But for them to tell everyone who is willing to listen that the system wronged them, that they've been railroaded, or the system's run amuck, or whatever terminology you want to use is not helpful either.

Not helpful to you, you mean. It is helpful to the case, because it was the truth.

When I read the Bell assessments, they talk about the fact we don't have any place to start from, and because of that, I don't understand what the big rush to unsupervised visitation is either.

There is a lot you don't understand Tracie, which is why I don't feel you are fit to practice law, much less prosecute anybody. The rush, my dear, is because parents are not accustomed to living without their children, and as it had already been seven months since we could live with them, it was our desire to reunite with them before they reach full growth. Only a dimwit would not understand that. Any parent does understand it.

Number one, we have parents who have not gone through all the psychological testing that I believe is needed, and that Mr. Ross has currently set up.

That you believe? Who the hell are you to evaluate what is needed?

Psychological testing (you mean more of it) is set up for Robert and Janet Coleman the first week of December, which is next week. We don't have counseling set up for Caitlyn, for any number of reasons, it just didn't get done. Most glaringly, it would appear that Caitlyn is being serviced through Medicaid dollars right now. (Maybe because Daddy lost his business over this?) Typically, when we have children who are in placement here, they have access to counseling that is paid for by DHS, and there's no waiting. They just get sent over to, it used to be Wendy Young, now it's Tara Miller, Doctor Brady, whoever because they're on contract with DHS. That's not the route that was taken with Caitlyn, she was sent through screening at North Care, and that's part of the reason this is taking so long. Because, as this Court is well aware, the State of Michigan as a unit, does not provide much in the way of counseling or mental health services for children. And that's the only service that Caitlyn is currently qualifying for. Yesterday Mr. Borth indicated that he was going to look for another funding source to try and get Caitlyn additional counseling, but right now, she hasn't even had one therapeutic session. And right now she's scheduled to a play date kind of therapy, so she doesn't even have the kind of counseling that she did have back when she was in Marquette. And part of the reason for that is because the CMH'S of this state don't recognize the glaring needs that children have sometimes.

Am I to gather from that, that you should be doing their CMH jobs? You seem to know so much about everything, other than prosecuting. Gives me the feeling you are in the wrong occupation.

The other reason is because they just haven't had enough contact with Caitlyn to figure out what she needs.

But you have, right? By the way, did you ever even meet Caitlyn or shake her hand?

What we do know is that she's doing abysmally in school ... she's got 25 time-ins this year. Apparently if you get one more, you get detention at the ripe old age of six; that's not normal six year old behavior.

You really should be a therapist instead of a prosecutor! And check your facts next time. My lawyer will address that in the forthcoming response he makes.....

Certainly, it's been pointed out by the parents' counsel that the whole reason Caitlyn is, you know, having all these problems, is because she was taken away from her wonderful, loving, perfect family, the Colemans.

Thank you. Those are the first nice words I've ever heard you say!

And that doesn't ring true.

Damn! And I thought you meant it!

Everyone in this room sat through the trial, and we knew all the other things that were happening in that household. So I think it's really too early to send Caitlyn into any kind of unsupervised contact with Robert Coleman. I'm less concerned about her having unsupervised contact with Janet, but because they seem to function as one, perhaps I'm just misguided and not perceiving her to be as much of a potential threat in brainwashing her child as her husband clearly is.

To teach is to brainwash. Remember that, all you parents, and never teach your kids. Remember also to go along with the state when they invade your home and take your kids by force. Oh, and isn't it interesting how she tries to pass along the subtle "suggestion" that maybe Janet should split from me. Well, maybe. But to do what? Go back to Wade? Isn't he married now? Or has anybody checked that out? In their zest to nail Robert, how many families is this prosecutor willing to disrupt? I used to think she did not like me and Janet. Now I realize it is just me she doesn't like. Good, the feeling is mutual!

I know the agency wants to move this case, move it forward, have this momentum, remove barriers. I'm not against that, but it hasn't happened yet. We can't fake progress just to make progress.

No, but we can sure fake everything else, like the true details of what happened, can't we Ms. Wittla? And now you are the expert at how much progress is being made? You really should have another job that fits your expertise, Ms. Wittla, because prosecuting is not it.

We don't have a counseling relationship for Caitlyn that has to happen first.

Who said so? You?

We don't have the psychological sessions back from Robert and Janet that needs to happen first.

You mean second report results that would perhaps reflect what you want to see, correct Ms. Wittla? Because for now, all you have is positive things pertaining to the Colemans, and that is not acceptable to you. And this case is about you—isn't it Ms. Wittla?

So although there has been unsupervised contact for short periods of time for Ashley, while the supervisor goes off to get Caitlyn, I'm not in favor of it expanding beyond that.

I completely understand, because it might get in the way of your own state brainwashing effort.

Yesterday Mr. Borth was trying to find middle ground amongst us, he suggested that perhaps there could be a 5 or 6 hour visit, which would be mostly unsupervised, and have the supervisor pop in a few times during that period of time. I can't say that I'm in favor of that, but I can see that would be the next logical step. I would be more in favor of that for Ashley than I would for Caitlyn, because Caitlyn has clearly been the target of most of the abuse as the step-child in this case.

Yeah, I really hate that. Which is probably why I try to do bad things, like teach her, and why I hug her, love her, all that rot. Step child or natural child, I love her as my own, and always have.

I know that the court is used to just checking one of the boxes on the form for either supervised or unsupervised visitation.

Yeah, unlike you, Ms. Wittla, the court is pretty stupid too. Help them out here, will you?

This is a case where I would request the Court to go far beyond that and spell out what is meant by visitation. Because Mr. Borth also made it very clear yesterday that semi-supervised visitation could mean half an hour without supervision, or out of a 6 hour block of time, only one half hour with supervision. That's just not acceptable to me at this point in time because of all the variables we just don't know, the risk factors that have not been identified, and the lack of any meaningful counseling.

And stop me if I'm wrong, Ms. Wittla, but because this is not acceptable to you, it should be recognized that you are the one making decisions here— right?

Connie Eltman has all these glowing reports. I don't have her records, I don't know what she based that on.

But it must be wrong because it is not your assessment—right, Ms. Wittla? So tell us clinically, what Connie Eltman's approach should be:

Typically, in these cases, we get the entire file, the Court's aware of that. We get all the case notes, we get all the progress notes, we get all the intake forms, and that's what we would need in order to see what's going on with these cases.

Uh.... So doctor-patient confidentiality should be thrown out in favor of you—right, Ms. Wittla? If that was typical, maybe you had some doctors in your hip pocket as you tried to assert your kidnapping ring efforts too! Is Connie to be assassinated because she would not play ball?

Until we get all that information, I don't know what Connie Eltman's letter really means. I do know that Connie Eltman told me that she thought that Robert and Janet were being, um, I can't remember the phrase she used exactly, but the gist of it was—that they were being taken advantage of by a system that was run amuck. Knowing that she had that predisposition to believe that gives me great pause in accepting her glowing recommendations of the Colemans; so I would be very interested in having her records.

I'll bet you would! But stop for a moment here. You don't have her records, and it is because people like you do their own interpretations of these things, that they keep these records on a confidential basis. I should add, you don't know that she had any predisposition about what she believed. You have no idea, she did not tell you. So to say that is a lie, just like so much else you have submitted to the court, in which you said, "we know."

I think this is moving just way too soon, way too quickly, and I'm very concerned that Mr. Wade has not been given much information or any kind of chance to be involved in Caitlyn's life.

He had six years and showed no interest.

Certainly this is not the place where he would fight out a custody battle, if it was to come to that with Janet Coleman.

No, but you are sure doing your best to see that it happens, aren't you?

But knowing he is out there, and ignoring that fact, I don't think is a precedent that the Agency has ever set in the past. So, at this time, I'm requesting, again, that the Court order a home study on John Wade's residence, and order a very strict parenting time schedule that does not leave these children in an unsupervised capacity with Robert Coleman for more than perhaps a couple of hours at a time.

THE COURT: All right, I'm going to completely side track before I move on. The reason the counseling is not available like it is locally, I mean, for instance Strong Family dollars couldn't be used is because that's only on contracts with the Dr. Brady's of the world. So that doesn't apply where they're sitting in foster care, right? I mean, that's why that's not an alternative source?

MS. WITTLA: Well, I would think that Menominee County would have a similar thing, but… .well, we would, I would think that Mr. Borth would pay for that from our county's dollars because they're our kids. (OUR KIDS—THE COUNTY OWNS THEM?)

THE COURT: But he couldn't pay out of the Strong Families because it has to be under a contact with a specific person, which is like Dr. Brady.

MS. WITTLA: Doctor Brady contracts… .

MR. ROSS: … Your honor… .

MS. WITTLA: … contracts with them as well.

THE COURT: Ok, wait, wait! All right, I'm just trying to feel out the… .

MS. WITTLA: … He was looking into the… you know there's the unlimited line item when kids are in care. The unlimited pot of money, so to speak?

THE COURT: Yeah.

MS. WITTLA: That's something he said he was going to look into yesterday.

THE COURT: All right, what I'm trying to ask is—and I'm going to get Mr. Ross and get to the agency's position in a minute—but I'm asking you, because you are making the argument.

MS. WITTLA: Yes.

THE COURT: The kind of counseling that she is getting or not getting is based on what they offer in Menominee, the country she's residing in.

MS. WITTLA: Based on Medicaid funding.

THE COURT: Okay.

MS. WITTLA: Not based on DHS funding—which you know is far expanded.

THE COURT: But we use it here with our Strong Families counseling dollars and we use it here in other things. Is there a reason they're not using it in Menominee County? Let me try to get my question more specific.

MS. WITTLA: I don't think they figured out they could.

THE COURT: Is that just the way they do things in Menominee, which is why she's like… .. It's happening there, as opposed to the way we do it in Gogebic?

MS. WITTLA: They said that they send all of their clients to North Pointe to get counseling, but my belief is that everything is, as you know, driven by money. Medicaid might only be able to pay for one session every two weeks because she doesn't need the priority population for anything more. But that doesn't mean that there isn't counselors' time available to be purchased through another funding source. That's exactly what Mr. Borth was looking into yesterday.

THE COURT: Ok, because like I....

MS. WITTLA: ... Can we buy more time with another funding?

THE COURT: He's going to Marquette, Craig Kitchen gets involved, I mean different—as we have kids in different positions around the state. Different places offer different services, and it's not all tied to CMH, which we all know, frankly, is not real good in terms of children services anywhere in this state. You know, we're darn lucky that we have the couple of... Doctor, Mrs. Doctor Cool. We're lucky we have a couple of specialized people here through CMH, some places they basically don't have anybody. So what I'm saying is CMH is not the good alternative, then why is it that Menominee County is only using CMH which I guess is going to jump us to Mr. Ross. Can you answer that question specifically?

MR. ROSS: The assessment, your Honor, is a starting point. We have to determine what type of diagnosis and what needs Caitlyn and Ashley had before we can apply the service. What we're looking for right now, and what they've decided right now through what North Pointe can offer as play therapy for both the kids to work on Caitlyn's behaviors at school and Caitlyn and Ashley's behaviors in the foster home, which are basic—Caitlyn's behavior at school is terrible; I mean she's got 25 write ups already this school year. Ashley continues to bang her head and stuff like that—the assessment is a starting point. North Pointe right now is offering play therapy to try to address some of these behaviors. What we're doing through our agency now is, we have Dr. Brady, Wendy Young, Tara Miller, some of these people that offer a fair market contract rate, paid for out of our unlimited foster care funds. What we are looking to do now is to supplement what we're getting from North Pointe with our fair market contractor in Menominee County to provide additional counseling for the girls. And we've contacted Len Welling who's a supervisor and Sue Aston, who is a supervisor in Menominee-Delta, to get a list of fair market providers in that area to see what we could do to dump extra dollars to help this—to provide additional counseling for the girls.

THE COURT: And your complaint is that it hasn't been done quickly enough, right?

MS. WITTLA: Yes, because they've been there since July, and this is November.

THE COURT: Okay.

MS. WITTLA: And honestly, it could be a bureaucratic snafu, and okay, so it is, but that still leaves these kids without a service, that, in my opinion, they need before we can take the next step to unsupervised parenting time.

MR. ROSS: Doctor Cools here has a six month waiting list. It takes that long to get kids in to some of these providers.

THE COURT: Yeah, I know, but like I said, here we got the other alternative; we've got Strong Families' money for instance, maybe I'm just obsessed because I'm on the Strong Families' committee. But I mean we have the ability to dump somebody fairly quickly with some other dollars, you know? We have another alternative, and we're not getting to that. But you're telling me we are getting to Menominee, but it's a process. You're telling me that we need to get to it and they haven't been listening to you?

MS. WITTLA: No, not exactly. I mean, they've been listening, it's just that until that gets done, from the parents' perspective, so much time has gone by they should have these kids back home. That's what Mr. Findlay essentially portrayed to this in October. From my point of view, it doesn't matter how much time has been, gone by, but if the kids never get the serices they need, we can't push them to the next step just because it's November. We have to get them the service first, before we can take the next step, and I'm not hearing that as clearly as I would like from the agency.

So now, we all work to do things to make it clearly acceptable to Tracie Wittla, right?

I think that they (the agency) understand my concerns, but I think that they feel that they're under this time crunch too; like so much time has gone by, we have to have movement. Movement just for the sake of movement is not helping anybody, we need to make sure the kids are okay first, and then have the movement.

THE COURT: Yeah, but you make too much sense. The problem is including with the settlement it's going to get worse, time crunch is going to keep going on. I mean, they are indeed under a time crunch, whether they like it or not, whether it makes any sense or not, whether it makes any sense that we can't use independent living as a goal anymore. I mean, that's what they've got to live with.

MS. WITTLA: That's what they have to live with through the bureaucracy and that's why the decision is being put in your lap.

THE COURT: All right, touche. Okay, so Mr. Ross then, back to the point, I guess you gave me an answer that you're working on the counseling issue, that you're getting to that, the other questions are what about Mr. Wade here, and a home study. Is (it) number one?

MR. ROSS: I'll take responsibility for the home study not getting done. Some of it's not been done because of my travel back and forth to Ontonagon and the other caseload that I have had. Another reason that it hasn't been done is because a lot of times we get a request from a parent for a home study. By not doing a home study we want to keep, we want to guage the parents' interest; we want to see how he's involved. Since July I've received three or four emails and one phone call from Mr. Wade. So we kind of delay some of these things to guage the other parent's interest in doing the home study. I don't mean to detract or get off the subject here, but why is it taking a CPS and a foster care case for Mr. Wade to now express an interest in Caitlyn? I mean, he's known where she's been in Ironwood for several years and has never approached becoming an active part of Caitlyn's life and we got a foster care case and a PS case, and it's being thrown in my lap to initiate contact between Mr. Wade and his daughter. I'll get the home study done, and I don't have an issue with that, that will be done next week, but....

THE COURT: Okay, and then the other part of it was what about, I guess specifically, what are the plans for parenting time between now and the next review, holidays, and what is the agency's position on how it should work?

MR. ROSS: I guess I got this whole ball rolling a couple of weeks ago because the Colemans have completed a parenting class; the Colemans have completed anger management and are ongoing with their counseling, their marriage counseling. I guess there's problems with the credibility of the person providing the service, but the parenting time appointments, according to Ms. Benson, who's my supervisor in Delta County, says the parenting time has been outstanding. They've acted appropriately, there's been no safety issues, at no time have the children been in danger or unsafe, and I thought as a way to move forward, I was going to reward the family with an overnight over the course of the weekend; allow them to spend Friday or Saturday night in a hotel, and have Ms. Benson do pop-ins and then allow the family some time alone to spend Thanksgiving together. That seems to be a problem for everybody, so I'm trying to work with Ms. Benson right now to arrange for some extended visits on a Saturday, in a semi-supervised state because that seems to be where the Guardian Ad Litem and Prosecutor are at, to allow the family to have five to six hours with their children and have Ms. Benson stop in every ninety minutes to two hours to make sure things are okay. She still does the pickups and still does the drop offs. The Colemans don't go to the foster home at all. Then, the other thing we've started in the last couple of weeks, are the Colemans are allowed now to call the foster home a couple of times a week to talk to the girls, and then once on weekends. It seems to have helped Caitlyn out a lot that if she has a good day at school or has a good day at the foster home. For her mom to be able to talk to her and give her some instant gratification, you know, if she has a good day at school. Janet is able to share with Caitlyn and say, "Hey, you had a good day in school, I'm happy for you," and it seems to have stabilized some of Caitlyn's behavior in the foster home. So the phone contact seemed to have helped stabilize some of the kids behavior, the more frequent contact seems to have been beneficial for the kids, and that's why I'm trying to arrange more time and some unsupervised time because the kids seem to be responding well to the time that they're spending with their parents. After every visit the kids cry and they want to go home, and I mean I'm in a position now where I understand everybody's concerns for their safety, I do, but there hasn't been any problems since these kids have been in Menominee County. The psychological assessments are going on next week, that's going to happen at Bell, and my concern is I want to get this done today because I don't want to come back here two days before Christmas and have to go through this again. But if it pleases the court to do semi-supervised with pop-ins, I can arrange whatever the bench desires.

THE COURT: Okay, Mr. Perhalla, what's your position?

MR. PERHALLA: I believe after meeting with DHS that they're not going to do the overnights, and I'm in agreement with the semi-supervised plan, that the plan is a place to start. I'll be very curious once we get the evaluation next week or whenever, however long it takes to type it up, to see what we can do from there, and that's the evaluation of Robert and Janet. But I don't want to do the overnights at this time. I think DHS assured, at least me, that they're not going to, at this time.

THE COURT: Okay, Mr. Wade, I've got off the track with you a little bit because I need to redo some history here, and I've probably asked these questions before, I'm sorry, but we have a lot of cases. So the history with you and Mrs. Coleman, you are not married, correct?

MR. WADE: Correct.

THE COURT: And you had Caitlyn. Did you live together for a period of time?

MR. WADE: No, we did not.

THE COURT: Okay, so have you had time with Caitlyn? Have you ever had a regular visitation or that sort of thing?

MR. WADE: As a matter of fact, your Honor, I've had roughly five visits and Caitlyn's mother, Janet, had brought Caitlyn to my U.S. Coast Guard unit in Duluth, Minnesota and taken pictures with she and I together, when she was feeding me, which I sent, copies via email to Mr. Ross, who claims that I have no interest in getting custody of my daughter, so on and so forth. We worked out an agreement to that when I was leaving the Coast Guard, when I ETS'd, I was going to be spending my free time with my son, and that she was going to eventually get married and you know, move to Michigan because she was graduating college soon and she was going to allow whoever the father is to be the father and she would update me via pictures, letters, and so on and so forth. And that's the agreement we came to. Then later on, after she did get married, I think it was about two years ago, they tried to acquire full custody rights to my daughter per Robert Coleman. I denied it and never heard anything since. So that's the arrangement that we had worked out. I've attempted to contact Wisconsin with no results whatever, because that's where my child support was going through. They never, ever contacted me back, and they keep changing the caseworker that's in charge of it, and that caseworker says, "I have no information yet, let me get back to you," and by time I call back, because I'm a patient person, I call back and "Oh, somebody else has your case, your daughter so on and so forth." I just keep getting the runaround. This came out of the blue. I got a letter from the Prosecuting Attorney, if I'm not mistaken, telling me the information of the state's removing my daughter and her little sister away from her parents due to severe physical abuse, stopping at physical abuse, and suggested child molestation.

There you have it! A complete lie from the prosecutor, and proof of it! Never has there been any form of child molestation, and that was born out in follow up examinations! But this prosecutor lied and suggested to him that this was happening! This prosecutor made up what she wanted the case to be, and put it out as if it were the case— and for that, she should be disbarred! Continuing:

MR. WADE: I called and even wrote for a request to get a copy of the case, and I received it and I perused it and agree that this is preposterous that they are even giving Robert Coleman any time alone with my daughter. This is ridiculous and concerning Mr. Ross, who I've emailed and pleaded with begging please get this home study done. I was under the impression it was court ordered this last time that I was part of this hearing via phone, and unfortunately, apparently it was a suggestion by the Court and he did not follow through. I sent toys to her. I've asked him to give me pictures of her, and he gave me the run around and told me that she's four hours away, and I haven't been there yet. This is the last email that he has gotten me, and I don't know how to breach this subject about her having another dad, you know, I have no confidence in Mr. Ross, who claims that they're trying to assess my interest when I've made it plain and simple that I want her. I'm doing what it takes to be very patient, waiting for my home study, sending pictures, sending toys, and I've gotten no responses whatsoever.... none. I don't have pictures. I don't even know what she looks like. Her mother hasn't sent me anything in the last two years.

THE COURT: Okay, was it a short type term relationship with her mother, I mean, the two of you didn't live together or have a long term.....

MR. WADE: It was a very short term relationship. We were intimate twice, and dated for a week, and she got back together with an ex-boyfriend who they thought the child was theirs, and they found out later it wasn't theirs because she came out blonde haired, and they both had black hair.

THE COURT: And when you said they tried to have a permanent custody, are you talking about out of this county or a different county?

MR. WADE: Out of your county. Unfortunately, through the way the paperwork works, I have to send a request also to Wisconsin because unfortunately that's where I've been paying my child support through, since Caitlyn was a year old, when I found out that she was mine.

THE COURT: What county in Wisconsin again?

MR. WADE: You know, I don't know the name of it. I've never lived there.

MS. WITTLA: Douglas.

THE COURT: Is it Douglas?

MR. WADE: Superior.

THE COURT: Yeah, right.

MR. WADE: The name of the town was Superior, Wisconsin.

THE COURT: Douglas County. Okay, and you now live in Durango, Colorado?

MR. WADE: Correct.

THE COURT: Okay, and that is where you're going to be for the near future? Is that accurate?

MR. WADE: That's true because I have a three and one half year old daughter and she lives here. I have joint physical and legal custody with her. So I'm staying in this area because of her.

THE COURT: Okay, I am going to order the home study. Mr. Ross has already indicated that he's going to get it done, so that's going to happen. The only thing I can tell you is you absolutely have rights to participate in this proceeding. You have rights to know what's going on with your daughter. But I don't want to delude you into thinking that his is going to be some kind of a permanent custody situation for you quickly and easily through this court. These kind of proceedings are generally regarded as temporary and we have to review them periodically and after a year it becomes critical to decide what's going to happen in the case. The point of these cases is to end. (As to) The evidence on the record, I know you got a lot of information, but there has been no adjudicated or found sexual abuse that you're referring to.

MR. FINDLAY: I'm going to raise that.

THE COURT: So anyway, when it comes to sexual abuse, it's the great horror of whoever knows, if anything happened or didn't happen. If it did happen it's a horrendous situation. If it didn't happen, it's a horrendous thing to be accused of. So the record does not show that. A jury found, in general terms, abuse, physical abuse, a belt issue, and I've said it on the record, that's what I believe. I believe it did happen and the Colemans continue to deny that, but I believe the jury believed that and everybody else in the room believed that. I think that is substantiated proven or whatever word you want to use. So that is a concern, but I guess I just wanted to clarify it to you, we're not looking to hand the child back to a child molester, but there is no evidence on that issue at this time. There is no proven case at this time. There is however, a proven case which emphasized a sorted home situation with some strange things going on with some people living there, and there was a belt issue that was a primary part of the case. You're interested in what really happened, and I'm sorry to be the one to speak to you, but I'm just telling you that I can't be finding that Mr. Coleman is a child molester because that has not been legally established in this case. But we're not sending your daughter home today, we're working out the details of what is going to happen. So anyway, my final words to you are we'll make sure the agency keeps in contact with you. I'm going to put orders in place to that effect. They're going to have to comply with them. But in terms of the whole legalities of the custody of your child, I don't know that that's going to be resolved in this case. If there are issues on what's called parenting time, visitation with your child, and you want to see Caitlyn, you need to communicate with Mr. Ross, whether or not the two of you are having words over today or not. I don't know. But I mean I would certainly, if arrangements can be made, arrange for you to see Caitlyn. You may have to come here to do it, because I'm not going to ship her off to Durango, Colorado at this point either without just cause. That would shake her up that much more. But I mean, you are entitled to see your child, so if you work that out with Mr. Ross, if it needs to be ordered, I'll consider that too. All right, let me just move on here now. Mr. Findlay, you're obviously on the adversarial side of the table. What do you want to say?

MR. FINDLAY: I appreciate the court clarifying that on the sexual abuse and reminding me that I wanted to raise that because there is that. I remember when the issue first came up and I used the phrase, "raising the horrible specter of it,"— and it has been raised and it was never substantiated. I believe in forensic interviews it was never substantiated. The State Trooper never followed up on it, never pursued anything more after conducting their investigation. But it's finding its way into everything. As the court indicated, it's a horrible thing to be accused of, and it's in the North Pointe assessment of the girls. It's in there; suspected sexual abuse. It's in the updated service plans and I guess I'm just mentioning that because it's unfair. I appreciate the court acknowledging on the record that it's never been substantiated. The court is going to order the home study of Mr. Wade. He's the biological father with respect to Caitlyn.... it is what it is. My only point was that it, up until this point as much as Mr. Ross has indicated, that Mr. Wade has not expressed interest in Caitlyn. Even here he said on the record that they had an agreement basically where he was , maybe not formally giving up his parental rights; giving up his practical parental rights and allowing whoever the husband was to be to act as the father. So that is what it is. Obviously, I think from my response, my concern is more on the visitation issue. I have throughout these proceedings expressed the concern that this case is personal for the prosecutor. I imagine it's gotten personal for all of us at times, but I think that in this case and even the prosecutor's comments here today have demonstrated that it's personal. You know from making comments to others outside of this court that Robert Coleman shouldn't be trusted to care for a gerbil or a hamster, she has an extreme bias against Mr. Coleman. For whatever reason it leads to basically ignoring of court rules in terms of filing pleadings. I just advise both the opposing counsel, and I use the term for the GAL too, because I believe he's obviously opposed to the Colemans as well, but MCR 2.114 is physically at C, indicates that when you sign a pleading that you know or should know the veracity of those pleadings. And that was not the case in their pleading on this unsupervised visitation issue, where they indicated that parenting classes have not been conducted and no progress has been made. That was in Court, on the record, with everybody present. It was said that on October 14th that they had completed their parenting classes, that they had been making progress. I think the court even recognized that they have done everything that had been asked of them up to that point. And to ignore that fact either willfully or even out of neglect, I think again raises the specter of a personal ammos that the prosecution has for these parents. The things the parents have done so far again are everything that the court has asked of them. They went to parenting classes, they went to anger management, they did all that. They're continuing with counseling. There's this issue with the education. Ms. Coleman has been engaging and emailing the teacher there in Menominee, with good results of her being involved in Caitlyn's education in terms of the teacher communicating that she'll be communicating to Caitlyn that she'll be communicating with Janet Coleman back and forth. Then the phone calls they had with Caitlyn, you know, addressing school issues, does, it seems, to be working. I also point out that in terms of this education, and how terrible she's doing in education, I remind the court that when Mrs. Semo, her Ironwood teacher, testified it was a com— about what her educational experience was. It was completely different before. Now I'm not saying Ms. Wittla mischaracterized what I said, this all because of them being removed from their parents. I've never said that and that's not what I'm saying, but I would think that there is an element of being, when you have been removed from the only people you know as your parents, that has an effect on a child. And it may attribute or contribute to some of these acting out issues. In terms of assessment, the girls were assessed on November 12th—and I'm not sure what the prosecution doesn't like about the services, but it's a pretty thick packet of an assessment. It's obvious the prosecutor doesn't like the assessment, and so, wants a different one that will give her the results that she wants. The assessment was basically a recommendation for play therapy with these girls. The prosecutor may not like that's what it is. I would submit that the people at North Pointe are more qualified to make an assessment of what these girls need than the prosecution. I would ask that the original plan for this Thanksgiving be allowed to take place, given the progress that's been made in this case, the significant progress on any objective standard. The parents have done, again, every-

thing that's been asked of them. The phone calls, I think are extremely illustrative of the change in the parents' demeanor and attitude towards this case. While it's true they haven't done a miacopa and admitted that they did something, again, that may never happen. That is what it is. But they have been calling because of Mr. Ross allowing it and arranging it with the foster care parents. They've been calling for a couple of weeks and that's gone well and it's had positive affects on these girls. Nobody would have dreamed of doing that previously because of the allegations that they had gone out and investigated the foster care parents. They're not doing that now, and they've been again, doing everything that they're supposed to do. The original plan was that the girls be allowed to spend Thanksgiving holiday and an overnight with their parents in a hotel. It was what Mr. Ross's comfort level was. He wasn't comfortable with them going home, although I had asked to have them go home. I would point out that actually, she's available by phone if the court wanted to hear from her. Sheri Benson is the hands on worker who is in complete support of the original plan of unsupervised visits. My understanding is, from everything I received, and again what Mr. Ross indicated, (it was) nothing but positive reports about the parenting time and how it goes, and they're appropriate. I ask the court to allow the visitation to continue in DHS, at Mr. Ross's discretion. I believe he is doing what he should do in moving the case forward, but moving it forward appropriately given the progress that's being made by all involved in this case. If Caitlyn needs some additional counseling, if somebody determines that, then that can be addressed, but at this point the assessment was done and is indicating play time for the girls to help them with their issues in terms of relating to others. Once every two weeks, I believe it is. As I've said before, and I think everybody acknowledged, this is a difficult case. It's been difficult for various reasons, in representing the parties that I represent. One thing that has been extremely difficult for me to do is to convince them (the parents) that this isn't all about termination. The prosecution and the state didn't go into this from the get go to terminate their parental rights. And my real concern is that pleadings like this, the allegations made, the statement that the prosecutor makes about these parents, whether on the record or off the record, indicates that that is her intention. That if she had her way, these children would never return to the Colemans. That isn't the law. The law is that reunification is supposed to be the goal and if the parents are complying with all the orders of the Court, and the services are provided, benefiting them to the court's satisfaction, the law says they're supposed to be reunified at some point. I think that the rather limited unsupervised visits we're talking about, at this point, are one overnight. You know, the children have been removed from their home since March. We're talking about one overnight now, and under the context of all that the parents have done, in terms of services to them, it certainly doesn't seem unreasonable and I ask the court to, again, allow the visitation to remain supervised by DHS, as it has been.

MS. WITTLA: Your Honor, may I respond briefly please?

THE COURT: With the qualifier you just threw on the end there, yes, briefly.

MS. WITTLA: Just because Mr. Findlay tries to paint me as a raving lunatic doesn't make it so.

It is interesting Ms. Wittla, that you used the words raving lunatic. Mr. Findlay never used those words, but I think you hit the nail right on the head. Perhaps, for once in your life, you were using a little introspect! Continuing:

MS. WITTLA: This case is no more personal to me than any other case I've ever dealt with.

I believe that too. It is my opinion you genuinely enjoy screwing people every chance you get, and that is why you remain a prosecutor. Continuing:

MS. WITTLA: The problem I suppose, from his point of view, is that all my cases are somewhat personal because I actually care about the outcomes.

Yes, winning is everything—right? But fairness is not in your thoughts, or you would consider first if your charges were even right, and you would not go out of your way to make them up or write unsolicited letters or make unsolicited phone calls to try to shape the outcomes in order to win.

MS. WITTLA: I suppose if I was a good bureaucrat that wouldn't be true, beyond that though, if things are so wonderfully well with this phone contact with Caitlyn and her mother, then why of 25 time-ins that Caitlyn has had, have 17 of them happened since the last court hearing? Two-thirds of the time-ins that this child has had at school, it happened in the last six weeks, since October 14th. This isn't a sign that everything is getting wonderfully rosy, or better. This is a sign that they are not. The parents haven't complied with everything that this court has asked of them, they went into the Bell assessment and they didn't tell the truth, that's what happened. The fact that the kids aren't getting as much counseling as I'd like to have through the local CMH provider is a fact. I'm not happy with it. I have no issue with the assessment, the problem is that CMH as a system is not a good service deliverer for kids. They don't give much service to kids. I don't have an issue with the assessment. I've never said I had an issue with the assessment. It's funny that an off-hand comment of mine can find its way into the court room because the person who is constantly trying to make this personal is actually Mr. Findlay. He's the one who is constantly trying his little barbs, trying to make me react, trying to get a rise out of me, and make this all about the crazy lady who works in the Prosecutor's office. And frankly, that's just not accurate; I've been doing this job for ten years almost, I do not feel any more allegiance to Caitlyn or Ashley than I do to any other kid I've dealt with. But I'm also not going to sit and pretend that they don't matter or that the services that I know exist and have been offered in other cases shouldn't be provided to them, because they desire to have a shot at a happy, healthy life, regardless of how much time has gone by or regardless of what the parents feel about the system. I can't get into Robert and Janet Colemans' heads and convince them the system isn't out to get them. They tell that to everybody they meet, it has nothing to do with me. The fact that Mr. Findlay is referencing the original plan for an overnight visit is shocking to me, considering that yesterday Mr. Perhalla and I were at a meeting with Mr. Ross, Mr. Borth, and several other caseworkers, and it was told to us point blank that there was never a plan for an overnight visit, and that we must have been mistaken. So the fact that Mr. Findlay is so adamant that we should go back to the original plan also points out to this court, hopefully, that there is a huge lack of communication between the DHS, the Prosecutor's Office, and the GAL. The only person who the DHS seems to feel the need to communicate with lately is the defense. That's unfortunate and that's unusual, but in the end it also leaves it back in the court's hands that unless you make very specific orders as to what's going to happen, I can't predict,I can't tell you that this is going to go along rosy like every other case, because of all the other caseworkers who were sitting in that room yesterday, not one of them raised their hand and said there should be unsupervised visits. So I don't want this court to come away with the opinion that DHS, as an entire entity, is in favor of overnight visits, because that's not the vibe I got.

THE COURT: Well let me flush this out. Mr. Ross, just directly, was there going to be an overnight or wasn't there going to be an overnight?

MR. ROSS: I started the ball rolling a couple weeks ago because I thought things were progressing and the kids were longing to spend an extended period of time with their parents. I tried to see if I could arrange an overnight visit at a hotel for the Colemans and their children provided I had Ms. Benson available to do pop-ins, semi-supervised. I was never going to give the Colemans carte blanche to have 48 hours alone with their kids. But I set the ball roll in motion, at least, to have the Colemans spend some type of Thanksgiving with their children.

THE COURT (to MR. FINDLAY): And did you think it was going to be 48 hours alone?

MR. FINDLAY: No, I didn't think it would be 48 hours alone.

THE COURT: So the operative words seems to have been semi-supervised, which I know you don't like, but that seems to be the new definition they're working under.

MS. WITTLA: Well, because it gives them cart blanche to actually do whatever they want, which honestly, Judge, I've never sat in front of this court and asked for you to give a super detailed order on visitation because I've never been in this position. I've never been completely in the dark. I mean, you can ask the GAL. We didn't know anything about this. This is really, really unusual. This is the most difficult case that we have ever dealt with. That's no secret. And to have this complete shut off of communication and all these things just kind of happening and finding out about them at review hearings isn't okay. I'm not happy with it, okay fine, but the child's attorney doesn't even know? How is that all right?

THE JUDGE: Okay, we're at an end here. No more words.

MR. FINDLAY: ... Just, could I ask a question of the court in terms of this last order?

THE COURT: Oh, a question. Sure.

MR. FINDLAY: If the court can confirm, my recollection of the hearing was that the court said once the counseling has been set up with Caitlyn, then it would be within DHS's discretion to allow the unsupervised visits anyway. Is my....

THE COURT: You know, a transcript was prepared for today. I don't know the answer to that.

MS. WITTLA: That's essentially what the court ordered and that's the reason for the motion today, your Honor.

THE COURT: All right. Okay, because frankly, I have a hard time piecing one hearing together without looking at notes or transcripts. So let's get the easy part out of the way. Within 30 days the DHS will complete a home study on Mr. Wade. Now when I say complete, you just told me you could get it done in a week or so, is that right on, or?

MR. ROSS: I can get the paperwork processed, it goes to Interstate Compact, it goes to.... from Lansing to Boulder I believe is the capital of Colorado to theirs, then they kick it to the local county.

THE COURT: All right, DHS will initiate within seven days, home studies. I just don't want to get into the nightmare of different counties or different states, I mean. California has been horrible. I don't know that we've dealt a lot with Colorado, so we'll see. But I want them to get it going pronto because they told me they could. DHS will also investigate and arrange for, expanded counseling for Caitlyn. What that means is beyond CMH counseling and we get into this problem because there's a case from Judge Hupy over in Menominee. Ironically, where he ordered specific types of counseling from non-CMH and for them to pay for it and it was eventually overturned in the appellate courts. I mean, I can't make them do a particular type of thing, I can make them go and look for it, and explain to me why not, so I'll say investigate it and arrange.

MR. ROSS: Your Honor, I'm just going to do it for both girls, if that pleases the court.

THE COURT: Yeah, yes.

MS. WITTLA: Your Honor, I understand the court's point regarding CMH, but I believe that DHS potentially does have funding sources for this.

THE COURT: But again, on the same basis of the same case, I can't say you're tapping this CHILD FAMILIES or tapping your particular slush fund, you know?

MS. WITTLA: Right, it's their....

THE COURT: ... it's their baby. It's fortunate because I don't know that I would ever understand all their funding sources, so they have to do those things as requested by the motion. Then what remains short of the actual issue on parenting time, was there anything else specific, I think I hit the kind of agreed to points? Because I had to do a little background explanation which doesn't always come through that clearly. I don't know, it may be the most difficult case that I've sat on. I've been here longer than most of you. Actually, longer than all of you. But it's in the top three in the sixteen years that I've sat on the bench. Frankly, you know, to deflect it, the little side bar battles that goes on between counsel both on the record and in writing. I don't believe that the Prosecutor knowingly or the Guardian Ad Litem facilitated or the Prosecutor had an ethical violation in the signatures of pleadings, etc. I didn't remember that the LVD things were here until I was reminded. I think that was kind of a missed point, and I guess that the argument that she makes is on quality not the fact that something that technically (had) been gone through, so I don't find this was like a deceitful attempt to get the court to do something. Frankly, as far as the Colemans go, you know, as I said it's one of the more difficult cases and I've said it on the record. I mean, this is not an off the cuff comment, this is on the record comment. You know Mr. Coleman is one of the most manipulative persons if not the most to ever come through the court. Last time he's trying to indicate Native American, and then I get very vague answers on that issue. I mean, it's like every angle that can be tried. You know I waxed on and on about the ridiculous nature of the Mormon argument that was put on the record. So what I'm saying is they start a lot of this stuff with the off the wall type of issues that come up, and should not be surprised when people look with somewhat of a jaundiced eye. Frankly, the Bell assessment I discussed last time on Mr. Coleman was real wishy washy primarily because of, apparently, his approach to the system. And

I believe it was a manipulative type of approach. So that assessor comes off with a fudgy, "geez I don't know what's wrong with this guy" type of analysis. Then we're taking the next step, which was the big argument at the last hearing, and Mr. Ross is doing that. He is setting up the next step, and I'm all for it. That being said, I always say in all cases, difficult or easy, that when people jump through hoops, you have to give some kind of a reward. And it has to be a kind and, you know, maybe Mr. Ross learned that at my knee, working in this court. Therefore, expanding things to them is something that has to happen, whether or not people personally like them or whether they're abrasive or manipulative. If, indeed, they have altered their behavior from claiming it's the state of Texas and the state of Michigan against the Mormon Church to okay, we'll at least go along with this, behave ourselves on visitations, I think they have to get something back for that. And when I've blocked visitations in other cases, the Prosecutors and Guardian Ad Litems have brought forward things like reports from counselors saying this is a danger to this child. And then I pretty much react to that, you know, as gospel. But I can't really go on a "what if here," regardless of whether or not the difficult nature of the Coleman family makes us all suspicious that something bad may happen. I just don't have the evidence to interfere. In the thirty years I've been practicing law, and I know my age analogies don't go over well, I've sat on the bench, I've been a Guardian Ad Litem, I've been a defense attorney, I've been a limited Prosecutor, on these types of cases. I have seen a few incompetent social workers and few entrenched social workers. Frankly, nobody currently at the DHS office fits that bill and I have to have some trust in their ability to manipulate their own cases. That goes for everybody that works there. So I'm not going to get into a custody structured divorce type visitation situation or parenting time situation. I have to allow some latitude to the DHS. Since the parties seem to have reached some kind of a compromise, I'm going to order that there could be semi-supervised parenting time between now and the next review hearing, and we'll see where it goes. As I said, they've made some of the steps, I don't concur with counsel that they've done everything, but I do concur that they have done things and made a more positive turn. I don't know that that means they're cured in our mind, if they have anything to be cured of. Or that they're locked step with the system. But they've toned down the behavior which caused these children to be moved from two or three different foster homes, all of which was their fault. They have to get something back for that attempting to be compliant, so we will see how the semi-supervised goes over the Holidays. Understanding that DHS, if we start getting "daddy says I can't talk to you" or "you know social workers, daddy says you're trying to steal me away forever" (comments).... If there's bad influences coming from the parenting time, then the DHS can pull the plug, any time. And I'm not going to hear any emergency motions between now and Christmas. It's going to come up at the next review hearing. So, in a sense, even though nobody feels they have a victory, I guess I'll call it semi-supervised so there is still some degree of supervision. I won't totally shut it down or make it totally supervised or chain DHS to some kind of a specific thing. I don't feel that the evidence or the arguments that I have, rise high enough, to do that even in a difficult case. So that's what we'll do, and I also mean what I said, if Mr. Wade somehow makes arrangements with Mr. Ross, parenting time with him can be arranged if it's safe and everything else—if it works. You know, I'm just not. This is not a case, let me say, where Caitlyn, who we are really talking about mostly, is like in a real good foster home and outside comment, influences from dad and mom, or a real or biological dad is going to throw things off. Where she is, is having lots of problems in her current foster home; I'm sure it's a good foster home, but visits with mom and dad are going decently and biological dad is out there and expressing an interest. I don't see that we are throwing her world into a turmoil other than the turmoil that it's currently in, because it is in somewhat of a turmoil in her school situation and I'm not sure why until we get to the bottom of this counseling. So that's where we'll go from here. Anything further for the record?

MR. FINDLAY: Just an additional question, your Honor. When you indicated that they have not done everything that they are supposed to, could the court indicate to me what else they need to do because I want to communicate to them what else they need to be doing.

THE COURT: I can't, okay, to be fair to the Prosecutor. I mean, she hasn't told me everything that's gone on, so I don't know if they really have done it. I'm talking historically they haven't done what they're supposed to. I mean they, they did a whole lot of what they're not supposed to (do) before.

MR. FINDLAY: I understand. Okay, I meant in terms of complying with the service....

THE COURT: ... No, not just complying with the service plan and everything else. At this point, we're not doing a review. I do not have any evidence that they've done anything wrong at this point, or not. The service plan and the quick report I got from Mr. Ross is that they're generally following, and I'm being a lawyer when I never say anything a hundred percent I guess. And I guess I want to tell everybody on the other side of the table, again, which I don't plan on really doing any good with, but the fact that the Guardian Ad Litem, the Prosecutor, the DHS are kind of in an argument and a turmoil here, sometimes that's what's got to happen. Sometimes that's what's got to shake up DHS to do it's job. Sometimes what DHS has got to stand its ground on, and not do everything that is being asked by the other side. That's somehow, hopefully, where we reach a position. If we don't, we do what we did today, we spill it to the court and the court makes a decision, and everybody lives with it from there. Hopefully, it's the right decision. All right, Happy Thanksgiving, we're in recess.

So there we were. The judge had personal feelings about me (Robert Coleman) being the most manipulating person he had ever met, and I had the personal feelings that he (the judge) was the most biased judge I had ever met. But at least, we could now see the light at the end of the tunnel, knowing full well if we worked with DHS, the conniving prosecutor and the lying Guardian Ad Litem would not win out in the end, in their goal to keep our children forever.

—Chapter Twenty–Eight—

Vindictiveness Knows No Bounds

With some people, vindictiveness knows no bounds. Such is the case with the prosecuting attorney in our case. It wasn't enough to try to snatch our children for life—she now found it necessary to go after Janet's child support, as she filed a complaint under the Status of Minors Act that would require Janet to pay back to the state of Michigan, a total of $138 per month for the support and maintenance of Caitlyn. There was a very brief pretrial hearing on the matter on January 5, 2009, but at that hearing our attorney (Michael Findlay) requested and received a continuance on the matter, and the matter was to be heard at our next scheduled court review hearing, a week later, on January 12, 2009. That date arrived without further incident, but as we were about to discover, there was still more vindictiveness planned by both the prosecutor and the GAL for this hearing.

The judge opened:

THE COURT: From the prospective of the DHS and the service plan, Mr. Ross, where are we at today?

MR. ROSS: Both Caitlyn and Ashley continue to reside in a foster home in Menominee County. Both girls are receiving mental health services and the counseling through the Northpointe Agency there, and that's been conducted bi-weekly, and according to the stats, the counseling is going very well. Ashley is now becoming involved with the Head Start, Early Head Start program in Menominee County to address some of the deficiencies we are noticing in her speech, because she's not quite speaking as much as a child of her age, a three year old (might expect to be). Since counseling started, Caitlyn went from about twenty behavioral referrals the first marking period, down to about three or four this marking period, and her behavior at school has stabilized. She's gotten a referral for throwing snowballs and other stuff that kids do, but the behavior has stabilized. She seems to be doing academically well. I think it's helped her to stay on task at school, to have the phone calls with the parents during the week, because they get to talk about what she did in school that day and she gets reminders or prompts from her parents as far as the things she's doing in school that she has a good day in school. She gets immediate, positive consequences from her parents if she has a good day, if she did something well. That's working out well for her. My visitation supervisor hasn't reported any issues since we've been in court last, as far as how the visitations have gone. She continues to report nothing but positive things with the visitations. I was alerted by email about an incident that may have happened in December with one of the visits involving Mr. Coleman allegedly swang (swearing) at Caitlyn at a Walmart store in Menominee, which was noticed by an Applebee's manager there who had an incident with the family at Applebee's. But other than that, I haven't had any other reports with anything negative going on, so we'll continue into the semi-supervised visitation. There's been a delay in the Bell Behavioral Assessments coming back; both parents were assessed December 1st by Doctor Moore from Bell Behavioral in Ishpeming. Doctor Moore went on personal leave the 15th of December and then with the holidays we had a little delay, and then, Doctor Moore was out on sick leave all last week, so I don't have anything written to present to the court today, as far as how the assessments worked out. The verbal stuff that I've gotten from Doctor Moore indicates that he didn't see anything what he termed as alarming. He noted some, what he called borderline obsessive, compulsive disorder situations with Mrs. Coleman, and he said that's due to the fact that she takes meticulous notes about what's going on with the case and everything that's gone on. But he says there's nothing alarming that's coming out of his report to me.

THE COURT: And that's the follow up to the reports where you were discussing the last time?

MR. ROSS: Yes, they went for a full psychological evaluation and included written interview or personal inter-

views and written psychological testing on a computer, and I'm just waiting for the hard copies of the results to come back.

THE COURT: A thought just struck me, not to interrupt, but I'm sure you folks have taken care of it. Last time we had a big issue with Caitlyn's dad participating by phone, etc.

MR. ROSS: You ordered an interstate home study be conducted on Mr. Wade in Colorado; that information is with Marlene Sodi at the Interstate Compact office in Lansing.

THE COURT: But I mean he hasn't taken any affirmative— as far as I know he didn't call and ask to participate today. He hasn't hired counsel or done anything to....

MR. ROSS: He sent me an email last week, basically asking what the status of the home study was and basically accused me of not doing my job, and a few other things. But that was done; I also received phone calls from Mrs. Coleman's parents regarding the status of the case; I deferred those to her because I'm not talking about confidential case requirements with third parties; and Mr. Coleman has got a sister and brother-in-law in Ohio that requested an Interstate Home study done for possible placing of the children, and I'm not going to do it because I can't place Caitlyn because she's not a biological relative to these people, and I'm not going to split these kids. So I'm rejecting the request for the home study in Ohio as well.

THE COURT: Okay, well, anyway, I just want to take care of Mr. Wade there, and I am not informed that he had contacted the court to participate in the proceeding at all, and nobody else has told me he did, so we'll go ahead. So then what's the plan from here I guess, I mean, what's the recommendation in terms of continued....

MR. ROSS: I guess we're going to have to consider the status quo until we get the psychological evaluations back. My concern is that March is the removal date, and we're coming up on permanency planning and I need to move this case forward, prior to March, so what I'm going to ask for is if I get a clean bill of health on these mental health evaluations, once all the parties involved look at them, I want to start towards unsupervised visitation, and I want to start turning the corner to hopefully a reunification here, because once March comes up, it becomes problematic for everybody involved.

THE COURT: All right. Mr. Perhalla, what do you recommend?

Brace yourself! Here comes another attack from out of nowhere!

MR. PERHALLA: Thanks your Honor. I'm going to recommend that the parenting time be fully supervised, though Mr. Ross talked about these incidences involving Applebee's and Walmart. I'm concerned with this type of behavior in public. There's a history of this family complaining to hotels, to various places which clearly indicates to me anger management issues that obviously aren't being resolved, and I believe there's a safety concern. Further, I'm concerned if these incidences happened outside of the presence of the supervisor. I'm assuming they did; one incident is—as Mr. Ross indicated—the family complaining at Applebee's, which is a long history of doing. The other incident was swearing at the child in Walmart. If this is happening out in public your Honor, I'm very concerned about the safety of these children when they're not out in public, so I'm asking that the visitations remain completely supervised and not semi-supervised any more. And this is us finding this out, way from Menominee. We don't have contacts there. I go and contact the foster parents now and then. What aren't we finding out that's not being told to us?

THE COURT: So what I'm getting on the record here though is bits and pieces that I'm not fully understanding. I mean, I understand the swearing at Walmart, what that would mean, but what happened at Applebee's? I mean you're talking about complaining to other people? What? What?

MR. PERHALLA: Complaining to the manager. My understanding is that the plaintiffs, this is hearsay, is complaining to a manager to get a free meal, which they've done in the past.

Oh? You know a lot about my life history, right Mr. Perhalla? Aside from not knowing the name of my step daughter (Caitlyn, who you refer to as "the girl"), I'd invite you to tell readers of this book where and when we complained to a restaurant manager, with an objective of getting a free meal! That simply did not happen, nor did the incident at Walmart. But now, for the sake of readers of this book, let me me tell you how this all really did go down: First, by this time, Janet and I had been given the courtesy, over the objections of Mr. Perhalla and Ms. Wittla, to have supervised visits with our children, in outside settings. This was such an occasion, and Sheri Benson was our designated supervisor on this visitation. We had decided to take our kids to a large mall for the day, which also included the Walmart store. We began in Walmart. Sheri had her child with her that day as well, and once inside, we separated to do our shopping, as Sheri allowed us to do. So although the visitation was supervised, we were granted some time to ourselves, an allowance Sheri was now giving us. So Janet, myself, and our three children shopped at Walmart, completed our purchases and went to the counter to pay. There were absolutely no incidences at the register. We simply paid and then took the kids on out into the mall, where we would meet up with Sheri later. We were enjoying ourselves in the mall, when Caitlyn spotted Lori, her current foster parent. We saw her two or three times while out in the mall, and I decided to call Sheri to tell her about this. "She is probably following you around," Sheri said, and indeed, it did appear she was stalking us. In any case, as we prepared to conclude the supervised visit, we did meet up with Sheri, and were in the process of preparing for our separation again, when Lori walked up to us. In the ensuing conversation she offered to take Caitlyn and Ashley home with her, and it was agreed she would do so. Lori instructed Ashley to put on her hat, and Ashley refused. "Just wait until you get home," she stated to Ashley. I said nothing, but wanted to go after her right then and there. I wanted to challenge her and say, "Or what?" But of course I could not, we had to maintain our cool if we ever wanted our children back. But that was it. There were no encounters with Applebee's managers or anything else. As a matter of fact, we had not yet been to Applebee's, which would be our next stop. When we did go, it was just Janet, myself, and our youngest daughter Brittney. We went in, ordered our steaks, and when the order came, they had reversed our orders, which Janet and I figured out and did mention to the waitress, but with no adversity. Applebee's gave us free desserts for having made the error, but there was nothing contentious in any of it. We did not even ask for it, they simply did this as a matter of their policy. Only Tracie Wittla could later twist this, and make it appear we were making a scene and that we were making demands, etc., when, in fact, none of this ever took place. There was no police report. There were no police brought out to the scene. So nothing ever took place with either Applebee's or Walmart, as was claimed by the prosecutors in this case. They made it up, in their efforts to keep our children. So would I say Mr. Perhalla lied? Yes! Continuing on with his ficticious account:

MR. PERHALLA (continuing): It didn't escalate to the level of the police being called because of the nature of the complaining, but there have been many incidences at hotels where police had to be called in because of, and I believe the Subway in Ashland, where the police had to be called in because of—and I believe it's mostly Mr. Coleman—complaining and raising a ruckus in front of that employee, and basically.....

THE COURT: You mean like because the food is bad or something? I get a free meal or what?

MR. PERHALLA: I assume it's... I don't know, I'd let Mr. Coleman explain it further.

You assume? You don't know? Then why are you making accusations in court?

THE COURT: Okay, all right. Then the swearing thing was what that was about?

MR. PERHALLA: He swore at Caitlyn, is my understanding, in line.

THE COURT: Anybody want to tell me what it was, or....

MS. WITTLA: I will.

Now it was her turn to join in this latest sneak attack:

THE COURT: Okay, why don't you pick it up then?

***MS. WITTLA:** Okay, it's very concerning to me that these behaviors are coming out, mostly because of the distance.*

What? You are concerned because of the distance? The distance?

***MS. WITTLA (continuing):** We are supposed to believe at this point in time that Robert and Janet Coleman are doing everything they could possibly do to comply with services and everything is fine, and this is just a system run amuck. The problem I have is that when this case first began there was obvious manipulation, which we're not supposed to talk about any more because that's supposedly in the past, and it's just not an issue.*

Wait, wait, wait!!!! It is true, the judge suggested that after hearing enough of the character assassinations from this prosecutor, but if we want to talk about the past manipulation, how about if we start where it primarily occurred, with the dummied up phony charges from a mental case, manipulated by an overzealous prosecutor and a lying investigator (Elizabeth Fyle) who invented the so-called evidence that led to the abduction of our kids to begin with. And then Fyle's lies about our flight as a reason raid our hotel while we were trying to enjoy a few days away from it all? If you want to address manipulation, let's go where the manipulation really took place! And from that point on, the prosecutor (Ms. Wittla) continued throughout our ordeal with manipulation tactics that make mine minute! Continuing with her manipulation:

***MS. WITTLA:** For me, it's always going to be an issue because it has the potential to come back up, and that's exactly what seems to happening here. We have a visitation supervisor who can see nothing, but, you know, wonder parents in front of them and that's okay—that's fine. (EXCEPT IT REALLY TICKS HER OFF, RIGHT?) But when they (the Colemans) are not with this lady, they're apparently going to places like Applebee's and you know, after they eat their entire meal, I'm told, then they throw a fit and they raise it to the point where it's just a conversation with a waitress, the manager has to get involved, it's this big scene, and for the manager to just make it all end, they just say "Okay, fine. We'll give it to you on the house, let's just be done here." As luck would have it, this same person (the manager) ends up seeing them in Walmart. (CONVENIENT, HUH?)*

I don't know if it was the same, different day or whatever. (SO YOU REALLY DON'T 'KNOW' MUCH) He sees and remembers them obviously, because this was a fairly noteworthy even in Applebee's because I don't think it's typical behavior of all the patrons there, and he notices that Robert Coleman is yelling at Caitlyn and telling her, "Come over here you little fucker." Now that's a problem for me, not because people don't swear at their kids, I've been known to swear at my own children.

What? What? Somebody should raid your house and take away your kids!!!

***MS. WITTLA (continuing):** I can't hold anybody to a higher standard than myself, but the problem that I have is that this is in Walmart for goodness sake! Five hundred people running around on a daily basis!*

Tracie, that should mean you would have five hundred witnesses who say that I said those things. WHERE ARE THEY? Yet, you produce one ficticious one—the one who didn't like our alleged complaint at the Applebee's (which would have to have come after Walmart, since we had not yet been to Applebee's. And Tracie, you are asking folks to believe this Applebee's manager complained about our Walmart behavior before we ever want to his restaurant. Isn't there something quite wrong in that assessment? How can he make a complaint before something ever happened? And he is the one, you say, who just happened to be the only one who said he heard me swear at my stepdaughter in Walmart. Sounds a little like manipulation to me, Tracie! And a bad job of it, at that!

***MS. WITTLA (continuing):** Most people treat their children differently in public than they do privately. If you're going to scream and holler, carry one, whatever, usually your behavior is a little more checked when you're in public. If this is what's happening to Caitlyn in public, then what on earth is happening at this hotel room?*

Well, following your logic, Ms. Wittla, which says you treat them differently at home than in public, and since I am so mean in public, it must mean I am a gentle, loving soul at all times at home (or the hotel)— right? Flash, Ms. Wittla, some people try to teach their children at both times.

MS. WITTLA (continuing): We don't know. Okay, now I'm supposedly trying to make a mountain out of this mole hill kind of situation, but this is very problematic for me because I don't know how Caitlyn interprets this. Maybe this is normal for her. Maybe this is just how she expects to be treated forever.

Or maybe you are just making this "problematic" because you are trying to manipulate the court, Ms. Wittla.

MS. WITTLA (continuing): The other thing that I have a concern with is the fact that Robert Coleman lied to Bob Ross when he said that he quit his job at KBIC. He was fired for poor job performance, I just found that out today. Now does that really mean anything, you know, as far as the safety of these kids?

No.

MS. WITTLA (continuing): I'm not sure because the manipulation and the lies are still there.

Are you referring to yours or mine, Tracie?

MS. WITTLA (continuing): I don't know where they're at. I don't know how they're paying their bills. Do I have to know all the personal details of their finances?

No.

MS. WITTLA (continuing): No, I don't, but at one point in time they had a thriving business in Ironwood, which they supposedly sold; was the court ever notified as to what those buildings were sold for? How did they qualify for court appointed attorneys? How are they paying for all the things that they have? I mean, if they're working and not reporting that to the DHS, that's a problem. If they're not working, the other question would be why not? As far as I know they're both able bodied people who could find employment somewhere. Obviously Mr. Coleman has some issue because he wasn't able to maintain his employment at KBIC, but the only information we got from there was that basically it was poor job performance. So there are still problems here; there are still things that are not being disclosed as truthfully as they could be, or should be.

Here is a news flash for you, Ms. Wittla! Your prosecutor's position does not entitle you to any type of disclosure where it comes to my personal life!

MS. WITTLA (continuing): Regarding Mr. Wade, I don't know if he's ever going to become more than just a figment for Caitlyn, but I also find it a little bit disheartening to know that even though Mr. Ross's job is to work with Robert and Janet Coleman, that the person who seems to get most of his negative comment is the guy who is never here, and that's Mr. Wade.

Does this mean that you are now tired of attacking Robert Coleman, Ms. Wittla, and will have more fun now attacking Mr. Ross for not going along with you on your crusade to support Mr. Wade's candidacy for substitute daddy, and abolition of Janet as mommy? Your "poor Mr. Wade" crusade is getting stale, my dear!

MS. WITTLA (continuing): I can understand that there may be a tendency to try and take a middle road or try to not say anything too terrible about parents when you have to work with them day in and day out on a case you're trying to resolve. But this March deadline is really a bureaucratic thing; we routinely go past permanency planning hearings and do not file termination petitions and do not make any kind of ground breaking decision because of these little factors that they have in the Federal Legislation that allow you to kind of by-pass it.

Yes, I think I understand Tracie. In other words, if it suits your purposes, it is okay to violate federal laws.

MS. WITTLA (continuing): So I'm not overly concerned about the clock. I'm well aware of the fact the court can order whatever it chooses, and has, and I expect will continue to. So I'm not in a big rush to go to unsupervised visits, and to have Caitlyn exposed to more of this behavior until we can find out first what those actual written reports say from the doctor in Ishpeming; and second, how Caitlyn is doing in counseling because I'd like these issues should be addressed with her in counseling so that the counselor can tell us. You know, "It's not a big deal that he swears at her" or "Yeah, it really bummed her out"— or whatever the answer is, so that we're not sitting here trying to guess.

Now came the most revealing part of this hearing, as the judge turned to Mr. Perhalla, and between him and my attorney, he had to explain his own relationship with Caitlyn, who he was expressing such grave safety concerns for:

THE COURT: Let me ask Mr. Perhalla, do you know what Caitlyn wants herself? I mean, you represent her best interest, I understand, you can recommend whatever you want. But what's her desire, what does she want?

MR. PERHALLA: She doesn't tell me, and I don't ask. I sit there with her. She doesn't say much.

So, in other words, sir, you do not know! Yet you can sit there, and characterize who I am, how vicious I am to her, but you cannot talk to her? That's the biggest bunch of B.S. I've ever heard!

THE COURT: You know what I'm getting at?

MR. PERHALLA: Yeah.

THE COURT: I'm going to be told "I wanna go home" and "Miss mom and dad" .... or?

MR. PERHALLA: No, I have not heard that and I've not heard that from the foster home either. She doesn't say much about her life prior to going into foster care to anyone, is my understanding.

Except for at the beginning when she just poured her heart out to Elizabeth Fyle, right??? That kind of goes against the grain of what you people have been trying to

put in a frame, doesn't it? She doesn't talk, but you have all this information about how bad I was?

THE COURT: And how about you, Mr. Ross? Do you get anything from the perspective from Caitlyn?

MR. ROSS: The only thing I get in perspective I get from the foster parents, and I get a little bit from the counselors—and that is that Caitlyn still blames herself for being in care.

THE COURT: Yeah, for telling.

MR. ROSS: For telling, she still carries the burden, and that's not fair for her.

THE COURT: No, but I guess I'm asking about her desire at this time?

MR. ROSS: The kids want to go home.

THE COURT: Yeah. All right. Okay, Mr. Findlay?

Finally, it was our turn to retaliate:

MR. FINDLAY: There's just two items that I just wanted to address in the updated service plan. They're on page 14 and 16, and I just would ask the court to strike them or amend them because I don't think they're correct. On the top of page 14, under B, it indicates, "neither parent accepting responsibility for striking and abusing the children, even after a jury trial for jurisdiction and dispositional hearing." I don't dispute that both Robert and Janet further take an adversarial position with DHS and that relationship remains hostile and mistrustful.

That's more a matter, I guess, of interpretation and I don't think that's completely true. I would direct the court's attention down to the bottom of page 14, the emotional stability, behavior, etc., indicates therein, which is the third sentence; "the assessments were inconclusive because the assessors felt that they were deceptive." Referring to the Colemans, "and they have yet to accept responsibility for their role in the removal of their children." I went back when I read that, it struck me as that it wasn't my memory. I went back and read both of the Bell Assessments; they did not say that the parents were being deceptive. With Robert Coleman, they said there were maybe some inconsistencies; I didn't read that "deception" was being used. It appears his answer to questions were vague and perhaps evasive at times. Other times he appeared quite candid. This left the overall impression of an inconsistency, but I don't think they used the word "deceptive." Deceptive is a completely different thing than inconsistency. Then, further down on the next paragraph, at a minimum it appears that Robert is struggling to cope and adjust to the recent ongoing events, the legal process, and removal of children from his home. I don't think it's fair to say he was being deceptive when the assessor himself didn't even say that. Then, on to Janet Coleman's assessment. Again, it did not use the word assessment at all. The first time that it came we engaged in a colloquy with the court about that they posed in a question: Is it a matter of that they are in complete denial or is it a matter that they're being run over by a system that they couldn't answer in assessments. So I would ask that that be removed in terms of use of the word "deceptive." That also appears again on page 16, in the second paragraph. "Those assessments came back inconclusive due to what assessors believed to be deception and the lack to accept responsibility." I'd ask the word "deception" be stricken, because I don't think that is accurate.

Having now admonished both the GAL and the prosecutor for having put language into the assessments that were not contained it them, our lawyer then proceeded to make a request that had not even been considered by the judge up to this point:

MR. FINDLAY: Obviously hearsay is admissible at this dispositional review hearing, and I would ask that these pictures be submitted. I'm passing them to everybody. I'd like them to be made part of the record. They are pictures of the children. Pictures with children with them on the visits they've had. I'd ask the court to judge for himself. You know, obviously the pictures don't capture everything, but these are pictures of children who appear to be happy with their parents and enjoying the time with their parents. I'd ask the court to start considering the wishes of the parents. I think it's a little bit troubling that Mr. Perhalla admits that he hasn't asked Caitlyn what she wants; I think the reason for that is because he knows the answer that she wants to go home… …

MR. PERHALLA: … no, the reason your Honor is that I'm not a psychologist or psychiatrist trained to get that information from a child.

THE COURT: Okay, keep on going.

MR.FINDLAY: I would point out that in terms of MCL 712 (A) (19) (6) the criteria that the court is supposed to review in these things is the likely harm to the child, if the child continues to be separated verses the harm to the child if returned, so that at some point, and I think these pictures are evidence of that, that what the harm of the children being continued to be removed from their parents is something the court should take a look at. Especially with the compliance that the Colemans; the objective compliance with everything the Colemans have been asked to do, have been done. Even waiting for these psychologicals, with the delay on these, the Colemans did everything they could to get these done as quickly as possible, and we've had a delay here, through no fault of their own. At least, from what Mr. Ross indicated, Dr. Moore has initially reported there's nothing alarming in these reports. I would point out that the visits are still supervised. Sherry Benson, we could get her on the phone if the court wanted to hear from her, is the one that's had the hands on face to face contact with the girls, and she reports no problems of any kind that I'm aware of. She reports that even when she first started there were some issues of the Colemans. Not disciplining enough, and kind of letting the girls get away with everything. She addressed those and those things were corrected. These hearsay allegations—how do you combat hearsay allegations? If, in fact, there was a disagreement with a meal at Applebee's, I find it hard to believe that that would be held against the parents. This history of this Ashland instance? When does that take place? What are these about? To throw stuff in the kitchen sink (is) basically to do whatever can be done to prevent the return of these children to the parents, it strikes me. I ask the court to allow unsupervised visits, within the discretion of Mr. Ross, that if he thinks its appropriate, that it's his call to make. I think the girls deserve to have time with their parents in this situation. I'm not sure what else that they can do. I am convinced that there's pretty much nothing they can do to make the other side of the table, not including Mr. Ross, satisfied with their ability to care for these children. And at some point, that has to be taken for what it is, but then the court has an obligation to rule on the legal issues of when they should get their kids back. I ask, obviously, for the return of the kids; absent that, I'm asking that we move this along to unsupervised visits. That is going on, we have reports from the counseling that they're doing well, nothing negative is coming out of the reports.

THE COURT: Okay now, do you want me to look at the pictures or do you want to keep them in the file, or what do you want?

MR. FINDLAY: I'd like the court to have everybody look at them please.

THE COURT: I mean, if you want them in the file, they'll stay in the file, it's just that.

MR. FINDLAY: Yes, I would like them in the file.

THE COURT: They tend to take up space.

MR. FINDLAY: I'd rather have the pictures... they're on a CD too.

THE COURT: Oh, I get you. So I'm acting like a middle aged person, thinking these can't be replaced easily, and they can.

MS. WITTLA: Your Honor, regarding the incidents that were mentioned in Wisconsin, there was a police report that was generated from an incident at the AmericInn in Wisconsin and it was in the year 2007. I want to say it was in the spring of the year. That incident involved Mr. Coleman arguing with a clerk at the registration desk, wanting an upgrade on his room and complaining that there was a shower head missing, I think, or a condom under the bed. One of those two things.

Which was it, Ms. Wittla? You know so much, surely you must have a report to read! Oh, but actually, you don't have a police report, do you, Ms. Fibber? I mean, Wittla? Possibly that is because the truth of the matter is that there was no police report. So let me now reveal to readers what this was all about and how deceptive efforts of the prosecutor once again came into play here. You have to go back to the year 2007, which obviously Ms. Wittla attempted to do to see if she could dig more dirt up on Robert Coleman. At that time, my family and I did stay at AmericInn in Ashland, Wisconsin, on our way home from a trip. They had a water park there, and Caitlyn, like all 5-year-olds, was excited about it. She began running, which the lifeguard did not like, so he grabbed her by the arm, and in my opinion roughed her up. Naturally, as a parent, I did not like that, so I did challenge him, and it went on to the manager. When the manager seemed unwilling to respond, I told them I would call the police. Not them. Me! Well, instead, they did it. That's fine. When the policeman who was sent out arrived, we all discussed it and the manager of the place asked me to leave. The officer confirmed I would have to do so, so even though we would then have to make a 5-hour drive home, we did so, in compliance with the officer's instructions. He was half apologetic, telling us this had occurred before, but insisted he had not choice but to adhere to the request of the manager. It was done and over. But there was no police report done, which is why Tracie could never produce one. Most likely it was on the log that the officer was sent out, and that's all. But everything Tracie said was a lie. No police report. No request for an upgrade by me. No condoms. No nothing! But these were the lengths this prosecutor was willing to go to try to nail me, including extra efforts she made to find any type of complaint from my sordid past! Anything she could to try to keep my kids!

MS. WITTLA? The reason I can't remember is because they day before they had been at another AmericInn somewhere in the state of Wisconsin and made the same kind of claim, and wanted an upgrade or a free room or something to that extent.

Hmmmm.... Ms. Wittla. Let me point out that first, there is quite a difference between those two types of complaints, they are not the same. Secondly, if you know so much about where I stayed and what I did, where is the police report on the first incident you are discussing? Or for that matter, why can't you read the one for the second day, which you say you have? Because you don't have them! Never mind, go on with your history, which in fact, has nothing to do with current events or this case in any regard:

MS. WITTLA: Certainly making these claims is not exactly a federal crime (BINGO!)—and it's not the sort of thing that would really take anyone's interest except for the fact that it's a continuing pattern.

Oh! And so, too, were the tantrums I threw when I was age two, right?

MS. WITTLA: As far as the claim that the parents have done everything that they need to do, the only response I would have is that swearing to that degree at your step daughter in Walmart for all in sundry to hear indicates a complete lack of control from my perspective.

Produce the other witnesses who heard that Tracie. So far, you have one fictional one. Again, because it didn't happen.

MS. WITTLA: This is a family that is presenting to this court as having everything under control, everything is fine and dandy, and if that's true, then the incident in Walmart is not true, it didn't happen.

You finally got something right, Ms. Wittla!

MS. WITTLA: It can't be both from what I'm saying here, and it's not that I want this to go on forever; but I also don't want to be tied to an expectation that this case has to moved forward just so we can say it's moving forward. If it's not time, it's not. If the counselors haven't said anything about how the kids are perceiving these visits, maybe it's because they've only had a couple of visits with the counselors. The counselors are only seeing these kids every other week; that's all the DHS was able to arrange; it's not weekly; it's not multiple times a week; it's once every two weeks. I would expect at this point that they're still at the rapport building stage with these children. It's fabulous that their behaviors are self-correcting, due to this counseling influence; but I don't think that it's reasonable for us to expect that they've completely spilled their guts to these counselors or counselor if they've only had two or three sessions.

MR. FINDLAY: Your Honor, may I just briefly respond.

THE COURT: No, no, because we don't need it. I mean, this case will go back and forth forever. I get what I need to get, so let's take it from there. Okay, first of all, we have a motion to strike certain parts of this service plan. It's denied because I just don't do that. A service plan is an opinion, and I have referred to this report, the Bell Memorial report, as fudgy, because you glean certain things from it, and I glean the sort of interpretation that the worker did, that there's a manipulative, or situation that the writer of the report, for whatever reason, I guess we debated before, whether it was fear or being PC or whatever. That's an opinion that's in the report. That doesn't mean it's my opinion, although it is probably closer to my opinion than is being argued. So, no, I don't alter service plans. I suppose in there, if there was some extreme factual question, like (for instance) they put in there that the Colemans shot the president, and that wasn't true, I would consider striking a service plan. But you know, it's a matter of interpretation, and it is what it is.

And what it is, to a prejudiced judge, is that anything the prosecution adds words to. Am I correct?

THE COURT: I asked about the pictures. Let me ask this about the Walmart incident, and it's a shame Mr. Coleman is not here. Do we deny that happened?

MR. FINDLAY: Your Honor, that's what I wanted to bring up, is the way this is being presented. It indicates the unfairness of the process. It's like a "gotcha" surprise moment. I would have thought that when this report initially came in, maybe the appropriate thing would have been to contact the Colemans' attorney and said, "Do you want to check with your clients about this and find out what is going on?" Instead, it's brought up like a surprise in court where there's no opportunity to investigate it, to look into it, and to see what the situation was. I'm assuming they would deny it. That it didn't happen that way. I find it interesting that it is apparently the same person that did not approve of what they did in Applebee's that was reporting it. So there might be some bias in the report of it.

THE COURT: Okay, let me ask Ms. Coleman. Did the "F" word get used in Walmart?

MS. COLEMAN: No. Whenever we've been on any visit, me and Robert have always been together, so there's been no swearing at any visit when the children are with us.

THE COURT: Well.

MS. WITTLA: Your Honor, when the incident was first brought to my attention, I requested that Bob Ross have this person interviewed by his counterpart in Menominee. To my knowledge that was done, but I have not seen any written report from this. This came to my knowledge at the end of last week and from that point until now I was gone.

THE COURT (to Mr. Ross): What is your counterpart; did they find anything out or....

MR. ROSS: I talked to Jennifer Savage; she's my co-worker in Menominee that's making my monthly contact with the kids. Ms. Savage talked to the manager of Applebee's, who because there's a confrontation over....

THE COURT: No, no no! I'm talking about the "F" word....

MR. ROSS: Apparently the manager at the Applebee's goes into Walmart, remembered the Colemans from the visit to the Applebee's restaurant and says he overheard Mr. Coleman saying to Caitlyn, "You little fucker, you need to get in line"—something of that nature. Then he says his memory of the incident really wasn't that good.

Why do you suppose he said his memory of it wasn't that good? Maybe because he, in fact, didn't ever make this complaint, because, as I pointed out before, it could never have happened! So when Ross says, apparently—what he really means, is that is the invented Tracie Wittla version, which in no way, reflects any accurate facts!

THE COURT: Okay, well, the only thing I wanted to say is that, everybody on or off the record has to agree that that is inappropriate language. What jumps into my mind is an individual who lives in this community, who regularly referred to his son as that, and the kid ended up in prison. Big surprise. So, I mean, it's not right, and I doubt very much I would be surprised, Ms. Wittla, if you have actually used that word on your children. Maybe it's a generational difference, but that's pretty extreme to refer to your kids as such. Anyway, it's not good, whatever we make of it. And I don't know about the Applebee's incident. Again, it's a shame. All right, get your client back in here. I shouldn't be talking about people that are not here, so please. Okay, I understand you are taking the child out Mr. Coleman; it's like taking a child out of church if things get riled and you probably did see me try to sort out what these folks were saying while the baby was chirping, but we're getting back to the point of things, and I asked your wife if she heard you swear, use the "F" word in Walmart—and she said, "no." And are you telling me you didn't say the "F" word at Walmart?

MR. COLEMAN: No, I did not use the "F" word at Walmart.

THE COURT: All right, I don't know. I don't ever know whether to, frankly, believe your credibility or not. I've talked about that in court. I've touched, said I believe you are manipulative—that's well established here. So maybe it happened, maybe it didn't. If it did, it's grossly inappropriate; I just gave a little story about the one guy I know from this community who would regularly call their child the "F" word, and that child ended up in prison. Big surprise. It's not indeed appropriate if that indeed happened. I guess there's some dispute factor here as there is in every fact in this case about whether it happened or not. That being said, this case has to proceed one way or the other and the burden look is always towards reunification. I've got recommendations from the DHS, I've got other recommendations, and while I don't like the behavior that the Colemans have participated in, while I clearly find them to be manipulative, maybe all the way to bringing the baby here, maybe you can't find another babysitter, but to some degree I find that child may be being used as a prop. I don't want to hear the argument to the contrary because it's just symptomatic. But the question is, are the Colemans a danger to their child to the extent that they should never have them back, and that's no where we are at. Therefore, I'm going to adopt the current service plan; I'm going to indicate that upon the receipt of the report, these Bell Memorials, they were still fairly new into them; is it Mr. Moore and MSW, or is it Doctor Moore?

MR. ROSS: Doctor Moore.

THE COURT: Okay, and he's a psychologist?

MR. ROSS: Correct.

THE COURT: Upon the receipt of Doctor Moore's report in the discretion of DHS, let me repeat, in the discretion of DHS, we can maintain a semi-supervised parenting time. In their discretion, thereafter, we can progress to unsupervised parenting time, for the fourth time, in the discretion of DHS. That means if DHS is having problems with manipulative behavior which could include swearing at a child and expressing anger; which could include raising ruckuses in public; you know, they can cut it off; but if not, and DHS continues to proceed towards reunification, then it can be unsupervised after the receipt of that report. And you're anticipating that's going to be in a matter of a week to weeks, right?

MR. ROSS: I'm going to demand that it be done in a week, because I've waited long enough, and I think the parties have all waited long enough.

THE COURT: Okay, so that's the road we follow. In the past when there had been major issues, and I know there's going to be disagreement on this—but the DHS has heard from foster parents and supervisors that, you know, things aren't going well, and the Colemans are manipulating the situation, and this is really bad, and that's happened to the extent early on, not to beat a dead horse, that the kids have had to be removed (from foster homes), two times I believe, all of which was the Colemans fault. If we are at a better point now, then we need to progress towards the unsupervised, if bad things start happening, like being called a little "F" in public places, or, you know, raising cane in front of the kids that's going to come back—I'm confident that's going to come back to the DHS. Either through a supervisor, and I know there's somewhat of a contradiction here that, if it's not supervised, there's no supervisor, but a store manager or somebody; it's going to get back to the foster parents; because we're still in a small enough scenario in Menominee County that the word will get around; if somebody isn't behaving properly. So that's why I'm deciding, because, under the law again, which is correctly cited, the court has to weigh each side, and at today's point we have completions of several of the requirements of the service plan. We have completed assessment which was the next step; the follow up psychologicals to the assessment, which was the next step; and then we should be following that pattern. And if that doctor says no red flags or whatever the term Mr. Ross used, then we should be proceeding towards reunification. So that is the order of this court.

After a bit more chatter, the judge prepared to end it on that note, setting up a permanency planning hearing for March 14th. And that would end this hearing, right? Not right! It seems that if your first surprise attack in court does not work, you pull out the next surprise attack—which is precisely what the prosecutor did next:

MS. WITTLA: Your Honor, I had a request regarding employment; I don't see employment addressed in the DHS service plan. Obviously that's going to be an issue at some point in time, assuming these children are going to be transitioned home, and I would request that it either be added to the service plan or put into the Court's document or the Court's order that employment needs to be sought out by this family.

THE COURT: That's pretty typical. (To Mr. Ross) What do you say about that?

MR. ROSS: Are you guys getting cash from DHS; is somebody as participating in work first?

MS. COLEMAN: I would have no problem getting a job. I've actually had some offers, but I can't when I'm taking all these days off to go see my children and going to Court and all that.

MR. ROSS: That has become a barrier your Honor.

THE COURT: I'm going to let DHS work their service plan the way they work their service plan. However, you do, by asking that, remind me—all right, we're on a new track here—where we're looking at protective cases as well as delinquency cases to recoup money, that the court and the county and the state have expended. Part of doing that is the potential of a tax intercept. Mr. Novascone gave me a form real briefly this morning; it's a form we used to use, I think, in terms of a juvenile delinquency. There's way too much to it. We don't need to do that. I don't care what their favorite TV program is, all these other things. I think what we did is did a kind of a short shrift here on what we had available; so I've drawn a line, and what I'm ordering is that the parties provide their name, social security number, which I'm going to indicate for the record is protected by State and Federal law, that's going to go into the confidential part of the file and it's going to be kept there. And frankly, if we start with a future collection support order, may be used eventually for a tax intercept. Address, phone number, date of birth and driver's license number, I drew a line under that point. Hair color, scars, tatoos, drugs, alcoholic, etc., you know those are all more rehabilitative questions for a juvenile delinquency case. So that's all I'm asking for is the top of that, which I think the DHS probably has much of that.

MR. FINDLAY: I believe you have the information already.

THE COURT: But to be sure, I'm going to have your clients fill it out. I'm going to order them to fill it out before they leave today, because it's going to take a minute and a half, and if they refuse to fill it out....

MR. FINDLAY: ... To be fair to my clients, they didn't even know about this. I'm the one who said get the court to order it if you want it because my contention was that this information is probably in the file multiple times, so please don't hold that against the Colemans; they didn't even know about it, so they didn't refuse.

THE COURT: Yeah, yeah, yeah. I know, but they do refuse because things happen....

MR. FINDLAY: ... if the court's ordering, they won't refuse, so that was me, not them.

THE COURT: The court is ordering, and again, I drew the line under the top items which is what we need for collection purposes. So we started a support case, Ms. Wittla do you have that with you?

MS. WITTLA: I do.

THE COURT: Okay, and can you give me the number again?

MS. WITTLA: I ran guidelines based on minimum wage for Mrs. Coleman. It came back to an amount of a hundred and thirty-eight dollars per month for child support.

THE COURT: Can you give me the case number? (after she produced it) Okay, basically this is what we do on a support issue: there's no question that there's money; the court takes judicial notice to the fact that there's an obligation back to the state of Michigan and Gogebic County; I don't know, Mr. Findlay, what kind of an argument you have.

MR. FINDLAY: Your Honor, I believe that I would just make sure, inquire that, the state is getting the money that was already previously ordered from Mr. Wade that he's been paying, and that should be going through, $167.53 a month. My concern was that there's not a double dipping with the fact that his is $167.52 a month; would that reduce the amount Ms. Coleman is required to pay based on money coming in.

THE COURT: That fact that we're plucking her support; the fact that we're intercepting her support; is that what you're saying?

MR. FINDLAY: Right. That's being intercepted and that's already being paid. Is that being taken into account and calculating the guidelines that have been arrived at to give the figure a hundred and thirty, whatever dollars it was?

THE COURT: So that's a technical question. What is your response, Ms. Wittla?

MS. WITTLA: Your Honor, my response is that I don't have the information as to what Mr. Wade is paying; that didn't come through my office; it's a support order out of the state of Wisconsin; it's my belief that the state of Michigan is intercepting it and to my knowledge it's the number that he said. When I ran the guidelines, I ran guidelines showing that Gogebic County was the caregiver for this child and put zero as the income for the county. One thirty-eight a month is, and it's difficult to interpret the new guideline forms, but it indicates on here that this is a low income transition equation, and that support calculated in the low income transition equation. I can rerun it if the court wants me to, just to double check to make sure that Mr. Wade's child support contribution would not affect hers; but typically, the computer or the state, from their perspective, is that each parent owes an obligation of support. So, at most, it may change her support by a dollar or two—would be my expectation—but it wouldn't negate her responsibility to pay child support.

THE COURT: Okay, and on top of that, we're running technical guidelines on that as if it was a paternity or divorce case. Within the context of a juvenile case, I can basically order her whatever I want; the statute also refers to state guidelines, under juvenile cases. Those guidelines haven't been updated in twenty years, and frankly they would be a lot more than $138 per month. I'd refer them in and then I always go low on them, when I do a strictly juvenile type of reimbursement. So what I am going to do; I am going to ask you to rerun them, just to be safe, because frankly I don't understand the new guidelines myself; I'm not sure I ever understood the old guidelines ever since we quit running the cross points on the graphs. So I'll ask you to rerun them, and I'll order whatever the guidelines determine, but if it doesn't change, then $138 a month commencing February first, to give a little time which is also what I typically do. It's not that much. I mean, I understand it may be a burden in a situation where there's limitations on income. But in general, it's not a whole heck of a lot of money, especially compared with what the state is spending on those children and the county is spending on the children. So we're going to recoup what we can, and we're also going to recoup from Mr. Wade, yes?

MS. WITTLA: Your Honor, there's two questions that I would have. Things I didn't have the answer to. One would be Mrs. Coleman's state of birth.

THE COURT: North Dakota?

MS. COLEMAN: Yes.

THE COURT: North Dakota.

MS. WITTLA: The other one would be if they have a phone number that they use.

THE COURT: And that's going to be on the form here.

MS. WITTLA: Okay, everything else that's in here refers to any kind of parenting time visitation, just says to refer back to the NA file case number. So it would all go back to the case we were just talking about previously.

There was a bit more discussion of the ins and outs of collection, but no more elements of surprise tucked away as "attack vehicles" of the prosecution, so the hearing, at last, came to an end.

—Chapter Twenty-Nine—

The Divorce and Return Of The Kids

On February 21, 2009, we were finally given our first *unsupervised* visit with the kids. Our kids met us at the car center because our van had broken down on our way to Menominee. Despite a problem which required a new alternator for our van, *the visit went extremely well. This was an overnight visit, and both our visitation* supervisor and the foster parents reported that the girls responded well to this visit.

This must have created great consternation for the two prosecutors, Tracie Wittla and Rudy Perhalla. (Oh, I forgot, Rudy isn't a prosecutor, is he?) Ok, the GAL then. It must have hurt them badly that our unsupervised visit went so well, because it would not be much longer before we would get our kids back, and it seemed apparent there was no intent on their part to ever let that happen! Then came the talk of that happening from the office of Bob Ross, so Tracie and Perhalla had to come up something quick to present at the coming review hearing, set for March 9th. Well, they came up with two plans to try to stop the direction it was all going. First, they would reintroduce John Wade, I'm sure behind the scenes doing all they could to get him to try to get custody of Caitlyn. So he would speak at this hearing, hopefully swaying the judge with that. Second, they would try to use late emails from Caitlyn's last foster parent, Lori Kopsi, to insinuate they needed more time with her before allowing her to return home to us. They would try to indicate bad behavior on her part, which was *of concern to them*. It seems the prosecutor, Ms. Wittla, surprised Bob Ross with this last minute subpoena of Lori. I don't know why this came as a surprise to Bob, because it was a habit of hers to bring something in at the last minute, as she did many times to my attorney during the jury trial. But Ross wasn't happy about it, as you will see. We will next present the entire transcript of this hearing, so you can see for yourself the nasty way both Ms. Wittla and Rudy Perhalla behaved to try to have their way, when it was clear Mr. Ross was interested in getting the reunification completed. As you will see this was the start of their divorce from Bob Ross; I mean, how could this man actually *try* to put this family back together again! His interest was in returning the kids at this point; their interest was to never do so. So let's pick it up with the judge:

THE COURT: Okay, we're on the record in file Number 08-19 NA, in the matter of Caitlyn Brag and Ashley Coleman. We're here on a regularly scheduled review hearing. The DHS is represented by Mr. Ross, Mr. Borth is also here; Mr. Perhalla is Guardian ad Litem, Ms. Wittla is Prosecutor, Mr. Findlay represents the Colemans. They are present and Ms. Kopsi is also here as foster parents; who do we have on the phone?

MS. WITTLA: The father, John Wade.

THE COURT: Oh, Mr. Wade, the father of Caitlyn is also on the phone. The DHS has last filed a service plan as of today apparently, ah: it's stamped March the 9th. Now, in the meantime, the Prosecutor, this morning, gave me a pile of papers constituting some school records of Caitlyn's, and some emails. I have scanned them, um, I'll summarize that in a minute. Um, Mr. Findlay has supplied me with three reports; one for LVD Behavioral Health, one from Catholic Charities as it's now referred to; used to be Catholic Social Services; and one from BHK Child Development which is a, ah, consortium in the Copper Country. So that's the information I have, although, as I said, the ah, service plan is just filed today, so I guess I need a summary of that from Mr. Ross.

BOB ROSS: Um, let me start your Honor, by saying I'm in a rather precarious position today because I feel I'm going to be involved in an adversarial relationship with what the GAL and the Prosecutor. Um, Kopsi is

my foster parent in Menominee today, and she was subpoenaed by the Prosecutor, um, and I wasn't even given the courtesy of being notified of the subpoena. So my foster parent is here to testi — who I believe, to testify to some of the behaviors of the children, but I was, I was unaware of the fact that she was coming until she called me yesterday.

So there you go! This prosecutor doing her *behind the scenes* sneaky work as she did throughout this case, but instead of doing it to us, this time, it was to Bob Ross. A *big mistake!* We had grown used to her last minute antics, but for Ross it was a new thing. But I would love to have had a tape on to hear the conversations between Lori Kopsi and Tracie Wittla as they hatched this plot! We will never know what they really said to each other in phone conversations, but we will see how they attempted to block the return of our kids at this late juncture by trying to say the kids were misbehaving, and therefore needed *more time* with Lori Kopsi.

THE COURT: Okay.

MR. ROSS: Um, Ms. Kopsi does a great job with the two, with, with the girls. Um, I couldn't, I couldn't find a better foster home either in this county or in Ontonagon County; she's doing a great job caring for the kids.

Well, some lies still must be told in order to appease the judge. I'll forgive you this time, Mr. Ross.

MR. ROSS (continued): Um, Caitlyn is in the first grade; she does struggle in school and receives extra help in school with her academics. Um, her parents help with homework during their home visits, um, Ashley is getting education services in the home through Early Head Start; um, both girls continue to have behavior problems in the foster home; um, Caitlyn is very defiant; she's very defiant with authority figures, um, she acts out in school; um, there's some behavior problems with Caitlyn.

Imagine that! She's been a prisoner for nearly a year for a crime she did not commit, she wants to be home, and you won't let her go home! Is it so surprising she would begin to rebel? Normal, I would say!

MR. ROSS (continued): Both girls are receiving counseling services through North Pointe. Um, Breanne Fountain, who does the play therapy with the girls, tells me that none of the girls' behaviors is very extreme or out of the ordinary for kids that are in foster care. Caitlyn tells the counselors, both of them, that she wants to go home. Um, she's very insistent about that.

What? Why would she want to do that? After all, isn't the ogre — the big, bad ogre — is just *waiting there* to chase her with a broom and a wooden spoon, and lash her with belts? And she *loves* the foster homes, according to Ms. Fyle! So how is it even *possible* she is telling an independent counselor something *different* than what she is telling Ms. Fyle? She wants to go home? Is my daughter *lying* to the counselor Ms. Fyle? You'd better go NOW and doe a Forensic Protocol Interview so we can hear a new story from YOU about what Caitlyn says!

MR. ROSS (continued): The parents are continuing to participate in marriage services; parenting classes, and services through BHK which is mostly a fathering program for Mr. Coleman; by the, by the name of Buck Folst. Doctor Moore from Bell Behavioral did a psychological assessment on both parents in early December and found nothing out of the ordinary.

Does that mean that neither Janet or I are radical killers, under disguise as parents, who lurk in the shadows, just waiting to tie our kids up and belt them to death? Or try to bring them back to life later with a vinegar bath to cover up the murder? It must be so disappointing for this prosecutor and her gang to hear that somebody regards us as *ordinary.*

MR. ROSS (continued): Um, Janet Coleman was diagnosed with some minor OCD, which is Obsessive Com-

pulsive Disorder symptom, but Doctor Moore, at the end of his report determined that he believes that the parents are of no danger to the children.

Now THAT is just crazy! After all, Tracie Wittla, who has no background in mental evaluations at all, said that *we were dangerous.* So did Rudy Perhalla, who also has no background for making such determinations. Both of them make horrible prosecutors — but despite that, should really stick to what they know best because they'll never make it in other occupations!

MR. ROSS (continued): It took ten weeks to get this report back from Doctor Moore, um, because of vacations and illnesses and different problems he was having. At the request of everybody kind of involved, I delayed going down supervised visits because of the fact that we didn't have the psychological evaluation; if I would have got this evaluation back sooner; I would have probably started unsupervised visits about six weeks earlier than I did. In the last three weeks of visitation, it switched from semi-supervised to unsupervised. Um, the parents spend a weekend with the girls in a motel in Menominee. The visit went very well, um, the visitation supervisor reported good things.

Yes, but I wonder if Ron Carpenedo was checking my cell phone calls to make sure we were in Menominee during all that time alone with the kids! I mean, we *could run!*

MR. ROSS (continued): Ms. Kopsi reported that the kids came back to the foster home and there were no problems when they came back. The last two weekends the kids have gone home to Calumet to their parents' home, and, um, I've gotten nothing but positive reports again from the visitation supervisor and the foster parents, as far as how the kids have transitioned back into care after the reports. Um, Steve Pellie from the Copper Country or Houghton County DHS makes monthly contacts with the Colemans in their home. Um, he reports no problems with the Colemans. Um, things are going very well with the, the new baby that they have, and Steve reports no issues. Jennifer Savage is my contact in Menominee County, she, she's the kids' monthly in the foster home, and she checks in with Caitlyn at school, and, um, in her contacts, she reports no major concerns. Um, my request today is that the children be returned back to the parents' care. In order to do that, I would make a Families First referral to help facilitate the reunification, help the parents get Caitlyn enrolled in school, and, um, Steve Pellie would continue to make contacts with the family. The girls counseling would be switched to either Copper Country Mental Health or a provider up there. I would anticipate if the court grants this request, that we don't transition the children till Friday of this week, in order to get some of these services lined up and coordinated ahead of time. Um, the Colemans have done a lot of stuff in anticipation of the kids' return; making contact with schools, kind of already starting the ball rolling as far as counseling for the girls. Um, and the parents continue to do a good job of working with Connie Altman and Carol Sabol and the other providers that they're working with. I think at this point in time, reunification with the family should be considered.

THE COURT: Okay, let me, ah, have you comment on this because I should have. I saw everybody perked up when I talked about that the Prosecutor has supplied some emails and, ah, school things this morning, but let me, let me summarize what I gleaned from them, as, again, they were, they were submitted this morning, and I only had time to scan them. Um, they were, um, Ms. Kopsi's emails with you and they were the actual; some school summary type of things; and the only red, the red flags that popped out from those emails were, um, Caitlyn's behavior in school; that she had pushed some kids or done some things, basically, it was a series of referrals on school problems. Um, then there was a discussion of, or trying to find the right word, in it, it talked about Caitlyn inappropriately touching a neighbor kid, a young, a boy; and then some talk about inappropriate, maybe sexual knowledge we'll say and using the word SEX when a TV incident popped up.

Remember in the earlier chapter when I indicated Caitlyn sat on my lap and made the statement, *Daddy can I have sex with you?* That jumped out at me also, because she had no concept of that, or the words, at least not at home! I wondered then just where she was getting this, and in further discussions with her since her return home, I have learned that it was something she heard from some of the kids in the foster homes. She does not know what it all means, even now, denies there was ever any kind of touching going one, or anything like that, but says she does remember them using many sexually oriented words in their everyday conversations. I don't know to this day if this was any of Lori's kids, or any of the other foster parents' kids, or just some of the kids they all had staying there with them. It doesn't matter to me. What does matter is that she was *not sexually abused* in the foster homes, as we once feared, the result of such incidents. She was abused in those homes in many other ways, however.

THE COURT: Then there was some, something about Ashley's behavior when she was being changed or some, ah, in terms of her presentation of her private parts. Um, and then there was some other references about that the, that her parents might get in trouble if something happened and that they may be killed or some, some such thing, and there was some reference to dad in there too. But those are, as I say, the high points of what would have jumped out as potentially negative issues, um, and I'm guessing that you were not — were you aware of all this?

MR. ROSS: Yes.

And like most ordinary people, he probably knew that two year olds don't get their nickname of "terrible two" for saint-like behavior! These are two year olds for crying out loud! Only this prosecutor would try to write something into these kinds of actions from kids so young! And remember, she's being exposed to the other kids and their bad behavior each and every day! You want to blame the PARENTS for what happens in the foster homes? Even Bob Ross didn't buy into THAT!

THE COURT: Info going to come through here or?

MR. ROSS: Uh-huh.

THE COURT: So what, what about that which would appear to be a red flag?

Even now, this judge was *trying* to find a way to side with the prosecutor! Problem was, Bob Ross was no longer playing their stupid game.

MR. ROSS: The stuff that I got from Breanne Fountain says that the behavior that they're exhibiting; a lot of this is caused by separation issues; from being; or from their parents. Um, the issues are continuing to be addressed in counseling, but the behavior issues of the children, as far as I'm concerned, are not a grounds not to reunify. These issues that the girls were having can be addressed through counseling and the parental home; and I think it would be to their advantage to maybe see if these behaviors cease — even exist; it's just maybe a reaction of the children being in care for a year.

THE COURT: Okay, the, the biggy though, let's; let's just say, you know, Caitlyn's misbehaving, fighting, whatever is just possibly that. That, that, like you say is attributable to that or maybe she's just a difficult kid or whatever; but there are, her getting in trouble in school is not as scary as the sexual specter which pops up in these things; so that's my, I guess, to make this record clear because the agency is on the hot seat; as is the Court in the event that something happened afterwards; I mean, what about the fear of a sexual perpetration or problem going on? What commentary do you have on that?

MR. ROSS: Um, the, the incidents that I've got is she's inappropriately trying to kiss boys or some —

THE COURT: —yeah, yeah. That was the other one.

MR. ROSS: Some, ah, touching, and Ms. Fountain told me I think that the report I got from Ms. Fountain kind of contradicts what we get from Angela, who is the actual counselor. Angela is a little bit concerned, um, Ms. Fountain is not as concerned and feels that those sexual boundary issues are going to be addressed through counseling.

THE COURT: Okay, has, has anybody indicated that this indicates that Caitlyn's been sexually perpetrated by anybody?

MR. ROSS: No, no.

THE COURT: Particularly, I guess, her parents?

MR. ROSS: There's no indication of that.

Good God! That issue was dead long ago when the prosecutor falsely tried to bring it then! I have no doubt she would still like to see it as an issue, even though her state has had control of my kids for a year! And this judge would love to see it too, I think, because neither of them like Robert Coleman. But it is not an issue, never was, never will be, so move on!

THE COURT: All right, all right. Well, Mr. Perhalla?

MR. PERHALLA: Thank you, your Honor. Your Honor, I had agreed with the Prosecutor to have, ah, Lori Foster, and I was going to have her testify as to some of the problems that are still going on with the children. Ah, they would be from the emails that you already had, as well as the, um, school reports that you had. But, your Honor, before your decisions are made, I mean, we still have a child, Caitlyn, who is, she's hollering every day. She's hitting people every day. Pinching every day. She's had aggressive behaviors every day. Angela is the counselor. Um, my understanding is Angela has not had enough therapy sessions with Caitlyn to come to any conclusions anyway, either way. This, this is realtively new counseling; ah, sessions that are going on. So we cannot get, one of the critical people we need to, to give us that information; is unable to do so today because she has not had enough sessions with her. Um, there's also some behavior problems with Ashley. She is sticking her tongue out, she's, she's basically mimicking her sister and her sister's behavior; ah, saying I hate you, getting a lot of sticking her tongue out. She's, I believe, three years old. So, um, that's why I ask the foster mother to be here today to give the court some information from her as to what problems she's still seeing with the children before the court made a decision.

Good God almighty! Parents! If your two or three year old is sticking their tongue out, that is considered unacceptable behavior! CPS will be coming after your kids!

I would think probably ninety-eight percent of kids that age do that though. Maybe more. But just think of it, from the CPS point of view! Almost a hundred percent of the kids in their state could be kidnapped because the kids stick their tongues out at age two! And those *uncaring parents* just allow it to happen! And I've *never heard* a kid of that age say to another kid, *"I hate you!"* Perhalla, what cave do you live in, man? Go to a school someday! Listen to all the *"I hate you"* comments! It is, sir, what is called *normal.* Should it be corrected? Yes, it should. And that is what parents do, throughout their lives. Correct their kids, teach them right from wrong, etc., etc. And some even believe as I do, that a spanking, applied with the intent to teach, is the proper way to effect change. To CPS though, it is instead viewed as an *opportunity to kidnap!*

THE COURT: Okay, well let's get that out in the open then before we make the — go around so; and that's right, Ms. Wittla, you subpoenaed her to testify today?

MS. WITTLA: Yes, I did.

THE COURT: All right, so ma'am, if you would raised your right hand. Do you swear to tell the truth, the whole truth, and nothing but the truth so help you God?

MS. KOPSI: Yes, I do.

THE COURT: I guess since you subpoenaed her Ms. Wittla, I'll have you question her, and then I'll let Mr. Perhalla and Mr. Findlay.

MS.WITTLA: Um, I'd rather defer to Mr. Perhalla, he has more of a relationship with her, I just met her first time today.

Nice touch, Ms. Wittla. But I'll bet you talked on the phone with her, didn't you? It is fine though, you and Perhalla are on the same team anyway.

THE COURT: Okay.

MR. PERHALLA: Yes, that's true, your Honor.

THE COURT: Go ahead then.

MR. PERHALLA: Well, state your name and address for the record?

MS. KOPSI: Lori Lynn Kopsi, and I live at 1032 Fifth Street, Menominee, Michigan.

MR. PERHALLA: Caitlyn and Ashley have been with you since when?

MS. KOPSI: Approximately eight months.

MR. PERHALLA: Now you provided the time-ins, the records, the behavior records from the Central Elementary School, correct?

MS. KOPSI: Yes.

MR. PERHALLA: And those were already provided to the court, and at this time I'd move that they be an Exhibit, or did the court already accept all of those as?

THE COURT: I just, I just got it given to me, I don't know what we've accepted them; did you get copies Mr. Findlay?

MR. FINDLAY: Ah, yeah, apparently I guess they were here on the table. I didn't know they were mine, but yeah. I see they're them.

Last minute, as usual, with no time to review anything of course. Normal when dealing with this prosecution team. Oh! I keep forgetting, Perhalla is not a prosecutor is he? My mistake, go on:

THE COURT: All right, this is a dispositional, this court can consider any and all written reports; I guess, I want to get to the point of them, you know, how they're going to be in the file, and if you can tell me what the highlights of, of what or whatever you want Ms. Kopsi to say.

MR. PERHALLA: Yes, it's your understanding that there is still, ah, behavioral problems with Caitlyn at school, correct?

MS. KOPSI: Yes.

MR. PERHALLA: And what are those problems that you are aware of?

MS. KOPSI: The ones at school are pushing kids, head-butting, um, mostly kissing the boys, she's been told repeatedly not to be kissing, um, she's had I believe we counted thirteen since January, time-ins and two detentions.

MR. PERHALLA: Now what's the difference between a time-in and a detention.

MS. KOPSI: Detention is more severe. You have to stay after school.

MR. PERHALLA: And the time-in is just short —

MS. KOPSI: — a short, ah, sit at the bench. Like at recess or any recess time, they'll make them sit on the bench or something.

MR. PERHALLA: Now the, ah, Caitlyn is in the first grade, correct?

MS. KOPSI: Yes.

MR. PERHALLA: And the teacher or teachers have been thinking that maybe she should remain in first grade next year?

MS. KOPSI: Yes.

MR. PERHALLA: So she isn't reaching the level she should be academically?

MS. KOPSI: Not yet.

MR. PERHALLA: Okay, and what are the teachers telling you the problems are with her academics?

MS. KOPSI: Ah, she just has trouble retaining everything; she does not sit still long enough to, um, to kind of comprehend everything. She's very active, she's ah, just basically that's — she's really behind in her math skills, her reading skills are poor, um, she, her problem is she doesn't want to sit down to do it; so she gets really mad instantly and start; will start pitching a fit. Um, some days are good, some days are bad. If she wants to do it, she'll try hard, and if she doesn't, she won't; she won't do nothing.

MR. PERHALLA: And your hus — and your husband and you, ah, have a foster home together, correct?

MS. KOPSI: Yes.

MR. PERHALLA: And the two of you have been working with her in any of these academic skills?

MS. KOPSI: Yes, mostly my husband, because she works much better with him.

MR. PERHALLA: And what is he doing with her at night, I assume it is?

MS. KOPSI: He sits and makes her read her books, her little books, she usually gets two now; we've asked for more. Ah, then tries to get her to do her sight words to memorize those, and then she has a spelling list of words and we try to get her to spell the words.

MR. PERHALLA: Now, in the home, you're still having problems with both children, or more so with Caitlyn?

MS. KOPSI: Well, I have trouble with both children, but more so Caitlyn.

MR. PERHALLA Let's first ask you what problems today is; are you still seeing with Ashley?

MS. KOPSI: Ashley does a lot of sticking her tongue out, spitting, ah, you know, I hate you mom, when she doesn't get her way, you know, she'll pitch a fit and take off running; stupid mom, she started that.

MR. PERHALLA: Is she hitting any of the other children in the home?

MS. KOPSI: Oh yes, she hits, ah, Brandy, like daily; she'll go up to her like she's going to give her a hug or talk to her, and she'll get a mean look on her face and smack in the face or she'll shove her down and —

MR. PERHALLA: And just so the, the court knows, ah, Brandy is how old?

MS. KOPSI: Two.

MR. PERHALLA: And that is your child?

MS. KOPSI: yes.

MR. PERHALLA: And you also have another son and daugher?

MS. KOPSI: Yes, I have a daughter who is eight, and a son who is twelve.

MR. PERHALLA: And then an older son in the home too?

MS. KOPSI: — he's been quite physically handicapped, he's twenty-seven.

MR. PERHALLA: And that's; and your husband and you; and that's the entire, um; everybody who is in the home?

MS. KOPSI: Yes.

MR. PERHALLA: So you see Ashley; is she mainly hitting your other, you, your youngest, your two year old?

MS. KOPSI: Yes.

MR. PERHALLA: Now what problems are you having with , ah, are you seeing with Caitlyn?

MS. KOPSI: With Caitlyn, she just, she'll, if she doesn't get her way, she'll go up and she'll pinch Sasha or hit Sasha, ah, Sasha will try and hit her back. Sasha is not really a fighter; she does instigate, don't get me wrong, she's not an angel. Johnny is a high functioning mild autistic and he likes to be left alone. He doesn't like anyone to interfere with anything, she'll go off and aggravate him, just to get him mad; she'll start calling him names; tell him I don't care about you, I don't like you, you're stupid; call him Johnny Tess, and that's one of his worst words to call him in Johnny Tess. Um, and I've asked her repeatedly just leave him alone, he won't even go after you, and she'll just; she won't.

MR. PERHALLA: Okay, and this is, is this a daily problem with Caitlyn?

MS. KOPSI: This is a daily problem with Caitlyn.

MR. PERHALLA: Has she ever struck any of the, ah, your youngest for example?

MS. KOPSI: Ah, she did; the worst she's ever done to her was maybe push her down, and then she did this one, two, three thing where she touched the finger to the cheek, one finger and she said one, and then two, then when the third one, she flicked her in the cheeks, which I thought was odd, but....

MR. PERHALLA: Is she hitting one or more; is it mainly the three youngest children of yours that she's hitting?

MS. KOPSI: Usually the, she hits mostly the two oldest. She, ah, will periodically hit Brandy or something, but not, not a lot.

MR. PERHALLA: How about you or your husband, has she ever?

MS. KOPSI: No, she don't hit me.

MR. PERHALLA: Now, one of your, and the emails that you sent to, I believe, mainly to Mr. Ross, you would document these behaviors that you were observing, to him, correct?

MS. KOPSI: Yes.

MR. PERHALLA: And those are the documents, the emails that you copied that we've provided the court with this morning?

MS. KOPSI: Yes.

MR. PERHALLA: Now one of them refers to ah, is it Caitlyn's telling Brandy that she's going to kill her?

MS. KOPSI: She told my son, actually my son Johnny, I thought she told the sitter but she told Johnny that with, because she was mad, and she told Johnny when Brian takes off, I'm going to kill her.

MR. PERHALLA: And that was just in February of this year?

MS. KOPSI: Yes.

MR. PERHALLA: Is that something she says to a lot of people?

MS. KOPSI: No.

MR. PERHALLA: So that was unusual?

MS. KOPSI: Yes.

MR. PERHALLA: It's a game about killing and stuff but — not where you think she might have meant it?

MS. KOPSI: No.

MR. PERHALLA: Do they, are — is Caitlyn able to share with the other children at all? Her toys for example?

MS. KOPSI: She has a hard time with it.

MR. PERHALLA: How is she with her sister with her — with Ashley?

MS. KOPSI: Um, lately, usually she doesn't like to do anything with Ashley. She — we've — she used to always say I hate you Ashley, I don't like you, and she still says that to her, but not as much. Um, lately, she's been real, getting a little more protective of her when she wants to be, um, but she still will go over and take something from her, and she'll still tell she hates her and gets her screaming in the bedroom, when it's bedtime and because they share a room.

MR. PERHALLA: Those two share a room with any other children or just to them?

MS. KOPSI: Themselves.

MR. PERHALLA: Do you see a close relationship between Ashley and Caitlyn?

MS. KOPSI: No.

Oh? Then what was all of that "lately she's been protective" crap? Seems you really don't see too much! Maybe you spend too much time writing emails and talking to prosecutors on the phone.

MR. PERHALLA: Now there was a; one of the; one of the emails you sent. There was a reference to where Caitlyn stated she touched your husband in his private area. What was that about?

MS. KOPSI: Sasha and Caitlyn were goofing around with him and horsing around, all of a sudden Caitlyn went up and squealing that she touched dad in his private, in his pee pee. She calls him dad, not Ken, and, um, Ken is like, what is she saying? I said, well, she said she touched you in your private area; he said she never touched me there; yes I did, she said, I touched him, ha ha. And she took off running.

MR. PERHALLA: Have you ever had any other sexual type of things that Caitlyn's done?

This state would never quit trying! They wanted so *badly* to make Robert Coleman somehow guilty of a sexual offense, that they would try their best to make a case out of every little comment Caitlyn would make. Like most six year olds, she loved to play, and comments like that for a six year old are funny to them. They see it on TV, they hear it at school, etc., etc., so why does this guy go on and on like it is really out of the ordinary? We know why, don't we? Well, darn it, why don't you just get Elizabeth Fyle to go do another unrecorded Forensic Protocol Interview for you in Caitlyn's bedroom? This time come out saying that she said her dad molested her! That way you can file a new case against me, and you can make it a criminal case! Oh! That's right! You have to PROVE a criminal case, don't you? Won't be so easy as this time! If it were not for that, you might have had Elizabeth slip that lie in with the rest this last time, right?

MS. KOPSI: She touched me one time, we were in counseling, the first I thought it was an accident; I knew it wasn't, um, and when I tell her about it, she says well you shouldn't have told me, and I did tell her because she touched the neighbor boy in his private area.

MR. PERHALLA: And when was that incident?

MS. KOPSI: I couldn't tell you an exact date; his name is C.J.

MR. PERHALLA: The; and what kind of discipline are you using with Caitlyn first of all?

MS. KOPSI: We do timeouts or to bed early.

MR. PERHALLA: Are you having to use discipline on a daily basis or?

MS. KOPSI: Yes.

MR. PERHALLA: There was an incident recently where she was at the dinner table and had to be removed from the dinner table?

MS. KOPSI: Yes.

MR. PERHALLA: And what happened there?

MS. KOPSI: Well, she refused to sit down and was — kept hitting her sister and they were sitting next to each other and we asked her repeatedly to stop and sit on her seat; and she said, no, I'm not going to. And so I picked her up to bring her in the other room, and she was like kicking and flailing, so I just put her on the floor, and then I grabbed her ankles and I pulled her into the living room; and she ended up with a rug burn.

So, in fact, you abused her, didn't you Ms. Kopsi? We got the whole story from Caitlyn, and it was much more than you were trying to indicate in this court room. You grabbed her by one arm and one leg, dragged her out of the room, up the stairs, and yes, she sustained rug burns due to your abuse. This is but one case of abuse at your hands, Ms. Kopsi, according to Caitlyn today, who also tells about you locking her in the dark basement among other things. But this doesn't bother her *protector,* Mr. Perhalla, does it? But an imaginary belt spanking by me, that did not happen or have any reliable witnesses? That bothers him, to the point he tries to make up other *imaginary* types of charges. Kids are far worse off, for many reasons, in foster care, than they ever are at home, unless the parents, of course, are, indeed, real abusers. But spankings, without belt use, do not fit that scenario. But go ahead, Mr. Perhalla, let her off easy!

MR. PERHALLA: Okay, so you had to physically remove her?

MS. KOPSI: Yes.

MR. PERHALLA: Do you see a — Caitlyn's behavior getting worse recently, then when you first had her?

MS. KOPSI: She's a lot more mouthier and cockier, yes.

That usually results with real abuse, Ms. Kopsi.

MR. PERHALLA: And you've talked, you've spoken with, I believe, Angela is her counselor?

MS. KOPSI: Yes.

MR. PERHALLA: And what has Angela told you?

MS. KOPSI: Angela has told me because of what I've told her with her behavior issues, they were going to have in-home services. I would have people coming to the home to work with her; um, it's more extensive than just regular counseling.

OK, and will you tell them about the locking of her in the basement as punishment at that time?

MR. PERHALLA: Okay, so if, if they are removed home, this is something we'd probably should schedule up in, in the Copper Country too; what you've been able to find out?

MS. KOSPI: Yes.

Except, remember, not everyone agrees with Angela, and this court never put Angela in charge.

MR. PERHALLA: Okay, is Angela with the Community Mental Health there or someone else?

MS. KOPSI: Community Mental Health.

MR. PERHALLA: And she's actually the counselor, right?

MS. KOPSI: Yes.

MR. PERHALLA: Did Breanne; the other lady; ah, what is her role?

Yeah, that's right Perhalla. Play stupid. That should not be hard for you. Bob Ross already told you he was working closely with her, so her role would be a lot more vital at this point than would that of Angela.

MS. KOPSI: Like a play therapy, um….

MR. PERHALLA: And that's ah, Breanne the Mr. ah —

MS. KOPSI: — Breanne Fountain.

MR. PERHALLA: That Mr., ah, Ross was referring to?

MS. KOPSI: Yeah.

MR. PERHALLA: I believe the children had longer time with Breanne, right? They started with her back in November or so?

Glory be! Perhalla is getting his memory back! He couldn't remember who she was, but he can remember the dates she was involved! Halleluyah!

MS. KOPSI: Yes.

MR. PERHALLA: When did Angela, when will she be able to get in the picture?

Why is that important Perhalla? Would it mean if it's soon enough you could put a stop to our kids coming home? I mean, you've pulled out all stops! Why not try this one?

MS. KOPSI: Angela, I think started after Christmas.

MR. PERHALLA: But she wasn't able to give you —

MS. KOPSI: — or before Christmas, I'm not sure.

Yeah, uh, and I paid my taxes either before the tax deadline, or after the deadline too — I'm just not sure which it was. Good answer though, Ms. Kopsi. You do know of course, you didn't answer the question Mr. Perhalla *wanted* you to answer though, and that is when she will be available! Ah, it's okay, I'm sure after he fumbles around a bit, he will find his way back to it.

MR. PERHALLA: Any opinions on what she's observed in Caitlyn?

MS. KOPSI: No, she says she has not had enough time to, because the first one was just to get to know the girls, what they were like and then I bombarded her with a couple of issues and she brought them up and that's as far as they went.

MR. PERHALLA: Okay, did she give you any idea how it — would this be weekly in-home sessions, or more?

MS. KOPSI: She didn't say.

MR. PERHALLA: Some, some therapist is coming in the home and working with the girls? At least Caitlyn?

MS. KOPSI: Yes.

MR. PERHALLA: Does she see Ashley?

MS. KOPSI: Yes.

MR. PERHALLA: Was she as concerned with Ashley, or?

MS. KOPSI: She said she's — Ashley is only three, she always has a hard time getting anything out of Ashley.

MR. PERHALLA: That's all I had your Honor.

THE COURT: Okay, Ms. Wittla, did you have any questions?

MS. WITTLA: A couple. Ms. Kopsi, did Mr. Ross tell you not to email me any more last week?

Oooooo….. now she's mad! She's forgetting to attack Robert Coleman and is going after Mr. Ross now, because he won't let her have her way!

MS. KOPSI: He just told me he wasn't, when he realized that I was emailing you at the same time I was emailing him and Jennifer Savage; he said he didn't know if it was the right thing to do; he needed to check with his supervisor to see if that was right or not.

It isn't! Prosecutors were *told* in court they were to leave this in the discretion of DHS and Mr. Ross! She didn't listen, and as always, tried to inflict her will in the procedures, which she was not given permission to do by the court. If she wanted to have her input, it would be at the time of this hearing — not in the period leading up to it when DHS was in charge!

MS. WITTLA: And when you became aware of Caitlyn's increase in behavior problems; did the Colemans tell you not to share that information with me?

MS. KOPSI: Yes.

Yes, for the very same reasons I just cited. It was for Bob Ross, not Tracie Wittla. Wittla had no business discussing anything on the phone with Lori Kopsi. I should ask Ms. Wittla, though, while you were sneaking behind the back of Bob Ross to get information you were not supposed to be seeking, did you also discuss Lori's child abuse of my daughter at that time? The dragging incident? The locking of Caitlyn in the basement? Or is child abuse only important if it is something you can point at Robert Coleman? Here's a news flash for Ms. Wittla: I'd tell anybody I know to not share anything with Ms. Wittla, because she will twist it and turn it and make it all her lie, far apart from what the truth is, so unless you wish to be caught up in that, it is best to refuse to deal with her. That is for future reference for anyone who might have to deal with this woman. Of course, that is only Robert Coleman speaking, but so far she has not been able to silence me as she has tried so valiantly to do! My freedom of speech still remains, Ms. Wittla, despite your efforts!

MS. WITTLA: Thank you, that's all I have.

THE COURT: Mr. Findlay?

MR. FINDLAY: I didn't understand. How many kids were in the home?

MS. KOPSI: There's six.

MR. FINDLAY: And what are their ages?

MS. KOPSI: Alan is 27.

MR. FINDLAY: And Alan is?

MS. KOPSI: He's mentally and physically handicapped. He's my oldest son.

MR. FINDLAY: Okay.

MS. KOPSI: And then we, um, Johnny who is 12; Sasha who is 8; and then Brandy who is 2; and then Caitlyn and Ashley.

MR. FINDLAY: And are these other four; they all your children?

MS. KOPSI: I adopted the last three; yes.

MR. FINDLAY: Okay, so John — they are your legal children. Okay. Um, Caitlyn's teacher's name is, um, is Kristen Sartorelli?

MS. KOPSI: Yes.

MR. FINDLAY: And are you; you are aware, aren't you, that, that Ms. Sartorelli and Ms., Ms. Coleman have been involved in email exchanges and addressing?

MS. KOPSI: Yes I am.

MR. FINDLAY: And that Mrs. Coleman is pretty; pretty involved with Ms. Sartorelli in terms of being up and checking in on the educational things and trying to address them when they have the visits as well?

MS. KOPSI: Yes, I gave her all the, Caitlyn's homework and everything else.

MR. FINDLAY: That's all I have, thanks.

THE COURT: I, I hate to go into this, but I feel that I have to, um, in terms of the sexual issues, there's the TV comment and the kissing; and the touching issues you've referred to; um, does Caitlyn engage in any other kind of obsessive sexual behavior? Masturbation or anything like that?

MS. KOPSI: Not that I'm aware of. She's always saying she's sore down there, and I just keep referring to it as she's not wiping. The other day she didn't have her underwear and her pajamas bottoms on. That was the first time, but other than that, I have not noticed anything, no.

THE COURT: Okay, or made any references to anything that would appear —

MS. KOPSI: The only reference was in the beginning when I was helping her shower, and she told me how good it feels; felt to be washed down there, and I no longer wash her. She washes herself.

THE COURT: And she hasn't made any reference to anybody else doing anything to her?

MS. KOPSI: No.

THE COURT: Thank you. Okay, um —

MS. WITTLA: Your Honor, I have one or two more questions for Ms. Kopsi based on what, um, Mr. Findlay asked her.

THE COURT: Okay.

MS. WITTLA: Ms. Kopsi, are you aware of a retention hearing that was held regarding Caitlyn?

MS. KOPSI: Yes I am.

MS. WITTLA: What was the result of the retention hearing?

MS. KOPSI: Um, from what Mrs. Sartorelli told me she had said that, ah, Mrs. Coleman, ah, they stated that there would be no problems when they got home; everything would be just fine; they didn't think there was a problem. But they do have a summer program set up for her.

MS. WITTLA: Okay, and why is there a retention hearing even held, I guess, let's start with that?

MS. KOPSI: She is really struggling, she's very behind, um, she has a very hard time staying on task.

MS. WITTLA: Is a retention hearing held then to determine if a child will be repeating a grade?

MS. KOPSI: Yes.

MS. WITTLA: Was that the recommendation from Ms. Sartorelli?

MS. KOPSI: That is, was my understanding; was her recommendations.

MS. WITTLA: And the Colemans' response was that everything would be fine when she came home?

MS. KOPSI: Yes.

MS. WITTLA: That's all I have your Honor.

MS. KOPSI: But I was not there; that's what Mrs. Sartorelli told me.

A very valiant effort to try to make it look like we just *tossed this off* Ms. Wittla. It was unfortunate for you that you were merely digging your own grave on this one. It just happens, as my lawyer pointed out, Janet was right on top of this. It was clear to us that the state was failing miserably, and could not get the job done. So we planned summer classes to catch her up, and knew full well *we could do it better* once the girls came home. It has proven to be the case.

THE COURT: Just out of curiosity because I had never heard of a retention hearing, is, is that something that's special education related or does everybody who is held back have a retention hearing nowadays?

MS. KOPSI: They now have a retention hearing; they just, so that the parents can be there, involved, and everybody makes the decision.

THE COURT: And they call it a hearing?

MS. KOPSI: Yeah.

THE COURT: You know, actually just sit down with the parents, like they did with my son, and say, hey, can we hold him back a year?

MS. KOPSI: Yeah. They said, it's just the, the school, the principal, the teacher, um, anyone that's helping Caitlyn out, and then the parents, yes.

THE COURT: Okay.

MR. FINDLAY: There's a; you said there's a summer program that the Colemans have indicated to Ms. Sartorelli they — would get set up in Calumet?

MS. KOPSI: They said they had something set up.

THE COURT: All right, Ms. Wittla? Anything you want to say?

Oh, Lord! Here we go with more of her rambling on, and more fairy tales:

MS. WITTLA: Yes your Honor. Part of the reason we're here today, ah, has to do with the settling of the lawsuit last fall. I called Bobbie Jo Ferguson this morning to find out what the consequences are if a child is maintained in foster care beyond the one year mark. And to put it bluntly, the agency becomes under an extreme amount of scrutiny if that happens.

Uh-oh! Brace yourself Bob Ross! It looks like her attack on you is about to come! It is apparent she wants to do *your job* and will do anything in her power to stop you from returning our kids to us! The fact she made this call just this morning, is a good indicator of her desperation to do so!

MS. WITTLA (continued): Next week is the one year mark for Caitlyn and Ashley, and so from the agency's perspective, these kids have to go home before that date. Because they do not want to have to shift this entire file down State, for a review, and essentially get slapped on the wrists for all the things they did not do on behalf of these children. Any mistakes that were made will become apparent to the higher ups. This is not just an in-house thing any more. It doesn't go to Scott Parrot, it doesn't go to the zone director, it goes to straight to, as Bobbie Jo says, the tower in Lansing. Once that happens there are monthly reports that have to be filled out by the caseworker's supervisor, and they have to document why they're not making "active" efforts to return the children home. That continues until the children are either returned home or another option is devised to give them permanency. Now some people would say that the settlement is designed to return children home faster, but in speaking to Mr. Ferguson, it became clear to me that it's not necessarily about shoving kids home so that the books look better. It's about making sure that kids are safe. Unfortunately, from my perspective, that's not what is happening today.

And that is the *only thing that ever matters* isn't it Ms. Wittla! *Your perspective!* It is *always* all about *you! You* wanted to do the job of the doctors because you did not like their reports. The same was true about the counselors. You were holding hands with Bob Ross every step of the way in this process until now — when he has decided the kids should go home! So now, you want to do *his job* as well because *you* do not like his decision! This case was never about child abuse of my kids, Ms. Wittla — it was about *you* and *your power!*

MS. WITTLA (continued): Today is the agency's CYA day; get these kids home, our case never has to go to Lansing; no one ever has to spot check our records and we don't have to fill out oodles and oodles of extra paperwork to justify why Caitlyn and Ashley are not at home. So it's easier to send them back, despite the fact that the counselor that they currently have has only had a handful of sessions, and can't possibly give any kind of a diagnosis or opinion as to how these kids are doing or why they're doing the things that they're doing. It's obvious from the records, ah, from the testimony of Ms. Kopsi, that things are not all wonderful, sunshine, and rosy or hunky-dory.

Why not Ms. Wittla? Why not? You have had them for almost a year now, and have had *plenty of time* to make it all so! Seems they have started to rebel, but it's not against us because *we don't have them!* I'd love to hear you explain *that,* Ms. Wittla, but of course you won't. You won't touch that!

MS. WITTLA (continued): But the agency — the first time the agency ever acknowledged any of this is by having Lori Kopsi in the room. I have yet to hear Mr. Ross indicate that these children were not doing wonderfully, perfectly fine, while visiting with their parents and everything was great, and everything's glorious. What's interesting to me as well is an email that I forgot to copy frankly for everyone, from Mr. Ross, dated Wednesday, February 4, 2009. Lori Kopsi had written to Mr. Ross saying just wanted to let you know, the kids seem to be acting up more; Caitlyn is more mouthy, Ashley; Ashley does a lot more spitting and sticking out her tongue at us when she doesn't get her way; she doesn't think she has to listen, and when she does something wrong, she always says it's someone else's fault. Mr. Ross' response starts off by saying how long has this been going on, has this been addressed at counseling? I'm hoping to finally have the psychological evaluations on the parents and be able to move to unsupervised visits. Once that starts, the transition home will move quickly. The interesting thing about this email is that it shows that even though Ms. Kopsi is emailing him with problems, he's still talking about as long as I get those reports back, the transition home is going to move quickly.

No it doesn't, Ms. Wittla! It shows no such thing! His first sentence you quoted of him handles the *problems* Lori cited. The answer was to address it in counseling. Are you so *blind* you could not see that Ms. Wittla? Or did your *opinion* get in the way? The second part of his response simply was informative, in order to bring Lori up to date on what the agency was progressing towards. And so long as he got the reports he was apparently *hoping for,* they would move on to unsupervised visits. If they had gotten reports that were not desireable, I'm sure Mr. Ross would have then contacted everyone to inform them of the problem with the evaluations. Doesn't it just *irritate you* Ms. Wittla, that those reports came back in our favor? You must still have bad dreams about that!

MS. WITTLA (continued): His focus has always been on getting these kids home before that magical one year mark.

That is because that is what his mandate is. It's called *doing his job.* Something *you* would know *nothing about* Ms. Wittla!

MS. WITTLA (continued): I'm not saying that's entirely his fault. His agency has made it very difficult for him to do anything other than what he's doing today, but he problem I have, is that well, I guess the biggest problem I have from the agency's perspective, is that I don't work for them.

Amen. So stop trying to do their job! Oh, and your biggest problem from the point of view of *others,* in case you care, is that you are full of yourself and don't really give a damn about what anybody else thinks.

MS. WITTLA (continued): I'm here to make sure these kids are safe, and I don't really care how many bridges I have to burn with the agency to do my job.

You don't care about the kids, so that is a lie. But you were right on the second part of your statement. But why limit that to the agency? It applies to everyone else as well. And what is your job? To enhance child kidnapping in the state?

MS. WITTLA (continued): Because I am aware of the agency's mistakes; not in this county but in several others where people have sat quietly by and pretended that everything was fine, and not ever dared to ask the question whether something else should have or could have been done. I'm not about to be that person, and I'm certainly not about to let these kids go home with unresolved issues.

YOU are not going to let them go home? YOU? Are YOU now the judge too, Ms. Wittla? I think this will be HIS decision — not YOURS! Of course if he rules against you, you will try to do HIS job as well! But God forbid! The thought of YOU as a judge is too frightening to even think about!

MS. WITTLA (continued): It bothers me tremendously that these children are only receiving CMH services; I was told once upon a time that that was going to be looked into; that maybe there were other funding sources, other services available. Maybe that's just not the case. Maybe this is the best that Menominee County has to offer, but when I talk to CMH workers in the past about in-home services and, you know, what that means if you're offered in-home, their response is then typically, you don't get to in-home services, because everything is great. These kids are about to be offered in-home services which is a pretty big step for CMH, who historically doesn't offer much of anything to children.

Yeah. So let's add CMH to your list Ms. Wittla. Another one *you* don't like. Just like Bob Ross, the doctors, the counselors, maybe the judge, etc., etc. Nobody is quite as smart as *you* are — are they Ms. Wittla? Except maybe Becky Payne, Bobby Payne, Elizabeth Fyle, and Ron Carpenedo. You haven't said anything bad about them yet, because they all despise Robert Coleman. Right?

MS. WITTLA (continued): The other disturbing factor is, is looking at this email that Mr. Ross did send to Ms. Kopsi last week, where he says we have court on Monday to decide about the kids going home, if I have my way, they're going home sometime next week. Why this bothers me personally is because I had a conversation with Mr. Ross last week, and I talked to him about transitioning these kids home, because typically when he's had other kids who have been returned home to their parents, it's not a couple of weekends and then they're back forever. Usually, there's more of a transition than that. But this case is different, this case is special because this case is being looked at or will be looked at under a microscope if it doesn't get resolved before next week. That's the scary thing; it's not me; it's not you; it's Lansing. They're going to be reviewing this file. They're going to be sending, you know, angry emails back saying why weren't more things done with these kids?

Tell me what is *really scary* about this to you, Ms. Wittla? So long as this carries on and the agency is placed under the microscope of the state, you are fine with that, right? But *what if — just what if* — Ross got his way, the kids were returned home, and all went well from there on? What might happen? *Maybe — maybe* — Robert Coleman might just write a book and expose everyone in the kidnapping ring for who they are. If that happened, it might happen that *you, Ms. Wittla,* might be under that microscope! Only it would not be only the state that was looking at you — it might be a lot of other people too! Maybe your law license might be looked at. Or your extracurricular activities that you may be conducting while under the cloak of doing your prosecutorial job. Who *knows* what might be found if the microscope were suddenly turned to *you?* Yeah, that *could prove very, very scary!*

MS. WITTLA (continued): I can't deny that the Colemans have gone and sought out their own providers and have several letters indicating what they've done, but what has the agency done for these kids? They have issues, why, I don't know, because the counselor hasn't had enough time to work with them. It's also interesting to me that Mr. Ross isn't the one bringing you records from the counselors; he isn't bringing you records from the school; I've asked for those, but they are not forthcoming. I had to rely on Ms. Kopsi for those, because Ms. Kopsi was willing to give me the rest of the story.

Was she willing to talk with you about the dragging of Caitlyn across the rug, leaving her injured? Or how about locking Caitlyn in the dark basement? Was she willing to tell you *that part of the story?*

MS. WITTLA (continued): Throughout this case I've been kept in the dark by the agency, and I believe that that's on purpose, and I believe that the agency's email to Ms. Kopsi just highlights the obvious; I'm not supposed to have access to information that they don't want me to have because they want this case to go away quietly.

Ho-hum! It's really becoming quite *boring* listening to *you* concern yourself with *you!* Let's remember, Ms. Wittla, this case is not about *you!*

MS. WITTLA (continued): It's unfortunate that the relationship between Mr. Ross and I has deteriorated to the point that I purposely didn't tell him that Lori Kopsi was coming; it's true; but I also told Ms. Kopsi in an email I sent to her, she's free to tell him or not; it's up to her.

You know, it's funny! If Mr. Ross felt as you do, that this case was about *him,* he would be crying loudly about it in this court now too! But he isn't. Maybe he knows the case is *not* about him. It is called being *professional.* I doubt you know about that though, Ms. Wittla.

MS. WITTLA (continued): I'm not trying to make this case last forever.

You know what? I agree with her! Wow! I don't think she is! But I *do think* she wanted to drag it out until the kids turned 18, because then the state would get more federal funding. The kids would be out on the street in a second, once they reached that age! Of course, as loving parents, we would still take them back, even then, so they would not be homeless as are many others are who this state makes its victims!

MS. WITTLA (continued): But I'm also not the least bit comfortable with sending these children home in this fast track way, up to Calumet where services will have to start all over again and hope for the besst that they even qualify for services in the first place. That services are actually offered to the family, that they attend them, and on and on and on.

Yeah. On and on and on. Will you ever shut up?

MS. WITTLA (continued): There won't be anybody who is watching this case the way anyone in Menominee County would; or that our country would. It's not their case. It's curtsey supervision.

Yeah. Your ruling with an iron hand would be very limited then, wouldn't it? Don't you just *hate it* when you don't have complete *domination* over people's lives Ms. Wittla? Most government people do! And if you are actually working for the state government, legally or logistically as a kidnapping ring specialist, it just galls you when somebody else steps in and puts a cog in the machine!

MS. WITTLA (continued): There isn't going to be the visitation supervisor any more to tell us what's going on; there isn't going to be the foster parents to tell us what's going on; and it wouldn't surprise me in the least if all of a sudden, these children just, were home-schooled kids, so that their teachers would be cut out of the loop as well.

But Ms. Wittla, you don't think her teacher did a good job detecting child abuse in our case anyway... remember? So what difference can *that* make to you? But just for the sake of information, students of home-schooled kids do better as a whole than do kids in public schools. So despite your efforts to make it look like we would try to keep our kids at home so your snooping into our private lives would not be possible, it has not been the way it all turned out. Not a bad idea for parents though, if they don't want the government in their lives. But in stark contrast to what is your apparent effort to try to scare the judge into thinking we might go that way, we did not. Our kids today are in public school, doing just fine. CPS still exists, much to my dismay, but we have no problems with them now. Nor do we expect to, since now, as it was in Ironwood, we don't beat our kids with belts. If they show up now, we will know it is because we wrote a book. But please, Ms. Wittla, do go on:

MS. WITTLA (continued): I'm not convinced that now is the time to send these kids home, and I really had hoped that the agency would have done more to make sure that they were safe before sending them back for their own convenience.

THE COURT: Okay, I guess, in general, Mr. Ross, any comments on the allegations about the lawsuits and the time limits of all that stuff?

MR. ROSS: That's not why I'm doing this. That's not why I'm making the recommendations I'm making. Um, I understand the issues at school, I understand the behavioral issues in the foster home, and I understand all that stuff, and I understand that that stuff can be addressed through counseling. But the behavior issues and the school issues and some of those issues have nothing to do with the primary issue of why we're here, that's child safety. There's been no allegations of neglect or abuse with these families; this family, for a year. I've got documented semi-supervised visits from a parenting supervisor that says the parents have been wonderful during their visits, and they've been appropriate when, with discipline with the children. Um, Doctor Moore, in a psychological evaluation says that he felt that the parents were of no danger to the children. I'm not minimizing the school issues and I'm not minimizing the behaviors in the foster home; but what's paramount here is child safety. And those issues, as far as the behaviors can go, could be a reaction to the kids being in foster care for a year; we don't know. But the counseling issues, I believe, can be addressed while the kids are at home.

THE COURT: Now how about the one year thing, I mean, is that now a big deal? Is that indeed —

MR. ROSS: It's a big deal, but it's not a driving force as to why I'm asking for reunification today.

THE COURT: What about the educational transition? I mean, what, obviously Caitlyn is in school, so what's going to happen to her, where is she going to go to school?

MR. ROSS: She'll be in the Calumet School District; it's not like we're moving a high school kid judge, where we're talking about dropping off credits and meeting criteria for criteria; she'd be enrolled in the Calumet schools, they've got after school programs there, they've got tutoring programs there. The parents are involved at BHK and then they're able to provide some school assistance, and then they're going to go to a summer school program for her as well.

THE COURT: What, what about the, ah, I mean we just thrown the potential of, ah, home schooling to hide the children?

MR. ROSS: Nobody has ever talked about home schooling their kids; that's never been on the table.

You see? The judge interpreted Ms. Wittla's sneaky little insertion about home schooling the same way I did. So it's not just Robert Coleman hearing her say "to hide the children" — it was also the judge! And Ross is right, nobody talked about it — except Ms. Wittla who was again trying to *fabricate something!*

THE COURT: Okay, Mr. Findlay?

MR. FINDLAY: Thank you.

THE COURT: No Rudy already — said, but he basically introduced what the petition was, called a witness, was there anything else you wanted to say?

MR. PERHALLA: Ah, no your Honor, unless you return the children home. I want you to make it clear to the Colemans that my, I will have to see the children. I do not make; I do not like to schedule them; I like to just show up, and when I do show up, if they're not there; if I leave a voice mail; they should call me back as soon as they can, but that's if you send them home; I want you just to make sure they know that I still have to see them.

Why don't you just say it the way you really mean it Rudy? "BIG BROTHER WILL BE WATCHING YOU!" He always wants us to know our kids are not ours!

They belong to the government! Consider us warned Perhalla!

THE COURT: Okay, has that actually been a problem or is that something you're just concerned about?

You mean just "paranoid" about!

MR. PERHALLA: I am; I went up there his; well, I went up there this weekend to see them; they didn't know I was coming; I was told they would be there; they weren't there; I left a voice mail; and they didn't respond to it, but to give them the benefit of a doubt, I want you to make it clear to them on the record, that that's what my purpose is here.

Your purpose? And what is that Rudy? Something like, "When I say you jump, you jump!"

THE COURT: All right, Mr. Findlay?

MR. FINDLAY: Your Honor, just to that note, is that there was a conversation that there may be a GAL visit; I instructed the Colemans that if, you know, I mean, you don't have to sit at the house the whole day for that; but if you get a call from him, then make yourself available, and I, I have no doubts that they will do that if that's necessary. Um, I guess I was struck when listening to Ms. Wittla's statements is that, um, and it sounded like more of a focus turf battle between her and DHS with the Colemans and the Coleman children, um, caught in the middle; and that because she's at odds and the DHS is, you know, towing her line on this that she is angry with DHS and it's the Colemans that have to; and their children; that have to pay the price for it. This isn't about the fight or feud between the prosecutor and the DHS; and it's about these children. Um, and as Mr. Ross indicated, all of the reports, I mean, I — the visitation supervisor, in terms of witnessing the Colemans' interaction with the children are all positive; I think he included them; just about all of them; I was going to reference them, and I think he included all of them in the updated service plan of all the visits. That's, you know, Sheri Benson has been participating with, um, they have done more than what was asked of them. The additional documents that were submitted and copies given to everybody; they've got BHK lined up and involved and in taking steps to do what's necessary. Um, the Bell Behavioral assessment, I mean, it comes back pretty positive if I, you know, nobody knew that was going to come back with the reading the last, I know, it's part of the records the court has, but reading the summary, the big questions in the examination is whether or not either parent poses any risk to the children; I have no evidence that supports such a conclusion. In addition to denying a history of harm to their children, both are too concerned about what others think of their behavior, have control over any impulse acting out, which is certainly within normal limits. And even if some impulse acting out did occur, both Colemans give evidence of understanding potential wrongfulness of their behavior and possessing a good ability to inhibit their behavior. That's probably about as positive as you're going to get in terms of, um, psychological evaluation. I would also point out that, that I think we probably would be further along in terms of unsupervised visits, um, if this psychological evaluation had not taken so long. I think that Mr. Ross, as much as our side of the table didn't like having to wait that long, wanted to have this recommendation or the evaluation back from the counselor before even going to um, unsupervised visits and it took a long time. It was done in December and didn't come out until February; it was, it was over two months before that was finally done. Um, the other thing I'd point out in terms of the educational issues, is that if the court remembers at trial, Caitlyn's teacher in the Ironwood School District, did testify and said that she was doing well in school. I don't think any of us, know here, for sure, um, but I would say that certainly, I think, there's certainly a good possibility that some of the educational issues may have to do with the separation, anxiety, and being apart from her parents, and the continued placement. There are reports that one email that was sent from Sheri Benson, the supervisor, after one of these recent unsupervised visits is that Caitlyn cried all the way home, saying that she wanted to go home. These girls do want to go home, um, I think at this point we're not talking about closing the case out; we're not talking about sending them to the Colemans and, and nobody is checking on them any more; they will be required to do things in, in the Copper Country, I mean, with the Copper Country Mental Health of whoever else they need to be involved with up in Calumet. They've expressed desire and willingness and motivation to get the girls into counseling, any kind of counseling that's needed. I know they will cooperate with; if there's in-home services for that therapy for these girls; I know they will cooperate with that. When I think of the issues that the girls were having, to the extent they're having any, um, the solution is services for these kids, not continued separation from their parents, and I'm asking the court to, to adopt DHS's recommendations; send these girls home with, you know, admissions and orders, I mean, if the court really orders on the home-schooling issue; if that's a concern, put it in the order, these children will not be home-schooled; they will, by, you know, be enrolled in a, in a public school system in, in the Calumet area. The orders for counseling? That's not a problem. Those are all appropriate orders and, and the Colemans are fine with that, as well they should be. I'm; I'm asking the court to send these kids home. Thank you.

THE COURT: Mr. Perhalla, let me, let me just ask you or Ms. Wittla, it's not in a lawyerly argument type of thing, but I mean, Caitlyn's behavior has gotten worse, that's documented, and Mr. Findlay gave his idea and maybe, maybe it has to do with separation. Have either of you got a theory maybe, what else it might have to do with?

Holy home wreckers, Batman! *Of course* Ms. Wittla is going to have a *theory!* That is, after all, what her entire case has been! No facts! No real evidence! Only her only theories, most invented and subscribed to! Why would this judge even ask for her *theory?* She is not a counselor or a psychologist! But keep trying to give her the edge judge, you've been doing that all along!

MS. WITTLA: Your Honor, I was lucky enough to attend, ah, um, seminar at the end of September, put on by a lady named Olga Truhilo,and she spent a lot of her presentation showing us home — photographs from when she was a child; which would indicate that, you know, if you just saw those pictures and didn't know anything about her story, that she had an ideal lifestyle. It wasn't until many years later that she was able to disclose the tremendous abuse that she suffered while she was at home, because her way of coping with it as a child was to disassociate, so that she actually compartmentalized these things and just flat out would not acknowledge that it happened. Wouldn't think about them; if someone asked her hey, I just saw you get hit or something; she would actually deny it to the — degree, because that was her mode of survival. I have no way of knowing, ah, because I don't have a counselor to tell me how Caitlyn is doing; I can't tell you that she's disassociating because that's a fairly extreme thing. But I also can't tell you that the reason that her behavior is getting worse is because she's in placement. I don't know the answer.

THE COURT: Well, but what I'm asking you is do you have a theory in place?

Why? Why, judge! What the hell difference does it make what her *theory* is? What are you trying to do?

MS. WITTLA: My theory is that, um, because of the increased contact with her parents, which is unsupervised, that her parents are showing behaviors that are upsetting to her.

Are you *crazy?* After all we had been through, just getting this process to this point, do you think *now* we would sabotage the entire course of progress so we could instill our comments to Caitlyn that would upset her more? Our goal was to get her home! Not to win a boxing match with Ms. Wittla or anybody else in the system!

MS. WITTLA (continued): And when she screams and, you know, makes statements about you're just like my dad, and things like that, it's because her dad really hasn't changed that much.

Where did you manufacture *this* up, Ms. Wittla? There has been no record of such a statement from Caitlyn presented to anyone! Never produced anywhere! How do you know there was such a statement? And even if there were, how would *you* know how much or in what way I might have changed? (Were a change necessary)

You do not talk with Robert Coleman. But you do have assessments. And you don't like them because they don't paint the villain you keep trying to describe to this court! Your *theory* Ms. Wittla is not even a good theory — instead, it is your *wish!*

MS. WITTLA (continued): We had a hearing a couple of months ago when it was brought to the court's attention that the Colemans were basically, ah, at least verbally towards hotel staff and restaurant people over in Menominee County which they flatly denied. To follow that up I sent Detective Sergeant Doane over there to interview those people, and they all said they dread dealing with him because he's awful. He screams, hollers, swears, throws things on the floor, he's abusive to them, and a very high maintenance customer, I guess you would say.

Hmmmm.... very interesting Tracie. What I wonder is why this is not all part of the record? I have seen no such reports. No police reports. Nothing ever presented to the court regarding this. And when you say, "they all said" Ms. Wittla — who is "they?" Names please. Places please. And locate it on the record. Because I can't.

Maybe this is all made up? Huh?

MS. WITTLA (continued): Now that contrasts greatly with the man that you're always presented with and with the stories that are always portrayed; you know, how wonderful he is at parenting time and this and that and the other thing. The thing that strikes me about it, is that those were the same kinds of incidences that were documented before the current CPS case, before the trial, before all the wonderful services were provided.

Oh, so now she doesn't like the *services* that are being provided either! Even though she *in-*

sisted that they be initiated! And the incidences she is referring to are of us using taping devices to protect ourselves against people like her and the rest of the state kidnapping ring! Not the same as throwing things at waiters, which by the way, only happened in the mind of Tracie Wittla.

MS. WITTLA (continued): So it's hard for me to accept that being verbally abusive to people because you're trying to get your way with your room upgraded or a free meal or whatever; it's not working out and your — in your favor — is the one thing that is a carry over from the way he was before, until the way he is now.

Hmmmm.... I'm observing you Tracie. You seem to be very *angry!* Let me suggest a great place to go for *anger management classes!* Trust me, Tracie, I went there at your request, and it was really a good class! And it seems to me that you are much more angry than I ever was! Try it Tracie. It might calm you down!

MS. WITTLA (continued): This thing with dealing with the kids. Oh, that's all changed and that's all wonderful and he's learned all these skills and everything is great.

Really gets to you, doesn't it honey?

MS. WITTLA (continued): Well, if he really has that much empathy and, and concern for other people, the way the Bell assessment claims, he would, well, he knows how to control his emotions; he wouldn't have these outbursts; he's too concerned about what other people think; then you wouldn't think that he would be doing these things in a public setting of a restaurant, in a hotel. But the detective is telling me that's exactly what's happening.

Ho-hum! Okay, Tracie — where is his report? Haven't seen it yet! The court has not seen it! Where is it?

MS. WITTLA (continued): So there are multiple sides to this case, and to these personalities, and it's knowing all these things makes it impossible for me to believe that this problem has been resolved. It's still there, it's just a lot better; it's hidden a lot better.

Oh! That might be because of the "How to hide things better" class I took along with my anger management classes. I have to ask you, Tracie, do you know what a schizophrenic is? Because it seems to me you might have a touch of that. You need to go see some professionals about that, because you live one life where you try to look at facts, and another life that is totally fabricated, and you seem to have a problem relating to which set of facts are real and which are fabricated in your mind. Try it Tracie, because I want to see you become a better person!

MS. WITTLA (continued): The only other thing I'd put on to the court is that I believe Mr. Wade is still on the phone.

Oh! Yeah! Gee, we all *forgot* about her other bargaining chip to try to keep this reunification from happening! Put him on judge! You have your orders from your prosecutor! She does direct you, doesn't she?

THE COURT: Oh! Well, let me, let me ask one more question that I was going to ask.

You *will let him,* won't you Ms. Wittla? Come on! Be nice!

THE COURT (continued): Ms. Kopsi, first of all let me tell you that I'm sorry that you had to be here today. The court appreciates your services of foster parent, and I know it's tough for you to be caught in between; because you had to deal with everybody here, and, you know, your job is to care for the children, not to be on anybody's side. So, um, I'm sorry that you had to be in that position, but I'm going to ask you a question, and I'm going to tell you if you feel uncomfortable, don't answer, and I'm not going to let anybody else ask you it either, okay? But I'm just fishing with this why is Caitly misbehaving idea. You got any ideas about it? Why Caitlyn is misbehav-

ing right now, or?

MS. KOPSI: I really don't. I really can't go there, um, she's got a lot of issues. She always has from the day I've gotten her; they have escalated since they've had unsupervised visits, and, um, the last few times she has stated she wants to go home.

THE COURT: I mean, when she says it, do you believe her? Is it, ah, zombie like statement or is it —

Say what you *mean* judge! What you really want to know is does it seem like she is saying this only because Robert Coleman has *programmed* her to say it? It's OK, judge, I will let this one slide, because at least it is an honest question. But you *are still trying to help that prosecutor in every way you can!* Trouble is, even *you* are finding it hard to support her failing arguments any longer!

MS. KOPSI: It's not a zombie. She's just mad, she says, "I just want to go home" — and then — and that's how she hollers at me.

Damn! This must have really been *hard* for Ms. Wittla to hear you say Lori. Not what she wanted you to say, I am sure! A *clincher,* for sure!

THE COURT: Mr. Wade, I'm sorry, you, you're on the speaker here, listening; is there anything you want to say?

MR. WADE: Ah, yes, your Honor. You know, unfortunately I can only address my daughter because she's my biological daughter, but, ah, both girls were removed for a reason, and parents under scrutiny will always, ah, be far better, ah, with their manners and so on and so forth, so the current, um, evaluations of the parents, is, to me, is irrelevant. You know, I mean, counseling takes a lot of time.

Yes, Mr. Wade. It does. So does being a parent. But you wouldn't know about that, where Caitlyn is concerned, would you? I mean, to you, what was it? A one night stand? Then she was out of your life forever? Or until now at least? Never did you show any concern until prompted by Tracie Wittla, did you? And it was also her and her band of kidnappers who brought about the dilemma I know you can't wait to talk about. So go ahead, Mr. Wade, convince us how much you care:

MR. WADE (continued): Now unfortunately, you know, my daughter's dilemma is pretty large because she's been removed from the home. She's in foster care, and thank God she is with these great foster parents.

Great? Is that because they drag her across carpets resulting in carpet burns? Or because they lock her in dark basements? What makes them great, Mr. Wade? Oh, and by the way, when do you plan to actually *meet them* before making such an assessment? For that matter, when do you plan to meet your daughter? I asked her about that scenario just recently, and her comment about you was, "He's stupid!"

MR. WADE (continued): But unfortunately, her social worker, Mr. Ross, just dropped the ball in many different ways. For example, everything that's been stipulated in court already and it's obvious that he just wants to sweep it under the rug, and get rid of the kids, and move on.

What everything, exactly, are you referring to Mr. Wade? Are you talking to the admitted motives of Becky? Or the lies the Paynes told to get this case started? Or the allegations Ms. Fyle *made up* from their list of claims, which are today, not even supported by your own daughter? What "everything" are you referring to?

MR. WADE (continued): I have been completely ignored, I am the biological father of Caitlyn.

What took you so long to acknowlege that, Mr. Wade? And where have you been for the first six years of her life? And is this case about *you?*

MR. WADE (continued): And I have an excellent background and it was ordered by the court to get me evaluated, be a home study, and an interview; it has not been done.

Well damn it! Let me help you Mr. Wade! I'll call Elizabeth Fyle and ask her to come to your place and do a Forensic Protocol Interview! If Ross won't do that, I'd be happy to do that! She'll probably charge you with child abuse for abandoning Caitlyn, and since Caitlyn lives with us, she will just take away your other kids. When do you want the interview Mr. Wade? And just to inform you it will be an unannounced visit in the bedroom of your kids. You do have kids now, do you not?

I can also suggest some places for you to evaluated. Bobby Payne knows one very well, as he spent a little time there. I can even have Bobby file false charges against you so Ms. Fyle has to do the interview. It is the law! As for a home study, I have to say I can't help you with that one. But two out of three ain't bad — right?

MR. WADE (continued): In fact, I called Social Services in my area, multiple times, and they said they have never been contacted by Mr. Ross or the connecting agency where he has to go through. They said he hasn't done anything. I've also made multiple attempts via email and phone conversations in the past with Mr. Ross; I have, I have asked and begged for her (Caitlyn's) contact information, and to get my home study done. He's done nothing. He's given me nothing. I have sent a letter, pictures, um, I've sent toys and I was told that he's not even going to introduce me as the father because he doesn't know how to do that yet. So I've not, I don't have her address, I don't have her phone number, you know, Mr. Ross just wants to sweep this under the rug, and, and this is a disservice to my, to my child. And I want this remedied, and if that means they have to stay in foster care for another year or whatever the case may be, then so be it.

Ah, the *truth* comes out! That sounds like a line right out of the Tracie Wittla playbook! Keep them in foster care! Don't let her mother, who you walked out on to handle this all by herself, keep her kid! Set it up so *you* can gain custody! That *is why you made this phone call wasn't it?* Is it *conceivable* that this was at the prodding of one Tracie Wittla? She seems to be the one most concerned about keeping these kids away from the Colemans!

MR. WADE (continued): But I'm going to do the best I can, ah, to eventually contact my daughter, which, you know, I can't; and if I'm not mistaken, you know, two hearings ago it was ordered that I was to be given the contact information and Mr. Ross completely ignored that.

No he didn't. That order was issued *at the discretion of DHS,* and apparently, after talking to you, his discretion was that it would be a bad idea. I concur.

MR. WADE (continued): It was also ordered by you, your Honor, that I get a home study done and that was also ignored. Mr. Ross is incompetent.

Did Tracie tell you to be sure to say that in your phone call? After all, she was mad at Ross!

MR. WADE (continued): I have worked for a juvenile prison here in Durango, as a supervisor, and I've dealt with social services, so I know when, you know, somebody is doing their job and somebody is not. And it's obvious he's not. I also have friends here that are psychologists and psychiatric partners that I've discussed the case with; with Bruce Herring, ah, Jamie Knight in my area, um, a child psychologist, and a child psychologist that deal with kids specifically in this predicament. And it's obvious my daughter should not be going back to her father, ah, her step father and biological mother. They were removed for a reason and nothing's been done; their evaluations have been abruptly cut short and restarted again.

Amazing Mr. Wade! You have so much information on this case! But what *kind* of information are you using that makes this case so *obvious* to you and your friends who are, what? Over a thousand miles away? Did you travel to this area to make your determinations? Just how did you get such marvelous input? Oh, wait! You have been on the *phone* with Tracie Wittla, haven't you? A *great source* for reliable, uncensored, unbiased information! And those juveniles you work with on a daily basis, Mr. Wade? How many of them have fathers who walked out of their lives at birth as you did? You are certainly the father figure they should now follow, are you not?

THE COURT: Mr. Ross, any comments about why Mr. Wade hasn't been given any contacts in the situation?

MR. ROSS: Paperwork was prepared you Honor, as you ordered, and it was sent to the Interstate Compact Office in Lansing. Um, once it's sent there, it's supposed to go to Colorado and he's supposed to be evaluated. It's been past experience dealing with other states, sometimes these take 6 to 8 months. When we dealt with one family in Colorado, it took six months and I believe the family we had in Hawaii took almost 8 months to get a home study back. There's a lot of bureaucratic nonsense that we have to go through to get these home studies done.

THE COURT: I guess, Mr. Wade, what is your idea about getting to see your daughter; would you be coming up here to see her? What, what is your situation?

MR. WADE: I work for a school district, your Honor, I don't make a lot of money. I work full time and I have a part time job, teaching kids how to work out. And I can't afford to go back and forth.

Whoa! Wait a minute! You started this off by telling us what an excellent background you have, and now you tell us you don't have that job any longer at the juvenile facility? What happened there? And now you work for a school district, but don't make much money? Why? Most of those jobs pay pretty well. What do you do there? Did you say teach kids to work out? Are you a physical education teacher? No, they make good money. And you need a part time job to get by? If you have such a great background, why would you have to settle for just that?

MR. WADE (continued): Right now, I mean, I can, what's the bear minimum; I want contact information so I can talk to her on the phone, write her letters, send her pictures. I, I just want the basics, you know, until this, this gets resolved, which, you know, it hasn't been.

With that, Mr. Wade's input was concluded. So we are back to Ms. Wittla's theory.

Forgetting the *theory crap* for a moment, let's just look at the *facts!* First, Caitlyn was now misbehaving a bit more than she was for the past year in foster care. If that is what they are saying, let's ask *why that would happen?* We can blow off Ms. Wittla's desired *theory* of blaming the Colemans again, because we were still under extreme scrutiny by Sheri Benson for what it is we are, or are not saying, to our kids. Her reports are totally positive! So that blows Ms. Wittla out of the water with just that. My lawyer says Caitlyn is crying and wanting to come home. That is logical. She's been imprisoned for a year, is tired of it, wants to be with her family, and the state won't let her. Would she rebel? You bet she would! I would! You would! The one unaltered fact, in all of this, is this behavior is happening while she is under state foster care control! Not while she is with us! So what does that simple fact, alone, tell you? You don't have to be a rocket scientist! Ok, that all said, we are back to the comments of the judge, once his conversation with Mr. Wade was completed:

THE COURT: So here we are again, um, and we are at odds as usual, and though the court has to sort out eventually in the end whether anybody remembers or not, it is my job to also keep the children safe, and when I get broadly divirgined opinions like this, and I have to find an answer, sometimes it's just a little bit of a difference between parties and compromise is possible; but here, it's pretty much across the board. So what I have to do, is look at the evidence that I have, and with all the emotion involved, um, that's what I have to stack up and weigh, somewhat mathematically, even though there is a lot of emotion involved here. All right. The case started as a, you know, clearly established, I'll say it again, ah, abuse case and the jury did not believe the Colemans and believed the witnesses and found that Caitlyn had been, basically, over disciplined; it was over discipline, involving a belt. There was, as I've referred to before, some sort of behavior by Mr. Coleman, but it has never

been established legally anywhere that there was any sort of a child perpetration going on. There is a version to that, or, or a reference to that, or I don't know what you call it.

Let me help you judge. *False accusation.*

THE COURT (continued): Um, the specter has been raised, but there is no evidence of any standard here, um, to establish that that happened, that sometimes when it happens there never is any evidence. The court also has to look at this major factor at the one year point of, and I'm not as concerned about the agency's, you know, paperwork after one year. I mean, I, I almost feel like I'm just making it drag a little longer just, just to tweak the system because while it's a good idea, and the law has long required that we evaluate kids at one year and look to either send people home or not, um, it appears that the settlement has resulted in even more scrutiny there, which has good points and bad points. But where are you at one year? You're either at return home or you're looking to termination; and when you look at termination, you look at, um, a higher standard of proof of clear and convincing evidence; we're not in a termination case, but when I'm trying to decide about which direction things are going, um, that's kind of the analysis I do in my head. So everything that's been laid out here, even the very scary specter with the sexual issues, would never qualify to bring a case to termination. I mean it would be thrown out at the close of evidence.

Ah! So in truth, these absurd allegations are not strong enough for a real case of child abuse! They could never pursue this ridiculous line in a court where they have to have hard evidence! It's just a *shame* that our system *ever* lets any form of child abuse charge be reduced to a *civil matter!* All that does is allow the Elizabeth Fyles' and the Tracie Wittas' of the world to operate unchecked! Where they could never get away with kidnapping kids in criminal court, where all child abuse cases should be placed, they are all too easily allowed to run amock in the civil courts.

THE COURT (continued): Ah, the documentation on the file that comes from the agency is, ah, the Bell Memorial report which says they're not a danger to the children. They have supplied documentations from more than one, from three professional agencies, and while I know that agencies are people of good will that can be snowed, um, not that diffi-cantly, difficulty, um, that's what the evidence is stacking up to be; the evidence stacks up that they have made the effort. They're not the typical re; refuse to rectify case where, you know, even though, defiant as they were at the beginning, they haven't continued to thumb their noses and say to heck with you or we're not going to do anything; they apparently have taken steps in that direction. So then we have to look at where we are in terms of whether the kids go home or not; and I guess, maybe I don't know, maybe I'm the guy that always rules for the agency; I don't think I am, um, certainly there are concerns expressed. But the problem I have with counseling and services, I got a case in Houghton County that I've been on for four years; the cases which have, a case which has serious allegations of sexual perpetration, where an "expert" has found in her, in their opinion, that there was such a thing. Experts on the other side found that there wasn't such a thing. I tried to enlist super counselor, I mean, the, one of the best counselors that I know to try to sort out the details, and in that case, after years we still haven't sorted out what really happened, and I don't know if we ever will. So while the services are beneficial in Menominee, I don't know that the counselor there in a month, six months, a year is going to reveal any other particular situations here, such as sexual perpetration, which apparently I'm obsessed with because that's the biggest fear here; um, had it occurred or not; so again, I have to look back at the evidence that I have. That evidence, certainly, as I said, leans in the direction of reunification verses termination.

So, in other words you *lose again* Wittla and Fyle, because despite all of your efforts to *create* such a case, you were simply unable to do so! The doctors, who I know you hated Ms. Wittla, said emphatically that no such thing occurred!

THE COURT (continued): So I am going to order that the children be reunified when DHS determines, and they're talking about within a week or two, whenever those things are set up. It will DHS's decision. It will not be today, obviously.

Hallelujah! It was our moment to rejoice! Finally, after all this pretensive state-sponsored injustice to our entire family, we could become one again! This must have rocked Ms. Wittla, but to tell you the truth, I was too busy rejoicing at this moment to even notice the expressions on her face! And it didn't matter! My battle was for my kids, not a personal battle with her! Of course the judge would have to issue his last warnings and intimidating threats, but at that moment I didn't even hear his final words. They didn't matter!

THE COURT (continued): I want to make it clear to the Colemans that that doesn't close this case, so regardless of everything else, you folks are still under scrutiny; and while it's pointed out by the people that advocate that your children not go home; that they think that you can probably hide it better; I don't intend to let that happen. I intend to keep this open for a period of time; I don't care what the lawsuit guidelines are; I'm not going to close it at the next, ah, at the next review, which is going to be in three months. I'm going to order after reunification that the DHS implement counseling services, that the children not be home schooled and be placed in a public education setting; and that the guardian ad litem be given access in this discretion to the children.

At that time, as I said, I paid little heed to what the judge was saying. All that mattered is that we were getting the kids back, and we were once again a family. But as I read his order in this paragraph now, I believe that again, this judge violated our rights. I don't believe he has the power to disallow a choice of school for our children. It would be interesting to see what the national home schooling organizations would say about this case, and his order from the paragraph above. As you know they have battled in court for years to allow parents who choose to do so to home school their children. They have won the battle, the kids in general who are home schooled have proven to score higher than their counterparts, and a lot of other interesting tidbits can be found on line regarding that entire fight as well. We have not insisted on this right, and did follow the judge's order then, but since the case was closed, have looked at the option, although not exercising it to this point. I do believe, however, that under the law, we have the choice.

THE COURT (continued): The only thing I want to say there is, I believe counsel can communicate, Mr. Findlay and Mr. Perhalla, you know, you don't want, we don't want to have an awkward situation; if they're hiding from you, that's important and I want to know. But then if you pop in and they happen to be out looking at ice sculptures, which are probably melted by now, you know, if they happen to be out of town at Bridge Fest or something where they couldn't have known you were coming, you know, there's some way you and Mr. Findlay are going to have to coordinate it so you're able to pop in, you're able to do it unannounced; but at the same time the Colemans, you know, have the ability to leave their home and go to community activities. So however you work that out, that's, that's what I fear here because what I'm hearing here is, I don't know if it was a dodging of you last weekend or not.

MR. PERHALLA: I had left a message, did you get the message? Well, there was a message.

Same old line Rudy! Worked last time with Fyle, why not try it again, right?

THE COURT: Well, you know, and I don't want to get into that if you, if you have an accurate phone number for them —

MR. PERHALLA: I used what is in DHS service plan.

THE COURT: Yeah. They have to give you a phone number, and I'm not going to buy if there's three or four contacts. Okay, I'm not going to buy it. What I tell the Colemans — three or four dodges that I didn't get your call.

MR. FINDLAY: That's an old phone number. We'll get Mr. Perhalla the current.

THE COURT: I also adopt the current service plan. Does anybody have anything else they want put in place? And I'm going to review in three months rather than six. Um, Families First shoud be implemented, that's another service that will be in place in the home, plus the fact that it is, in my opinion, the best service available; they help families in reunification. Anything else?

MS. WITTLA: Yes, a couple of things. Ah, the agency has told me several times that when the children were re-

turned to Houghton County that they expected you to be — you'd be transferring this case to Houghton County. I guess I'm just curious to know if that would be the court's intention?

THE COURT: No.

MS. WITTLA: Ah, the other question I would have would really, then, be on behalf of Mr. Wade. Obviously if the children were in foster care he would (need) a mechanism for contacting Caitlyn; since she's going to be with her mother, I guess, I'm just curious as the whether or not the court would encourage or allow Mr. Wade to have any court contact with Caitlyn since the agency has not made that happen.

You did so want to split this family up, didn't you Ms. Wittla? No matter what you had to do! And you wanted so badly for Mr. Wade to fight for custody! Why did you not just resign as a prosecutor, and then go into private practice and make Mr. Wade your first client? God, just think of how much *fun* you could have had in a nice, juicy *custody battle!* You tried your best to instigate it here, but I have some sad news for you Tracie: today, Janet and I and the kids are a very happy family, living in another state, and dear old John Wade has never made such an effort to get custody of his daughter! And I don't think she would give him the time of day if he did write her a letter! She might reply to him with two words: "You're stupid!"

THE COURT: Okay, what I'm going to put in the order, and thank you for reminding me, is the agency will immediately alert the counselor as to the issue as to Mr. Wade, get some feedback from the counselor, from the counselor that has implemented there; I mean, I don't want to — if Caitlyn has a natural father, I, you know, she's under a lot of stress with the move anyway; I don't know, I guess I want a counselor to tell me that she's ready to address that issue. Um, but I want to make it clear that I mean if Mr. Quade — Wade — showed up today which may be a financial problem for him — I would be ordering that he get some contact.

Yes, it does seem that if he was so all-fired concerned about his daughter, he would have found some way, even borrowing the money if necessary, to be in court and express that interest, doesn't it? I think that speaks for itself.

THE COURT (continued): I believe that this is probably going to have to be sorted out in some kind of a custody issue in the future, since no matter how long these cases drag on, protective cases are temporary. So whatever I establish would eventually go away no matter what it was, it would have to be addressed in a custody proceeding in whatever court had jurisdiction; which was Douglas County, Wisconsin, is that the last one? Paternity or whatever?

MR. WADE: That is correct.

THE COURT: Well, and I'm sorry Mr. Wade, I mean, it is legally complicated, but that's all I can say is that it is legally complicated and would have to be addressed either there or in Houghton County or wherever the parties end up residing under something called the Uniform Child Custody Jurisdiction Act, which follows the child.

In other words, Mr. Wade, you have to become *serious.* That did not happen during the first six years of Caitlyn's life (now ten years). Hard to believe it would happen now.

THECOURT (continued); All right, I'm going to get a calendar and set the review on it; and I do want to make it clear that I have no intention of ever greyhound this case; which is a fair term of art that has to do with moving things around, and we do dump cases out of convenience, and the people dump cases on us out of convenience, but this case has gone on too long and too complicated. All right. March, April, May, June; although I'm probably not going to be under anything but a six month requirement, so I'm going to review it on Wednesday, June the 10th, at 1:30 our time, Central, in the afternoon. Anything further for the record?

MR. FINDLAY: No your Honor.

MR. PERHALLA: No, thanks your Honor.

THE COURT: Thank you. We are all in recess.

Wait! Wait! We didn't hear from Tracie Wittla? Nothing? What? Are you *crying* Ms. Wittla? Well, in any case, the decision had been made. We were finally a family again! After almost a year in prison, my kids would be freed from this state at last! No longer could Elizabeth Fyle, Tracie Wittla, or anyone else hold them as kidnap vicitims of the state! It only got better from there and on March 11, 2009, one last Forensic interview took place with Mary Lou C. Nast of the Menominee County CPS doing the interview. Following that, on March 14, 2009, our children were finally able to come home permanently. And even though the case was not yet closed and this was all under the watchful eyes of all the mad bulldogs that took our children away in the first place, to say we were overjoyed would be the understatement of the century! Of course none of this came about without a last minute sabotage effort, however, as we were to learn later. It seems Lori Kopsi *tried* to throw a cog in the wheel on March 11, 2009, via her contact with Tina Hipenbecker. Kopsi told her about some comments Caitlyn had made the day prior, and thought Bob *should know about them.* The alleged conversation went as follows:

Caitlyn: My dad says I can't tell you.

Lori: Tell me what?

Caitlyn: I just can't tell you about the spankings.

(Lori stated that she proceeded to tell Caitlyn it is not a good idea to keep secrets and that's not OK. Lori asked her if Lori tells her to keep secrets from her parents about what goes on in the foster home and Caitlyn replied "no.")

Caitlyn: No, I just can't tell you.

(Lori said she did finally get Caitlyn to say the following: Dad told me not to tell you about the spankings because then we'll never be able to go home.)

Well, you could say that has shades of Elizabeth Fyle on it. But it was an effort that failed. By now Bob was sick of this case, and I would think did not want to be put in a position such as he was placed in with Elizabeth Fyle, the "she said she said" stuff. Interestingly, since Caitlyn has been home, we learned a lot more about what actually took place in the home of Lori Kopsi. Some of Caitlyn's bad experiences in Menominee County, at Lori's home, were described by Caitlyn in other chapters of this book. The dragging and the dark basement incidents. She describes vividly trying to escape and getting caught, and made to stay in a dark basement, a frightening experience that she still has nightmares about to this day. But just the sheer effort to try to throw a cog in the wheel at the last moment, to try to prolong our agony, shows what type of person the state of Michigan takes on as foster parents. In particular when you hear from Caitlyn what she had to endure while in the care of this family. In any case, we got the kids back, despite those attempts, on March 14, 2009.

On June 10, 2009, we had our final protective proceeding hearing, having had no other outstanding backlashes occurring that we were aware of, at least. And overall, this one was short and sweet. The judge began:

THE COURT: This is a child protective proceeding. We've been doing periodic reviews; this is a review hearing. The DHS has filed a service plan in the matter on June 9th and there was a follow up portion of that plan, the parent agency plan and agreement that was submitted today. I also received, just before coming in, various reports from BHK Child Development, the Western U.P. District Health Department, someone that administrates from a Life Outreach Center, the Calumet/Laurium Keweenaw Elementary School (from Karen King, a teacher of Caitlyn), and then a family contact report which frankly, I didn't really discern what it said because

it's written in kind of a fuzzy copy. But it looks like it's from a teacher named Sherry something or other. Canary, or....

MR. FINDLAY: ... your Honor, it's reports from BHK's activities, so, it's a little bit redundant in that it's somewhat covered, but it's just the actual reports of the ....

THE COURT: ... Oh, all right, so it's a follow up from BHK. All right, the Colemans are present, represented by Mr. Findlay, Mr. Perhalla is Guardian Ad Litem, Mr. Ross is the DHS worker on this file, and I guess then I would turn to you, Mr. Ross, and have you indicate the status of the case.

MR. ROSS: As the bench knows, the children were returned back to the Colemans' care on April 17th of this year. A Families First referral was facilitated to help the family with reunification, and Pam Pouttu from that agency in the Copper Country, reported that the Families First referral went well. Caitlyn was transitioned into the COK School District. The report from Ms. King indicates some academic concerns, but I spoke to Ms. King this morning and she indicated that Caitlyn was going to be promoted to the next grade, and that Caitlyn continues to be a good student, and has not displayed any behavioral issues, anything alarming while she's been in school. The service providers that we've received documentation from all indicated the family's continued participation in the Copper Country. Steve Pellie makes monthly contacts for me, through the DHS office in Houghton County and reports no problems with the family. I'm pretty pleased with the reunification and the efforts that the family has made to continue to keep their kids in their home, and continuing to work towards eventual closure of the case. My recommendation at this time is that we continue to monitor the case for another ninety days, and on or about the time that we have to review this case next, I will more than likely, if things continue to go well be submitting the recommendation that the court close the case.

THE COURT: Okay, Mr. Perhalla, Guardian Ad Litem, what is your recommendation?

Still as belligerent as ever, and never willing to admit he was wrong, it appeared he would try once more to throw a wrench into the mix, but it also appeared he knew at this point that he was defeated. Still, he had to throw out one last barb:

MR. PERHALLA: I would agree with that recommendation, though I don't know if we should close it that soon. I'd rather cross that bridge at the next review hearing.

I think that is what Mr. Ross said, stupid! But of course with your mouth always flapping, you probably didn't hear him say that.

MR. PERHALLA: Looking at the school report, I believe that looks favorable at least from a disciplinary standpoint. Caitlyn didn't have any disciplinary problems. I met with the family at their home and everything seemed to be going fine there. Caitlyn does have this reading problem and she will have help in the summer. I would like to see how that goes, and I'd like to have a review hearing. I don't think we are bound by a ninety day one, your Honor. So I'd rather ask for one like four months down the line so we can see how that went, as well as how she's doing in school when we get her in school for a good month before we come back. But it seems to be going fine at home, so that's....

THE COURT: ... Ninety, that's ninety-three days; it's either ninety-one or ninety-three; I always forget, but that is the maximum.

MR. PERHALLA: Oh, we don't have a six-month?

THE COURT: Six, it's six months with a — oh, wait a minute now. Kids are home; it is six months; when we're talking ninety days, that's when the kids are gone. Okay, but those numbers are the maximums, they can be done sooner.

MR. PERHALLA: Okay.

THE COURT: Ms. Wittla?

MS. WITTLA: Well, I have, I guess, a couple of questions for Mr. Ross. Are there reports back from counselors that have worked with the children?

MR. ROSS: I don't have any today. The information I've provided you is the stuff that was provided to me. I don't have any counseling reports for Caitlyn.

MS. WITTLA: Okay, is she seeing a counselor?

MR. ROSS: She was seeing somebody that was coordinated through the Families First referral. I just can't remember off the top of my head.

MS. WITTLA: Okay, would that be Doctor Robert Sharkey?

MR. ROSS: Yes.

MS. WITTLA: Okay, when you say she was, this is a past tense thing or she still is?

MS. COLEMAN: I know she is seeing the one at school, but Sharkey had decided to let her get into a routine, and then continue therapy later.

MR. ROSS: So it's a school counselor, and then Doctor Sharkey.

MS. WITTLA: Okay, so she was seeing Doctor Sharkey, now she's seeing somebody else. She's going to go back to seeing Doctor Sharkey at some point in the future?

MS. COLEMAN: Yes.

MR. ROSS: That's the plan.

MS. WITTLA: But we have no reports from Doctor Sharkey or a school counselor?

MR. ROSS: No.

MS. WITTLA: Okay, what kind of contact have you had with John Wade?

MR. ROSS: None. He doesn't call. The interstate home study for Mr. Wade was pulled from Interstate Compact upon the children being returned home.

MS. WITTLA: And what did you do to inform Mr. Wade that that happened?

MR. ROSS: Colorado told him.

MS. WITTLA: But you haven't had contact with Mr. Wade, so how do you know that?

MR. ROSS: Because Colorado emailed me requesting that the ICPC be pulled because the kids were returned home.

MS. WITTLA: Have you, yourself, initiated any contact with Mr. Wade, in this last three months.

MR. ROSS: No.

MS. WITTLA: Are you aware of whether or not Caitlyn has had any contact with Mr. Wade in the last three months?

MR. ROSS: He has not. He's been provided addresses, phone numbers, information as to where he can contact his daughter, and he has, to my knowledge, elected not to.

MS. WITTLA: Your Honor, in my opinion, the services that we do have reports on do seem to be going well. Obviously, I'm in favor of keeping this case open for another three months to monitor it; hopefully sometime during that period of time, we'll be able to get some counseling records back, describing how things are going with counseling for Caitlyn and Ashley. Aside from that, it appears that things are going as well as can be expected.

THE COURT: And just a follow up question, which I think has already been answered. Mr. Wade has made no efforts to contact you, because he had participated by phone before; he hasn't contacted you and asked to participate by phone or anything?

MR. ROSS: He's got my email address; he's got my phone number; he knows how to get ahold of me. We've provided him with Caitlyn's information upon return home; as far as addresses and phone numbers and, to my knowledge, he hasn't followed up on any of it.

THE COURT: Okay, as far as I know he has made no direct contacts here to make contact. All right, Mr. Findlay, on behalf of your clients?

MR. FINDLAY: Thank you your Honor. I don't have much to add to what everybody has indicated here. The court has the documents that I was going to present to the court. I think the Colemans, Janet and Robert, have done everything that's possible for them to do; and actually even more than has been requested. They've gone out and gotten a lot of these services on their own initiative and gotten involved with them. Assuming we have no reason to believe that the counseling reports will be anything of concern, given the school records; we would ask that, obviously, the case be closed out sooner rather than later. The only thing I would ask is, is Mr. Ross is in receipt of the counseling records and there is no problem indicated, and he feels it is warranted, that we could even come back in earlier than the set review date, and seek possible closure of the case then. Other than that, I think everything is going well.

THE COURT: Okay, just let me ask, as I was relating before we came in, I had been sitting for a number of years on a case in the Copper Country with mental health providers. I don't know Doctor Sharkey. Is he through CMH or something up there? Copper Country CMH, or....

MR. FINDLAY: I think through CMH, you drop some.

THE COURT: I don't claim to know everybody, but I do know of some of the health providers, and that's a new name, so I'm just wondering where he's from.

MR. ROSS: Copper Country Mental Health?

MR. FINDLAY: Yeah, I think it's Copper — that's what I remembered seeing there.

THE COURT: Do we know if he's a psychiatrist or a psychologist or what he is, or....

MR. COLEMAN: He's a psychiatrist, your Honor.

THE COURT: Okay, okay. As I said I was just unaware of him. Okay, what I'm going to do is I'll get a calendar. Now the out set requested is the ninety days, so we're in June today. July, August, September. I'll set a review in — oh, you were saying four months; you want it to go a little longer?

MR. PERHALLA: I just wanted to see how she was doing in school, next year too, after having a summer....

THE COURT: It won't be exactly ninety days; it will be, yes.

MR. FINDLAY: I do have one other comment. Caitlyn has been enrolled in summer school, so we'd have those reports available to us. So she'll be attending summer school.

THE COURT: I'll set it around ninety days. I'm thinking Michigan schools don't go back until after labor day, and that's going to be roughly at the beginning of school, but okay, so I will get a calendar; we'll set it for a review; I'll make other findings in a minute.

After more trivial discussions, the date was set. And on September 2, 2009, the court terminated the case and at long last, this case was behind us. For others, however, it is just beginning. Another Bobby or Becky Payne will emerge, make some false claims of child abuse against some unsuspecting parent, probably because of some personal vendetta, and there will be more over zealous public officials anxious to ride on the bandwagon so their state can profit from their false claims through the use of federal funding of programs like CPS. This will go on and on until, hopefully one day, Congress eliminates CPS funding in what would be a truly worthwhile cost-saving measure, as well as a much needed service to all American parents.

—Chapter Thirty—

In Conclusion:

What does it really mean when you have your children forcefully removed from you and you must be without them for over a year? What kind of emotions do you go through? How do you feel about the *kidnappers* who forced them away from you for such an extended period of time? How do you feel about the people responsible for this happening to you? How do you feel about a system, run amuck, which insists that you bow at their feet and compromise all of your standards in order to get your kids back? And finally, what can you do to fight back? Certainly, you cannot fight back at the time they are holding your kids for ransom, which is what the state does when it kidnaps your children. These are all good questions, which deserve to have good answers. I wish I had them, but I don't. It will take a united effort among people to first, *expose* the states for what they are doing in order to put federal dollars in their purses. Second, it will take a mass revolution on the part of parents to put a stop to the immoral, if not illegal actions of these states who are doing this. And third, it is a problem that can only be stopped with the abolition of CPS (Child Protective Services) which is the national arm that funds these state kidnapping rings. All of the corrupt judges, prosecutors, social workers, and people they buy must be brought to justice, not just with civil suits, but with criminal charges that put them in jail. Their accomplices, which include corrupt policemen, medical facilities and the corrupt doctors who man them, etc., must all be a part of the crackdown. The problem, as I see it, is that not enough people go through the agony of losing their kids, as we did, at one given time, for this to become a national issue, and for such a revolution to take place. It will take the mass media, who in themselves are so often corrupt, to put a stop to these practices. Will it ever happen? I doubt it. But I would bet if our congress were to stop the funding for CPS, you would all of sudden see the numbers of those charged with child abuse diminish demonstrably across the entire country! That would be miraculous in itself, because that would then force the states to charge only those who are truly abusers with the child abuse cases they are currently bringing, all in the name of money. Why? Because *the states* would then have to fund it all.

In our specific case, I have drawn the following conclusions:

(1) The judge was biased and in a hurry to conclude the case, with no regard as to if, or not, the case was heard properly. His main objective was to *move on* to what he considered more important matters. And while they may have been more important to him, nothing could be more important to us that losing our children!

(2) There is no way we could have had a fair trial. Every member of the jury was either employed in some form of law enforcement or had close ties to it. And with the bulk of the witnesses law enforcement or system related, what are the chances any of them would be willing to doubt the *system* stories and listen objectively to our side of the story?

(3) The prosecution case was built on lies. First, in accepting false claims by a less than stable couple who had every reason to bring false accusations built on their own revenge motives. Believe as you may about me, or my truthfulness, but the most convincing argument in all of this came in the testimony itself, when Rebecca (Becky) Petersen Payne took the stand and

admitted to my lawyer her complete lies and deception. (Read her testimony in chapter 20) Yet this jury insisted on siding with her false accusations, even after hearing her admissions. There can be but one reason for this: they had biased intentions even before this trial began. My lawyer was right when he pointed that out during the jury selection process. To ignore such direct admissions in court is remiss on the part of every jury member in this case. It should have been clear to all of them that if she would do all the things she admitted doing in court, that she would also fabricate the so-called *allegations* against me and my wife. But since most of them had law enforcement friends or relatives who were part of the budding little system in Ironwood, it was not too hard to predict what their verdict was going to be. But more than that, there was a state *investigator* who could not wait to pick up the ball and run with it when she saw the opportunity to exploit what these totally unreliable people had to say. And once the ball was in her court, *she* was the one to tell the lies, because nobody would be in a position, nor would they, challenge her version of events. Particularly when she had a vindictive policeman (Ron Carpenedo) who had been after Robert Coleman for some time because he simply did not like Robert Coleman. So Elizabeth Fyle lied, and she also lied about using the protocol they pushed so hard to exploit. She could not have used it. First, there was no way the protocol could have been used that would result in Caitlyn reciting so *perfectly* the entire Bobby and Becky manufactured script. Yet, essentially, if you believe her story, that is exactly what Caitlyn did. No six year old would be capable of that. But any six year old could be coerced into nodding yes to leading questions, especially if she was told she had to agree or never see her parents again. I know now, based on what Caitlyn says at age ten, at a time she is safely home with us, and is no longer afraid to tell us what really happened. Caitlyn could never, in a half hour interview, have had time to ramble and bring out every aspect of the Bobby and Becky list of accusations in a protocol manner, as both Fyle and Bob Ross claim the protocol procedure was based on. In order to cover that many facets that quickly, they would have certainly needed to ask *leading* questions, requiring very quick yes and no answers. Caitlyn tells us today that while in that interview, they told her she had to say we spanked her or she would be taken away. I'm certain there was much more. And while Bob Ross went to great lengths in court to point out how *articulate* Caitlyn was during this interview, at age 6, there were just too many words that she did not know, that still made their way into the supposed *quotes* that Elizabeth Fyle put into her findings report. And let's remember, the state tried to use Caitlyn's difficulties in school against us, saying we were at fault for her falling behind. But if she were so *articulate* at age six, as Bob indicated, why, when she was placed in *state custody* did she begin to experience difficulties in school? Let's remember, that did not happen while she was with us, because she was only in kindergarten, where grades are not kept. So there is no way the state can lay that one on us. Still in all of this, in Bobby and Becky's accusation list, all of the accusations appear, as Caitlyn was supposed to have expressed them, *exactly* as Bobby and Becky listed them, with Elizabeth Fyle confirming they were acknowledged by Caitlyn using this protocol method. Impossible. Oddly enough, even the words the state claimed Caitlyn used, were words used often by both Bobby and Becky, with many of them not even words recognized by Caitlyn at that age. Does all of this not ring a loud bell of total inconsistency?

And what about the judge? He let far too much go that should never have been allowed in this case. Why? Why would he not divulge who filed the complaint in the first place? He went out of his way to say it wasn't Becky and Bobby, but refused to divulge who it was. As a defendant, I had the right to confront my accuser. And if it wasn't Bobby and Becky, then who was it? It seems also he basically followed every command of the prosecutor. Friends? What do you think? And then there was the claim by Becky that she knew the judge and had, in fact, dated his son. Truth? Or another lie? The judge never denied it! I can't say for sure, but I do know she made that claim to Christine Towne and we have a recording of her conversation with Christine Towne to prove that. We should remember, it was on the word of this same Rebecca (Becky) Petersen-Payne that Janet and I lost our kids to the state. So is the judge also guilty of knowing Becky, as she claimed, and thus having a vested interest in the case? Perhaps a conflict of interest? Did his son, in fact, date Becky, as she claimed? If her word was good enough for a jury to convict us, then it would follow that her word must be good enough to incriminate this judge too, would it not? Just knowing that such false accusations from such unreliable sources as the Paynes — compulsive liars — could result in a parent losing their children should strike fear in the heart of any parent. More important, after seeing what happened to us in this case, combined with a review of so many other cases in the state of Michigan, which resulted in a class action suit the state lost, it should heighten that concern even more. And it's not just Michigan, as we pointed out earlier, and have invited you to follow the links of my website to read about. Viewing the vast number of cases of parents, all victimized by Child Protective Services (CPS) should leave every parent in the country asking themselves, "How safe is *my family?"*

Emotionally, I could never tell you what, as a parent, you feel. You can only imagine it, and it is probably much, much worse than you would ever imagine. The tears, the agony of it all is something Janet and I will carry with us for the rest of our lives. But we are only one case among the many wrongful cases that go down in Michigan each and every year, and we are only two of the victim. What it does to your kids can never be mended, and they are the ultimate victims in this. Caitlyn and Ashley still have bad dreams of people coming in the middle of the night to cart them away! They still have dreams of people locking them in basements, and in other ways being abused at the hands of foster strangers, who they did not ask to be placed with. During our own experience, apart from our kids, we began researching other states as well, only to find many other states who are on an abuse level comparable to Michigan, as I indicated above. I decided to start a website where ordinary people could link up and read about the many, many cases similar to or worse than our own. Cases where there really was no abuse, or the suggested abuse was so oversold by the states that there should never have been a case brought before the courts. What is most scary, I think, is that it shows what a true *police state* we live in, as you read the accounts of other people, and how the police behaved in manhandling them, as well as those who might come along and try to put a stop to them and their vicious kidnapping activities. They fight not only the parents, but lawmakers as well, who dare speak out against them, as you can read using my website and the links we have posted, with the most revealing case the one of Nancy Schaefer, the 50th District Senator in Georgia, who many believe was assassinated because of her fight against CPS. Another unbelievable case is that of Sarah Sandy, whose story is well told by Doc Bean, a well known radio talk show host. His interviews with her will make your hair stand on end. So will interviews conducted by another national radio talk show host Alex Jones. Just type in his name in your search box as follow: Alex Jones + CPS. You will spend hours listening his shows on that! Of course these corrupt figures have the welcome assistance of the courts and other institutions of government control. It is so reminiscent of other totalitarian governments that it is frightening to think we live under such a system, when our people are always led to believe that under the Constitution that was written to protect our people that none of this could ever happen. It is no small wonder that today, the common people are seeking to find any kind of governance which would shed us of this accepted form of corruption and wrongdoing, so prevalent now in our society. The only chance we have is for people to rebel, which I think is inevitable as things get worse. CPS is but one form of the mass corruption that pollutes our lives today, and nothing will change until people unite, fight the corruption, and stamp it out. Can it be done in a peaceful way? I hope so. But if not, trust me, one day, change will come.

AMERICAN HUMANE ASSOCIATION

Summary of the President's Proposed Fiscal Year 2012 Child Welfare Budget

CHILDREN'S PROGRAMS FOR 2012:

PROGRAM	AMOUNT
CAPT A State Grants	$ 27,000,000
CAPT A Discretionary	$ 27,000,000
CAPT A Community Based Prevention	$ 41,000,000
TITLE XX, Social Services	$ 1, 700,000,000
TITLE IV-B (1) Child Welfare Services	$ 282,000,000
TITLE IV-B (2) Safe & Stable Families	$ 408,311,000
TITLE IV-E Foster Care Assistance	$ 4,500,000,000
TITLE IV -E Adoption Assistance	$ 2,500,000,000
Child Welfare Training l Research	$ 27,200,000
Adoption Opportunities	$ 39,379,000
TOTAL	**$ 9,553,890,000**

Translated, this is 9 billion, 553 million, eight hundred ninety thousand dollars.

The national budget is $.3,729,000,000,000 or 3 Trillion, 729 billion dollars.

Child Welfare gets roughly 2.56°/o of the national budget.

Our national debt is$ 1,100,000,000,000 or 1 Trillion, 100 billion dollars.

Child abuse accusations can destroy your family in Michigan.

In Michigan, you can be investigated for — and charged with — Child Abuse, Child Neglect, or both. This article discusses Child Abuse in Michigan. If you need information about Child Neglect, please read about Michigan Child Neglect.

We will aggressively defend clients against Child Abuse and Neglect allegations by CPS in Lansing, Detroit, Grand Rapids, Ann Arbor, Traverse City, and throughout Michigan

It is important to know that the same allegations can lead to both a criminal allegation of abuse and a neglect petition. The petition in a neglect case is generally filed by a Children's Protective Services worker, although others can file as well. A neglect petition is an attack on your parental rights. If you need information about a criminal prosecution for the crime of child abuse, go to our criminal child abuse page.

What is Child Abuse?

In Michigan, the statutory definition of Child Abuse is:

"harm or threatened harm to a child's health or welfare that occurs from non-accidental physical or mental injury, sexual abuse, sexual exploitation, or maltreatment by a parent, legal guardian, or any other person responsible for the child's health or welfare."

Let's break that down. "Harm" to a child will likely be obvious, while "threatened harm" is when a child is placed in a situation where Child Abuse is likely to occur. A "non-accidental physical injury" is when a child is intentionally and severely hurt or temporarily disfigured, such as cuts, broken bones, poisoning, burns, and internal injuries. A "mental injury" is when a caregiver's physical or verbal acts or omissions cause the child to become chronically anxious, depressed, psychotic, or fearful. "Sexual abuse" includes sexual penetration (sexual intercourse or any other insertion into the private parts of someone's body) and sexual contact (the intentional touching of the child's or abuser's genitals or clothing covering the genitals for the purpose of sexual gratification or arousal). Finally, "sexual exploitation" occurs when a person responsible for a child encourages or allows child prostitution or child pornography. As you can see, the definition of Child Abuse includes many behaviors and actions.

Children's Protective Services ("CPS") is the part of the Michigan government that investigates allegations of Child Abuse. There are many ways CPS can become involved with your case. Certain people, such as doctors, teachers, and counselors must make a report to CPS if they have "reasonable cause to suspect" that a child is being abused. These people are often referred to as mandatory reporters, however, anyone can make such a report to CPS. Once CPS receives a report of suspected abuse or neglect, they will open up an investigation. The first thing CPS usually does is talk with your child at school. This can be done without your knowledge or permission. In fact, school officials are required by law to cooperate with CPS attempts to interview your children without your knowledge or consent, as long as CPS determines that the interview is a necessary part of their investigation (which of course, they always do.) CPS investigations can quickly become a disruption to your family life. Investigators often stop by the home or work at inconvenient times and demand to speak to you. They will often threaten to take you to court if you don't cooperate. Once in court, they often ask the court to impose burdensome requirements on parents already struggling to provide for their families. These may include attendance in parenting classes, meetings, and counseling. It is common for CPS to ask the court to take away your parental rights entirely!

The permanent loss of parental rights is most often sought by the Department of Human Services in cases where a parent or other responsible person in the home is accused of sexual abuse of severe physical abuse, such as cases involving fractures in babies, medical neglect, severe unhealthy conditions in the home and drug abuse by the parents.

Experienced attorneys fighting child abuse allegations in Michigan

If you let them, CPS will take control of your family. You need to hire an aggressive defense lawyer who will keep CPS at bay. At Kronzek & Cronkright, PLLC, we regularly defend our clients against CPS intrusions. We have years of experience fighting allegations of Child Abuse. Let us put that experience to work for you! Call today to meet with one of our very experienced CPS defense attorneys for your free initial consultation! We will meet with you to give you the chance to confidentially discuss your case and talk about your options. We can be reached at: (866) 766-5245 during normal business hours. After hours, our on-call attorneys are available to deal with emergencies.

Michigan CPS Attorney — Tips for Dealing with Michigan Children's Protective Services

Children's Protective Services (CPS), a division of the Department of Human Services, has been investigating allegations of child abuse and child neglect in Michigan for many years. CPS caseworkers have learned how to manipulate caring parents into doing or saying something that will harm the parents in the long run. That is why it is important to be informed on how to deal with CPS before having any contact with that agency. The CPS defense attorneys at Kronzek & Cronkright hope that you never have to deal with Child Protective Services, but if you do, here are some tips:

1. Don't tell your side of the story before talking to an attorney: Many people, especially those who are falsely-accused, think that if they could just explain their side of the story to the CPS caseworker that the caseworker would understand and agree and the entire misunderstanding would be over. In normal life, this may be true. But when it comes to CPS, anything you say can and will be used against you at a later date. What you may explain as disciplining your child, CPS could see as child abuse, and thus it is usually best not to even open up to them and tell them your justifications at all. They can't require you to speak to them. Just tell them you respectfully decline to speak to them until you have been told to do so by your attorney.

2. Request that interviews be recorded. If your school age children are to be interviewed, you should insist that those interviews be recorded. CPS workers will give their version of the interview in the report. However, the reports are often misleading as to what the child said and what the questions were. For example, the leading questions asked by the investigator have a way of appearing as statements made by the child. No investigator with integrity will ever deny the request to record the interview.

3. Keep a paper trail: You should keep a copy of all papers received from CPS. You should also request any records that CPS has on you. Knowledge is power. And you will have a stack of papers ready to hand to your attorney to help him or her prepare for your defense against CPS. Unlike the dramatic courtroom lawyer shows on television, much of the actual attorney work is done through paperwork, and having all the documents from CPS is essential to preparing a defense.

4. Don't agree to do anything before talking to an attorney: You should not sign any documentation, agree to take a polygraph test, submit to a substance abuse test, sign up for parenting classes, sign any HIPAA, medical or psychological records release, or do anything else for CPS without the advice of your lawyer. CPS caseworkers are counting on the fact that they can strong-arm you into compliance by threatening to take your kids away. A good lawyer knows simply telling CPS that you will not be doing any of these things until you are told to do so by your attorney is not grounds for immediate termination of parental rights.

5. Hire an attorney who has experience fighting CPS: Many parts of a CPS defense are a bit different than other types of defense law in Michigan. For one thing, CPS cases against parents are civil cases. This means CPS must only support the allegations of neglect or abuse beyond a preponderance of the evidence, which is much easier to do than with the beyond a reasonable doubt standard that is used in criminal proceedings. For another thing, the terminology used in CPS cases is much different than the terminology used in other areas of the law. For example, the word "jurisdiction" normally means that a certain court has the authority to hear a certain case, but in CPS proceedings, "jurisdiction" means that the court now has control over a child or family and can order services to be completed or termination of parental rights. Not all lawyers have experience defending clients in these types of cases. It should be important to you to find an attorney who does!

If CPS is intruding into your life, contact a CPS defense lawyer today!

THE DUVALL GROUP

INVESTIGATIONS

Duvall Group Investigations
Phone 1-800-681-0687
Cell 734-244-3865
Fax: 734-241-4068
E-Mail theduvallgroup@aol.com
www.Duvallinvestigations.com
Nationwide Coverage

The mission of the Special Investigations Unit is to identify, target, investigate, disrupt and dismantle criminal organizations and individuals engaged in fraud schemes that target the insurance industry. Special Investigations Unit is responsible for investigating select criminal matters involving public corruption, certain white collar crimes, and government and organized crime. Special Investigators provide assistance and expertise to agency divisions, assist law enforcement agencies throughout the State.

Made in the USA
Monee, IL
05 November 2026

67808172R00302